Fully Revised

The Encyclopedia

OF

Judging & Exhibiting

Floriculture & Flora-Artistry

A Classic

BY

Esther Veramae Hamél

Sketches by the Author

order form

PONDEROSA PUBLISHERS - KELLY INT'L

37522 21st Ave So.
Federal Way WA 98003
(206) 874-2592

Author's Other Books

"CREATIVITY WITH GOURDS" 1971 Ponderosa Publishers ($6.50 pp)

"CREATIVE DESIGN WITH DRIED AND CONTRIVED
FLOWERS" 1972 Simon and Schuster

"GESTALT AND FLORAL DESIGN . . . JUDGING"
1975 ($6.50 pp) (Isben #0-913162-03-5)

"HOUSE OF TERMITES" (1972 $6.50 pp Hamel-Kelly) (Isben #0-913162-02)

"BROOKLYN BOTANIC DRIED FLOWER DESIGNS"
(co-authored 1974)

"EDUCATIONAL EXHIBITS EXPLAINED" (1976 $6.50 pp)

"EXECUTIVE THINK LINK" (1990) $9.95 pp

"SEEING DREAMS" (1993) $4.00 PP

TABLE OF CONTENTS

FOREWORD

INTRODUCTION

DIVISION 1 — JUDGING PRACTICES

DIVISION 2 — HORTICULTURE

DIVISION 3 — ARTISTIC

DIVISION 4 — MISCELLANEOUS

INDEX

"HE THAT JUDGES WITHOUT
INFORMING HIMSELF TO
THE UTMOST THAT HE IS
CAPABLE, CANNOT ACQUIT
HIMSELF FOR JUDGING AMISS."

— **Locke**

TO ROBERT

FOREWORD

This ENCYCLOPEDIA OF JUDGING AND EXHIBITING FLORI-CULTURE AND FLORA-ARTISTRY is truly a textbook and ready reference that every Garden Club, Judge and Library should obtain for a more unified and comprehensive knowledge in the field of judging and exhibiting. Mrs. Hamel is a true artist and has endeared herself to thousands of women all over the nation through her artistry and originality in flower arranging and judging. This Ready-Reference should lead you to a fuller life and more personal enjoyment in the fields of judging and exhibiting.

Mrs. Daniel J. Mooney, President,
National Council of State
Garden Clubs, Inc.
1957-1959

Introduction

"FOR I, THE LORD, LOVE JUDGMENT AND I WILL DIRECT THEIR WORK IN TRUTH" — Isaiah 61:8
but
"WOE UNTO THEM THAT DECREE UNRIGHTEOUS DECREES" — Isaiah 10:1

What religion holds people together as closely as a common hobby? And the adhesive of joint garden interest is more binding than most, however, we too often evaluate the worth of any endeavor by the physical evidence and there is no physical evidence in the judging endeavor. Far more priceless, though, are the intangible values . . . the unmeasured worth that comes from concentrating on doing a public service to the best of one's ability . . . and the immeasurable stimulation derived from being a part of a successful affair, meeting exhibitors, discussing judging with one's peers and the general feeling of camaraderie which warms the heart and makes the considerable sacrifices worthwhile . . . the test of a hobby is to love even the drudgery it involves.

The various plant societies have given time and money to study soil, exposure, the needs of the plant relative to drainage, moisture and how to cope with the various hazards as well as encouraging hybridization and setting up standards of perfection. Every judge and exhibitor is strongly urged to seek out and join these societies, and to grow as many specialties as they possibly can.

Specialization seems to be the order of the day and oft-times the specialist thinks his plant is superior and can be judged by none but a specialty Judge. But realistically speaking, one realizes that no average show or fair could conceivably pay the expenses and hospitality of a panel of Judges for every one of the 38 society plants, and here the National Council Judges supplement the ranks to evaluate the hundreds of thousands of entries in the non-specialized shows and fairs throughout the nation.

Judges set the educative quality of the show by their choices and because of this importance, the National Council of Garden Clubs and some plant societies have set up more or less elaborate systems for training, qualifying, accrediting and refreshing Judges. Briefly, the National Council Judge-aspirant must complete five schools and attendant exams in theory and practice . . . theory in the fundamentals of art and the principles of growing horticulture and practice in exhibiting and winning ribbons in both horticulture and design, plus practical experience in judging both. The Judge is also required to pass a reading *examination based on some twenty books on both subjects and audit* three times on specified dates, spending a total of some nine years before receiving a Master Judge certificate. Merely growing 150 varieties of one plant or "knowing the powers that be" cannot earn one a Judge's *Certificate. Retired Masters may receive Emeritus standing.*

1

In order to aid the Judge in her studies, this book attempts to bring together in one volume that which formerly had to be sought in many places. The author is well aware that an attempt to consolidate the complicated techniques is to court criticism and the information is presented with the humility of one who knows that no evaluating criteria is infallible; that criticism comes easier than craftsmanship and with the full knowledge that presuming to state how to judge is risking censure . . . but Judges must have courage! It is recognized that the book can serve only as a stepping stone to individual search for more full knowledge of each subject here included. The deepest joy in life is to be creative. To find an underdeveloped situation, to see the need, to identify one's self with something worthwhile, to put one's all into accomplishment . . . this is a satisfaction in comparison with which superficial pleasures are of little consequence.

Any number of subjects covered in individual chapters have had whole books written on them. Those who wish to investigate one particular phase further have but to inquire at the nearest garden center, library or garden club to find what is available. There is no one perfect source which will answer all needs of all. As Samuel Johnson said: "There are no books not to be questioned . . . no men know for sure!"

Although the chapters are arranged according to a sequence of subjects there is often interpenetration of subject matter from one to another. Wherever deemed advisable, cross references have been inserted in the text and every effort made to guide the reader to the fullest. The text is slanted to include all degrees of expertness in staging, exhibiting and judging.

No attempt has been made to cover any subject except judging. The sketchy discussions of botanical backgrounds are not intended to be a scientific analysis for which the reader is referred to other and more technical texts. The families and species are discussed as a practical means of helping the Judge quickly refresh himself on the sometimes involved relationships within a plant family. All designs are covered in detail because many shows have a dominance of early 20th Century and modern designs with a few abstracts. Since the material used in the artistic section encompasses all the flora of nature, dried, dormant and discarded as well as flowers, it seems reasonable to refer to this section as flora or flora-artistry rather than the more restrictive "flower" arrangement.

One difficulty of writing such a text has stemmed from the peculiar unevenness of the quantity and quality of the references. They run the gamut from short, romantic, subjective, undependable little pieces about nostalgic beauty and elusive distinction and creativity to exhaustive, erudite and accurate (though often stuffy and self-centered) treatises on chromosomes, auxins and the all-exclusive merits of one individual species.

Notes from hundreds of lectures, books and articles as well as personal experience have provided this material. All have been rigorously distilled for relevance and authenticity but even so it is too much to hope that the book is without error. It has been the experience of everyone who cross-checks a number of 'authorities' on a subject such as horticulture, insects, birds or abstract flora design to find that even 'experts' do not always agree . . . in fact, the gulf of their disagreement is often wide, deep and confusing. However, "man would accomplish little if he waited until he could do it so well that no one would find fault with what he has done", and any corrections that a reader can provide will be welcome.

A detailed coverage limited to only judging in its entirety has been lacking and it is hoped this will fill the gap for Judges, exhibitors, Schedule and Classification committees whose caliber and capabilities *are admired and familiar to the author after nearly four decades in the* work. Those who enter the shows need to have a knowledge of judging to enable them to select and construct the best possible blooms and designs for their exhibiting. To have a really fine show the exhibits should be evaluated critically before they leave home. To do this the exhibitor must know the relative worth to be given each quality and the scales by which the exhibits are likely to be judged.

Equally the Judges, in order to do their best work, to avoid criticism, to assure no important points are overlooked, require standardized guidelines to facilitate fair and equitable awarding. By compiling in one book, all the judging information possible, the author hopes to make their decisions easier, more uniform and to lead new Judges into habits of procedure and thought which will result in greater satisfaction to them, to the exhibitors and the general public. No book of this kind is the creation of any one person, but owes its contents to hundreds of hybridizers, growers, instructors, exhibitors and judges of the past who have provided the laboratory for practical judging . . . it is hoped the text will be a help to those of the future!

No addresses of plant societies are listed, as these are subject to change. The current address of any society is available from the Plant Societies Chairman of the National Council of Garden Clubs, 4401 Magnolia Ave., St. Louis, Mo.

In presenting so many words on over 125 different subjects involving the multiple phases of a complex subject it is impossible to express adequately and in detail the thanks due so many. All that can be done is to name those who cordially supplied generous information which is herewith gratefully acknowledged.

Special thanks to a number of dedicated garden club members and friends, to the International Geranium Society; American Begonia Society; American Orchid Society; North American Lily Society; to Mrs. *A. Mabry, Lilacs; A. L. Levi, R. Clark, B. Bauers, Sr. of Holly Society of* America; Ruth Carey of African Violet Society; W. D. Morton, American Amaryllis Society; Mrs. R. E. Gaunt, American Poinsettia Society; Sibylla Young, Gourd Society of America; George Peyton, American *Peony Society; A. Tripple, H. Johnson, North American Gladiolus Council; E. Lloyd, M. Alger, American Dahlia Society; A. Hazzard, Japanese Iris; Ila Craw*ford, Spuria Iris; W. Welch, Dwarf Iris; Crescent Deru, Median Iris, and *R. Davidson, Species; W. Bledsoe, Rokki Rockwell American Iris Society; M. Brown, American Camellia Society; Mrs. J. Stanglin, National Chrysanthemum Society; Helen Link, Marie Bozievich, American Daffodil Society; I. Jones O. Evans, Jr., American Rose Society, Lillian Pethtel, Marigold Society, and H. Metcalf, Prof. Emeritus Horticulture. Appreciation is expressed to NCSGC Instructors Jolly Gardner, Hallie Brown, Betty Helme, Author Emma Cyphers and Ida Stowe.*

And I express thanks to good friends Betty Shryock and Evelyn Mooney (deceased) who always encouraged me, and to National Council of State Garden Clubs whose presidents Mooney, Johnson, Nettleton, Gose, Mauntel, Dean, Steel and Kittel gave me such responsible jobs I had to bring order out of chaotic notes collected in the years since 1945 on judging, exhibiting, instructing and serving on the NCSGC Flower Show Schools Committee and as NCSGC National Judges Chr., National Awards Chr. and National Landscape Critics Chr., and on the National Board for 19 years. I have been highly complimented that the "Ency" (since 1966) has served as a guide for re-structuring society manuals, show schedules and practicing judges, here and abroad.

To my children — Kay, who loves good design and Dennis, who reflected our home environmental emphasis on horticulture and judging by majoring in entomology and horticulture, becoming National President of the Junior Horticultural Association; and from the book's germination to full flower, my husband Robert has been a never-ending source of encouragement and help . . . has put up, put up with and *loved a Judge for thirty-seven of his forty-one married years . . . my* deepest appreciation.

Goals are made to be reached and once reached, remade to continue improvement. The information here is not an end in itself, as changes are continually being made. However, basic information is not so transitory and herein lies the value. Changes as publicized in garden club and plant society publications, trade magazines, current books and in seasonal catalogs issued by seed and nursery men should be drawn on in connection with and as a supplement to fundamental information provided in the **Encyclopedia of Judging.** Thus this book must end with the familiar phrase " . . . to be continued".

Esther Veramae Hamel

DIVISION 1 — JUDGING PRACTICES

In Defense of Flower Shows and Fair Floriculture Divisions

For the discerning visitor a Flower Show is a capsule education *in horticulture and design. To obtain such information elsewhere would necessitate* visits to many gardens. Even then, it is difficult to carry in one's mind from garden to garden and even plant to plant, the detailed qualities of a flower for comparison purposes. Flower Shows and Fairs are aimed at the general gardener rather than the professional grower. Quite often this gardener will see a flower in a display garden and be pleased with it until, in a show, he sees it side by side with a superior flower on the show bench.

Some breeders and Garden-Judges dislike the cut-specimen division of a show, maintaining that it does not give the public a clear, true picture of the flower in relation to the parent plant; that a plant may produce only a few good flowers, or hold its flowers in the foliage or has other undesirable landscape-worthy traits which are apparent when seeing the flower on the plant.

But a compromise must be reached. The cut specimen division serves the purpose of educating the public as to the individual color, *form, substance when cut, and to new introductions. It makes the public* cognizant of the cultural perfection which can be obtained with knowledge and care and inspires many a gardener to visit display gardens, thus seeing plants and flowers in their full perspective before making a decision as to whether the plant is the size and quality they wish to purchase.

Also many who visit shows are aged or handicapped or are apartment dwellers, having no wish or need to see the plant in full perspective, but come merely to visually enjoy, even for the brief duration of a show, the proximity of beautiful flowers their circumstances deny their growing. Should they be denied this vicarious pleasure? We think not and salute the hardworking men and women of the entire world to whom the flower show is the social and educational horticultural highlight of the year.

A show with both horticultural and artistic divisions points out that a cultural specimen is not the whole of natural beauty; it is only one manifestation of it! The person who delights in the perfection of a cherry blossom or a rose but sees no beauty in the dormant branch that will bear it, is in a rudimentary stage of aesthetic development. His attitude is like that of one who professes to love flowers but while admiring the rose, would despise the lowly forget-me-not. The true lover of Nature is he who gives interested attention to all natural effects and form, and finds beauty where the average finds none.

Every once in a while, someone decides to hold a flower show without ribbon awards. Well and good! However, the discipline exerted on the designer in following the scheduled theme and the point scale requirements is invaluable training and should not be dispensed with entirely.

The beginning arranger needs such controls to guide her designing; she and the horticultural exhibitor both need the trained eye of the Judge to point out failures and triumphs and to assess the degree of each. The show without awards lacks the educational advantages because exhibitor and public alike attempt to justify their own decisions against those of the Judges. Competition has been a by-word in the American system of things ever since the pioneer's first turkey shoot . . . or earlier!

Viewers should not sneer at the meager display in a small show, comparing it unfavorably to the riot of flowers in a florist shop or a test garden, but rather should appreciate the exhibits as samples of loving care lavished on a home garden and a home and brought to a show by women, men and young people who want their handiwork judged to see how much they have learned about the art of growing, showing and even of home-making because surely producing flowers and arranging them is an asset to any home, expressing a great deal about the people who live there; often making the difference between the group of people who merely live in a house and the family which has a HOME!

The Inevitablity of Change

Years ago the pace of change was slow and orderly but with the advent of communications media which span the world in a second, the pace of change has stepped up to breakneck speed. Years ago when one spoke of a rose, the hearer was able to picture the plant as a shrub about so high, flowers thusly shaped, probably red, white or pink.

Now a rose, through advances in horticulture, can mean anything from a climber to a Grandiflora, with colors ranging into the lavenders and sizes as varied as the colors. The general size and color of roses stayed pretty much the same for hundreds of years, then the pace of change quickened and within only the last few years all these variations have come about. Today we no longer think of time and the things associated with it in terms of a century, but as a fleeting few months. Art forms that must be grasped and used today are released tomorrow to make way for the new.

Thomas Hardy wisely observed that "time changes everything except something within US which is always surprised by change". Many people are even frightened by it or tend to drag their heels when new ideas change their ways of doing things. Some are in the paradoxical position of being 100% in favor of progress . . . it's just all this change they object to.

Now change, of course, has been with us since the world began; and the world has not only survived, it appears to have thrived! What concerns us then, is not so much change itself or the surging rapidity with which it is occuring, but how well we can adjust ourselves.

Today, as has been true through the ages, we find people who try to stop change or retard it by throwing all kinds of obstacles in its path. They stand like King Canute upon the shore, commanding the tide to turn back.

The fear of change . . . this nostalgic clinging to things as they are . . . is understandable and a pyschological characteristic of human nature. Studies indicate that from the time a technological innovation is proven in the laboratory to the time it comes into widespread commercial use, covers a span of five to seven years as a rule thus giving people time to adjust. However, in horticulture particularly, changes come with each new break, and are in commerce and grown by the general public within the next season, and it behooves the Judge to keep himself mentally ready to accept these changes. He cannot cling to that which is known and familiar . . . the graceful garden snapdragon, not the tetra, the pink rose and reject the lavender, the Period or traditional design rather than the abstract.

Changes take the effort of study to understand and many refuse to make that effort not realizing that it is just such change that adds vitality and zest to life.

Descriptive phrases, listings of standards of perfection and condensed scales of qualitative points can only be a foundation . . . these things are temporary and subject to change as new hybrid introductions further expand our variety lists, increase the color ranges and bring changes in what we now think of as "characteristic form" which are undreamed of today. Breeders are hard at work providing plants which have more flowers, larger flowers, miniature flowers, flowers that have different form, more fragrance, better or different color and a host of other different characteristics.

We can readily see that a variety which was recognized as outstanding in 1930 would ordinarily be considered as unworthy by today's standards. We can recognize that certain faults which were tolerated in the past are now considerd a reason for reducing points. Such changes come readily to mind, for instance, one remembers that not too long ago the non-branched quality rated a large number of points in the evaluation of Miniature Dwarf Iris. Now, through breeding advances the branchless factor has become an established standard of the type, and so emphasis has been shifted to other characteristics which are deemed more in accord with modern objectives.

The same is true of floral design. Many remember when decorative designs (and many of the set geometric forms can be classified as decorative) were all the Judge was called upon to evaluate. It was quite easy (we think now, looking back) to evaluate the pre-conceived perfection of a Hogarth or a Crescent line, easy to evaluate the visible relationships of materials, the rhythm of the color harmony or the contrasts of texture.

But then changes began to appear, more and more Schedules began to call for expressive designs with emphasis on the invisible . . . our feelings, emotions! Scales of points were adjusted to include such qualities as Schedule conformity and interpretation; we began to SEE and to use line and color for the pyschological message they impart which might be restful, or restless, exciting or soothing, inspiring a certain mood. We began to use accessories to supplement the story or mood and credit was given for original selection of materials.

We probed this field deeper and deeper, attempting to communicate subjective and objective feelings with plant material only and the emphasis in our point scales shifted again to include distinction, the technique or execution of the design and we began to hear about abstract and assemblages and dynamic balance.

The ability to communicate an abstract idea, the creativity and originality of the designer's conception, the perceptive selection of materials both in nature and industry to supplement the flora materials and the attention placed on space and spacial relationships once more necessitated an adjustment in the point scales . . . a shift in emphasis. Design and its principles, however, has always remained and always will remain stable on the artistic scales because it is based on age-old, fundamental truths.

In the light of this past progress and the anticipated changes, it is readily apparent that any judging criteria must have elasticity and a flexibility which allows it to absorb new standards of perfection which are imminent as a result of the brilliant and continuing research being done with intensified hybridizing, atomic bombardment of seeds and chemical applications in the horticultural field, and as a result of the creative search for ever deeper and more subtle communication through artistic design. We would have it no other way, for progress must have its day before becoming a part of the past.

A Judge must not only have a fact-laden knowledge based on the evolution of both Artistic and Horticultural evaluation, but must keep alert and learning . . . alert to new changes and learning how to incorporate these changes into new standards of perfection and to evaluate them as objectively as is humanly possible.

Each one must develop a flexibility in training, a willingness to adapt, and an understanding that the surest foundation for uniformity and progress in judging is the ability to contribute what one can to the inevitability of change by accepting, conforming to the majority and doing his part to further communicate that change by judging with the new standards in mind.

Within ourselves we must nurture an acceptability as we approach the challenging and disturbing world of change. Half measures are not enough. Question change if we must; not all change is progress or improvement. But learn to bow to the inevitability of change and judging will be enjoyed far more, and the decisions will reflect the times.

Judging Ethics, Conduct

One day Max's son asked him for a definition of ethics and Max replied "A customer once paid me cash for an order with a $100 bill. When I went for change, I discovered he had given me two $100 bills stuck together. With such a situation, you reach the heart of ethics . . . namely, should I or should I not tell my partner!"

Judging ethics are much more clear-cut and not so cut-throat. However, some are confused over just what ethics means. Webster defines it as "the science which concerns the laws of the actions of intelligent beings, these actions being considered in relation to their moral qualities . . . the science of human duty".

Ethics can thus be thought of as a part of our public conscience. Ethical standards are adopted to protect justice and to keep firm the integrity of a profession. It is a particular system of rules concerning duty, rules of practice in respect to a single class of human actions. For instance, we have social ethics and medical ethics as well as judging ethics. It is not so surprising then that one Program Chairman confused social ethics with Judging ethics and attempted to hire a speaker on "CHARM".

Judging ethics contains our particular terminology and outlines our particular duties and right actions toward the Flower Show personnel, our responsibility to the exhibitor, to the public and to our fellow Judges, as well as our personal actions as Judges. These are the principles of right action . . . ethics.

Judging maturity is based on:

SINCERITY: There is no sham, pretense, hypocrisy, apple-polishing, uncertainty, show, arrogance or equivocation in the mature Judge. We know where they stand. They possess a realness of character which is an essential ingredient in getting along with people.

INTEGRITY: Refers to very special qualities of decency, honesty, loyalty, fair-play and honor. A Judge with a real personal integrity has a deep sense of responsibility and dependability. He keeps his promises. He lives up to his commitments.

HUMILITY: One invariably finds this trait in the great of human past and present. Maturity is usually combined with modesty. It is never found in the smart-aleck, the know-it-all, the self-appointed saviours, nor the persons who know all the rules and the answers to questions yet unasked.

9

COURTESY: This goes beyond mere thoughtfulness and politeness. It means tolerance. It means respect for individual viewpoints. It means being gracious and considerate to the other person. In the intimate relationship of the three-judge panel, courtesy is indispensible.

PRACTICAL WISDOM: is needed to make the right decisions and actions most of the time, and to do the right things at the right time most of the time. A mature Judge is one who profits by experience. The chance to explore, practice and apply knowledge to real situations gives confidence which leads Judges to assume responsibility for actions.

CHARITY: In its broadest interpretation, this means the capacity of tolerant love. It implies the acceptance of the fact that we all have weaknesses; we all make mistakes. To be able to get along with other people requires the charity of forgiveness.

INTELLIGENCE: the ability to cope, to be articulate in communication; to be able to mobilize the resources of experience and opportunity to achieve a goal or complete a service.

EMPATHY: No human association is possible without empathy. The sign of its absence is misunderstanding. Empathy means the ability to correctly interpret the attitudes and intentions of others. To see things from another's standpoint.

AUTONOMY: refers to the degree to which one is self-directed and self-controlled in his actions by a stable set of internal standards. It refers to one's confidence in and reliance upon himself, and the degree of self-respect he maintains. All these attributes can be specifically applied to the art of judging ethically.

KNOWLEDGE AND EXPERIENCE

Knowledge and experience are the basis for practical wisdom. The art of judging ethically is skill in performance, acquired by experience, study and observation. Experience is a very important tool for the Judge. Familiarity with plant diseases, plant enemies and the effects of these, plus all the hazards of cultivation come with practical experience. These teach the Judge to recognize the nature of the blemishes and to appreciate near-perfection.

He must be familiar with the reaction of plants upon being severed from the parent. He must be able to appreciate the skill of conditioning and controlling these plant materials when they appear before him as specimens or in artistic design classes. The Judge must acquire a sympathetic alertness to grooming and execution tricks of the trade and able to decide fairly whether these tricks merit condemnation or praise.

A Judge can no more be a good Judge merely sitting in the back row at a lecture than one becomes a chicken by simply sitting in the henhouse. It takes work, experience. Judging is hard, exhausting mental and physical labor. Despite this, the good Judge judges every show he possibly can, large and small, important or unknown. Wise decisions come from experience. Judging standards must be stable but cannot stand still. This paradoxical dilemma can be resolved only if Judges continue to study. Judges must progress or retire! The time never comes when knowledge is complete! Success is not a destination . . . it is a continuing journey.

Tactful Decision-Making

Disagreeing on the color of a banner hung between them, two knights fought viciously. One insisted the banner was gold, the other that it was silver. Oddly, both were right. One side was gold, the other silver. Often, though convinced we are right, it pays to look again! See things from the other's point of view. One mark of the educated human is his ability to differ without becoming angry, sarcastic or disgruntled.

A Judge must at all times be courteous to his fellow Judges. Although he must be alert to point out reasons for his decisions, he must avoid an aggressively argumentive attitude. He must guard himself against any attempt to dominate the thinking of the other members of his team. And he must not assume a pouty attitude should the majority disagree with his decisions.

Each Judge should listen courteously to the other panel members and give their opinions due consideration. Of course, no attempt should be made to influence other panel members with impressions based on one's own personal tastes.

On the other hand, the Judge should not assume such a timid, and psuedo-modest attitude that his presence is of no help to the other members. He can overcome such feelings by sincere study as knowledge is a sure crutch for self-confidence. The Judge, inexperienced or otherwise, who finds himself unprepared to cope with an issue is stimulated to thought and research which brings a greater degree of justice next time.

The basic quality underlying all good Judges' public relations is the ability to work well with other people. Understanding, thoughtful and considerate Judges do not in any way offend their fellow team members or the Show personnel.

Andrew Jackson once said: "One man with courage makes a majority" and this is never more true than when the one vote we cast is the deciding one. The Judge's courage is rooted in knowledge. He quietly and modestly discusses after deliberate, private consideration. He speaks from an informed background and is prepared to back up his statements with facts and appropriate references if needed, never speaking from personal likes or dislikes.

He is prepared to give reasons for decisions and these reasons are so stated as to encourage rather than discourage. He is tactful when he must disagree and willing to hear the other side. Discussion should not become mere bickering, with disparaging remarks being bandied about. Point-scoring will clarify and point up merits and faults and put the proceedings on a factual, dignified plane.

Conflicts can be competently handled through adopting a peaceful, accommodating attitude. Accommodation or peaceful co-existence means striking an equilibrium in which the panel comes to tolerate opposing viewpoints. Accommodation permits certain differences of viewpoint to be tabled in the interest of a common goal.

Fallibilty

Of course, Judges are fallible! Questions should be asked if some point needs personal clarification. No one can be expected to remember everything. This is one of the reasons why panels are superior . . . three heads are better than one and why point scales are so helpful, no one quality is overlooked.

It is no reflection to admit the limits of knowledge . . . the error lies in the failure to do something about it. A Judge should conduct himself with humility, with full understanding of himself, his abilities and shortcomings, with the realization that he COULD be wrong!

If proven wrong or out-voted, the ethical Judge bows to the inevitable with humility, thus through amiable adjustment he maintains the unity necessary to proceed.

Doubt

There will ever be times when the humble, dedicated and ethical Judge will worry over a decision . . . and doubt his own choice. There will ever be the occasional exhibit which has undeniable distinction, although it appears to defy all the principles. There will ever be the scrupulously correct design which "fits" but the result is so undistinguished!

The wise Judge recognizes these complexities as one of the mysteries of design to which the answer can only be found in ceaseless comparison, extensive study, informed observation and deeper understanding.

CRITICISM OF FELLOW JUDGES

Criticism of another's decision is anathema! Judges must discipline themselves with great patience toward the few who do not heed this taboo, but they should let him know firmly that such criticism is out of order. However, discussion after the show, with only the Judges present can be a helpful and educational process, mutually beneficial.

No Judge should express an opinion on an entry he has not helped judge, unless requested to do so by the entire panel which did judge it!

JUDGING WITH THE LESSER EXPERIENCED JUDGE

When judging with a lesser experienced or student Judge, the Judge must allow the beginner to express his opinion. He should be allowed his say and deserves the chance to vote on the merits of the exhibit.

If anyone of the panel is not allowed to state his opinon and scoring, he is not a working member and the other Judges are going contrary to a theory that "a jury of three establishes justice". Ethically, the stronger-minded or more experienced Judge will not pull rank. Equally, the lesser experienced Judge will listen closely and learn from his more advanced companions.

Beginning Judges often have a tendency to be too strict and technical . . . to exert too many rules. Experience usually will bring a more tolerant understanding. A student or beginner should not make the mistake of trying to impress the other Judges or the clerks but should sincerely attempt to broaden her knowledge through the privilege of serving with an experienced panel. Equally obnoxious is the Judge who is an authority or Judge in another field of activity, but who attempts to impress the panel with his medals and background. True knowledge, like truth, will out!

EXPEDIENCY

While a Judge is friendly, he should stick to business at hand. A show is scheduled to be opened to the public at a certain time and social conversation with other Judges or the clerks is improper.

The Judge must not allow over-lapping personal appointments to hurry him through the judging. To leave the Show before judging the last class assigned to one is an unforgivable breach of judging etiquette unless actual illness intervenes to render one incapable of proceeding.

Some Judges are slow as new teeth! Each exhibit offered is lectured upon . . . complete with details of what "should have been done". A panel of Judges should be able to judge 16-20 classes in the two to two and one-half hours allowed in the average show.

RECOGNIZING CREATIVITY

A good Judge has an empathy for and a belief in the worth, dignity and creative capacity of every individual human being. He does not penalize originality and creativity. He makes no preconceived analysis of a class, expecting all entries to conform to his ideas and penalizing those which do not.

Judging is methodical reasoned appreciation with tolerance of minor infractions of a principle as he was taught it. If beauty and distinction have been achieved, he gives credit and appreciates the skill involved. He looks first to see and praise what has been done rather than criticizing. He analyzes what was done well, as well as what was not.

A good Judge does not look only for the discovered and ordinary use of the elements and principles. He no longer penalizes for infractions of set rules when judging modern or abstract interpretations. He conscientiously strives to catch the spirit of the design, to probe for the impression the designer is communicating, permitting imagination to function, participating in the discovery of relationships with the exhibitor. What may seem at first to be the design deficiencies he checks carefully to possibly credit a more creative approach. He fully understands the characteristics of the different designs from Periods to traditional through modern to abstract.

The too-conservative Judge is restrained by rules and maintains a level of mediocrity. The progressive Judge aids advancement and development through expert evaluation and the realization that there are manys ways the artistic exhibitor may treat a subject within the latitude of the principles. He is a thinking Judge, alert to correct inequalities and well-meant but mistaken and unworkable rules and to accept changes in standards of perfection.

COURTESY TO SHOW PERSONNEL

Invitations and Thank Yous

Invitations must be accepted or declined promptly and politely. Notification should be given immediately if something prevents serving. If emergencies arise to prevent appearance, the Judge may suggest a substitute, but he should never arrange for a substitute without the authority of the Show or Judges' Chairman.

No matter how small or insignificant the show may seem to be . . . courtesy is expected. A heartfelt thank-you for hospitality extended and clippings sent is also expected etiquette.

Assignments

Upon arrival, a Judge should not ask for or demand special assignments. His fitness for the task should have been determined upon acceptance at which time the ethical Judge refuses any assignment for which he feels inadequate or does not want to handle. He should allow the Chairman to assign classes upon arrival if this was not arranged previously.

In preparing for a Show, the entire schedule should have been studied because in a small show one panel may finish their assigned classes and be asked to judge others to expedite the opening.

In many Fairs, a Judge is often expected to judge alone and to judge both artistic and horticultural classes. Any Judge accepting such assignments should feel confident to serve in both divisions or gain the needed knowledge before officiating, otherwise he should refuse the invitation.

If, upon receiving a Schedule, the Judge finds classes beyond his ability, he must notify the Judges' chairman to get another Judge. He may ask permission to come as an observer-judge to gain experience. To judge without knowledge is unfair to the exhibitor, to the visitor whose education is thwarted and to the other Judges who suffer under common criticism.

Criticism of the Locals

The ethical Judge does not make fun of or make disparaging remarks about the way a show Schedule is written or the manner in which the show is staged. Constructive comments given to the Committee will be much more appreciated than tactless remarks within the hearing of the clerks during the judging process.

When judging in an area other than one's own, the Judge will control any tendency to imply that his home area is more advanced, that the area where he is judging is behind the times. Such action is rude and unworthy of the trained Judge. Courtesy must extend to the clerks; they deserve the Judge's thanks at the completion of their duties.

CONSERVATION LISTS

In preparing to officiate, the Judge should make himself acquainted with the Conservation List of the State where he will be serving so as to be able to recognize those plants which may be freely used, used if home-grown or are definitely restricted in the area.

COGNIZANCE OF SCHEDULE REQUIREMENTS

The Judges must have fortified themselves with a complete understanding of any terms used in the Schedule. If ambiguous terms are discovered, consultation with the Flower Show or Judges' Chairman during the in-depth briefing period should clear up confusion before judging begins.

The Schedule should be referred to often during the judging of each class and the Judges must abide by its every word. Otherwise, they will be cheating the exhibitor who did abide. Judges should not be guilty of overlooking the general rules. For instance, a specialty show (iris, rose) general rules may state the specialty flower need not predominate to give the exhibitors more varied materials for creative designing. Some Judges ignore the better design and award the less well-done design featuring the flower of the show. READ THE ENTIRE SCHEDULE!

The exhibitor is entitled to assume that the Judges are fully qualified to intelligently judge all the classes and to fully understand the use of the point scales which is the mutual measuring stick used by both.

SERVICE

Ethics also means giving aid in the preparation of schedules. "They have the right to censure that have the heart to help". Judging is expedited and shows are improved by adequate schedules. Judges owe loyalty and obligation to local clubs and Fair Boards, for without them a Judge's knowledge would be for naught.

With much work and worry they sponsor the shows. In return they look to Judges for help and guidance in the staging of more beautiful shows; in the writing of more understandable schedules and the exhibition of high quality designs and specimens their advanced training should enable them to achieve.

Often a Judge is faced with the decision of accepting a judging appointment in a show "not of the fold" so to speak! Judging should be regarded as a public service and an opportunity to raise horticultural and artistic standards through awards to superior exhibits. By remaining in contact with such groups, the Judge educates and promotes excellent public relations which may have far-reaching consequences.

SPECIALIZATION—Personal Preference

Some Judges are caught in the mesh of specialization to the extent that if they are modernists they can see no worthy distinction or interest in the traditional; or if they are traditionalists they see no beauty, unity or plan in the abstract designs. Only by acceptance of the value of traditional as a decorative asset and modern and abstract as expressive or pure design can they be judged fairly.

The principles absorbed in earlier forms are the best possible foundation for judging the new. Judges must examine themselves for defective judging habits and salvage and carry over only constructive effort. Constant study arrests the erosion of judging ability.

They must not accept only the ordinary use of elements and principles, but must keep informed through continual study of the new trends and freedoms or else restrict themselves to those traditional classes. The modern Judge realizes the ultimate in beauty and art has not yet been reached. And he keeps searching for the knowledge that will enable him to recognize its possible appearance. To this end, a Judge is a Judge for ALL seasons . . . not just the flower show season. In lull periods, he reviews and replenishes his library with current books.

Though the things we get for nothing are all too often scorned, no smart Judge will overlook the valuable, though free information offered seasonally by the seed houses and nurseries. A study of the catalogs eliminates the embarrassment of being confronted with a new variety or color not available last season.

A Judge never allows himself to be unfairly influenced by his prejudices against or preference for any quality of a bloom or design. "I like or don't like" regarding variegation, color, form, newness, rarity, familiarity are the remarks of an immature Judge (see Obstacles to Objectivity).

Awards are to be based on the superiority of the color and of the whole specimen. Of course, if all things are equal between a common and a rare or new specimen, the consideration of rarity, difficulty of culture or newness could be a determining factor.

The Judge is aware of the fact that the reason the public disagrees with the awards is that they judge on prejudice and emotion, an "I like" syndrome based on the visual impact of color, texture and design; while Judges reasonably evaluate by point-scored qualities according to accepted principles of design and standards of perfection. Judges supplement sight with informed opinion and consider creativity, distinction and interpretation based on experience and shows they have seen. As a rule, the general public ignores or misunderstands these last three qualities, which often determine the winners.

JUDGING JUNIOR-HIGH SCHOOL CLASSES

If it is likely the Judge will be asked to officiate in the Junior-High School division, he must familiarize himself with the age groups and anticipated ability. Juniors deserve the same attention given the adult section. In judging, there should be no let-down of merit! The competitive aspect which awards high quality is not furthered by Judges who mistakenly seek to "encourage" and fail to consider the deficiencies, though a Judge expects each exhibit to be of a quality commensurate with the age group in the class.

The indiscriminate awarding of ribbons in the Junior-High School division is not compatible with their daily school experiences where an English question or a math problem is either right or it's wrong. They know they don't get an "A" or even a "C" just for submitting a paper, though all the answers are wrong! Respect their feelings by honest awarding.

LOCALITY VARIATIONS

Judges should make themselves aware of the limitations of the area and the club in general. Upon being admitted to the hall, a quick glance over the whole show will give a general idea of the calibre so the Judge will not expect too much or too little upon turning his attention to the individual exhibits.

The show which has a number of outstanding exhibits is judged more tightly than one which is generally mediocre. A Judge must take into consideration the age, experience and size of the club. A group which has not had the years of exposure to top-flight instructors and regular meetings of flora-art group activity or the availability of superior instruction in the techniques of expert practice in horticulture requires a more tolerant approach.

A Judge should be willing to accede to special requests of the Show Committee unless such requests would conflict in some way with his training. "Acts of God" as concerns weather are taken into account as well as the cultural advantages of the area. On occasions where weather just prior to show time has been especially injurious to blooms, the Judge may be requested to be lenient in appraising physical damage and is justified in granting the request.

The cultural advantages vary greatly within just a few miles. A rose grown in an area where soil conditions, moisture and other factors are exactly to its needs will be a superior bloom to one grown in a less hospitable area. However, blue ribbons must be awarded to those roses which are the BEST grown in that particular locale. If a Judge is unfamiliar with local variations, he should request to be teamed with Judges who are and allow himself to be guided by their knowledge and advice.

OPEN JUDGING

While many Fairs and some Flower Shows still allow the public to be present during the judging process, such action does interfere with confidential deliberation which is not compatible with interference, whether active or passive on the part of the bystanders.

Many Shows and Fairs maintain that allowing the presence of people other than actual show personnel in the rooms is a means of educating the public. However, most Judges feel such education can perhaps be handled under more opportune circumstances.

It is the rare Judge who can effectively come to unbiased decision if, in the background, he hears groans and whispered comments. However, some Judges actually enjoy the challenge of making verbal decisions and if able to communicate clearly this will serve to educate the audience.

If a Judge accepts an invitation and then finds he is expected to judge with an audience, he should graciously make the best of the situation and avail himself of this chance to verbally show how judging is actually accomplished according to standards of perfection and not merely by Judge's whim.

ARTIFICIAL MATERIALS

Because the use of artificial flowers and foliage defeats the fundamental concept of educating through the use of plants, Judges should not themselves use artificial flowers or foliages when making public demonstrations.

EXHIBITING

A Judge can no more judge his own design than he can tickle himself and laugh! The ethical Judge should excuse himself from any class or better yet . . . any SHOW in which he has entries in competition.

If the remaining Judges are unable to agree on their choices, they should appeal to another panel of Judges. If no other panel is available, they should appeal to the Judges' Chairman to act or to appoint a deputy to serve in that particular class. If the exhibit in question enters competition for a higher award, the Judge must again step aside.

From a public relations standpoint, it is far better to refuse judging assignments in any show in which the Judge intends to exhibit, as such practice often leaves the Judge himself, his fellow Judges and the Show personnel open to criticism, however unjustified it may be. The public does not know which sections a Judge served or that he excused himself, and eyebrows are raised when a Judge's name appears among the winners.

A Judge will never judge a flower or design if he can in any way identify the exhibitor and FEELS THIS MAY INFLUENCE his decision either way.

APPEARANCE

Tastefully selected and appropriate apparel are prerequisite for the Judge . . . it should go without saying. A careless, untidy appearance often presupposes an untidy mind and is not conducive to respect of ability.

ATTITUDE

A Judge's attitude must complement his aptitude. To be knowledgeable is not enough . . . a dull, dead approach to judging can take all the joy out of a flower show for everyone concerned. A light touch based on deep understanding is emphasized. "Oh, Lord, keep me alive as long as I live" is an excellent credo for Judges.

Joy can be brought to judging by maintaining a sincere, enthusiastic approach. A grim and dictatorial attitude is as out of place as an insect on a specimen! If the feet hurt . . . slip on "flats" and SMILE . . . the whole Flower Show Committee will love you for it!

Joy in judging comes through enthusiasm . . .

> . . . enthusiasm comes through self-confidence
> . . . self-confidence comes through knowledge
> . . . knowledge comes through study.

Study of what?

> . . . the National Council of Garden Club publications
> . . . the Plant Society Handbooks
> . . . the current books relative to horticulture and design
> . . . the seed catalogs
> . . . the plants — growing and showing
> . . . the floral designs . . . yours and others.

And where will this lead?

> . . . to wisdom in conduct. With every Judge studying the same material unity and uniformity, which are the underlying goals, will be the evolutionary result. How expediently this will come about is each Judge's personal responsibility.

The ethical Judge remembers that his attitude and manners will affect the many others who serve as Judges. He keeps an open mind, avoids bias, examines himself before and after each assignment to discover if personal tastes or past experience influenced his decisions.

After some Judges attain a certain amount of status . . . a certificate or a title, they not only settle down, they "bog" down. For some, those titles are like a tranquilizing thalidomide . . . giving birth to an ill-formed infant of smug complacency. At this point, the three "I" sins usually show up; indifference, ignorance and indecision. Being complacent with one's ability and knowledge and indifferent to changing aspects is detrimental to the up-to-date application of justice in flower show judging.

It is the responsibility of the Judge to keep himself well informed. He must continue to mature in knowledge and experience by supplementing study with attendance at lectures and schools, by giving programs and exhibiting. He will gain much by exposing himself to the allied arts of painting, interior decoration, architecture and sculpture. The principles are the same, the freedoms are inspiring and the rewards are satisfying.

Only in this way can we conquer judging's new frontiers and cultivate the ability to recognize, appreciate, evaluate and give credit for the inspiration and creativity of the designer and the cultural skill of the grower. As Goethe so wisely said, "He who is ignorant of foreign languages knows not his own." Judgment without wisdom is impossible. As the Judge matures he will bring insight, sensitivity and understanding as well as self-control, kindness, discernment and humility to the task.

Perhaps the best full-scale definition is that Ethics is wisdom in conduct, which involves consistency, courage, tact, responsibility and most particularly up-to-date knowledge. These are the qualities of ethics.

Learning to judge isn't accomplished overnight. Beginning Judges should not be impatient for maturity. When Nature wishes to grow an oak she spends fifty years or more doing it . . . only little things like radishes can be matured in a month. Is your goal to be a radish or an oak-type Judge?

Obstacles to Objectivity

Judicial action at its best implies fairness, impartiality, utter lack of prejudice and a thoroughly objective approach to the problem at hand.

Though judgment must be based on objectivity to arrive at fairness, we must recognize that there are many obstacles to objectivity which can influence the mind without a Judge even being aware of them. Human nature cannot be changed of course; all that can be done is to expose these reactions in the hope that such exposure will aid in the examination of each Judge's judging patterns with improvements being made wherever necessary and possible.

These hidden influences include:

A—Personal reactions
       1) experiences (Lily of the Valley, death)
       2) preference (Mother wore pink, I LOVE pink)
       3) unconscious gravitation to color (human failing)
       4) familiarity

B—Cultural Background
       1) personal environment, education
       2) nationality traits
          (A Chinese might reveal his national preferences

for color and line restraint, or a German for order or an Italian for brilliant color)

C—Reputation, status
(of other Judges on the panel)

D—Resistance to Change
1) ego
2) mental laziness

E—Mood
1) dislike of a panel member
2) overdrawn at the bank
3) illness, discomfort (hurting feet)
4) poor working conditions (hot, cold, poor lighting)

It is always helpful to carefully examine one's motives from time to time, a practice which may reveal that the Judge is being influenced unduly by unconscious motivations.

Indications are that humans are naturally attracted to certain colors. For instance, the colors of yellow, lavender, blue, pinks and reds will draw the human eye quicker than others, and the Judge must be conscious of this human tendency and judge all qualities as objectively as possible. It is extremely difficult for some Judges to see the same beauty in darker varieties and brown and green flowers as in pastels. For this reason, some societies insist on schedule divisions between light and dark blends, and other color combinations.

A Judge, if he is normal, reacts very definitely to color; color is a very personal "visual sensation" and it takes training to divorce one's self from affirmative and adverse reactions to it. The bright, advancing colors in full chroma or tints usually impress an individual favorably, while the colors which lean toward the dark purple-to-black may cause a mental reaction tying the color to a mood of gloom, somberness, depression or melancholy or a funereal impression which will cause him to reduce points for color without really analyzing the reason or whether the reason is truly based on sound fact.

Strong opinions on the "place" of color also affect some Judges' opinions. Just as some people often feel "women's PLACE is in the home," these Judges FEEL the PLACE for Green is in trees and grass, not flowers, or they may LIKE any color "as long as it is red."

Flowers which contain two or more essentially unharmonious colors such as dahlias of full chroma red and yellow, or brown Iris with blue signals and orange beards may appeal to some and repel others. Such personal reactions are obstacles to objectivity and must be firmly put aside, while the Judge concentrates on the clarity and purity of the color, or lack of clarity and purity which affects the color.

Any preference is a kind of prejudice, prejudice is one thing, discrimination is something else. Prejudice is a matter of belief and discrimination is a mode of behavior. Prejudice can be FOR as well as

AGAINST. Discrimination is always AGAINST. Many variables enter into the equation, and strongest among these may be cultural background, environment and education.

Sociologists agree that involuntary group memberships and the ascribed status that accompany them in a given society are relatively fixed. They can sometimes be changed but in general it is difficult to withdraw from the ingrown reactions which are a result of group indoctrination. Middle "class" often has trouble empathizing with upper and lower "classes". Values and thought waves are different due to past experiences, environment and education.

Another influencing factor against objectivity is based on relationships. The reputation or status of a Judge on the panel can exert a subtle influence through fear of dissension or a desire to "be on the side of superiority." For instance, a known preference of the Senior Judge for abstract or pink might lead a less experienced Judge to vote up that particular exhibit because she thinks (albeit unconsciously) that the Senior Judge might select it also. A fear of dissension may keep a meek Judge from expressing an opinion when judging with an outspoken or dominant Judge.

Objective judgment leaves no room for being unduly swayed by another, if you are convinced otherwise. Of course, majority rules, but sometimes it is the dominant Judge, rather that the majority doing the ruling.

Resistance to change may be based on ego and pride of position. A position such as being the State's **first** Master Judge, or a Professor or a Specialized Society Judge or an author can so influence one that, if also connected to mental laziness and a failure to keep up, through disinterest or other reasons, judging and fair decisions suffer. It isn't enough to hold ground; we must progress.

A Judge must never allow himself to be unfairly influenced by a prejudice or preference for or discrimination against any quality of a bloom, such as a variation in form, newness, rarity or long familiarity with the variety. And the same applies to design. Many old cliches have more than a grain of truth in them, and the old one which says "Familiarity breeds contempt" applies here. Some Judges tend to go "overboard" for anything new on the basis that "if it's new, it must be better." This is not necessarily true, as some older varieties are still accepted as the standard of perfection while many newer ones have fallen by the wayside after being highly touted as "the best". The single Hybrid Tea Rose, "Dainty Bess", is a classic example. A Judge must learn moderation and to wait, to watch and to weigh each new introduction and not allow himself to be unduly influenced by what psychologists call the "obsolescence syndrome" in which everything must be the latest to be the best!

Fragrance in the horticultural specimens is a very subtle and vexing thing to evaluate. Memory comes to play a part in the judgment of fragrance, hampering the Judge's objectivity. Some treasured moment or some unhappy experience can trigger the memory and sneakily influence the Judge to regard the odor as unacceptable while others find it sweet and desirable. While the majority of the qualities on the judging scales are visually judged and glasses assist those who have poor vision, a sense of smell varies in individuals, and the Judge may not be conscious of any lack or lessening of the sense of smell due to olfactory damages, smoking habits or other limiting factors. However, if they suspect, or are aware of any handicap in this area, they should ethically defer the judging of flowers in which fragrance is a factor (lilacs, sweetpeas, etc.) to other Judges not so afflicted. Characteristic odor of a plant (marigold) or a tendency to get hayfever (goldenrod) can influence a Judge in artistic classes if he is not careful to avert such.

Long familiarity with a plant can affect judgment also. There is the classic example of the person who wouldn't give a blue ribbon to an arrangement of calla lilies "because they grow like weeds here!" Such discrimination is not only unfair, but it raises an embarrassing question regarding such person's qualifications to judge!

Trite as it may sound, the mood the Judge is in may play a part in his evaluations. Just as a quarrel before leaving home may upset a man so badly, he exhibits poor judgment and has a car accident, so the Judge may allow upsetting problems in his own life to influence his decisions. If the Judge who is ill, tired or his feet are hurting unbearably approaches a class in which one designer has created a very jagged, restless, modern design in brilliant orange-red (the psychological reaction to red is danger, orange is fight), his non-objective reaction might be very unfavorable.

Or tip the scale the other way, the feet are still hurting, but here's a restful design, in soothing colors, and without knowing why, the Judge might feel comforted and give the last a higher score.

Of course, it is not possible to limit judging only to those days when one feels on top of the world, or when working conditions and companions are congenial. But being conscious of how influences can affect objectivity is a long step in the direction of fair decisions.

Judgment must be on reason, not caprice. When decisions are based on appropriate standards, they represent wise judgment. Haphazard choices based on guesses, rationalization or whims are of little value.

Gestalt and Judging

Objectivity is mainly conscious trained effort in most people. During thirty-six years of close observation of Judges who had been similarly trained, this author isolated patterns of sub-conscious response apparent in all ages, and both sexes, of a non-verbal 'vocabulary' bespeaking definite reactions to color, lines, forms, textures, positions, space and motion which led to her popular lecture and book "GESTALT & FLORAL DESIGN . . . JUDGING." This original research and application was the first to apply gestalt to flower show design and judging.

In the early 1900s psychologists isolated a concept of human behavior they called 'gestalt,' defined as "the theory of visual perception and response to lines, forms, colors and how we organize what we see as a whole." The gestalt or whole effect is determined by the relationship of the parts perceived, and is unconsciously evaluated differently by all because of personal past life experiences, including education, religion, health, even right and left handedness. Research on right-left brain concepts also shows effects relative to gestalt perception.

Gestalt psychology has always been akin to art. Rudolph Arnheim ("ART & VISUAL PERCEPTION") writes "that the realization of a whole cannot be attained by adding up isolated parts is not new to artists. At no time could a work of art have been made or understood by minds unable to conceive the integrated structure as a whole."

We in floral design recognize in this comment the concept of "plastic organization" (p. 387) where careful selection and positions which carry the eye to all dimensions results not in confusion, but fusion into an aesthetic whole. Picasso said "plastic rhymes are forms that rhyme with one another." Arnheim's statement also accords with "distinction" (p. 336) where every detail contributes to the entire aesthetic effect while still emphasizing the beauty of the component parts. An object seen in conjunction with another may look different from the way it appears by itself, or as it would appear in companionship with yet another object. Advanced floral designers and Judges of this specialized art are fully cognizant that items used in design react upon each other, personal emotional involvement and reaction are added to what is seen . . . a magical alchemy takes place . . . an alchemy that changes a collection of disparate, eclectic objects into a work of art. In the same way, the combination of conscious and under-conscious motivations make up the Judge's personal 'gestalt.'

For many years Judges were instructed to be objective, to keep themselves above any personal reactions. The truth is that such action goes against the real purpose of all art, and further, is impossible to achieve. The point is that a Judge must be aware of metaphysical (hidden) motivations, learn to recognize deepest reactions and then moderate her behavior when judging someone else's artistic effort.

To modify is impossible unless the Judge recognizes her own personality type. A staggering array of research proves the introvert and extrovert evaluate and react differently to visual stimuli . . . even the number of ribbons given or withheld may hinge on personal gestalt. However, if a Judge knows how she reacts based on personality, she will be able to adjust judgments thus becoming more fair and objective. Judges with synthetic attitudes, a quality of extroverts, tend to see perceptual fields as an integrated whole. Their fault may lie in overlooking details. Whereas the introverted analytic fragments the whole, studies each detail separately and her fault may be in overlooking creativity of the whole in minute breakdown of parts. Most people have a tendency to find it easiest, by nature, to use one style over the other; neither is better . . . only different, and naturally as Judges, we arrive at different decisions. Native confidence and cautiousness interacts with decision-making. A confident person tries to see the entire design at a single glance and is sincerely confident she has seen it all; when challenged, will fill in more details than were actually included. A cautious, hesitating Judge takes one thing at a time, and may emphasize certain details over others, or the whole. Is it any wonder police have trouble getting the same story from several witnesses at an accident? Various traits isolated by psychologists are applicable to judging as follows:

INTROVERT
(also termed subjective, analytic, leveler, verbalizers, form-bounded)

- concentrates on details, is practical, passive, independent, drifts
- overlooks whole, uses reason, comparison, patient
- retreats into self, allows self to enter into decision, emotional
- sees more but sees less accurately, clearly; often diffident.
- eliminates complexity, cautious
- perceives color gradations less easily thus related harmonies less highly rated; prefers unified symmetrical, period, traditional, conventional designs and use of principles; smooth rhythm, contrasts easy, not jarring.
- prefers risk of saying "no" incorrectly to saying "yes" incorrectly thus gives fewer ribbons
- tend to see movement differently
- stickler for rules
- less appreciative of creativity
- may have difficulty in seeing through subtle theme interpretations and non-objective designing
- prefers cool, receding, passive colors; difficulty in judging abstract designs in which objects are barely recognizable or in unusual positions
- looks for something familiar
- tends to 'see' what expects to see; requires time to see complexity
- more conscious of, and influenced by intruding environment ('visual noise')
- disturbed if visual weight is equated, feels low center of gravity gives stability, thus has problem judging kinetic designs; feels threatened by 'loose ends;' prefers order and obvious harmony; tends to "tunnelize," sees all objects from frontal perspective
- sees a "wire" cube as having "walls" in practical sense of space
- tends to think they know best what "belongs;" mourns yesterday's "proper" proportion and scale; sees spaces as "holes" or "voids"; finds oral commenting and defending decisions difficult; good at writing comments

EXTROVERT
(also termed synthetic, sharpener, objective, form-labile, visualizer)

- sees whole, overlooks and modifies details; accurate size and scale judgment; active, energetic, competitive, quick; somewhat aggressive
- independent; confident; facile
- prefers complexity; highly rates subdivision, equated interest, plastic org.; emphasis on differences; stresses slant, obliqueness
- leans toward strong color, form, textural contrasts, asymmetrical designs stressing diagonal slanting lines, abstract in construction and concept; pointscores higher, gives more awards; less inhibited; shows and appreciates imagination, creativity
- more tolerant of use, even abuse of principles; unconsciously swayed by super theme interpretation to point of ignoring design or attention to details and rules; manipulates shapes, positions mentally thus less offended by imbalance, etc.
- responds to expressive communication
- prefers warm, advancing, active color
- accepts incongruous combinations, ways
- enjoys subtle repetitions ('hidden delights of design'); appreciates flora manipulation, unusual positions, strong tensional pulls; easily adjusts to space as a material thing having shape, texture, directions, etc.
- too contemptuous of 'status quo'
- constantly aware that solid objects have another 'side,' 'sees' other side in plastic manner
- applies closure to equate interest which vitalizes plastic organization
- denigrates some things as common, ordinary, unimportant; tend to think they know best what is "art;" likes surprises, dislikes sameness, monotony
- readily accepts today's exaggerations of proportion, scale; may 'talk' a good story, but fail to comment concisely, constructively

Either type may be creative to a more or lesser degree which also affects evaluation.

LESS CREATIVE
- concentrates, focuses too hard
- prefers order, sameness, practicality; sees "time" as slow serene movement, flat prairies, long sweeps of history; apt

MORE CREATIVE
- amplifies sights, sounds, stimuli
- feels shock, noise more intensely
- sees "time" as dynamic, fast paced, jet plane, events in history

to describe self as contented, rational, virtuous; suspicious, hostile to "new;" finds fault, analyzes defects; must check hostility toward "novel," giving creators credit; daydream at low alpha wave levels; honors conformity, "as-isness"

- apt to describe self as impulsive, uninhibited, enthusiastic; marked preference for odd, differences
- when faced with "new" gets excited, involved, overlooks, ignores difficulties; daydreams at high alpha wave levels; not intentionally accentric but do process information differently; treasure controversy, change

Buried in our subconscious is much symbolism and many superstitions relative to color and these overlap our emotional responses. Color engineers have found a cold cream in a dark brown package will stay on the shelf far longer than one in a delicate pink jar. Refer to Color, p. 331. Color blindness is a problem sufferers are aware of, but they may not know that with one form all colors appear greyed which presents unique difficulties for fairly assessing color relationships or purity and clarity in horticultural specimens.

It's been found that overweight people over-respond to color, texture and food clues in their environment. They are drawn to 'edible' colors. A lean persons sees only a green leaf, but a fat person sees a succulent minty leaf next to luscious berry-red dahlias intermixed with whipped-cream white baby's breath, and may be unconsciously influenced to place an award.

If a person finds it difficult to identify an object, she begins to feel doubtful, uncertain, uncomfortable and finally irritated. The next reaction is attempting to rid herself of unpleasant reactions by simply dismissing the whole thing. She doesn't even know that she is unconsciously ignoring the thing which seems to be out of place, upside down or too unfamiliar to identify adequately. Or a Judge may unconsciously give more credence to an accessory than it really has. For example, the class is to feature plant material, one design contains a Madonna. A devout Catholic Judge may feel the figure is dominating the plant material or throwing design off balance, while an agnostic Judge gives the Madonna less visual attention. The devout Judge may be unconsciously letting her personal emotional response interweave with fair objective judgment.

How many times have you heard an elderly Judge remark that she no longer drives at night, and you sympathize without realizing this can affect her judging ability. Details of shapes and colors and how clearly they stand out from the background, and ability to evaluate is impaired especially if the design is staged under low light conditions, the problem is maximized if the design is also complex or made up of many small objects or includes unfamiliar objects or positions, or if the Judge happens to also be an introvert! The solution is to request more light and take more time to fairly evaluate the design.

The "handedness" of people affects their perceptive reactions. Psychologist Gaffron says "vision to the right in the right-handed person is more articulate, objects on the right seem more conspicuous." Left-handed Judges should be aware that their position perception is unique, and quite often opposite of the majority of right-handed arrangers. Analyze your attitudes!

Closure, where the eye and psyche complete an interval, is absolutely necessary in designs employing the technique of equating interest and plastic organization as the eye must be directed to weave a visual path from one area of visual impact to the next in visually creating the whole. In one test, persons were shown a vertical and a horizontal line separated at their corners by a space. Some filled in the square corner, a few moved the horizontal up to meet vertical, others joined the two with a slanted line. This indicates we do not see closure and movement of line direction in the same way, therefore do not judge it the same.

Until this century's last few decades women were excluded from serious art, and surrounded by adjectives such as sweet, refined, emotional, pastel. The result of such stereotyping is an ingrained reluctance to take women artists seriously. The one area where women's art has increasingly refuted the stereotype of sweet harmony has been modern floral design. The 50's finally released creativity, and women used all types of materials to make designs that were major, direct, intellectual, primary statements . . . and worthy of the name "art." Judging floral art is done mainly by women . . . some of whom are still themselves cast in the stereotyped mold, thinking arrangements should only be sweet, refined, pastel, decorative . . . and not expressive of strong, private inner sensations and drives. Truth is, there is a place for both the decorative classics as well as the direct, intellectual primary statement, and Judges must be prepared to evaluate both equally well, fairly, objectively.

The gestalt way of perceiving floral arrangement is a plastic interplay between the design and the nature of the observer. Judges must train themselves to appreciate the object's influence in plastic organization and how it interacts with the other components. In applying the gestalt theory we have to relate back to the personalities of Judges which brings us to Hame'l's Law of Aesthetic Attitudes as applied to floral art. "The first observer finds it difficult to see beauty in the 'common' onion even if beauty is lent by position and companion parts. The second sees only a target form which looks the same each time, she does not downgrade it as a common onion, but merely accepts it as 'expected' of an onion of certain size and maturity. The third aesthetic attitude properly acknowledges the interplay between surroundings and object, fully appreciating, enjoying and analyzing the infinite and often profound, sometimes puzzling changes the design undergoes due to textural contrasts, repetitions, illuminations, afterimages, overlapping and positions. For her, the peeled white onion takes on red-violet reflections from red and purple companions. Shadows enhance the roundness, the glossy texture is enriched by the contrasting background's roughness. The interactions make the total more interesting and beautiful than any lone part. To this Judge everything interacts, reflects upon and contributes to the beauty and interest of every other thing."

Obviously the third type is the ideal visual attitude and can be termed the "bio-vert" type of personality, trained, observant and aware. Those Judges, having been made aware of their native tendencies which are apt to restrict fair judging, must adjust and modify their reactions to assure fair evaluations. Since some of us are more cautious and conventional, and others too quick and controversial we must retrain ourselves to strike a happy medium. The intelligent observer learns to modify inborn traits and to adopt those of others which prove beneficial. If we are too quick, we may overlook important details; if we are too detail-prone, overall perception may be restricted. If after honestly analyzing your personality type, you realize you incline to superficial scanning . . . modify, learn to search attentively, study closely, select particular details, mentally go through the principles, analyze the parts as well as appreciate the whole. This gestalt approach works when we come to know and understand our own subjective reactions, and knowing them, know enough to modify behavior in the interests of fair judging.

Judging Procedure

The borderline between ethics and judging procedure is thin and often overlaps. The actual act of judging is an operation of the mind involving comparison to an ideal, and evaluation of merit out of which definite conclusions are reached. When decisions are based on appropriate standards, they represent wise judging. Haphazard choices based on guess, psychological influences or whims have little value. Periodically, the Judge should check the standards by which his decisions are reached and check his ability to apply the standards efficiently.

The Judge should arrange to arrive on time and report promptly to the Chairman of Judges for the briefing period. He should be prepared with any points regarding the Schedule which he feels need clarification.

After the briefing session, when any special instructions have been absorbed, the Panel is escorted by their clerks to the first class. Having already become familiar with the Schedule and briefed, the Judge needs but a moment or two for a quick, comprehensive survey of the general overall quality of the Show. Judges are a bit more lenient with inexperienced or small shows, but it must be remembered that a drastic relaxation of standards will tend to defeat the purpose.

APPRAISAL AND DECISION

The first order of business is to carefully check the number of entries. If the class has been properly staged, it will appear as one distinct unit.

In fairness to every exhibitor, the Judges definitely examine each and every entry in the class before them. Each Judge approaches the adjudgment systematically without undue haste.

Elimination

In judging classes which contain many entries, it is usually comparatively simple and saves a great deal of time, to as rapidly as possible sort out those which appear to have the best chance of winning. Those eliminated must be carefully examined to make certain no qualities are missed. All misclassified entries, horticulture which is lacking in show quality due to age, immaturity and artistic designs which lack design or conformity are eliminated. This reduces the class to those which are qualified and reasonably normal or artistic.

The process of elimination can be handled either mentally or by asking the clerk (in horticultural classes) to move only those under final consideration to a separate table to be carefully appraised in good light and without crowding. If the Schedule requests named varieties in any horticultural class, the Judge must consider this in judging, deducting the amount listed in that plant's particular scale. He must be cognizant of the local variations in size and color, however, before declaring a specimen misnamed. A Judge is not required to NAME the varieties, but to know if the name given is correct.

The vast assortment of similar varieties within some plant families adds confusion. Some, under different names, are so similar that a microscopic examination by "experts" is needed to distinguish one from another. Faced with this flood of nearly identical varieties, the Judge must often trust the labeling and rely on the current standards of perfection.

Making the decision

Often, it is not easy to separate the top two or three entries for awards, but this difficulty is usually resolved after thought and quiet discussion, followed by point-scoring if needed. The time element does not always permit point-scoring of an entire show, but it must be resorted to in close decisions.

If each panel member is well trained, experienced and conscientious, there will be no irreconcilable differences of opinion between them regarding the merits of the entries. Such minor differences as do exist are simply reconciled by discussion and adjustment. If unable to convince colleagues of the justness of his own decision, the Judge should bow gracefully to majority rule, realized through point-scoring and try to support it.

Judges do not have time to sleep on their decisions. The cliche that time brings an uncertain situation to a head is not compatible to the procedure of judging in a Flower Show. There is not time for decisions to ripen, or feelings to jell or to call in other experts for advice.

Nor is there such a thing as a flexible decision. The first decision must be accurate and fair with little or no chance of retraction. Too much backing and forthing confuses the issues and reduces confidence in the Judge's ability.

Factual discussion among the Judges as to the merits and demerits eases the decision-making task. By having all the facts in mind, by talking over the entries with the Panel and by point-scoring, each Judge's thoughts are sorted out and clarified. In this way few points are missed and few poor decisions made.

INDICATING THE WINNERS

It is a safety procedure for the Senior Judge to note the award on each entry card. The ribbons can be placed later, thus speeding the judging process while minimizing the possibility of a clerk misplacing a ribbon in her hurry to keep up with the group.

REASONABLE SPEED

While a Judge should acquire reasonable speed in reaching a decision, it is discourteous to the conscientious Judge for his team to hurry on to the next class before his decision is made known. The head Judge of the Panel should make sure all Judges have given their decisions before instructing the clerks and marking the card.

Judges often spend excessive time on the first few entries, and may find themselves without enough time to give each deserving exhibit its proper consideration as they near opening time. Too much discussion over any one class is never desirable, or fair to all exhibitors. If the Judges know the number of classes (even approximately) and the amount of total time until opening of the show, they can determine whether five or fifteen minutes can be spent with each.

Because Fairs often provide only one Judge for an extensive number of exhibits, the judging must necessarily extend over a period of several hours. The Horticultural Judge can suggest that the awarding of the more fragile blossoms such as hemerocallis, roses, etc., be judged before drafts, heat and aging take their toll.

REMEMBER THE CLERKS: Conversation

Behind every successful man stands a surprised mother-in-law and behind every Judge stands a listening clerk whose ears are sharply attuned to every word.

Even if they could hear every word uttered, the clerks would unfortunately still get only hints of the Judges' reasoning because they seldom say aloud everything they think when the qualities of an exhibit are obvious. Often only the most trivial reactions are aired. Usually only in close competition are all decision-making aspects of the matter analyzed out loud.

These comments on often unimportant aspects, combined with comparative silence on obvious points often give an entirely erroneous impression of the points really under consideration and the reason for award placements. The Judge should be aware of this and try to avoid the impression of placing too much stress upon an unimportant point.

Conversation even in jest among the Judges, should be prudent, discreet and to the point. Caustic or sarcastic remarks serve no purpose and result in embarrassment and resentment. Such conduct creates disrespect for the Judges as a group. Clerks and Judges should regard discussions held during the process as confidential.

TOOLS

Judges must be provided with a Schedule, scales of points if not printed in the Schedule, any specific additional instructions, pencil and any other helpful item or information pertinent to the task. Measuring devices are not provided as Classification Committee will have passed entries for exhibit. If a measurement seems unreasonably over or under size as per scheduled requirements, Judges may deduct points wherever applicable (i.e. size in Hort. or conformity, interpretation in Artistic) Judge from distance of 3 feet.

RECLASSIFICATION

The reclassification of exhibits leads to confusion of records and lost time for all concerned, and it is hoped that the Classification Committee and Staging Committee have everything in order to avoid the problem. If the Judges do find an exhibit which does not fit the Schedule, they may, out of courtesy, ask the Committee to reclassify to a more fitting one. If there is no other class suitable or if the request is refused, the Judges proceed with the judging, removing enough points so the exhibit cannot win an award which it would not deserve because of lack of conformity or misinterpretation. Even artists must follow the rules. If the artistic scale supplied has no quality of con-

formity, points may be removed under distinction. Judges deduct under scale, proportion if design defies Schedule limits. A misplaced or misclassed exhibit should not be returned to a class already judged, nor should judging be redone to accommodate it. If all class requirements are met, Classification approves entry, Judges then evaluate, eliminate. See p. 40. Judges should not be expected to count stems, this is the duty of Classification Committee. Many Schedules state such exhibits will be eliminated with no attempt to adjust error if not discovered before Judges reach the class. Exhibitors often bring extra specimens and forget to remove, but the error is theirs.

JUDGING "AS IS"

No Judge should be expected to foresee when a flower will be past its prime and perhaps shatter, or if it will open to perfect form within the hour or the day. Nor can he be expected to evaluate a design as it was before a line shifted or a flower opened or withered to disrupt the balance. He must evaluate only as he sees the exhibit at the MOMENT OF JUDGING.

HANDLING

Sometimes the temptation to correct a leaning branch is almost *impossible to resist, but resist one must! Vibratiles may be touched to test sound, but no others. If an artistic design is crowded, Judges may ask clerks to rearrange the grouping so each can receive full attention without color or line intrusion from another.*

In most areas, the handling of horticulture is also frowned upon. The reason being that room temperatures plus heat and chemicals on the hands affect flower freshness and lasting quality. Textures can be seen as well as felt, freshness can be seen! Substance can be detected in the angles at which the petals and leaves are held in the bloom or on the stem. Light shining through the petals shows thinning of substance. If a closer look is needed, the container may be lifted or a pencil gently run under the petals or foliage. When qualities relative to the stem are concerned, it may be necessary to carefully remove the specimen from its container, clear glass alleviates this problem. Undue jostling or rough handling should be avoided.

One sometimes hears the statement that an artistic design should be viewed from at least three feet back, like a painting. Thus, the full beauty can be better appreciated. Certainly picayune faults apparent only upon "eyeball" inspection should not determine the placement. If wiring, soil or distracting mechanics are easily apparent deduction is made, of course.

THE "ANY OTHER" CLASS

Often a Judge is confronted with a class which is a hodge-podge of confusion . . . a class where there is no common basis for judging as happens in the "any other" horticultural class and often houseplants section in small shows. One type is never judged against the other. Each is judged against perfection for that particular plant and awards placed accordingly.

DECISIONS ARE FINAL

The Flower Show Committee can ask the Judges to review a class and if it wasn't done previously to point-score to make sure no quality was overlooked. However, it is the JUDGE OR JUDGES who decide if the award should be changed after careful review.

When a class has been properly judged, there is seldom any question by competing exhibitors or by a visitor as to the decision. But should a question be raised the careful, courteous Judge should be able to promptly point out valid reasons for his choice, using words and manner which are intended to be helpful rather that dictatorial or resentful.

The Judge should not permit the clerks to expose the names of competitors for special awards until after the judging is entirely finished.

WITHHOLDING AWARDS: COURAGE

Firmness and courage are necessary because an honest Judge will refuse to accede to improper requests. He will refuse to place unearned awards. But he will insist that real merit be justly rewarded. The worthy Judge will refuse to tolerate compromise with honesty and fair play.

He has the privilege of withholding awards if the exhibits are inferior generally. The best of a very poor class may not receive any ribbon at all, or only a second or third award may be made as merited in the Judge's opinion.

Various Plant Societies and the National Council of Garden Clubs have strict rules for the presentation of their coveted top awards. The Judge should not hesitate to withhold these if no exhibit meets the stated requirements. A "Recognition" award, given to an excellent exhibit which did not QUITE score high enough to merit the top award, carries with it at least as much prestige in the opinion of the general public. It allows some exhibitors to achieve the recognition her work deserves yet without making the Judge go against her training of giving the top awards only when they are truly merited according to the very high requirements. The Judge will not refuse to give a "Special Notice" in lieu of the other awards if it is listed in the Schedule and the entry merits this extra distinction over and above the other exhibits.

Special local awards may be given if merited and if listed in the Schedule. A Judge also needs courage to stand up and question any tradition or rule or idea and to ask "can the job be done another way". Look back, but look forward too!

OF NO CONCERN

The Judge does not concern himself with the following:

- who arranged the design
- who grew the material
- who is an amateur or professional
- the meaning of ambiguous schedule terms (get FS Comm. opinion)
- the Sweepstakes Awards
- such matters as counting, regrouping entries, division of classes, *misplaced entries. Refer to proper classification. p. 40.*

Point - Scoring

Point-scoring involves the use of a score card upon which certain qualities deemed important by the makers, are allotted points to total 100 points or ideal, perfection.

VALUE

Scales of points should be printed in the Schedule for the benefit of the exhibitors, Judges and the public. The exhibitors and the public are entitled to know the standards by which the exhibits are judged. They should know the relative weight to be given each characteristic of the entries. Exhibitors have the right to feel confident that the Judges use the same standards which they try to follow in selecting their blooms and constructing their design for competition. By studying the scales, the exhibitor forges a bond between her work and the Judge. Unless uniformity of ideals is established and followed, exhibitors will be increasingly less inclined to make the considerable effort required to exhibit.

In the act of judging, scales draw attention to details which might be overlooked. Since the most important qualities are emphasized the decisions are easier and more fair. Point scoring is the only device discovered to date which can reduce the possibility of personal prejudice. Scales serve a beneficial purpose as a limiting factor for avoiding extremes, and keeping a sense of order in a complex and confusing field.

Point-scoring as used by experienced Judges can be relied upon for logical decisions based on merit alone. It is the only method which can overcome the barrier of opinion differences and bring the Judges together on decisions. Every Judge must understand the mechanics of point-scoring and the necessity for using this system, particularly in close decisions. Writing comments (which see) in explanation of decisions helps the Judge to understand and become efficient in the use of point-scoring.

FLEXIBILITY

Standards of excellence shift as new varieties in horticulture and new trends in design make their appearance and the qualities in the scales must shift in response if the changes warrant the importance of emphasis.

Because of this needed flexibility to meet the demands of progress, and to fit specific artistic class problems, scales are used as patterns or guides, rather than being rigidly set. New artistic scales may be made by qualified persons to fit any situation. Those supplied by Plant Societies are official with those organizations and are officially changed from time to time to meet developments.

Authoritative scales may be made up by authorities in the horticulture field such as specialists, instructors, authors, officials of plant societies, experts in floral design such as instructors, authors; by National Council of State Garden Clubs' Flower Show Schools Committee and by local Judges or Flower Show Committees to fit specific schedule classes.

MAKING SCALES OF POINTS

Sometimes the elasticity applies only to the point values, at other times the qualities themselves are changed, depending upon where the makers wish emphasis to be placed.

Scale qualities and their point values must be carefully thought out. Care should be exercised so there are no repetitions or overlapping as deductions cannot be made for a fault more than once. Of course, there are exceptions, when two qualities are adversely affected by the same fault, points may be deducted from each for a total of the fault. Distinction is often difficult to appraise by the inexperienced Judges as it is affected by all the other qualities.

If color, or some other element is to be stressed in a class, it can be given a larger number of points. Perhaps the schedule makers want to stress space or a problem of balance or any other principle of design; these can be isolated with point value in relationship to their intended importance. Design is always included as a quality in artistic scale.

Care must be taken that the qualities stressed fit the style or type of design. To give creativity or originality a large number of points in a Period class such as the tussie-mussie or a Flemish defeats the purpose and confuses both Judges and exhibitors. Since the "formula" for a Flemish Period design is set as to colors, materials and form, much originality or creativity would not be possible without risking penalty for deviation from style.

A scale for a class of Abstract Non-Objective would not include communication as a judgeable quality because non-objective work has no subject beyond the design relationships . . . the organization of lines, shapes, angles, forms and areas of color, texture and space.

Rarity is an ambiguous word as plants are uncommon because of the exhibitor's or Judge's unfamiliarity with them. The word should be replaced with less illusive and questionable quality in point scales not approved by a plant's own specific Society.

Occasionally a scale of points is made in which design is given thirty points and each of the six principles is allowed an equal five points. Such breakdown is not recommended. A design with excessively poor scale and proportion could still win a blue ribbon if the other qualities were superior. Of course, some will argue that a designer with an inadequate sense of scale and proportion would not be able to make a design superior in other qualities. Granted, but a sliding scale would minimize the possibility of an unwarranted blue ribbon given because the Judge was limited in her deductions for a specific fault pertaining to a design principle. Leave it to the Judge how much she should deduct when she is actually confronted with the problem.

A study of the scales of points suggested in this book will reveal a number of applicable phrases to help in assembling a Scale of Points for Design.

There are a number of phrases, some are synonyms which express qualities indicative of today's designs:
— aesthetic compatibility
— superior execution
— skillful handling
— perceptive choice of materials
Phrases less binding than originality are:
— *uniqueness*   — *creative adaptations*
— unconventionality (the quality of being different)
— freedom from precedent
— individuality (one of a kind, different, quality which characterizes it as different)
— singularity (some quality of a thing by which it is distinguished from others, different, uncommon, rare, stands by itself)
— creativity (power to originate something new or to indicate something in an unusual manner through selection, perception)
— dramatic impact
Communication of individual expression is the key characteristic of modern and abstract designing, other phrases in addition to communication are:
— perceptive impact or perceptivity
— expressiveness
— individual or personal expression
— communicated inspiration, expression
— sensitivity of expression
— inspirational message
Any phrase used should be understandable, stimulating and challenging.

USING THE SCALES

The Judge must thoroughly understand and know how to use the scale of point system of arriving at a fair and complete decision. Even though he will not always find it necessary to actually add up the score of the leading contenders, he should habitually, even if unconsciously and instinctively, evaluate the entries according to the accepted standards.

After years of judging, the various accepted standards will come to mind upon viewing the specific class, even if no special effort has been made to memorize the scales. With experience it will not be necessary to actually add up the points, unless the competition is very close. In such cases, the Judge should break down the qualities and allot points to substantiate the fact that the decision is based on all the qualities as outlined in the scale. Usually only close decisions need be point-scored unless are Home Show exhibits in same class, different rooms.

For beginners it is suggested that one quality be considered at a time in all exhibits. In other words in considering a class of dahlias, the Judge would ask himself just how near to color perfection the specimen is and how much would the penalty be for its color defects. He would repeat this process regarding color on each exhibit in the class. Some entries may be equal in point value of a single quality, but variations will invariably show up in others, assuring a different total for each.

The Judge would continue to take all entries through the next step of scoring for form, then the remaining qualities. For some Judges, it is easier to quickly look over the class, pick out the entry with superior color and assign its points, then rate its less perfect competitors relatively. With practice and experience, the Judge will be able to point-score a single specimen through all its qualities accurately and mentally, without confusion or missing a quality.

Some Judges find it easier to use a minus system. Rather than GIVING a quality twenty of its twenty-five allotted points, they DEDUCT five. It is quicker for them to add a -5, a -2, and a -7 for a total of 14 and deduct this from 100 for a score of 86 than it is to add bigger figures in their heads.

In a panel decision, the point totals of each Judge are added together and divided by the number of Judges to arrive at the winner, as the Judges seldom arrive at the same total. Entries scoring at least 90 — first place. Entries scoring at least 85 — second place. Entries *scoring at least 75 — third place. If quality is very high, it is possible that all four placements score in the 90's. Honorable mention (75 at least) may be given to draw attention to some creative or superior aspect.*

MAKE SENSE

The relationship of the qualities to each other must be kept in mind. For instance, it makes no sense to give a near perfect score for form of a rose and take off half the points for substance.

If a flower lacks that much substance, it is bound to be losing form. This could be reversed, however. The bloom may be beautifully fresh with a perfect score for substance, yet is so malformed it must be heavily penalized under form.

If a quality being judged is reduced more than 40-50% of its points, the specimen is likely to be eliminated as lacking show quality. For instance, if the substance is fifty percent bad (even if only 20 points are allotted substance) it follows that the appearance of the specimen is such that it does not deserve an award.

Beginning Judges are sometimes disconcerted to find that after adding up the score, the exhibit believed at first glance to be blue ribbon comes out as a red ribbon. That first estimation may have been influenced by any number of personal, psychological and visual reactions. Rational checking of the qualities via the scales, barring prejudice and preference, has objectively indicated the real winner.

In using the point scales, the Judge should never have two exhibits receive the same total. Closer observation will surely reveal differences.

The total one-hundred points are rarely, if ever, given. Perfection, particularly in living material, is almost impossible to attain.

Snap judgments have no place in evaluating and the role of the scales of points is to assure that all important qualities are considered. Before totaling his score the Judge should pause to quietly double-check by asking such questions as "Have I given every feature the proper weight?", "Have I over-penalized the slightly open center of this rose?", "Have I been influenced by the outstanding color of this design?"

Beginning Judges often ask how much SHOULD be removed for a specific fault. There are no set rules specifying deductions. Points are deducted according to the deviation from perfection and variables involving locality, variety traits and other factors preclude set deductions.

Judging, even with point scales, is not a mechanical or automatic decision as with a mathematical problem. If this were so anyone could judge without training. Fair appraisal is informed opinion applied to the point scale qualities. It is something learned by experience, based on knowledge, taste, color and design sense, blended with the ability to discern differences and adjust the values as each exhibit and situation demands.

Constructive Comments

As Judges, communication is very important . . . involving our satisfactory public relations with Flower Show personnel, exhibitors and other Judges . . . involving our being perceptive enough to appreciate and evaluate what the designer is trying to express and involving our use of correct flower show terminology in writing constructive and descriptive comments that are helpful and not hurtful.

VOCABULARY

No Judge should give a lame answer to a challenged decision. He is prepared to quickly, intelligently and unemotionally retravel the road to his decision.

A vocabulary adroitly employed and richly varied is certain to be distinguished from one that is meager . . . containing only a small store of basic, abstract words that are rigidly and repeatedly applied.

In the five hundred most frequently used words in America there are only FIFTEEN even remotely related to vision! Of these fifteen, five apply to color. They are "color", "light", "white", "green", and "red". Obviously a Judge's sensory discrimination and the vocabulary to describe it MUST be superior to the average or he will find it impossible to judge fairly or to communicate his decisions. Almost everyone can see differences in successful and unsuccessful designs, but the Judge often must be able to see differences between two or three successful designs and be able to analyze the cause of these different effects and then put the analysis into specific terms.

Psittacism is a coined word which refers to the repetitious use of words or phrases in a parrot-like manner and derives from psittacosis or "parrot-fever". A Judge must examine his working vocabulary for symptoms of psittacism. How many times does he say emptily "good", "poor", "lacking", "satisfying", "beautiful". Wise men since the age of Athens have tried to describe beauty and failed! These are abstract terms which carry a vast difference in the mind of the reader or listener who applies the meaning in the light of his own understanding, experience, education and emotional development.

VARIED MEANINGS

One of the premises of modern linguistic thought is that NO WORD HAS PRECISELY THE SAME MEANING TWICE and certainly not when applied to such variables as living plant material.

Take the simple word "dog". To each the word conjures up a different picture. "Dog" has personality and character different for each. He is either smooth or rough, male or female, friendly or frightening, large or little, poodle or pooch! He must be described in these terms before the listener or reader SHARES the same picture of "Dog". If such a simple, well-known word cannot be communicated clearly, how much more difficult it is to explain a design fault or justify a decision.

THE QUALITIES OF CONSTRUCTIVE COMMENT

When an exhibitor reads specific words aimed directly at his situation, his design, his horticultural specimen he knows that some real, live HUMAN BEING has taken the trouble to search for phrases to convey a helpful message specially for him.

Good manners must enter into the Judge's choice of words partly because they are due in propriety toward the exhibitor and partly because the Judge's own dignity demands them of the writer. Clear, well-written comments compliment the exhibitor. Sarcastic comments demean the Judge!

Clarity, however, does not mean they should be simple like Simon or in a primer class. People who demand immediate intelligibility without giving thought to what they read should stick to comic books.

The time element necessitates concise, precise statements. Short and definite and pared down to the essentials! There is no time to write a lecture and the Judge should avoid giving one verbally that delays the judging. The written words should be definite, expressing the meaning as precisely as possible.

Lastly, the Judge is obligated to know the principles of design so well that his comments fit the subject or he will sound like the woman who tells the mechanic to fix her car horn as the brakes don't work! The statements must be logical, reasonable and tailor-made for the exhibit. They must be correct and lucid, and easily verified by observing the exhibit.

Thus it is apparent that the qualities of a constructive comment are that it be instructive, clear, concise and logical.

ABSTRACTS VERSUS SPECIFICS

To say "it is a good design" is really not a statement of merit, though it SOUNDS complete it conveys nothing and upon analysis it leads to questions of why and how? It is what one linguist refers to as a "purr" statement. If purr statements are accompanied by verifiable reports on the use of design principles, its distinction and creativity . . . the listener understands and (hopefully) comes to share the opinion.

The use of a sliding scale of generalized abstract words in addition to the present number (point-score) system would convey nothing more really helpful to the exhibitor.

To illustrate: A class is point-scored and the results may be 60, 67, 76, 89, 91. To use poor, fair, good, excellent, superior as well as the numbers still does nothing to help the exhibitor or the public to know WHY the design was poor 60, and another was superior 91. Constructive comments can bridge this gap between the Judge's experience and the exhibitor's wonderment and are an instructive, educational part of the show . . . the basic goal of the whole process is education! When the Judge explains the exhibitor learns far more than she ever could any other way. Imagine this exhibitor's confusion and frustration:

Judge's Comment	Question
— not according to schedule	— why?
— rose lacks form	— how?
— color poor	— what's wrong?
— lacks design	— what did I do wrong, where?
— fair balance, almost right	— what does THAT mean?

Here are some actual examples of constructive comments. Try to visualize the exhibit. You will be more successful than you imagine.

— Class requested only fresh-cut materials, the large pieces of wood are not in accordance with Schedule requirements.

— rose center split, several missing and twisted petals distort form

— color is streaked, outer edges turning dark

— interesting, triangular design but too many forms of unequal value and unrelated color disrupts dominance, gives a busy effect. One should be featured. Needs more plant material to be in proportion to container. Accessory too large.

— the heavy branch and bright flower on the left need items of equal INTEREST on the lower right to achieve better asymmetrical balance.

The score or ribbon given, plus the published point scale will further advise the exhibitor of the seriousness of his error.

Constructive comments by respected Judges give exhibitors encouragement, particularly if no award is placed. Those few extra words clarify, acknowledge effort made and help to channel creative power so future attempts will receive credit.

The Judges should agree on the comments to be written and one of the Judges should be designated by the Panel to do this, as the clerks may misunderstand or misinterpret.

Writing comments on one's own designs and garden flowers or at shows where not officiating is good practice. Remember constructive comments contain no "I's". . . . "I like or don't like", "I wish", "I don't feel happy with . . . " Good Judging is objective!

The Judge should not resort to slang phrases or any term that may be misunderstood by either the exhibitor or the visitor. Take an extra second to reread the written comment and ask yourself "Would I understand this?"

These few short phrases found on the judged exhibit card display to the exhibitor and the world in general the extent of that Judge's experience, knowledge, justice and tolerance.

Careless words written in haste on an entry card become the autobiography of the Judge who wrote them.

And they may very well be the obituary of the hopes of an exhibitor who tried and now no longer will have the courage to try again . . .

Schedules

The schedule has been properly called the law of the show — it controls all the details and the entries. Too frequently, Judges are severely criticized when the fault lay with an improperly worded schedule or a confused exhibitor or a less-than-knowledgeable Classification Committee.

The Schedule must be specific! It must be up to date! It must be correctly worded!

The inclusion of a few definitions will clarify design types, accessory, dried, fresh-cut, horticultural terms and Scales of Point qualities for the benefit of all concerned. Sufficient Scales of Points should be printed in the Schedule to notify exhibitors and Judges where emphasis will be placed in the exhibits of various classes and divisions.

Suggested classes for specific exhibits are listed throughout the text and can be transferred completely or in part to the Schedule as are needed.

The Schedule has a number of general rules, the following are suggested to ease the flower show process:

— the Flower Show Committee has the right to sub-divide or add classes in any division if the number of entries warrants.

— any and all designs using artificial flowers or foliage will be disqualified.

— handcrafted, contrived or manualistic flowers or figures constructed of RECOGNIZABLE PLANT MATERIALS are allowed in classes as designated.

— potted plants must be of show quality as regards maturity or show-size in relation to their type.

— exhibits which are not in accordance with specific schedule-listed sizes, lengths, number of stems and blooms or other specifications will be eliminated. (It is the joint duty of the Classification Committee and the exhibitors to see that entries comply with scheduled requirements.)

— creativity is restricted by too many limiting factors. To state "selection of and design pattern and form in all artistic classes may be made at the discretion of the exhibitor" frees her to use accessories, foliages, dried, altered, fresh-cut, bases, background and lighting as she wishes and needs. Classes designated for special awards can specify fresh-cut or other material be predominant.

— many Horticulture Scales of Points give a small number of points for correct labeling. Exhibitors should be advised of this fact in the Schedule. Either by stating "Horticulture must be labeled", or listing those types for which labeling is given a point value.

— the Schedule should specifically state that a small, neat, typed or printed card of explanation may accompany the interpretive design.

— artistic exhibitors should be allowed to place their own designs after going through the proper channels of classification, entry and staging direction. This precaution eliminates the possibility of incorrect staging and possible dissension.

— awards are by the Standard System and awarded only if merited IN THE OPINION OF THE JUDGES! Standard System is: only one blue, one red, one yellow ribbon per class. Several Honorable Mentions (white ribbon) may be awarded if others than the winners are of exceptionally high quality or distinctive in some manner. Other special awards are presented only as specified in the Schedule.

— anyone may enter, exhibit and receive any ribbon herein offered regardless of Club or Society affiliation. (To restrict non-member participation discourages potential memberships, leads to charges of exclusiveness, hard feelings and limits the educational possibilities.)

— the decision of the Judges is final in all matters within their jurisdiction.

— *novice, amateur, professional status defined.*

OBSOLETE TERMS, AMBIGUITIES AND INCORRECT INTERPRETATIONS

Many times lack of understanding the true or new meaning of a term is the cause of dissension and loss of an award. Actual examples show how classes written in good faith are unworkable in practice.

— a Class calls for a design using pine, etc. What does the etc. mean? It would have been better to specifically state "design using needleleaf (or narrow-leaf or conifer) evergreens such as pine". If it simply stated "using evergreens", both broadleaf or needleleaf would be accepted and judged.

— no differentiation is now made between the terms composition and design.

— "interpretive", "expressive", and "impressionistic" designs are generally interchangeable.

— "dominant", "predominant", and "featuring" mean "one that shows greater influence", "that which carries the most visual weight", "attracts and holds the eye". Easier detected by looking, turning away, then back quickly. That which is remembered and seen first is no doubt dominating the attention.

— "incorporating" means "a part of", "united with". The accessory cannot simply be sitting there, it must work in the design.

— holiday design classes often seem to inspire some entrants to make novelties, scenes and the like, rather than an arrangement as defined using a container, mechanics and plant materials arranged according to the principles. The schedule can alleviate such problems by simply stating "No scenes accepted except in Classes as designated".

— "THE LAST ROSE OF SUMMER", One rose with or without a bud".

Very difficult for the arranger and Judge to know what is expected. Is foliage or some other material permitted. No one can be sure unless the general rules so state. Very little designing can be done with one lone rose, even with a bud!

— "MINIATURE ARRANGEMENT, not over three inches high".

May it be more than three inches wide? The schedule should state "not to exceed three inches in **any** dimension". The size of small designs is now arbitrarily set at 8 inches or less.

— creativity is restricted by specific geometric designs (crescents, etc.) and strict color classes (analagous, etc., or white, etc.)
   When used, the color classification should be made more flexible by allowing "incidental" color not a part of the required "harmony". Incidental color includes small green leaves, bracts, calyxs, flower centers. All things being equal, however, the lack of any incidental color might be the determining factor.
— the following phrases may be used to request Period designs without demanding authenticity:
— in the manner of   — adapted from
— inspired by   — influenced by
— suggested by   — in the spirit of
— the number of stems requested for Horticultural classes should be more or less the same for all plants of a type. To request a different number for each, confuses and encourages mistakes. Ones, threes and fives used with size and staging in mind. To illustrate:
   Asters, 3 blooms; Zinnias, 3 blooms; Bachelor Button, 5 blooms; Dwarf Marigold, 5 blooms; Sweet Peas, 5 sprays; Delphinium, 1 spike; Glad, 1 spike; Snaps, 3 spikes.
— the horticultural section should be overhauled yearly to bring it into line with new developments.
— the term German Iris is obsolete, substitute "tall bearded".
— if the Schedule states "BEGONIA IN A HANGING BASKET" any type could be entered. If the class means pendular, trailing or basket type DISPLAYED in a hanging container, it should so state.
— do request the plant by the accepted classification or type rather than by colloquial or variety names except in rare instances as the "PEACE" rose. For instance:
   PANSY, a—Giant. b—New Variety.
      Confusing. What may be a new variety to one may not be to another. Does it mean new this year, introduced last year, or what? See Pansy for suggested entry.
   NASTURTIUM, 7 stems. a—Single. b—Double.
      Until hybridizers come up with a more distinctly double Nasturtium, it is best for everyone's peace of mind to simply request Nasturtium, 5 stems.
   PETUNIA, a—Dwarf. b—Multiflora. c—F1 Hybrid.
      This is duplication. See Petunias for suggested classes.

MARIGOLDS, 5 sprays. a—Single. b—Dwarf Single.

> Request blooms, not sprays. As yet, there are no Marigolds that are single and different from the dwarf single, so again the class is a duplication.

DAISY, Shasta, 5 blooms.

> Are we going to judge the Single, Double and Crested Shastas (Chrysanthemum Maxima) with each other and with the Painted or Ox-eye Daisy?

ROSE, Hybrid Tea, Collection, three sprays.

> Hybrid Teas are exhibited as one BLOOM to a stem, disbudded.

ZINNIA, Hybrid.

> Almost all modern Zinnias are hybrids, if Cactus is meant, say so. See Zinnia for suggested classes.

SNAPDRAGONS, 6 Spikes.

> To mix exhibits of tetra, double and common garden snaps makes for difficult decisions.

The Judge should tactfully point out to the Flower Show Committee wordings which make for misunderstandings.

Proper Classification

In General Flora Shows and Fairs it is a duty of the Classification Committee to disqualify exhibits. In the case unworthy exhibits slip through, Judges eliminate from consideration by penalization. Reasons for elimination or severe penalization should be marked on the entry cards for the edification of the public and the exhibitor.

Such duties as counting stems, checking lengths, measuring miniatures and glad florets are those of the Classification Committee. When they neglect this task or do it incompletely or carelessly the work of the Judges is tripled and the time it takes to judge is increased many fold. Often the Judges are criticized for being slow, when they have to practically reclassify the whole show while judging.

Judges are justified in eliminating from consideration a Floribunda that is entered in the Hybrid Tea class, or a cactus dahlia as an anemone or a giant single petunia entered in the multiflora class. It is the duty of the Classification Committee to check and make certain before the exhibitor leaves, or the judging begins.

Scheduled Rulings

Problems relative to who is a professional or if more than one entry is permitted per garden are not the concern of the Judges. These are problems of the Classification and Entry Committees, or if need be, of the General Committee. A Judge judges the entries placed before him as a class, assuming that all rule qualifications have been met as required by the schedule. The same also applies to the ruling that a plant be grown by the exhibitor or that it has been in the hands of the exhibitor a certain length of time.

One person may be pleased at an award given out of class, but the reputation of the Show and the Judges will be harmed because of the many others offended by such leniency and exception.

Labeling

Because so much horticulture judging is based on what is typical for the variety, the Show Committee and the Classification Committee should educate their exhibitors to correct labeling of entries. Not only does this ease the Judge's burden, but is so much more educational for the public. The exhibitor should be proud of how well he has grown that particular variety . . . proud enough to label it.

In plants such as gladiolus, marigolds and the like which are entered in size-of-bloom classes, the Classification Committee is expected to measure (not guess) each exhibit to make certain they qualify. If the Judge finds a spike of Joyous Glad (464) measuring only 3½" entered in the 300 grouping, six points would have to be levied against it for undersize (three points for each one-fourth inch). The Judge can usually be sure that the spike is Joyous if it has been named, and he has a basis from which to proceed on evaluation of trueness to type in size as well as color.

Who Did What And When?

The Classification Committee is expected to settle such questions as who grew what and who arranged the design, also such questions as "if a potted plant entered in a show earns a ribbon, should it be exhibited again in other shows?" and "is it fair that it win another ribbon?". The Classification Committee would have to disqualify if that is what they wished to do. The Judge would not, of course, know that the exhibit had won before.

But consideration should be taken of the fact that a well-grown plant is an asset to a show. A prize steer may win and win again and again. So may a horse or a beauty queen. Our goal is to grow the very best to attain the ideal of perfection and such a grower should not be honored with a ribbon in one show and penalized in another. It is not the same as copying a design and re-entering the same thing because while there can be many ideals of perfection in artistic design, there is only ONE for a well-grown plant. Let the others attempt to surpass it, but do not penalize the one who has, through care and attention, grown a prize-winning plant.

Conservation

It is the duty of the Classification Committee to disqualify any material on the Conservation Lists which is prohibited from competitive use in a show. They must also make certain that a verifying note accompanies any exhibit using material which is restricted but may be shown if grown by the exhibitor. The Judge cannot otherwise be sure it is eligible for competition.

Judge's Courtesy and Hospitality

Judges become Judges through a voluntary regime of many years of studious effort, rigid testing and grow-plus-show training. They are working guests of the club and deserve courtesy and consideration. There are several procedures to be followed which make things run smoothly.

Invitation

In the initial contact, the Judge should be advised of the classes he will be expected to judge and he should accept or decline on the information given at this time. Two or three weeks before the show, he should be sent a Schedule in which the classes are plainly marked. Usually at this time, the Judge is also advised of the names of the others with whom he will be working. Clear directions on how to reach the show building should be furnished and if he is coming by public transportation, arrangements should be made to have the Judge met.

When the Schedule is sent the Judge should be advised of a definite time specified for the starting and completion of judging. He has the right to expect that the show will be ready to start punctually, just as it is his obligation to be on time. Also since the Judge often comes some distance, he appreciates promptness in order to meet return schedules.

Assignments

Panels should not be assigned more classes than they can easily handle within the time allowed. Approximately sixteen classes (about 50 entries per team of Judges) in two to two and one-half hours is about average. Extra time must be allowed if comments are to be written.

Judges appreciate a briefing period in which their questions regarding the schedule are answered and any special instructions are given. They should be provided with the necessary equipment such as pads, pencils, rulers. A few extra moments should be given them to briefly ascertain the quality of the show as a whole before judging begins.

Clerks

Judges are often delayed by lack of direction in moving on to subsequent classes. Enough fully instructed clerks should be assisting each Panel so one can point out classes and check the count, one writes in the records and publicity book and one attaches awards to entry cards marked by one of the Judges.

The clerks also act as messengers between the Judges and the Classification Committee if needed. They should not intrude, never volunteer advice and give information only when asked. They should stand back to allow the Judges working room and to permit them privacy in their discussion — distance helps avoid misunderstandings.

Decisions

The Judges should not be expected to settle disputes concerning who grew what, where or the meaning of ambiguous schedule terms. These are matters for the Flower Show and Classification Committees to settle.

It is extremely poor taste for the Flower Show officials to make improper demands such as insisting on the placement of unearned awards. The conscientious Judge will ignore such requests.

The Judge/s must be extended the courtesy of having their decisions accepted. They may withhold awards if exhibits prove inferior. It is bad form for the show management to allow any appeal of the Judge's decision other than a request for the rejudging of a class by the ORIGINAL PANEL of Judges. It is interesting to note that some Fair schedules stipulate that any dissenter place a bond of a specified sum, which is forfeited if the former decision is upheld.

The Flower Show Committee should uphold the Judge's decisions. Those invited are a reflection of the Committee by reason of their choice and they must make the best of it this time. Incompetent Judges should not be invited. It is the club's privilege to refuse to arrange the return of a Judge whose work was not satisfactory.

Hospitality and Appreciation

Judging is exhausting for both clerks and Judges. A friendly "cuppa" and a cookie during the briefing and a lunch afterward is expected hospitality. To send the Judge any post publicity and a note of appreciation endears the club to him.

Expert Practice in Preparing Exhibits for Show

It's been said that dancing is wonderful training for girls in learning to guess what a man is going to do before he does it. Hardening flora is the same, despite promises of magic formulas, there are no guarantees, each must experiment; often two varieties of the same species will react different, and growing conditions affect keeping qualities. Read Judging criteria and scales herein before cutting. Grooming means to give a smart appearance . . . clean, perky, standing upright. Neat, correct labeling gives impression of expertise. Attention to details now can mean the blue rather than no ribbon.

Plants vary in their molecular structure being woody, bleeders or hollow stemmed and must be handled accordingly with varying preservative treatment due to their inner stem structure. Alum, vinegar, salt and detergents tend to 'set' the water conducting tissues in an open position speeding water intake. Bacteria retardants in mouthwash, vinegar, bleach and acids kills or prevent bacteria. Acidifying the water promotes water uptake, experience has found that pH4 satisfies most criteria, rainwater is low in pH and alkalinity. Your local spa dealer sells test strips and supplies, experiment with your water source. Chemicals lower the pH and inhibit bacteria, pH is lowered by adding sodium bisulfate and raised by adding sodium carbonate. Alkalinity is lowered with sodium bisulfate and raised by adding baking soda (bicarbonate of soda). One quart non-diet soft drink (i.e. Sprite, 7-Up), 1 qt. hot water, ½ tsp. bleach works well because the sugar provides energy, acidity retards bacteria and citric acid is present for metabolism of plant tissues.

Generally, unfertilized (pollen, not soil) flowers stay fresh longer, so cut daffodils, lilies, tulips, poppies, etc. just as showing color. Some winners swear by pre-conditioning; three weeks before the Show, water growing plants weekly with a solution of 1 tbs. saltpeter, 1 tsp. epsom salts, 1 tsp alum-free baking powder to each gallon water. Others rely on merely soaking the soil with clear water several hours before cutting to increase substance and turgidity.

Disbudding: *should have been done days/weeks earlier as soon as tiny buds appear so the wound heals and extra strength goes into making show-quality blooms. Generally remove all but terminal bud on singles (i.e. rose, dahlia, zinnia); cluster types (floribunda, etc.) should have misplaced stems and buds and the lowest bud in cluster center removed.*

Gathering: *Cut in late afternoon about sundown, after plants have 'eaten' and when the greatest amount of natural sugar is in tissues, this may extend life as much as ten hours. Those plants with little or no stem foliage may be cut in either morning or afternoon. Length of stem should be in proportion to flower/s. Remove foliage below water line to prevent decay which fouls water and prevents absorption. If stem grows with foliage attached, the exhibit must retain enough to balance stem and flower/s.*

Preparation: *The life of the flower is in the stem. Contrary to many opinions, water is not absorbed from the sides but from the bottom, therefore opening up or exposing the water tubes at stem bottom is crucial to extended life. Carry a pail of hot water and wrap each in wet newspaper as cut to avoid bruising. Using a sharp knife (shears may crush soft stem tubes) make a slanting cut to expose tubes and prevent from resting flat on container bottom which could block water and allow sediment on bottom to be taken up to clog tubes.*

Bleeders: *Squeeze liquid from lower 2", this sap seals off water ducts. Searing coagulates sap in the ducts before it can enter the water-conducting tissues to clog them. Searing is preferred to boiling as is more easily controlled. Rubbing alcohol in a small lid or metal container burns with hot flame and no steam damage to leaves, petals; hold 30–45 seconds. Sear immediately upon cutting or re-cutting. Do only 2–3 at a time.*

Woody: *Slit, scrape or hammer up 2–3", or peel back bark for 2" and crosscut before hardening.*

Hollow: *Cut under water, remove, fill with water, plug with bit of clay and insert into hardening medium.*

Hairy leaf: *Use hot water, cut under water.*

Cutting under water prevents air bubbles which stop absorption. Make several pin pricks near bloom to let air escape and water to rise. Keep all containers, pinholders, knife clean, contaminents clog tubes, shortening life. Warm water is absorbed more quickly than cold. Tepid means 75–90°F, warm: 90–110 (bath temp.), hot: to 190°F (just under bubbling).

Hardening off, conditioning: *is a warm-water, cool air technique which allows warm water to move into the stems faster while cool air around the flowers slows down evaporation from the tissues (transpiration). Holding temperatures should range from 33°F to 55°; 33° is detrimental to glads, orchids, geraniums and most tropicals which prefer to lower than 55°, flowers freeze at 27−31, not 32°F. If it is impossible to refrigerate, loosely drape bouquet top in cleaner's plastic bags and tie around bucket top, even at room temp. this reduces evaporation. Let stand 2−12 hours. Never put hardening flora in drafts, dry air, direct sun or heat. Never subject flora at any time to abrupt temp. changes.*

Grooming: *Foliage rinse of ⅓ vinegar and ⅔ water applied with soft sponge or nylon removes spray, soil, some mildew. Brush hairy, wooly leaves gently. No waxing, oiling, wiring or supports are allowed in horticulture specimens. Dampen fingers or use wet nylon gloves to help prevent oil transfer and bruising. Prevent design flowers (i.e. tulips, roses) from opening fully by applying egg white or matched color wax between petals. Drop a bit of same or glue on back of multi-petaled mums, etc. If browned petals or foliage is trimmed, additional discoloration is prevented by coating edge with egg white.*

Transporting: *Soft drink cartons aid in carrying single stems. Schedules usually allow some wedging materials, i.e. additional foliage, clear pliofilm (never aluminum foil) or collars cut to fit inside the container opening; insert stem through hole cut in center. If design seems shaky, pour a little melted paraffin on the water, when cool it helps hold stems in place.*

Reviving: *Recut ends of wilted blooms. Place ends in very hot (not bubbling) water for a few minutes, then plunge into cold water. Repeat hardening process in water to which 1 tsp. detergent for ea. qt.*

Acacia, Aconite, Arctotis: *harden in ½ cup vinegar, 2 qts. water 2 hrs., then spray with cold water, wrap in wet newspaper 4 hrs.*

Apple, Almond, Cherry, other trees: *crush ends, harden in 2 tbls ammonia, 2 qts water*

Amaryllis: *carefully wrap facial tissue around stamens to prevent staining. Cut under water, harden in ½ c. vinegar 2 c. water.*

Anthirrium: *cut ¼" off ends under hot water. Immerse flower and all in tepid water 2−4 hrs. Will hold in designs without water.*

Aster: *Cut when open. Dip stems in boiling water or sear. Stand in 5 drops peppermint oil to 1 pt. water for 2−4 hrs. Harden 12 hrs. in clear water.*

Aquilegia, Columbine: *stand 2 hrs. in 1 tbls. sugar, 1 tbls. salt, 1 qt. water or 5 drops peppermint oil to 1 qt. water. Then rub salt into ends and harden.*

Astilbe: *crush stems, harden overnight in 1 cap mouthwash, 3 gal. water.*

Aspidistra: *cut under water, harden in 1 cap mouthwash, 3 gal. water*

Azalea: *Crush ends, sear, stand in peppermint oil for 3 min., harden in 1 tb. alcohol per gallon hot water.*

Baby's Breath: *stand in 1 tsp. alcohol, 1 pt. water 2 hrs., harden in tepid clear water*

Begonia, Tuberous: *stand in 2 tbs salt, 2 qts. water 2−4 hrs., cover with damp tissues, refrig. till used.*

Bird of Paradise, Strelitzia: *Soak heads ½ hr. in tepid water. Harden in ½ c. vinegar, 1 qt. water 2−4 hrs. at 50°F, use stem slime to shine sheath.*

Bittersweet: *slit or crush ends, harden in ¼ c. sugar, hot water.*

Bleeding Heart: *split stems, dip in tincture of capiscum for a few seconds. Harden in clear water overnight.*

Bougainvillea: *slit ends, dip into peppermint oil a few seconds, harden in warm water 10 hrs.*

Boxwood: *submerge in tepid water 6 hrs., harden in 1 qt. water, 1 tsp. chlorine bleach, 1 tsp. powdered sugar for 6−10 hrs.*

Bamboo: *stand 3 hrs. in 3 tsp. salt, 1 qt. warm water, harden overnight.*

Caladium: *rub salt into ends, harden 10 hrs. Coat underside with thin glue or plastic spray to prevent curling in designs.*

Calendula: *cut under hot water, stand in hot water 2−6 hrs.*

Calla Lily: *hold upside down, fill stem with tepid 1 c. vinegar, 2 c. sugar, 2 c. water, harden in same mixture.* **Leaves:** *immerse in clear water 24 hrs.*

Camellia: *cover fingers before handling, harden between damp towels in refrig. 50°, add a few grains salt to vase water.*

Canna: *scrape ends, stand in 2 qts. water, 1 tsp. hydrochloric acid for ½ hr., harden in clear water 6−10 hrs.*

Canterbury Bells: *sear ends, stand in 2 tbs soda, 2 qts. water 2−4 hrs. harden.*

Carnation: *cut stems under water below node, stand in ⅛ tsp. boric acid, 1 qt. water 2−4 hrs., harden in clear, avoid abrupt temp. changes, do not store with fruit/veg.*

Cattails: *pick green or mature, harden in 1 tsp. vinegar, 1 qt. water, spray with clear plastic.*
Clematis: *harden in 3 tbs. alcohol, ¼ tsp. soda, 2 qts. water, or 3 tbs. gin, ¼ tsp. salt to 1 qt. water.*
Chrysanthemum: *break rather than cut, crush or slit ends, sear or dip in boiling water, harden 12−16 hrs. in 3 tbs. sugar to 1 qt. water, or, 8 drops peppermint oil to 2 qts. water, or 5 drops cloves to 1 qt. water.*
Coleus: *Dip ends 2−3 minutes in alcohol, harden in warm water 8 hrs.*
Cosmos: *Same as Clematis, harden in warm water to heads.*
Daffodils, Narcissus: *gently squeeze sap from lower 2". Dip ends in alcohol few sec., harden in warm shallow water.*
Dahlia: *cut fully open after sundown, sear ends, harden in pinch of potassium nitrate to 1 qt. warm water, or stand in tepid water 1 hr., then in ½ tsp alcohol per qt. warm water for 2 hrs.*
Delphinium: *cut when 1st floret opens, invert, fill stem with 1 tbs alcohol in 1 pt. warm water, harden in same.*
Dogwood: *crush, stand 1 tsp hydrochloric acid, 3 qts. very hot water for ½ hr., harden 2 hrs. in clear water.*
Evergreens: *crush, swish in warm soapy water, stand in 3 tsp. glycerine + 3 qts. hot water 2− 4 hrs., harden overnight.* **Christmas Tree:** *hammer end, stand in ¼ c. horticultural iron, 2 cups corn syrup, 4 tsp bleach per 1 gal. boiling water.*
Fern: *to enrich color add 1 tsp ammonia + 1 qt. tepid water, break stems, immerse in tepid mix 12 hrs.*
Forsythia: *crush ends, harden, caution: some commercial preservatives bleach color.*
Foxglove: *harden in 1 tb. alcohol to 1 pt. warm water.*
Freesia: *harden in ½ tsp alcohol to 1 qt. warm water.*
Funkia: *immerse in ½ c. vinegar, 2 cups tepid water 1 hr., harden.*
Gaillardia: *cut fully open, harden in 2 tbs salt, 1 pt. water.*
Gardenia: *cover fingers, float face down overnight, put pinch of salt in vase water.*
Geranium: *harden at no cooler than 50°, keeps 5−7 days without water.*
Gerbera: *dip end in peppermint oil for few min., harden.*
Gladiolus: *fluoridated water decreases life by 20%, discolors, burns sheaths, cut when lower florets opening, harden in 5 tbs. vinegar or ½ tsp. peppermint oil per qt. of rainwater, only 12 hrs. as will drink themselves to death, harden no cooler than 50°, avoid abrupt temp. changes, florets open best in dark.*
Hemerocallis: *cut night before in bud form, carefully wrap tissue around stamens after open, to avoid staining, harden clear water.*
Hibiscus: *cut in morning, rub stamens of 2 identical varieties together, harden in refrig. 6 hrs., will hold without water a few hrs.*
Hollyhock: *split stems 4", sear ends, harden in 1 handful rock salt per qt. hot water, or pinch of potassium nitrate per qt. water.*
Holly: *crush ends, stand in 1 cup white corn syrup, 1 tsp. bleach, 1 qt. hot water for 2 days, avoid fruit/veg. which cause defoliation.*
Hosta: *crush ends, dip in peppermind oil a few seconds, immerse 3 hrs.*
Hyacinth: *remove white end, gently squeeze sap out, sear, harden in 5 drops peppermint oil per pt. cold water 2−6 hrs., for designs, put tape around bottom to prevent splitting.*
Hydrangea: *drink thru their heads, split ends, sear, immerse in tepid water 1 hr., harden in ½ c. vinegar + 2 qts. hot water 12 hrs.*
Iris: *cut when 2 buds are size of hen egg. Leave brown husk on, harden in 3 drops peppermint oil to 1 qt. water, avoid abrupt temp. change.*
Lilac: *cut when ¾ to fully open, crush ends, immerse heads in tepid water, shake off excess, harden in deep hot water 12 hrs.*
Lily: *cut when lower flower fully open, gently wrap tissue around stamens to prevent staining, turn upside down, allow cool water to flow over, scrape stem ends, harden in 1 tbs. alcohol, 1 pt. water.* **Leaves:** *immerse 1−3 hrs.*
Magnolia: *cover fingers, crush ends, dip into boiling water, harden in tepid water with ¼ c. sugar 2−6 hrs.*
Marigold: *stand in 2 tbs. sugar, 1 tbs salt per qt. water or 8 drops peppermint oil per qt. 2−4 hrs., then harden, may be dry-stored in plastic 33−40°F for 16−21 days, recondition 12 hr.*
Oleander: *sear 15 sec., harden in ¼ c. sugar to 2 qts. hot water.*
Peony: *cut as showing color, split ends, stand in 3 tbs. sugar, 1 qt. hot water for 2−4 hrs., harden in clear water, will last 1 mo. if dry-wrapped in film and refgr'd, do not use with Oasis as 'allergic'.*
Phlox: *split ends, harden in 2 qts. hot water, ¼ c. sugar, ½ tsp. bleach.*
Poinsettia: *sear ends, hold upside down, fill stem with mix of 1 handful rock salt, 1 qt. warm water, harden in mix, sear end each time cut.*
Poppy: *cut just as opening, sear ends 30−45 sec., rub ends with salt, harden in deep warm water 10 hrs.*

Rose: Cut when ⅓ open, or 2nd petal unfurling, avoid fluoridated water which discolors and shortens life 18%, avoid fruits, veg., dip ends in 115° water briefly, stand in 2 tbls powdered alum, 1 qt. warm water 1−4 hrs., harden in warm rain water, or ½ part pop (i.e. Sprite), ½ part water, ½ tsp bleach, or harden in ½ tsp alum, ½ tsp. bleach, 1 pinch iron rust (ferrie oxide), 2 tsp. sugar per qt. warm water, dip end into alum before arranging, may be dry-stored at 45° 2−4 days after hardening, form may be altered before hardening by gently manipulating petals using wet fingers, brush, wrap in clear plio or yarn to retard opening.

Salvia: stand in 1 tbs. alcohol, 1 pt. water 2−4 hrs., harden 10 hrs.

Snapdragon: cut under water, cut when ¾ flowers fully open, scrape ends, stand in 3 tbs. salt, 1 pt. water, or 3 tbs. soda, 2 qts. water 2−4 hrs., harden overnight in clear water, avoid fruits/veg.

Stock: crush end, harden in 1½ tbs. sugar, 2 tbs. white vinegar in 2 qts. warm water, do not use with Oasis.

Sunflower: sear, boil end in vinegar or dip into liquid camphor 5 min., harden in 100° water for 6−10 hrs.

Sweet Pea: cut ends under hot water, dip ends into hot water, harden in 1½ tbs. sugar or 1 tbs. alcohol per qt. warm water for 8−10 hrs.

Tulip: cut just as shows color, wrap in wet newspaper to heads, tulips open by day, close by night for 5 days, thereafter stay open for varying times; for straight stems exhibit those opening for 1st or 2nd time, wrap each in clear film to preserve form, harden in 1 tsp gin to 1 pt. warm water, a piece of laundry starch may help keep stems straight, and a penny may straighten a curved stem.

Violets: drink thru their heads, immerse 1 hr., wrap in wet paper, submerge to flowers in ice water.

Water Lily: recut under water, drop bit of glue in center to keep open, stand in 12 drops alcohol, 1 pt. water 1−4 hrs., harden in clear water.

Wisteria: split ends, harden 12 hrs., to peel, boil in 1 tsp soda, 1 qt. water.

Zinnia: sear or dip in boiling water, harden in ¼ c. sugar, 1 cap mouthwash, 2 qts. hot water. Plants not listed; crush or sear and harden in warm water 10 hrs.

Forcing Blooms: The plant must have entered dormancy (frost or freeze). Best to choose those shrubs which bloom before leaves appear. Cut after a thaw and rain with outside temps. above freezing; if cut when frozen immerse in cold water 3−4 hrs. Cut at least 18" long from the south side of plant. Flower buds are plump, round; leaf buds slim, pointed. Crush ends, immerse in warm water 1−3 hrs. Place upright in deep warm water in 55−65°F lighted place. Higher temps may dry out buds. May be arranged in vase at this time. Flowering period is extended considerably if water is changed every 3−4 days and ends recut and crushed. The later the season, the more quickly they bloom. The later the species blooms outdoors, the longer it takes to force, but they last longer indoors. Preservatives may lengthen vase life, but also may bleach color if the shrub is dormant. Charcoal, etc. will help control bacteria.

To schedule forcing for Show and bloom progression mark calendar for each kind and cut 3−4 days before and after the minimum date, i.e.

Andromeda	12−20 days	Lilac	28−40 days
Azalea	16−20	Magnolia	20−36
Almond, flw'g	20+	Maple	12−18
Crab, cherry, quince	19−25	Mt. Laurel	30−40
Dogwood	20−25	Weeping Willow	10−16
Forsythia	12−21	Witch Hazel	3−8
Honeysuckle	10−15	Violets: place on pebbles	15−30
Horsechestnut	20−35		

Bromeliad: water well, place in plastic bag with an apple cut into pieces. Seal, place in shady spot 3 days. Remove bag. Put plant in usual place. Should bloom in apprx. 45 days.

DIVISION 2 — HORTICULTURE

SECTION 1 — HORTICULTURAL QUALITIES

The following are brief definitions of the various qualities appearing in horticultural scales of points. The same quality is covered under each specific plant or flower where the quality is important enough to be given a number of points. Not all scales have the same qualities, nor are the same number of points always given to the quality in each scale.

For instance, cultural perfection appears in the scale for Begonia Plants and Gourds but not in the scales for Geraniums, Roses or Chrysanthemums; distinction appears in some Iris types and not others. Color may be given more importance and more points in some flowers as in roses, orchids and peonies; and less importance and points in others such as lilies, gloxinias and others.

The quality of foliage is not considered in such flowers as tulips, iris, and daffodils where the stem rises free of the foliage. If no points are allowed for foliage by the official scale, but "other foliage" is exhibited with the plant, the Judge simply ignores the addition.

Distinction

Distinction, found as a quality in a number of Plant Society scales, is elusive and difficult to judge, especially when judging one variety against another, but as long as the word appears in official horticulture scales, Judges must try to pin it down.

Distinction is really a re-evaluation of all the other factors and involves any particular superiority or refinement of form, size, color, texture, stem and foliage. Even staging and labeling, as well as unique color breaks and interesting form variations, etc., may apply.

The distinctive horticulture specimen is better, more perfect or has some quality which sets it apart from its companions, but care must be taken so this quality does truly give distinction and not merely make it appear as a freak!

It might be helpful to divide the plants in a class into four groupings with a percentage of the points given for distinction as follows:
- easily distinguished from others in the class because of some outstanding difference or superiority . . . give 75-100% of the distinction points.
- distinguishable from others in at least one quality . . . give 50-75%.
- average to above average in at least one quality . . . give 25 to 50%.
- substandard, mediocre, unlabeled, carelessly staged . . . give no points under distinction.

It should be noted that these points may be used to increase the rating already earned for the other scale-listed qualities; if no quality is distinctive from any standpoint, these maximum or extra points are not given.

Flower Form and Inflorescence

Form is that shape which is the true or characteristic form of a variety in all its customary variations. The form may be better than average, but it must not fall short of the requirements for the standard of perfection as is habitually found in a certain growing area.

Form may be broken down into three categories:
1. *trueness to type which includes the generally accepted outline and any abnormalities or variations from the standards;*
2. *development, which covers over-maturity or immaturity;*
3. *distortion due to mechanical, disease or insects. Due to environmental concerns over spraying, less concern given than formerly.*

MATURITY CHANGES FORM

Over-maturity is indicated in many ways which alter form. It is sometimes difficult to draw the line between SUBSTANCE where one scores for turgidity and freshness; CONDITION where one scores for intactness of parts, and OVER-MATURITY which is often indicated by collapsing form, bald centers, stamens dropping pollen and other specific indications typical of the flower.

Since both substance and form are usually adversely affected by over-maturity, points are often deducted from both to a total of the fault.

The blooms of a plant or variety which are known to change form as the bloom continues to mature have as the standard of perfection, that form which represents its normal shape at peak of maturity. For example, certain rose-form Camellias open with bud centers, with petals filling in the space between the high centers and the outer petals. When past the peak of maturity, the flowers have a distinct division between the rosebud center and the flattened outer petals. Certain other formal Camellia flowers are frequently flat or with the petals slightly upturned when fresh and as the flower ages, the petals have a tendency to turn down. The normal shape at peak *of maturity is to be considered the ideal form. Popped or raised centers of marigolds, scabiosa and a number of other plants are examples of over-maturity.*

IMMATURE FORM

An immature bloom may hold attention momentarily for its fresh appearance, but such a partially developed bud, not yet opened into a flower, should not be eligible to be judged as a specimen or considered for an award. In many cases, such as the rose, the Judge must be able to recognize when the particular variety is at its most perfect form. Roses which have fewer petals are at their most perfect generally, when they are less than one-half open, while the many-petaled forms are most perfect at approximately two-thirds open.

MERGING FORMS

In some plant families, the form has evolved into infinite gradations as is found in the Dahlias and all manner of border-line cases are found. For instance, the semi-cactus Dahlia varieties merge with the decoratives, formals and informals on one hand, while on the other hand they merge with the true cactus, in curved and straight forms. Such involved form variations exist in similar or slightly lesser degrees in many plants such as the orchid, the camellia, the aster, etc. It is the duty of the Judge to score down any bloom which does not actually meet the formation requirements of the class, or which fails to come up to the approved standard of excellence of form for the type defined.

AREA VARIATIONS

A very slight allowance may be conceivably made for the vagaries of weather, soil, season, etc., but must not be carried to the extent of lowering the standards of attainable excellence in form. Such effects are usually more apparent in color, size and height than in form. The acceptable criteria for form of a certain variety or species should always be adhered to and deviations penalized in most cases.

HYBRIDIZING CHANGES FORM

Through hybridizing, form changes are continually occurring in the wonderful world of flowers. These new introductions show variations which are often both interesting and attractive. Such variations should be judged on the basis of whether or not they enhance beauty and form. Each part must be in balance with all the other parts and proportioned to the other parts. Each part must be consistent with a particular form. In other words, one fall on an Iris bloom cannot flare while another on the same bloom droops or is horizontal.

Form variations such as ruffling, crimping, lacing, flouncing, and fluting are not necessarily always desirable, nor do they necessarily merit more points. An occasional smooth flower is a welcome sight among its ruffled fellows whether they be daylilies, gladiolus or iris. The question is how to distribute the points allotted to form. Rather than GIVING additional ones for variations, reduce the number assigned to form if any of these variations or factors contribute to an impression which is not perfection for its style or type.

Crimping, ruffling, lacing, etc., should be refined and uniform, not giving the impression of damage, a bedraggled appearance or that "something has been chewing at the edges". The Judge must not allow a personal preference or familiarity with a plain edge to blind him to quality, however.

DAMAGE AFFECTS FORM

Insect damage and disease which has progressed to the point where it cripples or alters the shape is considered under form. The same applies to mechancial damage, a tear or a broken petal on an iris affects both condition as well as form. It is up to the Judge where he feels the most damage occurs or he may divide the points deducted under two headings. However, care should be taken that the FULL NUMBER of points deductible for a fault is not deducted under both headings which would be an unfair handling of the situation.

POTTED PLANT FORM

Most Judges have very little trouble in judging form of our more common houseplants, but due to cultural experimentation, the forms of some plants are altered by the exhibitor's efforts with grafting or training where a vining plant is grown as an unsupported vine, on a trellis, on a totem or even pinched back to form a bushy plant. The effect of such training or experimentation with grafting may be one of desirability and beauty, but if the effect is otherwise the Judge should penalize.

INFLORESCENCE CATEGORIES

Flowers entered in shows fall into three categories of inflorescence:

A. Round Forms both single and doubles (asters, zinnias, large marigolds, etc.).

B. Spike Forms (stocks, snapdragons, salvia, etc.).

C. Spray Forms (cosmos, sweetpeas, etc.).

Round Form

Singles are circular with a circular center. Ray florets should all be the same length, width, shape, equally spaced with smooth and even margins.

Doubles are circular with depth and fullness. Outer petals recurve slightly, inner rows cup. All petals in a given row should be uniform in length, width, shape, spacing. A too high or popping center is penalized.

Spike Form

With all spike types, the number of flowers and buds is the important consideration. Removal of a drooping stem tip is penalized if detected. Faded flowers and seed pods lower the score drastically and may be removed with less severe deductions, but with full knowledge of what is required regarding removal on a specific species. There should be a maximum number of open flowers, usually in the proportions of two-thirds open flowers to one-third developing buds and flowers, with an equal one-third for good stem proportion. The spike must be erect and straight to the tip, the stem sturdy and the flowers uniformly colored, sized and spaced.

Spray Form

Total form points are divided between general effect and individual floret effect. Under general effect consider the number of flowers and buds, branching, grace and vigor of the spray as a whole.

The other half of the points for form covers the separate flowers, their typical form and uniformity.

SYMMETRY AND CIRCULAR

There seems to be some confusion over the application of symmetry and circular. Circular means round either in the three-dimension sphere or two-dimensional round as in the ball-shape marigold and the round pansy. Symmetry means beauty due to a balance or harmony of parts. The form may be oval or square and still have symmetry. For instance, a Gladiolus floret is slightly elongated and the equality or agreement in the number and placement, arrangement of the petals and sepals gives it symmetry within the less-than-circular outline.

Color

Color standards are often difficult to define because in many cases the true color and quality of the color in a variety in one locality or cultural environment may vary due to amounts of moisture, types and fertility of soil, amounts and intensity of sunlight and the temperatures. A good Judge acquaints him/herself with the color CONSISTENT to the area. In extreme cases, two entries of the same variety at times may appear as hardly recognizable as the same variety.

Many scales previously grouped substance and texture, and it makes sense to team texture with color if texture hasn't been given its own amount of points in the scale being used. A Judge must consider if the texture enhances or detracts from the beauty and color of the flower under consideration.

Indications are that humans are naturally attracted to certain colors — yellows, lavenders, blues, pinks and reds being among those usually preferred and the Judge must be conscious of this human tendency, and judge all qualities objectively.

Some Judges still insist that color is a matter of personal taste, that they prefer any color as long as it is yellow, or that there is enough blue in the sky and that green should be reserved for grass and that all blends are "muddy", and that all flower color should be "advancing and stimulating". Color should be judged entirely aside from one's personal preferences by noting whether the purity and patterns are up to the standards of perfection for the variety.

The descriptive word "muddy" has been much used in the past to describe a color fault, but with the advent of certain colors which at their clearest literally LOOK like mud (i.e., the brown, fawn, russet, tan, sorrel and khaki colors), the growers and advocates of these varieties object to the use of the word "muddy" as a fault as being confusing and ambiguous. The same probably applies to the words "smoky", "shadowed", "dusky", "sooty", "creamy". These are not words which actually describe a fault, but rather are descriptive words which paint a picture of the color value.

A descriptive word to take the place of "muddy" as a fault term is not hard to find, but will be harder to graft into the judging vocabulary. Such possible substitutions include "murky", "obscured", "clouded", "dingy", "dismal", "spiritless", "dreary", "sullen", "flat", "dull".

A Judge must be careful in the evaluation of color as it is a visual sensation and each person reacts very acutely and in an individual way to each color. Some colors might impress the Judge as "gloomy, funereal, sombre, depressing, melancholy", but these reactions should be put aside and should not enter into the evaluation of color.

True color is that which is characteristic for a given variety. The markings, their amounts, their distribution, design and clarity must be considered, and any combinations must be evaluated on the basis of their harmony. Some very unpleasant combinations may occur, along with a lack of clarity. Where more than one color appears in a flower, the effect must always be harmonious and pleasing without violent or jarring contrasts. As hybridization continues, many such combinations are encountered in the search to present "something new and different" and the Judge must exert her color training to ascertain the color merits. Markings, patterns and contrasts should be clean, clear and the blendings smooth and pleasing.

Color fading is often but NOT always an indication of age. The Judge checks to see if a lack of substance, pronounced stamens or other indications accompanies a bleaching of color or lessening of intensity. Fading may not always be considered objectionable. For example, pale blues that fade to white, medium blues that fade to pale blues or medium pinks that fade to pale pinks may retain their attractiveness, all other factors being equal. But the typical color for a variety is always to be given credit.

Fading is usually more of a fault in red, yellow and in some browns and blends. Fading in dark colors may not be uniform and is sometimes accompanied by burning and water spotting which is penalized. Reds which have turned blue or are sunburned are to be penalized and any streaking or uneven fading is objectionable.

So many hues are represented in the flower world, and these hues vary widely in their values, from brilliance and degree of saturation or vividness to darkest tones and up to palest tints. When the Show Schedule sets up a class for yellow Iris, or Pink Iris or Red Roses, the Judge should expect to find a rather wide range of related color values, but he should not be tempted to rate one entry higher than another because it "seems" to him to be "redder" or "yellower". If, however, the color of one is more pure, and clearer, then it will deserve premium rating. Good books on color are available so it is only necessary here to point out that as far as specimens are concerned, the lighter tones of any color produced by reduction of the color content with white diminish the intensity of the color, changing the value, but without altering the purity or clarity. But if the color value is altered by addition of grey, the color loses not only intensity, but purity, clarity and brightness as well. The grey admixture contributes to the dirty, clouded appearance which is considered a fault. Clarity and purity are particularly important and this extends to any roughness or blurring of markings and patterns.

When rating color, the Judge must be alert to penalize for disagreeable fading, excessive color instability, burning, water spotting, spray deposits or mildew and for blemishes caused by careless handling. Insect damage which alters the color is penalized here, such as damage done by the obscuring of color by red spider and the whitening, lightening or color transparency caused by thrips; disease damage which alters or changes or obscures the color is also evaluated under color. The age and maturity of a bloom will also affect the color, being more intense when the flower is at its prime, and fading or bluing as the blossom ages. Recent advances through hybridization are opening whole new color and pattern ranges; such color breaks should be recognized and judged for their general attractiveness, clarity and purity.

COLOR QUALITIES SUMMARIZED

FRESHNESS: the color is not blemished by aging, fading, heat or refrigeration.

CLARITY: luminous, bright, rich, clear, not dull, murky or clouded.

PURITY: freedom from unnatural pigmentation, foreign color or grey. Evidenced by white streaks in red varieties, light spots in darks, or dark spots in lights, or an over-all greyed look. Self-colors should maintain uniform color throughout entire floret. Streaky unevenness is penalized. Purity also involves the absence or presence of discoloration on the surface from weather, insects sucking, dust or spray residue.

BRILLIANCE: that refractive characteristic which makes petals appear lustrous, sparkling, glittering, shimmering or glistening. Often looks like bright diamond dust when observed in the sunlight. Sheen means lustre.

ATTRACTIVENESS: degree of appeal.

Texture

Texture is at first a difficult quality to judge. Technically, it means the surface quality of a leaf or petal. It is the roughness or smoothness of the surface and can be silky, satiny, velvety, cloth or suede-like, leathery, etc. Anthuriums have a smooth, varnished texture, geraniums a velvety texture, poppies a papery texture and lilies a waxy texture.

Texture is closely allied to color and in some scales of points is actually listed with color. Rough textures absorb light, thus grey or darken colors, adding richness through the tiny shadows cast by the protrusions. Smooth textures reflect the light, making the color glow and giving it vividness. The texture should enhance the color.

Some flowers, such as poppies and sweet peas, are typically fragile and filmy and their textures should be delicate and refined, never coarse or ribbed. The texture should be consistent and unvarying over the entire surface of the flower or leaf.

Texture should be considered according to what is normal and typical for that particular plant being judged. Coarseness is often the result of over-fertilizing or improperly diluted and applied sprays. An aging, dull texture detracts from a color's appeal and makes it appear less brilliant.

Where variations, such as crepe-ing, leather or other differences appear in a hybrid of a species which is usually smooth surfaced or vice versa, the Judge must consider if the change enhances the color and appeal of the flower. If so, the variation can be considered an improvement. But points must be deducted if the appearance is marred. The Judge must be careful not to allow his own preference for the familiar to blur his judgment.

Size

Size must be as large, due to cultural excellence, as good proportion allows and that which is most nearly representative of the variety being judged; with consideration given to that specimen which is above average but not gross. Excessive extremes on either side of normalcy should be penalized. Large size is not desirable if form and substance have been weakened and texture coarsened.

Though extra size is usually considered an improvement, Miniature flowers without daintiness are devoid of charm and pleasing, typical "personality". Size, proportion and scale are of utmost importance and must be given discerning consideration, as the whole concept of these tiny flowers or plants is based on their miniature appearance. A Judge must not let a personal preference for small, medium or large flowers influence evaluation.

The question sometimes arises as to the point value of a "typical" size for a bloom. Certainly the same number of points are not given for both "typical" and "larger than average".

If the size is "typical" or "average", at least one point is deducted; if the size is larger that expected for the area and other circumstances, then the full quota of points allotted to size may be given, or the superiority may be figured under Distinction if that quality appears in the scale.

Substance

Substance is that quality of firmness or rigidity of the flower or leaf which enables it to retain its characteristic form and to retain an even freshness overall and brilliance of color. It is the material of which the flower is made, and should be strong, firm and crisp, but not so heavy as to give an appearance of coarseness.

Substance is recognized by the thickness and toughness of the floral parts, but involves more than this in that the flower parts must be turgid . . . the tissues filled with moisture. Substance makes the flower last longer, hold its shape and take adverse weather conditions. Turgidity will be high when the specimen is in its prime and when it has been well-conditioned or hardened off for showing.

Lack of attention to cultural needs with reference to water, fertilization, shading and other factors is reflected in the degree of substance. The degree also varies with varieties and species within a plant family.

Overmaturity often brings about a lack of substance, limpness and wilting or a thinning at the edges of the petals which can be determined by holding the specimen up to the light. A Judge should refrain from touching or feeling the petals between the fingers to determine substance. The heat and oils of the hand hasten deterioration. A pencil may be used, if necessary, and carefully run under the petals, or the specimen may be **gently** shaken to ascertain the presence of a crisp, turgid substance.

Substance is considered in most horticultural exhibits, being given a separate, though usually lower number of points. In some plants, substance may be considered under "freshness" or even under condition, or may be combined with texture.

Cultural Perfection

Here the Judge evaluates the effort, ability and knowledge of the exhibitor as a grower by the results he has achieved in the exhibit. Cultural perfection starts with good seed or plants, grown in properly prepared soil, watered, staked, divided, disbudded (if required), fertilized, sprayed, cut and hardened off at the proper times and in the correct way.

That the grower practices proven cultural techniques will be evident in the appearance of general good health, peak of perfection and prime maturity with no evidence of cultural neglect.

The Judge deducts for any injury caused by cultural neglect or malpractice. Cultural malpractice is the grower's lack of attention to, and neglect of a plant's requirements relative to environment, shade, light, humidity and needs, soil type, food, water, protection from insects and disease, staking, disbudding and division. Lack of attention in any of these areas is often reflected in small ways in a plant's appearance and are discernible to the knowing eye.

When all entries are of high quality, decisions must often be based upon minute details — a little lag in color, weakened substance, lengthened nodes, twisted placement all of which indicate treatment practices contrary to established rules.

The word "happy" is general and abstract, yet it does serve to aptly describe the state of a plant which is culturally perfect. If the specimen is or was in active characteristic growth, thrifty appearing and vigorous, fresh and turgid, showing no lack of attention as regards its needs or protection — if it seems "happy", the Judge can assume all its specific requirements are being met in the case of a potted plant, or have been met in the case of the cut specimen.

Throughout the text, the symptoms of insect and disease damage and nutrient deficiencies are described because a Judge is often asked to identify the causes of certain damage. The prevention and treatment of these ills may be found in many excellent books and have no place in a book on Judging.

The Judge must be able to recognize abnormalities due to chemicals, and nutrient deficiencies.

Chemical Spray Damage

Twisted, spiraling shoots, abnormal leaf, stem development

Elongated leaftips, "fern" leaf.

Prominent, swollen "varicose" veinings.

Scorching or burning of leaf margins and tissue.

Carbon monoxide from a car motor running near a plant bed results in similar symptoms, plus singed appearing leaves.

Nutrient Deficiency

Nitrogen: foliage light green, yellowing, growth stunted, stems weak.

Phosphorous: foliage dark green, retarded growth, leaf veinings often purplish.

Potassium: lower mature leaves mottled, with dead spots, yellowing margins.

Magnesium: leaf margin curling up or down, puckering, dead areas.

Iron: yellow between veins, green veins. Tip browning.

   (Overwatering, too high Ph, low temperatures and root nematodes cause similar symptoms.)

Boron: breakdown at leaf base, stem and petiole dry, brittle.

Manganese: bloom inferior in size and color. Dead spots but veins remain green.

Calcium: browning leaf tip and margins, hooked tip.

Insects

Judges eliminate from competition any infested specimens. Be sure aphids did not just "walk over"! In-residence aphids and scale and red spider show effects easily recognized by the Judge.

Damage caused by insects or any of the above symptoms receive greater penalties than tears or bruising, as they show long-standing cultural neglect.

Uniformity

Because single specimens of many plants look insignificant, the Schedule often requests several specimens. When judging such multiple entries, uniformity of all the qualities of size, form, color, stem length, stem and foliage characteristics, texture, cultural perfection, condition and grooming, facing and spacing must be considered if the Schedule has requested they all be of one variety.

However, if assorted varieties are requested, uniformity cannot be applied to ALL the qualities as these will differ according to that which is typical of the cultivar. In such mixed exhibits, the uniformity of stem length, cultural perfection, condition and grooming and color harmony is considered.

Judge the color by individual perfection and then by the harmony of the combination when more than one color is allowed or called for. Sometimes the addition of a white or a mutually harmonious intervening color is skillfully included to make the selection more harmonious.

While artistic effect is not judged as such in collections, the wise exhibitor will tilt the specimens or arrange them for more effective angle, in such a way that all face the Judge and each is as exactly alike the others as possible. Bonus points for uniformity may be used to break ties in close competitions.

If one bad bloom is too poor to be scored at all, the remaining blooms cannot save the entry. If the decision is close, score individual blooms and total.

Educational Value

LABELING

Since the purpose of flower shows and fair floriculture sections is educational, each exhibitor can do much by labeling his plant correctly. Growers themselves have caused confusion by selling plants under incorrect names that stick like second skins! For instance, Philodendron oxycardium, the common heart-shaped vining plant is often incorrectly called P. cordatum; Monstera deliciosa is incorrectly sold as Philodendron pertusum or Split-leaf Philodendron, and Peperomia argyreia (sandersii) is called Watermelon Begonia though it is related neither to watermelons or begonias.

Labeling has been encouraged not only as an educational aid to both exhibitors and the public, but as a help to the Judges and is often used to break ties. Specialized shows take labeling for granted and exhibits are disqualified if they are not named. In the general shows and fairs we have neglected this practice and the quality of our educational effort suffers for it.

When there are other specimens of the same variety shown, a comparison of the anatomical parts (leaf shape and edge, bracts, petal placement, etc.) will aid the Judge in arriving at a definite conclusion on correctness of labeling.

Any grower proud enough of his specimen to show it, should label it. Labels should be neat, small but not too tiny, inconspicuous but easily read, neatly printed. Whether or not they are waterproof is not considered unless the lack of waterproofing has resulted in a blurred, messy appearance. If the scale does not include the quality of labeling with its own number of points, labeling can be considered either under Distinction, Condition or Grooming, failing that, consider it under Cultural Perfection. Fancy lettering or decorated cards are not taken into consideration. Emphasis is on legibility and above all . . . correctness.

MATURITY

To have full educational value a plant should be grown to its peak of bloom or growth. Of course, the Judge takes into consideration the fact that many plants never can be considered truly mature when home-grown, they are mere saplings as potted plants. But with controlled pot care, they can be grown to be satisfyingly mature as house plants.

The Judge must penalize any plant which is immature or an inadequate example of the type. The plant must be old enough to show mature characteristics and to reflect the care which has been given it for a considerable period of time. A casual rule of thumb is that a plant should be three months to at least a year old, depending upon the type, before being exhibited. A carefully worded schedule and an alert Classification Committee can circumvent the exhibition of "baby" plants.

TRUENESS TO TYPE, TYPICAL

Educational value also includes consideration of trueness to type; is the plant typical in form, color, flowering, branching, spine and glochid formation, etc.? It will aid the Judge to determine what is typical for a variety in the area by comparing a dubious specimen with others of the same variety in the class.

To arrive at a fair and practical appraisal of type characteristics, the Judge must accept the normal expression as the standard. Season, climate, culture, fertilizer and various environmental conditions all enter into the growth, performance and appearance of the various expressions of a variety. If conditions are unusually favorable for excessive growth, this stimulates the expansion of size, height, the production of extra leaves and flowers and also intensifies the color, etc. Obviously this unstable situation creates much controversy and confusion. Under these contributary circumstances there is only one practical method to follow.

We can lay down approximate specifications based on a plant's NORMAL CHARACTER UNDER NORMAL CONDITIONS and expect such plants to vary within reasonable limits when conditions are abnormal for their natural expression. We must know and accept the normal expression as typical for the area and judge accordingly.

Color is an unstable factor in identifying varieties as it shifts due to weather, soils and cultural care including moisture, degree of shade and fertilizer available from garden to garden, as well as from area to area. Location, altitude and season also have a bearing. A Judge should not be dogmatic regarding what is typical color, and especially when judging flowers from areas other than his own.

Height is also a most undependable characteristic upon which to base a standard as it varies with season, climate, culture and weather. A variety or cultivar which normally has a height of 5-6" may grow to over 12" in a neighboring yard or in another season. So to arrive at any specification for height, it must be indicated as that which is "normal" . . . normalcy being SELDOM exceeding 6" or 12" or 24", or whatever the case may be.

SHOW QUALITY OF VARIETIES

No matter how much attention is paid to their cultural requirements, some varieties cannot successfully compete with superior varieties in respect to the general qualities listed in the respective scale.

It behooves the exhibitor to study up on the peculiarities of the varieties with which he hopes to win. And it must be remembered by both Judge and exhibitor that newness alone means nothing if the qualities listed on the scale are not ideal in the specimen. Some are just naturally "show quality" and a cultivar which consistently has mediocre form or consistently lacks substance or is weak-necked cannot hope to win over a proven "show quality" variety. Expert selection as well as expert cultural practice is a "blue ribbon" tool for exhibitors.

NEW VARIETY, RARITY, DIFFICULT CULTURE

The exhibit has educational value if it is a new variety exhibited in the area for the first time; or if it is a new species which has been discovered, imported or propagated; or if some new or unorthodox growing or training method was used to create successful results, or examples of cultural experimentation as the grafting of a pendulous form (Rattail Cacti) on the top of a tall, erect stem (Cerus).

In some instances, all things being equal, newness, rarity or difficulty of culture may be given a point or two to break a tie in a closely competitive class.

LATE SEASON EXHIBITS

Often it is noted that a rose or a columbine, etc., exhibited after the peak season is given a ribbon with the lame explanation that "for this time of year this is pretty good". It must be remembered that standards of perfection should not be unduly relaxed . . . that a specimen must rate at least 90 for a blue ribbon in any part of the growing season. Very slight variations of the standards are allowed from area to area, but not from week to week of the growing season. Such exhibits have little educational value, other than their mere presence, which is often quite sad!

Condition, Grooming

Here the Judge evaluates the effort, ability and knowledge of the exhibitor in selecting and showing worthy specimens.

CONDITION

Is based on the actual physical appearance of the specimen at the time of judging. Under condition, the Judge considers mechanical injury, bruising, immaturity, age, and weather damage. (Rain spotting and fading are deducted under color). Any torn or damaged parts are penalized here. Damage done by insects or disease is considered under cultural perfection if that quality is listed in the scale being used. If not, then consider such damage here.

The fragrance characteristic of some species or varieties may be considered as a part of condition when there is no separate spot on the scale for this quality.

GROOMING

Involves the care taken to have the specimen present the best possible appearance. Under grooming, deduct points for soil, dried florets, spray residue, careless labeling or lack of labeling, over-grooming such as trimming or polishing.

Since practices vary in the removal of spent blossoms, according to the type plant being judged, the Judge must be cognizant of what is acceptable for the specific family and judge accordingly.

Leaves, if present, should be clean. They may be wiped with a cloth, but not polished with any additives or preparations.

A good motto in assessing grooming is that the exhibitor should add nothing and take nothing away, including dried bracts from spring bulbs and rose thorns. With the exception, of course, of dried flowers and foliage as is permissible.

Detection of excessive grooming techniques is often difficult and the Judge is sometimes criticized by an "eyeballing" competitor who spots an attempt to "gild the lily," so to speak.

The expert exhibitor can improve and refine the form of a rose or other flower with careful training with brush and fingers, but when he goes the step further in surreptitiously trimming petals or foliage to remove defects or otherwise indulges in an urge to improve the appearance by any removal other than of foreign materials, thistledown, dust, spray residue, etc., he is courting detection and penalty. Trimmed edges often show burning or browning and an edge "slant" which is distinguished from the natural.

If the back petals of a many-petaled type such as a dahlia are any shorter than the others, it can be presumed that trimming has taken place. Since detection is difficult and the penalty if discovered probably no more than the presence of the defect, exhibitors often take the risk.

A Judge should be able to correctly assess the type of grooming and credit the exhibitor who takes every legitimate means, such as skillful re-arrangement of petals, foliage, wiping and removal of foreign material and spent florets as well as careful staging to have the exhibit present its very best appearance.

Summary Clarified

The lists of descriptive words are included in an attempt to train Judges to discard the over-used abstract terms such as "poor", "good", "superior", and substitute more descriptive ones which convey an educational word-picture of the quality under discussion. While these are more general and less specific than what is expected in constructive comments (which see), these summaries show that words other than "suitable" and "lacking" can be found to express a common fault or merit.

The words "well-shaped" are not specific unless one knows what constitutes a well-shaped form for the specific plant being discussed. Such words as "lovely", "magnificent" and "noble" can convey only a general impression. To say a flower is "immense" makes the listener or reader wonder HOW BIG? To say a flower is "outstanding" leaves one wondering in what way is it outstanding? The conscientious Judge will, no doubt, wish to add to these lists in a personal attempt to bring his comments down from cloudy abstracts to solid concretes, thus training himself to leave as few questions as possible in the minds of the exhibitor and the public.

The words and phrases in the PLUS-BONUS and MINUS-PENALTY portions of the summaries are not intended to be complete or applicable only to ONE type or to all types, but are cross-sampling of phrases which may be applicable. To show acceptability and to refresh the Judge's memory that such variations may be found, they are listed in the PLUS column. The PLUS column contains specific words and phrases to describe certain qualities which are acceptable generally as to form, color, etc., and for which no deduction is made. The MINUS groupings are specific words and phrases which describe undesirable qualities for which points will be deducted.

For instance, the descriptive phrase "irregular petal formation" of Japanese Iris refers to several varieties in which this IS a fault, but is not applicable to the Monstrosa type which normally have irregular petals.

The words "intense" and "delicate" may both appear in the PLUS summary of a flower. Now, obviously a color cannot be both, but both are listed to remind the Judge that both intense colors and delicate colors are found in the varieties within that particular plant family.

The same can be said of form and other qualities. The trusses of rhododendrens may be "conical", "globular" or "round-topped" according to variety, all are acceptable forms and are listed in the PLUS summary.

Lilac flowers are typically small in some varieties and large in others, thus the word "small" could be a fault in one and a typical, expected characteristic (relatively) in another. Fragrance is certainly a merit quality in Lilacs, yet there are several species (i.e. S. Wolfi and S. Juliane) which are not at all fragrant. And certainly no specimen should be penalized for not possessing a quality which is NOT typical of its type. The Judge upon viewing the specimen must know what to expect in each case. He must apply the proper characteristic to the individual specimen and variety being judged at the moment.

It will be noted that the summaries may also be used as a handy index to find under which quality a point is discussed. For example, to quickly find the discussion on tablecloth overhang lengths, one checks the table summaries to find this listed under Proportion!

SECTION 2 — GENERAL PLANTS

General Cut Flower Scales Of Points

For flower types not covered specifically apply the scale that fits their type of inflorescence.

In multiple-specimen exhibits any lack of uniformity of any one quality is to be penalized.

SPRAY FORM CUT FLOWERS

Amount of Bloom	25	Substance	15
Color	20	Size	10
Form	20	Condition and Grooming	10

*of spray, (grace, branching, placement and vigor)
*of flowers, (depth, uniformity, symmetry)

SPIKE FORM CUT FLOWERS

Spike —

Color	20
Substance	15
Form	15
Size	5

Florets —

Amount of Bloom, Floriferousness	15
Size, Vigor of Spike	10
Spacing	10
Condition and Grooming of Whole	10

ROUND FORM CUT FLOWERS

Form	25	Stem and Foliage	15
Color	20	Size	15
Substance	15	Condition and Grooming	10

Aster

SUGGESTED CLASSES:

Aster, 10 to 15 inch stem. 3 Blooms, same variety, same color.

1. BALL FORM — 3 to 5", Three Blooms
   (includes Peony Flowering, American Beauty, Giant Branching, etc.)

2 SHAGGY FORM — 3 to 5", Three Blooms
   (includes Crego, Comet, Calif Giant, etc.)

3. PINCUSHION, CRESTED — 3 to 5", Three Blooms
   (includes Sunshine, Needle, Anemone, Princess, Powder Puff, etc.)

4. SINGLE — 3 to 5", Three Blooms

5. POMPON BOUQUET FORM — Three Sprays
   (small flowers in cluster, use Spray Form Cut Flower Scale)

CHINA ASTER, ANNUAL

Ball Form

- globular, must have depth
- symmetrical
- circular
- incurved petals
- regularly spaced
- 3 to 5 inches

Shaggy Form

- symmetrical
- circular, must have depth
- petals, fine, ribbonlike
- curled and feathery
- 3 to 5 inches

Pincushion, Crested

- quilled, cactus-like
- semi-quilled
- sometimes combined with ray petals
- 3 to 5 inches
- must have depth

Single

- circular
- flat
- center bare surrounded by
- 2 to 3 rows of ray florets
- 3 to 4 inches diameter

SUGGESTED SCALE:

Form	25	Stem and Foliage	15
Color	20	Size	15
Substance	15	Condition and Grooming	10

Form 20 Points
*center well filled (except Singles) *graceful *round *globular (except Singles)
*symmetrical *according to variety and type *mature *¾ to fully open *puffy and full (except Singles)
-flat, thin (except Singles) -scanty -immature -fullness not uniform from center to edge
-malformed due to tarnished plant bug or yellows virus -misshapen -not round
-centers bald, split, depressed in doubles, -irregular -lopsided -off center
-lacks uniformity -too few petals in double types
-singles petals unequal lengths, gaps between petals on singles

Color 20 Points
*rich *lush *pure *bright *clear
-weak -dull -faded -greenish (due to yellows virus) -lacks brilliance, sparkle

Substance 15 Points
*turgid *crisp *fresh *holding well *strawlike
-flaccid -drooping -wilted -limp -soft

Stem and Foliage 15 Points
Stem — *wiry *strong *supporting bloom *long *straight *disbudded *well posed
blackened (due to stem rot) -weak -spindly -short -twisted- coarse
-cut too long for size of flower -damaged -disbudding recent and apparent -pose of bloom too upright -unequal stem lengths -cut too short
Foliage and bracts — *fresh *clean *strong *typical green color
-weak -scanty -small orange patches (caused by rust fungi) -wilted

Size 15 Points
*larger than average for type and area *typical
-small -dwarfed -different sizes -freakish

Condition and Grooming 10 Points
*intact *undamaged *clean foliage, stem, bloom
-damaged by blister beetles or grasshoppers -torn -soiled

Bells Of Ireland

SUGGESTED CLASS
Three spikes, displayed with foliage removed.
SUGGESTED SCALE: Use Spike Form Cut Flower Scale.
BRACTS (Florets)
Color 20 Points
*translucent *green *delicately veined *lively
-weak -watery -bleached -whitened -dull

Substance 15 Points
*fresh appearance *crisp *strong
-thin -drooping -wilting -drying -petioles relaxed allowing bracts to droop -floppy

Form 15 Points
*mature *all bracts uniformly fluted *uniform
-deformed -loose

Size 5 Points
*bracts uniformly sized *above average size bracts
*almost all the same size all the way up the spike
-bracts size varying -small overall

SPIKE
Number of Bracts and Spacing 25 Points
*closely set all the way up *all the way around *profuse *graceful
*spike form symmetrical *cylindrical *bracts touching but not crowded
-scanty -inadequate -skipped placement -bunched on spike -clubby effect

Size and Vigor 10 Points
*strong *plump *curved stems -allowed as grown primarily for interesting effects *long
-weak -thin -skinny -short

Condition and Grooming 10 Points
*foliage neatly, completely removed *clean *mature *unmarred *secondary laterals removed
-streaked -soiled -bracts torn, hanging -stem scarred -brown spotted -mildewed -foliage left on and bracts obscured -side branches need disbudding

Calendula (Pot Marigold)

SUGGESTED CLASSES:
Five Blooms
    A: one color, one variety
    B: assorted colors, one variety
Sub-divisions may be added for
    1. Crested, Quilled
    2. Doubles
    3. Singles
SUGGESTED SCALE: Use Round Form Cut Flower Scale

Form 25 Points
*crested, single, double according to variety
*deep *circular *symmetrical *centers filled *uniform *mature
-distorted -lopsided -immature -pollen drop

Color 20 Points
*rich *clear *desirable combinations *pure
-weak -blurred -faded -streaked

Substance 15 Points
*fresh *crisp *perky *appealing
-wilted -drooped -spikey -centers bolting

Stem and Foliage 15 Points
*long *uniform *strong *straight *proportioned to flower *bright green
-short -crooked -yellowing -scarred -thin -weak -should be disbudded

Size 15 Points

Attains at least 3 inches in some varieties
*larger than average *typical
-small -inadequate

Condition and Grooming 10 Points

*intact *unmarred *clean
-missing petals -foreign matter -scarred calyx -soiled -damaged

Celosia

SUGGESTED CLASSES:

1. CRESTED COCKSCOMB (Cristata) 3 flower heads

   Tall A: one color, same variety; B: assorted colors, different variety

   Dwarf C: one color, same variety; D: assorted colors, different variety

2. PLUME, FEATHERED (Plumosa) 3 spikes

   Tall A: one color, same variety; B: assorted colors, different variety

   Dwarf C: one color, same variety; D: assorted colors, different variety

Schedule to specify if exhibits are to be fresh, dried or either!

SUGGESTED SCALE:

Crested		Plume	
Color	30	Color	30
Condition and Grooming	25	Form	30
Form	25	Condition and Grooming	25
Size	20	Size	15

CRESTED

Color 30 Points

Head — *brilliant *showy *lush *rich *striking *pure *positive
-harsh -bluing -faded -dull
Foliage — *fresh specimen *some varieties are typically light green, others dark bronzy

Condition and Grooming 25 Points

*clean *dustfree *mature *intact
-wilted -limp -dusty -containing seeds -immature -chaffy

Form 25 Points

*typical 'cocks comb' *full *dense *plushlike *broad *corrugated *interestingly flattened, ruffled *firm *stem straight *side or secondary laterals removed *stem proportionate to flower head
-loose -thin -head divided deeply -weak stem -long, awkward laterals

Size 20 Points

"TOREADOR" makes a 6 to 9 inch crown
*larger than expected for the area *average
-stunted -small

PLUME CELOSIA
Form 30 Points
*long *feathery *spire-like *chenille-like *full *symmetrical *side and secondary plumes removed
-ragged -clubby -spindling -thin -blunt -immature -long, low side shoots

Color 30 Points
*brilliant *clear *lush *rich *pure *showy
-dull -faded -streaked -discolored

Condition and Grooming 25 Points
Fresh: — *soft *silky *mature *foliage present, green and clean
-limp -wilted -tip drooping
Dried: — *crisp *clean *foilage rubbed off *completely dry
-dusty -webby -shedding

Size 15 Points
*large for area and season *typical
-stunted -below average

Columbine (Áquilegia)
SUGGESTED CLASSES:
Three sprays (corymbs) 12 to 15 inch stems

Separate classes may be made for Doubles, Long Spurred, Short Spurred.

SUGGESTED SCALE: Use The Spray Form Cut Flower Scale
Number of Flowers 25 Points
*at least 6 to 8 open *more than average *adequate amount
-scanty -sparse -too many buds in proportion to flowers open

Color 20 Points
*clear *combinations pleasing *unique *striking combinations *rich *pure
-dull -faded -blurred -murky -weak -uneven
-seedlings often produce unclear, impure colors

Form 20 Points
Spray — *gracefully branched *airy *strong, wiry stem *bushy *balanced *flowers gracefully uptilted, well posed *vigorous
-crowded -too loose -overlong -too short -thin -weak -lop sided -cut off above foliage (some should be exhibited on the stem) -foliage too heavy and obscuring flowers

Flower — On some varieties the spurs incurve slightly, on others they flare. The length of spur varies, some varieties may have 4 to 6 inch spurs.
*graceful spurs *slender spurs *uniform on all *widely flared sepals *sepals tapering *petals broad *petals open, some overlap
-spurs crumpled -uneven -sepals and petals gaping -petals too narrow -form not uniform in all flowers

Substance 15 Points
*spurs plump *fresh *crisp *holding well *stamens fresh
-spurs collapsed, shriveling -pollen drop -limp -thinning -thin -crepey -coarse

Size 10 Points
Some varieties exceed three inches.
*larger than expected *typical *uniform
-small -less than average

Condition and Grooming 10 Points
*undamaged *clean *well groomed of all foreign matter, dried petals, seed pods
-foliage blemished -foliage shows serpentine tunneling of leaf miners -foliage shows evidence of mildew (greying) -soiled -dried florets present -seed pods present -spurs or petals torn, or bruised

Cosmos

SUGGESTED CLASS
Three sprays 10 to 15 inches long, one variety, one color

SUGGESTED SCALE: Use Spray Form Cut Flower Scale
Amount of Bloom 25 Points
*plentiful *profuse *adequate *well placed over spray
-scanty -lacking

Color 20 Points
*uniformity of center zoning in Radiance Variety *definite pattern *clear *bright *pure
-dusty -faded -streaked -discolored -color chewed away by sucking insects

Form 20 Points
Spray — *¾ of the flowers should be open *well branched *robust *airy *balanced *adequate to support laterals *typically wiry
-crowded -sparsely branched -lop sided -weak, thin stems

Flowers — *prettily fluted *ribbed *slightly overlapping petals *typical of variety *double or single *uniform over the plant spray
-loose -petals gaping at base -lack symmetery

Substance 15 Points
*upright *petals and stamens fresh, crisp *turgid *perky
-aged -wilting -thin -petals curling, drooping

Size 10 Points
Sensation variety achieves 4 to 6 inches *larger than expected *typical
-small -weak -immature

Condition and Grooming 10 Points
*undamaged *clean *prime
-centers popped -insect chewn -seed pods present -brown spots on stem indicating blight -spent, dried petals or flowers

Gourds

SUGGESTED CLASSES:

1. DECORATIVE SPECIMENS (uncured, natural)
   A: 3 specimens, same varieties
   B: 3 specimens, assorted varieties
2. DISPLAY (uncured, natural)
   At least five varieties, displayed attractively in designated area. Judged for perfection of specimen and beauty of display.
3. GOURD CRAFT (cured)

GOURDS

Generally inedible members of the Cucurbitaceae family which includes the cucumber, squash, pumpkin and the melon.

Properly cured gourds have been known to last for 100 years or more. The Japanese treasure them as sake bottles, they are used as flutes by professional Indian snake charmers, as drums, and novelties and as utility utensils and toys. In Chinese symbolism, the gourd represents longevity because of its durability; fecundity because of its large number of seeds and is thought of as a magic charm.

Cured gourds are not displayed as au-natural specimens as they become brown and uninteresting unless color-altered or in craft work.

Ovifera (small decorative gourds) are most decorative in color, texture and shape; Lagenaria (large gourds, bottle) are easiest to cure and are used extensively for craftwork. The latter includes the "dishcloth", utensil, calabash, and snake gourds. Lagenarias dry brown and are often shown as cured and painted, dyed, or designed. Designs may be burned on, indented or other and shapes altered to use or beauty.

The Judge of such cured specimens expects to find experimental shapes — carved while still on the vine, grown in flasks or moulds or by taping or tying to alter form. Mold produces a mosaic-like design on the surface.

While small size is preferred in the ornamental specimen classes of complete form, large sizes are often found in the craft section, reconstructed as masks, jugs, other.

Natural means ornamental gourds displayed unpolished or unvarnished. Polishing is easily detected as it removes the natural bloom and imports a lustre which gourds do not have when merely washed with water and wiped.

The Judges, of course, do not touch or handle the exhibits.

Identifying Ornamental Gourds

Any gourd has three characteristics . . . shape, color and texture. The names given ornamental gourds are descriptive of their shapes. Varying color combinations of greens and yellows may be found in most of these classes. Textures include smooth, ribbed, warty or combinations of these. Finger and Spoon gourds are apt to come true to form and are very durable when properly cured.

EGG — white, size and shape of a common hen's egg.

APPLE — nearly globular. About 1½ to 2½ inches high. Ribbed or plain. Light yellow to white.

ORANGE — globular, resembles an orange. Dull or light yellow.

BELL — rather bell shaped. Yellow marked with green. Slightly ridged.

BIG BELL — large, heavy, smooth or sparsely warted. 4 to 6 inches across and nearly as high. Dark or dull green, or sometimes white.

WHITE PEAR — pear-shaped with well marked narrow part at

least ⅓ as long as the body. 3 to 5 inches long. Surface smooth. Familiar as pioneer darning ball.

STRIPED PEAR — shape and size similar to above, but length-striped in yellow and green.

BI-COLOR — similar to white pear, lower half green with dark stripes, upper half striped in shades of yellow.

SPOON — brilliant green and yellow with extended handle 5 to 6 inches long, 1 to 1½ inches thick at spoon end.

MINIATURE — Smallest of these gourds, 1 to 1½ inches across and ½ inch high. Deep green marked with a thin, lengthwise band and flecks of lighter green.

BROAD STRIPED — flattened endwise. 3 to 4 inches across and approximately 1½ inches high. Dark green marked with whitish stripes or flecked and broken-striped.

LADLE OR SCOOP — 6 to 8 inches long with a handle. Often warty. Yellow on upper half. When dried may be hollowed out to make a scoop.

WARTY HARDHEAD — Globular. Green. 3 to 4 inches across. The seeds are often mixed or cross pollinated so frequently they do not run true to form.

FINGER GOURD — also called Holy Gourd, Crown of Thorns, Gourd of the Ten Commandments, Sugar Bowl. White, turning creamy as it dries. Has ten fingers or prongs if perfect, in five groups of two each.

TOP — rather small gourd which is large at the stem end and pointed at the other end. Shaped like a toy top. As these gourds cross, many mixed forms and colorings tend to make them unique and fascinating.

SUGGESTED SCALES OF POINTS

ORNAMENTAL SPECIMENS — Natural, uncured

Cultural Perfection	35	Color Interest (varietal)	15
Shape Interest (varietal)	15	Nomenclature	20
Textural Interest (varietal)	15		

ORNAMENTAL GOURD DISPLAY

Cultural Perfection	30	Quality and Suitability of	
Staging and Arrangement	30	accessories	20
Color Effect	20		

GOURD CRAFT — (Cured and/or Crafted)

Practicality and/or Interest and/or Beauty of item produced   45

*may be floral design featuring color-altered gourds; dolls; dippers; bird feeders, houses, kitchen utensils, planters, figures, doorstops, massage mitts, scuffs, others.

Individuality   30
*originality, uniqueness of item produced, contrived shape

Distinction   25
*consider craftsmanship

SUMMARY OF NATURAL UNCURED SPECIMEN

Cultural Perfection 35 Points

*blemish free *colors distinct *ripe *no indication of excess grooming *characteristic as to size, texture, shape, color *stem present *shells fine, thick *small (small sizes are more useful, with heavier skins, thus keep better) -overlarge -ungainly -fungus present -hail pitted -bruised -thin, weak shell -lustrous polish (indicating bloom removed by hand buffing, serious fault) -scarred -peeling -stem absent -color not typical, blurred, stained -finger gourd lacking a 'finger' -immature, underripe

Shape Interest 15 Points

*according to variety *interesting
-flattened unpleasantly by prolonged contact with ground -immature

Textural Interest 15 Points

*smooth, ribbed, warty or combination of these, according to variety *mature "bloom" retained (not buffed away, serious fault)
-defaced by insects, disease or mechanical injury -polished or varnished (deduct severely in this class)

Color Interest 15 Points

*according to variety *clear *pure if self-colored
-blurred -stained -moldy -impure -lacks clarity

Nomenclature 20 Points

For educational purposes, gourds should be labeled.
*correctly labeled *neat label *ease of reading *appropriately sized
-no label (deduct all points -incorrect (deduct all) - carelessly labeled

SUMMARY GOURD DISPLAY

Cultural Perfection 30 Points

*blemish free *stems attached *colors distinct *characteristic as to size, color texture *no indication of excess grooming *shells fine, thick, *size small as preferred in specimen classes
-immature -overlarge -thin, weak shell -fungus present -hail pitted -moldy -lustrous polish (indicating hand buffing, serious fault) -scarred -peeling -stem absent -color stained, blurred, impure

Staging and Arrangement 30 Points

*background color in keeping with season (fall, autumn) *background cloth textures appropriate (burlap, monk's cloth, cotton, other) *background colors appropriate (green, brown, yellow, orange, black, other) *grouped attractively *in suitable containers, (baskets, pottery, copper, gourds) *originality of theme (Mexican market, home kitchen, historical, other) *number of varieties *distinctive, artistic utilization of area allowed *correctly labeled *varied selection of varieties for textural, shape, color interest
-no apparent design or theme -inappropriate choices of background color, texture -lacking in interest -no labels -incorrectly labeled -carelessly printed -display lacks scope -crowded -poor use of space allowed

Quality and Suitability of Accessories Used in Staging 20 Points

*appropriate in color, texture, simplicity, season (evergreens, autumn leaves, cornhusks, straw, corn ear swags, vines, other)
*accessories subordinate to gourds which must dominate the display
-artificial plants, grass, leaves, flowers used (reduce points drastically or eliminate) -accessories dominating (the beauty and usefulness of gourds are of primary import.)

Color Effect 20 Points

*interesting *varied with some contrasts *harmoniously selected *colors grouped

-monotonous -spotty -lacks harmony -lacks imagination

Larkspur (Annual Delphinium)

SUGGESTED CLASSES:

Three spikes

a. one color — b. three colors

SUGGESTED SCALE: Use Spike Form Cut Flower Scale

FLORETS

Color 20 Points

*clear *desirable *delicate or intense *pure
-faded -bleached -streaked

Substance 15 Points

*holding well *fresh *turgid *perky
-thin -drooping -shattering -relaxing -curling back

Form 15 Points

*broad petals *well formed *touching to over-lapping petals
-loose -deformed -gaps between petals -not uniform up the spike

Size 5 Points

*larger than average *typical
-small -puny

SPIKE

Amount of Bloom 15 Points

*18 inch of flowering portion is ideal *profuse *adequate
-scanty -too many buds for amount of open florets -bloomed out

Size and Vigor 10 Points

*strong *tapered *straight *long *sturdy *wandlike *side branches removed
-thin -weak -short -clubby -long side laterals

Spacing 10 Points

*closely spaced *symmetrical *well placed all around the spike
-thin -gaps between florets -loose

Condition and Grooming 10 Points

*foliage soft grey green, typical *clean *unmarred *spent florets and leaves neatly removed
-dry -Blackspot damage -mildewed -dead tissue at point of leaf attachment (evidence of Diaporthe Blight) -stained -foreign matter present -hanging petals -seed pods

Marigolds (Society est. 1978)

SUGGESTED CLASSES:

A. TAGETES erecta Giant: over 3½" Large: 2½–3½"

1. Carnation or Peony Flowered, three blooms, same color.
2. Chrysanthemum Flowered, three blooms, same color.

B. T. Patula
Double
1. French Harmony, five blooms
2. Hybrids
   a. over 1", five blooms, same variety, same color.
   b. under 1", five blooms, same variety, same color.
Single
3. T. Signata, five blooms
4. Mexican Signet, five blooms

C. Triploids ('Mules') three blooms, same color.

Limited Schedules *often request by size:*
Giant 3½–5" Large 2½–3½" Small 1–2½" Petite under 1"

Classification *of Marigolds is according to their bloom formation, color, and height as follows:*

A. MARIGOLD AMERICAN (formerly African) TAGETES erecta, Large Flowered

1. Carnation and Peony Flowered

- ruffled or frilled, loose
- petals broader than 'mum flowered
- fully double
- often deep as diameter, perfect ball
- *Giant: 3½–5" Large: 2½–3½", according to variety*
- some varieties odorless
- more graceful, informal than 'mum type
- *Example: 'ALASKA' (short plants, 'LADY' series (med.) 'SIERRA' (tall)*

2. Chrysanthemum Flowered

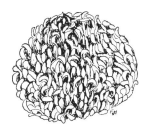

- relatively tight ball
- petals finer, narrow
- fully double, often deep as diameter
- smaller generally than carnation-flowered
- *2½" to 5" and over*
- *Example: 'FANTASTIC'*

B. MARIGOLD TAGETES patula

1. Double
A. French (Harmony Type)

- compact, tight ball
- less frilled and ruffed than African, some crested
- bicolor shades of yellow, orange, red-mahogany
- 1½ to 2 inches

B. Hybrids
- large types have broader petals
- *rather loose 'carnation' form*
- *less frilled than American*
- often in solid colors, as well as bicolored, yellow, orange, mahogany, *short reddish stems*

- two sizes, large 2 to 3 inches Example: "Red and Gold" dwarf ½ to 2 inches. Example: "Rusty Red," "Butterball"
- dwarf are very tight, compact, ball

2. Single: TAGETES signata
- wide open
- single row broad
- slightly ruffled petals
- blotched or contrasting edges
- crested center
- *include T. signatua tenufolia (pumila) the Mexican Signet Marigold*
- French 1½ to 2½ inches
- Signet under 1½ inches
- *Example: "NAUGHTY MARIETTA"*

C. Triploid hybrids ('Mule')
- *cross between Erecta & Patula*
- *neat, compact growth*
- *yellows, oranges, reddish*
- *Example: "NUGGET"*

- *vigorous, short stemmed plants*
- *double blooms 2–3"*
- *early flowering*

D. Tubular Trumpet
3–4 rows of tubed petals, 3" Ex: "GOLDEN TRUMPET"

E. T. Filifolia
Pot grown for feathery foliage effect. 6" plants Ex: "IRISH LACE"

SUGGESTED SCALE OF POINTS

Form	30	Size	20
* stressing depth, filled center, *symmetry; calyx intact*		Stem and Foliage	15
		Substance	5
Color	20	Condition and Grooming	10

Form 30 Points
In ball form, depth equals bloom width

*doubles deep as diameter *sufficient depth for type *typical depth *fluffy, globular, balled or loose according to variety *no disc florets evident in center *centers well-filled with unexpanded florets *some small singles and doubles have crested centers *symmetrical

-flat -off center -misshapen -depressed center -divided center -center popping -center bare -center bloomed out -irregular depth -shallow double -falling open -calyx split so deeply form is affected, loosened

Color 20 Points
*clear *bright *vivid *lively *pure *unstreaked *French harmoniously combined

-dull -blurred -unpleasant combinations -greenish -green center (serious fault) -impure -murky

Size 20 Points
*larger than expected for type, and variety *typical

-small -dwarfed -stunted-appearing

Stem and Foliage 15 Points

Five to fifteen inches of stem depending upon type
Stem — *straight, strong *able to balance bloom *proportioned to bloom size *bloom well posed on stem *disbudded *expect short stems on Triploids* -coarse -not disbudded -overlong -weak -short -spindly -crooked -too recently and carelessly disbudded *Giants, Large: remove side buds*

Foliage — *size and amount proportionate to bloom *typical green -too much foliage for size of bloom -yellowed -dull -elongated -deformed -no foliage (should be at least 2 true leaves

Substance 5 Points

*firm *turgid *crisp
-limp -relaxing -soft -aged

Condition and Grooming 10 Points

*unmarred *intact *clean *calyx unsplit
-calyx split slightly (if serious split which affects form, deduct there) -soiled -foreign matter clinging -edges dry, scorched -grey mildew evidence -bruised

Pansy, Viola and Violettas

SUGGESTED CLASSES:

Due to identification difficulties, Pansies and Violas are shown together.

1. PANSY and/or VIOLA — five blooms, a. same color, b. assorted colors. Over 2"

2. VIOLETTAS OR VIOLETS — five blooms, a. same color, b. assorted colors. 2" or less.

Best displayed flat, with stems put through a velvet-covered piece of cardboard over water, with only the flower faces showing above. Schedule may call for 6 blooms of same color or variety, or different varieties. Judge on uniformity, overall perfection and balance of exhibit.

PANSIES, VIOLAS AND VIOLETTAS

Until 1839 Viola and Pansy designated the same flower, commonly called **Heartsease.** Then the first blotched flower was found and designated as the Pansy. Both come from one parent genus, botanically called Viola Tricolor. Viola is called "tufted" because of its compact, mounded growth habit and is also referred to as "bedding" pansy.

Previously pansies have been exhibited without foliage and violas with, it seems this designation could easily be dispensed with. The suggested scale allots the former foliage points to form and color which are, along with substance, the most important characteristics of a pansy or viola.

Authorities say that botanically there is no difference and then proceed to point out differences and similarities as follows:

PANSY	**differs from**	**VIOLA**

PANSY differs from	**VIOLA**
• sprawling habit	• compact habit of growth. Stems wiry, erect, flowers carried well above the foliage
• imperfectly perennial, usually treated as an annual or biennial.	• perennial. 'MAGGIE MOTT', 'AMY BARR', 'PINKIE' remain free-flowering for 10 year period
• very short, blunt spur	• longer spur
• much-divided stipules (leaf-like) appendage at top of petiole (stem)	• less divided stipules
• blooms in excess of 4½"	• generally smaller blooms, but still should measure at least 2"
• pansies have 'faces', are blotched and banded. Even most self-colors have a lighter band around the edge.	• violas usually have more definite ray markings, and usually a slightly darker band around the edge, or else the color flows over the edge with no marked change in value. Color may be suffused at the center, but not definitely blotched, no definite 'face'.
• pansy substance is generally thick, velvety	• viola substance is more fine, delicate.
• pansy is a cool-weather plant	• viola withstands warmer, drier conditions.

PANSY is similar to	**VIOLA**
• form is symmetrical and circular	• form is symmetrical and circular
• are often self-colored	• are often self-colored
• measure from 2 to 5"	• according to English authorities must measure at least 2 to 2½"

Modern hybridization has made the size and colors so similar that for many show classes it might be less confusing to request two classes

1 — Pansies and Violas measuring at least 2½"
    A. Blotched
    B. Self Colored
2 — Violettas measuring less than 2½"

VIOLETTAS & VIOLETS differ from	**PANSIES & VIOLAS**
• tinier, often only 1" long and ½" wide	• 2½ to 5"
• form is oval, longer than wide	• form must be perfectly circular
• must be fragrant	• some are fragrant
• no definite ray or blotching, though may be bi-colored	• according to variety and type

SUGGESTED SCALE OF POINTS

Form	30	Substance	20
(stressing roundness and symmetry)		Size	15
Color	20	Condition and Grooming	15

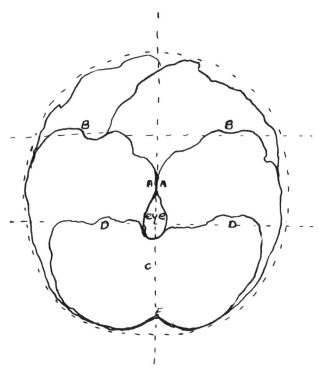

Form 30 Points

*symmetrical *circular

All petals should be broad and flat, lying upon each other in such a way as to form a perfect circle. The face of the bloom should be slightly arched, and have a small eye.

The two center petals should touch above the eye at A and reach well up on the top petals.

The lower petal (C) should be sufficiently deep and broad to balance the others.

The two center petals should be arranged evenly on either side of an imaginary vertical line drawn through the eye. Top of both these petals (B) should reach the same height on the upper petals.

The top of the lower petal (D) should be horizontal. The B and D lines equally divide the flower into thirds. There should be a definite indentation at (E).

-aging, drawing in upon itself -lacks symmetry -not circular -lacks indentation at bottom -gaping petals -asymmetrical -lower petal too narrow or too deep thus failing to balance the others -eye too large -off center -center petals fail to meet eye, especially on smooth petaled types, is more difficult to judge on ruffled types.

Color 20 Points

*eye bright, clearly defined *blotches, if present, well defined, dense, solid and in good proportion to the petal size *margins definite and of uniform width *bright *clear *pure *unusual *texture velvety *texture typical . . . heavier in pansies *color deep.

-ill defined margins -fading -murky, dull -edges whitening -coarse texture -crepey -weak -off color -streaky -watery -wishy washy -lifeless -inharmonious color combinations.

Substance 20 Points

*fresh *perky *firm *jaunty *thick, especially in pansy *velvety.
-wilting -limp -curling -shrinking -loose -soft -thinning, particularly at edges

Size 15 Points

Pansy, Fancy varieties 2½" and up — Swiss Giants 4" — Steele's Jumbo 5" — Violas at least 2" and up — Violettas approx. 1"
*larger than average for variety *typical
-less than expected for type -small -puny -underdeveloped

Condition and Grooming 15 Points

*intact *undamaged *clean *mature *properly displayed
-soil markings -water spots -torn petal -split petal -bedraggled -bruised
-scarred -water soaked.

Petunias

SUGGESTED CLASSES:

1. MULTIFLORA — Size: up to 3½" (includes Bedding, Cascade, Dwarf, F Hybrids) One spray (no part of primary plant, any side branches should be smaller than main one)

A. single   B. double

2. GRANDIFLORA GIANT SINGLE — 3 blooms on 1" stems appropriately displayed. (Includes ruffled, fringed or plain edged), Size: 3½" or over.

3. GRANDIFLORA GIANT DOUBLE — 3 blooms on 1" stems appropriately displayed. Size: 3½" or over.

4. CALIFORNIA GIANTS — 3 blooms on 1" stems, appropriately displayed. Size: 3½" or over. (Heavily veined, frilled, ruffled, etc.)

In the accompanying suggested scale, the stem is considered under Cultural Perfection. Multifloras have thinnest stems, Cal. Giants the heaviest, Cascade stems often twist. Grandifloras and Cal. Giants are requested on 1" stems because cutting a spray takes much potential bloom. Form is given less points as Petunias are quite typical, less subject to form changes. Substance is less enduring, requires special attention, so considered important as color. F Hybrids are expected to have better substance than open pollinated. Stems of Multifloras should be sturdy, cylindrical, unscarred. Must support the blooms. Check front and back of the flower.

SUGGESTED SCALE

Color of Bloom	30	Form of Bloom	15
Cultural Perfection		Size of Bloom	10
. substance, vigor, etc.	25		
. condition, grooming	20		

Color 30 Points

*bright *clear *typical *harmonizing markings and shadings *sparkling
*sharp color patterns
-dull -weak -watery -flat -bleached -low intensity

Cultural Perfection — Substance, Vigor, etc. 25 Points

*vigorous *abundance of bloom and buds on Multiflora *foliage bright to dark green on Multiflora *substance crisp, turgid, perky
-scanty bloom on Multiflora -rank foliage -leggy -foliage weak, small -foliage shows chlorosis, yellowing -edges of petals thinning -limp -water soaked

Condition, Grooming 20 Points

*well groomed *well displayed *Grandifloras and Cal. Giants on short stems *clean* unmarred *sturdy *free of aphids, thistledown, soot, etc. *spent flowers neatly removed from Multiflora spray
-soiled -torn petals -bedraggled -mud spattered -dried petals, leaves -bruised -spent

Form 15 Points

*typical *Doubles are full, compact, fluffy *⅔ to fully open *slightly asymmetrical to symmetrical (upper part may be slightly larger)
-abnormal -loosely formed double -straggly -poorly placed on spray (Multiflora)

Size 10 Points

*large for type *conforms to show class and type
-stunted -puny

PETUNIA

A: Multiflora

B: Grandiflora Giant Single

C: Grandiflora Giant Double

D: California Giant

77

Phlox

SUGGESTED CLASSES:
1. PERENNIAL 3 heads (stems, cymes) 12 to 18"
   - A. one variety   B. assorted varieties
2. ANNUAL 5 heads (stems, cymes)
   - A. smooth margin, all of one variety, same color.
   - B. starred or fringed varieties, assorted colors.

SUGGESTED SCALE OF POINTS

Form	25	Substance	15
Color	25	Foliage and Stem	10
Size	15	Condition and Grooming	10

. individual florets
. flower head

FORM
of flower head
*symmetrical *abundant florets *mounded or conical *solidly filled *heavy truss *full *broad *deep *lateral characteristic (Some varieties typically make the flower head out of long tightly bunched laterals, forming a conical or pyramidal truss; others hold the flowers on shorter laterals, forming a solid flat-top, mounded head.)
-skimpy -uneven outline -missing florets mar form -one sided -thin -loose -shallow -immature -crowded -sparse

form of florets
*symmetrical *wheel-like *petals evenly spaced, touching or overlapping
-petals too widely placed, gaping -lop sided -off center

Color 25 Points
*eye neat and distinct (if present) *margin of eye sharp, clear *color brilliant *pure *clear *uniform throughout cluster *color fast *vivid *interesting, desirable combination *alive *striking
-streaked -bleached -eyes varying throughout cluster -faded -dull

Substance 15 Points
*crisp *turgid *perky *holding well
-limp -droopy -thinning -wilting -dull sheen -shriveling -drying

Size 15 Points
Individual Florets
Often 1¾" in Plain-edge Annual and Perennial, smaller in Starred.
*larger than average *typical *uniform in all
-below average -small -varying

Flower Head
Some Perennial varieties exceed 1½" when ideally grown. Starred are smaller than Smooth-edge Annuals Grandiflora and Gigantea
*massive *typical for variety and type *larger than expected *thickly studded with florets

Foliage and Stem 10 Points
Perennial foliage may be 3-5" long, Starred Phlox has typically finer foliage than Smooth-Edge. Some perennial varieties have a bronzy-green foliage rather than the typical deep green. Some have a leathery texture.
*rich green *stem straight *vigorous *well formed *sturdy *cylindrical *stiff stem *proportioned to flower head and floret size
-foliage dominates flower head -stem crooked, weak, short -inadequate stem and foliage in proportion to flower head -mildewed -brown spots (Leaf Spot damage) -crinkled (Leaf Nematode damage) -yellowing, webby under leaf (Red Spider infestation) -yellowing (nutrient deficiencies)

Condition and Grooming 10 Points

*intact *flower head well groomed of faded, dried florets *clean
-faded florets hanging -dirty -dusty

Salpiglossis

SUGGESTED CLASSES:

Three sprays

    A. one variety   B. assorted varieties

SUGGESTED SCALE OF POINTS: Use the Spray Form Cut Flower Scale

Amount of Bloom 25 Points

*numerous *profuse *more open flowers than buds
-scanty -sparse -too many buds

Color 20 Points

*attractive interior netting and veining or ribbing *colors pure *brilliant
*veining definite *combination appealing *rich
-faded -dull -murky -blurred -veining not uniform -yellowed foliage

Form 20 Points

Spray

*well branched *airy appearance *graceful *vigorous, wiry stem *stem
straight *typically slender
-unbalanced -lopsided -top heavy -crowded -weak stem -crooked

Flower

*trumpet shape *petals uniformly flared *tubes well proportioned *sym-
metrical *petals equally spaced *petals same length and width *uniform
-lopsided -deformed -petals fail to overlap, gaping

Substance 15 Points

*holding well *crisp *well poised *fresh *velvety
-limp -collapsing -shriveling -thinning -excessive curling

Size 10 Points

Two and one-half inches wide and deep is ideal
*above average *typical
-small -stunted

Condition and Grooming 10 Points

*clean *intact *groomed of spent flowers, dried foliage, pods
-petals split -dried flowers, pods, foliage -foreign matter -soiled -torn
-broken stem or flower petiole

Scabiosa

SUGGESTED CLASSES:

Five Blooms

    A. one variety   B. assorted varieties

SUGGESTED SCALE:

Form	30	Substance	10
Size	25	Stem	10
Color	20	Condition and Grooming	5

Form 30 Points

*circular *symmetrical *ball or cone shaped *uniform *good depth *fully
double *broad *frilled petals *pins conspicuous
-flat -thin -lop sided -petals lacking -center popping

79

Size 25 Points

Expected size Large: 2½ to 3" Dwarf: 1 to 1½"
*above normal *typical
-small -puny

Color 20 Points

*clear *pure *rare *showy
-faded -dull -weak -bleached

Substance 10 Points

*stamens erect *petals, all parts crisp *fresh
-limp -loosening with age -thinning

Stem 10 Points

*sturdy *erect *bloom well posed *graceful
-contorted -weak -not proportioned to bloom -coarse

Condition and Grooming 5 Points

*clean *unmarred
-soiled -scarred -torn petals

Snapdragons (Antirrhinum)

SUGGESTED CLASSES:

A. TETRA, F HYBRIDS, three spikes (racemes)
    A. one variety   B. three varieties

B. DOUBLE, three spikes (racemes)
    A. one variety   B. three varieties

C. COMMON GARDEN, three spikes (racemes)
    A. one color   B. three colors

SUGGESTED SCALE: Use Spike Form Cut Flower Scale

FLORETS

Color 20 Points

*rich *solid or attractively combined *pure *brilliant *harmonious shadings
-murky colors often appear in self sown -weak -bleached -fading

Substance 15 Points

*plump *glistening *lustrous *heavy texture *turgid *velvety
-thinning -limp -dull -shriveling -crepey -edges thinning -lacks sheen
-marginal burn

Form 15 Points   May be frilled, ruffled or plain edged according to variety

*gracefully flared *broad, prominent lip *uniformly reflexed *'snapper'
sac well puffed
-sac limp -sac not puffed -sac dimpling -form varies in florets on spike

Size 5 Points

*larger than average *typical *uniform
-small -varying

SPIKE

Some types such as 'SKY SCRAPER' reach 3' or more, some doubles 2-2½',
Tetras approximately 2'. Ideal stem to inflorescence proportion ½ to ⅔ open
florets, ⅓ buds with buds at the top showing color and perfectly formed
flowers at the base. Some new introductions boast 100 flowers and buds
with 40 fully open at one time.

Amount of Bloom 15 Points

*profuse *typical *loaded
-scanty -sparse -skimpy

Size of Spike and Vigor 10 Points

*inflorescence well proportioned to stem length and diameter *massive or graceful according to variety *open florets nicely balanced by bloom to come *stem straight *strong *canelike *foliage clean, green *robust *strong tip *side laterals previously disbudded
-short -clubby -weak -thin -twisted stem -unhealthy appearance -tip curved, limp, weak, drooping, undeveloped -unthrifty -crooked -long, awkward side laterals

Spacing 10 Points

*symmetrically full all around *tapers to top *evenly set *florets well placed *no skips *closely set or slightly open arrangement according to variety
-bloomed out -crowded -loose -voids -too widely spaced -missing florets

Conditioning and Grooming 10 Points

*unmarred *fresh *clean
-floret detached, hanging -bruised -pods forming or removed -tip broken -spent florets -soiled -rust spores under leaves, on stem -dark spots (Blight) -water soaked spots (Blight) -insect damaged -anthracnose -caused white spots on leaves, with reddish borders and sunken area on the stem

Stocks (Border Grown)

SUGGESTED CLASSES:

Three Spikes

    A. one color   B. three colors

SUGGESTED SCALE:

Florets		Spike	
Color	20	Floriferousness and spacing	20
Substance	15	Size and Vigor	10
Form	15	Condition and Grooming	10
Size	5		
Fragrance	5		

FLORETS

Color 20 Points

*true *appealing *clear *pure
-streaked -dull -greying -mottled

Substance 15 Points

*fresh *velvet-like
-drooping -withering -flaccid -crepey

Form 15 Points

*well rounded *fully double *rosetted *uniform
-flat -misshapen -thin -lack symmetry

Size 5 Points

*larger than average *large *typical
-small -inadequate

Fragrance 5 Points

*strong *apparent *heady *pleasant
-lacking -weak

SPIKE

Floriferousness and Spacing 20 Points

*½ to ¾ open flowers to ⅓ buds is ideal proportion *cylindrical at base to slightly domed at tip *well filled *round *no irregular placements or omissions *fully expanded flowers at the base, none missing
-bloomed out -crowded -sparse -straggly -one sided -lanky

Size and Vigor 10 Points
*sturdy *heavy *long *straight, graceful stem
-weak -thin -curved or bent tip -clubby stem -crooked

Condition and Grooming 10 Points
*foliage and flowers clean *foliage must have characteristic grey-green 'bloom' *florets well attached *undamaged
-soiled -torn -burned -poddy -evidence of flea beetle or other insect damage

Sweetpeas

SUGGESTED CLASSES:
Five Sprays (sub-divided into color classes)

SUGGESTED SCALE:

Amount of Bloom	20	Substance	15
Color	20	Size	10
Form	20	Condition and Grooming	10
. of spray	. of florets	Fragrance	5

Amount of Bloom 20 Points
Some authorities state the number of blooms seems to vary with the color. Six to eight florets is ideal, four to five open florets in prime condition is average.
*above average number *average amount *uniform number on each spray
-too few -not uniform

Color 20 Points
*bright *pure *lively *luminous *clear *marginal contrast interesting and in proportion if present
-streaky -uneven -water spotted or soaked -blurred -dull -lifeless -faded
-edges blued, whitened (particularly in red and purples)

Form 20 Points
Spray
*graceful *petioles holding flower out from main stem *balanced *symmetrical *evenly placed up main stem *stem vigorous, long, straight, wiry, may be 14-18" in some varieties under optimum conditions. Bush types 7-12". *top buds in active development, developed blooms in center and fully expanded bottom flowers with no keels present *approximately three-fifths of the entire spray length should be florets and buds
-petioles overlong or too short -stem looped, contorted, weak -poorly disposed blooms (e.g. two at bottom, an empty space, then three more) -hanging florets

Flower Form
*sepals (center) uniformly out-thrust *uniform, symmetrical form in all florets *margins equally ruffled, plain, frilled, waved, duplex *well proportioned as to parts and stem
-ill shaped -torn sepals or petals -overmaturity altering form -keel forming

Substance 15 Points
*crisp *turgid *waxy, satiny texture *fresh *firm
-edges thinning -flaccid -soft

Size 10 Points
Some varieties exceed 2"
*above average for area and variety *large *typical
-small -below average

Condition and Grooming 10 Points
*unmarred *intact *stem unscarred *clean *well groomed
-keels (seed pods) present or removed -petals, sepals split -bruised petals
-damaged by pea aphid -frayed margins -stained -edges burned

Fragrance 5 Points

*strong *decided *evident
-weak -absent

Zinnias

SUGGESTED CLASSES:

A. DAHLIA FLOWERED
1. Giant, over 4½", three blooms, one color
2. Medium, 2 to 4½", three blooms, one color.
(includes 'PEPPERMINT STICK', 'POLKA', 'CUT AND COME AGAIN', etc.).
3. Dwarf Ball, ½ to 2", five blooms, one color.
(includes Lilliput, Cupid, Pompon, etc.).
4. Multicolored Dahlia Flowered, five blooms, 1½ to 2½".
(includes 'PERSIAN CARPET', 'NAVAJO', etc.).

B. CACTUS FLOWERED (includes Fantasy, Quilled, etc.).
1. Giant, over 4", three blooms, one color.
2. Medium, 1½ to 4", three blooms, one color.

C. CRESTED (Sabiosa, 'RED LADY'), 3", three blooms, one color.

DAHLIA FLOWERED ZINNIA

- petals overlay each other in regular manner
- sizes range from Ball ½" to Giant over 6"
- includes Ball Lilliput and Cupid in which petals are very compact and form is deep as wide
- Medium and Giant should be ¾ deep as wide
- symmetrical, circular
- some petals are blunt, others rounded according to variety
- includes California Giants in which
  . petals are slightly reflexed
  . are 5 to 6" in diameter BUT
  . are typically only about 1" deep
  . often unusually soft color combinations

MULTI-COLORED

- includes Multi-Colored which
  . have overlapping
  . pointed petals
  . tipped in contrasting colors often yellow, gold or white
  . includes 'PERSIAN CARPET' and 'NAVAJO'

83

CACTUS FLOWERED

- includes Fantasy, F Hybrids, etc.
- petals twisted, tubular, quilled, ruffled
- up to 6", often about 2" deep

CRESTED

- full cushiony centers
- surrounded by broad guard petals
- approximately 3", 2 to 3" depth

SUGGESTED SCALE OF POINTS:

Form	25	Substance	15
(stressing depth, center filled, symmetry)		Stem and Foliage	15
		Size	15
Color	20	Condition and Grooming	10

Form 25 Points
*depth should be ¾ the diameter of Medium and Giant Dahlia Flowered, equal in Ball, and at least 2" in Cactus *round *full *center free of pollen and carpels *calyx unsplit *petals emerging in a symmetrical manner *form true to variety
-shallow -center hard, bare -misshapen -flat -popped -advanced carpels -bolting -off center -irregular development of disc florets in center -calyx split -irregular depth -center unevenly developed

Color 20 Points
*clear *back fresh *back full colored * vivid *glowing *pleasing blends *interestingly mottled according to variety *showy
-yellows showing greenish cast -whites dull, greyed -reds age blued -backs brown, scorched -margins browned, scorched, -discolored

Substance 15 Points
*crisp *fresh *properly conditioned (ends burned or scalded) -advanced age -limp -withered -wilted -petals hanging

Stem and Foliage 15 Points

Stem

*straight *strong *good proportion to flower and foliage *evenly round with no crimping *disbudded *stiff, erect
-crooked -weak -distorted -knotted -damaged -too short -needs disbudding

Foliage

*clear *bright green *size of leaves in good proportion to flower and stem *removed below waterline to prevent deterioration and odor *vigorous *foliage of certain varieties of Cactus-Flowering typically curl and twist -light green -small -overlarge -dominates flower -mildewed -distorted by red spider

Size 15 Points — According to variety.

Giant Dahlia Flowered, up to 6" diameter, ¾ as deep: Cactus, 3¼ to 5" diameter, 2" deep;Cut and Come Again, 2½"; Crested, 3"; Peppermint Stick, 1½ to 2"; Mexican, 1 to 2½"; Persian Carpets, 1½"; Lilliputs, 1 to 1½"; Cupids, ½ to 1".
*typical to slightly larger for variety *according to schedule
-smaller than average -freakish

Condition and Grooming 10 Points

*undamaged *clean *intact *foreign matter removed
-bruised -sunburned -insect chewn -spray evidence -scorched -dried margins -presence or evidence of earwigs, grasshoppers -dirty -torn

SECTION 3 — SOCIETY PLANTS

African Violets (Saintpaulia)

SUGGESTED CLASSES
1. Potted plant, single blooms
2. Potted plant, double blooms
3. Potted plant, Supreme, Amazon, duPont, single blooms
4. Potted plant, Supreme, Amazon, duPont, double blooms
5. Potted plant, Novelty types (Green edged, Scallop-edge Girls, Geneva white-edged flowers, Miniatures, Albino, Varigated)
6. Potted plant, Trailer
7. Collection: Three potted plants, different types or varieties

All plants to be single crown with exception of Class 6 Trailers. The Schedule can include a class for double crowns, but these are not ideal and their exhibition should be discouraged. Class sub-divisions can be made for colors. A: White B: Pink C: Red D: Orchids and Lavenders E: Purple and Blues F: Bicolor, multicolor and varigated.

AFRICAN VIOLET (Gesneriaceae Family) 10 species.

Actually this plant is not a violet, but is related to the Gloxinias.

Single Crown Species

S. ionantha is the parent species of many modern specimen plants. It grows as a single crown with ovate leaves (new introductions have many leaf variations). Petioles seven to nine inches long and leaves three to three one-half inches long. 15-25 blooms ¾" to 1½" in diameter. A well grown plant will measure overall 18-21."

Other single crown plants the Judge might find entered are species **S. confusa:** 8-10" overall plant size. 15-20 1¼" flowers. Very thin leaves with serrated edges.

S. difficulis has long 4-6" crowns, open growth habit. 1" flowers and an overall plant size of 10-15". **S. orbicularis** has 20-25 cupped ¾" multicolored flowers. Thin leaves. Overall size of plant 12-14". **S. shumensis** has leaves only 1" long, petioles 1¼". 5-8 ½" flowers with 4-5 per stem. Plants measure 10-12" overall.

Trailer Species Include:

S. amaniengsis with 1¼" wide leaves and 12-20 ¾" flowers. Overall 9-14" depending on the number of crowns. It has a trailing growth habit arising from multiple crowns and the Judge should not expect to find any of these trailing species or their hybrid grown as a single crown. **S. Grotei** trails and climbs. Stems are often very long with clusters of leaves on the ends. Leaves are very flexible with open spacing. Mature plants often 38" overall. Hybrids 7-15", 20-25 1¼" blossoms. **S. Magungensis** has a creeping and trailing crown on crown growth habit. Overall size 7-12". 15-20 1" flowers. Leaves in cluster on stem ends. **S. Goetzeana** has no real leaf pattern, is a pincushion type. A 3" pot may contain 21 crowns, 6-7" overall plant size. Poor bloomer, small flowers.

SCALE

Cultural Perfection	50	Bloom Quantity & Quality	50
. symmetry of leaf pattern, plant form	30	. floriferousness (number of blooms)	25
. condition	20	. bloom size	15
		. bloom color	10

Leaf pattern, condition and floriferousness are given the most points because these are indicators of the grower's ability. Size of bloom and color are varietal qualities to a great extent, bought in the variety, thus are not clear indicators of grower skill and so receive less points.

SYMMETRY

The leaf pattern should be completely circular, wheel shaped with strong healthy vigorous foliage evenly distributed around and over the entire "wheel". There should be no gaps or wide spaces between the leaves or between the rows of leaves, but there should be room enough between the leaves for the flower stems to emerge above the leaves. Each leaf should overlap the one in front and fit fairly close to the one beside it, so that no soil or petiole (leaf stem) shows. Points are to be deducted for this fault according to the degree the symmetry is disturbed by the missing or ill-placed leaf or leaves, and the number of resultant gaps per plant.

The single crown plant is the ideal show plant. The quality of symmetry is based on a single crown. There is no symmetry or perfection of leaf form and pattern in a multiple crown plant. It ordinarily takes much less effort on the part of the exhibitor to produce a multiple crown plant in comparison to the properly shaped, single crown specimen. All points for symmetry of leaf pattern are deducted if the plant is multiple and the schedule requests a single.

The hemispherical form of the plant when viewed from the side will vary as the foliage of some varieties have a tendency to grow out horizontally, others bend downward around the container and in some varieties the foliage stands almost upright. The health of the plant is often evidenced by abnormalties in foliage form and these are discussed under condition where points are levied against them unless the actual symmetry is affected. If such is the case, points are also deducted here.

The size of the plant is not considered generally, but all things being equal, the larger plant according to type will receive the higher placement. The average size of a mature miniature may be up to 6"; a semi-miniature up to 8"; a regular 15-21". Of course, the Judge will deduct points for immature plants, a "baby" plant has no real educational value and no place in the show.

There are many varieties known as the duPont, Amazon and Supreme strains. The one characteristic these have in common is the thick, hairy, heavy foliage with some variation in the other characteristics. The Girl varieties have a common characteristic in that the leaves are deeply scalloped, some are almost ruffled, and all have a characteristic white spot at the base of each leaf blade.

If young plants are left attached to the petiole without division, they become crowded and result in unsatisfactory plants. Plants with leggy petioles and ragged or irregular symmetry will be penalized under form.

A nicely rounded symmetrical circular form, developed evenly and uniformly on all sides, resulting from ample spacing and quarter turning twice weekly is the ideal show form.

CONDITION

The overall impression must be one of symmetry, sturdy, vigorous attractive foliage and numerous flowers, clean and bright.

The plant should show no evidence of disease or insects. The Judge is permitted to pick up a specimen plant and turn it so he or she may view it from all sides and below, but if it is necessary to handle the foliage to determine disease, insects or abnormal thickness, great care should be taken to avoid bruising the sensitive leaves. The use of pencils or fingers to lift up the foliage should not be permitted as the petioles are normally crisp and will snap.

Check the new growth and on or near the bloom stalks for evidence of aphid sucking the sap and substance away. Check underneath the flowers and petioles for the powdery growth of fungus Botrytis. Malformed leaves and flower stems and leaves that exhibit a grayish webby appearance leads the Judge to suspect Mealybug infestation.

A threadlike growth, whitish appearance, deformed flowers and dwarfed stems results from mildew. If the center leaves appear stunted with a puckered appearance, distorted and curled up, the Judge will suspect Cyclamen mites though they are too tiny to be seen. Mites work on the tender growth in crown, bloom stalks and blossoms. One side of the leaf will be smaller than the other side, hard, and shiny and untypically thick and brittle.

Thickened flower stems, short distorted flowers that are blotchy, small and either fail to open or open incompletely can be attributed to mite damage. Its big brother, the Broad Mite also interferes with normal growth, especially of the lower leaf surface, causing the leaf to turn downward.

Plants infected with nematodes have a dulled appearance, the leaves droop as if needing moisture and the plant produces an abnormal amount of suckers. White or brown streaks plus pit-like scars on the backs of the leaves may be caused by thrips. The symptoms of virus parallel those of the Cyclamen mite with leaves broader, shorter and thicker than normal. The leaf edges roll upward, the surface is smooth and the hairs are much finer than is typical.

Evidence of such carelessness and neglect in disease and insect control should result in the severest of penalties. No insecticidal residue should remain on the plant. Clean foliage shows evidence of careful grooming. The leaves should have a bright appearance, a natural sheen and glow. The use of any liquids or preparations to cleanse the foliage which imparts an unnatural shine, etc., is considered over-grooming and is penalized.

The color or markings of the foliages range from light yellow, all white, olive, pine and dark green to variegated with many varieties that are an interesting purplish red underneath. Variegated foliages range from green and white combinations to those of rose, red, coppery pink, chartreuse and brown tones. The Judge takes off points if variegation of the foliage is lacking in varieties which are expected to have this characteristic, according to the extent it is absent. Proper attention to the plants' needs for light, food, etc. intensifies the colors and all things being equal the one with the most brilliant foliage will capture high awards. For instance, a coppery pink foliage variety may be faded while its competitor is a brilliant intense green indicating prime health and so would place higher.

The Judge is aware that too much sun or high light intensity scorches the leaves or will harden their texture as well as yellowing and bleaching the color. The petioles will be shorter than is typical for the variety, the leaves will cup or turn down around the pot edge and the center leaves tend to curl upwards.

Insufficient light over a long period of time will lengthen the petioles excessively, the leaves will be a very deep green and the stems spindly and weak with less than the expected amount of bloom.

In judging African Violet specimen plants, no special consideration is given any particular method of lighting . . . the end result only is evaluated. Bleached foliage, if accompanied by center leaves which look hard and deformed, is caused by fluorscent light being left on for too many hours each day.

Plants which have been chilled will carry the effects in fewer blooms which lack quality, shorter flower stems and brittle leaves which curl down. The flowers may also be discolored and deformed.

Excessive heat causes center leaves of Girl types to grow too tight and compact. Careless watering is the cause of leaf spotting as well as putting wet plants in strong light. If the plant droops unnaturally for the variety, they show evidence of neglect to moisture needs because after excessive dryness the weight of the leaf will be too much for the foliage to be raised again.

All plants have a sign language to which the Judge can 'listen' by sight. He can be sure that attention to an African Violet's nutritional needs have been neglected when plants are spindly indicating excessive nitrogen. When the older leaves are yellowed (usually the outer leaves) but still clinging to the plant, nitrogen is lacking.

Weak foliage color and sappy growth that lacks substance so the entire plant has a droopy appearance, with leaves a dull, dark green and petioles having a purplish cast leads the Judges to suspect a lack of phosphate.

Plants signal a lack of potash when the lower leaf margins are yellow with the leaf veins mottled, and a lack of boron when bud opening is poor, flower bracts and leaf petioles are short and thick, with narrow, puckered, misshapen leathery leaves. The leather-like texture distinguishes this from mite infestation where the leaves are brittle.

When a plant has yellow leaves in the center, with veins still green, an iron deficiency is indicated. A bowl of ripening apples placed near a pot of African Violets gives off a poisonous gas which will also turn the leaves yellow.

Examine the soil surface, there should not be an accumulation of mineral salts. The soil should be up to where the petioles meet the stalk, with the plant firmly anchored in the center of the pot.

In considering the pot in proportion to the plant, the Judge must remember that Saintpaulias do not require as large or deep a pot in order to develop a sturdy, symmetrical, healthy plant and the normal bloom crop as with other flowering plants. No flared top pots, supports or collars under the foliage should be permitted. A three inch pot is proportionate for a plant with an 8" spread, a four inch pot for a larger plant. The six inch miniatures are best in two and one-half inch pot sizes. Check for adequate drainage.

The Judge remembers that a quantity of flowers sometimes camouflages a badly shaped, off center plant or damaged foliage. The condition of the entire plant must be considered.

BLOOM QUANTITY AND QUALITY

Floriferousness

A mature plant is considered to have an average number of blooms when there is a total of 20-25 blossoms. Miniatures are prolific bloomers with 6-20 flowers per one small six inch plant. Semi-miniatures are expected to show 6-20 flowers per eight inch plant. And 10-15 blooms are average for a single crown duPont, Supreme and Amazon with the Supremes being expected to have a greater number than the other two. All three of the last mentioned bloom better in small pots, a characteristic they share with all other Saintpaulias which bloom best when pot bound.

The size of the plant or amount of foliage should be considered in determining the number of blossoms it should have. There should be a balanced appearance between the amount of flowers and the amount of foliage, with neither over-powering the other. Only open blossoms are counted, buds are not blossoms as yet.

Saintpaulias are varied of flower form, including singles, doubles and semi-doubles, star shapes, fringed and ruffled forms. Double flower varieties hold their blooms longer than singles and usually have more blooms per plant than singles. For best flowering effect, the flowers should be concentrated at the plant's center.

Sparse bloom may be caused by insufficient light, excess nitrogen or aphids. Bud and blossom drop results from insufficient light, lack of humidity, drafts, chilling, thrips. Poor quality flowers lacking substance result from drying out. Mildew and Cyclamen mites cause deformed flowers and the Judge is expected to recognize and deduct for these faults.

Each plant should have an abundance of blossoms with two to three flower stems rising from between each leaf, with flower stems strong enough to support the flowers well above the foliage. Flowers hidden below the foliage are considered faulty, regardless if this is a varietal characteristic.

BLOOM SIZE

Judges should be familiar with the varieties, because if an exhibitor grows a plant with blossoms exceeding average size, the Judge should recognize this accomplishment. Supremes, duPonts and Amazons produce flowers approximately two inches in diameter, most other varieties average three-fourths of an inch to one and one-half inches. The blossoms of Miniatures and Semi-Miniatures vary in size and are often larger than expected on such small plants.

Cyclamen Mite infestation and virus stunt reduces the flower size. Special growing lamps often increase individual flower size.

COLOR

The African Violet color range includes purple, reddish purple, medium and light blues, lavenders and orchids, pink, rosy red, white and variegated (spotted, mingled or mixed), multicolored (two or more colors), bicolors (two values of the same color) and Geneva varieties which have a white edge or band around the petals.

The color of the blossoms should be clear and fresh in appearance, though soil, fertilization, light and water do influence color to a certain extent, color is a built-in characteristic. A variety which does not reproduce true should be disqualified by the Classification Committee. Varieties whose colors vary back and forth should be considered characteristic of that variety.

Flowers fade quickly on aphid infested plants. Cyclamen mites cause the flowers to become blotched and thrips infested plants have gray-streaked bloom that fall off prematurely.

Plants grown under special growing lamps produce flowers more brilliant, intensely colored than ordinarily. Plants which have received the amount of potash they required will carry flowers with a desirable, clear lustrous look and intensified color.

SUMMARY

Symmetry 30 Points

*circular *space enough for flower stems to emerge *single crown *overlapping neatly *full leaf pattern *even, uniform on all sides *compact -excessive crown development -irregular -gaps -soil and petioles showing -leggy petioles -ragged appearance -sparse leaf pattern

Condition 20 Points

*fresh *healthy *clean *normal *intensely colored flowers, foliage *vigorous appearance
-broken foliage -flowers, foliage lacking substance -dulled appearance -deformed flowers -hairs finer than normal -leaves abnormally hard, shiny, brittle -off center -spindly -center leaves puckered, curled, deformed -pot too small, big -artificially supported -foreign matter present -yellowed foliage -spotted foliage -over groomed -drooping foliage -extra long, weak petioles -weak bloom stalks

Floriferousness 25 Points

*semi and miniatures 6-20 flowers *regulars 20-25 blooms *duPonts, Amazons, Supremes 10-15 flowers *foliage and flowers balanced *flowers well held, centered in plant *flower held above foliage
-sparse -bud and blossom drop -spent blossoms -hidden blossoms -less than normal

Size 15 Points

*large *distinctive *duPonts, Amazons, Supremes 2" *others ¾ to 1½" -stunted -small

Color 10 Points

*clear *fresh *brilliant *intense *lustrous *typical
-dull -faded -weak -spiritless -blotched -grey streaked

Amaryllis

SUGGESTED CLASSES:

1. Cut Scape
2. Single Floret, three different varieties, exhibited singly in small glasses
3. Potted Plant
   a-one scape
   b-two or more scapes
4. Collection
   a-three or more potted plants
   b-five or more cut scapes
   c-five or more single florets, exhibited singly in small glasses
      1-different colors
      2-different shapes
      3-different sizes

Classes separating hybrids and species must be listed if expected competition warrants. Collections of color, shape and size classes add much interest and educational value. The exhibits must have been grown by the exhibitor for at least two months prior to the exhibition dates to insure that the plants were brought into flowering by the exhibitor. An exception may be made for pretreated bulbs, which can be brought into flowering in less than two months.

AMARYLLIS

Amaryllidaceae family. The Amaryllis are perennial bulbous plants bearing several lily-like florets on a single, leafless scape. The American Amaryllis Society has classed cultivated Amaryllis in nine divisions. Amaryllis can be fairly judged for flower structure and flowering habits by the Division standards only. See sketches below for general flower structure.

DIVISION 1: CULTIVATED WILD AMARYLLIS

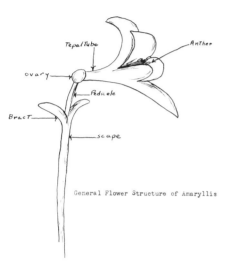

General Flower Structure of Amaryllis

- Includes approx. 45 wild sub-species and varieties
- no sketch
- **Example: 'Striata'**

S – seTsegs
P – PeTsegs

DIVISION 2: LONG TRUMPET

- resembles Easter Lily in form
- tepaltube long, 4½ to 5½"
- pedicels relatively long
- flowers distinctly drooping
- several flowers per scape
- **Example: 'Ambiqua Sweet'**

DIVISION 3: A. BELLADONNA

- tepaltube less than 4"
- Pedicels long
- flowers usually droop
- vanilla scented
- tepalsegs (floret segments) are rather widely spaced and relatively long and slim.
- **Example: 'Garfield Triumph'**

DIVISION 4: REGINAE

- tepaltube less than 2" long
- pedicels shorter than Div. 2 & 3
- moderately open-faced, but not flat
- tepalsegs broader
- viewed in profile the flower length exceeds 4"

TWO DIVISIONS:

A — Markedly imbricated (overlapped petals)

- tepalsegs overlap ¾ or more of their length
- tips rounded or slightly pointed
- **Example: Herman Brown un-named white**

B — Less imbricated

- tepalsegs overlap less than ¾ their length
- tepalsegs sometimes reflexed
- tips rounded or pointed
- **Van Tubergen un-named Picotee**

DIVISION 5: LEOPOLDII

- pedicel shorter than Div. 2 & 3, same as 4
- tepaltube less than 2" long
- wide open, flat form, largest diameter of all
- flower profile length must NOT exceed 4"

TWO DIVISIONS:

A — Markedly imbricated

- broad tepalsegs overlap ¾ or more of their length
- tips rounded, blunt
- **Example: 'Doris Lillian'**

B — Less Imbricated

- tepalsegs often overlap over ½ their length
- tips less blunt, rounded or slightly pointed
- **Example: Un-named Mculloch Clone**

DIVISION 6: ORCHID FLOWERING

- tepalsegs long and slender
- variously shaped, twisted or extremely reflexed
- **Example: 'Cannae Butterfly'**

DIVISION 7: DOUBLE

- includes double and semi-double forms
- flowers have 2, 3, or more rows of tepalsegs each which
- narrow and shorten toward the center
- there may be petaloid 'ears' in the center.
- **Example 'Helen Hull'**

DIVISION 8: MINIATURE (includes Gracilis Hybrid)

- flowers smaller than Reginae and Leopoldii
- scapes and foliage scaled down
- various flower forms
- **Example 'Graceful'**

DIVISION 9: UNCLASSIFIED HYBRIDS

- meritorious specimens not easily fitted into any preceding Division

Scales

Qualities Considered	Cut Flower	Cut Scape	Potted Plant	
			One Scape	2 or More Scapes
FLOWER				
• color	45	45	45	35
• form	25	15	15	15
• size	20	15	15	15
• fragrance	2	2	2	2
SCAPE				
• number of florets per scape	—	6	6	6
• length and character	—	5	5	5
• number of scapes per plant	—	—	—	10
FOLIAGE	—	—	2	2
CONDITION-grooming of flower	8	12	10	10

In single, individual flowers cut from the umbel, the points given to scape and foliage are spread among the qualities of form, size and condition as the choice offers more chance of picking the most perfect from a number produced.

COLOR

The word Amaryllis is derived from the Greek word "amarysso" meaning to sparkle or twinkle and refers to the irridescent gold or silver "dusting" or texture on the surface of the Amaryllis blossoms which contributes to its color richness and appeal. Any dulling or lack of this sparkle due to aging or other causes is to be penalized.

The colors range from pure white, pink, red, scarlet, yellow, pastel tints, feathering and stripes, and whites with other colors. Long lists of color classes would be required only in advance shows. Amaryllis flowers need to expand in half or direct light to insure typical flower color.

No flower of inferior color should be considered as the total number of points allotted color is exeedingly high (35 to 45 points). Some of the flowers should be fully expanded to show the typical color. Inferior color is that which is bleached, faded, dull or unnaturally streaked or smeared, lacking in clarity. Any of these listed faults deserves severe penalty under color.

Throat-greening is acceptable if the variety description so states. In varieties not so described one to two points should be deducted for throat-greening if in competition with flowers in which no throat-greening is apparent.

FLOWER FORM

The accompanying sketches show the distinct and varying forms of the Amaryllis flower, ranging from the long trumpet-like Easter lily form to the huge open-faced Dutch Hybrids; from the irregular orchid shapes to the double forms. Rating for form is to be strictly within these standards in classes differentiating between the divisions.

The portions or segments of the blossom, usually called sepals and petals are called tepalsegs. There are six tepalsegs in each blossom in Division Two through Five. The outer ones are called setepalsegs (abbreviated to setsegs) and these are usually broader and heavier than the three inner portions which are called petepalsegs or petsegs for short.

The upper, center setseg is usually larger than the other two OUTER setsegs. The lower, center petseg is smaller than the other two INNER petsegs. Observe these differences in size in the sketches. These size generalities make up the characteristic form and if not apparent the Judge should exact penalty under form.

The tepalseg tips should be uniformly pointed or rounded and the tips all reflexing at approximately the same degree. While not circular, the Amaryllis blossom should be symmetrical with the same size petals placed the same distance apart on each side of the flower.

Any twisting or deformity of any segment or of the whole flower is reason for deduction of points; with the exception of Orchid and Double types. Leopoldii Hybrids should be almost flat, Reginae are usually less flat. The tepalsegs in both may be either rounded or pointed.

Blooms with anthers and pollen are more beautiful than those denuded and in close competition, the blooms with anthers and pollen should be given preference. Anthers may be removed, without penalty, to prevent staining the petals in transit to the Show or for other prevailing reasons if **prior** permission is granted by the Show Committee. A card signed by the Show Chairman should accompany such exhibits.

FLOWER SIZE

The Amaryllis provides almost the largest flower possible to grow in the home. Some individual blooms measure as much as ten to twelve inches across. Miniature sizes have been added through the efforts of hybridizers. Excessive size may contribute to a gross, coarsened appearance, all out of proportion to the scape and foliage, which will require a point deduction.

There are several measurements involved in the size of Amaryllis. The lengths of throat (tepaltubes) vary and should be typical of the variety.

> TRUMPET — 4½ to 5½" throat tube
> BELLADONNA — less than 4" throat tube
> REGINAE — less than 2" throat tube

When viewed from the side, in profile, the flower of the REGINAE HYBRIDS should exceed 4"; but the flower of the LEOPOLDII HYBRIDS should be less than 4".

Flower diameter is dependent upon the variety and the general sizes recognized in each Division should govern.

LEOPOLDII:

if the floret is 6-7" across the face, 13 points are allowed

if the floret is 7-9" across the face, 14 points are allowed

if the floret exceeds 9" across the face, 15 points are allowed

In all other Divisions, a 6" flower rates the full 15 points, provided it meets the throat-tube and profile measurement listed above. Any size less than these listed is scored down commensurate with the degree of the fault.

FRAGRANCE

Two points are allowed for fragrance and both of these points are to be deducted if no hint of fragrance is discernable at the distance of approximately five inches from the flower. The fragrance should be pleasingly delicate and light; if it is too strong, the Judge is to deduct one point. The Belladona Division has a typically vanilla-like scent.

NUMBER OF FLOWERS PER SCAPE

Often considered almost as family heirlooms, when properly handled Amaryllis bulbs have been known to continue to grow for 50-75 years and usually produce a greater number of blooms each season. The normal flowering season is February through May though the bulbs can be forced into bloom earlier by special treatment.

In determining the number of florets per scape, both expanded and unexpanded flowers are included. If the scape carries four or more flowers, allow 6 points, if the scape carries three flowers, allow 5 points, if the scape carries only two expanded, allow 3 points.

In Miniatures, allow 4 points for two expanded flowers and the full 6 points if the scape carries three or more flowers.

SCAPE LENGTH AND CHARACTER

The length of the scape is considered in relation to the size of the flowers. Tall growing scapes average more or less 20-28". A tall scape topped by a small flower will be penalized as will the short stem topped by a 9" flower.

The character of the scape means its coarseness of fineness; its weakness or strength. The scape should be strong, erect and straight. It should have enough substance to hold the several flowers erect and well posed without excessive nodding or bending.

SCAPES PER PLANT

For potted plant exhibits, allow the full ten points only when three or more scapes are present. Deduct one point for two scapes and two points if the plant carries only one scape.

As long as there is at least one scape in bloom on a potted plant, any earlier scapes with faded blooms may have been removed without losing any points because of their removal.

FOLIAGE

Amaryllis plants produce strong, strap-like foliage with a healthy, glossy texture, but the foilage is given only a total of two points because it may be only just developing at the time of flowering, or it may disappear before the plant blooms. Leaf growth that is present with the flowering scape is very desirable and indicates proper cultural practice relative to temperature control in the potted plant exhibits.

If the foliage is entirely absent, deduct the full two points. If the foliage is only slightly developed, allow one point. For well-developed healthy foliage, allow the full two points.

Of course, the leaves must be a healthy, typical green. Ripening apples in the same room with the plant, give off an ethylene gas which may cause a yellowing or bleaching of the foliage, this or any other disease or insect damage is to be deducted.

CONDITION

Specimens in prime condition, healthy, properly cultured and fresh should receive the full number of points allowed for the specimen classes. Those failing to come up to the standards should be penalized accordingly.

Amaryllis are blessed with exceedingly heavy substance and long-lasting qualities. Under 75 degree daytime temperature, blooms will last approximately three weeks. In a cool window or room (65 degrees), flowers often last ten weeks. Spent flowers or scapes with spent flowers may be removed, but the removal must have been done carefully, leaving no unsightly stubs or scars.

Amaryllis scapes and foliage grow tall and it is often necessary to stake them. If the stake is green in color, does not protrude above the flower or foliage, is not too heavy or unsightly or conspicuous and is tied with green string or twisting wire, no points are deducted. But if the stake does attract attention to itself, then some deduction must be made. Care should have been used in applying the string or ties to avoid scarring the scape.

A pot only slightly larger than the bulb is used. A pot may be considered large enough if there is room for an inch of soil between bulb and pot. At least one-third of the bulb should protrude above the soil. The pot should be deep enough so that at least one inch of space is left between the soil surface and the rim for watering.

The petals should be completely free of pollen stain or other soil. Leaf scorch, fuzzy gray mold sometimes affects leaves and flowers. If the flower stalks are bent or deformed with foliage red-spotted, the damage was probably caused by Red-Fire disease. Evidence of such disease must be severely penalized. Mechanical injury, such as torn leaves or petals, etc., is penalized less severely.

SUMMARY

Bloom Color

*irridescent dusting present and lively *color rich *clear *glistening *vibrant

-texture dulled -aging -inferior -bleached -lacks clarity -throat green -darkening with age '-unnaturally streaked or white spotted

Bloom Form

*outer setsegs (petals) broadest *upper, outside setseg biggest *lower, inside petseg smallest *tips uniformly pointed or rounded *reflexing approx. same degree *Leopoldii flat *Reginae less flat *anthers, pollen present, or card of permission for removal

-deformed twisted petals (Exception: Orchid, Double) -one pedicel shorter -upper, outside setseg too small -lower, inner petseg too broad -irregular form -Leopoldii too cupped -anthers removed without permission -not symmetrical

Bloom Size

*Leopoldii: 6-7" allow 13 points: 7-9" allow 14 points; over 9" allow 15 points — if all other standards of measure are met *all other Divisions for a 6" bloom allow 15 points *Reginae profile must be 4" or more *Leopoldii profile must be less than 4" *Trumpet . . . 4½ to 5½" throat tube *Belladonna less than 4" throat tube *Reginae less than 2" throat tube

-excessively gross -out of proportion -coarsened -deviations from standards as to profile, throat tube length, and diameter

Fragrance

*present *delicate *pleasing

-absent -strong Note: Judge from a distance of 5" from bloom

Number of Flowers Per Scape

*four flowers, allow all 6 points — Minatures: *three flowers allow 6 points

-deduct one point for scape carrying only 3 expanded flowers -deduct three points for scape carrying only 2 flowers — MINIATURE: deduct two points for scape carrying only 2 flowers.

Scape Length and Character

*length proportionate to flower *straight *sturdy *erect *regular pose

-rust scars -scape split -too short -too long -weak -coarse -crooked

Foliage

*strong *healthy *glossy *well developed (allow all points)

-absent (deduct both points) -slightly developed (deduct 1 point) -yellowing

Condition

*healthy *fresh *stakes green *stakes inconspicuous *ties harmonious color *well groomed * pot size appropriate (1" between bulb and pot) *1" of watering space allowed

-pollen stained -wilted, spent florets -stakes unsightly -stakes protruding -ties conspicious -scape scarred -stub of removed scape remaining -over potted -deformed by Red Fire -gray mold -leaf scorch -petals showing slug damage.

Begonias

SUGGESTED CLASSES:

A: Tuberous
1. Large Flowered Branching
2. Pendula (Hanging)
3. Multiflower

B: Rhizomatous
1. Beefsteak, Trout, Star, etc.
2. Rex cultorum

C: Fibrous
1. Cane, Angel Wing, Steel, Fernleaf, etc.
2. Herbaceous Bareleaf: Wax, Calla, etc.
3. Hairy type: **scharffi, phyllomaniaca,** etc.

D: Bulbous, Christmas

Because of the great variances in types of Begonias, they will be considered here first as potted plants which includes all classifications and second, as specimen blooms of Large Flowered Tuberous, which see.

This is only a partial listing of the species which includes approximately 12,000. In a show in which Fibrous, Rhizomatous and Rex are in competition in the same class, the only way they can be fairly judged is to identify the plant and judge according to the scale for the specific type.

A: TUBEROUS

1. Large Flowered Branching
   - summer blooming
   - flower forms of rose, camellia, carnation, daffodil, crested
   - blooms 4-8". Circular Single & doubles
   - plant 1', leaves 6-8"
   - leaves flat or crimping downwards
   - all warm colors, plus white and
   - picotee, mottled as well as self
   - stems erect, but may droop under bloom weight.
   - use Scale Number 1 or 2.

2. Pendula
   - flowers smaller than A. single & double
   - allow to cascade on fine stems
   - profuse bloomers, small leaves
   - use Scale Number 3.

3. Multiflower
   - exceedingly floriferous
   - small flowers carried above foliage
   - yellow, orange, red
   - small leaves, compact branching plant
   - use Scale Number 1 or 2.

SCALE 1
Specimen Plant, Tuberous

Quantity of Flowers	30
Cultural Perfection	25
Foliage	25
Quality of Flowers	15
Erect Flowering Stems	5

SCALE 2
Collection Tuberous Plants

Cultural Perfection	20
Foliage	20
Quantity of Flowers	20
Staging and Arrangements	15
Color Effect	10
Erect Flowering Stems	5

SCALE 3
Specimen Pendula Tuberous

Number and size of blooms in proportion to plant size	40
Cultural Perfection	25
Foliage	15
Drooping Flower Stems	10
Quality of Flowers	10

B: RHIZOMATOUS: (Includes the following plus many species and hybrids many with hairy stems. Mostly winter and spring flowering)

1. 'Beefsteak' **(B. feasti)**
   - both foliage and flower value
   - erect
   - succulent, water storing leaves
   - l e a v e s roundish, water-lily shaped
   - hairy leaf margin, red below, pink flowers
   - easy to grow, includes
   - 'Lettuce Leaf' **(B. bunchii)** in which leaves are crested, ruffled.
   - 'Trout' **(B. argentes-guttata)** leaves oval, pointed coarsely toothed; shining olive-green with white spots, pink flowers
   - Mexican specie leaves 2' wide, flower stalks 4'
   - use Scale Number 6 or 7.

2. 'Star' **(B. heracleifolia)**
   - leaves silver, red, blue-green
   - resembling cow-parsnip
   - 8" in diameter
   - white and rose colored flowers
   - flower stalks 2-4'
   - easy, blooms February-April
   - use Scale Number 6 or 7

3. Rex cultorum **('Painted Leaf')**
   - grown for foliage beauty
   - colored, patterned leaves, striped, spotted, plain
   - small, medium, large leaf types
   - extraordinarily varied l e a f forms, including Spirals in which leaves curl and recurl near leaf apex.
   - creeping and upright habits
   - difficult to grow, over 50 varieties
   - example: 'Can Can' (has oakleaf foliage)
   - use Scale Number 4 or 5.

C: FIBROUS

1. Cane
   - tall woody species often over 3'
   - more or less shrubby habit
   - bare leaf, no hairs
   - stems swollen at nodes, similar to Bamboo, many species, hybrids
   - three different heights: pendula, under 2', over 2'
   - example: 'Dancing Girl' (Hybrid, no two leaves alike)

SCALE 4
Rex Cultorum Begonia Plant

Cultural Perfection	45
Foliage	40
Difficulty of Cultivation	10
Correct and Suitable Labeling	5

SCALE 5
Rex Cultorum Collection of Plants

Cultural Perfection	25
Foliage	25
Staging and Arrangement	20
Color Effect	15
Difficulty of Cultivation	10
Correct and Suitable Labeling	5

SCALE 6
Cane-like, Shrub-like, Thick-stemmed and Rhizomatous Plants.

Cultural Perfection	35
Foliage	30
Quantity of Flowers	10
Quality of Flowers	10
Difficulty of Cultivation	10
Correct and Suitable Lebeling	5

SCALE 7
Collection Cane-like, Shrub-like, Thick-stemmed, Rhizomatous.

Cultural Perfection	25
Foliage	20
Quantity of Flowers	10
Quality of Flowers	10
Color Effect	10
Correct and Suitable Labeling	5

SCALE 8
Specimen Plant Basket or Pendula, other. than Tuberous.

Cultural Perfection	40
Foliage	15
Cultural Difficulty	15
Quantity, Quality Flowers	15
Plant Habit	10
Correct, Suitable Label	5

- includes 'Angel Wing' (**B. coccinea**)
- tall cane
- oblique leaves approx. 5"
- coral red flowers in drooping clusters
- some leaves have silvery spots
- example: 'President Carnot'
- **includes** 'Steel' (**B. metallica**)
- tall woody, exceeds 3'
- metallic glossy olive - green sheen on upper leaf surface, purple veinings beneath.
- pink-white flowers
- **includes** 'Fernleaf' (**B. foliosa**)
- small plant, slender stems
- smallest begonia leaf, glossy, drooping
- almost invisible flowers
- good basket plant
- use Scale Number 6, 7 or 8.

2. Hairy Type

B. haageana or B. scharffi (same plant)
- large rose flowers in hanging clusters
- very floriferous
- everblooming but most prolific in summer
- upright
- hairy olive-green leaves, red beneath
- use Scale Number 6 or 7

B. phyllomaniaca
- thick, fleshy hairy stems
- large fringed leaves on which young plants are produced
- profuse small pink flowers
- many other hairy types
- use Scale Number 6 or 7

3. Herbaceous Bareleaf (**B. semperflorens**)
- single and double flowering types
- green and bronze leaf types
- three height types; Dwarf: 6-8", Medium: 10-12", Tall: 12"
- includes Wax, Calla, etc.

Wax
- polished leaf surface
- summer bloomer, single, double flowers
- likes sun, fairly easy
- example: 'Ballet' (dwarf,

(Continued in next column)

SCALE 9
Begonias with Semperflorens Characteristics.

Quality of Flowers	30
Cultural Perfection	25
Foliage	20
Quality of Flowers	20
Correct and Suitable Labeling	5

SCALE 10
Collections Begonias with Semperflorens Traits.

Cultural Perfection	20
Foliage	20
Quantity of Flowers	15
Quality of Flowers	15
Staging and Arrangement	15
Color Effect	10
Correct and Suitable Labeling	5

SCALE 11
Collection of mixed types of Begonias.

Staging and Arrangement	20
Cultural Perfection	20
Variety	20
Foliage	15
Color Effect	10
Quantity, Quality Flowers	10
Correct, Suitable Labels	5

---

brown leaves and double white flowers)
- use Scale Numbers 9 and 10

Calla
- mature leaves veined white, variegated
- center cluster of new leaves pure white, and shaped like a calla lily
- red flowers (one double variety called 'Calla Red Jewel')
- dislikes moistness, humidity
- use Scale Numbers 9 and 10

D: BULBOUS: CHRISTMAS
- small flowers, single, semi, double
- produced in clusters
- Hybrids of this and Tuberous produced Heimalis (Winter) Begonias
- flowers resembling Tuberous, some larger, some smaller
- sturdy, erect compact plant
- dark green foliage
- winter blooming, florists' favorite
- use Scale Numbers 6 and 7

The so-called Strawberry Begonia with white flowers and leaves red below and green above and strawberry-like runners is really **Saxifraga Sarmentosa.** It is also sometimes called the Strawberry Geranium.

CULTURAL PERFECTION

Cultural perfection is the evaluation of a number of qualities which indicate the health of the plant and the care it has been given. The qualities below are listed in the order of their importance to cultural perfection.

Plant Form (Balance and Symmetry) is allowed approximately 20% of the points for cultural perfection. Begonias may be low mounds of foliage and flowers, foliage only, thick bushes, treelike or vines, and so must be judged according to their growth habit.

All Begonias are asymmetrical in their growth as each stem is one-sided. The leaves and side shoots are produced alternately at the nodes, always facing in one direction so it is only when a number of stems have developed that the plant form takes on a symmetrical appearance such as is ideal. The plant should be well-centered in the pot for perfect balance.

Because most Begonias lack woody fibre in the new growth, the stems snap off easily and each such accident gives an unbalanced appearance.

Plant Fullness and Bushiness is allowed approximately 20% of the points for cultural perfection.

The public may question the apparent number of plants in a pot when the schedule stipulates "one plant to a container". But knowledgeable Judges and exhibitors know that such Begonias as Rhizomatous and **Rex** often give the appearance of several plants since the stems creep as well as branch and another rhizome takes off at right angles to the main rhizome, also in repotting buried rhizomes often break into new growth.

A well-grown, full, symmetrical plant of this group will of necessity be made up of a number of such rhizomes in vigorous growth. Shoots of Pendula types should be pinched, trained and developed into compact plants, drooping over the pot equally on all sides.

Staking and Tying is allowed approximately 15% of the points for cultural perfection. Staking and tying is often advisable as the stems are brittle but it should be inconspicuous and neatly done with appropriate materials. Paper clips, colored rubber bands or anything which detracts from the plant's appearance should be discounted. Unpainted sticks will at times blend in with the stems better than highly finished ones. No stakes should protrude above the top of the plant. Stakes should be proportioned to the plant, no huge "clubs" in a pot with a small plant. Of course, Pendula types should not be staked, but allowed natural growth lines.

Clean Containers are allowed approximately 15% of the cultural perfection points. No soil, moss, fungus or foreign matter should appear on the container or the exhibit must suffer deductions.

Suitable Container is allowed approximately 10% of the cultural perfection points. The size of the container should be proportioned to plant size. The plant should not look lost in the container, nor should it be over-grown. While many Begonias would grow in a hanging basket, the Pendula types are most suited to this pot design. Low bush types such as Tuberous multiflower, Wax, Calla, etc., are most suited to smaller clay pots and decorative pottery. Tall growers show best in large jars, wooden tubs, etc. Pots simulating ludicrous animals, heads or coy designs usually detract from the plant they contain, as does the addition of figures such as animals or birds stuck on the plant or placed in the soil. The plant is best shown without such additions.

Proper drainage must be a consideration in all types of containers. Pots that are simple and similar do not detract from the plants in grouped collections.

Plant Vigor is allowed approximately 10% of the cultural perfection points. The Judge should be able to recognize the short, regular nodes of a well-grown Cane Begonia; the lush leaf color of a healthy Hairy Begonia; the sturdy stem and unblemished leaf and blossom of a well-grown Tuberous; the well-placed, many leaved Rhizomatous plant. He is able to appreciate the pinching which produces a stocky, well-developed Semi-Tuberous Christmas Flowering Begonia or Pendula. He will recognize that spindly, leggy Tuberous Large Flowered, with weak stems and bud drops is a result of over-fertilization and that longer stems, better branching and a greater number of shoots results from large healthy tubers. And that a stunted plant may be the result of a too-porous pot which has been allowed to dry out, thus chilling the soil and roots. Or that a stunted plant may be caused by Eelworm infestation, this or any evidence of Bacterial Leaf Spot and resultant defoliation or Botrytis Blight must be severely penalized.

The plant should not be in a static state of growth, but new leaves and/or buds should be apparent. The pot should not be soil-depleted nor contain any weeds or other type plants. Tuberous Large Flowered stems should be erect, but bearing a heavy flower will naturally cause some bending, this should be penalized when excessive.

Size of Plant is allowed approximately 10% of the cultural perfection points. Immature plants add very little that is of educational value. The Judge, however, must take into consideration the fact that many plants can never be considered truly full-sized or mature as pot plants; especially mature in view of their growth in native habitats. But with controlled pot care, they can be grown to be satisfactorily mature as house plants. Refer to Classification for approximate heights.

QUANTITY AND QUALITY OF FLOWERS

The quantity of the flowers must be in proportion to the foliage and also as is characteristic of the type. For instance, Tuberous Multiflower and Pendula are extremely floriferous; Large Flowered Tuberous bear fewer individual flowers but their size and distinctiveness makes each one stand out and for this reason each should be of high quality with colors clear, substance heavy and with no blemishes caused by bruising, cuts, disease, insects, sunburn or age. At least two sets of flowers should be shown on Tuberous Large Flowered. Flowers of all types should be clean, fresh and with colors pure.

In such plants as are grown for both flowers and foliage (i.e. 'Beefstake', etc.) no penalty should be taken for flower lack if the plant is shown out of bloom season. Special consideration, however, can be given to a plant showing bloom out of season.

FOLIAGE

Begonias are truly mimic plants for there are variations of leaf shape which resemble the palm, ivy, elm, maple, oak, pond-lily, lettuce, woodbine (**B. cirumlobata**) and the fern with the tiniest leaf of all (**B. foliosa**). Leaf texture varies from the sheer silk of the **Rex** 'DEWDROP' to the heavy, blistered seersucker of **Rex** 'TWISTY SPOT'. Foliage can be found in all shades of green, red, brown and endless combinations of these, plus white variegations (Calla).

Common Begonias grown primarily for their foliage include 'Trout', 'Beefsteak', **Rex** and **B. sunderbruchi.** In such types, the Judge must assess the quantity in relation to size and length of stems. Long stems, lengthy internodes with sparse, unbalanced leaf placement are faults to be penalized.

In those types which are shown for both flowers and foliage ('Star', many Fibrous, Wax, Calla, etc.) the flower and foliage should be well-balanced in area, neither overpowering the other. The Judge should not penalize such a plant for not being in bloom when it is not its season to bloom.

One of the outstanding characteristics of all Begonias is the high development of their stipules and bracts. These appendages protect plant parts during early development. Some types shed these parts quite early and are called deciduous. In Judging these Begonias, the Judge will penalize any loose or dried stipules lying about on leaves or soil. Some Begonias have non-deciduous stipules which remain firmly affixed and such stipules which have dried but are still attached should not be penalized.

The foliage must be dust and spray free, fresh and undamaged. Examine the reverse sides for Eelworm damage (small dark brown spots), Mealybugs, Red Spiders. Stunted leaves may be the result of mites and defoliation may be caused by Bacterial Leaf Spot. Any evidence of insect or disease deserves deduction. All old, dried foliage should be groomed away.

CULTURAL DIFFICULTY

Begonias are judged as to how exacting in its cultural requirements the plant is according to several categories:

1. Very difficult
2. Difficult
3. Fairly Difficult
4. Medium
5. Easy
6. Very Easy

It is unrealistic to state that it takes no effort to produce a healthy plant and some points should always be allowed for such occurence. It is difficult to assess this quality as a type may succeed easily for one grower and environmental circumstances and yet be fairly hard for another.

Begonias vary in ease of culture as they originate in a wide range of habitats being native to sub-tropical and temperate zones from Africa to Mexico; from low to high altitudes; along streams or high rocky mountainsides. When a schedule is not detailed, easy culture Begonias may have to compete with those which take patience and skill. A large handsome specimen of a comparatively easy to grow type competing with a touchy type makes judging difficult, thus a well-grown small specimen of a "difficult" should rate higher than a large, well-grown specimen of an "easy".

The area in which judging occurs must also be taken into consideration. What may seem a rare occurence in one area, may be the norm in another. The wise Judge should consult the other panelists or the Classification Chairman for information on local norms when judging in unfamiliar territory. Calla Begonias are considered difficult in most areas except in certain New England circumstances. Wax are considered fairly easy, Beefstakes are considered "easy as a geranium". Star Begonias are thought to be easy and Steel as medium easy. Tuberous Large Flowered are considered easy in coastal areas and fairly difficult inland. Of course, varieties differ within a species. For instance, the Wax Begonia variety 'WESTPORT BEAUTY' is considered difficult to grow and many of its sisters are not.

DISTINCTION

Distinction is a most difficult quality to judge in horticulture, especially when judging one variety or one species against another, but as long as this word appears in the official scales Judges must try to pin it down.

Distinction involves superiority; that which is better; more perfect; or has a quality which sets it apart from its companions. Any superiority of form, color, leaf pattern, size, even staging and labeling can be noted here, especially if all are the same variety.

All Begonias have interesting qualities of leaves but some have small idiosyncracies which set them apart, indeed from all plants. For instance, in the Rhizomatous variety, 'PAGE 13' on a large mature plant the stems will develop lateral lens-shaped splits.

Sometimes large stipules (**B. venosa,** etc.) can lend a plant distinction. Hairy appendages on various parts of the plants, small plants growing on mature leaves (**B. phyllomaniaca)** add interest. **B. plantanifolia** and **deliciosa** exude small crystals resembling insect eggs on the leaves.

While typical to type, these things add a difference which is often distinctive. Of course, a plant, no matter how interesting, cannot be given full points here if it lacks cultural perfection or a high count on all the other qualities in the scale as distinction is also tied in with its superiority as a plant overall.

Begonias can be judged according to difference as follows:

Easily distinguished from other types	Not the common run
	Common
Distinguished from other types	

CORRECT AND SUITABLE LABELING

Much educational value is lost by lack of correct labeling. Many Standard Shows and Fairs are lamentably lax on this point and Classification Committees should be responsible for tightening standards in this area.

Labels should be neat, small but not too tiny to read. Whether they are waterproof or not is no consideration unless the lack of such has resulted in a smeared, messy appearance. Then deduction should be made. Incorrectly named species of which the Judge is SURE should be corrected after at least 60% of the total points for labeling are removed. Printing should be neat, legible and the label itself clean and unwrinkled.

STAGING AND ARRANGEMENT

The artistic placement of the various exhibits in a collection is considered here. The Schedule should specify the minimum number of feet allowed and the minimum number of plants to the collection (usually five).

The rhythm of color, textural interest; the contrast of form, color and texture; the balance of color and size are all considered in judging the staging, as well as the scale of each plant to the others and to the area the total exhibit occupies. A huge Angelwing displayed with four small Wax, Calla and Cane types would make an exhibit which is unbalanced and out of scale. Spacing is also considered, each plant should have been selected in view of the total overall space allowed and within that space each plant should be uncrowded. A large plant drooping over a smaller one or placed in front of a smaller one is reason for penalty here. The plants should be displayed in the manner most suited to their growth habits. For instance, pedestals or shelves should be provided for the Pendula types. Any unique staging should be rewarded.

Pots should be simple and similar so they do not detract from the plants in the collection and destroy the unity of the arrangement and staging. Judges should deduct for garishly colored pots which are inharmonious with the plant in them and the others in the collection. The entire staging should present an orderly, harmonious, balanced apperance.

COLOR EFFECT

The Begonia family is without doubt the only plant so common yet so varied in color, both of leaf and flower as well as form. The Judge should penalize any inharmonious inclusions in a collection. For instance brick-red flowers of one variety will "fight" with the coral-red of another, thus reducing the score for color **harmony.**

The delicacy of Calla will be over-powered by the colorful exuberance of a **B. feasti (Beefsteak).** The same principles of color design as are used in floral arrangements apply here. Large areas of white and pink flowers perked by a smaller area of brilliant red for **balance. Contrasting** many brilliant leaved plants with a plain green increases the color effect of both. The colors should be placed so the eye travels **rhythmically** over the exhibit. Several-level staging is an aid here. The Judge should reward the exhibitor who places his Tuberous Large-Flowered reds so they blend into pink which blend into white. If it is necessary to show a brilliant orange and a full chroma red Tuberous Large-flowered in the same collection, the exhibitor who tones down the contrast by placing a white flowered plant between will be rewarded under color effect by the Judge.

SUMMARY　　　(points allotted vary according to type, refer to individual Scales.)

CULTURAL PERFECTION

. Plant Form 20% of points allotted
*fairly symmetrical *balanced *uniform growth habit
-one sided -off center in pot

. Fullness & Bushiness　　　20%
*mounded *compact
-loose -leggy

. Staking and Tying　　　20%
*inconspicuous *adequate *trained
-obvious -needed -inappropriate materials

. Clean Container　　　15%
*scrubbed *clean
-salt stained -dirty -mossy

. Suitable Container　　　10%
*suitable size, design *drainage provided
-too small, large -coy -broken, chipped, cracked -lack drainage

. Plant Vigor　　　10%
*healthy *normal *well developed *stems vigorous *well nourished *actively growing *T.B. stems erect
-diseased -weak -spindly -static state of growth -T.B. stems excessively bent (T.B. Tuberous)

. Quality of Flowers   60%
*area of flowers proportioned to foliage area *typical number for type

-sparse -hidden -too few for amount of foliage -overloaded

. Quantity of Flowers   40%
*firm, crisp substance *backs unblemished *undamaged *colors clear, attractive *edges crisp unburned *texture sparkling

-soft -thin -wilted -texture dull -color dull, faded -torn -bruised -soiled -diseased

FOLIAGE

. Quantity   20%
*proportionate -sparse

. Vigor & Substance   20%
*healthy *firm -weak -succulent

. Color   20%
*rich *interesting *typical -dull -discolored

. Cleanliness   20%
*wiped -dried stipules on leaves

-soiled -over groomed

. Blemishes   20%
*unscarred *perfect -torn -marginal burn -brown spots -underneath (eelworms) brown spots, on top (sunburn)

CULTURAL DIFFICULTY

. Very difficult   100%
Example: Rex

. Difficult   90%
Example: Calla

. Medium   50%
Example: Steel, Tuberous (according to area)

. Easy   25%
Example: Star, Trout

. Very Easy   15%
Example: Beefsteak, Wax Angelwing

STAGING AND ARRANGEMENT

. Balance   20%

*fairly equal placement around vertical axis (imagined) *well chosen, harmonious containers

-unbalanced by large plant on one side -too many large or small plants in exhibit.

. Rhythm   20%

*repetition of color, texture, size, etc. *gradation of color, texture, sizes, etc.

-spotty placement

. Spacing   20%
*orderly uncrowded
-mixed up appearance -crowded

. Contrast   20%
*different, harmonious sizes, textures, colors, etc.
-monotonous -all the same

. Scale   20%
*fits space allowed * proportionate to each other

-too big, small for space allowed in schedule -some plants too large or small in proportion to others

COLOR EFFECT

. Balance   25%
*law of areas observed -disorderly color placement

. Contrast   25%
*some contrast *interesting -all same
-monotonous

. Harmony   25%
*harmonious pots, flowers, leaves
-clashing -pots garish -unharmonious

. Rhythm   25%
*eye travels easily over colors
-eye stopped by spotty placement

Tuberous Large Flowered Single Specimen Blooms

SUGGESTED ENTRY: 3 blooms on 1″ stems, shown with 2 mature leaves.

SCALE

Form	25	Size	15
Color	20	Foliage	10
Condition	20	Staging	10

FORM

The Large Flowered Branching species of Tuberous Begonia is sometimes referred to as the mockingbird flower because it has successfully mimicked the form of the camellia, the rose, the carnation, daffodil and the hollyhock.

The blooms must be symmetrical of form, circular and have depth in the doubles. The singles should have petals of equal length, evenly dispersed in a circular manner with no excessive gaps between the petals. All petals of singles should be approximately the same size.

The Rose double form should have a high center typical of the classic exhibition rose. There should be no separation between the center and the outer petals but an even full transition from the high center.

The Crested form should be perfectly centered in the petals, with the tuft held pert and crisp and in good proportion to the length and breadth of the petals which surround it.

The petals of all forms should stand at right angles to the stem and not droop or reflex back toward the base. The blossoms should be fully open to display the form. Distorted form which may be caused by cyclamen mites is a serious fault.

COLOR

Few flowers produce such clear, intense colors as do the Large Flowered Tuberous Begonia. The warm advancing oranges, reds and yellows from full chroma to the palest tints plus pure glistening white make up the color range.

Most outstanding and well-known contrast is the Picotee in which a narrow brilliant, rick-rack-like band of color edges each ruffled petal. This band should be narrow and even and there should be no bleeding into the white background or points are deducted.

Variegated, mottled, feathered and striped varieties are available. These combinations must be pleasantly harmonious, not smeary-appearing and with margins clean-cut. Each color should maintain its true clear value. The whites should be pure and clean. The texture of the Begonia lends an irridescent glistening refractive quality to the color and any dulling of this is a fault.

Burning and browning of petal edges are deductible under color to the degree that this fault affects its beauty and clarity. Any transparency caused by insect rasping away the substance or thinning and fading due to age are also deducted under color.

CONDITION AND GROOMING

Each petal should be clean and crisp and at its peak of perfection. While Begonias naturally have heavy substance, bruising, careless handling and water soaking soon destroy the fresh appearance and any such damage should be penalized. The Judge also deducts for any cuts, tears, or soil on the blossoms. Signs of wilting and aging are faults.

SIZE

Tuberous Large-flowered Begonias normally bear three blossoms on each stem, a large male flower and two smaller female flowers at the sides. When exhibiting blooms are desired, disbudding results in larger, better developed flowers. A Judge should recognize the superior attention to the production of an exhibition bloom by giving extra consideration to those blooms that have been disbudded. A well-grown carnation or rose form often reaches 5-6".

FOLIAGE

It is customary to show two fully developed leaves with an exhibit of three large-flowered Tuberous Begonia blooms. The foliage should be typically dark green, heavily substanced. There should be no marginal burning or crisping. The leaves must be free of dust, spray residue and soil, but not with the help of artificial dressings.

Deductions will be taken for scarring, tears and blemishes of any sort. Thrips, Red Spider and Mealy Bug evidence is seriously penalized. Small brown spots on the leaf undersides are often eelworm damage. The size of the foliage displayed with blooms should be in proportion to their size. If the leaves are dark green in color and tend to crimp downward the Judges can be sure satisfactory growth has been made. If the leaves are light green or yellowish and tend to cup upward, it is evident the plant was suffering from lack of food and appropriate penalty is taken.

STAGING

A Judge can justifiably deduct points for blooms displayed with side buds and for blooms cut with long stems that allow the blooms to droop. Extra consideration is given for blooms displayed face up in a low, flat container, in such a way that the blooms and/or leaves are not under water or in danger of becoming water-soaked.

Uniformity of size, color and form is always a consideration in multiple entry exhibits and all things being equal will often be a deciding factor. Unharmonious colors such as full chroma red and orange displayed as close companions may cost points in close competition.

SUMMARY

Form 20 Points

*high centered rose *uniformly ruffled camellias, carnation forms *petals of singles evenly spaced *well centered on stem *circular *full *deep (doubles) *fully open

-lopsided -off center -flat (doubles) -separated center and outer petals -poorly developed center -voids -reflexing excessively -too tight bud form

Color 20 Points

*clear *bright *picotee narrow, clean edged *harmonious combinations *intense *pure *glistening

-sunburned -browning -thinning -fading -bleeding -streaked -dull

Condition 20 Points

*clean *crisp *fresh

-water soaked -soiled -wilted -torn -bruised

Size 15 Points

*normal *slightly larger than normal

-small -stunted

Foliage 10 Points

*healthy green *heavy substance *clean *fresh *turgid *crimping downward

-scarred -soiled -edges burned -leaves spotted -mealy bugs -webby -crimping inward

Staging 10 Points

*well displayed *face up *disbudded *uniform in size, color, form

-drooping out of container -underwater -waterlogged -varying size, color, form -unharmonious color choices

Tuberous Begonia — Flower Forms and Foliage

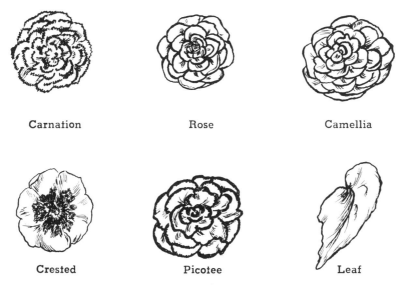

| Carnation | Rose | Camellia |

| Crested | Picotee | Leaf |

Camellia

SUGGESTED CLASSES:

A. 1 bloom, grown outdoors

B. 1 bloom, grown indoors

C. 1 bloom, chemically treated, grown outdoors

    1 bloom, chemically treated, grown indoors

D. 3 blooms, one variety

E. Collection, at least five blooms, named varieties

F. Pot-grown plants

    1. outdoor grown

    2. indoor grown

    3. miniature (50% of blooms less than 2-2½")

In Shows where numerous entries are expected, subclasses as to variety, color, size, degree of protection and treatment for:

    1. **Japonica**

    2. **Reticulata**   4. *Hybrids*

    3. **Sasanqua**   5. *All other species (Vernalis, etc.)*

Such subclasses can be combined at the option of the local sponsoring group, eg. **Japonica,** grown outside, chemically treated; **Japonica,** grown inside, etc.

It is not the responsibility of the Judges to determine if a bloom in a given class (grown inside, outside, chemically treated) has been placed in the proper class.

DEFINITIONS:

Blooms Grown Outside: *Blooms that have been grown in the open, without protection other than that furnished by an unheated slat house where slats have no covering whatever over them or any substance between them. Schedule should define unprotected blooms.*

Blooms Grown Inside: *Blooms from plants in enclosed structures grown and/or bloomed under artificial conditions where temperatures and/or moisture can be/is largely or completely controlled.*

Chemically Treated Blooms: *Blooms which have been treated with any chemical substance for any purpose other than prevention, suppression, or eradication of fungus, other diseases, insects or any pest. Blooms which have been treated with gibberellic acid or any of its derivatives or similar type chemicals are specifically acceptable. No such treated bloom (otherwise qualifying for exhibition) shall be disqualified from its class.*

Mutant: *Is defined as a flower possessing a distinct break in color or form from normally accepted parent bloom. The 'break' must hold true when propogated. Variations attributed to virus not recognized as mutants. Entrant must state how grown and treated.*

CAMELLIA, Theaceae Family

The Species most ofen encountered are: **C. japonica, C. reticulata** and **C. sasanqua.** The majority of cultivated Camellias are **C. japonica.**

C. japonica: Color range includes white, pink, red-purple; striped, margined, marked, self, blotched, contrasted, shaded, blended, flushed, variegated. Naturally more stiff and formal than **Reticulata.** Flower forms include single, semi-double, anemone, peony, rose form and formal double. Foliage is glossy. Species size was 2", and modern day **Japonicas** range to 8".

C. reticulata: The flower form, resembling semi-double peonies rather than the more formal **Japonica** may be loose, petals revolute, waved, smooth, imbricated, according to variety. Form is usually high-centered and open. Colors range from pale pink through carmine to purple-red, may be naturally a marbled, self, variegated, according to variety. Sizes range up to 9". Foliage is naturally a dull green, not glossy.

C. sasanqua: Graceful shrubs, small glossy leaves, profuse flowering. Small blooms. Forms as varied as **Japonica.** Colors are white through purple; may be margined, self or variegated. Flowers are often creped in texture and cupped in form. The petals shatter easily.

Hybrids: Defined as plants (not sports) grown from a cross between two or more species, or between hybrids, or hybrids and species of the genus Camellia. At this time, Camellias do not include the color blue or pure yellow, though yellow is present in some **Japonicas** as 'FRANK GIBSON'. Only a few cultivars emit a faint fragrance 'HERME'. Shows using the ACS Seal and awards please refer to the American Camellia Society Handbook for detailed judging standards.

POINT SCORING SCALE

Form	20	Texture and Substance	20
Color and Marking	20	Condition and Distinction	15
Size	20	Foliage	5

FORM:

Camellias are classified by form as follows:

1. Single

- all stamens central and obvious

- one row of not over eight petals

- Example: 'AMABILIS'

2. Semi Double

- conspicuous stamens

- two or more rows of regular loose or irregular petals

- Example: 'AKEBONO'

3. Anemone

- center composed of intermixed petaloids and stamens

- one or more rows of large petals lying flat or undulating

- Example: 'ELEGANS'

4. Peony: Incomplete Double

- center composed of mixed petaloids, stamens and petals

- or center composed of irregular petals of full form with no stamens showing

- deep, rounded shape

- Example: 'KINGS RANSOM'

5. Rose-Form: Semi Double

- *9–20 petals*

- stamens form a concave center when fully open

- imbricated petals

- Example: 'ROSEA SUPERBA'

6. Complete Double

- stamens never show
- numerous petal rows
- fully imbricated
- Example: 'SWEETHEART'

NOTE: Any form falling within the description of the named bloom as set forth in the Camellia Nomenclature or known to be not a freak within the experience of the Judge shall be deemed typical.

Camellias are exhibited and judged when fully open. A partially developed bud, not yet opened into a flower shall not be eligible to be judged as a specimen. Proper disbudding results in a bigger, more perfectly formed bloom on the large-flowered cultivars of **Japonica.** 'PINK PERFECTION', 'COVINA', 'COUNTESS OF ORKNEY', and 'MONJISU' are seldom disbudded. **C. sasanquas** also are seldom disbudded.

The bloom of a variety known to change its form as it approaches maturity, shall have as the standard of perfection that form which represents the normal peak of maturity. For instance, certain rose form flowers open with bud centers, with petals filling the space between the high center and the outer petals. When past prime, the flowers have a distinct division between the rosebud center and the flattened outer petals. Example is 'MATHOTIANA'. The first form is ideal.

Points are to be removed under form if the condition has altered the form, otherwise points are removed under condition or substance, or the amount of points removed may be divided between the qualities affected to total the degree of fault.

The petals of some formal flowers are frequently flat, or are slightly upturned when fresh. As they age the petals of certain varieties turn down toward the calyx and stem. Example: 'ALBA PLENA'. The first form is ideal. Points may be taken off under both form and condition to total the degree of fault.

Anemone, peony, rose and formal forms should have depth, thinness is to be penalized.

As the season advances, flowers of some varieties, which earlier in the season are formal double, will exhibit stamens. Experience in such varieties shall guide in judging. For instance, if most of the flowers of these varieties exhibited still retain ideal furled bud centers, those showing stamens are less than ideal. Example: 'MATHOTIANA'.

Some varieties, under certain conditions fail to attain the form described as typical. The form described in ACS Nomenclature as typical for that variety or sport shall be considered as the ideal.

Variations in form are consistently caused by climatic and soil conditions peculiar to the locality where grown. This fact should be understood by the Judges, and judging should be according to what is typical of the locality. Example: 'ELEGANS'.

Other varieties are subject to distinct form changes caused by adverse growing conditions such as temperature extremes. These variations are to be penalized. For example, the variety 'LALLAROOK' may produce some flowers with incurved petals and others with flat petals. The flatter form is considered more desirable for this variety as described in ACS Nomenclature. A flat form would not be ideal for 'TEUTONIA' the petals of which normally curve upward at the tips. The petals of 'DUTCHESS DE BRABANT' are notched, 'EDELWEISS' should have a high center.

The form of some cultivars is indeterminant, being by nature not settled or fixed in one form regardless of the growing conditions. For instance 'SNOW PALACE' is listed as having Peony to Anemone form. 'STELLA SEWELL' has Semi-Double to Peony form. 'CAMELLIAN' has Semi-Double to Rose-form double, etc.

Failure to attain symmetrical form in outline is a fault. Leaves which cramp or crowd the flower are faults to be deducted.

Form should be understood to mean that which is true or characteristic of a variety in all its customary variations. The form may be better, BUT must NOT fall short of the requirement except as in **habitually** found in a certain growing area.

CAMELLIA FLOWER COLOR AND MARKINGS

Color should be that which is characteristic or better for the variety and should have clarity and attractiveness. The markings and variations should be in the amount, distribution, clarity and design characteristic of the variety with no unpleasant qualities.

The flowers of some varieties are subject to distinct changes in color, resulting from adverse growing conditions such as temperature extremes and these variations must be penalized. Example: 'MATHOTIANA' tends towards a darker purple, the color is not ideal regardless of the cause. White cultivars discolor from excess exposure to sunlight, and deduction must be made if this fault is present.

Variations in color are often **consistently** caused by climate or soil conditions peculiar to a locality. This fact should be recognized by the Judges and judging adjusted according to what is typical and normal **for the locality.** Example: 'ELEGANS'. Browning may be the result of thrips, blight, cold or age and is to be penalized commensurate with the fault.

SIZE

Miniature	2½" or less	Medium-large	3½-4"
Small	2½-3"	Large	4-5"
Medium	3-3½"	Very large	over 5"

There are some good miniatures available. 'CORNISH SNOW' has bloom 1-1½". Plants entered in the Miniature Classes are often required by the Schedule to carry 50% flowers less than 2-2½" in diameter. This allows competition only of naturally small Camellias and eliminates underdeveloped blooms of average-size cultivars.

Maximum points for size are alloted when the specimen is fully as large as can be grown in the area and the conditions prevailing relative to protection.

Chemical treatment may bring increases in size of some varieties which are truly amazing, increasing some regular 4" flowers to 6-7" size. **C. Reticulata** flowers normally are large, up to 9".

SUBSTANCE AND TEXTURE

The texture (surface quality) and the substance (holding quality) should be characteristic of the variety being considered. 'MASTERPIECE' may last up to ten days. 'SNOW PALACE' and 'WHITE VELVET' have a velvety texture. 'MARIE BRACEY' has a satin sheen.

Substance and texture reduce as the season advances and the same high quality will be unavailable.

CONDITION AND DISTINCTIVENESS

Condition. A Judge shall never touch or otherwise handle a Camellia on exhibition. A bloom shall be judged as exhibited without regard to **HIDDEN DEFECTS.** However, in the event that several blooms are in such close competition that consideration of defects of any kind is desirable, the Judge should request a clerk to move the bloom in its container so it may be examined more critically.

The petals of some formal types are frequently flat or are slightly upturned when fresh and turgid. As the bloom grows older, the petals of these varieties have a tendency to turn down towards the calyx and stem, indicating weakened substance and advancing age. Points are to be removed under form if the condition has altered the ideal form; otherwise points are removed under condition or substance, or the amount of points removed may be divided between the qualities affected.

Freshness is indicated by crispness, turgidity, color and firmness of the stamens and anthers. Blooms are to be exhibited at the peak of physical condition.

Distinction. The quality of elegance and finish is that which makes a bloom stand out above the others. Labeling, because of its educational value, may be considered here. Good staging contributes to distinction. Containers for camellias should be individual, low, "bottom-heavy", wide-necked, clear and spaced at least five inches apart to lessen any possibility of bruising.

FOLIAGE

In order to prevent premature dropping or shedding of blooms of some single and semi-double varieties that have this tendency even while quite fresh, such blooms may be wired **TO THEIR OWN WOOD**. A Judge should be able to recognize, within limits, leaves typical of a variety and observe and penalize any infringement of the rules that the flowers MUST be wired to their own wood.

Only **C. reticulata** may be judged without wood or foliage IF so stated in the Schedule. In such an event the five points allotted to foliage may be given to distinction.

Growth buds may be removed without penalty. One or more leaves should be attached to each bloom. Foliage crowding or cramping the flower are faults.

The foliages of some varieties have idiosyncrasies which distinguish them from the ideal of perfection, but since these are characteristic no penalty is taken. The foliage of 'FROSTY MORN' is exceptionally long and narrow and slightly twisted. The foliage of 'KUMASAKA' typically curls, giving the impression of needing water. Plants of 'MARY CHRISTIAN' are distinguished by yellow-green leaves, so it is obvious that the Judge must be familiar with foliage characteristics to avoid taking unfair penalties.

Several chewing and sucking insects feed upon Camellia foliage and deductions must be made for evidence of damage. Curling foliage may be harboring aphids.

SUMMARY

Form 20 Points

*symmetrical *true *characteristic *fully developed *prime *well proportioned *petals uniformly placed *no space between high center and outer petals

-irregular outline -ungainly -malformed -ill formed - distinct division between center and flattened outer petals -exhibiting stamens (other than normal for form type) -not typical -lacks described form characteristic of the variety -petals turning back toward calyx (age) -lacks depth (doubles, anemone, etc.)

Color 20 Points

*color true to variety and season *clear *bright *delicate *glistening *pleasing *attractive *rich *striking *distinct *luminous *strong *novel *desirable *intense *markings well distributed

-dull -faded -displeasing -burned -browned -weak -pale -uneven -off color -lacks sparkle -watery -blurred -darkening -bleached -muddy -discolored -wind damaged -cold browned -markings not balanced

120

Size 20 Points

*larger than average expected *generous size *typical of variety *maximum potential in all parts

-too small -stunted -overlarge (in miniatures) -less imposing -inadequate -abnormal

Substance and Texture 20 Points

TEXTURE
* smooth *sparkling *has sheen *brilliance *silken *refined
-dull -coarse -rough

SUBSTANCE
*firm *crisp *turgid *heavy *fresh *perky *strong *substantial *holding shape well
-wilting -limp -droopy -flabby -shrinking -thinning -relaxing -curling -soft

Condition and Distinction 15 Points

CONDITION
*prime *unmarred *stamens fresh

-blemished -petals torn -bruised -petals creased -spotted -residues present -scarred -old -diseased

DISTINCTION
*has overall charm, quality *finesse *unique *well staged *labeled

-mediocre -plain -poorly staged -lacks grace -falls short of ideal in any quality

Foliage 5 Points

*color characteristic of variety *vigor typical of variety *form typical of variety *clean *undamaged *bright *healthy *surface texture typical of variety

-scale present -insect damage -disfigurement due to weather, mechanical injury, disease -dust or spray residue -unthrifty -not typical -cramping flower

Carnations

SUGGESTED CLASSES:
1. Large flowering hardy Carnations, disbudded
2. Miniature, cluster of two or more
   A. Single
   B. Double

CARNATION   (Dianthus, Clove Pink)

Carnation is the common name for the **Dianthus caryophyllus,** also known because of it fragrance as the Clove Pink. While general usage associates the name "carnation" only with the florist type, it properly belongs to all forms of the species.

Carnation plants are 5" to 3½' tall, with brittle, slightly branching stems and narrow, opposite, grey-green foliage. The terminal flowers are often ruffled or toothed.

121

Botanically, there are two main groups of species. Group one includes the Grass Pinks **(D. plumarius),** Sweet William **(D. barbatus)** and Annual Pinks **(D. chinensis).**

Group Two includes two main groups of highly developed LARGE-FLOWERED forms.

1. The Florist or Greenhouse Carnation **(D. caryophyllus),** including the perpetual-flowering American Carnation and

2. The Outdoor or Border Carnation, including the "marguerite" types. Large-flowered Outdoor or Border Hybrids are the result of crosses between **D. plumarius** and **D. caryophyllus.**

In shows, a class is made for standard, large flowered disbudded blooms and one for clusters. Miniatures are defined as Carnations produced in a spray. The spray is a cluster of blooms produced by a lateral growth; the terminal flower may have been disbudded or be intact. By greenhouse standards, the stems of Miniatures should have at least three flowers, the stems not exceeding 24" and the individual flowers not over 2½" in diameter.

SCALE OF POINTS

LARGE FLOWERING, Disbudded

Bloom	75
. color	25
. size	20
. substance and condition	15
. form	10
. calyx	5
Stem	20
Fragrance	5

MINIATURE, Cluster

Blooms	75
. condition including substance and calyx	35
. form, including size, shape and placement	25
. color	15
Stem	15
Fragrance	10

BLOOM COLOR

Traditionally red, white and pink predominate with occasional yellow, purple and tangerine (orange) blooms. Many variegations occur but usually on body colors of yellow, white and pink. In Carnation color class,

"Selfs" are the flowers of one solid color

"Flakes" are striped with one color

"Bizarres" are striped with two-three colors and

"Picotees" have petals edged or banded with a second color.

The centers may be of a different hue. For instance, 'DINAH' is a deep rose with a maroon center.

Textures vary considerably, the smooth waxy texture of 'CYNTHIA' gives a glow to the color, and the velvety texture of some varieties adds richness and depth. The color of "Selfs" should be even throughout. The color of both "Selfs" and variegates should be fresh and clear.

122

BLOOM SIZE

The size of the individual flowers in the Miniature cluster is not to exceed 2½" in diameter in official Carnation Shows. The size of garden grown clusters is considerably less. The size of all the flowers in the cluster should be uniform, any extreme variability should be penalized slightly.

English Cottage Carnations grown in pots often measure 2-2½" and 3" as do well-grown, large-flowered Hardy, garden-grown Carnations. The size should be judged according to what is optimum for garden-grown Carnations in the area.

SUBSTANCE AND CONDITION

Carnations are time-honored for their substance which makes them so long lasting and popular as cut flowers. The substance should be crisp, the petals firmly turgid.

Wilting or yellowed leaves indicates that stem rot or wilt disease has attacked. Yellow swollen areas on the leaves and stem which may have burst to expose brown spores is rust. Leaf spot or blight and red spider damage cause yellowing, drying or drooping of the foliage. Any of these symptoms is severely penalized.

FORM

The Flamands have large flowers, always double and with a higher center than other varieties. Chinensis (Annual Pinks) throw flowers that are very loosely assembled. The petal edges may be laced, fringed, imbricated (overlapped), notched, entirely wavy or even entirely smooth at the rims as in 'CYNTHIA'.

The general flower form should be symmetrically circular with enough petals in the doubles to appear well-filled and form a full-rounded center. The bottom petals should extend out horizontally to form a relatively flat base on the flower. However, some varieties do characteristically hold their petals a bit lower than a right angle and if the incline is not excessive, the form should not be too severely faulted.

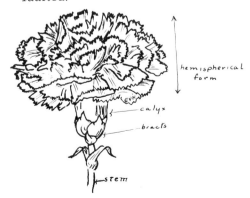

The petals should regularly overlap each other and be of similar size and shape in each ring or row. The optimum stage of openness is that in which the flower is approaching maturity with some of the center petals not yet fully developed. The form should be hemispherically shaped or like a half a ball when viewed from the side at eye-level. No large, irregular voids should be present on the face or in the outline.

In the disbudded, single-flower-to-a-stem exhibits, the bloom should be placed on the stem in such a manner that the plane of the outer petals is at right angles to the stem. A flower whose pose is inclining excessively is to be penalized.

In multiple-flowers-to-a-stem, the form of the overall spray is considered, including the size, shape and placement of the flowers. The flowers and buds should be uniformly distributed along the main stem to produce a somewhat loose, but well balanced spray with each flower showing off to the best advantage. At least two of the top flowers, preferably more, should be fully expanded with the remaining buds showing varying degrees of color.

The condition called 'sleepy' results from physiological and environmental conditions such as high temperatures, over-maturity and other factors. The tips of the petals curl toward the center and the whole flower appears cup-shaped or partially closed. The fault is serious and points should be deducted accordingly.

CALYX

The calyx should be strong, with the sides ideally nearly parallel or slightly funnel-shaped. The bracts at the base should closely adhere to the calyx.

A split calyx is defined as a slit of the calyx lobes due to excess number and pressure of the petals. The tendency toward calyx splitting has been bred out of some hybrids as for example 'OLD SPICE' and 'EVANGELINE'. Three degrees of splitting are recognized.

1) Minor splitting to less than ½ the length of the calyx, with no resultant flower form damage. This is not considered serious. Deduct 1-2 points.

2) A long separation extending down to the calyx base, but without any apparent flower form deformation. Deduct 3-4 points.

3) A long split extending down to the calyx base, with the petals protruding through the split and a resultant loosening and deformation of the flower. Deduct all five points.

As is seen, a bloom can have a major split and still win a blue ribbon if color, condition, size and form are of high quality; many Judges tend to penalize a split more than the maximum five points. Of course, it follows, that if the split is caused by over-maturity (usually the case) then substance and condition will be altered, color fading and certainly the form will be other than ideally symmetrical, and the bloom will usually deserve its ultimate elimination from competition, or at least for a top award.

STEM

Outdoor grown Carnation stems range from 12" long in 'SALMON UNIQUE' down to the 5" stems of 'HER MAJESTY'. The stems may support only one terminal bloom or two to six flowers on a single stem.

The schedule should provide enough classes so one is not judged against the other.

The stem should be of sufficient strength and stiffness to support the flower or flowers in an upright position without excessive bending or swaying. The stem should be straight, not dog-legged. Side shoots should not be present nor evidence of recent, incomplete disbudding. The leaves should not be torn or removed in the process of disbudding.

In the Miniature or spray classes, disbudding is for a different purpose. Instead of a "mechanical" culture to produce one large flower, the procedure is taken to create a loose, uncrowded spray of flowers by removing the main central bud. The bud removal should have been done at a relatively early stage to allow for scar-healing and to encourage strong stem elongation of the auxiliary buds.

While lack of disbudding does not eliminate a Carnation exhibit in a Standard Show, the Judge will use it as a means of breaking ties in close competition.

FRAGRANCE

It is interesting to note that annual American Carnation Society Greenhouse Shows offer a special award for fragrance. Winners of some recent shows are 'BASCO', 'LORETTA', 'DARK PINK AURORA' and 'STARLITE'.

The Grenadins include very strongly perfumed flowers of a single color. Many varieties of Carnations are not naturally fragrant. However, a hint at least is traditionally expected in the blossoms. In all fairness, it is suggested that no deduction be made for lack of fragrance and that a sliding scale be applied for existing fragrance as follows:

Faint — allow one point

Obvious — allow 2-3 points

Prounouned or penetrating — allow 4-5 points

SUMMARY

COLOR: Disbudded: 25 points   Cluster: 15

*clear *fresh *tips fresh, clearly colored *marking distinct

-dull -faded -petal tips darkening -not optimum for variety

SIZE: Disbudded: 20

*two to three inches *optimum possible for the area

-small -scant -undersized

SUBSTANCE, CONDITION: Disbudded: 15   Cluster: (including calyx) 35

*crisp *firm *turgid

-flaccid -limp -curling -overripe -insect, disease injury -spray residue -wilting

125

FORM: Disbudded: 10   Cluster: (including size, shape, placement) 25

*hemispherical *circular *base fairly level *petals overlapped evenly *petals have similar size and shape *high crowned *center petals still undeveloped

-'sleepy' -cupped -large, irregular voids -not fully expanded -spray crowded -one-flower pose inclining -irregular petal size or arrangement -flat flower top -too few flowers open in cluster -misshapen -lacks symmetry -petals drooping down around the stem

CALYX: Disbudded: 5

*complete *no splitting

-minor splitting (less than ½ of the calyx length) deduct 1-2 points
-medium (no petals extending thru split) deduct 3-4 points
-major (petals extending) deduct all 5 points

STEM: Disbudded: 20   Cluster: 15

*sturdy *stiff *erect *straight *timely careful disbudding

-side shoots -recent disbudding -incomplete disbudding -leaves torn -leaves removed -weak -dog legged

FRAGRANCE: Disbudded: 5   Cluster: 10 points

*faint: allow 1 point *obvious: allow 2-3 points *penetrating: allow 4-5 points

Chrysanthemums

SUGGESTED CLASSES:

Sections have been abbreviated for Standard Show and Fair Schedules. Consult the National Chrysanthemum Society Handbook for detailed scheduling. Classing should be by bloom type and color in most shows. Specialty Shows are often classed by variety. Cut blooms and sprays should measure 15-30".

SECTION 1. SPRAYS
    a. Pompon
    b. Decorative
    c. Spoon
    d. Quill

All types above may be further classed as
        1. Small up to 1"
        2. Medium 1" to 2½"
        3. Large 2" to not over 4"

SECTION 2: INDIVIDUAL BLOOM
    a. Regular Incurve
        1. Small . . . over 4" but not exceeding 6"
        2. Large . . . over 6"
    b. Irregular Incurve
        1. Small . . . 5" but not over 7"
        2. Large . . . over 7"

c. Regular Reflex
    1. Small . . . 4-6"
    2. Large . . . over 6"
d. Irregular Reflex
    1. Small . . . 5" but not over 7"
    2. Large . . . over 7"
e. Pompon (disbudded to one bloom to one stem)
    1. Small . . . less than 1"
    2. Medium . . . 1" to 2½"
    3. Large . . . 2" to 4"
    Top size limit is 4". Larger Pompons go into the incurve or reflex classes of 4-6"
f. Large Spider ('er 6") Thread (over 6") Quill (4") (Each to be judged against its own type and ideal)
g. Single, Semi-double, Anemone, Spoon (each to be judged against its own type and ideal)

SECTION 3: POT PLANTS
A. Bush   B. Standard   C. Bonsai   D. Cascade

Color classes may be made following divisions found under Color, which see. A spray is defined as a "cluster of blooms led by a single crown or terminal bud". Separate classes can be made for terminal (preferred) and crown sprays. Disbudding may be permitted in terminals or may not be permitted in crowns. Disbudding is preferred in Quill Sprays.

It is understood that the specimens have been grown in the open. Temporary protection is permitted, after color shows, to guard against wind, rain, frost damage. Any further protection should be agreed upon and stated in the Schedule.

The practice of disbudding garden varieties to a single bloom, to create bloom sizes which do not fit any regular class in the schedule should be discouraged. Sprays may be disbudded to one bloom per pedicel if the schedule permits. Where climate or special conditions make an early show a necessity, the schedule should rightfully include a class for disbudded varieties of 4" or more in diameter. Any disbudding under 4" should be discouraged and the practice discontinued (except for Pompons, which may be disbudded to a single bloom and entered thusly).

CHRYSANTHEMUM

A herbaceous, bush type perennial of the Compositae (Daisy) family. Variable hardiness, good greenhouse and garden subject.

Species originating in China, Japan and India have been hybridized into innumerable varieties. The Chinese and Japanese species gave us the tall (4') erect, many branched plants. The Japanese types have the largest blooms of all, composed of irregular, loosely arranged, curved, or twisted petals. The Chinese types are distinguished by their large blooms resembling huge, compact balls and are composed of regularly placed petals in the Incurve and resemble huge asters in the Regulars. Indian (Pompon) species and varieties have smaller flowers and characteristically lower bushes.

Many variations are available and fancifully named by their originators. These include the Korean, Arctic and American Hybrids, Bird, Football, Space Age, Button, Azaleamum, Million and the Atomic Age Daisies, (such as 'MIRAGE', a semi-double) etc. These can all be placed in the classes given under suggested entries. Classing by bloom form and size is preferred to listing classes according to such fanciful naming. No radical changes in form have come about. The changes have been according to growth height, flower size and hardiness characteristics.

Most garden cultivars mentioned above are Decorative or Aster-Flowered Reflexes and Pompons. Cushion Mums are a type of growth in which cultivars are "self-pinching" or natural branching and because of this have a low, spreading growth habit.

Feverfew (single and double), Pyrethrum and Marguerite are also Chrysanthemums as are some plants called Daisy, such as Crown, Nippon Shrub, High, Ox-Eye, etc. The Shasta Daisy is Chrysanthemum maximum, single and anemone, which may be crested or double.

Chrysanthemum bloom types can be grouped according to form similiarity

> A: Conspicuous Disk—single, semi-double, anemone, regular and irregular, and a few Spiders
>
> B: Disk concealed by strongly incurved petals—Pompon, Incurve both regular and irregular and Decorative.
>
> C: Petals reflexed, turned back—Decorative Reflex Aster Flowering, Regular and Irregular Reflex, and some Irregular Incurves.
>
> D: Tubular petals—Spoons, Quills, Threads, Spiders.

DIVISION A: CONSPICUOUS DISKS
1. Single

- strap-like ray florets
- evenly spaced, formal or
- subclass with florets fewer and much broader
- florets stand at right angles, do not reflex around stem
- not more than five rows of florets
- prominent "eye" or disk, with no ligulate petals in disk
- "eye" or disk flat
- size: small, not over 2"; medium, 2-4"; example: 'SYBIL': large, over 4", example Strap, 'BAMBOO', Broad, 'PALOMA'

2. Semi Double

- more than five rows of ray florets
- petals more irregularly placed, informal
- petals may or may not be at right angles to stem
- same size divisions as Singles
- prominent eye, clear of ligulate petals
- example: 'HAPPINESS'

3. Anemone Regular

- five or less rows of ray petals
- broad, flat to the tips, evenly spaced, equal in length
- standing at right angles to the stem
- disk in center is main feature
- disk formed of short ray petals
- disk raised to form a hemisphere
- disk must be free of ligulate petals
- or holes where such were removed
- example: 'POWDER PUFF'

4. Anemone Irregular

- ray petals irregular in length
- ray petals may be flat, twisted, somewhat tubular
- or quilled
- any spoon anemones are included here
- disk same as for Anemone Regular
- example: 'TUXEDO'

DIVISION B:

Disk may be present or concealed or the disk florets may be scattered singly or in small groups among the ligulate florets or be entirely absent. In any case, if present, the disk florets must be concealed by the many ligulate florets that give the bloom character.

5. Pompon

- globular form, equal in width and depth
- s m a l l sizes are acceptable though flatter
- ray florets may be incurved and broad or
- may be reflexed, broad, short and center may be incurved for a short distance
- size: small, less than 1" in diameter; medium, 1-2½"; large, 2-4"
- if over 4" place in the Regular Incurve class
- example: 'BRIGHT FORECAST'

6. Incurve: Regular or Chinese

- globular form, equal width and depth
- ray florets broad, tips rounded and incurved
- regular, even, smooth, overlapping

- bloom full-centered, compact
- if disk shows, disqualify specimen
- length of each petal should be such that each forms a graceful curve
- penalize loosely incurved petals lack of depth
- size: small, over 4", not exceeding 6"; large, over 6"
- example: 'KIDDER'

Subclass: SKIRTED INCURVE
- lower rows of petals not incurved but stand at right angles like a ballerina's skirt; or hang down to form a skirt that conceals the upper part of the stem
- other characteristics including size same as incurves
- example: 'THE INDIANAPOLIS GROUP'

7. Incurve: Irregular

- ray petals broader than the regular incurve
- ray petals twisted, incurved
- lengths intermingled, irregular, overlapping
- as a class are larger than INCURVE REGULAR
- size: Small: 5-7"
       Large: over 7"
- Example: 'ANNE,' plus many Japanese varieties

DIVISION C. PETALS OF TYPES 8-11 REFLEX OR TURN BACK FROM THE CENTER

8. Pompon: Reflexed or Decorative

- globular form, equal depth and width
- ray florets reflex as a rule
- ray florets broad, short
- centers may be incurved for a short space

9. Reflexed: Decorative or Aster-Flowered

- ray florets longer, narrower than Pompons. Petals often pointed
- blooms are flatter
- may be incurved at the center

- may have pinked, lacinated edges, (carnation-flowered)
- reflexed as a rule, regular or irregular petal arrangement
- size: Small: less than 1"
   Medium: 1" to 2½"
   Large: 2" but not over 4"
   Blooms over 4" are placed in Type 10 or 11 according to regular or irregular petal arrangement
- Example: 'AVALANCHE' Most double garden cultivars fall into this group

10. Reflex: Chinese or Regular

- strap-like petals strongly reflexed in a more or less regular manner
- spherical form, full centered
- diameter and depth equal
- size: Small: over 4" not exceeding 6"
   Large: over 6"
- Example: 'MOHAWK CHIEF'

11. Reflex: Japanese or Irregular

- strap-like petals broader than Reflex Regular
- petals reflex but are irregularly placed, presenting a shaggy, mop-headed appearance
- larger than Reflex Regular
- size: Small: 5-7"
   Large: over 7"
- Example: 'GREER GARSON'

131

DIVISION D: TUBULAR PETALED

12. Spoon: Single

- ray florets regular and tublar, opening at the end to form a spoon-like tip
- not more than five rows
- right angles to the stem
- disk conspicuous and flat
- size: Small: less than 1"
    Medium: 1" to 2½"
    Large: 2½" and up

- Example: 'CHARM SPOON'

12A. Spoon: Double or Semi Double

- more than five rows of ray florets, spoon tipped

- right angles to stem

- disc may be less apparent than in Single Spoon

- Sizes same as Single Spoon

- Example: 'YELLOW SPOON'

13. Quill

- ray florets elongated and tubular
- tips usually spoon-like but may be closed at tip
- curved or slightly hooked tips
- bloom fully double, globular
- no disk showing
- size: Small: not over 2"
    Medium: 2-4"
    Large: over 4"
- Example: 'INCA'

14. Thread

- ray florets long, may be unequal length
    slender
    closed and tubular
- ray florets may be straight or slightly curved
- delicate, willowy appearance

15. Spider   So-called Fuji

- ray florets long, irregular lengths
    tubular
    more or less curved, twisted
- tips may be open and spoon-like or closed
- tips MUST be coiled, sinuous, or hooked at tip
- petals may hang down or spread, according to cultivar
- Example: 'BUNBU,' 'LORRAINE'

NOTE: Some novelty forms defy classification; if need be special classes can be made if entries are worthy, rather than be judged with unlike types. Ex: 'Saga', a thistle-like form where fine, long tubes stand up parallel to the stem like a brush. Disk nearly concealed.

The terms COMMERCIAL, generally designating large disbudded REGULAR Incurves and Reflexes and

EXHIBITION, designating large IRREGULAR Incurves and Reflexes should be discontinued and the blooms referred to by form and approximate size in inches, according to the accompanying sketches.

JUDGING SCALES

NOTE: All disbudded blooms to be 4" or over except pompons, decoratives or their lacinated counterparts, which may be any size. Pompons should be grown less than 4" with emphasis on form and substance.

Scale 1 — All Disbudded Blooms

BLOOM QUALITY	55
. color 10	
. form including fullness 20	
. size 15	
. substance incl. freshness 10	
STEM	10
. size and substance 5	
. straightness incldg uniform internode lengths 5	

FOLIAGE	10
. color and size 5	
. substance, incl. freshness .. 5	
EXHIBIT AS A WHOLE	25
. cleanliness and absence of damage 15	
. pose and proportion 10	

Scale 2 — All Sprays

BLOOM QUALITY	40
. color 10	
. form incldg fullness 10	
. size 10	
. substance incldg freshness 10	
STEM	10
. size and substance 5	
. straightness of main stem 5	

FOLIAGE	10
. no true leaves on pedicels 4	
. color and size 3	
. substance incldg freshness 3	
EXHIBIT AS A WHOLE	40
. spray form 15	
. spray grace and number of blooms 15	
. cleanliness and absence of damage 10	

Scale 3 — Pot Grown Specimens

BLOOM QUALITY   45
. color 5
. form 5
. fullness 5
. size and number 15
. substance incldg freshness 15
STEM   10
. size and substance 5
. straightness 5

FOLIAGE   10
. foliage to soil distance 4
. color and size 3
. substance incldg freshness 3
     10
EXHIBIT AS A WHOLE   35
. appearance 15
. balance 20

COLOR
Bloom Color Classification

White
(cream
(white with yellowish center
(pure white
(white with purple or pinkish cast

Yellow
(light
(medium

Green
(white with greenish cast

Purple and Pink
(true pink
(lilac
(lavender
(orchid
(purple

Bronze and Orange
(peach
(apricot
(orange
(bronze
(buff

Red
(scarlet
(crimson
(purplish red

Any Other Color
(a. splitting any of these color groups to make additional color classes may be done upon the wishes of the Show committee provided circumstances warrant such
(b. true pinks may be classed separately
(c. when the inside (obverse) or front of the petal is bi-colored, it is placed in the class of the most prominent or dominant color
(d. indeterminate colors are placed in the color group they most closely resemble
(e. blooms should be placed in the color class most fitting at time of classification, without regard to their color before or after that time, or according to typical color of cultivar.

Color must be characteristic of the cultivar (variety) and can only be judged on the basis of comparing the entry to an ideal bloom of the same variety.

Poor culture, soil conditions and too intense sunlight can affect the color. Penalize Pompons, particularly for clouded, dingy, murky hues. Color intensity varies greatly in Chrysanthemums and the Judges should not expect to find the adjective applies to all shades and tints. There are soft and delicately tinted yellows, as well as bright, intense, gay yellows and so on throughout the color range. Whatever the intensity, the color must be clear and pure. Diluted, weak, faded, dingy colors should be penalized. The color should be evenly distributed out to the tips of all the ray petals.

The combinations of colors in the bicolors or two-tones must be harmonious and pleasing. Disks should be clear, freshly colored, not dull or darkened with age. A greenish color indicates immaturity.

Multiple entries or multiple-plant pots should be selected with an eye to color harmony. Color of all the flowers in a spray should be uniform with no flower faded or variously hued. Of course, partly open buds will show more intense hues.

SIZE:

The size of the variety will vary with the number of flowers permitted to mature on the plant. Size is measured by the diameter; breadth is the horizontal diameter measured from side to side. Depth is measured from the top to the bottom, called vertical diameter. Specimens should be fully expanded to determine size.

Singles, Semi-doubles, Anemones, Spoons, Quills, Threads and Spiders are measured from side to side (horizontal diameter) because of their lack of depth. Extend the petals of Threads and Spiders to measure full size.

Doubles like Pompons, Incurves, Reflexes, Decorative Pompons and Decoratives are classed according to their largest diameter which is usually horizontal, but the depth and width should be approximately equal. The exceptions are Small Pompons and Decoratives which may be rather flat.

Judges should realize that while size is important, it is only ONE of the major qualities and must not be given undue consideration. However, if a particular cultivar, because of good culture, exceeds typical size, all other qualities being equal, it should be given special consideration. Generally the largest size consistent with the quality is desired, as growing to extreme size is sometimes accomplished only at the sacrifice of substance, stem strength, leaf health, etc.

Disbudding (rubbing off tiny side buds) is done to increase size. Pinching (taking out terminal growth) is used to control the size of the larger Incurves and Reflexes and to increase branching in small sizes, such as Pompons and Decoratives and also to control the number of blooms per plant in exhibition specimens.

As noted in the suggested classes, there is overlapping between the size of small and large Pompons. The reason being that in crown sprays the topmost blooms will be open and larger than the lower blooms, but in disbudded terminal sprays the single bloom on each pedicel would definitely be easier to place in a size class.

FORM OF BLOOM:

Bloom form is the approved shape for the type and variety. Every Chrysanthemum bloom in its prime assumes a form characteristic of its type, but for various reasons, it may not assume the ideal form for its type. A good specimen will contain the necessary number of florets required to complete the form, whether the characteristic form is a single, semi-double or double.

Some petals are lacinated (notched and fringed) like a carnation. Some petals are ligulate (straplike), others are broad and flat; others are tubular (for all or a portion of their length). Any abnormal distribution which creates faulty form should be penalized. Imperfect florets may be present surrounding the disk and are to be penalized.

In double forms, the breadth and depth which determines the size and fullness, also sets the form which must be globular or spherical (except in Small Pompons and Decoratives) when viewed at eye level or looking down upon the bloom. A pencil or ruler laid over the middle of the bloom helps to determine the balance and fullness on either side. Any lopsidedness, one-sidedness or imbalance or uneven development or deformity must be penalized.

Regular, even petal spacing to produce a firm, closely overlapping bloom in the Regular Incurve and to some extent in the Pompons and Regular Reflexes is a requisite. Any misplacing or unevenness of petal placement is a fault in these types, as well as in the Singles and Spoons.

A disk that shows in a normally double form is reason for disqualification; or if passed by the Classification Committee, is eliminated from competition by the Judges. The center should be fully filled in with petals, usually incurving but sometimes tousled (particularly in the Irregular Japanese Reflex).

In the Single and Anemone forms, the disks are conspicuous and should be radially symmetrical, with an even, not bumpy surface. The disk is to be flat in Singles, Spoons and Threads and relatively small in comparison to the bloom size. There must be no ligulate petals in the disk of Singles and Semi-Doubles. If removed with tweezers several days before, the hole will close. If a hole is apparent, penalty is taken. The disks in Anemones are raised, cushion-like and hemispherical in form and relatively large in comparison to the bloom. Florets in the disk may be of varying lengths, but must maintain a tufted appearance in the flower center. The presence of ligulate florets interspersed among typical disk florets is a serious fault, as are holes in the disks which indicate plucking of such florets.

Chrysanthemum blooms develop slowly to peak bloom and before reaching optimum perfection it is referred to as "green" and is subject to penalty. A bloom mature enough to show all fully developed ray florets in the center, or "green" are equally faulty.

Ascochyto blight affects the form, causing poorly developed, discolored, one-sided blooms. Excessive watering and crowding contributes.

FULLNESS:

Fullness is closely tied to form, though it is possible to have a satisfactory bloom form for any type without sufficient petals to complete the ideal of a perfect bloom. The number of florets can be affected by the type of bud which developed the bloom. For instance, disbudded crown buds develop the greatest number of petals, while a late terminal bud will have many less petals. The variety 'AMBASSADOR' may throw so many ray florets from a crown bud that crowding results. Others ('GRACE STURGIS') may not produce enough to hide the disk, if a terminal bud is used. So the experienced exhibitor should select the type of bud most suited to produce the best bloom for the variety.

Petals or ray florets must be evenly disposed over the receptacle which is the expanded, enlarged portion of the stem that carries the florets. In close competition, the fullness of each entry must be carefully considered. Remember, the diameter should equal the depth in all doubles except Small Pompons and Decoratives.

SPRAY FORM:

The NCS standard of excellence is the terminal spray and culture should be geared to this type. Mixed classes of TERMINAL and CROWN sprays are impossible to judge properly, and if entered as a mixed class in a NCS Show, the crown sprays could earn no more than a Red (2nd place) Ribbon. When a crown bud appears it is recognized by its encircling leaves. This should be pinched out. The terminal bud, which comes later, is readily identified by the circle of small buds around it.

Terminal Spray: (Ideal Type)

- develops from a terminal cluster of buds
- is led by the terminal, i.e., central bloom
- a single stem carrying a number of blooms on pedicels which may carry miniature leaflets or bracts, BUT does not carry true leaves

- acceptable type: terminal bloom set lower than others by not more than ½ its diameter.
- a single stem runs through the spray center as a vertical axis
- this stem carries true foliage continued by the pedicel of the lead or terminal bloom
- this stem terminates in, and is leaves
- the lead bloom is the apex of the spray and the
- auxiliary blooms are accepted as belonging to the terminal spray IF their origin is continuous from that of the lowest bloom of a terminal cluster AND
- as long as the blooms are carried on a pedicel rather than on a secondary branch
- sprays having at least 5 well-placed, uniformly open blooms are most acceptable.

Crown Spray:

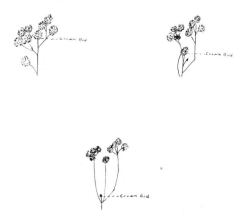

- crown sprays are led by the bloom of a crown bud which is lower than the auxiliary bloom of the spray
- the crown bud is a flower bud whose development has been interrupted. The interruption may have been of long or short duration or permanently stopped. note sketches
- blooms are carried on secondary branches rather than on pedicels (stems supporting a single bloom, no leaves)
- a class of crown sprays can be scheduled, but these are not accepted by NCS nor is it recommended they receive Society awards. In order to educate the public along the lines of the Society the schedule and Judges should give preference to terminal sprays.

Branch:

The branch usually (not always) is an entire plant, with multiple sprays attached. The branch is definitely not a horticultural triumph, it does not conform to the definition of the acceptable Terminal Spray, and its presence in the show should be discouraged by the Classification Committee at the time of entry.

Spray Grace:

Grace is defined as the beauty of the overall form through the pleasing relationships of the characteristics of parts which go to make up the flower. The spray may take one of three forms; cylindrical, conical (where the base is broad) or round-topped, but the overall effect must be one of grace.

Terminal sprays of Chrysanthemums will vary between cultivars in the placement of the blooms. While two entries may both conform to the definition of a terminal spray, one may have a more tapered, open, graceful overall appearance resulting from more widely spaced blooms held separate by properly spaced pedicels and balanced bilaterally (alike on both sides). The other entry may appear crowded, clubby or squat. Naturally the last mentioned spray will lack the grace of the more open spray and be penalized accordingly.

The entire spray should appear as an entity. The blooms should be well-distributed, and the overall form well balanced and defined. The spray should have blooms of similar size and maturity. In terminal sprays, the superfluous buds are removed, leaving only one bloom on each pedicel, thus giving all a chance to develop fully, evenly and without crowding.

Crown sprays generally lack grace; are jointed, unbalanced, branchy and angled. Reduce points proportionate with the degree of fault when considering crown sprays.

Number of Blooms:

Terminal sprays of Chrysanthemums vary between cultivars in the number of blooms. Some varieties may produce only five or six blooms on a whole terminal spray whereas others may develop many more. Buds not yet fully developed and open should not be referred to nor counted as blooms.

The number of blooms should be in proportion to the stem length. A spray may win with fewer blooms than its competitors if color, grace, etc. are superior.

Substance:

Perhaps the most valuable quality of Chrysanthemums are their characteristic substance to which color, form, and freshness are so closely allied, for without substance these qualities are very short lived.

Substance is that quality which makes a bloom long-lasting and combined with attention to cultural requirements produces a firm textured bloom that remains in perfect condition for several weeks, in many types of Chrysanthemums.

The degree of substance begins with varietal selection, progresses through culture and is strengthened by proper hardening off. Any deterioration of substance evidenced by thinning, translucence, limpness or softness or a papery texture will be penalized. Petals should be thick, firm; with disks (if typical of variety) showing no evidence of breakdown.

Freshness: (Condition)

Petals of a perfectly fresh Chrysanthemum possess a glistening texture. Petals should be fresh and crisp clear out to their tips; disk florets must be bright and maintaining typical stance; and not be darkened by age.

The physical appearance of the bloom (s) should be such that it gives an overall impression of freshness and cleanliness. All blooms on a spray should be as uniformly developed as possible, with none overly immature or aged. Wilting, withering, browning, and bruising must be penalized and deductions made for soil. The presence of disease or insect damage is severely penalized. Mechanical damage less so. Botrytis first appears as small water soaked brown spots and develops grayish brown mold, infecting the entire flower-head. White flowers should have a crisp shining quality and be free from pink streaks which indicate the bloom is past prime.

139

Stem:

Exhibits of cut blooms or sprays should be 15-25" long. Height is measured from the table top to the top of the highest flowers. When the stem length is not specified in the schedule, its graceful relationship to the sizes and weight of the bloom/s is considered AS WELL as the characteristic height of that cultivar. The stems up to and including the individual pedicels should be firm, straight, relatively sturdy and capable of supporting the weight of the bloom/s gracefully and without undue bending and nodding but not be so heavy as to seem misproportioned to the flower/s. Crooking, offset curves, angles and knotty effects are faults. Acute angles or "dog-legs" are the result of improper handling, usually severe or poorly timed pinching.

Disbudding to a single bloom (except in Pompons) is discouraged in types normally 4" or under. Disbudding should be clean, leaving no evidence and with scars neatly healed. Untidy disbudding, stubs and evidence of recent disbudding are penalized commensurate with the faults. The stem should carry healthy, typical true foliage, which see. The bloom should sit squarely on the stem. If it leans to one side, the form of the flower is often lop-sided.

Foliage:

Foliage quality is usually in direct proportion to bloom quality, and for this reason the number of points allotted are lower than warranted, considering its importance in producing a quality bloom. Foliage should extend from the bloom to the container lip in cut, disbudded specimens. Lack of **own** foliage is penalized full count.

True leaves are not present on the pedicels of terminal sprays, though leaflets or bracts may be present. Where size is at a premium as in both Regular and Irregular Incurve and Irregular and Regular Reflex, the typical foliage leaves below the bloom may be replaced by bracts (modified leaves) for a few inches. However the bloom should appear well-shouldered in foliage. If the bracts extend over a considerable portion of the stem, this is a fault and is heavily penalized. The specimens MUST have some true, typical leaves.

Foliage should have substance, be firm, not limp. It should not be mechanically torn, or bruised, withered or damaged or spotted by spray or dust.

Abnormal form, color, size, texture and distortion, discoloration, due to insects or disease will be subjected to severe penalty. Most Chrysanthemum disease and insects affect the foliage.

Rust: blisters or powdery masses on leaf undersides
Leaf Spot: dark brown disfigurations and defoliation
Mildew: whitish surfaces
Stem Rot: slow leaf fading and withering
Nematodes: wedge-shaped areas, drying, shriveling
Midges: galls

Aphids, Red Spider, Four-lined Plant Bug do chewing, sucking damage.

Light or dark green foliage may indicate an imbalance in the chemicals required for true color and leaf perfection. The size of the leaves should be neither too small nor overly large for the bloom, nor should the foliage be too sparse or abundant as to overpower the bloom/s.

Exhibit as a Whole, Cleanliness, Pose ,Proportion

Foliage, stem and bloom/s must be free of spray, webs, disease, bruises, tears, insect and pollution damage; oiled or polished leaves, scarred stems, auxiliary shoots are penalized. Blooms should be poised perpendicular to stem with graceful proportion between stem length and bloom weight. Foliage evenly spaced around stem; 'neck' (between bloom and first leaf) should not be elongated proportionately. When exhibit is turned, leaves' upper surfaces should be in view. If leaves all face one direction deduct points. Multiple bloom exhibits should be uniform in type, bloom size, stem length and same or harmonious colors.

POTTED CHRYSANTHEMUM PLANTS: Standard, Bush, Bonsai and Cascade Potted plants should not exceed 30" from top blossom to table top. Shorter exhibits (22"-25") show superior culture. Size of pot should be specified in the Schedule. Many cultivars do not adapt themselves readily to this type of handling, so care should have been exercised in selection. Staking of growing plants is permitted. There are several types of potting procedure as follows.

1. Disbudded Standard or Tree

Made from Decoratives of high quality and ample bloom. Flowers should have uniformity of size, form, and freshness. The plant should be on a single main stem usually bare of foliage 18" to 24" above the soil. The head should be symmetrical, the sprays of bloom well balanced and graceful. Foliage should be abundant, true green and free of disease, insects, soil and other foreign matter.

2. Informal Bush:

The horticultural perfection of the plant, bloom and foliage is emphasized. The plant should have been disbudded enough so remaining blooms have good size; and the flowers should have good uniform color and freshness. Foliage should be ample and healthy.

3. Multiple-Plant Pots:

Usually a commercial potted plant practice using 3-7 cuttings in a 7-10" pot. Plants are allowed to grow without pinching. Each plant is disbudded to a SINGLE bloom. Sprays may also be grown in this way and a single pinch is given. All blooms should have uniformity of height and size and should not exceed 22" from pot bottom.

4. Cascades

This group denotes a trained plant which flows or cascades over the pot edge; and must be staged on a shelf or table to show off this downward rhythmic flower flow. The waterfall shape is the most popular, but stylized hearts, fountains and fans are also done. All laterals and sub-laterals must be stopped and controlled so a symmetrical flow results. Length generally is 2½ to 4' but skillful growers may attain 6-8'. A straggly unsightly plant is the result of stopping pinching too soon. The growth will be short and tidy if the plant has been facing South or South-East during the growing season. Many cascades are made of Anemone and Single cultivars with typically thin, wiry stems such as 'DIADEM', 'FORTUNE', 'SOZAN', 'ANNA', etc. These same varieties are also grown normally as bushes.

5. Bonsai

When applied to Chrysanthemums this means a dwarfed plant, rather than a tree. The plant is sometimes grown on a dead tree stump or on a stone and is acceptable thus. A well-executed Bonsai should represent naturalness, the entire scene is judged according to Bonsai standards of excellence, which see. A small, neat-leaved variety such as 'BO-PEEP' should have been chosen for this type training.

SUMMARY

Size: Blooms

*full size *over size *approximately equal breadth and depth in doubles (except Small Pompons and Decoratives)

-undersize (except Small Pompons) -unequal breadth and depth in doubles -not fully open

Color: Blooms

*disks florets clear *pure *typical *combinations pleasing *even *vibrant

-lacks clarity -dull -weak -faded (disk and petals) -diluted -not typical -off -unharmonious combinations -disc greenish (immature) -tips faded -browning -sun or wind burned

Form: Blooms, any size

*approved form *overall symmetry *center filled (doubles) *equal width, depth (doubles except Small Pompons and Decoratives) *regular, even petal spacing in types 5-11 * disk conspicuous in Singles, Spoons, Threads *disk even, flat *disk raised, hemispherical, relatively large (Anemones)

-uneven development -irregular symmetry -lopsided -uneven petal placement (Regulars) -one sided -off center -disk showing (doubles) -center depressed, open (doubles) -disk uneven, off center (Singles) -ligulate florets in disk or holes where removed -promiscuous ray arrangement -not fully mature.

Fullness: Blooms

*sufficient petals to fulfill excellency standards *not crowded or sparse *petals evenly disposed over the receptacle *proper bud selection

-sparse -uneven floret distribution -insufficient petals to cover disk (doubles) -crowding -odd tufted center petals

Spray Form:

*lead bloom rising above auxiliary *approved terminal form *single stem forming vertical axis

-crown spray -crown bud or terminal bud low or buried in auxiliary blooms -branch rather than a spray

Spray Grace:

*balanced *open *symmetrical overall *loose *blooms widely spaced *airy *blooms uniformly opened *tapering

-crowded -clubby -squat -unbalanced -leggy -jointed -bunched

Number of Blooms:

*well proportioned to stem length *adequate for variety (some only carry 5-6 on terminals)

-sparsely flowered -too many buds in relation to open flowers

Substance: Bloom

*long lasting *petals firm *petals thick *prime state of maturity

-thinning -translucent -limp -soft -papery -disk showing breakdown -'green'

Freshness: — (includes condition)

*glistening texture *crisp *blooms uniformly developed *clean

-wilting -aging -withering -browning -bruised -insect, disease damage -past peak -torn -shattering -falling petals -overripe -drying

Stem:

*stem firm *straight *relatively sturdy *supporting bloom *clean disbudding *disbudding scars healed *carrying true foliage

-crooked -knotty -dog-legged -thin -too thick for bloom -untidy disbudding -recent disbudding -undue nodding of bloom -curving

Foliage:

*true green *clean *undamaged *sufficient amount *firm

-absence of own foliage (deduct all) -limp -withered -dry -diseased -insect evidence -torn -bruised -soiled -too small, or large -bracts extending a considerable distance below disbudded bloom on large types (Severe penalty)

Dahlia

AA—GIANT, over 10" diameter, 1 bloom

A—LARGE, 8–10" diameter, 1 bloom

B—MEDIUM, 6–8" diameter, 1 bloom

BB—SMALL, 4–6" diameter, 1 bloom

M—MINIATURE up to 4", 3 blooms, may be any form

POMPON under 2", 5 blooms. Must be Ball Type

OTHER TYPES include Balls, Miniature Balls, Single, Orchids, Collarettes, Anemone, Peony and Waterlily types. Schedule # by size. In Shows where numerous exhibits are expected, Schedule can provide for sub-classes under types and colors.

DAHLIAS

Dahlias are classified according to form as follows.

BALL (Ba), MINIATURE BALL (MB), & POMPON (P)

- fully double, ball shaped or slightly flattened
- must be finely quilled throughout, with absolutely tight center, no dimpling

- rows of ray florets (petals) evenly spaced around a fully developed center of tubular disk florets
- uniformly elongated disk florets
- quills uniform, well rolled, not flattened out
- Ball: over 3½" Ex: 'DOTTIE D' Miniature Ball: 2–3½" Ex: 'GADGET' Pompon: under 2" (1½ ideal) Ex: 'SMALL WORLD'

ANEMONE

- open center
- one or more rows of rays regardless of form and number of florets, no size criteria
- evenly spaced around a fully developed center of tubular disk florets
- disk florets uniformly elongated and measuring ⅔ to ½ the length of the florets for a pin cushion effect
- Example: 'COMET'

COLLARETTE

- a single row of petaloids usually of a different color which form a collar around a central disk

- open center
- single row of 8 florets of regular size, evenly overlapped
- florets flat or nearly so
- ideally the disk carries no more than two rows of pollen-bearing stamens, more indicates over-maturity
- sizes: may range from less than 2" to more than 6"
- Example: 'COTTONTAIL'

SINGLE

- open center
- *more than 8 florets are an aberration, hence less desirable*

- single row of 8 petals with rounded, pointed or lacinated *tips, no size criteria*
- petals overlap uniformly, ⅓ of the petal tips may recurve slightly
- petals are flat rather than involute*
- must contain no petaloids
- more than 2 rows of pollen-bearing stamens in the disk indicates over-maturity
- *Example: 'TUPI'*

Sub-Class: MIGNON — *single flowering; plants 12–18" high, flowers up to 2" dia. Ex: 'JET'*

ORCHID FLOWERED

- *open center, single row of petals, no size criteria*
- evenly, symmetrically spaced
- petals involute, margins meeting and overlapping AT LEAST ⅔ their length from tip to base
- *with margins meeting or overlapping for some portion of their length*
- *Example: 'MARIE SCHNUGG'*

PEONY FLOWERED

- *open center, no size criteria*
- 2-5 rows of twisting curling ray florets
- with or without the addition of smaller curled or twisted floral rays around the disk
- Example: 'BISHOP OF LLANDAFF'

CACTUS FLOWERED

(Straight)

- *fully double, depth ⅔ bloom dia.*
- narrow petals which should be revolute* ½ to full length. The *rays being straight or slightly incurved or recurved*
    - *involute: petals rolled spirally inward
    - *revolute: petals curled or rolled backward or downward
- may be lacinated
- cone-shaped center breaks gradually, evenly into fully developed, revolute petals
- Example: 'JUANITA'

DAHLIA

145

SEMI-CACTUS

- fully double
- *petals broad at base, usually pointed at tips, may be lacinated*
- margins revolute less than ½ of their length
- *Example: 'SURPRISE'*

INCURVED CACTUS

- fully double
- more or less regularly arranged narrow, long, pointed petals
- petals fully revolute for well over ½ length
- petals strongly incurved toward flower center
- may have a "stag-horn" half-twist in petals
- must have a high center
- Example: 'DANNY'

DECORATIVE (Formal)

- fully double, deep, symmetrical *bloom, depth ¾ bloom diameter*

- formal, regular arrangement of broad petals
- petal tips may be round or pointed but can not be revolute
- *outer petals may recurve toward stem*
  ball or globe
- center well formed
- *petals may emerge cupped but must flatten and broaden in less than ½ the length*
- Example: 'FIRST LADY'

DECORATIVE (Informal)

- *fully double, depth ¾ bloom dia.*
- irregular arrangement of
- broad, twisted, ruffled petals

- must be deep, massive bloom with high center
- petals may be pointed or deeply lacinated (cut)
- petal tips may be revolute at tip, but not over one-fourth the total length
- not to be confused with Semi-Cactus which petals are broader at the base with margins *fully revolute one-half their length*
- *Example: 'WALTER HARDISTY'*

WATERLILY

Fully double dahlia form with broad ray florets giving flat 'waterlily' look. Rays may be straight or incurved. Depth not more than ½ dia. of flower head. Ex: 'APOLLO'.

MINIATURE

(noun) is a size classification of fully double blooms of the standard forms of Formal & Informal Decorative & all Cactus forms. The word is used as an adjective in size classification of Balls (e.g. Miniature Balls 2–3½"). These flowers must not simply be stunted specimens but true miniatures.

AMERICAN DAHLIA SOCIETY SCALE OF POINTS

M	BB Small	B Medium	A/AA Large	CHARACTERISTICS
Max. 20	Max. 20	Max. 20	Max. 20	COLOR -|- Clean -|- Bright -|-Attractive -|-Pleasing Blend. — 2 Dull — 2 Fades — 4 Burns — 4 Unpleasing Blend.
Max. 20	Max. 20	Max. 20	Max. 20	FORM -|- True to Type -|- Good Contour -|- Full Petallage. — 2 Varying Type — 3 Gaps in Contour — 3 Sparse Petallage. Deduct up to 5 pts. for Hard or Green Centers.
Max. 5	Max. 5	Max. 5	Max. 7	SIZE—Diameter -|- Credit Poms and Ms up to 5 pts for diminutiveness. -|- Credit BBs and Bs up to 5 pts for good proportionate dia. and depth. Credit As up to 7 pts. for extra size.
Max. 3	Max. 3	Max. 3	Max. 4	SIZE—Depth -|- Ideal is ¾ of dia. Deduct up to 3 pts. for depth less than ¾ of dia., all sizes except A's. In A's, deduct up to 4 pts. for depth less than ¾ of dia.
Max. 15	Max. 15	Max. 15	Max. 15	SUBSTANCE -|- Thick -|- Firm -|- Non-wilting -|- Back holds firm. - 3 Thin — 3 Soft —5 Wilts —5 Back falls.
Max. 10	Max. 10	Max. 10	Max. 10	STEM -|- Strong -|- Straight -|- Graceful -|- Good Proportion. —3 Weak —3 Crotchy —3 Crooked —3 Poor Prop'r'n.
Max. 5	Max. 5	Max. 5	Max. 5	BLOOM POSITION -|- For Bs and As, ideal is 45 degree angle. — Deduct 1 to 3 pts. for Top Blooming—EXCEPT no penalty for —Top Blooms in Poms, and Balls. DEDUCT up to 5 pts. for Down Facing—all sizes.
Max. 10	Max. 10	Max. 10	Max. 10	FOLIAGE -|- Healthy -|- Vigorous -|- Good Color -|- Uniform. — If Diseased, DISQUALIFY — 3 Weak — 3 Soft —- 3 Succulent. Deduct up to 5 pts. for unbalanced form.
Max. 5	Max. 5	Max. 5	Max. 2	UNIFORMITY -|- Except in As, Credit up to 5 pts. for ideal similarity. — Deduct up to 5 pts. for varying Size, Color, Form, except in As. In As, — Deduct up to 2 pts. for varying size, color & form.
Max. 7	Max. 7	Max. 7	Max. 7	DISTINCTIVENESS -|- Add up to 7 points to emphasize superior Form, Color, Depth. Contour, Extra Petallage, Substance, Stem, Bloom Position, Uniformity, etc.

If any specimen shows disease, deduct 5 pts. from final score.

COLOR

Color ranks equally with form as the two most important attributes of all Dahlia types. In a class designated by color e.g. yellow or red, the Judge must guard against rating one entry higher than another because it SEEMS "redder" or "yellower". The value of the hue is not under consideration, however, its intensity is! If it appears more clear, bright, pure, then give top rating. Most Dahlia colors contain more or less grey . . . only when this grey factor contributes to a "dirty" or murky *color is it significantly penalized.*

A tint of yellow or cream in the young center rays of a white is not to be construed as impure color. If green tones are present, however, purity is impaired and penalty issued. Conspicuous green bracts among the petals are penalized.

"Wolf" petals (individual petals of a different color than other floral rays) disturb color purity and are scored down.

Petaloids of a different color from that of the principal floral rays in Double varieties do not make the variety a bicolor or a blend. However, they do detract from color purity and should be scored down.

Texture is judged under color in Dahlias. A sparkling, satiny, cloth-like texture (according to variety) can make the color vibrate and sing.

Self-colored Dahlias should have an even color spread overall; blotching, streaks and veins produce a muddy effect. **Blends** should have an even merging of harmonious or pleasingly contrasting colors, otherwise harshness results and is penalized.

Bicolors should have sharp separation of contrasting color, with minimum bleeding. Floral rays should be uniformly marked, each carrying a substantial proportion of color on its face. Petals merely tipped with white should rate less than those whose outer one-quarter to one-sixth is white. Score down heavily any specimen if bicolored and self-colored rays are intermingled. Variegates should be sharply contrasted.

The rules of color harmony should prevail in the case of those varieties which conspicuously expose reverse petals of contrasting color to the face petals and in blooms in which the petaloids are of a different color from that of the principal floral rays. If the result is in any way displeasing, harsh, inharmonious, points should be deducted.

Judges are often unconsciously more favorable to light blends over dark blends and bright red or dark red in Dahlias, and to prefer self-color to bi-colors. This natural tendency must be recognized and controlled.

Any fading, burning, water spotting, spray, mildew, bruising, browning, transparency, or obscuring with dust or soil which alters the color is penalized.

If blooms of more than one color are exhibited together in any multiple bloom class, harmony or pleasing contrast of the specimens as a whole is essential for a high color rating.

FORM
CONTOUR AND CENTER
Under FORM is considered the center, contour, condition as affects form, bloom development and trueness to type. Examine the bloom from every angle, the front should be approximately circular with due allowance for informality of certain types. The floral rays should radiate approximately the same distance from the center in every direction in all types. *Blooms are asymmetrical if petals below center are longer than those above, or if petals are more numerous and thicker. Such are penalized. The petals should rise from the center at a graceful angle. The center and the petals must not look like two distinct parts put together. Wide open blooms which show carpels in the center are referred to as "popped" and are eliminated from consideration. The center of doubles should have "more to come". Depth of bloom should be at least three-fourths its diameter in Decorative and Semi-Cactus and at least two-thirds its diameter in the other Cactus types.*

DEVELOPMENT
Even development of the petals "completing to the stem" in fully double contributes to desirable depth. Varieties having relatively few, very large petals present an undesirable coarse appearance.

Definite evidence of removal of petals or other floral elements (nubbins, adventitious buds) is to be regarded as though these were still actually present and in poor condition, therefore are penalized.

A suspiciously clean back on a well-developed bloom where outer floral rays fail to roll back toward the stem may indicate dropped or plucked spent petals. A variety well-known for petal droppage, an asymmetrical form plus back bracts with corresponding floral rays in them, indicates excessive grooming or over-maturity and a lack of prime condition.

Glue or shellac used to hold falling petals is penalized no matter how skillfully done. If the back petals are any shorter than others, are browning at the edges or (under hand lens) show a cut edge, trimming is presumed. Exhibitors often risk loss of one-half to one point for trimming against stiffer penalties for defective petals.

TRUENESS TO TYPE
All manner of borderline formations are found, e.g., some Semi-Cactus varieties merge with either Decorative or True Incurved or Straight Cactus. But it is the Judge's duty to score down any bloom which does not ACTUALLY meet formation requirements of the class or which fails to come up to approved standards of excellence of form for the type.

The majority of "type" petals (involute, revolute, etc.) determines classification as to type. But the entry which is "typey" in all petals scores higher than the one which has only a "majority".

STEM

Stem refers to the support of the bloom from its base to the first *fully developed pair of leaves . . . below this is the "stalk" in Dahlia parlance. When show rules specify a certain length stem for a Dahlia, the intent is presumed to be combined "stem and stalk".*

There can be no absolute rule as to proper length proportion to bloom size because the formation and character of the bloom definitely affects the pleasing proportion as do the character of the underlying foliage and length of stalk between sets of leaves (internodes). A small, unpaired leaf on a stem slightly longer than ideal tends to lessen the *disproportionate effect. Ideally, the large bloom stem length should equal one and one-half times the diameter of the bloom.*

Smaller flowers permit a somewhat longer stem without apparent disproportion, especially in the multiple-bloom classes.

All things being equal, a too-long stem is preferable to a short, crotchy one.

FOLIAGE

The specimen must bear sufficient foliage to permit proper evaluation. Two sets of fully developed leaves is adequate. Their size, formation, substance, texture, color and arrangement in relation to the bloom are to be considered. In stiff competition, the rating given foliage may actually determine the winner.

SUBSTANCE

Soft, limp petals are penalized. Stiff, firm petals indicate superior keeping quality. Shedding is a serious fault in all types, but especially in Balls and Pompons. Petals lost long before entry are scored down under FORM as noted previously. Petals dislodged on show table indicate defective substance, or over-maturity and are down-rated under SUBSTANCE.

CONDITION

Condition of the petals as it affects their substance should rate one-half the maximum allowed under SUBSTANCE. Condition as it affects color and form, foliage and stem is discussed under those headings.

Substance and condition are affected by over-maturity, immaturity, improper feeding and watering, careless or inexpert handling after cutting.

Perfect conditions exists only when the bloom is clean without the slightest trace of wilting, fading, burning, spots or deposits. In fact . . . the stem would not even have the characteristic "bloom" or fine powdery covering marred, and this would be quite a feat as it comes off at the slightest touch.

In open-centered types, over-maturity is indicated if more than two rows of pollen-bearing stamens are present in the center disk.

BLOOM POSITION

Bloom position is related to the entire stance of the flower and is an element in giving it distinction.

The preferred Dahlia position is a forty-five degree angle between bloom and stem, holding the flower towards the viewer.

Side facing, with the bloom parallel to the stem is acceptable in medium sizes, cut-flower and florist varieties.

Downfacing in any size, EVEN TO THE SLIGHTEST DEGREE, is a serious fault, penalized from at least three to all five points, depending *upon the degree of fault. Top facing is penalized one to three points, except in Balls and Pompons.*

SIZE

The AA Giant Dahlias should be measured with the utmost care, preferably using large calipers or a ring gauge. Official scoring is based on the diameter times the depth.

The Schedule is the Law of the Show, and the Classification Committee places the properly measured entries. The A.D.S. recommends that each variety be entered in the size class to which that variety has been assigned, e.g. a dahlia classified as a medium-flowered variety is to be entered in the B class. If such a bloom is oversize (in excess of 8″) it is not penalized unless in the Judges' opinion the size has contributed to undue coarseness. Undersize is penalized as being under-grown, a horticultural deficiency. Numerical tolerances for over-size are discouraged.

Size is important in AA Giant Dahlias and these big ones should be scored down for any faults, but give proper advantage to size. In spite of this advantage, a smaller bloom may win with superior form, color and condition.

Since the size range of B-Medium Dahlias is fixed at 6–8″, the scale does not allow points in this category.

In order to call attention to the exquisite beauty and usefulness of the many varieties in the 4-6" range, the Society provides special *classes in official shows for these, designating them as BB-Small.*

When judging Miniatures and Pompons, smallness contributing to daintiness is rewarded, carrying a maximum of three points. Thus in two exhibits, all other things being equal, the smaller entry wins in the Miniature and Pom-pon classes.

Pompons are rigidly limited to two inches in diameter. Smaller size is rewarded as it contributes to daintiness. Pompons over two inches must be exhibited as Miniature Balls in the M-Small Class.

DISTINCTION

Distinction refers to the staging of the exhibit as well as to the rather intangible attributes which make the exhibit stand out supreme, loudly proclaiming **Quality.**

The Judges are justified in up-pointing a specimen carefully staged, with the stalk placed in a container of a size correct for its diameter, the whole perhaps tilted ever so slightly for best possible display of the bloom, thus enhancing the general excellence of all its good qualities.

Any superior difference in color, form, size, etc., which is an advantage to beauty, as well as use and purpose, is rewarded. For instance, the lacination of petals in a straight Cactus type is considered distinctive, as is a superior bloom position, etc.

Labeling, important from an educational standpoint, is considered here as encouragement in setting habits beneficial to public and exhibitors alike.

UNIFORMITY OF MULTIPLE-BLOOM DAHLIA CLASSES

Uniformity, all things being equal, may be the deciding factor in *determining awards in multiple-bloom exhibits.*
Since the Schedule usually calls for a single bloom of AA Giant Dahlias, uniformity has been deleted from that scale.

If the Schedule requires three or more in the A-Large or on the other hand, single bloom exhibits in the B, BB or M classes, the five points for UNIFORMITY can be shifted to meet the demand.

Therefore, it is recommended that when judging single-bloom classes of M-Small or B, BB-Medium, the 5 UNIFORMITY points be disregarded, leaving a total of 95 for perfection. In multiple-bloom *classes of M-Miniature or BB-Small, the 5 UNIFORMITY points be disregarded, leaving a total of 95 for perfection. In multiple-bloom classes of AA-Giant, the 5 UNIFORMITY points are added for a total of 105 for perfection.* in an entry, COLOR HARMONY would replace COLOR UNIFORMITY.

If the Schedule requires or allows blooms of more than one type, uniformity of form would be omitted. If one bad bloom is too poor to be scored at all, the remaining blooms cannot save the entry. If the decision is close, score individual blooms and total the score.

SUMMARY

Color

Quality *clear *pure *intense *even color spread *vibrant *lustrous *Blends merge evenly *Bicolor sharp, clean-cut, uniform separations *pleasing color harmony in multiple-bloom exhibits

-maximum deductions 12 points -dirty greyed -central rays green tinged -green bracts conspicuous -'wolf' petals -harsh contrasts in Blends -color spread uneven, blotched, streaked, veined giving muddy effect -Bicolors merely tipped -intermingled bicolored and self-colored petals (serious fault) -magenta hues excessively greyed -unpleasant reverse petal contrasts -Bicolor variety showing few normally bicolored petals

Blemishes — maximum penalty — 8 points
-fading -water spotting -spray deposits -mildew -discoloration -browning, whitening, transparency or obscuring color by thrips, red spider, soil, other

Form

Contour, Symmetry
*symmetrical *centered *circular *adequate depth for type *calyx well hidden *completes to stem *back finely finished *petals uniformly flat, quilled, *according to variety *Decorative and Semi-Cactus should have depths ¾ths their diameter *Cactus should have depths up to ⅔ diam. as ideal*

-asymmetrical -lop sided -irregular -dish faced -sloppy -gaps present -coarse -thin -malformed -insufficient petals -uneven development of disk -missing florets -missing petals -trimmed petals -insect injury -insufficient depth -calyx bare -nubbins, adventitious buds present or removed -artificial control of petal drop (serious fault) -wilting -drooping

Center
*round *fairly tight *good proportion *doubles should have more to come, full *singles must not have more than 2 rows of pollen-bearing stamens

-large -clumsy -bull center -too high -depressed -center isolated -hard -green -oval -oblong, misshapen -open -weak -small -hole in center -blown or popped (serious fault) -double, triple, monstrosities (serious fault)

153

Bloom Development

*fully developed *mature *prime *peak of development *petals same length, width attachment in singles

-maximum deductible 2 points -over-mature (indicated by weak center) -center too tight (immature) -impaired color -shriveled petals present or removed -coarse

Trueness to type
*true *meets perfection standard of type

NOTE: For specific indications of type trueness refer to listings of types.

-maximum deductible 5 points -deduct any deviation from the norm

Ball & Pompon -bottom petals fail to reflex to stem -lacinated petals -imperfect quilling of back petals

Collarette -petals cupping or quilling excessively -unevenly overlapped or gaping

Single -contains deformed, hair like, pin petals of petaloids -gaping at base too many ray petals

Orchid -off center asymmetrical -petals fail to quill at base

Cactus Straight -petals fail to be revolute one-half to full length

Cactus Semi -petals fail to be revolute at least ¼ but no more than ½ their length

Cactus Incurved -fail to quill over ½ their length -petals merely curve instead of incurve toward center -petals too wide, lacination obscures form -petals too long, twisting, overlapping obscuring form

Peony -too much center disk showing

Decorative Formal -excessive lacination detracts from formality -tips revolute rather than flat
-uneven petal placement

Decorative Informal -petals quilled more than ¼ back from their tips

Stem

Strength *strong *erect *graceful *round *straight *fairly rigid

-maximum deduction 7 points -weak -willowy -too flexible -rubbery -wilting (last 2 are serious faults)

Stem Form
*meets bloom squarely *gracefully arched *disbudding scars well healed

-maximum deduction 3 points -irregular -crooked at neck -crooked elsewhere -clubby -faulty disbudding -faulty disbranching

Stem Proportion

*length adequate in proportion to flower *diameter in proportion to stem of larger blooms (measure from calyx to first pair of leaves), should equal one and one-half times diameter of bloom

-maximum point deduction 5 -too long -too short -crotchy -too heavy -too thin -gawky -diameter too heavy -fragile appearing -has side bud -sways a bit -too slender in diameter for bloom size -stem oval or longitudinally ridged

Foliage

Quality
*rich *clean color *pleasing texture *attractive formation *firm *turgid *crisp *vigorous

-maximum point deduction 5 -faded -bleached -coarse -deformed -succulent -thin -folded -crinkled -limp -droopy -unthrifty -unduly stiff -shows rust

Proportion
*correctly proportioned to bloom and stem *adequate amount of foliage for bloom *well placed and spaced

-maximum deduction 5 -stunted -too large -leaves missing -too abundant -sparse -inadequate -bunched

Substance

Inherent Quality, freshness
*thick *heavy *crisp *firm *turgid *uniform quality front and back *finely textured

-maximum point deduction ½ the amount allowed on the scale -lacks body -thinning -relaxing -back soft -petals clinging

Condition as affects substance
*fresh *thrifty *all petals retained

-maximum point deduction: ½ the amount allowed in the scale -petals dropping -withered -shriveled -shrinking -more than 2 rows of pollen-bearing stamens in disk of open-center types

Bloom Position
*45 degree angle *side facing acceptable in mediums

-maximum deductible 3 -top facing (-1 to 3 in all but Ball, Poms where no penalty is taken) -twisted -down facing (deduct all points)

Size
*fits A.D.S. size for variety *according to Schedule

-appears coarse -undersize, indicating cultural deficiency

Uniformity
*uniform, same in respect to color, formation, size, stem, foliage, substance, -lacks uniformity in any of the following, points may be deducted accordingly:

Color	(1 point)	Substance	(½ point)
Form	(1 point)	Bloom Position	(½ point)
Size	(1 point)	Foliage	(½ point)
Stem	(½ point)		

Distinction
*outstanding color *superlative form *at attention pose or stance *unusually strong substance *perfect proportion of parts *overall superb condition *artistically effective staging *well posed *stalk-stem properly proportioned *outstanding in all qualities listed on score card *properly labeled

-mediocre -plain -inharmonious -poorly posed -poorly staged -lacks outstanding characteristics in the qualities on the score card

Hemerocallis (Daylily)

1) Scape not to exceed 36"
2) Individual Flower
3) Collection of Scapes (at least five)
4) Collection of individual flowers (at least five)

Individual flowers, cut off the scape and displayed in appropriate containers, may be shown and judged at the discretion of the local Show Committee. The American Hemerocallis Society recommends that only the newer, named varieties be entered in such a class. Age limitation is left to the local Show Committee.

Hemerocallis (Daylily) are hardy, herbaceous perennials belonging to the Lily Family. Growing on scapes 12-48" in height, each scape carries a number of flowers. The flowers are short-lived but many open over a long period, usually four to six weeks per plant. Some varieties (Example: 'NIGHTHAWK', 'VESPERS') are nocturnal bloomers, opening in the evening and remaining so throughout the following day. Most are diurnal, day bloomers with a one-day life. Flowers of the Common Yellow Lemon Lily (**H. flava**) and some of the newer varieties may exceed the usual one-day life. Foliage may be evergreen or deciduous.

Bloom season is from June to October, with varieties listed as to Early (Spring) Midseason (Summer) and Late (Late Summer and Fall) blooming.

SCALE OF POINTS (Scape)
The Total OVER-ALL Perfection Is To Be Considered

FLOWER	50	SCAPE in harmonious relation to flower size	35
. color	10		
. form	10	. height and strength	15
. texture	10	. number of buds	10
. substance	10	. branching	10
. size, according to variety	10	CONDITION AND GROOMING	15

SCALE OF POINTS (Individual Flowers)

COLOR	20	SIZE, according to variety	20
TEXTURE	20		
SUBSTANCE	20	CONDITION	20

COLOR

Color of Hemerocallis varies due to weather and cultural conditions. The Judge should be cognizant of this influence on Hemerocallis in the area in which he is judging. Color is judged on front only.

Color patterns vary greatly in Hemerocallis, including the following:

Predominant color: Self (solid except for throat); Petals one color, sepals another; Tips of petals and/or sepals different color.

Eye Zone: No eye; Faint eye on petals; heavy eye on petals; Eye on both petals and sepals.

Throat: Confined to center of flower; Extending fingers or triangles into petals.

Midrib: No rib markings; Prominent ribs on petals; Prominent ribs on petals and sepals.

Veins: Vein coloration not noticeable; Prominent vein markings.

Edging: No edge marking; Light edge on petals; Light edge on petals and sepals.

The vibrancy of the color is important, particularly in blends, bicolors, bitones and patterned varieties.

Brightness is to be desired in the browns, tans, mahoganys, mauves, etc. New color breaks frequently appear. The Judge must not be swayed whether by personal like or dislike, rarity or newness, but must endeavor at all times to judge for clarity, vibrancy and trueness to variety.

Fading is not objectionable provided substance remains intact and the altered color is equally pleasing.

All color combinations should be attractive and pleasing.

FORM

The shape or form of the Hemerocallis varies greatly with the variety and includes:

1 Trumpet
2 Full Cup
3 Flaring Star
4 Recurving Sepals
5 Flat (Example: 'Cartwheels')
6 Recurving petals and sepals
7 Spider (narrow petals and sepals, twisted and reflexed. Example: 'Summer Orchid')
8 Double: consistently more than 6 segments. Ex: 'Darling'

Flower form is altered by broken sepals or petals and must be penalized commensurate with the degree of impairment.

The removal of the pollen tips is considered a fault under form, as these are an integral part of the flower make-up, and their color and movement add much to the flower's grace and charm.

Petals and sepals must be of uniform length, evenly placed and spaced. If crowding has altered true form, it must be graded down. If several flowers are open on the scape, form of all should be similar. Petals are normally wider than sepals.

The contour should be generally symmetrical, each petal and sepal reflexing at approximately the same degree. The lower or bottom petal is typically a bit larger and a bit more out-thrust in some varieties, but it must be in proportion.

The ends of the petals may be rounded, pointed, twisted or pinched, according to the characteristics inherent in the particular variety. The flowers may exhibit smooth petals and sepals, or ruffled petals with smooth sepals or ruffled petals and sepals both. The degree of petal and sepal reflex or twisting, anther length, placement and angle, ruffling, frilling and petal width are to be judged as to trueness to variety, not personal preferences.

TEXTURE

Texture is the surface quality, the smoothness or roughness and varies decidedly from variety to variety in Hemerocallis.

Some have a smooth, lustrous finish, others crepey or ridged. Some are fine textured, others are coarse. Some are veined or creped while others are marble-smooth, or waxy and carry an irridescent dusting.

Some have heavy ridging or midribs, others exhibit a level appearance. It is apparent, therefore, that texture must be assessed according to variety, and whether the surface appearance does or does not add beauty and distinction to the specimen.

SUBSTANCE

Substance is the thickness, firmness, crispness of the flower. The evenness of the substance (lack of thinning toward the edges) can be ascertained by holding the specimen up to the light and deducting points for any unevenness or transparency.

Turgidity, the amount of moisture present in the parts, is a part of substance. Turgidity will be high when the specimen is in its prime. Lack of attention to cultural needs with reference to water, fertilization, shading etc., is reflected in the degree of substance. The degree of substance also varies with the variety.

SIZE

Size must be that which is most nearly representative for the variety with consideration given to that specimen which is above average but not gross. Extremes on either side of normalcy should be penalized.

Size variations due to geographical location are acceptable but size variations due to cultural malpractices must be penalized heavily. The Judge must not only know the variety, but must know how it performs in the area in which he is judging.

Miniature Hemerocallis must not exceed 3" in flower diameter and must be a true miniature variety and not merely a poorly grown regular.

The size of the flowers vary with variety from 2" or less in diameter in the Miniatures (Example 'BONANZA') to medium (Example 'MOROCCO BEAUTY') to large, over 5" (Example 'HYPERION'). Some of the tretraploid Hems reach over 7". Size should be in proper proportion to the length and diameter of the scape.

SCAPE

Height and Strength

Hemerocallis vary in height of scape from dwarf (under 2') to tall (over 4'). The height and strength of the scape must be in proportion to the size of the flower. A weak, whippy stem supporting a full complement of overlarge flowers will be penalized even though this condition is characteristic of the variety.

Height of a scape entered in a show, should not exceed 36" and may be much less, according to flower size and variety.

Accordingly, a thick, heavy stem supporting small, delicate flowers is not artistically proportional and should be penalized.

Fasciation (two scapes grown together) is a deductible fault.

Number of Buds

Do not expect of a variety that which it cannot do. If all the Judges on the panel are unfamiliar with the variety, use discretion, especially in evaluating the number of buds on older varieties.

But if there are less buds and flowers per scape than is known to be typical, either age, spent or 'gone' flowers or cultural malpractices should be suspected and deductions made accordingly. When Daylilies are planted in dense shade, the amount of bloom is considerably reduced.

Some varieties normally throw 25 to 50 buds and flowers. A scape with several flowers open should be considered superior to a scape with only one open flower, all other qualities being equal.

A scape is in the prime of blooming when it has several open flowers, numerous buds and no spent flowers. A scape in its prime shall be considered superior to one that has half, or more than half of its buds bloomed out.

If the over-all attractiveness of the scape has not been marred by dropped flowers and the remaining blooms are still of show quality, the scape should still be considered for top honors.

Branching

Branching is influenced by the variety and consideration should be adjusted accordingly. A proliferation may **not** be removed. If a scape with a proliferation is shown, the Judges will decide if the over-all perfection or appearance is altered and if the size or form of the flower is altered. Proliferations are structures that arise as buds on the scape and may be handled as cuttings to produce more plants.

Branching should be sufficient to allow the full flower form to show without crowding against the scape or against other flowers or buds. Flowers should be carried at such an angle that their beauty can be appreciated.

Branching and over-all form should be balanced. A scape unbalanced by crowding or dropped flowers is less than ideal.

Hemerocallis blooms face in the direction of the strongest light, those planted in mid-to-full shade may produce an unbalanced inflorescence.

CONDITION AND GROOMING

This includes merits and faults incurred in growing, spraying, dressing, transporting to the show, and even accidents during placing, as well as care taken in preparing the entry for exhibit.

If the over-all perfection of the flowers or scape has been altered more than 15 points, it will have to be reflected in the judging of the quality which is infuenced most adversely, i.e., form, color, substance, number of buds, etc.

Holes and tears in petals, soil, spray residue, spent flowers, seed pods, scape scars, and proliferations removed are all faults. Each specimen should be presented in the best possible condition and the backs of the flowers should be as clean and perfect as the fronts.

SUMMARY
Color   10 points
*clear *true to variety *vibrant *unusual depth *harmonious *sunfast

-lacks clarity -deviates from typical for variety -streaked -blurred -dull -bleached -edges browning -water stained (particularly on dark colors)

Flower Form   10 points
*true to variety *uniformity of all open blooms *uniformity of petal and sepal placement, length and width of individual flowers

-deformed -dissimilarity of flowers on scape -petals and sepals on individual flowers lacking in uniformity -broken petals or sepals -lacking substance (wilting) so severely as to affect form

Flower Texture   10 points
*typical *pleasing *glistening *lustrous *velvety *uniform on all parts and in all flowers

-not typical -lifeless -dull

Flower Substance   10 points
*crisp *fresh *turgid *firm *holding up
-edges thinning -edges melting -limp -collapsing

Flower Size   10 points
*characteristic of variety and area *proportionate *above average

-not typical -undersized -gross -puny

SCAPE
Height and Strength   15 points
Height *Proportionate *adequate *erect *graceful *according to variety
     -not typical -too tall -too short for flower size -crooked
Strength *proportioned to flower size *firm *sturdy
     -weak -limp -fasciated -coarse

Number of Buds   10 points
*typical for variety *unusually floriferous *adequate *prime *profuse *less than one-half bloomed out

-scant -not typical number -few -over one-half bloomed out

Branching   10 points
*typical *adequate *not crowded *well-spaced *unusually well-branched *artistic carriage

-untypical -inadequate -crowded -short -unbalanced

160

Condition and Grooming   15 points

*clean *well groomed *overall vigorous appearance

-seed pods present -torn flowers -scarred scape -careless grooming -proliferation removed -stubs left on after flower removal

Delphinium

SUGGESTED CLASSES

    A. Hybrid (**D. elatum**) cultorum. (Pacific Giant, etc.)

        1. Massive column. One spike

        2. Slender column. One spike

    B. Belladona, Bellamosa

        1. Three spikes

    C. Annual Delphinium, Larkspur

        1. Three spikes

Sub-divisions according to colors listed under Color and single or double forms may be added if expected competition warrants.

DELPHINIUM

Hardy perennial and annual herbs of the Buttercup Family, producing spike inflorescence made up of many individual florets. The name is derived from the Greek 'delphin' meaning dolphin and refers to the buds' resemblance to the dolphin.

There are three generally recognized groups:

1. **Belladonna, Bellamosa:** Belladonna is an older type which grows to a height of 2-3'. The plants produce more spikes than Hybrids and are very useful for cutting and flower arrangements as the florets are smaller and the spikes more dainty and graceful. Color range originally was limited to clear, sky blue. Bellamosa is a dark blue form.

2. **Annual Delphinium, Larkspur (D. ajacis):** Blooms earlier than other types and continues to produce flower spikes throughout the summer and fall on dwarf (8-10"), intermediate (15") and tall (4') plants. The blue, white, lavender, purple and pink flowers are borne in great profusion.

While there is no particular structural difference, the Larkspur is smaller, of looser form and less imposing than its perennial relatives.

3. **Hybrids (D. elatum) cultorum:** Hybrids such as the Jackson and Perkins Strain and the Pacific Giants have nearly supplanted earlier Wrexham (Hollyhock flowered) and Blackmore, Langdon English Hybrids in popularity. The Hybrids are the most popular group for production of fine exhibition specimens. Spikes are 4-5' and often quite mildew resistant. The color range includes white, lavender, maroon, pink, red, orange, blue, purple, violet and many degrees of color value and many contrasts in both single and double floret forms.

POINT SCALE

Floret	60	Spike	20
. color	25	. length	10
. form	10	. symmetry	10
. size	10	Foliage	10
. placement	10	General Perfection and	
. substance	5	Fragrance	10

FLORET
Color

There are two color divisions in Delphiniums. The **SELFS** refer to florets which are of but one single color, tint or shade. Those with a slight suffusion of a closely related tint or shade are also classed as SELFS.

BICOLORS are those florets which are composed of two distinct colors, either on the sepal or on different, individual sepals.

There are fourteen major color classes within the two color divisions.

Classes 1, 2, 3 light, medium and dark blue selfs;
4, 5, 6 light, medium and dark purple selfs;
7, 8, 9 light, medium and dark bicolors;
10 light, mauve (a greyed lilac);
11 medium mauve (a greyed violet);
12 dark mauve (a greyed purple);
13 pure whites or creams with or without bees;
14 any other which includes the Astolat Series of pink shades with large fawn, brown and black bees.

Delphinium colors generally have a glistening, irridescent quality and often are more delicate and refined in appearance than the same color appearing in the bloom of a different plant, due to the fine texture. The Judge does not expect to be able to apply the word "bright" as effectively, nor, particularly in the mauve and some bicolor classes, the word "pure".

The colors, however, should appear fresh, alive and unvarying. The contrasts, if present, should be harmonious and the blendings smooth. Whitish streaks which mar the color should be noted and deducted.

Form

The florets of a delphinium are composed of one or more rows of enlarged colorful sepals which the layman often calls petals. Petals may be present. If present, they form the eye or "bee" in the center of the floret. The sepals should be broad and fairly circular.

Single florets have one row of sepals and at least five petals forming the bee. Semi-double florets have two rows of sepals and may or may not have bees. Double florets have more than two rows and may or may not have bees.

Size

The size of the individual floret varies with the group, being relatively small and dainty in the Annual and Belladonna types and large in the Hybrids, often exceeding 2½" each floret and with the spike measuring up to 4-5" in diameter.

Floret Placement

The floret placement is closely related to spike symmetry. The florets must be evenly spaced along the stem, leaving no voids or open spaces. Placement should be such that each floret shows off to the best advantage without crowding.

The pedicels (stem) of each floret should be of such length that it neither holds the florets too tightly to the main column nor so long or weak that it allows the floret to droop or obscure any other floret.

In the Belladonna, Bellamosa and Annual groups, the florets are more loosely attached and arranged on the slender, graceful spires.

Substance

The substance of a delphinium floret is naturally thinner than that of a rose, for example, however, it should be such that the individual florets as well as the entire spike presents a crisp, perky appearance, with no relaxation of form. The florets, though thin-walled, should not be flabby, soft or crumpled appearing.

SPIKE

Length

The length varies from the eight inch spikes of the dwarf annuals through the two-four foot spikes of the Bellamosa to the towering spikes of some of the new Hybrid Strains which often exceed five feet.

Maximum spike length for type indicates ample water has been provided during the growing season.

Symmetry

The Delphinium florets are produced on a long florescence generally referred to as a spike, which may include laterals. The spike is called a column if it is very slightly tapering, with the tip being nearly as broad as the base and quite blunt. It is called a spire if it has a pronounced taper.

Secondary or lateral spikes which crowd the primary or otherwise obscure or detract should be penalized according to the degree of fault. The score should be reduced if large conspicuous laterals are present which impair the symmetry of the spike.

The Pacific Hybrids particularly often need staking and the Judge will deduct for any crookedness or off-sideness which affects the symmetry adversely. The symmetry of the spike is closely allied to the floret placement, which see.

FOLIAGE

Vigorous, unblemished foliage indicates proper attention to cultural requirements and insect and disease prevention. Aphids feed on the undersides of Delphinium leaves and their presence is severely penalized. The Judge should carefully inspect any leaves which cup downward in an unnatural manner.

The cyclamen mite curls and distorts the leaves while also stunting the plant and blackening the flower buds. Chlorosis or stunt also dwarfs the spikes and mottles the foliage. The white, powdery covering caused by mildew is evidence to the Judge of careless watering and over-crowding. Shiny, irregular, tar-like spots are caused by a bacterial disease called Black Leaf-Spot. Such damage is to be deducted commensurate with the degree.

GENERAL PERFECTION AND FRAGRANCE

All florets, including those at the bottom should be fresh, crisp, and glistening without spent or brown sepals (petals). General Perfection includes the quality, appearance and appeal of the entire inflorescence, its fragrance and any unique or distinctive types of sepals, bees, or colors. Seed pods should be inconspicuous, preferably absent.

Points for General Perfection are reduced if growth appears weak and spindly, with generally inferior blooms. The Judge suspects over-fertilization of small-flowered, small spike types if the growth is floppy or leggy.

SUMMARY

FLORET

Color 25 Points
*fresh *alive *unvarying *blendings smooth *contrasts harmonious

-faded -streaked -weak -dull

Form 10 Points
*sepals broad *circular

-irregular form -sepals narrow, fine (Hybrids)

Size 10 Points
*typical to types (Annual, Belladonna small, delicate 1")
(Hybrids, large, 2½")

-smaller than average for area

Placement 10 Points
*florets evenly spaced *Belladonna, etc. are looser *spike well filled

-voids -crowding -cramped (too short pedicels) -weak pedicels

Substance 5 Points
*firm *crisp *perky

-crumpled -flaccid -soft

SPIKE
Length and Symmetry 10 Points Each
*straight *long (according to type) *column tip blunt, tip and base nearly equal (Hybrids) *taper pronounced (Belladonna, etc.) *well-filled with florets *few or no laterals

-crooked -stunted -voids -one sided -large laterals -crowded florets

Foliage 10 Points
*vigorous *clean *healthy *fresh *undamaged

-diseased -mildewed -weak -distorted -mottled

General Perfection and Fragrance 10 Points
*maximum development *fragrant *distinctive bees or colors *rigid *strong *top condition overall

-spent florets -wilting -lacking fragrance -conspicuous seedpods -spindly -floppy

Geraniums, Pelargoniums

SUGGESTED CLASSES: Single Potted Specimen
1. Zonal Hortorum (House)
   A. Single Flowering
   B. Double Flowering
2. Zonal Fancy Leaf
3. Zonal Dwarf
4. Ivy Leaf, Trailing
5. Scented Leaf
6. Lady or Martha Washington
7. Any other species

Plant or plants must have been in Exhibitor's possession 60 days prior to show date.

Any or all of the above classes may be used, depending on expected competition in a given community. The Schedule may request pot size limitation or increase classes by having a section for 8" or less pot size and another identical section for pots over 8". Classifications can also be included for Hanging Baskets, Standards, Espalier, Bonsai and other trained specialties where competition warrants.

GERANIACEAE: Geraniums, Pelargoniums
Sometimes common usage of a name becomes so much a part of our society that it is difficult to change. So great is the power of the common name "geranium" for all species of this plant, that even the International Society calls itself the Geranium Society. Actually, the **Geranium** (Cranebill) is a group of relatively unknown and unused species plants, many hardy and native to North America. Flowers are ½" to 1½". Plants are 1 to 3 feet and are useful in rock gardens and flower borders. Several have "fernleaf" foliages.

PELARGONIUM: (Storkbill) is the genus which includes six common types.

1. **P. hortorum** — the common house geranium
2. **P. zonale** — fancy leaf, variegated
3. **P. domesticum** — Martha or Lady Washington
4. **P. scented leaf** — **P. odortissi-sum** (nutmeg) **P. gravealens** (rose) etc.
5. **P. roberanium** — Robers miniatures, dwarfs
6. **P. peltatum** — ivy-leafed, trailing

The genus also includes some odd and unusual plants, some of which grow from bulbs, some have thorns like cactus **(P. echinatum)**, some have scented flowers, one has swollen joints **(P. gibbosum)**, some are succulents, others are semi-climbers **(P. tetragonum)**. The so-called Strawberry Geranium is really **Sasifraga sarmentosa**, a completely unrelated plant.

Zonals: House or **P. Hortorum.** Also called Bedding, Horseshoe and Fish. Approximately 400 known varieties. This is the common house and garden variety which in its native habitat had a dark horseshoe-like zone on its foliage, thus the name. Hybridization has produced many without the identifying "horseshoe" but they still belong to the Zonals.

The **Fancy Leaf Pelargoniums** are also Zonals, as are the Dwarf (also called Pigmy, Miniature, Elf). These two are usually put in separate classes for judging and commercial use. All are easy to grow and flower with singles, semi-doubles and doubles, as well as cactus (poinsettia) and rosebud in the Hortorums.

P. domesticum: These are commonly called Lady (or Martha) Washington (also Regals and Show). Semi-double flowers, sometimes 3-5" across. Free-flowering. Veined and blotched colors or "faced", resembling pansies which gives rise to a colloquial name of Pansy Geranium. Not perpetual bloomers, normal season in the spring. More difficult than Zonals. Less erect stems and wrinkled foliage.

P. peltatum: Ivy Leaf. These are easily distinguished by their long, trailing branches with considerable space between the glossy leaves which have pointed lobes in the manner of ivy. Semi and double flowering. Excellent for hanging baskets, window boxes and ground covers. Self colors, pencilings and veinings in white and various shades of pink, purples and red flowers. More difficult and generally less floriferous than Zonals. Normal bloom season early spring through fall under ideal conditions.

Scented Leaf: More than fifty species and hybrids. Easily grown. Minor floriferousness, flowers smaller and less showy than Zonals. Emphasis on scent and form of plant. Includes growth habits both compact and vining **(P. crispum).** Foliages vary, including oak-leaf 'CLORINDA' which has eucalyptus scent. Several well-known species are listed under foliage, which see.

P. hortorum (House) are judged with emphasis on floriferousness.

Fancy Leaf are judged with emphasis on leaf color.

Dwarfs are judged with emphasis on dwarfness.

Lady Washingtons are judged with emphasis on low bushiness and floriferousness.

Scented Leaf are judged with emphasis on leaf scent.

SCALES OF POINTS

Number One

Zonals, Lady Washington
Ivy Leaf and Dwarfs

Plant	30
. form . vigor . container . size . condition	
Umbel	25
. size . form . number flowers	
Flowers	25
. form . size . color . substance	
Foliage	20
. form . size	

Number Two

Fancy and Scented Leaf

Foliage	50
. fragrance (Scented) . color (Fancy)	
Plant	40
. form . vigor . size . condition . container	
Umbel	5
. size . form . number of flowers per	
Flowers	5
. form . size . substance . color	

PLANT

Form. Plant habit of growth varies greatly in Geranium Pelargoniums, ranging from dwarf plants about five inches tall ('PIGMY') to tall Zonals which attain heights of three to four feet and the spreading, trailing forms of the Ivy. With the exception of Ivy the form of the plant should be a symmetrical, compact mound of foliage. In all types, the plant should be well filled in and shapely, bushy and sturdy appearing.

If pruning, training, pinching and cutting out of weak shoots has been neglected, the plants will be leggy specimens with leaves at the ends of the shoots only. Zonals which "go every which way" indicating a lack of attention to pruning and quarter-turning are penalized, no matter how floriferous they are. The most compact varieties will become tall and scraggly with lack of attention. Stumpy, awkwardly branched old plants should be severely penalized.

The pots containing Ivy Leaf plants should be well filled with branches trailing evenly over the pot sides. There should be no bare spots, as often occurs if the planting has been done at the edge of the container and the plant has not been pinched and trained. Long, spent branches should have been neatly pruned out. The specimen should be a short-jointed, many branched variety with fairly dense growth and several bloom heads. Most geraniums are at their best when viewed below eye level and the trailing or basket types should be displayed to show off their individual growth habits.

In considering Dwarfs, the emphasis is on the dwarfness of the plant. The flowers of some varieties ('BLACK VESUVIUS') are surprisingly large for the five inch plant. In general, the flowers, leaves and overall plant size should be relatively small regardless of varietal characteristics, and should be potted in a proportionately sized container.

The Judge must not allow himself to be influenced by the fact that a variety is unusual or the color is different. He must remember that awards are based on the best **Specimens** grown. Of course, if **all** things are equal between a common and a more rare specimen, the consideration of difference, rarity or difficult culture could be the determining factor.

Suitable Container is also considered under this heading. The size of the container should be in proportion to the size of the plant. If the Schedule has restricted the pot size, recheck by measuring. Classification Committes **DO** slip up. Plants which do not conform to Schedule and classification types required should be eliminated.

A plant which belongs in a four inch pot should not be shown in a six or eight inch container (this is called over-potting), or vice versa. The container should be of harmonious color, deduct a point or two for such "clashing" colors as scarlet flowers in a brilliant orange glazed pot. Shiny foils often detract from the plant colors and should be discouraged. The material from which the pot is made is immaterial as long as proper drainage has been arranged. The container should be perfectly clean, no clinging salts or soil apparent.

Floriferousness is also considered here. Hortorums, Dwarfs, Ivy and Lady Washington types must show bloom. Judges can deduct only five points if no flowers are present on Scented and Fancy Leaf types. There should be sufficient numbers of umbels according to variety and type. Hortorum and Lady Washingtons are the most floriferous, often with up to fifteen umbels on a prime Hortorum plant. Lady Washingtons are not perpetual bloomers as are the Hortorums. Their bloom season is early spring around Easter time. Scented and Fancy Leaf are expected to produce the least number of umbels.

Vigor, Condition and Size. The size of the plant should be mature. An exhibit that is no more than a slip should not be considered. The overall impression should be one of health and vigorous, active growth with new leaves and buds forming; not static, deteriorating, debilitated or sick-looking. The plant should be completely free of insects and diseases. Check carefully for aphids, mealy bugs, red spider, Cyclamen mites, garden slugs and termites. A Judge should recognize the brown or yellowish circles of Bacterial Leaf Spot, the soft gray mold of Botrytis and the brownish red spots of Ceriospora Leaf Spot and the irregular yellow spots and abnormally ruffled, dwarfed foliage caused by the virus disease called Leaf Crinkle. A starved and yellow plant indicates cultural neglect.

Dead leaves and spent florets or umbels should have been carefully razored out, the plant should be clean with no foreign matter, dust, or spray residue apparent. But any artificial dressing applied to create shine, etc., is considered over-grooming and should be penalized.

Any staking or tying should be done inconspicuously as possible and should be unnecessary on properly grown plants with the exception of espaliers, totem-poled or other specially trained plants.

Fancy training such as espaliering, bonsai, standards, etc., should be judged according to perfection of the training, technique and cultural perfection, including floriferousness in those types where such is of prime consideration.

The specimens should be labeled as an educational feature to help the public learn more about the plants. The labels should be neat, clean, legibly printed. Insufficient or inaccurate labeling should be penalized.

UMBEL

Is defined as a mode of inflorescence in which a number of pedicels rise from one level on the main axis and each pedicel terminates in one floret. The form of an umbel is more or less rounded or flat topped. In judging Geranium umbels the size, form and number of flowers are evaluated.

The umbels should be of proportionate size to the plant, well filled with fresh appearing flowers and buds. Any spent flowers should have been neatly removed including the pedicel, leaving no unsightly stub.

The umbels should be fairly compact, but each floret should show to the best advantage. Any gaps, "holes" or voids left by plucking spent flowers or by poor pedicel placements are penalized. The size of the umbel should be typical for type and variety and may exceed seven inches in some (Hortorum 'MAGNIFICANT') or be less than two inch clusters (Scented Leaf 'CAPRI'). Generally Hortorum umbels are the most compact and upright. Lady Washingtons have more flowers per umbel, those of Ivy Leaf vary from clusters of tight, rose-shaped blossoms to large, easily shattered blooms. Scented and Fancy Leaf are expected to have less showy blooms, generally. A plant with many smaller umbels should rate as high as one with a few large umbels in all types of Geraniums.

The main stem of the umbel should be straight and sturdy enough to support the blooms without excessive nodding. Lady Washington stems will be less erect and straight than Zonals. The stems of all types should be of a proportionate length, neither holding the flower head too far out from the foliage or too short, thus crowding the florets down in the foliage.

Destroyed flower buds may be the result of Red Spider invasions or Botrytis Blight. Over-potting (too large a container for plant size) causes Geraniums to produce lush foliage and few blossoms, as all types do best when pot bound. Excessive shade and too much fertilizer, especially nitrogen, also encourages lush growth and less flowers.

FLOWERS

It is necessary to evaluate the individual flower as well as the umbel as a whole. The individual flowers of Fancy and Scented Leaf varieties are less profuse and eye-catching, therefore rate only five points in their scale as against the twenty-five points in Hortorum, Lady Washingtons, Dwarfs and Ivy Leaf.

Four qualities of the flowers are considered: 1. Form; 2. Size; 3. Color and 4. Substance and condition.

1. **Form:** the structure of the florets is divided into three groups:
    1. Single flowering with five petals.
    2. Semi-double flowering with five to ten petals.
    3. Double flowering with over ten petals.

The single individual Pelargonium floret has been divided into primary and secondary petals of which the upper two are of a slightly different shape and in some varieties even of different color (Ivy Leaf 'ADMIRAL BYRD') or different color design (Lady Washington 'EDITH NORTH').

The Doubles have subdivisions Cactus and Rosebud. The Cactus (formerly called Poinsettia) has numerous narrow flat petals (Zonal 'NOEL') or petals curled and twisted ('MORNING STAR'). The rosebuds hold a rosebud form even in the mature flower (Zonal 'APPLEBLOSSOM ROSEBUD' and Ivy Leaf 'THE BLUSH'). The Ivy Leaf 'MRS H. J. JONES' has serrated petals which lend it a carnation-like appearance. Petals of many **P. domesticums** (Lady Washington) are ruffled, wavy, and frilled as for example the variety 'PINK GARDENER'S JOY'.

The **size** of the floret varies with the type. Since the quality of dwarfness is emphasized in the miniature Zonals, the flowers should be proportionately tiny in keeping with the smaller leaves and bush. Lady Washingtons often exceed three inches but some varieties such as 'MRS LAYAL', a pansy-flowered type, are only about one inch in diameter.

Colors of florets are excitingly varied, no yellow has yet appeared and the Hortorum 'MONTMORT' is often called the Purple Geranium. Color classes can be made for Zonals: dark and bright red, white, deep and light pink, salmon; Ivy Leaf: red, purple, orchid, lavender, pink, white; Lady Washingtons: red, salmon, white, light and deep pink, lavender-orchid and purple.

Color patterns range from selfs to bicolors through multi-color, and many different designs.

For example: Hortorum —
    'BETTER TIMES' has scarlet splash in the floret center.
    'SENSATION' has red flowers with white on reverse side.
    'PINK PHENOMENAL' has pink flowers with a white eye.

'MR. WREN' has a white edging around a red flower.

'BAUDELAIRE' Birds Egg, has tiny red dots, speckles on pink flowers.

'NEW LIFE' has red flowers with white pencilings and stripes.

Ivy Leaf includes selfs, bicolors and multicolors, sometimes with veining, markings or pencilings on some or all petals as in 'JESTER'.

Lady Washington color designs include: upper petals blotched 'GRANDSLAM'; black centers, 'BURGUNDY'; veining and petal edging 'CONGO', as well as the interesting pansy-faced designs from which the name Pansy Geranium is derived ('MRS. LAYAL').

Whatever the pattern, the colors should be clear and fresh appearing without fading and non-varietal streaking. The colors should be harmonious when more than one appear in a floret. Water spotting or any other damage to color pigment should be penalized. The texture should be fine and velvety.

The substance of the flowers should be crisp, turgid, with no evidence of wilt, thinning or drying. Any collapsing or change from the typical shape will be penalized. Each floret should be perfectly clean and free of dust or soil. Any shattering is a fault to be deducted.

FOLIAGE

Hortorum, Ivy Leaf and Lady Washington: While foliage color is important in these types as concerns their health, it is considerably more important in the Fancy Leaf. Generally, the leaves should be a bright, rich green of typical form and size.

Hortorums may or may not retain the horseshoe marking and may be quite flat or ruffled. The Dwarf 'BLACK VESUVIUS' has small, almost black foliage. Foliage of all dwarfs must be small and in proportion to miniature plant and flower size.

Ivy Leaf should have shiny and crisp foliage quite different in texture from other types. Some varieties have variegated foliage, edged or mottled with yellow and cream ('SUNSET').

Lady Washington foliage is wrinkled rather than ruffled, and deeply veined.

Scented Leaf. The Scented Leaf section is fascinatingly large including such well known scents as **P. scarboroviae** and **P. fragrans** which are strawberry scented.

P. nervosum — lime scented.

P. citriodorum — orange.

P. scabrum — apricot.

Many Scenteds also have foliage distinction in addition to their scent interest.

P. tomentosum, peppermint with a velvety, hairy leaf surface.

171

P. graveolens, rose scented, variety 'FILBERT' has lacy finely cut foliage.

P. capitatum, rose scented, has a trailing habit.

P. odoratissimum, nutmeg scent, and also an apple-scented and variegated foliage variety.

P. denticulatum, pine scent and finely cut leaves which led to its name "Skeleton Leaf".

P. filicifolium, rose scented has finest cut leaves of all, is called "Fernleaf".

P. rapaceum, pungent scent has small ruffled, deeply cut leaves similar to parsley.

Many other species and hybrids come into this classification. In judging these, the scent must be pungent and distinctive. One leaf may be plucked and placed beside the pot to be pinched by the Judges and later by the viewers in order to control the handling of many different leaves with resultant damage.

Fancy Leaf. The leaf forms vary from ruffled ('PRINCE RUPERT'), deeply cut ('LADY PLYMOUTH'), to deeply toothed ('SKIES OF ITALY') and are divided into two classes, Bicolor or Gold Leaf and Tricolor.

Bicolor or Gold Leaf have either yellow or white edges ('Mme. LANGUTH'), and Tricolors come in several combinations of three or more hues. For instance, the vivid 'MRS COX' has yellow edged green leaves and large zones of red and brown. The more sedate 'MRS. POLLOCK' has yellow edged green leaves with reddish bronze zones, and the striking 'HAPPY THOUGHT' (Butterfly) whose large irregular ivory zone resembles a butterfly, hence the name Butterfly Geranium.

The markings should be uniform, distinct and typical on all leaves of a plant. Judges should obtain specialty catalogs and study the illustrations of new introductions as well as attend shows and grow the varieties in order to be well acquainted with the different types and varieties.

All foliage must be clean, fresh appearing, not wilted or soiled and dusty. Leaves should be vigorous and healthy; not weak, succulent or diseased. Examine closely for mealy bug, red spider, etc. Review the disease evidence as concerns foliage in the Plant section under condition and assess severe penalty when the leaf actually shows a change in form, color, etc., due to the presence or destruction by insect or disease, otherwise deduct points only under Plant, as the same fault should not be deducted for twice unless as described above.

SUMMARY

Plant   (refer to scales for points allotted).

*bushy *well balanced *compact *well filled mound *shapely *sturdy *vigorous *container proportionate *pot color harmonious *actively growing *typical to type *short jointed (Ivy) *abundant umbels (Zonals, Ivy, L. Washington)

-lacks miniature characteristics (Dwarfs) -leggy -rangy -scraggly -pot too big, small -pot color clashing or too dominant -pot dirty -diseased -insect damage -dead leaves -spent flowers -over dressed -conspicuous stake, ties -incorrectly or inadequately labeled -few umbels

Umbel

*umbels well filled *compact *rounded *typical to type *stem sturdy *correct proportion of flowers to foliage *umbels held close above compact plants

-gaps -spent florets -blighted blossoms -excessive foliage -too small -sparse -stem too long, short -umbel outline irregular

Flowers

*form typical *normal or slightly larger size *dwarf flowers proportionate *colors clear *fresh *harmonious *clean *crisp *turgid

-incomplete form -petals missing -puny size -faded -dull -soiled florets -water spotted -thinning -wilting -collapsing form -shattering

Foliage

*vivid *rich *bright (depending on variety) *distinct markings (Fancy) *uniform markings (Fancy) *richly fragrant (Scented) *typical scent *easily detected scent *glossy, crisp (Ivy) *healthy

-weak -succulent -diseased -dirty -broken foliage -not characteristic -dull -lacks uniform markings on all leaves (Fancy) -scent weak or absent (Scented) -foliage too small, dwarfed (except on Dwarfs) -foliage too large (Dwarfs)

Hortorum Umbel

Single-Flowered

Cactus-Flowered

Fancy Leaf (Butterfly)

Gladiolus

SUGGESTED CLASSES:

A: 1 Spike (100) Florets measuring up to 2½".

B: 1 Spike (200) Florets measuring 2½ to 3½".

C: 1 Spike (300) Florets measuring 3½ to 4½".

D: 1 Spike (400) Florets measuring 4½ to 5½".

E: 1 Spike (500) Florets measuring over 5½".

Classes of color divisions may be made following the classifications listed under Color (p 177). In limited Schedules, combine 'Pale' and 'Light'; 'Medium' and 'Deep' and/or closely related colors, i.e. orange with salmon.

GLADIOLUS:

Are a spike inflorescence of the Iridaceae (Iris) family composed of individual flowers closely attached to the main stem with a definite frontal placement. The individual florets rise from the axil of a bract, and consist of three each sepals and petals, very similar in color, form and size.

Hybrids of the numerous species make up the bulk of garden glads which fall into two general types of large flowered and miniature. These have been crossed to give us specimens carrying characteristics of both, further increasing the range of variety and adding interest and beauty. The term "formal" and "informal" are now obsolete.

The title Gladiolus is correct for both singular and plural. Gladioli is horticulturally correct as the plural. No authority can be found for "gladiola" as a plural form. The word is derived from the Latin 'gladius' meaning sword which gives rise to the common name 'Sword Flower'.

The North American Glad Council issues annual lists of classified varieties, and the Classification Committees and Judges will find these a great aid in determining placement. The official North American Score Sheet is one of the very few horticultural point scales in which the familiar words "typical of variety" are not found. The official score sheet may seem complicated at first glance but a bit of study will reveal that it is far easier to use than the so-called simplified scales, as each item is clearly covered and nothing is left to chance.

The best Gladiolus catalogs list each corm by size of floret and color code. For instance 'ELFJE' (330) means the size of the floret is 3½ to 4½" and the color is a light salmon. The 300 designates the size code and 30 designates the color. The numbers in the color code are given under color, which see.

BASIC DATA CHART

Code Number	Diameter In Inches	Buds	Open Florets	Buds In Color	Stem Length
100	up to 2½"	15	5	4	17" max. height
200	2½" to 3½"	18	6	5	18" max. height
300	3½" to 4½"	19	7	5	20" max. height
400	4½" to 5½"	20	8	6	20" max. height
500	over 5½"	19	7	5	22" max. height

Refer to Fixed penalties and deductions, p. 176

By using the Basic Data Chart and the Color Code jointly, we find that 'LANDMARK' (512) should have florets measuring 5½" or more; *that it should be judged as a yellow, with a 22" minimum stem and have at least 7 open florets, five more buds in color and at least 19 buds and flowers on the stem. 'POLAR CUB' (200) is a white flower between 2½ and 3½", 18 buds and flowers ideally and with six of these open with five more showing color on an 18" stem.*

SCALE OF POINTS
North Am. Gladiolus Council

FLORETS Color and Structure 40 Points

Color 30 Points

Item			
	1: clarity		5 points
	2: saturation		5 points
	3: harmony		5 points
	4: uniformity		5 points
	5: beauty and appeal. Refer to p. 182		10 points

Structure 10 Points

Item		
	6: form	5 points
	7: substance and texture	5 points

SPIKE Structure and Balance 60 Points

Structure 35 Points

Item		
	8: total buds	4 points
	9: open florets	7 points
	10: buds in color	4 points
	11: floret attachment	6 points
	12: facing	5 points
	13: floret uniformity	4 points
	14: stem	3 points
	15: grooming, condition, health	7 points

Balance of Spike   25 Points

Item		
	16: floret size to flowerhead	8 points
	17: inflorescence to flowerhead	6 points
	18: taper	6 points

SUGGESTED
SIMPLIFIED SCALE

Color, Beauty, Appeal	*30*
Floret & Bud Num. Size, Uniformity	*25*
Balance and Taper	*15*
Floret Form, Attachment, Spacing, Pose	*10*
Stem Length, Crooking	*10*
Grooming, Condition, Health	*10*
	100

−1 each lacking
−2 each lacking
−1 to −4 each lacking

−2 ea. inch over or under
−2 ea. inch over or under

In judging a multiple spike class, award up to 15 points for the matching quality (uniformity) of the exhibit as a whole.

FIXED PENALTIES AND DEDUCTIONS
(All others are Judge's opinion)

Item *8:* Deduct 1 point each bud short of required
     9: Deduct 2 points each open floret short
    10: Deduct 1–4 points each bud in color short of required
    16, 17: Deduct 2 points each inch over or under

NOTE: *One point removed for the first gone or completely deteriorated floret, and four points for the second.* −2 *for any further infraction.*

Wilt: varying degrees of wilt are penalized under:
    Length and balance of flowerhead (Items 16, 17)
    Structure (Items 6, 7)
    Grooming and Appeal (Items 15, 5)

EXTRA DEDUCTIONS

A spike may also be penalized up to 10 additional points for **each** of the following serious faults:

A: Deformed Florets
    Not to be confused with petal folding, Item 6. } *(see Items 6 and 7)*

B: Irregular Opening
C: Adventitious Buds
D: Attachment
} *(see Item 15)*

E: Stem Short and Weak
F: Stem Crooking, Curving
} *(see Item 17)*

G: Condition
H: Health
} *(see Item 18)*

Floret Color

Item 1 — **Clarity** means the absence of any vagrant color that causes a dull, murky, clouded, flecked or smeared appearance. Any tinge, infusion or stain of another color reduces the clear, clean purity. Flaking or flecking is undesirable unless the variety is known to be naturally striped. A murky, smeared appearance on this type is also debited heavily . . . up to the full five points.

Item 2 — **Saturation** is the amount of vividness, intensity, vibrancy and brightness. Saturation is that point where further increase of intensity produces only an equal increase in density. Deductions are made for peeling, bleeding of blotches, weakness, or fading as in some orange varieties. Fading can be ascertained as such if the floret still retains its substance, is not wilted. Peeling is often due to water damage. Transparency is due to thrip damage. See Health.

Item 3 — **Harmony.** In the pursuit of 'difference', growers often introduce color combinations which are incompatible. The color class lists many varieties with conspicuous markings on throat and lips and these must not be objectionable, either in size or color. Bizarre or discordant blotches and combinations which lack a pleasing harmonious relationship should be penalized.

Item 4 — Uniformity. The color on each floret should be the same degree of clarity and saturation with uniform markings. If one floret is faded or the color is less intense, or is not as pure and clear as it appears in the other florets, then points must be deducted. The most open petals are sometimes of a less intense color than those above. The size value and general area of the markings, etc, must be similar.

Item 5 — Beauty and Appeal. See page 182

COLOR CODE

COLOR CLASSIFICATION

Color	Pale	Light	Medium	Deep	Other
White	00				
Green		02	04		
Yellow	10*(1)	12	14	16	
Orange	20 (2)	22	24	26	
Salmon	30	32	34	36(3)	
Pink	40	42	44	46	
Red		52(4)	54	56	58 Black Red
Rose	60	62	64	66	68 Black Rose
Lavendar	70	72	74	76	78 Purple
Violet (Blue)	80	82	84	86	
Smokies		92	94	96	
Tan	90				
Brown					98

*Includes (1) Cream (2) Buff (3) Orange Scarlet (4) Red Scarlet

Classification numbers ending in an odd digit, 1, 3, 5, 7, 9, indicate "with conspicuous markings" for the color indicated by the even number immediately preceding the odd number.

Floret Structure

Item 6 — Form. Hereditary characteristics are strongest in the col- or of gladiolus, but a few such as lemonei and primulinus breeding pass on a variation of form known as hooded; while crosses of childsii and cruentus had the form characteristics resulting in a large, round, flat flower. Much interbreeding has led to a form being accepted as ideal in which any evidence of cupping, hooding, clawing, excessive reflexing or ragged effects are penalized. Form cannot be ascertained unless the floret is fully open.

The form should be properly shaped to conform to floret arrangement on the flowerhead. The hood or top petal should not conceal the center of the floret, the Judges should be able to see into each floret.

The petals and sepals on each individual flower should be uniformly developed with the segments regularly placed in the same pattern. There may be either one or two lip petals. Some double forms are available.

Florets are classed as either plain petaled or ruffled and the degree should be consistent on the segments of each floret and on all the florets. Ruffling naturally will be more intense on freshly opened or partially opened florets. Schedules sometimes attempt to class glads according to the ruffling. This is the road to drive everyone close to the brink of insanity. Classification should be by size, then by color and let the ruffles fall where they may; being judged on their uniformity and contribution to the general beauty and appeal of the floret.

Petals which excessively reflex or turn back sharply will be penalized. If any florets or petals have collapsed, wilted or drooped so badly the form cannot be seen, points must be deducted under form and condition.

Up to 10 additional points may be taken for deformed florets, petals or sepals which are twisted, malformed, distorted, whether by insect, disease or cultural accident.

NOTE: EXTRA DEDUCTION A: **Relative to floret structure.**

Up to 10 additional points may be taken for deformed florets, petals or sepals which are twisted, malformed, distorted, whether by insects, disease or *cultural accident. Not to be confused with petal fold. Item 6*

Item 7 — Substance and Texture

Substance is the heavy, crisp, firm tissue construction of the petals which permits it to withstand handling and weather and which gives the floret lasting quality. Substance should be heavy and thick, giving the petals a springy quality. Softening, curling, limpness or thinning are faults to be penalized. Examine the edges of the florets for evidence of thinning.

Over-maturity and over-feeding cause weak substance. Texture and color are both dulled and adversely affected by the loss of substance.

Texture is the surface quality which ideally has an irridescent sheen that contributes greatly to the color appeal to which it is closely allied. When the texture is dulled or coarsened, penalty is taken.

Spike Structure

Item 8 — Total Buds:

According to the Basic Data Chart, each size classification has an ideal number of total buds and flowers as follows.

Code Number 100	ideally has	15 buds
Code Number 200	ideally has	18 buds
Code Number 300	ideally has	19 buds
Code Number 400	ideally has	20 buds
Code Number 500	ideally has	19 buds

No penalty will be levied for having more than the recommended ideal except as this affects a deviation from standard for the *flower head. (Item 16, 17). For instance, if a 200 has 20 buds and exceeds an 18" flower head, the exhibit will be penalized.*

A deduction of one point is to be made for each bud lacking. For instance, if 'NOLA' (330) has only 16 buds, the Judge would deduct 3 points. There is no penalty for too many buds.

Item 9 — Open Floret

According to the Basic Data Chart, each size classification should have an ideal number of florets open, as follows.

Code Number 100	ideally has	5 open florets
Code Number 200	ideally has	6 open florets
Code Number 300	ideally has	7 open florets
Code Number 400	ideally has	8 open florets
Code Number 500	ideally has	7 open florets

Note that size 400 (florets 4½ to 5½") has the most bloom potential for an ideal spike.

Two points are to be deducted for each floret short of this standard of perfection. For instance, if 'BURMA' (556) has only 6 florets open instead of the ideal 8 for its size class, then 4 points would have to be deducted. And 'SNOWSPRITE' (200) would have to be reduced 2 points if it had only 5 instead of 6 florets open.

A floret shall be considered open if it is one-half or more the diameter of the next LOWER open floret.

Item 10 — Buds in Color

According to the Basic Data Chart each size classification has an ideal number of buds showing color.

Code Number 100 ideally has 4 buds in color
Code Number 200 ideally has 5 buds in color
Code Number 300 ideally has 5 buds in color
Code Number 400 ideally has 6 buds in color
Code Number 500 ideally has 5 buds in color

One to four points are deductible for deviations. Penalize 2 pts. max. for too many buds in color. For example, 'ELIZABETH THE QUEEN' (556) ideally has 5 buds showing color, but supposing it has 7 showing color, then at least two points can be reasonably *deducted in the Judge's opinion. Those with many buds and open florets may exceed the norm here without penalty.*

Item 11 — Floret Attachment

Deduct for split calyx, long, tubular-necked florets and for weak, loose attachment. By viewing the flowerhead from the rear, the Judge can ascertain whether the florets are loosely or tightly attached to the spine. Drooping enhances danger of floret loss with handling. This is inherent with some cultivars.

Item 12 — Facing

All florets should uniformly look out toward the viewer, showing a face-front manner. Viewing the spike from the side and back helps determine the degree of fault, or perfection of this quality. Any floret which faces completely around is deducted the full 5 points. Some spikes exhibit an irregular facing which must be penalized commensurate with the fault.

Item 13 — Floret Uniformity

The form of the gladiolus floret is such that it may have a two-petal lip structure or a one-petal lip structure. Neither is superior. However, points are deducted if some of the florets exhibit a single petal while others on the same spike carry two or vice versa.

The florets should not show varying degrees of rotation. All petals and sepals should occupy approximately the same position in relation to each other in each floret and should have the same degree of openness and reflex. And they should be of such shape that they conform to their arrangement on the flower head.

Item 14 — Stem.

According to the Basic Data Chart, each size classification has an ideal length of total stem. Schedules may set length of stem below flowerhead. The lengths given in the Data Chart are encouraged as these sizes contribute to balanced spikes. Refer to Item E. Crooking p. 181 and Item F. Stem Weak p. 182. Anything more or less than the required length, stems too weak or heavy for floret size, are penalized.

Item 15 — Grooming. *Every specimen deserves to be shown to the greatest advantage, free of soil, dust, and with foliage, florets and stem all clean. Side shoots should be removed, two points are deducted if the side-shoot sheath is also removed. There should be no pollen stains. Penalize one point for removal of bottom floret or bud sheath. Remove four points if second floret or calyx is missing. An additional two points deducted for further infractions. If more than two florets are gone, the specimen can hardly place due to total deductions involving other Items, plus extra deductions (see) Eliminate any spike carrying wire, cotton, pins, or other foreign objects.*

Spike Balance

Balance of the spike is based on (1) floret to flowerhead (2) proportion of florets to stem and of open florets to buds and (3) taper.

Item 16 — Balance of Floret Size to Flowerhead. *The length of the head should be 5—6 times the breadth of the inflorescence at its widest point. The goal is horizontal mass at the bottom. See Sketch. No bloom should hide more than ¼ of bloom below. Spacing of the florets is best determined by examining the spike from the back, as well as the front. Ideally, there will be no stem showing between the florets when examined from the front. A 'loose' appearance should be penalized. If the 'spine' shows on the front in the open floret area, this is considered a serious fault. Florets that are too large or too small for the length of the head are faults. Deductions should be made for gaping between florets (except in 100, 200) as well as crowding or overlapping. The size of the first open floret establishes the size classification. There should be a gradual decrease in size up the spike. Deduct two points for each inch over or under. Classes 100 and 200 should maintain the general dainty and symmetrical appearance characteristic of the type. For example, if the Judge finds a spike of 'ATOM' which normally should measure 2½ to 3½" which has been forced by feeding to a size of 3¾", and which generally exhibits a less dainty appearance two points will be removed for oversize. Points under balance (florescence to flowerhead) might be removed as well. The small 300 Series is sometimes called the Butterfly or Table Glads by certain suppliers. The Miniature and Baby gladiolus are the 200 and 100's. It is advisable that the Judge use the official number code rather than calling these by such trade names, and that they encourage Schedule Committees to do the same.*

NOTE: EXTRA DEDUCTION B, C, D

B—Irregular Opening
Up to 10 additional points may be deducted for irregular opening of the florets. Sometimes a less-open bud or flower will be found lower than some more fully-open flowers; or a half-open floret will be found high up in the green buds. This is a serious fault. The degree of openness should diminish uniformly and evenly from the green buds at the tip, down through the half-opened florets to *the wide open ones at the broad massed base of the flowerhead.*

C—Adventitious Buds
An additional 10 points may be deducted for any buds out of their usual place, arising sporadically from between or behind their normal placement. Two buds or florets will sometimes be found *growing from the same bud sheath. Minus 1—2 points for first one either removed or left in place. Increase penalty if more.*

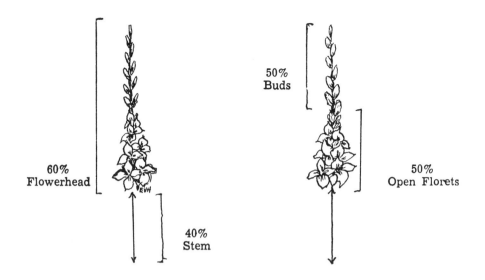

60%
Flowerhead

40%
Stem

50%
Buds

50%
Open Florets

Item 17 — Balance of Inflorescence to Flowerhead

The balance of the buds to open florets should be in proportion, giving an overall pleasing appearance of balance. Inflorescence is the continuous mass of color made by open and half-open florets and is measured in inches from the first open floret up through the half-opened buds and should be 50 to 55% of the overall length providing the spike is not thrown out of balance, depending on floret width, flatness. This relativity is important to overall symmetry of the flowerhead.

Too many buds in relation to too-few open florets will be penalized as immature. Too many open florets with too few buds will be penalized as bloomed out. The spike whose tip has been broken immediately loses points since it throws the balance of florescence off, as well as causing a lack of the required number of buds to open flowers. Deduct 2 points for every inch over or under. Even though the spike may carry insufficient buds and open florets for its length and size class (with resulting deductions there), the balance may be in good proportion, earning full points under this item.

Item 18 — Taper

An imaginary axis drawn down through the center of the spike from the green buds at the tip, to the lowest florets will indicate the approximate amount of spread on each side which must be as nearly equal as possible. Viewing the spike from the back helps.
From the tip down to the half open buds there should be a gradual separation, lowering and movement of the buds to alternate sides to give room for the opening flowers.
A crooked stem is closely tied to taper, as the crooks or curves will throw the vertical balance off, giving a lopsided appearance *which is penalized. Balance (Items 16 and 17) is also closely tied to taper as irregular spacing and arrangement can throw the visual weight to the right or left, destroying the vertical balance and uniform tapering. The bottom should be rounded, and the overall flowerhead should present appearance similar to an elongated teardrop. Deduct for clumps of unseparated buds at tip, or lack of gradual grading of open color to green buds.*

NOTE: EXTRA DEDUCTION E, F, below re **Taper.**

E—Stem Crooking

Additional penalty up to 10 points can be levied for a stem that is crooked and which adversely affects the vertical balance (taper, *Item 18) of the flowerhead. Sometimes the crook will be only in the lower stem, below the lowest floret and does not affect the* taper. Points up to 10 are deductible commensurate with the degree of crookedness and the area involved.

F—Stem, Short and Weak

Additional penalty up to 10 points can be levied for a stem that is too short or weak. The stem must be straight throughout its entire length and strong enough to support the flowerhead. The size of the flower is in direct proportion to the length and diameter of the stem. A large flower measuring 5½" needs a longer, stronger stem to appear at its best. The stem should not be so slender and whippy that it cannot adequately support the full complement of flowers in a gracefully erect position. The stem should not be so long that it destroys overall balance. A good rule of thumb proportion is 60% flowerhead and 40% stem (see sketch under Item 15). The Judge expects 100, 200 and 300's to have more slight, slender stems in keeping with the flower's more dainty proportions.

NOTE: EXTRA DEDUCTIONS G, H, below re **Overall Appearance.**
G—Condition and H—Health

Up to 10 additional points may be deducted for each general condition and health of the exhibit. A general limp, flabby condition indicates poor culture. Any evidence of damage either mechanical, by insect or disease must be deleted. Wilted florets still attached are penalized here. Those removed are penalized under grooming as directed.

Thrip damage is evidenced by scars on the surface of the leaf and flower. Flowers may be distorted at the edges with much coloring matter removed. Sheaths may become brown or silver-streaked white and the flowers misshapen and discolored.

Botrytis may cover the buds with grey-brown spores. Flowers showing slight color change or if streaked greyish, light green *areas show Mosaic damage. Browning of the bud sheaths may indicate poor growing conditions, especially lack of water. Eliminate if damage is extensive.*

Some **foliage** should be present on the stem. Excess foliage should be discouraged as the corm should be left with at least four leaves to mature properly. Excess foliage should be no problem if the stem is in the proper proportion lengthwise to the flowerhead, I.E. 40% stem and 60% flowerhead.

Beauty and Appeal. *Refer to Item 5, p. 177. 10 points*

This is the sum total appearance of the color qualities, plus the form and balance. Any qualities for which deductions were made reflects on both beauty and appeal.

Any lack of vibrancy, clarity, harmony and uniformity reduces the distinctive appeal of the exhibit. The beauty of the specimen also means the eye appeal of the flower considered as a whole. The form of all florets should be uniform and the ruffling or blotching, if present, should add to the beauty and appeal. **Form** distortion, a ragged appearance, any lack of perfection, or general freshness reduces the attraction.

Familiarity with a variety should not blind the Judge to a spike's beauty, nor should the novelty of a new introduction influence his evaluation. An older variety, such as 'BURMA' (556) should be given its due, despite new competitors in its size and color class of 5½" up and rose-red coloring.

Color relationships and value must be judged fairly with no prejudice against or preference for a certain combination or hue. Salmon smoky (83), black red (54) and (90) any other color are gladiolus colors which have their champions and their critics. But Judges must be above such selection based on discrimination.

SUMMARY:

Florets

Color

Clarity:
*pure *clean *clear *living

-murky -clouded -diluted -smeared -bluing -dull

Saturation:
*intense *vibrant *bright *distinct

-flat -weak -peeling -blotches bleeding -faded -watery -flaking (except where typical)

Harmony:
*pleasing *blotches proportionate *striking

-incompatible -bizarre -discordant -objectionable

Uniformity:
*clarity, saturation and harmony must be uniform on all florets

-uneven saturation, clarity -blotching not uniform on all florets

Form and Structure of the Florets

Form
*centers exposed *symmetrical *regular *fully open *uniformity throughout *equal ruffling or plain on all

-severely reflexed petals, sepals -uneven development -hooded -ragged -lacks uniformity -irregular outline -petals obscuring centers
Note: additional 10 point penalty may be taken for deformity of any floret or bud.

Substance and Texture
Substance: *springy *crisp *firm *heavy *thick
-curling -softening -wilted -weak -flaccid

Texture: *crystalline *glistening *sheen
-dull -rough -coarse

Spike Structure
Total buds
*ideally has 100-15
           200-18
           300-20
           400-22
           500-20

-lacks buds − 1 each short of required
No penalty for too many buds except as it affects balance, etc.

Open Florets
*ideally 100-5
       200-6
       300-7
       400-8
       500-7

a floret is to be counted as open if it is one-half or more open

-lacks: deduct 2 points for each lacking

Buds in Color
*ideally 100-4
       200-5
       300-5
       400-6
       500-5

May exceed norm without penalty

-deduct 1 to 4 points for too few

Floret Size
*ideally 100 — up to 2½"
       200 — 2½ to 3½"
       300 — 3½ to 4½"
       400 — 4½ to 5½"
       500 — over 5½"
*first floret open establishes size

−2 points off each inch over or under

Facing and attachment
*all florets facing front *no split calyx, elongated tube
-irregular facing -floret on back (deduct all 5) -florets facing different directions -downward nodding

Floret Uniformity
*equal lip petals (either all one-petal lips, or all two-petal lips)

-varying number of lip petals -differing petal-sepal arrangement

Length of Stem
*ideally 100 — *17"* maximum height
       200 — *18"* maximum height
       300 — *20"* minimum
       400 — *20"* minimum
       500 — *22"* minimum

-weak -too heavy, thick
-deduct points for any deviations commeasurate with the degree of fault

Spike Balance

Balance of Floret to Flowerhead
*well spaced *no flower obscuring another

-gaping -overcrowded -overlapping -unevenly spaced -too widely spaced -distribution irregular on stem -stem 'spine' shows
Note: up to 10 point penalty each for:
    1. irregular opening
    2. adventitious buds
    3. loose attachment

Balance of Inflorescence to Flowerhead
*well proportioned *buds equal to open florets *50% buds to 50% flowers *symmetrical

-too few flowers open for number of buds -lacks buds -bloomed out -out of proportion

Taper

*vertical balance equal on each side of imaginary central axis *bottom *rounded *elongated teardrop form *even transition green into color*

-lopsided -unbalanced -florets swing too far left or right -clump of buds at top
Note: Up to 10 point penalty extra each for
1. crooked stem, curving tip
2. short, weak stem

Grooming

*clean *all florets present *lateral spike correctly removed

-lateral spike present or incorrectly removed -pollen stains -soil, dust, spray -floret sheaths removed
— 1 floret wilted or removed (deduct 1)
— 2 florets wilted or removed (deduct 4)

Note: Up to 10 points are deductible for each condition and health

*normal *healthy *vigorous *undamaged *intact

-spotted foliage -foliage lacking -excess foliage -torn, split petals -scaled, brown bud sheaths or foliage -general limp, aged, beat-up look -foliage streaked -color removed (thrips) -color change (greenish) Mosaic -spores on buds (grey-green) Botrytis

Beauty and Appeal

*color clarity, saturation, harmony, uniformity at their best establishes beauty and appeal
*general overall perfection, balance, freshness, floret form and spacing reinforces beauty and appeal

-any deductions in quality reduces beauty and appeal commeasurately

Holly, Ilex

SUGGESTED CLASSES:

A. Evergreen, Red Fruited, Branch 18-24"
1. English Holly, **I. aquifolium**
2. Chinese Holly, **I. cornuta**
3. American Holly, **I. opaca**
4. Any other

B. Deciduous, Red Fruited (Sawtoothed, **I. serrata**. Winterberry, **I. verticillata**).

C. Evergreen Black Fruited (Japanese Holly, **I. crenata**. Inkberry, **I. glabra**).

D. Yellow Fruited Specimen

E. Orange Fruited Specimen

F. White Fruited Specimen

G. Non-Fruiting Branches (male)

HOLLY

185

HOLLY

Holly belongs to the Family Aquifoliaceae and is a group of deciduous or evergreen shrubs and trees with watery sap. The leaves are *of alternate placement. The fruit is a berry-like drupe. There are three genera of which Ilex is the most important.*

The leaf margins may be entire, crenate, serrate, serrulate-ciliate. Fruits are red or black with a few yellow, orange and white fruiting types.

There are between 400 and 500 species of holly found in the flora of all continents except Austrialia. Nineteen species are native to the *Eastern and Southern United States, and I. decidua in Illinois.*

Hollies are divided into four groups based on fruit color and persistence of foliage. Asterisk (*) designates the species most commonly cultivated.

1. Evergreen Black Fruited which includes:
   I. coriacea (native), **I. crenata*** (Japanese)
   I. glabra (native Inkberry)
2. Deciduous Black Fruited, only type grown in U.S. is **I. macrocarpa** from China which has large black fruits approximately ½ inch long.
3. ..Evergreen Red Fruited which includes
   Native I. cassine, I. myrtifolia, I. opaca*, I. vomitoria, *I.x Meservae*
   Exotics I. aquifolium, I. centrochinensis, I. chinensis, I. corallina, I. cornuta*
       I. dipyrena, I. fargesii, I. integra, I. latifolia, I. paraguariensis (Mate Holly) I. pedunculosa, I. pernyi, I. rotunda, I. rugosa, I. sikkimensis, I. yunnanensis
4. ..Deciduous Red Fruited includes
   Native I. ambigua, I. amelanchier, I. Busellii, I. curtissii, I. Cuthbertii, I. de-*cidua, I. laevigata, I. longpipes, I. montana, I. verticillata* and *Exotic I. serrata plus interspecific crosses.*

AMERICAN HOLLY   (I. opaca)

The species known as American Holly has evergreen foliage, with bright red berries generally, but with some varieties bearing orange or yellow fruits. The leaf blades are variable, flat, keeled or twisted. The *leaf color may be dull or glossy green depending on the cultivar. The fruit matures in October and November. 8–12 mm in size. The native I. opaca has contributed a large number of fine horicultural varieties.*

ENGLISH HOLLY   (I. aquifolium)

The title "English Holly" is used to designate a particular group of green and variegated leafed Hollies. These Hollies are particularly *well adapted to the Pacific Northwest and the over thirty-six cultivar* now available are planted freely there. Some are narrow and upright, others columnar, conical and a few are weeping or pendulous. There is varied berry placement and leaf forms.

CHINESE or HORNED HOLLY

Among Chinese Hollies, the most common in the U.S. is the Horned *Holly, Ilex cornuta, (red berry, evergreen) and its cultivars. It is superior* in its glossy, dark green foliage and showy bright red, abundant, clustered fruits. On some specimens fruits reach full color by Mid-November, others delay until mid-January. Cv. 'BURFORDI' is a well-known variety.

JAPANESE HOLLY   (I. crenata)

This constitutes a very important group of garden plants with black fruits. New varieties are compact, dense with closely spaced twigs and foliage which is small and closely resembles Box. Heights vary from *dwarfs only a few inches in height to 4' or more. Cv. 'CONVEXA' is reported to* have lived through temperatures 18 degrees below zero.

DECIDUOUS HOLLY

These are not widely used. I. verticillata (common name: Winterberry) is reported to withstand the lowest temperatures of all such Hollies. Its abundant red fruits brighten snow covered gardens from Ontario south. Several yellow fruited plants are known. I. serrata, 'SIEBOLDII' is a red-fruited deciduous Holly commonly used. Its small, glossy red, abundant fruits drop early in the winter.

Holly orchardists in commercial production often plant **I. opaca** varieties such as 'OLD-HEAVYBERRY', 'SLIM JANE', 'CROONEN-BERG', and **I. aquifolium** 'BROWNELLS SPECIAL', 'FIRECRACKER', 'SILVARY', etc.

POINT SCALE FOR HORTICULTURAL SPECIMENS

	Berried Branch	Non Berried
Vigor	10	15
Foliage		
. spacing	10	15
. color	15	25
. freedom from blemish	15	20
. texture	10	15
Fruit		
. size	10	—
. color	10	—
. spacing	10	—
Correct Labeling	10	10

VIGOR

A sturdy, but flexible branch with several twigs evenly covered with large, firm fruits and clean healthy leaves is ideal. Excessive fruit-shedding is a fault to be penalized.

While fruits may form without pollination, particularly on Chinese variety, 'BURFORDII', they are not nearly so satisfactory. Fruits with seeds are larger, firmer, less prone to drop in handling and generally superior.

The ethylene gas given off by ripening apples and pears and by oil and gas stoves causes premature defoliation of Holly.

The vigor and general appearance of well being may be marred by scale, insects, or disease. Vigor often influences spacing, which see. Extreme vigor or shade results in widely or unevenly spaced leaves and branches. To rate high, all portions should have uniform spacing of leaves, balanced on both sides of center. Excessive or weak growth is deducted. Deduct or eliminate for missing or malformed leaves.

A brittle, dried appearance is to be deducted. The branch should appear healthy, lively, strong with typically colored bark. The Judge is often asked why a Holly has not produced fruits. The reason may be:

1. The plant is too young.
2. The flowers were injured by frost or cold, or were not pollinated owing to unfavorable weather conditions or absence of bees.
3. The tree is male.
4. The female tree is too far from the male tree.
5. Male and female trees did not bloom at the same time.
6. Slight or no crop may follow a year of heavy fruiting.

FOLIAGE SPACING

The characteristics of Holly leaves have led to the use of some descriptive terms. A **curved** leaf is one in which the midrib and blade of the leaf are curved from base to apex or part of that space. A **keeled** leaf is one in which the halves are set at an angle from the midrib like the keel of a boat. Most are keeled. **Divaricate** leaves have spines pointing in different directions. The whole leaf may be twisted or only the upper part.

The number of spines on different leaves of **I. opaca** and other species may be different, one side having five and the other six, etc. The Chinese Holly **I. cornuta** has a typical leaf shape likened to a flying bat, though the number of spines and the shape of the leaf varies in some other Chinese species. The variety 'NATIONAL' has a smooth-margined foliage with a single spine at the tip.

The spacing and placement of the foliage on the branch varies with the variety and the species. For instance, the leaves of **I. pernyi** fit closely to the branch and to each other while those of **I. opaca** 'CROONENBERG' are farther apart and less precisely placed.

However, the Judge must decide if, regardless of varietal characteristics, the spacing is too dense, or closely spaced or spotty. Excessive or bunched leaves interfere with the display of bright fruits.

The branch should be well-clothed, neat and compact appearing with the foliage uniformly spaced all along the specimen's length.

FOLIAGE COLOR

English Holly variegates include both gold and silver blotch and gold and silver edged. In some, the edge may be yellow or silver and in others the edge will be green with the center yellow. The variety 'GOLDEN QUEEN' may be entirely golden yellow.

Petioles and twig color in the species and cultivars varies from purplish to tan. Deduct yellowed, bronzing, partial mutation (mixed variegated with green) or evidence of removal of variant leaf.

A Judge will recognize that intense green color is the result of efficient cultural and feeding practices. Variegated colors should be distinct and clearly defined, not 'smeared-looking. The color should be uniform on all leaves of the entire specimen. Leaves attacked by Red Mites lose their lustrous bright sheen, becoming gray or grayish brown.

FOLIAGE: FREEDOM FROM BLEMISH

The perfection of the foliage, thus the general appearance of the specimen, can be marred by disease, insects, dehydration and weather damage. Wind damage resulting in spine punctures are faults, as is a *dried appearance or marginal burn. Examine both sides carefully.*

Several different insects and diseases attack Holly. Black mold caused by a fungus is sometimes present on the leaves, making them unfit for ornamental purposes. Leaves may be yellowed, stunted or deformed through Leaf Miner attacks. Their tunnels and blotches show on the surfaces of the foliage and so destroy its beauty and appearance.

Attacks of the Spittle-bug also discolor, distort and stunt Holly foliage. Wax scale evidenced by a soft, waxy white covering exudes honeydew and the leaves are blackened by a fungus which feeds on the honeydew. Several other types of scale also may be present on the *leaves and twigs which deserve penalty. Wax or other leaf-shine additive causes elimination. Deduct for too thick, thin, dull, glossy, rough, smooth, ridged if not typical of cultivar.*

FOLIAGE: TEXTURE

Some cultivars such as American Holly 'CANARY', 'BAKER', etc., are naturally less glossy with a more leathery texture than others such as 'ELEANOR', 'OLD FAITHFUL' and others. The texture should be firm and fine, and the substance crisp and turgid.

The H.S.A. also refers to sprig foliage balance and spacing (overall formation) as 'texture'. Lateral growth is to be proportional to terminal growth. In this context, texture is influenced by branching, leaf size, and leaf spacing. Culture influences both vigor and spacing (which see). A mature, but dwarfed leaf is a fault.

FRUIT: SIZE

*The size of fruit varies among plants of the same cultivar due to poor culture. The black fruits of the Japanese I. crenata, variety, 'CON-*VEXA' are small, 5mm in diameter. The red-fruited English Holly berries are from 6-7mm in size. American I. opaca's red fruits range from *up to 11mm long and 9 mm wide to 10mm long by 12mm wide. The shape of the fruits range from round or globose to ellipsoid or oblate (oval, flattened at each end). Any shriveling or size reduction due to dehydration should be noted. The size of the fruit should be uniform over the entire specimen.*

FRUIT: COLOR

The color of Holly fruit varies from yellow through orange, orange-red, light red, brilliant scarlet, deep red to black and even white.

The fruit color should appear brilliant, glistening and carry an attractive sheen. *If the berries are old, blemished, spotted or appear* soiled, the Judge will down-grade as much as he deems necessary.

All fruits on the specimen should have full color, and are uniformly colored over the entire specimen.

FRUIT: SPACING

The ultimate purpose of the cut Holly specimens for decorative use governs the decision. The Judge must not expect the same position, as the spacing and placement varies according to the species and variety. See the accompanying sketches for fruit position of some of the more common types. It will be noted that some Hollies produce fruit on short peduncles (stalks) or on long ones and that sometimes the fruits are in groups or held singly. Excessively long twig or branch growth with the fruit only at the bases is not desirable for ornamental use. The branch should be heavy with abundant fruit, well placed *throughout. If the placement is spotty, berries missing, spacing bunched or sparse, penalty is taken. Short twig growth with uniform, conspicuous berries is most desirable. Too much fruit may be atypical of the cultivar, and produced at detriment of fruit and foliage size and color.*

SUITABILITY, LABELING

H.S.A. recommends entry be eliminated if entered in wrong class. If entered in proper class, but mislabeled, it becomes a matter of point reduction. Points could be taken off for misspelling.

The branch should be symmetrical, well-shaped and well-balanced. A branched specimen rates higher than an unbranched one, but excessive wide forking reduces the use to which it could be put.

SUMMARY
VIGOR

*sturdy *flexible *healthy *lively *fresh *short 'handle' achieved without removal of lateral branching or leaves
-fruits dropping -dry, brittle -stunted -diseased

FOLIAGE

Spacing

*well clothed *compact *neat *uniform spacing *symmetrical
-too dense -uneven -partially defoliated -spotted (lacks, nutrients) -unbalanced -atypical -leaves missing -deduct if laterals are unequal or exceed terminal growth

Color

*intense *uniform *variegations clear *lustrous

-discolored -dull -streaked -weak -yellowed -mined (Leaf Miner damage) -gray, grayish brown (Red Mite damage) -bronzed.

Freedom from Blemish

*unmarred *perfect *all parts intact

-dried -margin burn -spine punctures -blackened *leaf Miner tunnels -stunted -distorted

Texture

*sheen *glossy *firm *fine *crisp *rigid *stiff

-dull -not typical -limp -roughened -coarse

FRUIT

Size

*typical *larger than normal for season, area

-stunted -small

Color

*glistening *ripe *brilliant

-dull -blemished -spotted -soiled

Spacing

*uniformly spaced *abundant *short twig growth *heavy crop *conspicuous berries

-excessively long twig growth -fruit clustered only at base -sparse -spotty -uneven -bunched -one sided -hidden in foliage

SEEDLING

Distinction of vigor, foliage texture and color; color and size of fruit is considered in seedlings.

FRUIT POSITIONS   (Variations appear within specie) 6

1. I. opaca   2. I. cornuta   3. I. aquifolium   4. I. verticillata

5. I. pedunculosa   6. I. coriacea   7. I. serrata   8. I. pernyi
                                                      deciduous

191

Holly Leaf Variations

1. I. opaca

I. cornuta

I. aquifolium spiny

I. opaca

I. cornuta

I. aquifolium

'E. PALALTKA'

I. cornuta

Japanese I. crenata

IRIS

The Iris family is divided into Bearded, Beardless, Bulbous and Miscellaneous types and are one of the most common, yet diverse show plants with at least six active sub-societies within the American Iris Society.

Bearded Iris are divided into two sections including the (1) True Bearded and (2) the Arils and Arilbreds. The True Bearded are sub-divided into:

    A. Tall Bearded, over 28"
    B. Medians which include:
        Standard Dwarf, *8–15"*
        Intermediate — *16–27"*
        Miniature Tall (Table) — *16–27"*
        Border Bearded — *16–27"*
    C. Miniature Dwarf, *0–7"* '

Beardless Iris are sub-divided into:

    Japanese
    Siberian
    Spuria
    Louisiana
    Species

Bulbous Iris are sub-divided into:

> Dutch and Spanish
> English
> Reticulata

Iris are classified as to height and other characteristics as follows.

1. BEARDED IRIS

A. Tall Bearded, TB

- medium to late blooming
- *28" and up*
- repeated branching, stiff, erect stems
- *large flowers, 4" and up*

B. Border Bearded, BB, Median

- early to medium season, blooms with Tall Bearded
- *16 to 27"*

- stiffly erect stems
- branched, sometimes clubby
- *numerous blooms up to 4½" or 7–8" combined height and width*

C. Miniature Tall Bearded, MTB, Median

- often called Table Iris
- early
- *16–27"*
- slender, graceful, undulating stem
- Branched, Blooms with TB
- 3-4" flowers

D. Intermediate Bearded, IB, Median

- early
- *16–27"* stiff, nonflexuous, well-branched stems, floriferous
- 4-5" flowers

- so named because it blooms between Talls and Standard Dwarfs
- diverse color patterns and forms, including Onco
- * see Tall Bearded

193

E. Standard Dwarf Bearded, SDB, Median

- very early
- may be branched or unbranched
- *8—15" tall, straight stems*
- 3-4" flower diameter
- many blooms per stalk

F. Miniature Dwarf Bearded, MDB

- earliest bloomer of all Bearded
- unbranched ideally
- sickleshaped foliage no taller than bloom

- *0—7" tall*
- flowers 2-3" but less than 2" is ideal
- * see chapter on MDB

G. Arils and Arilbreds

Oncocyclus

Regelias

Oncocyclus
- globular form
- signal spots
- circular segments
- *large flowers (4¼") standards larger than falls*
- bearded on falls, very heavily
- 8-28" tall, unbranched
- *early*

Regelias
- heavily veined or self color
- heavy beard on BOTH standards and falls
- bloom long, pointed at top and bottom
- flower parts long, pointed
- *early*

Arilbreds
- *may be branched*
- taller, up to 36" or more
- large flowers, some in excess of 8½"
- typical aril form, rather than bearded
- several flowers open per stalk
- *early*

2. BEARDLESS
H. Japanese

- *6—14" blooms*
- forms loosely grouped into singles, doubles, peony and Monstrosa, fanciful, no beards
- colors and patterns vary
- *15—60", but dwarf varieties being developed*
- blooms late spring, summer

I. Spuria

- orchid-like flowers with narrow, erect standards, oval falls, no beards
- blooms on short branchlets
- stems are dwarf up to 6 feet
- 3-6" blooms
- also called Butterfly Iris but Spuria preferred

J. Siberian

- erect stems
- *under 10" to over 48"*
- *foliage erect, grasslike, branching*
- general airy, light appearance
- size varies, falls may be 2" wide
- *5" max. bloom size*

K. Louisiana

- native to U.S.
- flexuous, graceful stalk
- *branching*
- *diverse form, flower size and height*

3. BULBOUS

L. Dutch and Spanish

- up to 30" stalk
- wiry stems
- Dutch well-known
- Spanish short-lived

M. English

- similar to Japanese in culture preferences

- wide falls, slender standards

N. Reticulata

- earliest bloomer of all Iris
- under 6"
- reed-like foliage
- both standards and falls upright

O. Other Iris

- varying height, forms
- bloom seasons vary

- includes Vesper, Crested, Roof, etc.

IRIS COLOR GLOSSARY

Note: The color of the standards is taken to be the background color.

SELF: An Iris all one shade, or tint of any color.

PLICATA: An Iris which has standards and falls of a self color, overlaid with stitching, stippling, veining or mottling.

BI-TONE: An Iris all of one color, but having the standards a lighter color than the falls.

BI-COLOR: An Iris having its standards one color and its falls another (If a signal, thumbprint or other mark occupies more than one-half the area of the falls, the Iris is listed as a Bi-Color).

BLEND: An Iris having an infusion or overlay over the basic color, self or other.

CM (Conspicuous Marking): An Iris on which conspicous marking signals, thumbprints, other) occupy less than one-half the surface of the falls.

CB (Constrasting Beard): An Iris on which the beard is contrasting and very prominent.

AMOENA: Any Iris having white or nearly white standards and *colored falls. Also reverse Amoena and Varigata*

NEGLECTA: Any Iris having standards of any shade of blue and falls of a much darker tone of the same hue.

FLOWER STRUCTURE DEFINITIONS

FALLS: Those three petals of the Iris flower which lie parallel to and below the three style arms. They are usually held lower on the flower than the other three petals, which are called standards.

STANDARDS: The three inner petals of an Iris flower. Usually upright in position and usually carried higher than the falls.

BEARD: On Iris of the Bearded section of the genus there is a characteristic beard on the haft of each fall. This may take the form of a thin line, a multiple row, or a large patch. It may appear to be hairy or furry. Sometimes it stops on the exposed portion of the haft, and sometimes it extends down into the heart of the flower.

BLADE: The widest portion of the standard or fall.

STYLE ARMS, CLAWS: protrusions on or above falls

CRESTS: The appendages just above the STIGMA on the STYLE ARMS.

SPECIES

Wild, native species, long ignored as too plain or common for the show bench are receiving more show space. HORTUS III lists many in addition to those on pages 194, 195, 196.

Long established guidelines for judging cultivar color and condition are applicable, but the major difference is in form where diversity reigns and cannot be over-emphasized. Extremes in size, shape and proportions which are verboten in cultivars must be accepted as worthy in species. Falls may twist or tuck ('Regal', Jap); standards reduce to tiny bristles ('Alaska Blue'); with signals rather than beard (I. verna). Moderate petal width and smaller flower size is typical of species compared to cultivars. Standards and falls may be on same plane, or standards may be semi or fully erect. Falls may be semi-flaring to drooping. Expect strappy petals, twisting, tucking, crowding, all at variance with cultivar criteria. Height, bud count, and branching vary. Stems may be thin, willowy (Spanish), reedlike (Reticulata), black (I. virginica); may really be long perianth tubes in shorter species while branching stems may reach 20" in others. Some dwarf species have little or no branching where a lone flower is typical, while others have very complex structures and several dozen flowers per stem.

Foliages are also different, i.e. Junos sometimes are called "cornstalk iris" because of wide, rippled leaves, and Xiphium foliage is typically folded, silvery. Colors vary, Californicae probably exhibit the greatest color range and pattern among beardless groups. Cal-Sibe hybrids (ex: 'Swirling Mist') exhibit these traits on more easily grown plants than Siberians.

Many Species are elegantly proportioned, others seem very inferior. Therefore, A.I.S. suggests classes for "Iris Ancestors" or even "Unidentified Wild Types" especially in bearded species. Judge species with respect and tolerance for diversity so all groups retain their individuality of size, form, color, pattern.

COMPARISON OF IDEALS FOR BEARDED IRIS

Iris Class	Height	Branching	Stem Diameter	No. of Buds	Flower Size	Bloom Season	Form of Flower
STB	Over 28 inches	three or more branches	proportioned to stem length and flower size	3-4 per branch 3-4 open	4 to 7" depending upon the variety	medium to late	similar form, three upright standards and three falls either flared, pendant or horizontal.
BB	16" to 27"	three or more branches	3/16" stiff, erect	2 per branch and 6 per stalk with 2-3 open	not exceed 4-6"	early to medium	
MTB		three or more	¼" or less at stalk bottom and ⅛" or less at flower base	2 per branch with 6 or more per stalk 2-3 open	2-3" no more than 6" overall	early	
IB		three or more	proportioned to stem length and flower size	2 per branch	4-5"	early	
SDB	8" to 15"	may or may not be branched	fine	2 or more terminal buds	3-4"	very early	
MDB	0-7"	un-branched	fine	1-2 terminal buds	under 2"	earliest	

MEDIANS — Flower must exceed 7-8" (measuring width plus height)

The chart indicates, not the average, but the IDEAL. Anything less than this IDEAL would be penalized with a reduction of points commeasurate with the degree. Qualities equal to or exceeding these ideals receive the full quota of points for that quality as listed on the scale for the class being judged.

198

Tall Bearded Iris

SUGGESTED CLASSES:

A. 1 Stalk

B. 3 Stalks, same variety

C. Collection, 5 different varieties, displayed in separate containers

SCALE OF POINTS FOR TALL BEARDED IRIS SPECIMEN

Flower	35	Stalk	30
. form	10	. number of open flowers	15
. color	10	. branch balance and bud	
. substance	10	placement	15
. size	5		
		Condition	35
		. cultural perfection	20
		. grooming	15

SCALE OF POINTS FOR TALL BEARDED IRIS COLLECTION

Condition	30	Flower form, color, size	25
Spectacle Value	20	Stalk, uniformity, branching	25

Flower Color

Iris have a most unusual color quality . . . a shimmering changeability under varying lights and positions which has given our language the word "irridescent". All Iris should be staged under adequate light.

Color standards are difficult to define because of the innumerable values of the more frequently occurring hues and because in many cases the true color of the variety in one locality or cultural environment may vary due to amounts of moisture, types and fertility of soil, amounts and intensity of sunlight and temperatures. A good Judge acquaints himself with the color **consistent** to the area.

The trend has been to favor bright, clear colors even on the Show Bench, but soft, subtle, muted colors should be encouraged also, and the Judge must put aside prejudice. Iris of certain colors . . . yellows, lavenders, blues and pinks seem to receive awards more frequently than others and Judges must be conscious of any tendency for preference, judging all qualities objectively.

Fading is not always objectionable. For example, pale blues that fade to pure white, medium blues that fade to pale blues or medium pinks that fade to pale pinks may retain their attractiveness, all other factors being equal; substance tells whether the fading is due to sunlight or age. But the typical listed color of a cultivar is always to be given credit.

Flowers that sunburn easily or fade poorly are objectionable. Fading is more usually a fault in reds, yellows, some browns and blends. Fading among dark colors may not be uniform and is sometimes accompanied by burning or water-spotting and must be penalized. Soil deficiencies (chlorosis) cause colors to be paler, washed out. Paleness or lack of depth that is streaky is penalized.

Texture should enhance color and is considered here. Extreme smoothness is the preference, especially on the haft. Texture veining over most of the flower, as in some of the Arilbreds or textural grooving below the beard, giving a pleated look, etc., may be considered a pleasing, desirable trait. Lined hafts ordinarily detract from the finished appearance of a TB.

Texture may be silky, smooth, or velvety as in Dominion breeding, crepey as in the 'CHANTILLY' variety or leather-like as in 'BEDDING BOUQUET'. Rough texture is rarely pleasing, therefore penalized.

Form

Iris flower form may be flared, horizontal or gracefully pendant, depending on the pose of the falls. No one form is superior to another except that the beauty of the flower must be enhanced and each part consistent with a particular form. One fall cannot flare while another on the same bloom, droops or is horizontal as might be caused by crowded blooms, defective development or mechanical damage. The parts must be uniform, whether flaring, horizontal or pendant. 'OLA KALA' normally holds its falls almost horizontal, while 'TECHNY CHIMES' tends to drop its falls considerably below the horizontal position. Yet neither should be penalized for this dissimilarity which is consistent with the ideal acceptable for TB Iris form.

Petals may be smoothly tailored, laced, ruffled, fluted, or crimped. Nobody expects a variety in which the petals are normally ruffled to be tailored or a "long-flowered" Iris to be flared, and to find such means that the specimen is either mislabeled or the form is abnormal.

The key to evaluating novelty forms with horns, spoons, flounces or additional petals is the retention of a balanced flower of pleasing proportions, uncrowded and with a typical "Iris" look. Many novelties lack form, colors are mediocre and branching high or bunched. The Judge must check these and other qualities and not be swayed by uniqueness.

The standards may vary according to variety from conical and closed to well-domed and touching or overlapping or held slightly agape. Such open standards are not necessarily a fault. They may be a pleasing feature if interesting center color contrast or uniquely designed style arms are revealed. Regardless of pose or shape, the standards must be strong, firmly held erect and should have a sturdy but not coarse midrib. They must not lean to one side or the other.

The falls also vary in shape and pose. They may be circular, pointed or triangular, but must never be "strappy" or shaped or hung like a hound dog's ear. Both haft and blade should be broad, smoothly spread, not pinched at haft or elsewhere. Pose of the falls may be gracefully pendant, or slightly to almost horizontally flared. To tuck under at the tip is a characteristic inconsistent with the ideal of a TB Iris.

There must be good proportion between size of standards and size of falls; standards may be larger than the falls or vice versa, but the flower as a whole should be symmetrical and well-balanced. If the substance is still firm, one can be reasonably sure the form is according to variety.

Below freezing conditions can cause deformed flower shapes, lacinations and other abnormal conditions. Form must be judged according to what is the **known** or normal form for the variety. A bloom in the first stages of closing or a partially open bud cannot receive full credit on form.

Substance

Substance is the quality of firmness or rigidity which enables the Iris to retain its characteristic form and symmetry and to retain color freshness and brilliancy. It is what makes the specimen seem alive though cut! Substance should be strong enough to keep the flower in good shape for at least 3 days; a Judge should give full consideration to flowers holding their shape and substance on the show bench.

The thickness or toughness of the standards and falls is influenced by varietal characteristics as well as climate, soil and other cultural conditions including fertilizers. Weak substance is indicated by blooms which crumple, tear, droop and are thinning at the edges. Falls sometimes have heavier substance than standards, and dark colors may have the heavier substance when compared to lights. Loss of substance usually shows first in the standards . . . they begin to sag and collapse. Blooms should never be touched or felt between the fingers to determine substance.

Size Of Flower

A Judge should not let a personal preference for either medium or large, full flowers influence valuation. Consideration is for what is normal for the variety not comparison to other Iris. In collections and multiple entry classes, uniformity of size and all other qualities are considered if all the specimens are of the same variety. In such mixed exhibits, the uniformity of stem length, condition and grooming are considered.

TB flower sizes normally range from 4-7", measured in width, not top to bottom. Extra points can be given if the grower has obtained extra size for a particular variety, if all other factors are equal. However, large size is not desirable if it weakens form and substance, or coarsens texture.

Number Of Open Flowers

The number of blooms varies with the variety, some may hold 15 or more buds. Three or more open blooms should receive full credit. Specimens showing two open blooms or one open bloom should receive approximately 12 points or 7 points respectively.

If the season is late or generally bad and all exhibits show less than three or four flowers, leniency is suggested. It is not enough to have five flowers open if those five are crowded together in a shapeless blob. Two, three or four well-spaced, well-angled flowers might present a better appearance and thus win after due consideration of other qualities.

The terminal bloom is usually the best the cyme will produce but its presence is not essential. In a late show, it is possible most specimens will lack the terminal bloom. A stem with three to four open flowers is superior to one or two open flowers, unless the latter are far superior in color, form, and other listed qualities.

Varietal traits, as well as advanced season and other factors also determine the profusion of bloom. Some will have four to five open at the same time, and others will naturally have no more than two or three. The Judge must be aware that the number of flowers open counts only 15 points against 85 for other qualities!

Branch Balance And Bud Placement

If the specimens are viewed from a distance before examining them in detail, one may stand out for quality. Refer to the sketch for typical branching form. Stems of TB are held stiffly erect, repeatedly and alternately branched. Spathes should be neat and inconspicuous.

The stalk, branching and bud placement are judged as a unit and according to variety. The stalk as a whole should give a well-balanced, alternating effect. The stalk should be sturdy, without bending, capable of holding up the heavy flower display. The stalk thickness and height should be pleasingly proportioned to flower size.

The first branch should be far enough below the terminal, so that its bloom does not crowd the terminal flower. Branches should be well-spaced along the stem and placed at such an angle as to allow each flower to open freely without crowding against another flower or the stem. Four-way or candelabra branching, with at least three well-placed branches of sufficient length, plus the terminal, alternately spaced along the stem, is ideal.

Top Branching

If a stalk rises up with no branching on the first 2/3 of its height this is referred to as top or high branching. Top branching is objectionable, but short branching of the pallida type is not necessarily so, if adequately spaced and long enough to hold the flowers away from the main stem so they are displayed to advantage without crowding. High branching may be caused by adverse weather conditions or a locality variation as well as varietal trait as in 'WABASH', for example.

Many Iris specimens are not cut tall enough to satisfactorily exhibit good branch balance and proportion. While a specimen lacking the top or terminal flower is acceptable, seldom does such a stalk present a pleasingly balanced appearance and so is penalized here.

Buds should be poised on the branch in such manner that they open without obscuring any part of any other flower. Twisted buds pressed to the stem are faulty in comparison to shapely, divergent buds.

Cultural Perfection

Here the Judge evaluates the effort, ability and knowledge of the exhibitor as a grower by the results he has achieved in the exhibit. The specimen should show no disease or insect damage, must be in prime, peak condition and fully mature; the flowers fresh and turgid. Cultural malpractice involves lack of attention to the plant's requirements as to environment, soil, food, humidity, division, staking, disease and pest control. Aphids and thrips disfigure flowers and stems. Improper growing conditions and lack of staking results in unbalanced stalks.

If a defect is due to rain or some such thing beyond human control, the Judge will be lenient providing all entries show the same difficulty. However, if some do and others do not, those which do are penalized accordingly.

The growers should be proud enough of their specimens to label them which aids the educational factor of the show. Labeling is required in official Iris Shows.

Condition, Grooming

Condition is based on the actual physical appearance of the specimen at the time of judging. A specimen with proper branching and five flowers open will be scored down here if it is limp, soiled, water-spotted, torn or bruised. Careful judging is required to determine how much should be removed in accordance with the damaged appearance.

Grooming involves the care taken before judging begins, to have the specimen present the best possible appearance. Faded, spent flowers are removed. The spathes should not be injured in the removal of a flower but folded neatly back over the scar. A specimen is not eliminated because of removed flowers, but points are taken off for broken or damaged buds or flowers not removed or any evidence of damage to flowers or other parts. Broken branches may be neatly cut off the main stem, but penalty would be assessed under branch balance and bud placement.

Spectacle Value Of Collections

Evaluate the general, collective beauty of the combination as shown by good proportion of the flowers in relation to each other and to their stalks. Judge the colors by individual perfection and the harmony of the combination when more than one variety is allowed or called for. Staging should be neat, effective, labels present, correct and neat. Clashing colors, impaired form and/or substance adversely affects spectacle value.

SUMMARY
Color 10 Points
May be soft, subtle, delicate or brilliant and intense
*clear *pure *patterns distinct *contrasts harmonious *blendings smooth
*attractive textural veining if present *plain haft *texture typically irridescent *glittering, scintillating *texture may be satiny or velvety, other

-unpleasant fading -spotting -sunburned -badly faded -uneven fading -dull -murky, impure -jarring contrasts -rough textured -veined, lined haft -lacks sheen, life

Flower Form 10 Points
Standards may be conical and close, or well-domed or touching, overlapping or slightly agape showing interesting interior
*firmly held *sturdy midrib *upstanding•*proportional

-weak -flopping open -tipping sideways -one or more collapsed -sagging -limply set, loose -coarse midrib

Falls may be circular or pointed or triangular. May be gracefully pendant or flared or slightly flared or almost horizontal
*proportional *same size, length *same amount of angle

-strappy, doggy -hanging limp -too long -tucking under at ends

Haft & Blade
*broad *smoothly spread *proportional *sprightly

-haft pinched -parts not in proportion

Overall
*all parts well balanced *symmetrical *overall voluptuous look *faultless

-overall form inconsistent -unbalanced -lacks symmetry -irregular placement of any part

Substance 10 Points
*strong *crisp *fresh *jaunty *most perfect phase of possible beauty *pleasing finish *lots of "starch"

-coarse -wilting -thinning -shrinking -limp -crumpled -overage -sagging standards due to substance loss -papery

Flower Size 5 Points — 4-7"
*above average for variety *typical *proportioned to stalk, stem, parts maximum potential in all parts

-below average -dwarfed -abnormal -oversize -overblown -ungainly

Number of Open Flowers: 3-4 open with some buds is ideal. 15 Points
*more than normal *typical

-less than accepted standard -scant -deduct 5-8 points for only one open

Branch Balance, Bud Placement 15 Points
*alternating *well balanced *branches well spaced *candelabra branching *branches sufficient length *buds and flowers well poised *spathes neat, inconspicuous *stem cut long enough to display good branch balance *sturdy *proportioned *stem stiffly erect

-stem "snaked," crooked -stem weak, bending -spathes ragged -one-sided branching -flowers crowded -bunched placement -high or top branching -awkward branching -branches too short -branches too widely held -branches overly long, off balance -buds twisted -buds pressed to stem -toed-in branching

Cultural Perfection 20 Points

*thrifty *vigorous appearance *disease and pest free *well-grown *labeled

-unthrifty appearance -stunted -disease or pest evidence -unhealthy appearance -disfigured stalks (aphids) -disfigured blooms (thrips) -curved or bent, crooked stems (failure to stake, other)

Condition, Grooming 15 Points

*unmarred *prime *clean *spent flowers carefully removed *spathes neatly refolded

-overmature -undermature -broken -bedraggled -spent -damaged parts -blemished -soiled -scarred -bruised -foreign matter present -disfigured -wind-weather damaged

Spectacle Value . . . Collection

*attractive overall appearance *well staged in appropriate container or containers *harmonious color combination *labeling present, neat, appropriate

-jarring colors -poorly staged (leaning, poor container selection) -lacks labeling -labeling poor -incorrect

Median

Median classifications include

STANDARD DWARF BEARDED	SDB
INTERMEDIATE BEARDED	IB
MINIATURE TALL BEARDED	MTB (Table)
BORDER BEARDED	BB

Medians are small-scaled Iris which normally grow taller than the 10" of the Miniature Dwarf, but less than the 28" of the Tall Bearded. These 'half-way' Iris are divided into the above four classes according to height, bloom season.

Emphasis in exhibition judging is on awardable qualities that distinguish these from Tall Bearded Iris. Extraordinary color is not enough to win recognition. All judging should be against standards of perfection as outlined for each class. Misclassified specimens should not be considered for awards. Specimens which are coarse or oversized are eliminated from consideration for awards.

Most Medians are particularly responsive to various climatic and food growth factors which affect not only height but also size and color of bloom, branching and substance. Such variances cause confusion, a Judge should be cognizant of what is typical and normal growth behavior for an area and penalize accordingly.

Colors and forms may be varied, including species, Onco and Regelia influences. Small flowers require slender stems, shorter lengths and larger flowers require heavier stems and longer lengths for good proportions.

Standard Dwarf Bearded SDB   NOTE: Refer to page 213 footnote. *

Suggested Entry:
A- 3 stalks 1 variety
B- 3 stalks, assorted varieties
C- Potted

Because a single specimen of SDB looks insignificant, three stalks as one entry is encouraged. Height range 10-15". Flowers 3-4" across; stalks branched or unbranched.

Scale for SDB

Flower
. proportion, scale, size 15
. color 15
. form 10
. substance, texture 10
Stalk
. scale, proportion, size,
  branching 10
. number of buds 5

Condition   F
. grooming 15
. cultural perfection 10
. age of bloom 10

Haft striations are objectionable under color. Slightly open standards are not objectionable if the effect is pleasing. Branches, if present, should hold the flowers at nearly the same level as the terminal flowers, spaced to avoid bunching. Successive bloom should rise a bit higher to present a clean appearance. Flowers should be above the foliage and the foliage should be fine, erect and true green in the potted plants. All parts must be well-proportioned to other parts. Overall appearance must be one of slender, refined charm.

When judging multiple specimen entries of one variety, uniformity of all factors is considered. In judging assorted varieties, uniformity of stem lengths, condition, grooming, distinction and color harmony are considered.

INTERMEDIATE BEARDED

Suggested Entry: Same as Tall Bearded

Flower—maximum 40 points
. proportion—flower parts to each
  other and size of bloom to
  stalk. Typical of variety   10
. color—clear, clean, typical
  of variety   10
. form—best variety can
  produce, fully open, no
  malformation or tears   10
. substance—crisp, firm,
  evaluate at time of judging
  as is   10

Stalk—maximum 25 points
. proportion—diameter and
  height in scale to flower,
  typical   10
. branching—well spaced, no
  bunching, bloom balanced   10
. number of open blooms—3
  open, or 2 open plus well
  formed bud   5

Condition—maximum 35 points
. grooming—clean, spent or
  damaged flowers, buds,
  branches removed   15
. cultural perfection—absence
  of disease, insects; well grown
  but not overgrown   10
. age of bloom—fully opened,
  fresh, peak condition   10

MINIATURE TALL BEARDED (Table)
Suggested Entry: Same as Tall Bearded
SCALE OF POINTS FOR MTB

Flowers	50	Stalk	35
. scale, proportion, size	20	. scale, proportion, size	10
. color	10	. branching	10
. form	10	. floriferousness	5
. substance	5	. condition, grooming	5
. texture	5	. freshness	5
Conformance to Class	10	Distinction	5

MTB

These Iris are miniature replicas of Tall Bearded Iris in size, proportions and conformation, the whole plant must be relatively small in proportion throughout. Standards for flower size and stalk height are very rigid, so conformance to class is given 10 points in MTB scales. Proportion is of crucial importance.

Ideal bloom stalk height is 15-25". Flowers no larger than 6" overall combined dimensions (height plus width). Stalks slender, wiry, graceful.

A wide variety of form is encouraged, the standards may touch, overlap, be erect or gaping to reveal contrasting style arms, giving an air of jaunty charm. Falls may be down-hanging or slightly to horizontally flaring; either rounded or triangular shaped. Color breaks are encouraged, veined patterns must be sharp and clearly defined. Yellow standards with falls marked with violet or violet with white are undesirable.

Stem

A straight stiff stem or one with high branching is undesirable. The stem must be branched as in the Standard Talls with numerous buds, three or more branches with two or three buds per socket. Seven to nine buds is ideal, six is the minimum, penalize for less.

The stem should have a diameter of $\frac{1}{4}$" or less at the base of the flower stalk, tapering to 3/16th of an inch or less, to $\frac{1}{8}$ of an inch or less at the base of the flower. Coarseness is indicated, for instance, if dimensions are 5/16th" to $\frac{1}{4}$ to $\frac{1}{8}$" plus. The stem should be wiry, slender and graceful.

BORDER BEARDED BB
Suggested Entry: Same as Tall Bearded
SCALE FOR BORDER BEARDED

Flower	50	Stalk	25
. scale, proportion, size	20	. scale, proportion, size	10
. color	10	. branching	10
. form	10	. floriferousness	5
. substance	5		
. texture	5		
		Condition	10
Class Conformance	10	. grooming	5
Distinction, labeling	5	. freshness	5

Proportion in judging Border Bearded iris is of utmost importance, but proportions are larger than that of Miniature Tall Bearded in both flower size and bloomstalk thickness. Height range, 15-28". Flowers mostly 4-6" across. Stalks stiffly erect, branched, sometimes clubby.

The stems are held stiffly erect, ideally with 3 branches and 2 buds per socket may be expected and 2 to 3 open blooms in prime condition. A flat flared flower form, giving short measurement in height and greater breadth is not necessarily ideal in Border Bearded; a non-flaring form, measured only in width, giving a smaller measure is not superior. For more accuracy a steel tape hoop is used and width plus height of flower is totaled. Border Irises usually have good substance because of their compact structure.

The normal Tall Bearded size bloom on a short stem, regardless of beauty of the individual flowers, should not get awards in the Border classes. A flower that belongs on a 40" stalk is too large for a 27" stalk . . . it lacks proportion and balance.

Qualities Applicable to All Medians

FLOWER PROPORTION, SCALE, SIZE. Refer to scale for each for number of points. Proportion of all Medians is of utmost importance and must be given discerning consideration. Small flowers require slender stems and neat foliage in keeping with small plants. Large flowers on short, slender stems or small flowers on thick stems are faults.

The Iris flower should be symmetrical regardless of its shape or the shapes of its individual parts or its size. Each part should be in proportion to each other . . . standards to falls, flower size to height and slenderness of stem.

Size of flower figured only on diameter is misleading as a horizontal form will measure more than a flaring to pendant form. Generally, a measurement of width plus height which exceeds 5-6" will be penalized in Medians.

Color

Many hues are represented and they vary widely in brilliance and vividness, ranging from very delicate, soft and subtle to intense and vivid. Marking, pattern and contrast variations should always produce a harmonious effect. Colors should be pure, and clear with typical irridescent texture.

Form

Form involves the concept of a pleasing, standard shape. No attempt should be made to dictate a single perfect form as being horizontal or flared or other. For low-growing Iris which are usually seen from above, flaring form may be preferable, while for taller varieties a partially drooping form is less objectionable. Form variations often add to distinction. If the substance is still good, the Judge can be reasonably sure that the form is according to variety.

Hafts that are too wide may detract from an impression of daintiness in Miniature Tall Bearded and Standard Dwarf Bearded and are penalized. Bloom should be at the most perfect phase of its possible beauty, fully opened, not collapsing.

Substance and Freshness

In an Iris Show held during normal Tall Bearded season, Judges should show leniency in judging Intermediate and Standard Dwarf classes which have been refrigerated in order to exhibit after their normal blooming time. The grower should not be penalized for trying to assist the promotion and comparative study of Medians. The flower, however, must have sufficient substance to retain characteristic form and symmetry. Darker blooms sometimes have greater substance. The average flower should last at least three days.

Stalk

The bloom stalks should be strong enough to carry the normal complement of open flowers for the particular class being judged. The Judge should not penalize a Miniature Tall Bearded for slender stem when this is characteristic. The stems must be in pleasing proportion to the size and shape of the flowers. Overall appearance of all Medians must be one of slender refinement.

Branching

Branches, if present, should hold the flowers at angles to avoid bunching. See branching sketches.

Distinction

Any loss of daintiness means a loss of distinction in the low-growing, small-flowered types. Daintiness may be visually reduced by a heavy look imparted to dark variegated types that have ruffled or laced edges. Such colored flowers often look more petite in tailored (plain edged) form.

Staging in appropriately sized bottles with appropriately sized openings so the exhibits stand erect makes the show more attractive and reduces the chances of bruising or breaking if tipped or touched, as well as making the judging easier. Foliage must not be jammed into the neck of the bottle too large for the stalk, as the Judge is permitted to take the specimen out of water to examine the size and length of the stem in the Median classes.

SUMMARY

Color

*clear *pattern distinct *blendings smooth *contrasts harmonious *bright *markings clean *neat *stable *indelible

-dull -murky -unpleasant -jarring contrasts -haft markings, striations -wind marked (reds particularly) -wishy washy

Form

Standards may be domed, arched, slightly open
Falls may be pendant, or slightly to horizontally flaring; round or triangular
*symmetrical *typical for variety

-narrow, strappy falls -tucked falls -pinched hafts -droopy -standards twisting -standards collapsed -immature -haft too wide

Substance

*strong *pleasing finish *crisp *perky *fresh

-coarse -wilting -thinning -shrinking -limp -transparent

Texture

*smooth *glistening *fine *silky

-crepey -grainy -crinkled -dull -rough

Condition and Grooming

*unmarred *clean *disease and pest free

-bedraggled -torn -broken -bruised -soiled

Stalks   Proportion, Scale, Size

SDB
fine
wiry
slender

IB
stems stiff
non-flexuous
straight
slender

MTB
slender, wiry
flexuous
graceful, undulating, curved
not exceeding ¼" at cut base

BB
stiffly erect
sometimes typically clubbv

*spathes neat *spathes inconspicuous *well proportioned to flower

-heavy -weak -twisted -too short -too tall -bent -thick -stubby -floppy

Branching

See ideal Bearded Chart for comparisons
*bloom sequence balanced *well spaced *well placed

-crowded -lack of ideal branching -bunched -stubby -high branching

Floriferousness

Refer to Ideal Bearded Chart for general comparison and to official classification for individual varieties.
*more than expected

-less than accepted standard

Distinction

*interesting variation (ruffling, lacing, other) *superior quality in all parts *unusual bloom season or rebloom characteristic *fragrant *unique color break *labeled *well staged

-plain -substandard -poorly staged -falls short in any quality

Conformance to Class

*easy fit to all class requirements

-does not conform or is misclassified . . . eliminate from award competition in both instances

Miniature Dwarf

SUGGESTED CLASSES:

A- 3 Blooms 1 variety
B- 3 Blooms Assorted varieties and colors
C- Potted Plant in Bloom

Separate scales are proposed for Dwarfs which are more in accord with modern objectives and dwarf characteristics, such as no branching, dainty flower size as well as height which are the determining factors in Dwarf Iris.

Miniature Dwarf Iris plants do not measure more than 10" according to the American Iris Society standards. The Dwarf Iris Society measurement, based on botanical classification, states "seldom attaining 12", however the official 10" height is used herein.

The stems ideally are unbranched with one or two terminal blooms, not over 3" wide, 2" or less is ideal. The overall impression must be one of petite daintiness and miniature charm.

If multiple branching is present, the specimen is blooming later than normal season and exceeds 3" the specimen is disqualified as an MDB.

It is suggested that classes be set up for potted blooming plants. Normally Miniature Dwarf Iris bloom the earliest of all Bearded Iris. Because a single specimen of MDB may look insignificant, 3 stalks as one entry is encouraged. When judging such multiple entries uniformity of all the qualities must be considered if the schedule requests one variety. If assorted varieties are requested or allowed, uniformity of bloomstalk length, condition and grooming are considered.

SUGGESTED SCALE FOR DWARF IRIS SPECIMEN

Flower	60	Stalk, Branching (if typical)	15
· color	25	Height (0–7")	10
· form (flaring, domed)	15	Stem	5
· substance	10	Condition, Grooming	10
· fragrance	5		
· texture	5	Uniformity	5
Uniformity	5		

SUGGESTED SCALE OF POINTS FOR POTTED PLANTS DWARF IRIS

Flowers	65	Plant	35
. color	20	. cultural perfection	15
. size	20	vigor, including stem, foliage, condition, grooming	
. form	10	. inflorescence	10
. substance	10	flowers in relation to foliage (not buried)	
. fragrance	5	. floriferousness	10

Color

Color patterns include spots, borders, contrasting beards, self-beards, halo-ed beards, selfs and veination. Ideal spot pattern, if present, is a solid spot with sharply defined margin on falls, not weak or diluted.

The color is important in these wee plants, clarity and purity being the goal. The color should have carrying power since the blooms are small and limited to one or two per stalk, though on plants there will be a number of stalks in bloom at once.

Some cultivars, 'BUTTERBALL' for instance, change color according to conditions being yellow-orange turning to chartreuse during rainy periods. In 'GAY LASSIE', 'SNOW FAIRY', 'CHERRY SPOT' and others, coloration also varies with weather and soil. Such variations in color are often **consistently** caused by climate and soil conditions peculiar to the locality. This fact should be recognized by the Judges and judged according to what is **typical** and **normal** for the locality.

Where multiple colors appear in the blooms, the effect must be harmonious and pleasing, anything less is deductible. In multiple entries of assorted colors, care must have been taken in the selection of the colors of individual stalks which harmonize with each other.

Size

A Miniature Dwarf Bearded Iris without daintiness is devoid of charm and pleasing "personality". Size, proportion and scale are of utmost importance and must be given discerning consideration when evaluating MDB as the whole concept of these tiny flowers is based on their miniature appearance which ideally is less than 10" high and with flowers 2-3" wide. Any variation from these ideals is to be penalized commensurate with the degree.

Form

For MDB Iris, which are usually seen from above, a flaring form is preferable to a drooping form. Due to rapid and hybridal changes, form may be unique as in 'CUP AND SAUCER'. Any form known not to be abnormal within the experience of the Judges shall be deemed typical. Slightly open standards are permissible if they reveal interesting color or design of style arms.

Substance

This may vary with locality and cultural conditions. Falls usually have more substance than standards. Flowers should have sufficient substance to retain characteristic form and symmetry. Lack of substance is first evidenced in the softening of the standards and thinning of the edges.

STALK Height, Proportion

Height is probably the most undependable characteristic upon which to base a standard as it varies with the season, climate, culture and weather. A variety (e.g. 'PROMISE') which normally has a height of 5-6" may grow to over 12" in a neighboring yard or another season.

So to arrive at any specifications for height, it must be indicated as what is "normal" . . . that which SELDOM attains 12", which is an approximation.

A false impression of squatness and poor bloom proportion is given cut specimens when dropped to the neck in a container. Displaying in containers filled with commercial products (vermiculite, plastic foam, other) helps Miniature and Standard Dwarf Iris appear in better proportion and is easier to judge without handling.

Height of potted or garden plants is measured as the distance between the soil and the highest part of the plant at time of blooming, whether bloom or leaf is the highest point. Bloomstalks should hold flowers just above the tips of the foliage.

Stalk

Where Tall Bearded furnish only one bloom stalk from a single rhizome, and this bloom stalk has lateral branching to provide a number of flowers carried high and free; in dwarf pumila, a single rhizome will grow many stalks, each with a terminal bud, thus profuse bloom is obtained by an entirely different method other than the branching of the TB. The MDB in full bloom of terminal buds practically hides the foliage and if the side branching flowers are forced to bloom down among the thick and compact clusters of leaves and bloom stalks a messy appearance and malformed flowers would be the undesirable results.

Typical MDB Iris are thus without branching, but instead have terminal buds. In order to maintain this class of Iris according to type character, the undesirable trait must be discouraged, by outright elimination as not a true MDB or a reduction of points commensurate with the fault.

Single and terminal bud clusters are typical while terminal and lateral branching are **not.** Where a single stalk with a single terminal bloom would be penalized in a TB, this is typical of a Miniature and marks a major difference between the two types of Iris.

---

* STANDARD DWARF BEARDED: Page 206. Crosses of the miniature dwarf I. Pumila. Sometimes called Lilliput. Have as many as 7 bloom stems per rhizome, each stem having 2-3 flowers. Blooms after the MDB. From their tall ancestors they inherit the full bloom form and more buds and branches per stem. From their miniature ancestors they have distinctive color not found in other bearded iris.

ILLUSTRATIONS SHOWING BUD PLACEMENT VARIATIONS

Sketch 1 and 2: Ideal

Sketch 1 shows a stalk with a single terminal bud, enclosed in its individual spathe valve

Sketch 2 shows a stalk with two buds enclosed in a single terminal cluster and spathe valves

Sketch 3: Penalize

Sketch 3 shows 2 spathe valves at different levels on the stalk with a short piece of stem between them. By strict ruling this is branching of a terminal form rather than lateral branching. Such variations of the terminal cluster should be penalized but less heavily than the following

Sketch 4: Penalize Severely

Sketch 4 shows 2 buds in the terminal as is ideal, but has in addition a distinct lateral branch. There can be no question that this is undesirable branching

Sketch 5: Eliminate

Sketch 5 shows definite lateral branching

SUMMARY
Color

*neat color patterns *clear *brilliant *smooth blendings *has carrying power *fresh *immaculate white *neat, even border *has depth *neat spot *beard cleanly contrasting *beard harmonious *beard well proportioned *exact border *texture fine, glistening

-dull -weak, diluted -uneven -thin -blurred border -harsh -streaks badly -coarse, crepey texture

Form
*symmetrical *well-balanced *standards well domed or arched or overlapping, touching *falls may flare or be horizontal *falls broad, wide without sacrificing daintiness *smoothly tailored *finished appearance *leaves nothing to be desired *beards neat

-narrow parts -falls tucked under -elongated petals -petals too narrow at haft -doggy -droopy, hanging falls -ragged -crowded -standards too short -standards collapsing -standards and falls too long -haft rough

Substance
*crisp *pert *heavy *typical

-thin -relaxing -curling -limp -wilting

Fragrance
*sweet *definite *penetrating

-faint -lacking

Stalk
*good proportion to bloom size *cut long enough to display specimen bloom properly *cut to uniform length for multiple specimen exhibits *bloom well posed *slender *sturdy *neat spathes, tightly wrapped *valves inconspicuous

-too short in proportion to flower size -too long -weak -not uniform length (multiple exhibit) -too heavy -coarse -spathes ragged, out of proportion -valves prominent -spindly

Terminals
*terminal blooms *terminal bloom cluster *well carried *good stance

-terminal branching present -lateral branching present (eliminate) -crowded -twisted -bloom cluster variations

Condition and Grooming
*fresh appearing *clean *disease and pest free *malpractice free

-soiled -aged -spent -marred -torn petals -bruised -disfigured

POTTED PLANTS OR GARDEN GROWN
Foliage
*often curved or sickle shaped *narrow *neat *short (blooms must be carried above) *proportional *graceful

-foliage rising above flowers -overpowering flowers -too wide -coarse -diseased -browned, withered tips (Soft Rot) -blighted -too long

Floriferousness
*numerous enough to give nice color effect *profuse *plentiful

-predominance of green leaves -scanty number of blooming stalks

Vigor
*increasing *healthy *disease free *thrifty

-straggly -unhealthy appearance -blemished

Arils and Arilbred Iris

Arils include Oncocyclus, Regelia and hybrids of such species. Arils are so named for the light colored collar on the seed. Aril Medians and Dwarfs are appearing. The Judge cannot expect to judge these types by the same standards of color, form, branching and proportion as Tall Bearded. Pure arils will have only one to two blooms per stem, unbranched. Stems are generally short, ranging in height from 6" to 20" according to type, variety and culture.

	Oncocyclus Species, True Hybrids	Regelia Species True	Hybrids	Arilbreds
Flower				
. form	20		15	—
. color	10		10	15
. substance, midrib	10		10	10
typical type . characteristics	15		10	25
Size	10		10	10
Number of buds	—	1, 2 or 3	10	—
Stem	10	12"-24"	10	Stalk branching 15
Culture	15		15	15
Condition, Grooming	10		10	10

Oncocyclus:

Colors include selfs, bitones, blends and delicate or strong veining may be present. Some color patterns are dotted or stippled. Signal patches are present in some species. Color clarity, pattern clearness and prominent contrasted signal patches should be rated highly.

Form is globular, often with prominent, attractive style arms. Unicellular beards are broad, diffuse and prominent on the falls only. Standards are very broad, nearly circular, strongly arched or domed and usually much larger than the falls. (4½" across)

Falls are broad, nearly circular, may be recurved or slightly flaring. (3") It is these things which give Oncos their exotic, globular appearance.

Stalks are strong, straight, unbranched with a single terminal bloom. Height of the stalk is 8-28" with the average about 20" and is often influenced by culture and climate. Hybrids may have some branching. A 4½" x 3" bloom on the top of a 20" stem may look out of proportion when considered in the same light as used in judging Tall Bearded and so these standards cannot be applied.

Regelia, Hybrids and Crosses

Colors patterned on white or colored backgrounds include conspicuously veined patterns, blends in most species and self-colors in the hoogiana types, noted for their lustrous, satiny texture which should be penalized if rough and coarse. The unicellular beards are more narrow, colorful, well-displayed and prominent and appear on both standards and falls in all but one species . . . the Korolkowii.

The bloom is typically pointed or triangular with conical standards and long, narrow falls, sometimes meeting in a point around the stem — an elongated "arrowhead" overall effect. The margins of the petals may be nearly smooth, waved or ruffled. The falls should not pinch at the haft.

The stalk 12-24" though the average is about 20" and may be branched or unbranched with 2-3 terminal blooms placed close together, but which open at intervals rather than all at once. The stems must be straight and strong. Regelia and Oncocyclus crosses have incredible colors, beards, signal veining, dotting, and colorful style arms. The stalks vary from 7 to 20", fairly strong, though may be a bit too slim for the bloom size. The stalk may bear 4-5 flowers. The flowers show characteristics of both species.

Arilbreds

Includes a confusing complex involving crosses within species, with other species and with the resulting hybrids. In show classification, if an Arilbred does not show strong aril character, it should be entered in the appropriate True-Bearded class which fits its height, i.e., median, tall, other. The bloom in the Arilbred classes must be distinguishable from that of the true-bearded types.

Ideally such iris form should be extremely large, boldly rounded. Beards are huge, wide, colored. Some are fragrant. The style arms should be large, long and are often lacy, extending out over the falls or upright. The falls are broad, either flared or pendant and in some cases carry a signal spot. Falls may roll under or curve outward, but the test is balance. Standards should be domed and have broad, strong midribs. Substance must be heavy, strong. Stalks are generally strong, and with 5-8 blooms with adequate branching according to breeding. Bloom sizes are often in excess of 8". Colors clear or muted, unusual, veined, etc.

In an effort to clarify data a number of groupings have been made, Group Number ABIII, involving the famous Mohr family, is the most generally known and most widely grown and all too often, because of the influence of the more dominant True-Bearded traits, they come close to having lost characteristic 'aril' attributes.

The ideal objective, according to knowing irisarians, is to have aril-like blooms, with if possible the oncocyclus signal spot and with bearded-type branching, plants, disease resistance and floriferousness.

ARILS

SUMMARY: ARILS AND ARILBRED

Arils have typically short stems; are typically non-branching; have typically reflexed or rolled-under falls; have typically open standards (must be erect).

Oncos and Regelias should be judged in separate classes.

Beardless: Japanese Iris

SUGGESTED CLASSES: Same as Tall Bearded

SUGGESTED SCALE OF POINTS

Flower	80	Flower Stalk	15
Form and Size	30	. branching	10
Color	25	. height	5
. clarity	12		
. harmony	8	Condition	5
. novelty	5		
Substance	5	. cultural perfection	3
Texture	5	. grooming	2
Distinction	15		

FLOWER: Form and Size 30 Points

The size varies from three to twelve inch blooms and the form is also diverse. The form of a Japanese Iris is the most important feature and there are an unlimited number of possible forms. All types of form including the present-day singles, doubles, peony and fanciful and any other forms that may appear in the future should possess pleasing proportions, refinement and beauty. The value of the arrangements of the various parts is in direct proportion to their distinction. The forms are grouped into four types, single, double, peony and monstrosa (fanciful).

SINGLE (three petal flowers) may vary from those with petals held reflexed, forming a more or less ball-shape, through those with pendant or flaring to horizontal form. Petals may be of varying widths and shapes from narrow to broad over-lapping. The three standards are of varying sizes and lengths and may be held upwardly, or flaring or the shorter forms may combine with the styles to form a cup shape in the center of the flowers. Drooping is considered a defect.

DOUBLE (six or more petals) have forms ranging from a deeply convex shape through flaring, or stiffly horizontal to saucer or flaring cup shape with preponderance of the convex-shaped varieties.

PEONY (six or more petals) heavily ruffled. Double and peony types of nine to twelve or more petals have no standards. In these types the standards have been transformed into petals.

MONSTROSA (Fanciful) are those in which the styles or stamens, or both (which may be more than the three normal for Japanese Iris) are partly or wholly transformed into petaloids and which are sometimes arranged in an interesting pattern such as rosettes in the center of the flowers.

The form of all types must be symmetrical; any flower lacking symmetry will be penalized commensurate with the degree of fault.

The form should possess pleasing proportions and refinement. The flower parts must be evenly, uniformly and symmetrically placed, i.e., the spacing between each petal should be approximately the same width or penalty is the result. The petals must be of regular length and width with the exception of the Monstrosa forms. The proportion and balance of all the parts must form a pleasing ensemble which possesses character and charm. No one form should be taken as the only correct one, each is judged on its own merit.

Color 25 Points
Clarity 12 points
Whether the color is solid or a blend or any combination, the distinction of the markings, pleasing arrangement of the color pattern and delicacy and refinement of the lighter valued patterns are essential features. The patterns should be distinct and fading or smearing is penalized. The color must be clear, not murky, clouded or spiritless, dismal or dull; and the markings must not be blurred. A degree of smokiness is allowable if it lends attractiveness to the flower and in such instances should not be penalized.

Harmony 8 points
Where more than one color appears in the flower, the effect must always be harmonious and pleasing. The various colors of the flower should associate well together and complement each other without violent or jarring contrasts. As breaks appear, the Judge must exert his color training to ascertain the color harmony merits.

Patterns of color which will be inspected for harmony, novelty and clarity include:

(1) splashing as is sometimes present on the standards.

(2) blending which occurs on the petals as a halo of color surrounding the signals and extending to a greater or lesser degree over the petals.

(3) veining, white or colored, which may be normal width or more narrow or broad than usual and which may radiate in varying lengths on the petals.

(4) sanding which may form a light or heavy, but uniform blending or striated deposit between the veins and/or on the styles.

(5) sippling which is a finer grained deposit of color than sanding and consists of minute dots.

(6) dappling which consists of spots of color and may occur in varying sizes from mere flecks to more or less prominent marbling and may extend throughout the entire flower, including the styles, forming a self-colored flower.

(7) edging, the standards generally though not always have a more or less prominent edging of white or color and the petals may have an edging of white extending throughout the flower, varying from hairline to a more prominent feature.

Novelty 5 points

Consists of "entirely new and uncommon features"; some color change which is interesting, new or novel gains points under novelty. But unless the change is pleasing and adds beauty, it does not add to the distinction of the specimen and therefore should suffer point reduction.

Substance 5 Points

Substance may be starchy or more light and filmy but should be consistent with the form and sufficiently heavy to maintain the flower's normal form for the duration. If substance is light and filmy, this feature should contribute to the particular shape or character of the flower. The same must be found if the substance is starchy.

Texture 5 Points

If velvety or satiny, it should possess richness and depth. Other types of surface quality i.e., organdy-like, fragile, should possess delicacy and refinement.

Distinction 15 Points

Distinction is that quality which sets a particular flower apart as being superior because of the excellence of all its parts. Distinction may also be imparted by any unique color break, interesting form variation or some other admirable characteristic that makes the specimen stand out and adds to the general beauty.

Superiority of any or all of the qualities listed in the Scale must be evident in a specimen which receives full recognition for distinction.

STALK   15 Points

Branching 10 points

The stalk should have a minimum of two branch placements, preferably more. The branches should be well spaced and long enough so the buds and flowers are not clustered or crowded.

Each branch should present at least two buds. One open flower on a stalk at a time is normal for Japanese Iris. The stem should be strong, erect and stiff-necked enough to hold up the bloom it is bearing and must be in a diameter which is proportioned to that of the bloom. The perianth tubes must be sturdy.

Height 5 points

The height of the stem should have been cut to be in proportion to the size of the flower, which ranges anywhere from three to twelve inches. A three inch flower on a three foot stem would obviously be out of proportion. The stem must be long enough to adequately show the branching.

CONDITION   5 Points

The specimen must present evidence in all its parts that it has had the proper care and attention during its growing. Its parts must be unmarred, clean and turgid. Spent flowers should have been removed and the spathe valve carefully folded back into place. The label should be carefully attached and well printed.

SUMMARY

Form and Size 30 Points

*well proportioned in all parts *well balanced *typical of type (i.e., double, fanciful, etc.) *symmetrical

-bunched or crowded -drooping -lop sided

Color 25 Points

*clear *attractive *clearly defined *distinct *pleasing, harmonious combinations *unexpected *novel

-faded -murky -spiritless -dull -patterns blurred -unpleasant combinations -variations of pattern, combinations lacks beauty, refinement -indefinite

Substance 5 Points

*may be light and filmy or more starchy according to variety *consistent *firm *tough

-limp -wilting -droopy -thinning -shriveling -flabby

Texture 5 Points

*fine *rich *depth *delicate

-coarse -rough -varying

Distinction 15 Points

*superior in some or several qualities *interesting new color or form

-substandard -falls short in a number of qualities

Stalk 15 Points

Branching: *two or more branches *well spaced *flowers well poised *one bloom typical *of sufficient length *erect *well proportioned to flower size

Height: *shows proper branching *proper length in proportion to flower size
-cut too short or too long for flower size -not long enough to show branching

Condition 5 Points

*thrifty *disease, pest free *clean *labeled

-unhealthy appearance -soiled -spent floret still retained -stained -bruised -torn petals -unlabeled -spathe valves carelessly handled

Siberian

SUGGESTED CLASS: Same as Tall Bearded

SUGGESTED SCALE OF POINTS

Flower	25	Stalk	20
. color, texture, haft pattern	10	. branching, angle bud placement, stem slenderness, attractive bracts, foliage	
. form	10		
. substance	5		
· horticulture quality (grooming)	20	*Overall Effect*	35
		. grace	15
		· proportions	10
			20
		. individuality	10

Form

A diversity of shapes is expected. The standards stand erect, projecting triangular stigmas. They may be broad and rounded, or short, narrow and erect, or they may form a "double" in which the standards lie down in the manner of the Japanese type making a wide flat flower.

The falls should be broad and may be gracefully down-hanging or flaring or stand out horizontally. Any appearance of looseness or irregular development is penalized.

Color

New color patterns and types are desirable and should be rewarded. Hafts bear veination and an interesting pattern should result. Colors should have clarity with patterns and markings distinct. Clarity and intensity of color should be stressed.

Colorful bracts, stems and leaf bases are desirable qualities except when they clash with delicate flower color. Bracts and spathes should not be dry or fade before the bloom does. A lack of clarity, and any fading is to be penalized.

Size and Proportion

The flowers should give a delicate, light and airy appearance, rather than a heavy, floppy effect. Bloom size varies. It should be reasonably in proportion to the stalk. Coarse, over-large or heavy appearing flower size should be penalized. A maximum Siberian size (5") can appear graceful if it's substance is light, has a wide, flaring form and is poised on a tall, slender stalk. Three or four such flowers carried on one stalk, may appear and behave in a top-heavy manner. Flowers near three inches are well proportioned to stalks of medium height and to stalks with two well-placed side branches.

Substance

Substance in Siberians should be firm enough to hold the bloom for several days, yet be soft enough to flutter charmingly in the breeze. Tissue-paper thinness or cardboard stiffness is to be penalized, as well as any indication of thinning or wilting due to age, lack of moisture, others.

Stalk

The stems are erect, fine, almost dainty though measuring from 10 to 48" tall. Lateral branching is preferable to lack of branches. These should be well positioned along the upper one half of the stem. Where there are two branches, the top one should be about one-third down from the top, the second about one-third below the first. They should be well positioned along the upper one half of the stem. The angle of branching is as important to the pleasingly balanced appearance as the branch placement. Branches leaving the stem at 20 degrees should then curve in slightly so the top section is held parallel to the main stalk. Bracts that are too wide or long look clumsy and should be penalized. Spathe valves may be red or purple instead of green, unless the colors of the spathe valves clash with the flower colors, this trait is rated as desirable.

Spuria Iris

SUGGESTED CLASSES: Same as Tall Bearded

SUGGESTED SCALE OF POINTS

Flower	*30*	Stalk		**30**
. color and texture	10	. number of open flowers	10	
. form	10	. bud placement	10	
. substance	10	. foliage, stalk	10	
		Cultural Perfection		**25**
Condition and Grooming	*15*	. quality overall	25	

Color

Spurias normally show a color pattern made up of hues and reticulations, thus requiring more careful analysis than judging some other Iris class colors. Recent crossings are opening whole new color and pattern ranges in Spuria, such color breaks should be recognized. The color should have brilliance, delicacy and clarity and be generally attractive. Some varieties sport signal patches.

Texture enhances color . . . a smooth enamel-like texture is a normal characteristic of most Spurias, therefore desirable as typical. Where variations such as a velvety texture or ruffling appears, the Judge must consider if the characteristic enhances the color and beauty of the flower. If so, they should be considered an improvement. Evidence of disease often shows up most markedly in a change of texture in Spuria, so a Judge must be certain a change from typical smoothness is not a disease symptom.

Form

Through hybridizing, form changes are occuring, but the form should show good balance between standards and falls. Standards have become erect to slightly flaring, narrow to broad, closed or open, peaked or domed, spatulate-shaped. Falls should be arched, broad, curved down and outward, or flaring. The falls should not tuck back. Broadness and flatness of segments is preferred. The standards and falls should be well proportioned to each other and of consistent flare and angle. The style-arm should arch in such a way that it places the style-crest firmly against the fall just below the shoulder of the haft of the fall. If the style-arm arches high above the fall, it gives the effect known as "gaposis" and the appearance that the flower is falling apart.

Falls are made up mostly of an oval blade, separated by a narrow, constricted neck from the long, oval haft. Some have an indentation at the lower edge, creating an inverted heart shape. Hafts and style arms have become short and broad instead of narrow and spidery. The claw is the long, narrow part of the fall which connects the broadened part to the base of the flower. If too long, it holds the fall too far from the flower center for good proportion. The shortened claw usually gives the best overall flower form.

Some cultivars show form variations, both interesting and attractive such as the spurred types, a "corsage" form with both standards and falls nearly horizontal, and an informal form which is not starched and crisp-looking, some are laced and there are other variations. Such should be judged on the basis of whether or not the variations enhance beauty and form without sacrificing typical Spuria look.

Size

The size of Spuria flowers varies considerably with the variety. Size should be in good proportion to stalk height and strength. Since stalk length varies in lengths up to six feet, the flower size and proportion must be judged according to variety. The average flower size is approximately 4".

Substance

One of the great advantages of Spuria for cut flowers is their remarkable substance. Any diminution of this characteristic should be penalized. Though the Spuria flower typically gives an elegant, delicate appearance, the substance must be such that it holds the flower in typical form for several days. A lack of substance which alters form is considered under that heading.

In fresh flowers, copious amounts of nectar accumulate as droplets on the outside of the upper portion of the perianth tube and on the spathe valves; this has not been observed in other Iris.

Bloom Stalk, Bud Placement and Floriferousness

Stalks should always be straight and erect with sufficient strength to support the ideal complement of blooms. Bud placement is often fastigate, in a pyramid-like shape. The buds are not widely held, but are erect and close to the main stem by subtending bracts or branchlets producing the effect of the flowers being borne one above the other on a single terminal spike. The buds may be single or in pairs and should not be clubbed together at the top, but spaced down the stalk so the open flowers do not touch each other.

Varieties with longer branchlets or true branching, as in some introductions, should not be preferred over the non-branched stalks with good spacing.

No points should be deducted for the removal of the spent flower of the top pair. The more open flowers, the more points for floriferousness are allowed. However, only one flower is inadequate, three to four is the **average** and six would be outstanding in present day cultivars.

Cultural Perfection

Any specimen must be in prime condition, fully mature, reflecting in every part, the care and knowledge of its grower and presenting a thrifty, vigorous, disease-free appearance. Spuria are not usually noticeably fragrant, so the presence of a pleasant odor should be considered a definite asset. The Spuria stalk carries foliage which should be present and in good health and upright or slightly arching. The specimen should be labeled for educational purposes.

Summary
Color 10 Points

*pure *clear *bright *harmonious combinations *texture typical, pleasing

-weak -faded -spiritless -uneven -gritty texture -faulty -textural change due to disease, penalize severely if positive

Form 10 Points

*well proportioned in all parts *standards erect, spatulate *falls oval *symmetrical *widely spanned falls *unique, beautifying variations (lacing, other) *shortened claw

-untypical -deformed -bunchy -falls tucking badly -irregular development -"gaposis" -form altered due to lack of substance -hafts narrow -standards collapsed

Substance 10 Points

*turgid *enameled *fresh *strong *starched *tough

-limp -wilting -thinning -relaxing -soft

Stalk 30 Points

*fastigate *columnar *flowers not touching *well placed, well spaced flowers *proportional length *straight *erect *cane-like

-whippy -weak -coarse -crooked -massive -lopsided -crowded -uneven -clubbed together at the top -too long or too short

Number of Flowers 10 Points

One open is inadequate, three to four is average, 6 outstanding
*more than expected *average

-inadequate -scant

Cultural Perfection 25 Points

*thrifty *vigorous *well grown *fragrant *labeled *unmarred *clean *spent flowers neatly removed *foliage present

-stunted -diseased -unhealthy general appearance -unlabeled -old -broken petals -tears -soiled -scarred -virus evidence

Louisiana (Native)

SUGGESTED ENTRY: Same as Tall Bearded
SUGGESTED SCALE OF POINTS

Flower	55	Stalk and Foliage	15
. form	15	. balance and bud place-	
. color	20	ment	
. substance	10	Open Flowers	10
. size	10	Condition	20
		. cultural perfection	15
		. grooming	5

Form

Diversity of form and stature is desirable. Forms vary, some being flat and large with drooping standards similar to Japanese Iris; others have pendant or flaring to nearly horizontal falls with upright standards.

Falls, depending on species or hybrid are medium narrow to wide, some are triangular, and larger than the standards. Standards are narrow to broad. Ruffling, showy crests and style arms often add interest. The current ideal is a wide, flat and flaring showy form. Those of Abbeyville lineage tend to have flat flowers with wide floral parts carrying width well to the base of each floral segment, branching, heavier substance, rich, velvety texture and increased size are the basis of many improved Louisiana Iris.

Color

There is a wide color range including red in the species. Signal patches may be present. Crests of contrasting or self-color add interest. Veination occurs. Textures vary, may be velvety, smooth, leathery. The color combinations must be harmonious and stable. Clarity and purity are important. Penalty is taken for a faded, vague, smeared appearance.

Stalk Balance and Bud Placement

While the stalk of a Louisiana Iris is flexuous and may be gracefully curving, if it bends or curves and then straightens out an undesirable condition is the result and penalty is meted out. The short branchlets must be well placed on the stalk and not bunched at the top or held appressed to the main stalk. While the diameter must be in proportion to the flower, not massive or coarse, neither may it be weak or penalty is taken.

Ideally the stalk will be balanced with alternating placement of buds, though the buds may not be evenly placed. Basic species and most natural hybrids have three flower positions with two buds at each position. In garden hybrids it is ideal to have four flower positions. Very narrow angles on the branch, even though the branch itself is long, give poor distribution of flowers along the stalk.

Floriferousness

Basic species and natural hybrids carry six buds, while garden hybrids ideally carry eight. Less than six buds per stalk is considered a fault. Full points for floriferousness are given if over six buds are present.

SUMMARY
Form 20 Points

*symmetrical *similar petal conformation *well proportioned falls to standards *wide floral parts carrying width well to segment base

-narrow hafts -standards not uniformly erect (or flattened) -segments narrow -bunched

Color 15 Points

*signal patches clearly defined *vivid *clean, clear markings *stable *rich

-off -uneven -weak -dull -streaky -lacks sheen

Substance 10 Points

*heavy *holding well *perky *turgid *substantial

-wilting -limp -thinning -collapsing -papery

Size 5 Points

*above average *proportioned to stem *typical

-dwarfed -not according to type -ungainly

Stalk Balance and Bud Placement 10 Points

*strong *flexuous *gracefully curved laterals well angled, well spaced *3 bud positions (species and natural hybrids) *4 bud positions (garden hybrids)

-stalk snaked -crooked -weak -laterals bunched -laterals held too close to stem -flowers crowded -flowers pressed too tightly against the stalk

Floriferousness 15 Points

*six or more buds present *typical

-less than six

Condition and Grooming 10 Points

*unmarred *clean *spent flowers carefully removed

-overmature -bedraggled -spent -damaged -soiled -bruised

Cultural Perfection 15 Points

*thrifty *disease free *blemish free *well grown *labeled

-unthrifty appearance -disfigured blossoms -disease or pest evidence -stunted

Bulbous Iris and Miscellaneous Species
Dutch, Spanish, English, Reticulata

DUTCH AND SPANISH

The flowers of the Dutch and Spanish do not differ greatly in appearance, though the Spanish standards are prominent compared to the falls.

Dutch varieties are best known . . . being an improvement over the older, shorter-lived Spanish Iris. Both have thin, scanty foliage. Both have broad falls compared to the standards. Both have prominent style arms, upright open standards, heavy waxy substance. They may have signal patches or stripes or ruffling. Falls and standards of the Dutch may be different colors. The Dutch is highly prized by florists. Heights up to 30", comparatively sturdy stems.

ENGLISH

Actually, the so-called English Iris is a wildling from the Spanish Pyrenees "rediscovered" in England. Its culture is different from the Dutch and Spanish, requiring a more acid, heavy, moist soil. It has a heavier foliage and the flower has short, erect standards, and broad falls which are much larger than the standards. The falls may be pendant or flaring. Colors range from whites, blues, values of red violet and lavender, and color patterns include signal patches or stripes as well as self-color. The English bloom after the other bulb Iris and before the Japanese. Vigorous.

RETICULATA (Basic Species)

Very dwarf, under 6", with reed-like fine foliage. The flowers are very fragrant, deep purple with orange veins. The standards are upright and the falls upright also, excepting for the tips which droop or flare. Blooms in early April, too early for most show judging unless by pot culture.

OTHER IRIS

Many species belonging to various subdivisions of the genus Iris are grown in gardens and cherished for their unique and distinctive qualities. They contribute novelty and interest to flower show Iris classes.

Such Iris include the Crested 'EVANSIA' in which the beard is replaced by a toothed ridge, resembling a rooster's comb. Best known Crested Iris are **I. cristata** (native) which is a dwarf type and **I. tectorum** (Japanese Roof Iris) and even one double form, 'GRACILIPES', which has 30-40 petals per bloom.

Other rarities include Juncea, Snake's Head, Peacock and the Vesper Iris which is summer blooming with tall, slender branched stems, and small dainty blooms which last only one day, opening late in the afternoon; it is purple and easily grown from seed.

Most autumn bloomers can be judged by the same standards as the Tall Bearded. In judging species, correct identification is a prerequisite and Bearded, Beardless and Bulbous species and hybrids should be judged on the basis of a standard of excellence required by the particular type. Standards and rules for judging will become more specific as these plants become more widely cultivated and hybridized.

SUGGESTED SCALE OF POINTS

Flower	50	General Condition	40
· form	20	· condition ·grooming	
. color and texture	20	· cultural perfection	
. size	10	Stalk	10

JUDGING SPECIFICS FOR SPECIES (refer to p. 197)

The standards should be erect, if typical, not leaning to one side or the other. Falls should flare outward or hang gracefully pendant to the same degree, well displayed. Standards, falls may be strappy, tucked, twisted (i.e. Spuria species) but are considered less desirable. If substance is so far gone it alters flower form, deduct severely. The substance of Spanish and Dutch is very heavy and similar to Spuria and any reduction of this typical characteristic should be penalized. Substance may appear fragile, almost transluscent, yet be leather-strong. Flopping is penalized. Doubles should be complete with six falls, not irregular (5, etc.). The color should be uniform, clear, smooth rather than streaked or flecked, excepting English, other where regular even flecking is accepted and typical. Size should be typical to larger than average, though expect to be smaller than cultivers. The bloom should be posed squarely on the stalk which should be relatively strong and erect. Faded foliage or leaf tips that are dead, brown or dried over ⅛" from tip are penalized.

All parts must be intact, clean, fresh, and the specimen appear well-grown and at peak condition. Dwarfs are typically unbranched, with perhaps only one flower, while others may exceed 20" carrying several dozen blooms.

The Judge will remember there is an ideal form which any prize winner should emulate regardless of whether the fault is characteristic of the variety or not. To condone a fault for this reason defeats furtherance of appreciation for the typical form.

Lilacs

SUGGESTED CLASSES:

A. 1 truss: colors blue, violet, purple — Single Flowers

B. 1 truss: colors pinks, reds, red-violet — Single Flowers

C. 1 truss: color white — Single Flowers

D. 1 truss: colors blue, violet, purple — Double Flowers

E. 1 truss: colors pink, red, red-violet — Double Flowers

F. 1 truss: color white — Double Flowers

G. 1 truss: color yellow (Ex: 'Primrose' variety)

For Advanced or Specialty Shows the Schedule can be set up to include classes for 1. Species, 2. Hybrids including Dilatata, Giraldi, French, Chinensis, etc.

LILACS

Lilacs (Genus Syringa) are a large and varied group with interesting species and hybrids which show various bloom, fragrance, size and leaf traits. Though fragrance is the most popular characteristic of Lilacs in general, it must be noted that varieties vary widely in depth of scent; some being heavily perfumed, others typically faint, while some lack any fragrance.

S. vulgaris is the well known Common Lilac with either white or lilac flowers. It is highly perfumed. There are several hundred named forms commonly called French Lilacs including several originated by Lemoine and other foreign hybridizers and loosely extended to include **S. vulgaris** varieties which are by far the most widely known and grown. Single, semi-double, double hybrids have larger flowers and heavier trusses, not quite as fragrant as the type. **S. giraldi** and **dilatata** have rather more loose trusses. The **Persian** Lilac has slender spreading branches. The blossoms are fragrant; the individual flowers are small, trusses are open. The species color is pale lilac, delicate as old lace and there is also a cut-leaved Persian. The Hybrid **(Persian x S. vulgaris)** **S. chinensis** which is the same plant as the Rouen or Rothomagensis has larger, more compact trusses, larger, broader leaves than the Persian, but finer, more thinly filled panicles than **S. vulgaris,** its other parent.

S. microphylla has a graceful spreading habit and is appropriately called the Little Leaf Lilac. **S. villosa** has erect, clubby branches and an odor unpleasant to some rather than a fragrance. **S. henryi** has no fragrance, a trait shared with species **S. wolfi** and **S. juliane,** plus several others. **S. oblata** has large, leathery leaves that turn red in the fall.

Chinese Lilacs, **S. pekinensis** and Japanese, **S. amurensis** are listed by the French Lilac authority Mr. Lemoine as Ligustrina, an intermediate between Syringa (Lilac) and Ligustrum (Privet). These are often termed Tree Lilacs. The plant Buddleia (Butterfly Bush) is often called Summer Lilac, though it is not of the same family.

SCALE OF POINTS

Color	25	Substance and Texture	10
Size	25	Foliage and Stem	10
Form and Structure	20	Condition	10

COLOR

It is nearly impossible to divide Lilacs into precise color classes. Not only do they combine several colors and shades in individual blooms, but they vary again each day, beginning with the unopened buds and ending with the spent flowers.

The moisture available, the amount of sunlight and the soil nutrients have such a definite effect, also, that any definite opinion as to the mobile color depends upon which day, which time of day and which season the bloom is observed.

The individual flowers which go to make up the truss may have varying intensity from the just-opened buds to the wide-open flowers.

The buds on a truss are often one shade with the opened flower another such as **S. microphylla** in which pink blossoms mingle with dark red buds. The exterior of an individual floret may differ from the interior, either as a contrast of color or a blend.

While some varieties may cast a bright or rich color, others are delicate, soft and fragile appearing as befits their characteristics.

Age and intense sunlight are the worst enemies of Lilac color and any bleaching, dullness or fading should be penalized. Age and sunburn can also burn and crisp the edges, as well as cause a brown cast and is likewise penalized. Whatever the characteristic intensity, the color must be clear, typical and attractive.

SIZE:

The Judge takes into consideration two things relative to size:

A. Truss (panicle) size

B. Floret size

Hybridization has changed the size of both truss and floret which varies as follows: **S. vulgaris** hybrids (French Lilacs) have larger florets and heavier trusses than the **S. vulgaris** parent. Individual florets of the Persian are the smallest of all while the variety 'CAVOUR' has florets measuring up to 1½" in diameter and trusses over one foot. The flower and truss size should be normal or slightly above normal, indicating superior cultural care, including proper pruning.

FORM AND STRUCTURE

The Form and Structure encompasses three considerations:

A. State of development

B. Truss shape

C. Branching and floret arrangement

A. A truss has begun to lose its individuality and beauty when all the florets are at the fully opened stage. The most perfect phase of panicle beauty is when there are approximately two-thirds fully opened florets combined with one-third buds. A panicle exhibiting more buds than one-third is considered immature and points deducted according to the degree of fault.

B. Each species has a distinct form, but with intermingling of characteristics brought about through hybridization, clear-cut lines are difficult to draw. The variety will usually take the form which is typical, barring accident or disease. Some varieties carry a thick truss, broad and with several ramifications which fork. This growth habit, plus the floret size and overall truss size give these a massive, broad appearance. The Common Lilac, **S. vulgaris** and its French Hybrids often present this truss form, as well as sometimes presenting a single, long, high-shouldered, closely packed, pyramidal truss. These may be held militantly erect, or gracefully curving. The tops of some are distinctly pointed, while others are rounded or domed.

Persian (Persica) Lilacs carry large, loose clusters of small flowers which have a charming, graceful fragility which takes a rather drooping stance when held erect. The overall apperance is narrow and slender, and not too solidly filled when compared to the French Hybrids.

S. giraldi and **S. dilatata** hybrids are also rather loosely held and open appearing. **S. chinensis,** rothomagensis and Rouen (all the same lilac) have larger clusters than the Persian, more rounded, but held similarly. **S. oblata** has compact, roundish trusses, plump and well-filled. **S. oblata dilatata** hybrids have a looser, more wide-spread truss. **S. microphylla** has fine, lacy, open trusses.

Individual floret form may be symmetrical, unsymmetrical, flat or incurled. The long tube and narrow petals of some varieties give a distinct, plumed and fleecy effect.

Generally the truss should stand well above the foliage, and not be dominated by it. Judicious pruning increases the size of the blooms and the number per panicle and plant.

SUBSTANCE AND TEXTURE

When cut when two thirds open and conditioned by crushing the stems, Lilacs have substance to last for several days. Some species and varieties are naturally thicker walled than others **(S. vulgaris)** while others are more fragile (Persian). The florets should be turgid with moisture, not drooping or thinning or wilted, or excessively curling.

The texture of Lilacs is usually glistening, not dull. Each individual floret has a smooth surface, which is somewhat mitigated by their size and grouping in the panicle. There should be no wrinkling or drying of the surface, though the petal edges may turn in, this is a different matter than texture.

FOLIAGE AND STEM

The characteristic foliage of Lilacs varies with the species and variety. Some are smooth, others are hairy such as **S. pubescens** which is sometimes called the Hairy Lilac. Some have a fine dark green on top and are paler with a slightly velvety texture below. Persian leaves are small and narrow and one variety has divided leaves. **S. oblata** has broad, leathery leaves, **S. microphylla** species have small leaves. **S. villosa** may have leaves up to seven inches long.

The foliage should be placed symmetrically on the stem, neither too little or so rank that it dominates the specimen.

Stem strength also varies according to species and variety. For instance, the species **S. microphylla** has stems so slender they bend under the blossom weight. Pubescens also has slender stems. The stems of Common Lilac **(S. vulgaris)** and its French Hybrids have relatively sturdy and smooth barked stems, while **S. villosa** has a warty stem, and the bark of the **S. pekinensis** Tree Lilac breaks in thin flakes similar to the habit of birches.

The stem should be approximately one and one-half times the

length of the truss for good proportion and should carry the bloom well whatever the truss size.

CONDITION AND GROOMING

The exhibit should be clean with all twigs and dead leaves removed. No dried or browning florets should be present. A general overall lack of condition indicated by relaxing tip and a droopy appearance is a fault. Some insects chew and scallop the leaves and points must be deducted if such damaged leaves remain on the exhibit.

Cultural malpractice resulting in disease or insect damage deserves severe penalties. Dark brown or black spots on the leaves may be the result of Blight. Presence of scale on the stem or twigs and stunted buds are serious faults. No spray, soil or foreign matter should be present. The foliage should be whole and wiped clean, but not artificially polished.

SUMMARY

Color 25 Points
*clear *attractive *typical (see text)

-bleached -dull -fading -browning

Size 25 Points   (Both flower and truss size considered)
*normal *slightly above normal

-small -dwarfed appearing -stunted

Form and Structure 20 Points
*⅔ open florets *typical for type *symmetrical *foliage held well *evenly distributed bilaterally

-foliage interfering -bloomed out -too many buds -lop sided -unbalanced -crowded -bunchy -voids

Substance and Texture 10 Points
Substance: *crisp *turgid *perky
         -limp -drooping -curling petals
Texture: *luminous *glistening *smooth *fine
         -dull -grainy -lifeless

Foliage and Stem 10 Points
Foliage: *characteristic *true colored *healthy appearing *sufficient
         -sparse -lacking -not typical in size and color -dwarfed -deformed

Stem: *characteristic *relatively straight *sturdy *bloom well carried despite size *stem 1½ times panicle length

         -weak -scarred -crotchy -stem too short -too long

Condition and Grooming 10 Points
*clean *attractive overall appearance

-disease -scale -blight -soiled -dusty -artificially polished leaves -mildew -insect damage

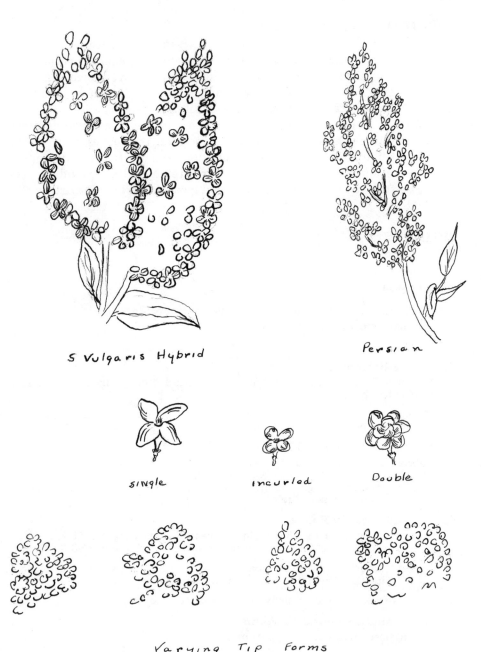

S Vulgaris Hybrid

Persian

single

incurled

Double

Varying Tip Forms

Lily

SUGGESTED CLASSES:

1. 1 stem Reflex
2. 1 stem Bowl
3. 1 stem Trumpet
4. 1 stem Upright
   (named if possible)

or

1 stem each Species or Hybrid in which competition is expected. For instance,

1 stem **L. martagon,** Olympic, etc. Named if possible.

LILY: (Lilium)

Perennial, erect, leafy-stemmed herb rising from a scaly bulb. Flowers reflexed or bowl shaped and erect in dry, moderate climate species and drooping, trumpet-like in heavy rain climates to protect the pollen. Solitary or clustered inflorescence. Six segments (three petals, three sepals, very similar) each with a nectar groove at the base. Six stamens. Varied heights and bloom periods and seasons. Family includes the curious apple-green **L. arboricola** which lives in trees in the manner of Orchids. The Cardiocrinum was formerly classed as a Lily, but is now listed as a separate genus. It is distinguished by broad heart-shaped leaves and grows up to 12' with approximately 20 six inch trumpet flowers. Many plants are called Lily which belong to other families or genus, the Day, Glory, Mariposa, Plantain, Lily of the Valley, Torch do belong to the Lilium family, but Sego and Zephyr, Calla, Pond and Water lilies belong to other families.

A "strain" means a group of lilies grown from seed which will be alike in general characteristics. flower form, season of bloom but with some variation in height, time of flowering and depth of color (Example: Cascade Strain) Named clones , ('ENCHANTMENT') of course are always true to type having been propagated vegetatively. A group of lilies of common ancestry composed of different individuals are referred to by a fancy name followed by the word "hybrid" such as Olympic Hybrids which are usually easier to grow than the parent species.

SCALE OF POINTS

Condition	30	Flower Substance	10
Vigor	20	Form	10
Placement	20	Color	10

CONDITION

Condition includes maturity and grooming in judging Lilies. Best condition is when the lower flowers are open, but not faded and the upper ones are still in bud. The more open flowers, with none faded, the higher will be the score under condition.

Any flowers indicating sun-bleach, wilting, thinning, or broken petals and anthers or other such damage will suffer penalties commensurate with the degree of fault.

Any specimen showing disease or insect damage must be penalized. Virus (mosaic) is manifested by curious mottling of the leaves and stunted growth with distortion of stems, leaves and flowers. **L. formosanum** flowers will show splits caused by virus. Chlorosis (a deficiency disease) is evidenced by pale yellow-green foliage either total or in patches. Disease and deficiency damage receive higher penalties than mechanical damage such as tears, etc.

The anthers should be present on locally-grown specimens. Anthers may be removed without penalty from flowers which are shipped in for showing.

The flowers and foliage should be clean, free of any foreign matter, dust, webs, thistledown and dropped pollen. Some hybrids (Example: 'CORSAGE') normally produce no pollen. The Judge deducts for pollen stains or an unsuccessful attempt to remove a pollen stain which has resulted in a large ugly blemish. Dull, dry pollen indicates age, an overripe condition. Though the scent of many lilies is delightful when the flowers are fresh, it can become anything but as they begin to fade and this characteristic will be a help to the Judge in evaluating age after a bit of experience.

If the exhibitor has not removed aborted buds and spent flowers close to the main stem, or has left a stub, penalty should be taken. A stem that is bruised and scarred or crooked and bent by improper staking will also be subject to penalty.

PLACEMENT

Placement refers to the arrangement of the flowers on the stem. Superior placement occurs when the pedicels spiral on the stem vertically, rather than crowd together at the same level. The length of the pedicel is important. They may be too long, allowing the flower to droop or too short to be ideal for the particular type being shown.

Spacing should be such that the bloom head is attractive from any side and the blooms positioned so no flower crowds or interferes with another. None of the lower flowers should touch each other.

The inflorescence should be well balanced; if removal of spent flowers has altered the balance or left ungainly voids, points should be deducted.

Unopened buds low in the cluster of open flowers are a fault. The angle of attachment and pose (drooping, out-facing, up-facing) must be typical of the variety and uniform in all flowers of the specimen. In judging Hybrids competing against each other, the spacing and attractive angle may be considered. Placement and form give dignity and stateliness to some (as Regals) and on the other hand, may give a pixy sprightliness to others (Martagon types).

VIGOR

Three things are considered under vigor:
1. Length and strength of the stem
2. Number and size of the flowers
3. Size and Attractiveness of the foliage

1. The length of the stem should be proportioned to the bloom head. A too long or short stem makes the specimen look awkward. Cutting over one-third of the stem and foliage reduces the bulb vigor and should be discouraged.

   The strength of the stem should be typical for the variety, some stems are thin and wiry; others are thick, heavy and give a stately appearance. The diameter of the stem should be in proportion to the size of the flowers and length.

   The stem should be sturdy enough to support a full complement of bloom without undue bending. Points should be deducted here for weak, fasciated (grown together), crooked, twisted, bruised or diseased stems in the degree that the fault has affected the length and strength. Mosaic virus and nematode infestations cause short-ened stunted stems and weak sappy growth which are serious faults.

2. Number and size of flowers should be typical for variety (see chart). The more open flowers there are, with buds still to come, the higher will be the score here. There should be no extremes on either side of normal size. Refer to the chart for examples.

   Reduced flower production may be nematode damage especially when in the company of stunted growth and smaller-than-normal leaves. Fasciation is an abnormal condition where the lily stem flattens out and seems to be composed of several stems grown together. The number of flowers is generally much increased and may be several times the normal crop. Since such condition produces abnormal ugly specimens they should not be exhibited and the Judge should eliminate them from competition if they have been passed by the Classification Committee.

3. Size and attractiveness of foliage: foliage should be well scaled to flower size and stem. It should not be either coarse or under-sized; undersized leaves may be a result of nematode damage.

   Foliage should be well-balanced on the stalk, either in whorls or scattered as is typical of the type. There should be no evidence of disease or mechanical damage. The foliage should be typically green out to the tips with no browning, drying, tears or soil.

FLOWER SUBSTANCE

Substance is that degree of matter and moisture in the petals which keeps them crisp, firm and turgid and is what gives the flower its ability to withstand exposure and aging for greater periods of time. Thinning substance is indicated by a melting or "drawing-in" of the petal edges. Most lilies are blessed with a heavy degree of substance and thus are longer lasting than many other flowers.

FLOWER FORM

True Lilies are divided into four distinct forms, as follows:

1. TRUMPET: Funnel

- petals overlap for greater part of their length, reflexing only slightly at the tip
- bases of petals are elongated into an extended "throat"
- Example: 'MADONNA'

2. UPRIGHT: Erect or Star

- Wide flower segments are broadest above the middle and then narrow abruptly toward their base
- each flower is held upright, erect and wide open
- Example: **L. umbellatum** and Hybrid 'GOLDEN CHALICE'

3. REFLEX: Recurved

- usually pendulous or nodding
- petals are broadest approximately in the middle and curl back toward the pedicel (stem)
- stamens protrude conspicuously
- Example: **L. speciosum** and **martagon.** Hybrids 'FIESTA' Strain

4. BOWL:

- petals broadest below the middle
- tips recurve slightly
- pose of the flower is out-facing (termed horizontal)
- Example: 'GOLD BAND'

The accompanying chart has been prepared according to flower form as many find the species and hybrids easier to remember when grouped by the shape of the flower.

Form is judged on conformity with that which is typical of the species or variety. The form of each flower to another on the same stem should be uniform. Sepals and petals should be of uniform length, width and degree of reflex on each individual flower. In general the petals should have bold, unbroken curves, not unduly twisted or rolled and relatively broad; but overly broad, coarse appearance is a fault.

Stamens and anthers should be present and centered in the flower. The color and movement of the anthers adds so much to the form and beauty of the flowers that their proper handling and retention should be encouraged and their lack penalized except on shipped specimens.

Blooms just opened may deviate slightly from the typical and the Judge should take this into consideration. If the form is flawed by torn segments, deformed parts, missing segments or crowding, the flower should be penalized commensurate with the degree of impairment.

COLOR

Because of the multiplicity of interbreeding, resulting in hybrids and strains with no recognized typical color, color in Lilies should be judged on the clarity, attractiveness and freshness.

Any dullness or cloudiness or spiritlessness should be penalized. Lily texture usually possesses a sheen and if this is dulled or roughened, the impairment should be deducted from the total score.

The color should be evenly spread in selfs and uniformly spread in suffusions. Dotting and spotting with another color should be attractively and uniformly placed. Bands and spots should be fairly equal in size, color value and dispersement. The margins should be definite, without smearing or bleeding into the background color.

JUDGING POTTED LILIES

The Judge will expect to find the plants to be a bit less vigorous and perfect than when the same varieties are grown outdoors, but the flowers are often more softly colored, more perfect than when exposed to wind, sun and rain.

The Schedule rules may permit lilies to be dug from the garden at bud stage and potted. Such late-potted specimens will have more vigor and larger flowers than those pot-confined for the entire growing season.

JUDGING LILY COLLECTION AND DISPLAY

In placing the entries in a collection, the quality of the flowers, the number of species shown (unless limited by the Schedule) and the horticultural difficulty of raising the species and hybrids exhibited are considered.

In judging displays, the preceding applies plus the consideration of artistic effect, such as the balance, scale and proportion of the exhibit parts to each other and to the space the exhibit occupies which is usually designated in the Schedule. Suitable foliage and accessories may be permitted. The Judge must check the Schedule closely in determining how well the exhibitor has conformed to the listed requirements.

SUMMARY

Condition 30 Points

*numerous open flowers and some buds *no faded flowers *clean *careful grooming

-disease or insect damage -dropped pollen -spent flowers present -bloomed out -too few open -scarred stem -crooked

Placement 20 Points

*well spaced *inflorescence well balanced *flowers opening evenly *pose (facing) typical *gracefully arranged *pedicels holding flowers apart

-entire inflorescence crowded -blank spaces -lopsided -buds low in inflorescence

Vigor 20 Points

Stem: *proportionate *sturdy *straight

-overlong -too short -weak -fasciated -crooked -bruised -diseased

Number of Flowers: *typical *adequate number open

-scant -small -excessive number accompanied by fasciated stem

Foliage: *well proportioned *well placed *uniform color *clean

-weak -lacking -dominates bloom -yellow -tips brown -diseased -soiled -dwarfed -mottled

Flower Substance 10 Points

*edges firm *petals crisp *thick *turgid *waxy

-limp -thinning -edges curling

Flower Form 10 Points

*typical of variety *uniform one flower to another *uniform each part to another *stamens centered *reflex typical and uniform

-form flawed by crowding -petal missing or torn -not representative of variety or specie -deformed -overly broad, coarse -twisted excessively

Flower Color 10 Points

*fresh *attractive *clear *even *uniform on all petals *sparkling

-faded -bleached -streaky -uneven -dots or spots or bands unevenly distributed beyond the general area

LILY FORMS

Type of Form	Variety Example	Color	Height	Ease of Culture	Bloom Season	Number of Flowers	Size of Flowers
Species: L. martagon (Turks Cap)		white, purple	3-5 ft.	easy	June	up to 30	medium
L. cernuum		orchid, lilac, old rose	1½-3	easy	July	up to 40	small
L. davidi	formerly willmotiae	red, orange	5-6	easy	July	up to 50	small
L. amabile		red	1½-3	easy	June — July	numerous	small
L. hansoni		orange, yellow	3-4	fairly easy	June — July	numerous	small
L. pumilum	Coral Lily	coral red, yellow	1½-2	easy	May — June	numerous	small
L. tigrinum	(wholly white stem hairs) Common Tiger Lily	pinkish orange	4-6	easy	Aug. — Sept.	up to 20	medium
L. tigrinum flora-pleno	Semi-double form	orange-red	4-6	easy	Aug. — Sept.	numerous	medium
L. pardalinum giganteum	Sunset, Leopard, Panther Lily	red-orange	6-9	medium	July	12-20	large
L. henryi		yellow-orange	6-8	easy	July — August	15-20	medium
L. speciosum, rebrum, album	'White Pearl,' 'Red Champion'	white, rose	4-5	easy	Aug. — Sept.	up to 30	med. to large
HYBRIDS Bellingham	'Shuksan'	yellow, orange	5-6	fairly easy	June — July	10-20	large
Harlequin (cernuum ancestry)	'Corsage,' 'Lemon Queen'	lilac, old rose	2-3	fairly easy	July	numerous	small
Fiesta (davidi ancestry) etc.	'Dr. Abel'	amber, sand, browns	4-6	easy	July	up to 20	medium

RECURVED Petals Broadest About The Middle, Stamens Protrude Conspicuously, Nodding, Pendulous

241

Type of Form	Variety Example	Color	Height	Ease of Culture	Bloom Season	Number of Flowers	Size of Flowers
BOWL Petals Broadest Below the Middle: Tips Recurved Slightly: Horizontal Out-Facing							
Species **Auratum platyphyllum**	'Gold Band'	white, yellow bands	6-12	fairly easy	Aug. — Sept.	15-20	10 inch
Auratum rubro-vittatum	'Red Band'	white, red bands	6-up	fairly easy	August	numerous	large
HYBRIDS Parkmanl	'Jillian Wallace' (flat form)	white to red	4-6	medium	August	up to 30	5-11"
Empress etc.	Jamboree and Inspiration Strains	pinks, red, silver, red dots	6	medium	July — August	10-40	med. to large
TRUMPET or FUNNEL Petals Overlap the Greater Part of the Length, Extending from a Long Throat							
L. longiflorum	Common Easter, Croft, Estate	white	2-3	fairly easy	July — August spring forcing	up to 10	4-6"
L. regal	'Royal Gold'	white, inside, rose purple outside. Yel., pink hybrids	4-6	easy	July	18-20	large
L. canadense		orange-yellow, red	2-5	easy	July	many	small
L. brownil		cream inside, red-lavendar outside	2-3	medium	August	1-3	large
L. japonicum	Bamboo Lily	pink	2-3	difficult	June — September	5-7	large
L. formosanum	St. Louis Strain	white, green outside	2-6	subject to virus	July, Sept., Dec.	5-7	large
Hybrids Olympic		white, purple	4-6	easy	July	numerous	large
Golden Clarion Strain		yellow	4-6	easy	July	numerous	large
Pink Perfection Strain		pink	5-7	easy	July — August	5-7	large
T. A. Havemeyer		ivory	6	easy	July — August	18	5-7"
Red Gold Strain		near red	5	easy	July	numerous	large
Species **L. candidum**	Madonna	white	4-6	easy	June	up to 12	miniature to medium
Hybrid Cascade Strain		white	3-5	easy	June	up to 12	miniature to medium
Species **L. nepalense**		green, purple	3-4	regional	June — July	5	large

Type of Form	Variety Example	Color	Height	Ease of Culture	Bloom Season	Number of Flowers	Size of Flowers
UPRIGHT Wide Flower Segments, Broadest Above the Middle and Narrow Abruptly Toward Their Base. Held Upright.							
Species							
L. croceum	Orange Lily	orange	6	medium	July	several	medium
L. concolor	Star Lily	yellow, red	up to 2	easy	May	several	small
L. dauricum	Candelabra 'Candlestick'	black spots red, orange	2-3	easy	May	several	medium
L. elegans	Peach	many	2-3	easy	June — July	several	8"
L. philadelphicum (Eastern Native)	Flame Lily	red-orange	2-3	regional	June	many	medium
L. umbellatum (Western Native)	Flame Lily	red-orange	2-3	regional	June	many	medium
Hybrids							
Golden Chalice		many yellows	2-4	easy	May — June	4-8	medium
Rainbow Strain		many	2-4	fairly easy	May — June	many	medium
FORM VARIED							
Hybrids							
Aurelian	'Sunburst,' 'Golden Clarion'	many	5-7	easy	July — August	varies	med-large
Mid-Century (Tiger ancestry)	'Enchantment'	many	2-4	easy	June — July	many	6"
Hollywood	'Joan Evans'	orange to dark red	4-5	easy	July	many	medium

The purpose of this chart is not to cover the entire range of species, but a brief survey of the better known and available species and some hybrids to orient the Judge according to flower forms. The time is not too far distant when the species will be grown only by specialists, having given way to the vigorous, easily propagated, colorful hybrids, but a foundation of knowledge of the species is necessary to any Lily Judge.

Narcissus (Daffodils)

SUGGESTED CLASSES:

1. *Single Specimen, Divisions 1, 2, 3, 4, 5, 6, 7, 8, 9, 10, 11, 12. (Schedules may further divide into Colors, listed below)*
2. *Three Stems, one variety. Divisions 1 through 12.*
3. *Three Stems, different varieties. Divisions 1 through 12.*
4. Miniatures, three specimens, 1 variety.

Daffodil is the English name for this entire group of plants, Narcissus is the Latin and correct botanical name so the words mean exactly the same and are used interchangeably. It is incorrect to call this *entire group of plants Jonquils. The Jonquil is merely one of the twelve divisions (see Division Seven).*

Daffodils are members of the Amaryllis family and each division contains many varieties, particularly in the Trumpet, Long and Short Cup Divisions.

Separate listings may be found for: 1. Exhibition and 2. Garden Varieties. Exhibition is defined as having a smooth texture, heavy substance, overlapping perianth segments, good balance, and fast, clear color. Examples being: 'VIGIL', 'KINGSCOURT', 'CEYLON', 'GREEN ISLAND'.

Garden varieties are chosen for reasons of hardiness, floriferousness, low price and color. Examples are: 'BEERSHEBA', 'POLAR ICE', 'SHOT SILK', 'MRS. R. O. BACKHOUSE', etc.

Some varieties fit both classes. Examples are: 'KINGSCOURT', 'TROUSSEAU', 'SPELLBINDER', and 'GALWAY'.

Daffodil classification includes twelve divisions, all of which are based on distinct flower forms. Familiarity with the flower and its parts is necessary to intelligent evaluation.

DEFINITIONS

CORONA (cup or trumpet): The center portion of the flower which varies in length and shape, from long and tubular to a flattened eye.

PERIANTH: The circle or wheel of petals and sepals surrounding the central corona.

COLOR: White or whitish, green, yellow, pink, orange, red. Color is fickle, varying with stages of development.

CORONA LENGTH: is measured from the junction with the perianth *to the end when the edge is flattened out. Divided into 'eye', mid-zone and to edge of rim.*

tion with the corona along the mid-rib to the extreme tip.

SKETCH "A"

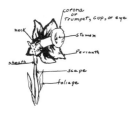

SKETCH "B"

DIVISION 1: TRUMPET NARCISSUS

Garden Origin (Hybrids)

- one flower to a stem
- corona is as long or longer than perianth segments

Color Classes:
- perianth colored, corona colored, not paler than the perianth. Example: 'KING ALFRED'
- perianth white; corona colored, bicolor. Example: 'ALL GLORY' (Pinks may be shown here, if no special class for them)
- perianth white; corona white, 'BEERSHEBA'
- any other color combination
- *perianth parts flat, overlapping, may be shovel-shaped, oval or pointed*

DIVISION 2: LONG CUP—
Garden Origin

- one flower to a stem

- corona, more than one-third, but less than equal to length of perianth. *See Perianth parts, Div. 1.*

Color Classes:
- perianth colored, corona colored, not paler than the perianth
- perianth white, corona colored
- perianth white, corona white
- any color combination

DIVISION 3: SHORT CUP—
Garden Origin

- one flower to a stem

- corona not more than one-third the length of the perianth segments

Color Classes:
- perianth colored, corona colored not paler than perianth
- perianth white, corona colored
- perianth white, corona white, not paler than the perianth
- any other combination
- *perianth parts flat, overlapping, may be shovel-shaped, oval, pointed*

DIVISION 4: DOUBLE —
Garden Origin

- flowers are double or semi-double in corona of perianth or both
- may be self or bicolored. Example: 'TWINK'

DIVISION 5: TRIANDRUS —
Garden Origin

- more than one flower per stem

- pendant, drooping pose or carriage
- slightly reflexed perianth
- *silky texture*

DIVISION 6: CYCLAMINEUS —
Garden Origin

- one flower to a stem (exceptions such as 'TETE-A-TETE', 'QUINCE'

- perianth completely reflexed
- corona straight, narrow
- nodding, pendant carriage

DIVISION 7: JONQUILLA (Jonquils) —
Garden Origin

- usually more than one flower per stem
- round, dark green, reedlike foliage
- sweet scented

DIVISION 8: TAZETTA (Poetaz)
Garden Origin

- *2–6 or more flowers per stem*
- perianth flat, circular, star-shape
- corona short
- umbel (umbrella) like inflorescence Exception: 'MARTHA WASHINGTON'
- does best in the South

DIVISION 9: POETICUS
Garden Origin

- *Perianth parts flat, underlined{overlapping}, shovel, pointed or oval shaped*
- one flower to a stem, fragrant
- glistening, white petals, slightly recurving
- very small, buttonlike, red-edged eye
- does well in North

DIVISION 10: SPECIES, WILD FORMS AND HYBRIDS

- N. triandrus L. variety 'ALBUS'
- N. poeticus L.
- N. odorus L.

- Tazetta L. sub species papyraceus including the scented 'PAPERWHITE' variety valuable for *forcing, etc. Doubles included.*

DIVISION 11: SPLIT CORONA FORM
Corona split for at least one-third its length, separating into six segments, three large and three small which are flattened back against the perianth. If cups are not split to the base, exhibit is placed in appropriate division as determined by corona length. Ex: 'EVOLUTION'.

DIV. 11   **DIV. 12**

DIVISION 12: MISCELLANEOUS

All narcissus not falling into any of the foregoing divisions
Includes N. bulbocodium hybrids ('Hoop Petticoat') such as NYLON,' 'TAFFETA'
MINIATURES are defined as narcissus with stems usually not exceeding 8-9"; proportionately tiny parts and may be found in all the preceding divisions. Examples are 'RAINDROP' (6") and 'APRIL TEARS' (4")
INTERMEDIATES are 8-14" and include all preceding divisions. *Example 'COBWEB' 9". All MINIATURES, INTERMEDIATES and PINKS must be placed in proper division according to characteristics. SEEDLINGS are any unregistered, unnamed cultivars.*

SCALE OF POINTS

Condition	20	Color	15
Form	20	Pose	10
Substance and Texture	15	Stem	10
		Size	10

In judging multiple entries, points should be subtracted from the total if the collection is not uniform. All like specimens should be of (1) Uniform size. (2) Uniform stage of development. (3) Uniform stem length. (4.) Uniform stem diameter. (5.) Uniform form (6.) Pose.

In judging unlike multiple entries, numbers   2, 3, apply with attention being given to compatible colors.

CONDITION

The flowers should not be immature or aged, but should be in their prime. Clean and free of all damage, blemish or soil. Check the back as well as the front. The tips of the petals show age first by melting and thinning. They should look fresh and normal.

*Brown anthers, wilting, dropping pollen and a large, rather well-developed seed capsule also are age indicators. Immature blooms may show an ex-*cessively crinkled texture with short stems and unclear colors. The sheath of the flower, which is the brown remains of the modified *leaf which covered the bud, should not be removed, nor mutilated. Rain spots, sunburn, and sunfading are penalized, as are tears.*

FORM

Although form is dependent upon the nature of the variety, in general the outer contour of a show daffodil should be circular with the corona well-centered, and standing out from the perianth. The cup, trumpet, corona should be in good proportion to the perianth.

The width of the petals and sepals which form the perianth should be typical. The perianth segments should all be fairly flat, not cupped in over the corona, but posed uniformly around it and overlapping at the base. The perianth segments should not be more than slightly reflexed in Divisions (1) Trumpet (2) Large Cup (3) Small Cup and (4) Double. The perianth segments should be typically reflexed in Divisions (5) Triandrus and (6) Cyclamineus.

Nicks or notches in any segment or part which alters the form should be penalized in proportion to the damage. The corona brim may be ruffled, wavy or fringed, but should not have a ragged or split appearance except in the "SPLIT CORONA" varieties. Any ruffling, etc., at the corona brim should be even and uniform.

The base of the corona should taper smoothly into the perianth. Though a star-shaped form is the most generally accepted, new forms resembling waterlilies (Example: 'Pucelle') foretell the inevitable change in standards that underlines the need for Judges to keep abreast of new horticultural advances.

Petals of a show specimen should not twist excessively. In double varieties, the segments should by symmetrically arranged. Also, either the midrib of a sepal or petal of the perianth should be in a vertical line with the stem. This is called axis balance. Fusarium basal rot often causes deformed flowers.

SUBSTANCE AND TEXTURE

Substance refers to the ability of the flower to withstand cutting, to "hold up" well. While one of the valuable characteristics of daffodils is their heavy substance, the degree varies according to species, variety *and cultural conditions. Texture should be crystalline, moist, fine.*

A well-conditioned daffodil will be turgid, crisp, firm, but not so excessively strong, thick and heavy as to give a coarse appearance. Any transparency or thinning is a fault.

Texture refers to the surface of the perianth and corona. Texture of a show specimen should be smooth with a waxy appearance. Ridging, crinkling or crepeiness are to be demerited. Cutting flowers in the bud and refrigerating them often results in an undesirable ribby texture.

COLOR

Color on the perianth and corona must be even, clear, pure; free from streaks and dullness, and indefiniteness. Faded color due to age is penalized under condition. Some varieties (mainly red cups and those with red edges) are particularly susceptible to sun-burn and sunfade.

In double varieties, the color should be symmetrically arranged. Combinations should be pleasing and attractive. Green at base of cup or eye is a merit in white varieties. Narcissus Fire (botrytis) causes Tazetta species and hybrids, particularly, to throw spotted blooms. Cutting the blooms in the bud often results in a reduction of color clarity and sparkle.

Colored trims, borders and edges should be uniform, definite and even without bleeding or blurring. Staining on the petals radiating from the base of corona is not undesirable if normal for variety and the effect is pleasing. (Example: 'EFFECTIVE').

POSE

Refers to the manner in which the flower holds itself. In types having a single bloom, it should be held so the face can be seen, generally just off a 45 degree angle with the stem and when viewed from its own level, should look you in the face in Div. 1, 2, 3, 9; also for Div. 4 except for SPORTS that normally droop ('CHEERFULNESS', 'WHITE MARVEL'); Div. 5, 6, 7 heads may droop; Div. 8 should be dome-shaped. Pose depends upon the length and strength of the neck. If the neck is weak, or too long the bloom droops and a penalty must be taken unless such pose is typical as in the triandrus and cyclamineus families.

A short neck, such as is characteristic of 'GOLDCOURT' presents a squat, hunch-back effect and may make the flower face upward. A pleasing normal is the objective and the wise exhibitor will show those varieties which come the closest to the ideal of perfection in all the qualities. This is the sort of "one-upmanship" that brings home the ribbons.

STEM

The stem of the show daffodil should be straight and strong enough to support the bloom (s) but should not be coarse, thick, clumsy or spindly. It should present a circular, rather than flat appearance. A stem shorter than normal may indicate that the flowers were cut in the bud and held under refrigeration, as the stem normally lengthens (sometimes as much as 6") as the bloom continues to mature.

Normal height of Trumpets, etc. is 15-24", though some are taller *or shorter than normal ('BEERSHEBA'). Miniatures are proportionately tiny, usually not exceeding 8". 'WEE BEE' is 5"; 'MINOR' is 4" and 'KIDLING' is 7".*

Intermediates, 8 to 14", are too big to be miniatures, but too small to stand much chance against big brothers where they are usually placed, i.e., ('PEPPER', 14"). There is some overlapping in Intermediates, especially in the triandrus, cyclamineus and jonquillas.

Stems cut from clumps with dense foliage may exhibit bleaching near the base which is not a fault. Some twisting of the stem is normal in most narcissus, therefore, caution should be used in penalizing severely a flower which is otherwise excellent. Foliage displayed with the specimen is not judged. Foliage does not grow attached to the stem therefore is not included in the judging scale. Foliage is needed to mature the bulb, to show it with the bloom indicates poor cultural practices.

SIZE

It is hoped that the Schedule will allow enough classes so smaller *daffodils do not need to compete with larger. The size, of course, varies with the variety and should be typical. Grace and charm have been sacrificed for size, coarse appearance is penalized.*

The size should be according to variety and as large, due to cultural excellence as good proportion allows; there should be no extremes on either side of normalcy. Flowers vary from thimble size, singles and in clusters to blooms five or six inches in diameter.

The bloom continues to enlarge after the bud opens; too early cutting reduces size. A size a bit larger than the norm, yet falling short of blowziness will often be the deciding factor, all other qualities being equal. For instance, in a class of 'ULSTER PRINCE', all other qualities being equal, the largest one usually wins. This does not apply of course, to miniatures, where larger size destroys the petite proportions.

Excessive nitrogen fertilizer decreases floriferousness, and may cause basal rot.

SUMMARY:

Condition 20 Points

*normal *fresh *mature *fragrance typical *clean

-wilting -over-developed seed capsule -pollen drop -soiled -bruised -fading -*spathe removed -anthers brown -torn -nicked -sunburned*

Form 20 Points

*corona well centered *corona and perianth well scaled to each other *axis balanced *outer contour circular *perianth fairly flat *segments overlapping at the base *reflex typical *ruffling and colored trim even *doubles *symmetrical *indentations even*

-torn or split parts -excessive petal twist -corona brim split -corona off-center -petals or sepals lacking uniform pose -doubles lop-sided -deformed -spaces between perianth segments -perianth cupped excessively

250

Substance and Texture 15 Points

Substance: *turgid *crisp *firm

-transparent -thin -limp -flabby -papery

Texture: *smooth *waxy *fine

-ribby -crepey -rough

Color 15 Points

*even *clear *bright *pleasing combination *fast *sunproof *unusual *luminous

-weak -uneven -diluted -indefinite -sunburned -spotted -streaked -flat -dull -clouded -bleached

Pose 10 Points

*45 degree angle to stem for Div. 1, 2, 3, 9 *typical for type

-drooping (not typically) -too upright -neck too short (squat appearing) -neck too long -neck too thin

Stem 10 Points

*straight *proportionate to flower *typical *strong *cylindrical *ridges down sides

-weak -flat -spindly -coarse -thick -abnormally ribbed -crooked -badly twisted -too long or short

Size 10 Points

*slightly above normal *typical *maximum potential in all parts *petite

-puny -not typical -stunted -ungainly -topheavy -overlarge (especially in miniatures) -coarse

ORCHIDS

Orchids

SUGGESTED CLASSES:
1. Cut Flower or Spray (sub-classes for species, varieties)
2. Collection of cut flowers (three different)
3. Potted Plant (sub-classes for species, varieties)
4. Display of Potted Plants

ORCHIDS

The Orchidaceae are an exceedingly involved family of particularly showy flowers with remarkably distinctive form. The family includes both epiphytes (air-growing) and terrestrial (land-growing) plants among its 500-600 known genera of which only about 25 are of practical value.

The flower form is entirely different from any other family of plants. They are irregular, but symmetrical in shape with three sepals and three petals, only two of the latter being alike. The third petal which is lip-shaped (called the labellum) has many distinctive forms some of which are pouch or sac-shaped, spurred, fringed or compound.

The flower stems differ in that some, such as Cattleya have a short, husky flower stalk compared to others such as Phalaenopsis which have long, wiry, arching stems.

KEY TO VARIOUS ORCHID PARTS

A—appendage

P—petal

L—labellum or lip

LS—lateral sepal, in some called the ventral sepal (VS)

DS—dorsal sepal

T—throat

M—mask

C—column

The following classifications cover the major horticultural types.

1. CATTLEYA labiata

- common corsage orchid
- large, 5" to 9" spread depending on variety
- grown on fairly short, sturdy stems
- trumpet lipped, prominently colored
- fairly flat
- many crosses cause form, size and color and substance variations

SCALE OF POINTS FOR CATTLEYA

Form	30
. general form	15
. sepals	5
. petals	5
. labellum (lip)	5

Color of Flowers	30
. general color	15
. sepals and petals	7
. labellum	8

Other Characteristics	40
. size of flower	10
. substance & texture	20
. floriferousness & stem	10

Form 30 Points

*carriage and proportion of petals, sepals, lip according to variety *circular outline *wide, full *sepals filling gaps between petals and lip petals and lip to form an equilateral triangle *petals erect *slightly arching *petals broad, rounded *petals undulated, ruffled at margin according to variety, uniformly *sepals stand out straight horizontally from base *do not bend back toward stem *lip end rounded *symmetrical *closed toward the base (tubular) *lip rolled into a column *wide open at lower end

-lopsided -oblong -sepals too narrow -petals too stiff -petals drooping -petals crumpled -petals folded -petals and sepals reflexing excessively toward stem -lip jutting out at right angle when viewed from side -lip poorly shaped -lip gaping at base -trumpet off center -flower as a whole lacks compactness

Color 30 Points

*clear *bright *strong *intense *vibrant *evenly dispersed throughout *of a hue in keeping with variety *in a balanced, harmonious pattern *lip more prominently colored *lip more richly colored than petals, sepals *symmetrical pattern if additionally marked *lip blends or pleasantly contrasts with rest

-weak -dull -muddy -color washed out at mid-veins -spotted -color breaking -color "splashing" -pale -scarred -bleached

Substance and Texture 20 Points

Texture: *sparkling *crystalline *velvety *waxy *fragrant according to variety
-coarse -dull -grainy

Substance: *thick *crisp *turgid
-thin -shrinking tissues -flabby

Size of Flowers 10 Points

*5 to 9" according to variety *maximum potential in all parts *larger than average *typical

-small -dwarfed -less imposing than expected

Floriferousness and Stem 10 Points

Labiata Cattleyas two or more flowers, though a single, exceptionally well-formed and large flower is judged. Bifoliate Cattleyas several flowers should be open. 2-25 in a cluster up to 5" in diameter, according to variety.
*stem strong *upright *flowers held at best advantage *flower posed to

face straight out at viewer *flower well held on stem
-weak -crooked -deformed -flowers crowded -not holding flower erect, straight out

2: CYPRIPEDIUM   Pouch lip

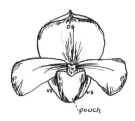

● includes Paphiopedilum, Phagmopedilum, Selenipedium
● also includes native Ladyslipper (Moccasin Flower)
● pouch lip is distinguishing feature
● also the large, often brilliantly marked dorsal fin at the top of the flower
● heavy substance taken for granted
● flower stem bears 1 to 4-5, depending on variety
● stem is short and of a diameter according to type

SCALE OF POINTS FOR CYPRIPEDIUM

Other Characteristics	20	Color	40
. size	10	. general color	20
. substance & texture	5	. sepals	10
. stem	5	. petals	5
		. pouch	5
Form	40		
. general form	20		
. sepals	10		
. petals	5		
. pouch	5		

Form 40 Points

General *full *segments well balanced and in proportion *neatly formed -loosely formed -ill posed -off center

Sepals *dorsal sepal (top) large, rounded *slightly concave *not reflexed *prominent *broad *wider than tall *ventral sepal (lower, behind pouch) *inconspicuous *forming a harmonious background for the pouch

253

Petals *narrow at base to broad at tip *proportioned to parts, though one group has elongated twisted petals *fairly horizontal *slender in proportion to dorsal

-narrow tip -too short in proportion to flower -too narrow or wide compared to dorsal

Pouch *in proportion to rest of flower *slipper shaped *conspicuous *stands sharply forward *may be eared, notched *approximately equal in length to ventral sepals

-poorly shaped -off center -loose -ill posed -irregular development

Color 40 Points

General *well-defined areas and patterns *exotic or subtle combinations *definite

Dorsal Sepal *brilliantly marked *striking *vivid *bold *may be barred, striped, spotted, veined, reticulated, tipped, contrasted, etc.

Other *pouch often brilliantly marked, colored *must be harmonious *two sections of the genus may have mottled, varicolored foliage

-weak -greyed -faded -streaky -lacks brilliance -lacks sparkle -plain -browning

Other Characteristics 20 Points

Size 10 Based on width of dorsal sepal and the proportions of the rest of the flower parts according to variety. Some petals may extend to 5" with a 2" tall dorsal (praestans) to 1½' in P. sanderianum. Callosum may have a 3" dorsal. 1-5 blooms per stem, according to variety

Substance and Texture 5 Points

Substance: *heavy *firm *strong *plump

-flabby -limp

Texture: *waxy *varnished in petals and pouch *plastic-like *may be warty, shiny or hairy, according to variety

-coarse -dull

Stem 5 Points

*proportioned to flower size *strong

-short -weak -bending

3: PHALAENOPSIS   Moth Orchid

- 'moth' orchid, so called because of its shape similarity to that insect
- long, arching sprays, sometimes branched

- strap-like foliage, long clinging roots
- many blooms per spray 4-20 depending upon variety and breeding
- all flowers face same direction
- flower size 1" ('Esmeralda') 1½-2" ('Lowii') to 5" ('Aphrodite')
- flower structure forms two groups
1. Euphalaenopsis (most widely grown) with petals broader than sepals and antennae-like appendages on the lip
2. Stauroglottis with petals similar to sepals in size and a lip without appendages

SCALE OF POINTS FOR PHALAENOPSIS

Flower Form	30	Other Characteristics	40
. general form	15	. size of flower	10
. sepals	5	. substance & texture	10
. petals	6	. habit and arrangement of	
. labellum (lip)	4	inflorescence	10
		. floriferousness	10
Color	30		
. general	15		
. sepals and petals	10		
. labellum	5		

Form 30 Points

General *full *circular *symmetrical *flat

Sepals *dorsal sepal larger, broader than lateral sepals *sepals arranged in equilateral triangle

Petals *broad *flat *fill gap between sepals *mid veins preferably horizontal

Lip *form varies according to variety. Most flowers of this genus have antennae-like appendages (cirri) or horns at lip base (Exception is P. Lowii)

-torn or missing parts -malformed -bunched -crowded -twisted petals or sepals -irregular development -lacks symmetry

Color 30 Points

*lip distinctively marked or colored *clear *definite *markings harmonious *pure *contrasting or blended over flower *sparkling *lustrous *alive

-lacks sparkle, brilliance -dull -pale -off

Size 10 Points

*flowers 1½ to 5" diameter depending upon species, etc. *larger than average is ideal *typical

-retarded -smaller than is typical

Substance and Texture 10 Points

*waxy *heavy *crisp *sparkling

-limp -thin

Inflorescence 10 Points

*gracefully arching *flowers well spaced *long *single or branched *each flower faces in same direction

-stiff -poorly placed -ill posed -crowded -twisted placement -short

Floriferousness 10 Points

*3-4 on Lueddemanniana to 15-20 on Esmeralda

-skimpy -lacking -inadequate

4: CYMBIDIUM

- tall, arching sprays
- grassy foliage
- 5-30 blooms per spray, several sprays per plant
- simple, serene form, petals and sepals form a wide X
- margins generally smooth
- very waxy substance, lasts 1½ to 3 months

255

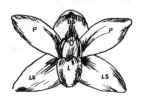

- delicately colored, yellow, green, rose, white, plainly or subtly blended
- some have star-like form, some more cupped
- size: plant up to 5' spread, leaves 1½ to 3' long, flowers depending on variety, etc. Grandiflorum measure 5" Insigne 3-4" etc.

XX SCALE OF POINTS

This Scale is used for Cymbidiums, Ondontoglossum, Miltonias, Dendrobiums

Flower Form	30	Other Characteristics	40
. general form	15	. size of flower	10
. sepals	5	. substance, texture	10
. petals	5	. habit and arrangement of	
. labellum (lip)	5	inflorescence	10
		. floriferousness	10
Flower Color	**30**		
. general color	15		
. sepals, petals	8		
. labellum	7		

Form 30 Points

*symmetrical placements *more or less rectangular outline *more or less pointed sepals and petals or nearly equal size and shape, similar color *dorsal (top sepal may be curved, hooded) *sepals broad filling gaps between petals and lip *sepals and petals arranged in nearly equilateral triangle *petals broad, slightly arched *minimum of narrowing toward petal tip *column erect *lip proportionately sized *side lobes erect *front lobe gracefully curved

-excessively cupped overall form -sepals too narrow -petal tips too blunt -front lip iobe abruptly turned under -front lip pinched, narrow at top -off center -irregular development -torn

Color 30 Points

*definite *clear *suffusion of one color over another regular, harmonious *color veining (if present) definite, distinctive *veining in regular lines and patterns *lip as distinctively colored as sepals, petals *lip markings in definite, distinctive patterns *throat and crests clear white or brightly colored

-mottled -muddy -greyed -uneven -faded -lacks harmony, uniformity

Size 10 Points

*3-5" depending upon variety, etc. *considerably larger than average for variety *typical

-small -dwarfed

Substance and Texture 10 Points

Substance: *crisp *fresh *perky *fleshy

-thinning -limp -flabby

Texture: *sparkling *waxy *heavy *lip may be downy

-crepey -dull -rough -coarse

Inflorescence 10 Points
*erect *tall *gracefully arching sprays *flowers well spaced *well displayed

-crowded -bunched

Floriferousness 10 Points
*each spray (according to variety and breeding) bears 5-30 blooms with one to several sprays per plant

-scanty -inadequate number

5: VANDA

- over 25 species
- gracefully arching sprays
- 3-80 blossoms
- foliage usually strap-like, tho some (terete species) have cylindrical, fleshy leaves

SCALE OF POINTS FOR VANDA

Flower Form	30	Other Characteristics	40
. general form	15	. flower size	10
. sepals	7	. substance, texture	10
. petals	5	. habit and arrangement of inflorescence	10
. labellum	3	. floriferousness	10
Flower Color	**30**		
. general color	15		
. sepals	7		
. petals	5		
. labellum	3		

Form 30 Points
*flat *full *spreading *no pointed tips on sepals or petals

Sepals: *broad *rounded *arranged in equilateral triangle *all 3 the same size

Petals: *slightly smaller than sepals *rounded *broad *fill gaps between sepals

Lip: *very much smaller than 2 other petals (except in V. Hookeriana terete where lip is as large) *harmonious in size, shape

Generally: -twisted -narrow -lip ill formed -loosely put together

Color 30 Points
*definite *pure *clear *suffusions regular *harmonious *color veining definite, distinctive *color veining in regular lines and patterns

-mottled -muddy -blurred -dull -not typical

Size 10 Points — 2-5" according to breeding
*larger than average is the ideal *typical

-small -stunted

Substance and Texture 10 Points
*heavy *crisp *long-lasting *fragrant *waxy

-flabby -limp -thin -dull -coarse

Inflorescence 10 Points

*erect or gracefully arching according to variety *flowers well-spaced

-straggly -bunched

Floriferousness 10 Points — (3-80 blooms per spray according to variety)

*more than expected for variety

-scanty -sparse

6: MILTONIAS   Pansy Orchid

- numerous
- called 'pansy' orchid, has "blotch face"

- lower petal (lip, labellum) is most prominent feature
- oval, symmetrical, flowers open flat
- softly colored, varied shades
- 1-10 flowers per spray according to species or spectabilis with up to 50 flowers, each on its own stem, all open at once
- foliage short, often yellow-green
- flowers 2" (Roezlii) to 4" (vexillaria)

USE XX SCALE OF POINTS — (See Cymbidiums)

Form 30 Points

*full *flat *sepals and petals slightly reflexed *two upper petals rather blunt "squared off" *lip (lower petal) predominantly large *flat *indented as in the pansy *lip spreading, oval or fiddle-shape according to variety

-lip too deeply indented or not enough -sepals, petals excessively reflexed -deformed -off center -lip too small -lip must balance whole upper part of flower

Color 30 Points

*free of blemish *distinct *varied, generally soft *mask, if present, should be symmetrical, well-defined, similar to pansy "face"

-dull -fading -weak -blemished -browning edges

Size 10 Points — 2-4" according to variety

*larger than expected *typical

-freakish -stunted

Substance and Texture 10 Points   (lasts for four weeks)

*glistening *firm *perky

-curling -shrinking -limp

Inflorescence 10 Points

*gracefully erect or arching *flowers well displayed along the stem

-crowded -stiff -flowers hiding each other

Floriferousness 10 Points   1-50 according to species

*more than expected *typical

-skimpy -spindly

7: DENDROBIUM

- over 1,000 species, both deciduous and evergreen

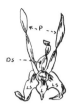

- form varies from similar to Cattleya (use that scale) similar to Phalaenopsis (use that scale) petals and sepals more or less equal with broad lip (use **XX** scale, see Cymbidiums)
- generally more delicate, fine
- 2-5" according to variety and breeding
- drooping sprays or upright clusters
- 2-50 blooms per spray or cluster

USE XX SCALE OF POINTS — (See Cymbidiums)

Form 30 Points

While the 1,000 species provide varied form, characteristically the lateral sepals are united at the base to more or less form a spur and the lip or lower petal narrows at the base to a mere stalk. Top petals may be erect, twisted or fringed.

*proportioned to rest of flower *symmetrical *typical

-squat -out of proportion -off center -lopsided

Color 30 Points   May be in spots, eyes, margins, tips, streaks

*pure *bright *clear

-dull -weak -streaky

Size 10 Points   2-5" depending upon breeding

*larger than average *typical

-small -stunted

Substance and Texture 10 Points

*waxy *some varieties have a downy lip *luminous

-dull -grainy -rough

Inflorescence 10 Points

drooping sprays or upright clusters according to variety

Floriferousness 10 Points

2-50 or more blooms per spray
*more than expected *abundant *typical

-too few for type -scanty

8: ONDONTOGLOSSUM   Oncidium

- over 100 species
- arching sprays
- 2-200 flowers per stem or panicle according to species, etc.
- 1-9" diameter
- varying colors

USE XX SCALE OF POINTS — (See Cymbidiums)

Form 30 Points

*petals and sepals each form overlapping equilateral triangles *sepals are more narrow and pointed than petals *circular outline *full *flat *spreading *petals bluntly rounded *base of lip (lower petal) parallel to column *generously rounded lip may be narrow, heart-shaped, kidney or shield-shaped *O. crispum is lacy, borders notched, toothed *flower parts well proportioned *well set

-too arched -divided appearance -torn -too narrow

Color 30 Points

*striking *well-defined patterns may be tinged, spotted, speckled, barred *clear *bright

-blurry -lacks brilliance -off color -fading -browning edges

Size 10 Points   1" up to 9" (O. grande)

*above average *typical

-stunted -less than average

Substance and Texture 10 Points

*long lasting *thick *waxy *crisp *may be downy in texture

-thinning -crepey -rough -coarse

Inflorescence 10 Points

*simple or branching *flowers well spaced *flowers well displayed

-crowded -stiff

Floriferousness 10 Points   2-200 per stem on panicle according to species

*profuse *more than average *typical

-sparse -less than average -too few

POTTED PLANT

Most Orchid exhibits in regular shows are potted plants, judged for cultural merit, for which the following scale may be used. For details on flower form, color, quality, size and floriferousness according to species, see the preceding breakdowns under name as for instance if the plant is a Cattleya, see that coverage.

SCALE OF POINTS FOR POTTED ORCHID PLANT

Flower	70	Plant	30
. form	25	. floriferousness	15
. color	20	. cultural perfection including	10
. quality (substance, texture condition)	20	: freedom from blemish, disease, insects	
. size	5	: well groomed (dust, dried leaves removed)	
		: size in relation to container	
		: in active growth	
		. labeling	5

Flower 70 Points   See specific species
Plant 30 Points

*sturdy *clean *well rooted *thriving *vigorous *free growing *in active growth *free of disease, pests, cultural malpractice *normal, characteristic foliage *supports and ties used sparingly *supports and ties inconspicuous supports and tie color compatible to leaf, stem *spent leaves, flowers neatly removed

-retarded -stunted -aged -needs repotting -succulent, soft growth -poorly developed -disease, pest or cultural malpractice evident (see breakdown following) -foliage yellowed -burned -drying -needs supports -foliage artificially "glossed"

Cultural Malpractice

(environmental — soil, temperature, light; disease, pests)

Environmental

. foliage yellowed, burned .... too much sun or light
. sepals dried .... too much sun or light
. foliage succulent, too dark green .... plant lacks sun
. poorly developed, leaves falling .... temperature too high
. yellowing .... may be excessive over or under-watering
. yellowing .... lacks nutrition (repot in osmundine)
. scars, wounds .... carelessness
. flowers spotted .... humidity too high

Disease

. foliage oozing drops, spots semi-transparent, later brown or
  black .... bacterial disease, Leaf. Spot
. foliage drying .... Orchid Wilt
. foliage browning at tip, progressing down to base .... Die Back
. foliage discolored, falling off .... Heart Rot Fungus
. foliage with sunken spots (red, yellow, dark green and a water
  soaked appearance .... Fungus Diseases
. flowers spotted and blotched with transparent spots, bordered
  in pink .... Fungus Petal Blight
. failure to flower (one cause), with orange yellow spots .... Rust
. foliage flecked and streaked with yellow .... Mosaic (Virus)

Pests

. swollen pseudobulbs .... Cattleya Fly
. root die back, spoiled blooms and foliage .... Orchid Weevil
. scaly, yellow mottling .... Scale
. circular spots, transparent, white or brown on flowers and
  foliage .... Thrips
. white spots on thin-leaved foliage and on Cattleya flowers .... Red Spider
. minute punctures on leaves, flower parts .... Springtail
. chewed flower parts .... Slugs, mice

Orchid Blooms Are Past Prime When —

. petals shrivel and pull together
. petals are excessively transparent
. the green where the sepals and petals join together fades out
. the tip of the sepals show dryness

SCALE OF POINTS FOR DISPLAY OF PLANTS

ARRANGED FOR EFFECT

General Arrangement	35	Variety	20
Quality of Flowers & Plant	35	Labeling	10

Peony <small>(Herbaceous)</small>

SUGGESTED CLASSES: Stems 15-18"

A. Single — 1 bloom, any color
B. Japanese — 1 bloom, any color
C. Semi Double — 1 bloom, any color
D. Double — 1 bloom, any color
E. Collection of Blooms — 3 blooms, different colors, same type
F. 3 blooms, different types

In areas where enough exhibits are anticipated sub-classes can be made for colors and a special class made for Hybrids.

PEONY

The Peony is a hardy perennial or small shrub (Tree Peony) of the genus Paeonia of the family Ranunculaceae which also includes buttercups (type), anemone, larkspur, etc.

The genus is divided into three section:

1. **P. moutan,** the tree Peony species (**P. suffruticosa** designates those from China and Japan).

2. **P. onaepia,** two species both native to America (West Coast) having sepals and petals the same length.

3. **Paeon,** all European, African and Asian herbaceous species from which have evolved our present-day plants.

Peonies are classified according to the form the flower takes. There are five distinct types as follows:

1. SINGLE

- five or more petals
- one or two rows
- arranged around a center of pollen bearing stamens and carpels
- center filaments are fine, threadlike
- center generally yellow, sometimes red in the red varieties
- Example; 'SEASHELL'

2: JAPANESE

- 5 or more petals
- a center of stamen bearing abortive anthers which may be thread-like or thickened. May present a tousled appearance in the center

- center cushion frequently a different color from outside collar of petals
- main difference from Singles is that the Japanese are nearly or completely devoid of pollen. The pollen test must often be used to distinguish fine-filament varieties such as 'WHITE GOLD' and 'ISANI GIDUI' from the singles
- Example: 'WHITE GOLD'

3: ANEMONE

- usually listed in catalogs as either Japanese or double rather than Anemone. e. g. 'GAY PAREE' is listed as Japanese and 'CAROLINA MOON' as a double

4: SEMI DOUBLE

5: DOUBLE

- five or more guard petals
- center of stamens and carpels more or less fully transformed into petals

- to avoid confusion it is best to eliminate the class from regular Shows
- 5 or more guard petals
- arranged around a center of stamens fully transformed into small, narrow petals called petalodes
- usually the center cluster is yellow or the same color as the guard petals, though novelty types may have contrasting-colored center and guard petals

- five or more guard petals plus
- several rows of petals and stamens intermixed
- the stamens may be all grouped in the center or may be mixed in among the petals
- distinguishing feature is that the stamens **must** be prominent
- Example: 'RARE CHINA'

- of varying widths and degrees of serration which make up the bulk of the flower
- distinguishing feature is that the stamens **must** be completely buried
- doubles are sometimes sub-divided into globular, bomb, and rose forms (also crown, conical, etc.) However, these forms are unstable, may vary with age, weather and other conditions and are best not used as a classification in the average show. The same may be said of the Hybrid Class.

CUT FLOWER VARIETIES

These are defined as dependable varieties which consistently give strong stems, lovely flowers and abundant blooms; have both commercial and home landscape value and are generally lacking in tempermental qualities such as weak stems, hard openers, weak plants, poor growers and shy bloomers. The list includes such as 'MONS JULES ELIE', 'FESTIVA MAXIMA', 'REINE HORTENSE', RICHARD CARVEL', 'EDULIS SUPERBA', etc.

EXHIBITION VARIETIES

These are defined as varieties in which the plant must produce a flower of extraordinary beauty and form. The show bench bloom is of paramount importance. Special emphasis is on perfection of form. Any relaxation of the rules for judging conditions as altered by adverse climatic conditions is discouraged in this group. The presence of fragrance might be the deciding factor — all other qualities being equal. The list includes such as 'ANN COUSINS', 'LE CYGNE', 'MRS J. V. EGLUND' as top-rated Double exhibition types. 'MISS AMERICA' is a top-rated Semi-Double exhibition type. 'TAMATE BOKU' is a high-rated Japanese type with 'ISANI-GIDUI' noted for having very fine purity of color. 'SEASHELL' and 'PICO' represent top exhibition form in the Singles.

Some varieties possess qualities which class them as both ideal cut-flower and exhibition plants, these include such doubles as 'DORIS COOPER', 'LA LORRAINE', 'HANSINA BRAND', 'MARTHA BUL-LOCH', 'RED CHARM', 'MRS. F. D. ROOSEVELT' and 'SARAH BERN-HARDT'.

HYBRIDS

Hybrids are produced by crossing one species with an entirely different species. Example is the pale yellow hybrid 'CLAIRE de LUNE' which is a cross of the **P. mlokosewitschi** and **P. lactiflora.** Hybrids are generally earlier blooming than the lactiflora and one of their main claims to recognition is a clarity and brilliance of color not generally found in lactiflora. This clarity and brilliance of color is a prime characteristic to be judged along with perfect form. Hybrids top-rated as exhibition flowers include 'RED CHARM' and 'CARINA' (for excellent color) and 'LAURA MAGNUSON' for color and top form.

SCALE OF POINTS
CUT FLOWER SPECIMEN

Form	30	Condition & Freshness	10
Color	30	Stem & Foliage	10
		Size	5
Substance & Texture	10	Distinctiveness	5

Form 30 Points

Unstable Forms. Perfection of form is of main consideration in judging Peonies. The characteristics of single, Japanese, semi-double and double vary in the same variety due to maturity, weather and other conditions, including the fact that first and second year blooms are often not typical of the form for the variety.

There may be several different type flowers on the same plant at the same time, such as happens on 'CHOCOLATE SOLDIER' and the old Red lactiflora 'ADOLPHE ROUSSEAU'. Some varieties ('A. J. PERRY', 'ELIZABETH HUNTINGTON') may vary in form from semi-double to double with stamens visible (semi-double characteristic) at one time and stamens completely hidden (double characteristic) another time.

The Classification Committee and the Judges must therefore place and the judge exhibits in that class which most closely **fits** the form of the individual flower **in that instance.**

While botanically a semi-double is any flower in which stamens appear whether hidden or prominent, the American Peony Society limits classes to those varieties in which stamens are **prominent!** And class those in which stamens are hidden or not easy to see as double, though botanically a double flower is one in which all the stamens have been completely transformed into petals. Many of the reds have hidden stamens.

For instance 'TEMPEST' often shows its stamens quite prominently and is judged as a semi-double; while another specimen of the same variety may have the stamens completely hidden and be judged as a double.

Judges do not eliminate a flower when its form complies with the class specifications regardless of the name its label gives. Form variations can be expected in Hybrids; point tips are quite pronounced in some hybrid bombs and are sometimes referred to as jappy bombs.

Centers

Not all doubles are high centered. Varieties like the famous 'JUBILEE' are quite flat when fully open which is the way they should be when shown.

Informal

An "informal" flower is one that often has its inner petals not symmetrically arranged. An example is 'GEORGE W. PEYTON' which though beautifully formed, seldom wins if the Judges are too strict about symmetry within the circular form.

Notching or Crimped Petals

This is usually due to weather, freezing and thawing. The condition is not 'normal', however, seldom is a single found without this flaw.

DOUBLE SUB-DIVISIONS

The division of doubles into sub-groups is confusing and difficult as this is an unstable characteristic of form with the same variety often assuming more than one of these forms at various stages of maturity of the bloom. However, they are briefly defined here for the Judge's edification should he encounter these sub-divisions.

Globular: is spherical, completely ball or half a ball. The outer guard petals are shorter than the inner ones. This is further divided into —

Crown Several rows of guard petals with a center in which the stigmas and often the whole carpel (pistel) have been transformed into a central tuft of petals which form a crown or nest above the other petals. Example 'JEANNE d' ARC'

Conical several rows of guard petals with a center that forms a cone. Example: a **fresh** specimen of 'BLUSH QUEEN'

Bomb Most florist cut blooms are bomb shape. With one or more rows of wide, flaring guard petals with a center of narrow petals formed into 'bomb'. Outer petals are much longer than inner petals and are held in a horizontal position. Example is a **fresh** bloom of 'MONS JULES ELIE'

Rose   one in which all parts have been transformed into petals, symmetrically arranged and forming a rosebud-like center. The Judge must not select any one of these as the ideal form and penalize everything that does not comply. It should be noted again that such varieties often lose these forms with a bit more maturity and become the simple globular type

Cupped Singles

If cut too soon the guard petals of Singles, Japanese and Semi-doubles may lock, preventing opening; a rigid cupped form or resemblance to a tulip is severely penalized under form.

A bloom of any of the types may be distorted by careless bagging (using too small a bag or carelessly placed bag). Petals of any of the types may be wavy, ruffled, other according to variety.

Color 30 Points

If the schedule calls for white with no incidental colors, very few will fit. 'MISS AMERICA' and 'ISANI GIDUI' are examples of **pure** white. Most so-called whites have a tint of some kind. The Schedule or instructions to the Judges should advise leniency in the average show regarding color flecking of whites or infusions. Dinginess or impurity is penalized however.

Red and its values are apt to show impure infusions of magenta, bluing and dark murky tones which are to be penalized.

Deductions must be made for weakness or fading. Fading can be ascertained as such if the petals have retained their substance and crispness, are not limp and soft.

Color varies in different localities and under certain show lights, so the Judge must exercise due caution in penalizing.

Condition and Freshness 10 Points

Carpels (pistel) are usually some shade of green but may turn to other colors with age. In some Anemone types, the transformed stamens (petalodes) fade from yellow to white with age.

In judging exhibition flowers, relaxation of rules for judging condition as altered by adverse climatic conditions, is discouraged.

SUMMARY:
Form 30 Points

*circular *fits class Singles with pollen: Japs with no pollen: Semi with stamens prominent: Double with stamens hidden *petals attractively placed *depth of flower typical of variety *well posed on stem *center well developed *refinement evidenced by a delicacy of petal form and placement *center built up uniformly *erect carriage *outer petals uniform length *mature enough to show true form *double center fully incurved with no sign of breakdown or separation

Single and Japanese should be *graceful *circular, saucer shaped *guard petals broad *guard petals same length *may be overlapped or more widespread according to variety

-lopsided -irregular development -irregular depth -distorted -center opening (Double) -excessively cupped (locked or tulip-like Jap. Single or Semi) -guard petals severely crimped or split -guard petals uneven lengths -abortive petals in the collar of guard petals -looseness -falling apart -shedding -coarse -ungainly -rough -guard petals relaxed, drooping, altering form -separation, weakness in the collar -opening anthers -stamens breaking down

Color 30 Points

*brilliant *clear *harmonious *rich *true to variety *pure *luminous *bold

-faded out (should have been bagged) -bleached -blotched -streaked (other than typical) -defacing marks -lack of beauty -pronounced magenta tones in pinks, reds -muddy dark tones in red -bluing -washed out appearance in near whites -dingy whites -insipid -weak -uneven -off -reds greying -dull -plain

Substance and Texture 10 Points

Substance: *long lasting *perky *fleshy *turgid *crisp *heavy
-relaxing -wilting -thinning -flabby

Texture: *silken sheen *velvety *suedelike *glistening *translucent *satiny *luminous
-dull -coarse -crepey -rough -lacks sparkle

Condition and Freshness 10 Points

*unmarred *prime *correct degree of maturity *healthy *clean *turgid *Japanese type nearly or completely devoid of pollen

-holes in petals (Rose Bugs) -mould caused by bagging wet blooms or careless storage -wilting -relaxing -water spotted -dust, soil or spray residue -pollen stains -over or under age -indications of poor culture -shriveling -crinkling -torn petals or foliage -dried foliage -bruised foliage or petals -creased or bent guard petals

Stem and Foliage 10 Points

Blooms that have been kept in cold storage are not penalized for damage to foliage or lack of foliage

*strong *adequate stem to support bloom *sturdy stem, starting at base of flower *disbudded to get full varietal size *1-2 upper leaves present *stems erect *in proportion to flower and type *green, luxuriant foliage

-stem or leaves marred by long, brown spots (Peony Measles, caused by Botrytis or similar Blights) -Leaf Spot evident -not disbudded -too recently disbudded -stems weak -damaged -scars left by careless disbudding -all foliage below water line should be removed, (leaving at least two upper leaves) -foliage damaged by insects or disease -weak neck -whippy

Size 5 Points

Peonies measure two inches up to 12 inches under optimum conditions. Average size it five to eight inches. The only way the smaller peony wins over a larger is if the smaller has more perfect form and color.

*well above average size *slightly above average *normal for variety and locality *no penalty for oversize except in miniatures and at the expense of other qualities *maximum potential reached in all parts without sacrificing perfection of form

-undersize for variety and type -big miniature -stunted -less imposing -ungainly

Distinction 5 Points

*overall charm and quality *well staged *labels legible and correct *has class *refinement as evidenced by a combination of delicacy of petal formation and outstanding color *unique color contrasts, or blends or glow *distinction in shape, form, placement of individual petals and/or petalodes *fragrance may be mild, pleasing, strong roselike or slight

-poorly staged -labels carelessly printed -label incorrect -mediocre -plain -has many faults which reduce appeal and distinction

Poinsettia (Euphorbia pulcherrima)

SUGGESTED CLASSES:

Note: **Named varieties** are subdivided according to variety (i.e. 'ECKE'S FLAMING SPHERE', 'ELIZABETH ECKE', 'PAUL MIKKELSEN', 'ECKE'S YELLOW', etc.) **Unidentified varieties** are subdivided according to wide or narrow bracts.

1. SPECIMEN BLOOM ON A STEM

A. Red

1. Singles
   a. named variety

   b. unidentified variety

2. Double
   a. named variety

   b. unidentified variety

B. Pink   1. named variety   2. unidentified variety
C. White   1. named variety   2. unidentified variety
D. Yellow 1. named variety   2. unidentified variety
E. Others

2. COLLECTION (5 blooms on individual stems)

1. named varieties
2. unidentifed varieties

3. CONTAINER GROWN PLANTS

A. One Poinsettia Plant
   1. Branched
   2. Unbranched
B. Two or more Poinsettia Plants grown in a single container.

POINSETTIA: (Euphorbia pulcherrima)

A perennial plant belonging to the extensive Euphorbiaceae or Spurge family. It is characteristic that Poinsettias do not always remain stable or true to type. If a plant, sold as a named variety, does not develop known characteristics attendant to the name, it should not be entered in a class for that named variety, but should be entered as an unidentified variety.

SCALES OF POINTS
By American Poinsettia Society

Specimen Bloom on Branch		Container Grown Plant	
Bloom	80	Bloom	60
. form	20	. size	25
. size	20	. form	20
. color	15	. color	15
. substance	15	Plant	30
. bloom position	10	. cultural perfection	15
Stem and Foliage	10	. foliage	10
		. stem	5
Condition	10	Grooming	10

COLLECTION OF SPECIMENS

Bloom	55	Uniformity	30
. form	15		
. size	15	Stem and Foliage	5
. color	10		
. substance	10	Condition	10
. bloom position	5		

NOTE: Allowance should be made where Poinsettias are grown in experimental locations, but not carried to the extent of lowering the standards of attainable excellence in form and substance.

BLOOM FORM

The form of Poinsettias is unique in that the bracts (modified leaves) are the showiest part, being large, white or highly colored and closely resembling petals. A bloom (as correctly defined) does not ordinarily include the bracts, but for ease of identification the word "bloom" herein will denote both the actual flowers and the colorful bracts of the Poinsettia.

The actual Poinsettia flowers are very tiny and are contained in small red or green cup-like structures called cyathiums; a number of which appear in the center of the encircling bracts. A well-grown Poinsettia need not necessarily be round, but will be uniformly symmetrical.

Currently, there are three distinct form types:
1. the double
2. the single with wide bracts and
3. the single with narrow bracts.

DOUBLE Poinsettias are made up of numerous, narrow, overlapping bracts which form a compact, symmetrical bloom. Any loose attachments or lopsided appearance is to be penalized. The points for form must be reduced if any bracts are missing, deformed, contorted or too few in number. Over-maturity rates a more severe penalty than immaturity.

The Double form has a high full center, formed by many small, short bracts under which the flowers and cyathiums should be completely hidden. The bracts diminish in depth from the center to a thin

269

layer around the outer edges. 'HENRIETTA ECKE' is a common double red variety, but its greenhouse-grown plants have a tendency to drop bracts prematurely.

SINGLE, WIDE BRACT Poinsettias are composed of one or more layers of wide bracts, which stand out horizontally from the stem. The bracts encircle a group of almost stemless greenish-yellow cyathiums which enclose the flowers.

The length of the bract varies; for instance the bracts of 'ECKE WHITE' are unduly short. They should be wide, closely spaced or overlapping, and should have nearly uniform size and angle in relation to the stem. The bloom should be symmetrical. Penalty is drawn if there are spaces caused by too few or irregularly spaced bracts. If a bract is drooping or distorted, it is considered a fault; all bracts should stand at the same angle from the main stem.

The cyathiums, containing the flowers, should be large and close together, forming a compact center cluster. The pollen should appear fresh. The varieties 'BARBARA ECKE SUPREME' and 'ECKE WHITE IMPROVED' are examples of type.

SINGLE, NARROW BRACT types are similar to the above with the exception of the compared width of the bracts which are more strap-like. The bracts stand out from the center in flat formation. The individual bracts will be more irregular in size, width and angle in relation to the main stem.

The center, comprised of numerous small cyathiums, should form a compact cluster and the cyathiums should be reasonably open. There will be some openness around the center, between the cyathiums and the bracts. The variety 'OAK LEAF' typically has long thin bracts that droop when mature. The bracts of the pink varieties are thin and not particularly large or showy.

BLOOM SIZE

Poinsettia size is influenced by season, growing conditions and geographical location. Prolonged high temperatures in the fall delays bloom development. Highly saline conditions during the growing season may produce smaller blooms. Some varieties such as 'ALBERT ECKE' and 'ALBERT ECKE IMPROVED' are particularly noted for their large bracts in relation to height. 'INDIANAPOLIS RED' produces bracts of a very good size in relation to the height of the plant. A bloom size out of proportion to the stem is considered a fault.

BLOOM COLOR

The depth of all colors in certain localities may vary with the geographical area in which the specimen is grown. The color in the whites and pinks is more affected by conditions during the growing season than that of the reds.

The bracts are a rich, true red in the double Poinsettias and in most singles of the wide bract type. 'BARBARA ECKE SUPREME' has an exceptionally brilliant red that the Judge should consider. The red of the single, narrow bract Poinsettias is characteristically less intense and light. 'INDIANAPOLIS RED' has the advantage of showing color as soon as the topmost leaves become reddish in color. The variety 'PINK' is a medium to dark hue and is not particularly showy.

The texture (surface quality) has a bearing on the color and should be such that the color is enhanced. The texture may be velvety, silky, satiny or crisp, but should not be coarse, rough or dull.

White and pink Poinsettias are often subject to infusions of green or yellow which should be penalized; the nearer to pure white or pink, the more desirable it is. If there is yellow apparent in a pink, it should be a smooth faint blending, since evenness of color is especially sought in the pinks.

BLOOM SUBSTANCE

A cut specimen of Poinsettia may be taken from the container for closer inspection by the Judge. This is not usually necessary if the specimen is properly staged — size, stem, foliage and substance can be easily detected without touching or handling in any way. If, however, the Judge does think it necessary, handling must be kept to a minimum and limited to the stem only. Neither bracts nor foliage should be touched as one break or bruise may cause the entire stalk to wilt. The Judge courts criticism even if he **does** observe all caution. An exhibitor may unjustly blame him for abusive handling when actually inadequate conditioning may have been at fault. To be safe . . . just look!

The thickness or crispness of the substance varies with the variety and type. It does not necessarily follow that the bracts must be stiff, thick and fleshy as in 'ALBERT ECKE' to have substance and adequate holding qualities. 'OAK LEAF' and 'PINK' have typically thin bracts. 'BARBARA ECKE SUPREME' and 'INDIANAPOLIS RED IMPROVED' have stiff bracts and those of 'ECKE WHITE' are crisp with excellent holding quality.

Bracts of proper substance stand out from the center, maintaining a horizontal angle to the stem and remain on the bloom without premature shedding or dropping. The substance should neither be softened or wilted by lack of conditioning nor thin, withered or shriveled from over-maturity.

The substance should be crisp and firm enough to maintain a symmetrical shape, high and full in the doubles and horizontal to the stem in the singles. The exception is 'OAK LEAF' in which bracts droop or reflex when they reach maturity.

BLOOM POSITION

Position refers to the angle the bloom takes in relation to the stem. If the stem is too weak for the size and weight of the bloom, allowing it to droop or bend, penalty must be taken. If the stem is crooked, it holds the bloom at an unnatural angle, a deduction is made. The position should be such that the full beauty of the bloom is evident.

STEM

Poinsettias should be exhibited in containers approximately ten inches tall with a small neck and of sufficient weight to balance the large, heavy flower head. There should be at least 10" of stem in the container with at least three fully developed leaves above the container rim.

The stem length and diameter should be in proper proportion to the bloom, straight and sturdy enough to support the head without bending. 'HENRIETTA ECKE' has thinner, finer stems than other varieties. Stem height varies with some, 'ALBERT ECKE', 'ECKE WHITE' and 'INDIANAPOLIS RED' have fairly short growth, while 'OAK LEAF' is a tall-growing variety.

FOLIAGE

The foliage on pinks and whites is characteristically lighter in color than on the reds. Foliage on reds should be a rich, dark green. Each Poinsettia entered must have at least three mature leaves above the container, 10 inches of stem in the container stripped of leaves. The lowest leaf **must not** touch the mouth of the container.

The size of the individual leaves should be in proportion to the stem and bloom according to variety, some, such as 'HENRIETTA ECKE' have naturally small leaves. The substance of the leaves should be firm, not soft or thin. Coarse texture is a fault. The three leaves should be fully developed in size and maturity and be reasonably well-spaced, alternately on the stem.

CONDITION

Special care in conditioning Poinsettias is to be expected on the part of the exhibitor. Evidence of wilting is cause for elimination from consideration of any award.

Some varieties such as 'BARBARA ECKE SUPREME' and 'INDIANAPOLIS RED' are more subject to bruising than others such as 'ECKE WHITE' and 'OAK LEAF'.

The specimen bloom or plant should be clean and well-groomed with no evidence of insects, disease, soil or damage to any part of the bloom, foliage or stem, not already considered in judging other qualities. Dropping, yellowing leaves may be the result of chilling or over-watering.

PLANT

Some varieties such as 'ECKE WHITE' and 'INDIANAPOLIS RED' make excellent small-size plants, while others such as 'SAINT LOUIS' are better as cut flowers. 'PINK' and 'ECKE WHITE' respond well to the pinching required for a well-shaped, symmetrical plant.

The Judge will expect Poinsettia plants which have been cut back (rather than propagated from new cuttings) and grown as branched plants to produce more than one bloom. The blooms will be smaller in size, however, than one bloom to a plant. The two should be exhibited in separate classes.

SUMMARY   (Refer to individual scale of points for each quality)

Form

Double
*symmetrical *numerous bracts *no flowers or cyathiums visible *compact *high, full center *graduated depth from full center to thin outer layers

-lacks symmetry, lopsided -open center -loose -lacks fullness -over mature -cyathiums and/or flowers visible -missing bracts -deformed bracts

Single Wide Bract
*bracts wide *uniform bract width overall *broad *horizontal to stem *close or overlapping bracts *symmetrical form *cyathiums conspicuous *compact cyathium cluster

-lacks bracts for symmetry -bracts too narrow -bract width varies -too widely spaced -deformed -missing -drooping -pollen darkening -cyathiums loosely grouped

Single Narrow Bract
*symmetrical *bract width, size and angle regular *numerous cyathiums *cyathiums reasonably open *space between cyathiums and bracts

-lacks symmetry -irregular bract spacing -missing bracts -malformed -too few bracts -bracts undersized -center too open for types -too few cyathiums

Size
*slightly larger than average for type, season and area where grown *in proportion to stem

-small -stunted -bloom too large or small for size and strength of stem

Color
*pure *smooth blending, if any yellow in pinks *clear *white true *lively *intense red in Doubles and wide bract Singles

-excess yellow or green in pinks or whites -blotched -streaked -faded -dull -burned

Substance
*firm *crisp *holding well

-thinning -soft -shriveled -withered -wilting

Bloom Position
*bloom's beauty fully visible

-bending -drooping -looking down

Stem
*sturdy *length according to schedule *stiff *proportioned to bloom

-crooked -weak -too slender

Foliage
*rich color (particularly in reds) *firm *at least 3 fully developed leaves
*well spaced, alternately

-lacking one or more leaves -too small -thin -soft -pale colored -coarse -damaged -torn- malformed -burned

Condition

*absolutely no sign of wilting *clean *well groomed

-damaged -torn -soiled -wilted (may eliminate)

Plant

*culturally perfect *vigorous growth *blooms well developed *bloom size normal *well shaped *symmetrical

-stunted -diseased -weak growth

Rhododendrons and Azaleas

SUGGESTED CLASSES:

Rhododendron, one truss, foliage attached

A. Hybrid   B. Species   C. Container-Grown Plant
                1. Dwarf 2. Other   (size set by Comm.)

Azalea, one spray, not exceeding 16"

A. Hybrid   B. Species   C. Container-Grown Plant
                1. Dwarf 2. Other   (size set by Comm.)

Sub-classes can be provided for deciduous, evergreen and varieties as needed.

RHODODENDRONS AND AZALEAS

The plants are so closely related that all are regarded by botanists as members of the genus Rhododendrons, but most amateur horticulturists distinguish between the two. Only a few plant families, such as Orchids and Iris are so involved.

The genus is called Rhododendron and within that genus, which is made up of some 800 different species, is found the more than 70 Azaleas and at least 10,000 hybrids have been named and added to the lists.

The most common Rhododendrons are usually broad-leaved evergreens and the most common Azaleas are deciduous, though they overlap both ways and some of the plants are dimorphic or semi-evergreen which means they have large leaves in the summer and smaller foliage in the winter. Rhododendrons are tree-size down to dwarf with thick leaves and with the flowers carried in compact clusters at the end of the stem (called a truss) and are often considered more "fussy" culturally than Azaleas.

Azaleas have a more low, spreading growth, with thinner leaves and a profusion of flowers carried irregularly in umbel-like clusters and a more airy appearance. The plants bloom at an early age, and usually are considered easier to grow than Rhododendrons and are slightly more alkaline tolerant.

Rhododendrons are divided into two rather overlapping, poorly defined groups; the Large or Standard and the Dwarfs.

Azaleas fall into either evergreen or the more hardy deciduous grouping. Each of these groupings is broken down into species and varieties. Those with persistent or evergreen leaves include Kurume, Dale, Korean, Gable Hybrids, 'BOUDOIR', 'ROSEBUD' and others.

Those with deciduous foliage include Appalachian natives and their hybrids with Asiatic species; Mollis with yellow, apricot and red flowers; Ghent Hybrids with bold white to red flowers and Knap Hill pastels. Deciduous varieties carry the yellow color range in Azaleas as well as the high autumnal coloration.

Kaempferi has semi-persistent leaves which hold to about zero temperatures. The evergreen Belgian Indian Hybrids are usually used for forcing and are the varieties sold in full flower in florist shops. Also, there are nine native American Azalea species which include the Flame, Western Azalea **(R. occidentale),** the native North Carolina 'PINK SHELL' **(R. vaseyi)** and **Schlippenbachi** the native 'ROYAL AZALEA' which is deciduous with four inch flowers and considerable alkaline tolerance.

Because both Rhododendron and Azalea plants are extremely shallow-rooted, they make fine subjects for show gardens and booths; they may be moved in full bloom, set in, watered carefully for 3-4 days and returned to the garden with no appreciable set-back.

While fragrance in both flowers and foliage is found in some, it is generally not noted and if found is considered as an unexpected bonus. Therefore, no specimen is penalized for its lack, though a specimen may receive a point more if the fragrance is present and pleasant. Scents of the flowers vary from heliotrope-like to clove-like.

SCALE OF POINTS FOR TRUSS

Truss		Foliage	15
Size	25	Substance	10
. truss		Condition, grooming,	
. flowers		label	10
Form	20	Color	20
. individual flowers			
. overall truss			

SIZE
Truss

Truss sizes vary from miniature with veil-like florets less than a dime in diameter to massive clusters larger by far than a human head, exceeding twelve inches, with florets in excess of six inches.

The number of flowers in a truss depends somewhat on the size of the individual flowers. For instance, if the individual flowers average four inches, the truss is apt to contain only ten or twelve of the florets. If the individual flowers average two inches, the truss may contain 12-20 or even 30 florets.

The overall truss size should be in good balance and proportion to the leaves and the plant. Because Rhododendrons grow so slowly, the stem is necessarily cut short to preserve as much growth as possible.

Flower Size

The size varies greatly and of course must be judged as to what is typical for the variety, season and area where grown. Generally speaking, the flower sizes of the various types can be averaged thusly:

STANDARD RHODODENDRONS: up to 7" ('LODERI')

EVERGREEN AZALEAS: range from ½" to 3"

DECIDUOUS, species and Hybrids: up to 4".

Flower Color

There is a great range of color interest with markings and patterns which include blotches, throats, flushings, margins and dotting in various sizes as well as self or uniform colors and varied blendings. Unusual effects are present with markings which include greens, browns and even near-blacks.

The colors should be clear, bright or soft and mellow according to variety. The blendings should be smooth, the contrasts harmonious, the markings clean, the combinations desirable. Eyes should be well-defined, clear cut and accented. Age-blueing, "washy" purples and off-colors are to be penalized.

Long, contrasting anthers offer color interest and should be present and in good condition. Some mauve or magenta colors are often murky and objectionable.

FORM

Truss

Contrary to the usual, multiple terminal flower clusters, leaf size and so on, the Judge may find exhibits of unusual variations as hybridizers introduce new crosses. For instance, 'GABLES PIONEER' possesses the rare trait of blooming in the axils of its leaves as well as the terminal trusses; an average plant may carry 400-500 individual florets on a 15-18" plant.

Many descriptive phrases can be found to describe the varied forms of truss modeling which, true to variety may be globular, flat topped, candelabroid, and umbel-like. The Rhododendron truss should be well balanced and resting well on a rosette of typical leaves. The flowers should not be buried in, but held above the foliage.

For the first few years of blooming, vigorous hybrids may partially conceal the trusses of flowers with new growth, which emerges simultaneously with the blooms; such vegetative growth is undesirable. Vegetative growth around the flower buds is to be penalized. A lax truss with flowers tending to hang down rather than stand upright is objectionable. Trusses are at prime when approximately one-half the flowers are open and the rest are in bud.

FLOWER FORM

While the usual form of the flower is open-faced and flaring, the forms vary between the varieties and both Singles and Doubles are represented, though Singles predominate.

Petal margins may be only slightly crinkled, or frilled or more deeply so. The wings and falls may reflex slightly. The forms include hose-in-hose, long tube, star-like, rosebud, coneshaped, campanulate (bell-in-bell) and funnel or trumpet-shaped as well as open faced and flaring. The petals of the individual flowers should be uniformly margined and imbricated (over-lapped).

FOLIAGE

The foliage should be sufficient to clothe the framework of the branches but should be subordinate to the flowers.

The size of the foliage is dependent upon the variety. Some are really spectacular; from three inches up to two feet, six inches wide, though it must be noted that such varieties usually have flowers somewhat less spectacular than the smaller-leaved types.

Shapes of leaves are varied also according to variety, being long and lance-like in one, narrow to ovoid in another, while a third variety may have leaves that are small and rounded and some are typically curled.

Coloration is different, too, ranging from glaucus (waxy white) to light green to dark green to near-black. Leaf indumentum (undersides) add considerable interest to some; such coloration may be white or brown with textures varying from suede-like to wooly or felted.

Nutrient deficiences and cultural malpractices show up very distinctly in Rhododendron and Azalea foliage. Refer to the list appearing under PLANTS, Cultural Perfection-blemishes in this chapter.

Some varieties hold their leaves in a drooping position, others stand upright. Specimen trusses should have some leaves present around the truss to give a general impression of their size, color and indumentum. Leaves immediately adjacent to the flower head are sometimes undersized and deformed. If no leaves are present, the Judge deducts all foliage points.

The foliage must be well balanced and proportioned to the size and habit of the plant and to the flowers.

SUBSTANCE

Substance varies from thin and veil-like to thick ('CAROLINE'), crisp ('COUNTY OF YORK'), fleshy with great substance and durability accompanying a lace-like daintiness ('PINK TWINS'), velvety ('ROCHELLE') or waxy ('C. B. VAN NES'). The petals should be turgid, fresh appearing and not limp or wilted, curling or collapsing.

CONDITION, Grooming, Label

The condition of the whole truss should be one of prime maturity, with all the parts intact, spent flowers removed and foliage attached and unblemished. All parts must be clean and the label correct, neat and legible. The pot must be clean, of a size correct for the plant it holds and in good repair.

STANDARDS OF PERFECTION FOR POTTED RHODODENDRON AND AZALEA PLANTS

SCALE FOR POTTED PLANTS

Cultural Perfection	35	Floriferousness	30
. form	20	. color	
. blemishes, condition	10	. quality	
. grooming	5	. quantity	
Foliage	10	Size	20
Label	5	. plant	
		. trusses	

CULTURAL PERFECTION

Form

In temperate and alkaline regions Rhododendrons and Azaleas make very successful pot plants as the shallow, contained root system adapts easily and the requirements for soil acidity, humidity and temperature are easily controlled. Varieties in tubs or pots should be selected with consideration to type of growth and leaf characteristics as well as bloom. Any variety which does not exceed four feet in ten years could be considered a likely subject for potting. Numerous Dwarf varieties are available also and are usually distinguishable by their smaller leaves, relatively small flowers, less height (average about 3') and a compact, mound shape, rather than a spreading form.

The pot should contain only one plant which may have one or more basal stems. Two or more plants in the same pot will seldom produce the same effect as a single plant and should be penalized. Strong sunlight is usually associated with a rather short, stubby growth, profuse flower bud formation and a tendency to yellowish leaves. Too heavy shade results in tall, spindly growth and relatively few buds and should be penalized heavily.

The shape of the plant should display the flowers to best advantage, and the trusses should be distributed evenly and uniformly over the plant. Flower and bud potential should be equal to leaf and plant size, the general effect should be of flowers dominating the plant, rather than foliage. Proper pruning will improve the form, and its lack should be deducted.

Varieties in which the flowers hang pendant ('FABIA G.') are a poor choice for potted plants as the full beauty of the flower face cannot be appreciated under the usual placement. Stunted growth may be the result of scale attacks. The plant must be well established in the pot, and any evidence otherwise is to be penalized.

BLEMISHES, Condition

The plant should appear vigorous, thrifty and actively growing with no lack of attention as regards light intensity, temperature extremes, humidity, soil moisture, improper acidity or nutrient dificiencies. Where such conditions prevail, a general "dwindling" begins which results in an unthrifty appearance and eventual death. General physiological negligence makes itself apparent readily in Rhododendrons and Azaleas. Lack of, or inadequate blooming can often be traced to inadequate light or too vigorous vegetative growth.

PEST AND DISEASE (evidence may be checked against the following as they affect Rhododendrons and Azaleas).

. grey mottled evergreen leaves (lace Bug, White Fly)
. holes in leaves (Inch Worm, Root Weevils)
. pests in residence (Mealy Bug, Thrips, Aphids, Spider Mites, etc.)
. leaf discoloration, white, then brown and dry (Spider Mites, Thrips)
. leaf spots (Fungus Diseases)
. leaves dull, curled, crinkled (Aphids)
. stunted growth (Scale)
. twigs dying back (Branch Blight)
. leaves swelled, thick, fleshy (Leaf Gall, Azalea)
. orange or yellow eruptions (Rust)
. buds blighted, killed (Bud Blast, Botrytis, Winter injury)
. petals covered with white or brown spots, later wilted, slimy (Azalea Petal Blight)
. flowers distorted, off-color, growth distorted, stunted (Cyclamen Mite)

PHYSIOLOGICAL ILLS

. leaves small, pale, dull stunted growth, burned (lack of moisture)
. leaves dull, pale, drooping (poor drainage, or root rot)
. tall, spindly growth, few buds (lack of light)
. short, stubby growth, yellowish leaves (too strong sunlight)
. girdling, leaves drooping, curled (Wire label strangulation or Animal gnawing, or insects, Winter injury)
. leaf spot and margin burn (High heat, frost, wind damage from bruising)

NUTRIENT DEFICIENCIES (reveal themselves in various ways on Rhododendrons and Azaleas)

. the effect of acidity is to make the iron available to the plant
. pallor, yellowness, a sort of anemia (is due to iron deficiency and a lack of soil acidity)
. pale leaves (other than according to variety) (Too acid or Nitrogen lack)
. weak, spindly growth, more than normal red pigment in new growth, failure to bloom normally (Phosphorous deficiency)
. leaf spot and margin burn (Potassium deficiency)
. leaves 'herringboned' with yellow or cream color lines (Magnesium deficiency)

Refer to Truss coverage for details on flowers, size, foliage and grooming.

SUMMARY   (Refer to Truss and Plant Scale for Points)

Size

*larger than average for the area *typical *generous *Standard Rhododendron: up to 7" *Evergreen Azalea: ½" to 3" *Deciduous Azalea: up to 4" flowers

-stunted -inadequate -undersized

Color

*pure *intense or mellow according to variety *rich *pure *interesting *novel *clear *fresh *smooth blending *harmonious contrasts *eyes well defined

-blueing -murky -fading -burned -off color "washy" purple

Form

Truss: *well shaped *conical, rounded or flat-topped according to variety *high centered *upstanding *tall *½ open flowers, rest buds *compact, close-fitting or loose according to variety *full

-flowers hanging down -lax -foliage concealing flowers (immature plant) -skips -bloomed out -lacking open blooms -vegetative growth around flower buds

Flower Form

*uniformly open faced and flaring OR according to variety, hose-in-hose, star, etc. *neatly formed *typical *wings and falls may reflex slightly

-malformed -crowded -loose attachment -irregular development -any deviation from the norm

Foliage

*may be dark or light green or glaucus *may be flat or curled *may be lance-like or round according to variety *may be large, small, medium *should be firm *glossy *lustrous *luxuriant *thrifty

-sparse leaf cover -bare -indications of cultural malpractice, disease, insects -mechanical damage -weak -thin -misshapen -undersized -plant lacks lower foliage

Substance

*turgid *durable *pert *may be thick, fleshy or waxy or fine according to variety

-limp -thinning -curling -wilted -flabby -relaxing -collapsing

Condition, Grooming

*unmarred *fresh appearing *all parts intact *spent flowers removed *foliage unblemished *all parts clean *label neat, correct

-tears -anthers hanging or missing -bedraggled -soiled -spent florets present -foreign matter present -damaged -pot overly conspicuous -pot soiled -pot cracked

Plant Form

*one plant, well centered *neat framework *graceful *mounded *compact *floriferous *desirable stature *symmetrical *well balanced *uniform truss distribution over plant *floral effect well displayed *well established in pot

-stubby -spindly -twiggy -coarse -leggy -too open -floppy -stunted -distorted -pruning inadequate or careless -lacks vigor -form high above pot -too few flowers in bloom- multiple plants in pot -lacks substance -irregular flower distribution -pendant flower variety

Plant Size

*proportioned to pot *adequate stage of development

-overlarge for pot -inadequate size -too heavy -too spreading -immature -pot over-large or too small

Roses

SUGGESTED CLASSES:
1. Hybrid Tea (see below) — (disbudded)
2. Hybrid Tea Singles — (not disbudded)
3. Floribunda and Polyantha
   (naturally grown spray and/or naturally grown individual bloom)
4. Grandiflora
   A. One spray with 2 or more blooms and side buds
   B. One stem with 1 bloom, no side buds. Naturally grown or disbudded.
5. Miniature Rose
   A. Individual bloom
   B. Spray
6. Old Garden Rose
   (one naturally grown stem)
7. Climbing Rose
   (1 stem or lateral)
   A. Hybrid Tea Climber, disbudded
   B. Hybrid Tea Climber, single, naturally grown
   C. Large-flowered Climber, other than Hybrid Tea ('BLAZE'). Naturally grown.
   D. Small-flowered (Cluster) Climbers. Naturally grown.

Sub-classes may be added for different colors and collections. Hybrid Teas may be further separated with classes for:
   A. Exhibition
   B. Decorative, full-blown

ROSE

The many kinds of roses may be roughly grouped into three main types based on distinct characteristics as (1) Bedding (2) Climbers and (3) Shrubs. The Bedding types are by far the most varied and include:

Tea: Vigorous bushy type, attractive disease-resistant foliage, fragrant, abundant, continuous bloom. Color range limited, no really good reds or rich yellows. Wrinkled, dull green foliage. Form is open cup, stem often weak. Tender. Shown disbudded except when exhibited in Old Garden Rose Section. May then be exhibited as naturally grown, if the Schedule permits.

Hybrid Perpetuals: Profuse early summer bloom. Large, fragrant flowers of good substance, vigorous. Outstanding example: 'FRAU KARL DRUSCHKI'. Bloom form is generally rather flat when open, except for 'FRAU KARL DRUSCHKI' which exhibits classic exhibition form. Shown disbudded except when shown as Old Garden Roses. May then be exhibited as naturally grown if Schedule permits.

Hybrid Teas: Offspring of the delicate Tea and the vigorous Hybrid Perpetual. Fairly large bushes, more or less continuous bloom. Flowers large, excellent form in exhibition and decorative. Long stems. Shown disbudded. Exhibition forms of proven show quality include 'PEACE', 'POINSETTIA', 'TIFFANY', 'CHRYSLER IMPERIAL', etc. These have flowers which are pointed or high centered. Decorative forms are less formal and regular such as 'HERBERT HOOVER', 'CURLY PINK', 'MICHELLE MEILLAND', etc. Hybrid teas are also available in single form and may be shown naturally grown, individual, 1 bloom, disbudded or as clusters. 'DAINTY BESS' is a popular example. A single-type hybrid tea is one having 5-8 petals in a single row.

Polyantha: Small flowers borne in large sprays or clusters. Continuous bloom, hardy and vigorous. Shown naturally grown, without disbudding.

Hybrid Polyantha or Floribunda: Plants are generally larger than Polyantha; medium to large, short-stemmed flowers grown in clusters or sprays and sometimes one to a stem. A spray of Floribunda is defined as one cane showing at least two or more true leaves (may be 3-9 leaflets) at the base of the cane above which many bud-eyes produce growth terminating in a cluster or clusters of bloom having approximately the same stage of development. The terminal (center) flower may be removed before mature to increase size and improve cluster form.

A spray that is unbalanced, uneven, one-sided, or out of proportion cannot score as highly as a spray having one cane of uniform and regular branching; terminating in an even, symmetrical shape of uniform heights and equal spacing of florets. Near-perfect sprays are rare, the closest example of this perfection is to be rewarded.

Vigorous growth, taller than the main spray and terminating in small tight buds (usually due to excess fertilization) will throw the spray out of balance so it could not score as highly as an even, uniform spray.

Such secondary growth, branching from any part of the main spray, may be removed but if recently done, it requires penalty in proportion to impairment. Such a recently disbudded spray cannot rate as high as one not requiring removal. Removal may further unbalance the appearance requiring a heavier penalty than if not removed. If such removal was carefully executed early enough (as in regular disbudding) it is accepted and not penalized.

The presence of immature growth originating from the base of the first leaf on the stem below the point of origin of the peduncles bearing the mature bloom, will not bring disqualification, but the Judge may assess a penalty severe enough to eliminate the specimen from winning an award.

While Hybrid Polyanthas and/or Floribundas should be displayed and judged as a cluster, some varieties frequently produce only one flower to a stem without any cluster or side buds ('FLORADORA', 'FARMERS WIFE'). Such specimens should be accepted and judged in competition **just the same** as if they were the usual cluster type inflorescence. Form of these singles is judged as in the Hybrid Teas and **a** penalty is to be taken for the lack of side buds. Since so few Floribunda produce these single specimens, it is not yet necessary to judge these in separate classes as is now required for Grandifloras.

Hybrid Polyantha/Floribunda clusters are judged by the same scale of points as in scoring exhibition types excepting under form where the **entire inflorescence** is considered. The form of the individual flowers, however, may closely resemble that of Hybrid Teas but on a smaller scale. The spacing and arrangement, without crowding of the individual florets, the number of blossoms from bud to full-blown and the attractiveness, balance and symmetry of the spray as a **whole** are considered.

The highest rating specimen spray is one having the greatest **number** of fresh, full-blown blossoms along with several buds and a few between bud and full-blown with no spent blooms. Spent blooms may be removed if this was done without leaving a "hole" or void thus destroying symmetry, even spacing and balance. However, non-removal of the spent bloom will likely receive penalty for fading color.

The condition of the stamens (as in the single Hybrid Teas) are excellent indicators of freshness. Color, stem and foliage parallel exhibition rose judging. A larger spray with proportionate flowers and foliage will naturally score higher than a small-scaled spray.

GRANDIFLORA

Off-spring of the Hybrid Tea and the Hybrid Polyantha, with characteristics of both. Blooms generally in group clusters. Usually tall growing, free flowering with long stems. The true Grandiflora possess-*es long, individual stems in a more-than-one-to-a-stem inflorescence. Exhibits of naturally grown or disbudded individual specimens should not be judged against the naturally grown mass inflorescence types. Separate classes should be provided.*

Grandifloras produce cluster inflorescence but also may flower singly, or with immature side buds. The specimen with mass bloom will score the highest if the classes are not separated. An acceptable spray must show two or more blooms.

When evaluating Grandifloras, the **whole** inflorescence (as in Flori-

bundas) is not considered alone. Rather the form of the mass of inflor-escence and the form of each individual bloom are of equal value.

The competent Judge should be able to detect a single individual specimen Grandiflora, entered in that class but cut from a group of more-than-one-to-a-stem by the insufficient number of true leaves and the overall length of the stem.

MINIATURES

The height of the bushes varies, but generally falls within the 6 to 15" range. Blooms are in cluster and single-stem inflorescence for which sep-arate classes should be provided in the extensive show. Criteria similar to H.T. is used for judging Miniatures. Form is one-third to fully open, symmetrical, with no gaps. Center well formed, not split, snubbed or confused. Miniatures are shown naturally grown, not disbudded. Elfin daintiness rates high, coarse heaviness is penalized. Size should be typical. The wee blooms are generally smaller than 25¢ piece, 'RED IMP' is usually smaller than a nickel. May be dec-orative, exhibition or open form according to variety.

Stem length in proportion to the flower will vary from four to six inches. Form of the one-to-stem specimens need not be the classic high-crown of the exhibition Hybrid Tea, but must be typical of the variety. Foliage is petite, slim, tapered and rarely exceeds two and one-half inches; it is rather thick and stiff. The substance must be crisp and the pollen (if showing) must be fresh. All entries in the Miniature classes must be varieties of the type and classification and not undersized specimens of Polyanthas.

CLIMBING AND TRAILING

These roses fall naturally into two groups, those with large flowers and those with small flowers in clusters. There are climbing Floribun-das, Polyanthas, Ramblers (i.e., 'DOROTHY PERKINS') and even climb-ing Miniatures in the small-cluster types. In the large-flowering group are the Climbing Teas, Climbing Hybrid Teas, Climbing Hybrid Per-petuals; some varieties are the American Pillar such as 'DR. W. VAN FLEET'.

The large, more vigorous climbing form of the Hybrid Tea will produce better disbudded specimens for the show table than the bush plants of the same variety. Therefore they should be classed and judged separately. Climbing Hybrid Teas, as well as Climbing Hybrid Per-petuals and Climbing Teas are shown disbudded.

Floribundas, Polyanthas, Miniatures, Hybrid Perpetuals, and Teas of the climbing type should be exhibited in the classes for their bush types if special classes are not provided for them.

In judging Large-flowering Climbers and Cluster-type Climbers, the Judge checks to see that only one bloom-lateral with no portion of the main cane is included. If not a true bloom lateral, the exhibit is penalized or disqualified, depending on the specimen.

OLD GARDEN ROSES

Old Garden Roses are defined as all those classes which were introduced prior to 1867, which was the year of introduction of the first Hybrid Tea 'LA FRANCE'.

Old Garden Roses includes Species Briar, Noisette, Tea, China, Gal-*lica, Centifolia ('CABBAGE'), Alba, Damask, Bourbon, Moss. These are shown naturally grown. Certain Hybrid Perpetual varieties, if not disbudded, may be exhibited in the Old Garden Rose Section. Floribundas, Grandifloras, Hybrid Teas and their climbing forms cannot be entered as Old Garden Roses.*

The term "Old Garden Rose" is now preferred to "old-fashioned" or "old rose". At times, long stemmed Teas, short-stemmed Gallicas and naturally-grown Hybrid Perpetuals may be in competition, but as each rose is judged according to its approach to perfection for that variety, the task is not too great. Substance and color are more fragile. Button centers are acceptable.

"Shrub" is a loose term which is hard to define and generally includes Hedge, Briar, Rugosa and many Species and Species Hybrids such as 'AUSTRIAN COPPER', 'HARRISON'S YELLOW', 'SWEET-BRIAR', 'GROOTENDORST', **R. multiflora** *and others. These are the sole exception to Rule #5 stem-on-stem elimination. New introductions are more compact and everblooming and are sometimes referred to as Park or Dooryard roses. These are shown either with or without side buds. The inflorescence may resemble H.T., Old Garden or Floribunda, and are judged similarly.*

FRAGRANT ROSES

A few shows add classes for the most fragrant rose or the most fragrant rose of all those entered. A rose that is delightfully scented to one Judge (or exhibitor) may be nothing to sniff at for another, so judging for fragrance is a tricky thing. Smoking and olfactory disorders may create scent blocks so a list of those roses considered most fragrant by several authorities will be a help to the Judges. The ARS BUYER'S GUIDE leaflet lists the fragrance quotient of hundreds of varieties having moderate to strong scent.

Most Old Garden Roses such as China, Musk, Rugosa, Scotch, Damask and Centifolia (which is also known as the Cabbage Rose) are well known for their fragrance but newcomers, too, have this quality in abundance. Climbers such as 'GOLDEN SHOWERS', 'ORANGE EVERGLOW' and 'DR. J. H. NICHOLAS'; familiar Hybrid Teas such as 'CHARLOTTE ARMSTRONG', 'OKLAHOMA', 'THE DOCTOR', 'TIFFANY', LAVENDER CHARM', 'ARLENE FRANCIS', 'KING'S RANSOM', 'CHRISTIAN DIOR', 'CHRYSLER IMPERIAL', 'DAINTY BESS', 'HAWAII', GRANADA', 'TROPICANA'; Floribundas such as 'FASHION', 'GINGER', 'JIMINY CRICKETT', 'SARATOGA' and

Grandifloras such as 'CAROUSEL', 'CHERRY GLOW', 'QUEEN ELIZ-ABETH' and 'PINK PARFAIT' are highly fragrant.

'TIFFANY' and 'CRIMSON GLORY' are the first two roses to win the coveted James A. Gamble Award for Fragrance. The winners must have outstanding merit in addition to strong and delightful fragrance. These listed varieties make up only a tiny portion of modern-day roses whose fragrance equals or exceeds that of their ancestors.

SCALE OF POINTS — Am. Rose Society

Bloom	70		
. form	25	Stem and Foliage	20
. color	20		
. substance	15	Balance and Proportion	10
. size	10		

Roses are eliminated from competition for following reasons:
1. Lack of required disbudding (see disbudding under Stem, p. 291)
2. Generally lacking in all or most of the qualities listed in Scale.
3. Incorrect or lack of labeling (in official Rose Shows, especially).
4. Use of any foreign substance such as green clay, ink, oil, vinegar, etc.
5. Any entry with part of the stem attached to main primary cane.
6. *Any specimen entered by exhibitor in incorrect color and class.*
7. Side growth with or without buds, but showing leaf formation.

The judging of roses is based on a comparison of the approach to perfection of the individual varieties. Difficulty of culture of a variety must not be a factor in judging; the rose is judged, not the grower's skill.

Judges in Rose Shows are required to disqualify unnamed or mis-named exhibits, and Shows often have classes for unnamed specimens. Because color varies due to conditions, it is an unstable factor in identi-fying varieties. The various anatomical parts of a rose (sepals, petals, calyx, thorns, bracts, peduncle (neck), foliage, etc.) provide verification. When there are other exhibits of the same variety shown, a compari-son of these parts will aid the Judge in arriving at a definite conclu-sion on correctness of labeling. Of course, a Judge's personal preference must not lead him to discriminate between types and colors.

Since the bloom accounts for eighty percent of the score, faults on or near the bloom (on the stem and foliage) are most serious and pen-alized more heavily than the same faults farther down the stem.

FORM

Form refers to the shape of the bloom and its circular outline. Gen-erally rose forms are classified as (1) Exhibition and (2) Decorative, with Exhibition preferable for show purposes. The rose of exhibition form has elegance, formal dignity, regularity and the perfection of shape. The highest type of exhibition rose has many petals forming a circular contour and a well-formed, high center. 'POINSETTIA' is a typical example.

A decorative type rose is more informal and less regular in shape, often with the center merely rounded or even depressed, ('HERBERT HOOVER'). A single Hybrid Tea Rose is one having only a single row of *5 to 12 petals ('DAINTY BESS'). Award for most perfect phase for variety.*

Semi-double roses have approximately 9-20 petals, ('AUDIE MUR-PHY' H. T.) and their most perfect stage is likely to be when the *flower is fully open to show the contrasting "heart" of stamens, but the outer petals must be in perfect condition. Sometimes an individual flower will score above a spray in the single Hybrid Tea (which may be shown disbudded unless the Schedule specifically requests a spray-type inflorescence. The climber 'ROYAL SUNSET' carries both semi and double blooms on the same plant. Many Grands are decorative form.*

Judges in Standard (non-specialized) Shows and Fairs are often *instructed to select the "Best Rose In The Show". The ARS recommends that the best rose should preferably be one of exhibition quality or the bloom most nearly approaching this standard. This form may occur in other types than H.T. and all things being equal other types, including singles could be awarded Best.*

The specimen rose at the time of judging should be in a stage of development that:

1. Shows the variety at its most perfect phase of possible beauty of all qualities on the Scale. Perfect form is generally when bloom is ½ to ¾ open. Heavy petalled varieties should be ⅔ to ¾ open with 4 to 5 rows unfurling.

2. With a typical number of petals that

3. Are symmetrically and gracefully arranged in an orderly, circular contour around a well-formed high center.

(1) "The most perfect phase" varies according to variety and Judges should be flexible in their demands that it be one-half to three-fourths open. Many present-day exhibition blooms are at their best when only *one-third to one-half open, with two to three unfurling ('SISTER THER-ESE'* 25 petals) while the many petaled ones ('MEMORIAM, 50-60 petals) approach perfection at the three-quarters open stage. Each variety is measured against its own ideal and not that of some other variety. The rose, regardless of variety, must be sufficiently open so that the Judge can see:

A. the arrangement of petals with even spacing, no gaps
B. the outline of its form which is to be circular
C. the center form, well defined, high, pointed

Form is deteriorating when the rose has opened to the stage in which the symmetrical petal arrangement and the well-formed center are altered, and when this condition is reached, points must be deduct-*ed. A tight bud with sepals down is not yet an "exhibition" bloom, and a full-blown rose is beyond perfect form unless it is a single or Old Garden.*

(2) Judges should be as familiar as possible with the characteristics of the varieties judged because there is so much variation of the "most perfect phase" dependent on whether the rose has a lot or less petals

and dependent upon the natural characteristics of each variety. A rose normally carrying twenty-five petals should not be expected to carry sixty. A partial listing of the expected petalage is placed at the chapter's end to assist the Judge in determining form. Too many or too few petals would result in a form not typical for the variety. A specimen lacking a sufficient number of petals for the variety will be unable to hold proper form. Too few petals on a variety known to be full-petaled might indicate "over-dressing". The American Rose Society permits the removal of a malformed or misplaced petal if the natural character of the bloom is not altered. Such grooming or dressing is allowed if it is done so skillfully that it is not evident and if it improves the quality. If dressing is not done carefully, leaving a torn part of petal remaining, or if it is evident that the character has been altered, then points are deducted.

(3) An Exhibition Rose of top quality has a number of petals regularly arranged to form a circular outline while maintaining a high, pointed, well-defined center. A specimen which lacks symmetrically arranged petals is penalized. The ideal symmetry means that the petals are well-proportioned and in orderly placement; well-balanced and well-arranged, all firmly attached to the calyx.

Some varieties retain full, rounded, smooth petals ('TALLYHO'), others furl the edges to form a point ('D. A. VICTORIA'), some varieties combine furled (outer petals) and smooth (inner petals) 'POINSETTIA'. None of these should be favored, but their degree of symmetry judged against the ideal. Deformed or misplaced petals are subject to penalty, the degree commensurate by the severity with which it (they) affect the symmetry and circular outline. The petals should form a perfect circle when the Judge looks down upon the rose.

A split or confused center is the faulty arrangement of petals in the center of the bloom which gives the appearance of a division or double center. A prominent split center is penalized more heavily than one which is just beginning to be obvious. To determine the form of the center, it is imperative that the specimen be sufficiently open so the petal placement, the form of the center and the whole outline may be evaluated. If it is not possible to ascertain these, then the form is penalized. The balance of the circular outline can be more easily determined by laying a pencil over the center and comparing the halves.

Buds and blooms may be dwarfed and distorted by the ravages of mildew. Excess rain or careless sprinkling causes some varieties to "ball", or open improperly. Form may also be damaged by the holes in petals caused by Rose Curculio, Japanese Beetles, Climbing cutworms and earwigs; thrips may discolor and "ball" the blooms. The Rose Midge leaves a "burned-to-a-crisp" appearance. Evidence of any of these is cause for penalty in proportion to the impairment.

Refer to the sections on Grandiflora, Floribunda and Miniature at the beginning of the chapter for notes on form relative to these types.

COLOR

Recognized rose color classes are:

1. White or near white	Example:	'SNOWBIRD'
2. Medium Yellow	Example:	'ECLIPSE'
3. Deep Yellow	Example:	'LOWELL THOMAS'
4. Yellow Blend	Example:	'PEACE'
5. Apricot Blend	Example:	'ANGELS MATEU'
6. Orange, Orange Blend	Example:	'FRED EDMUNDS'
7. Orange Red	Example:	'HAWAII'
8. Light Pink	Example:	'RADIANCE'
9. Medium Pink	Example:	'SHOW GIRL'
10. Pink Blend	Example:	'TIFFANY'
11. Light Red, Deep Pink	Example:	'TALLYHO'
12. Medium Red	Example:	'POINSETTIA'
13. Dark Red	Example:	'CHRYSLER IMPERIAL'
14. Red Blend	Example:	'FORTY-NINER'
15. Mauve	Example:	'STERLING SILVER'
16. Russet	Example:	'ULSTER MONARCH'

The ARS "GUIDE FOR BUYING ROSES" is excellent reference material for checking the correct color placement.

The ideal rose color encompasses five qualities. These are freshness, clarity, purity, brilliance and typical of variety.

FRESHNESS means that the color is not blemished by aging, fading, heat or refrigeration. 'SATURNIA' and other reds blue from cold. In judging floribundas and other multiple bloom types, penalty will be leveled against any having a faded or spent floret in the cluster.

CLARITY is the bright richness which gives the appearance of being luminous or transluscent. Points are reduced for a murky, dull look.

PURITY is freedom from unnatural pigmentation, evidenced by white streaks in red varieties, light spots on darks or dark spots on lights; self-colors should maintain uniformity and streaky unevenness is penalized. Purity of rose color involves the absence or presence of discoloration from weather, insects or dust and spray residue.

BRILLIANCE is that refractive characteristic which makes petals appear lustrous, sparkling, glittering, shimmering or glistening.

TYPICAL OF VARIETY. Rose color is not stable but varies with different varieties and shifts in the same variety due to weather, soils and cultural care including moisture, degree of shade, and fertilizers available. Location, altitude, season and chemicals applied also have a bearing. Judges should not be dogmatic regarding color when judging roses from an area other than their own.

The green or contrasting blotching sometimes found on the outer petals of red, pink and some yellow roses is inherent in the variety and while not considered a major fault, is undesirable and subject to penalty.

Some of the five qualities just covered may overlap in meaning and a rose's color may lack one or more of these. A Judge should decide what is typical and score accordingly. Petal texture also affects the color, some varieties are smooth and velvety, others are prominently veined ('LADY ELGIN'). These are varietal characteristics and points are not removed for any lack or addition unless such adversely affects the overall beauty or is not typical. Stamen color typical, not browned.

BALANCE AND PROPORTION

Refers to aesthetic overall impression of bloom, stem and foliage in relation to each other. Stem must be right length and diameter to complement and support bloom size. Foliage must sufficiently frame bloom without crowding, overpowering or seeming skimpy and awkward.

SUBSTANCE

Texture, crispness, thickness, firmness, stiffness of the petals and stamens are all involved and these things must be sufficient to give stability and durability of form, texture and finish to the rose.

Judges should never touch or otherwise handle the bloom as heat, oil and pressure of the fingers will quickly deteriorate and bruise the flower. Texture and sheen can be determined by holding the rose up to the light to observe thickness, firmness and life. Crispness and stiffness can be observed or determined by **gently** shaking the holder containing the bloom. Any deduction on substance causes color and form deduction.

Lack of substance and loss of moisture (turgidity) shows up first in the extreme tips and outer edges of the rose petals. This petal-edge deterioration should not be confused with the petal-edge damage caused by thrips. Loss of substance is a wilting, drying, thinning of the petals and thrip injury is caused by the rasping away of petal fibre. Each requires a penalty commensurate with the extent of the injury.

SIZE

Size refers to the actual dimensions of the bloom only. However, the Judge, finding average size for variety, gives only 7-8 points, not the full 10 points. Thus he has extra points to award a superior-sized bloom. Depending on the degree of deviation, 7-8 points can be deducted for undersize. All things being equal, the big rose wins over the small, or over a typically large bloom of average size, thus size often determines the winner.

Some varieties, as for example 'PICTURE' carrying 34 petals, are much smaller even when perfectly grown than others such as 'PINK FAVORITE' though it carries only 21-28 petals. Size is not only the total number of the petals but the length and breadth of each individual petal. For instance 'OREGON CENTENNIAL' is listed as large though it has only 30 petals to 'KARL HERBST'S' sixty. 'NIGGER BOY', however, with 56 petals is referred to as a medium-sized double. Refer to petalage table at end of chapter.

The general rule is that the size must be typical of the variety at its optimum. The Rose of much less than normal size and number of petals for the variety may be suspected of being a victim of "over-grooming", the removal of too many damaged petals. Stunted flowers, pale and dull in color may be the result of a lack of nitrogen.

STEM AND FOLIAGE

These two items combined tell a Judge a very great deal about the skill and cultural finesse of the grower and the size and health of the plant that produced the specimen.

A stem is defined as "the main stalk from the point of detachment from the plant to the base of the peduncle." The stem must be a primary one only, without any part of the cane from which it originated. If part of the cane is included the specimen is eliminated from competition.

If a Judge finds it is easier to evaluate stem with a score of ten and foliage with a score of ten, separately, this is permissible. Please refer to the outline on Floribunda, Grandiflora and Miniature at the beginning of this chapter for the standards of perfection for a spray.

The stem should be in proportion to the flower. A small bloom on the upper end of a great, long stem will appear even smaller than it really is; or a large beautifully formed and colored rose will look top-heavy and awkward if supported by a short or weak stem. Stem and bloom should tend to balance each other. If the stem and foliage seem to be the dominant part of the specimen, rather than subordinate to the bloom, Judges are justified in removing points, even though such a condition may be typical of the variety.

The stem should be of sufficient size and strength to support the bloom without undue bending. Most varieties nod slightly, adding to their grace and charm.

When looking down on the exhibit, you should see a somewhat circular green frame setting off the bloom. In profile, the leaves should appear evenly spaced, symmetrical, in stacked sequence. Single leaflets or bracts below the bloom are a fault if they detract from symmetry when viewed from top or side.

The stem should hold the rose so the horizontal axis of the rose coincides with the vertical axis. Nearly every rose has some thorns (prickles) and these should not be removed or clipped on the major portion of the stem, though removal from that part of the stem which is below the container top (to facilitate placement in slender testtube containers) is permissible. Stem and foliage should complement the bloom.

Too much fertilizer may result in the production of abnormal sepals or a cluster of bracts instead of the normal bract on the neck of the specimen. These are defects and are penalized accordingly. An unsightly curve in the neck of the stem is a more serious fault than a like curve farther down on the stem.

DISBUDDING. Specimen blooms of Teas, Hybrid Teas and Hybrid

Perpetuals and their climbing sports must have been grown disbudded. See exceptions under Old Garden Roses.

Side buds, accompanied by leaf/s causes elimination. Side buds alone are penalized. Recent and improper disbudding is graded down in relation to the tardiness and the degree of impairment. Late disbudding, indicated by a visible stub would be penalized more than if the stub has been neatly notched. Green clay or ink to conceal disbudding scars will cause disqualification or elimination from consideration. Disbudding is defined as "removal of immature growth". Removal of spent blooms is thus not dsibudding, it is grooming. Grandifloras are shown and judged either as naturally grown or they may be disbudded. They grow naturally, either *as one-to-a-stem, several-to-a-stem, or mass inflorescence. Any class for one-bloom-per-stem must be disbudded, this may include Grandifloras, Floribunda, etc.*

Single-type H.T. with less than 12 petals ('INNOCENCE') may be judged as naturally grown or disbudded. A single large perfect bloom may score higher than a cluster of single-type Hybrid Teas, unless the latter are all of exceptionally high quality.

All other classes, such as Polyantha, large-flowered climbers such as 'BLAZE', small-flowered climbers, Miniatures, Old Garden Roses, etc., *are shown and judged as naturally grown. Schedules may call for H.T. sprays of two or more blooms to show natural beauty.*

FOLIAGE

Ideally, the entry shows three-leaflet leaves above at least two sets of five or more leaflet sets as typical. Size of foliage should be in proportion to the bloom and stem, uniformly and regularly spaced; not too far or near the bloom and typical of the variety in quantity, size, color, substance and shape. Note the sketches of the types of leaf shape. Foliage may be thin and flexible; thick and leathery, wrinkled (rugose) according to variety and only experienced observation can bring this knowledge. Texture of the foliage may be glossy, waxy or dull and the typical color may be a medium or dark green.

The foliage should be free of discoloration, due to dust, sprays, disease, insects, nutritional deficiencies and weather, both on the top and beneath. Leaves which buckle excessively may be the result of excess water. Black Spot causes black irregular circular areas and the leaves may yellow and drop off. Dwarf, distorted leaves may be mildew damaged. Orange-brown spore masses on the undersides of the leaves is Rust. The substance may be sucked away by Aphids and Sawfly larvae. Light green or yellowed foliage may be a symptom of nutrient deficiencies — Chlorosis. A lack of Boron causes leaves to stunt, and become cupped, appearing scorched. Soft, sappy growth may be the result of excess Nitrogen.

Damaged leaflets may be removed entirely, leaving no stub, or may be unobtrusively trimmed to remove blemishes. Mars on the stem or foliages near the bloom are marked off more severely than comparable defects farther down the stem. For instance a torn, soiled leaflet on the first set below the bloom would draw more attention (thus a greater penalty) than would the same faults in the leaves just above the container.

The foliage **must** be free of additives such as oil (detected by residue), gloss (detected by minute raised crystalline particles), vinegar (detected by smell). Such artificial dressing is prohibited and results in disqualification or elimination from award consideration. If the Judge is dubious about a change in the appearance he can penalize for a deviation from "typical for variety". Points for foliage, stem, balance and proportion go to uniformity, overall appearance and balance in English box staging (i.e., 6 of same variety or mixed types).

Bloom Form

*most perfect phase of possible beauty *formal *circular outline *symmetrical *petals well-proportioned *well-balanced *well-arranged *center well-formed *center pointed *high-centered (Exhb) *regular in shape and petal placement *number of petals typical *no voids or holes in the inflorescence Flori: *uniform heights *cluster includes some open, half-open, buds (some varieties bloom out at once)
-fewer than 5 pts touching imaginary circle perimeter (full double) -crippled or torn petals -evidence of petal removal -artificial dressing (eliminate) -split or confused center -insufficiently open -full blown (exhibition class) -center unfurled (exhibition) -petals missing, misplaced -lacks regular petal placement -off center -irregular outline -improper stage of development (still a bud) -center low -overall symmetry disturbed by outer petal removal -outer petals waning affecting symmetry -lopsided center -blunt snubbed center -loss of substance

Floribunda, etc. -vigorous secondary growth or recent removal -unbalanced -one sided -spent flowers -lack of regularity in profile -bloom atypical for variety (may be dec. exhib. sngl.) -bloom stage atypical for variety

Bloom Color

*fresh *clear *bright *rich *luminous *translucent *pure *uniform *clean *brilliant *lustrous *sparkling *typical
-stamens darkened -eliminate if wrong color class for variety -aging -fading -blueing -bleached -murky -dim -weak -dull -insipid -streaky -unnatural pigmentation marks -not according to variety -lifeless -lacks brilliance of the variety -faded florets in cluster -white, green streaks -soiled -loss of substance -marred (disease, insects, spray)

Bloom Substance

*turgid *crisp *fresh *holding *firm *stiff *stamens alert, crisp (Singles, etc.) *starchy *irridescent
-lacks stability of form -wilting -limp -thinning -flabby -loose -soft -stamens indicating age, folding over (Singles, Polyantha, etc.) -petal edges shrinking -creped edges

Size

*truly representative of the variety *above average *no extremes *maximum potential in all parts   Miniature: *tiny *dainty *less than 1½"
Flori: *typical (some have 12, some only 3–5 per cluster)
-coarse -overgrown -blowsy -small -puny -stunted Miniature: -overlarge -eliminate Flori: if only 1 bloom and 1 or more side buds on spray Grandi: if less than 2 or more blooms.

Stem and Foliage

Stem: *well proportioned to flower and foliage *straight *strong *carrying several five-seven-nine leaflets sets *naturally grown (Floribunda, etc.) *properly disbudded (Hybrid Teas, Hybrid Perpetuals, Teas & climbing sport) *thorns intact above vase rim *Flori: view bal/prop in profile *no missing leaves *2 or more leaf sets

-stem over long -too short -coarse -weak neck -thorns removed -abnormal sepals or bracts -side shoots (eliminate H. Teas, Perpetuals) -recently disbudded-stem out of proportion to foliage and bloom. Unwanted growth of any kind may be removed, but then is subject to penalty for impairment of natural form, color, scars. *-Items 1, 5, 7 (p. 286) ignored*

Foliage: *well placed and spaced *in proportion to stem and flower *clean *free of any disfiguration *typical (gloss, etc.) *evenly stacked

-too dominant -lacking foliage -yellowing -too close or too far from bloom -blemished -torn -distorted -weak -thin -small (except in Miniatures) -succulent -cleaning or shining additives used (eliminate) -blistered -buckling -foliage damage close to bloom *(more penalty than further down)* -single leaflets *(if detract from bal/prop.)*

Balance and Proportion

*bloom of such size that long stem and large foliage complements it. *stem right length for bloom size *pleasing proportion *foliage *large enough, not overwhelming *may have less than ideal # leaves if in balance & proportion *bloom framed by foliage*
-stem too long, short -too weak, heavy -foliage excessive, too large. -foliage too small -neck barren of leaves for too many inches -disturbing proportions.

TYPICAL PETALAGE OF SOME VARIETIES:

VARIETY	TYPICAL PETALAGE	USUAL CATALOG DESCRIPTION
RED HYBRID TEA		
AUDIE MURPHY	18-20	large
CHARLOTTE ARMSTRONG	35	large
CHRISTIAN DIOR	50-60	large
KARL HERBST	60	large
MISTER LINCOLN	40-45	very large 6"
NIGGER BOY	56	medium
OREGON CENTENNIAL	30	large
RED AMERICAN BEAUTY	30-35	large 5"
TEXAS CENTENNIAL	25	large
PINK		
BROCADE	60	large
COUNTESS VANDAL	30	large
CHAMPAGNE	35-40	large
DAINTY BESS	5	medium
KORDES PERFECTA	45-50	large
MEMORIAM	50-60	very large
PICTURE	34	medium
PINK DAWN	60	large
PINK FAVORITE	21-28	
The DOCTOR	25-30	medium-large
YELLOW		
BURNABY	55	large

ECLIPSE	25-30	medium
KINGS RANSOM	40-50	very large
LOWELL THOMAS	35-40	medium-large
McCREDY'S YELLOW	30	large
PEACE	40-50	very large
SISTER THERESE	25	medium-large
EBB TIDE	40	large
COVER GIRL	28	medium-large
CONDESA de SASTAGO	50-60	large
MME. HENRI GUILLOT	25	medium-large
TALISMAN	25	medium
WHITE		
FRAU KARL DRUSCHKI (**H. perpetual**)	35	very large
McCREDY'S IVORY	25-30	very large
SNOWBIRD	30-35	medium
VIRGO	30	medium-large
WHITE PRINCE	50-60	large
LAVENDER CHARM	50	medium-large
TROPICANA		large
GRANDIFLORA		
JOHN ARMSTRONG	35-40	large
PINK PARFAIT	30	medium-small
QUEEN ELIZABETH	20	large
MONTEZUMA	40	large
CAMELOT	40	large
FLORIBUNDAS		
EUTIN	20	small
FLORADORA	25	medium
BETTY PRIOR	5	medium
GOLDEN SLIPPERS	18-25	medium-small
FUSILIER	40	medium

A comparison of measurement with adjective reveals that:

- very large generally means five to six inches

- large generally means four to five inches

- medium generally means three to four inches

1. Hybrid Tea   2. Floribunda   3. Grandiflora

4. Exhibition Form

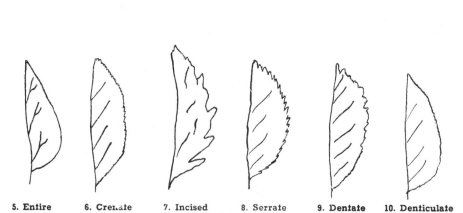

5. Entire   6. Crenate   7. Incised   8. Serrate   9. Dentate   10. Denticulate

Rose Leaf Margins

Succulents and Cacti

SUGGESTED CLASSES:

1. 1 pot, under six inches
2. 1 pot, over six inches
3. 1 planter (containing at least three different species or varieties)
4. Desertarium or Dish Garden
5. Collection (at least five different species or varieties)
6. Display (at least five different species, artistically displayed)

SUCCULENTS AND CACTI
SUCCULENTS

A true succulent is a plant which has fleshy leaves, stems and/or underground tubers of greater thickness than the average, serving as storage organs for water, thus enabling the plant to withstand prolonged periods of drought. Approximately 900 species are found in Mexico alone.

The varied families and species of both Succulents and Cacti are too involved to go into here, their diversity of form is so great and their variety of kinds so immense that a lifetime of study is needed to become acquainted with all. Many fine books are available for such botanical study.

The Succulents which appear frequently as Flower Show exhibits include the Agaves, Aloes, Crassula, Echeveria, Euphorbias, Hoyas, Haworthias, Kalanchoe, Sedums, Sempervivums and Mesembryanthemums. Yucca, including the Joshua Tree, and Agaves, etc., are common landscape subjects.

Many well-known plant families have succulent members such as the Milkweed (Hoya, Rosary Vine and Stapelia Carrion Flower); and the Lily (Aloes and Yuccas, Sansevieria and Haworthias). The small, spiky zebra-striped plant often seen in Succulent collections is the Zebra Haworthia, thus is a member of the Lily family.

The Compositae (Daisy) family gives us the "Pickle Plant Cactus" and the families of the Grape, Pelargonium (the family to which the Geranium belongs), Portulaca, Wandering Jew, Peppers (Pepperomias) and the Pineapple families also contribute succulents to horticulture.

Many Succulent members of the Euphorbia group (Spurge family) resemble Cacti as they have grotesque shapes and spines, but close observation will disclose the fact that the spines do not arise from areoles, thus identifying them as Succulents, not Cactus. The Crown of Thorns is an example, it is a succulent often mistaken for a Cacti.

The Agave group (Amaryllis family) is of American origin and includes the well-known Century Plants. The Mesembs belong to the Fig-Marigold family and includes the fascinating "Pebble", "Stone" and "Window" Succulents.

Sedums (not all of which are Succulents) Sempervivums (Houseleeks) Crassulas, Cotyledons, Kalanchoes and Echeverias (Hen and Chicks) all belong to the Orpine family. The well-known and often-seen Jade Plant is a Crassula.

CACTI

Not all Succulents are Cacti, but **all Cacti** are Succulents, being one part of that large family which includes 2,000 well-defined species, besides a great number of varieties. The word "cacti" with a long "i" is the plural form now universally favored. There are no annual Cacti.

Cacti are distinguished from Succulents in that they have areoles, a unique cushion-like organ on the stems and branches from which the spines, joints and flowers grow. It is the position and number of these areoles and the number, form and position of the spine forms which are the determining factor in differentiating between species.

The Cacti group is divided into three main tribes:

1. PERESKIAE, most primitive and least resembling Cacti as we know them but have instead, deciduous or evergreen foliage or leaves. Some Pereskiae trees could be easily mistaken for Lemon or Apple until close examination reveals areoles from which the growth arises.

2. OPUNTIEAE, which have spines and bristly hairs in clusters or bundles called "glochids". Includes Prickly Pear, Cholla and many native to U.S.

3. CEREEAE, Cereus, plants are usually leafless and the flowers have definite tubes. These fall into the following groups. Tree (Sahuaro), Columnar (Old Man), Barrel, Hedgehog (Lobivia), Pincushion (Mammillaria), Button, Thick Root (Rattail Cacti), Climbing, Creeping, Mistletoe and Orchid (Christmas and Easter Cacti).

A loose, cultural distinction often groups Cacti into:

1. Desert types which require arid conditions and sun (Barrel, etc.)

2. Jungle or Tropic types which require some shade and moisture (Christmas, Easter, etc.).

SCALE OF POINTS

Interest	45	Staging	10
. shape interest	15	. pot size relative to plant	5
. surface interest, textural	15	. pot choice	5
. coloring interesting		. condition	20
(flowers, pads, stems,		actively growing, typical	
etc.)	15	Educational Value	15
		. plant size and degree of maturity	
		Nomenclature	10

INTEREST

. species   . common name

Interest is of three kinds in judging these plants: shape, textural and coloring.

SHAPE INTEREST

Shape interest is evidenced in the multitude of interesting, even bizarre shapes found. Many Sedums and Sempervivums are cushion-like. Some, like the Prickly Pear have flat, oval pads; others, like the Fishbone, Elkhorn and Cowhorn Euphorbias and the Pygmy Joshua have interesting, almost grotesque shapes. The Tiger Jaw Faucaria and the Pyramid Crassula have toothed or bristled margins; the Peppermint Stick (**Senecio gregori**) is spiked. The Night Blooming Cerus has triangular stems, the Crested Opuntia has weird fluted pads and the Pine Cone Cacti, the Rick Rack Cacti, the "Windowed" Mesembryanthemum and the Inch Worm Succulent are names which aptly describe these interesting forms. This apt and interesting naming is a charming part of the study of Succulents.

SURFACE INTEREST

The surface texture is as varied and interesting as the shapes. One may expect to find thick, waxy cuticles (skin); thick leaves, bluish waxy "bloom" (**Echeveria gibbiflora,** abundance of hairs, felt, wool (**Kalanchoe tomentosa, Crassula Tecta** and **Echeveria pulvinata**)*;* filmy webs spun by the plant itself (**Sempervivum arachnoideum**)*;* plushy or velvety surface (**Kalanchoe beharenes**) or long, papery ribands instead of spines (Paper Spined Opuntia Cacti).

COLORING INTEREST

Direct sunshine and perfect ventilation will stimulate growth and tone in desert Cacti, often resulting in "sun coloring" (brighter spines, pads, stem colorings) on plants usually described as "green" and should not be penalized as "scorching". The high color of a healthy plant is easily distinguished from the rough yellow or brown of genuine scorching. Interest through color can be obtained through selection of plants which have colored spines, flowers, fruit or berries, colored leaves and stems. The coloration patterns include variegations, spotting, marginal markings, striping, etc.

STAGING

Staging includes consideration of pot size relative to plant size, the care evidenced in the selection of the pot and the general condition of the plant or plants.

POT SIZE. For globular Cacti or Succulents, the pots should not in general, be less than the diameter of the plant itself, including spines and should ideally be larger. Besides giving plenty of root space, the larger pot furnishes protection for the spines if the pots are placed close together and permits easy access to soil for stirring from time to time. The pots should always be in good proportion to the plant size in all cases. For plants with shallow root systems (Mesembs, etc.), half pots (height is one-half the top diameter) present a better appearance while giving ample root space. Half pots are also less easily tipped over.

For those varieties having longer tap roots, full pots are essential for proper growth.

POT CHOICE: Authorities differ greatly in their recommendations for choice of pots. Clay pots are cheaper, but less attractive, their porosity assists drainage and root aeration, but some authorities point out that this is not needed if a proper soil mix is used. Clay pots are not very resistant to heat and may if dried out, cause excessive root burn. Glazed and decorative pots are more attractive, but often lack proper drainage and are more expensive; if proper drainage is allowed for and proper soil tilth is used, drainage is no problem and roots near the outside of a glazed pot are not so readily damaged by heat. Since there are about equal advantages and disadvantages, both should be acceptable to the Judges unless the Schedule definitely states a type, then the Schedule must be adhered to by the Judge. Combinations can be used with a clay pot inside an ornamental pot as a "topcoat". The choices of glaze, texture and color should be complementary to the plant or plants used or the Judge may deduct a few points. Coy copies of ladie's hats, cowboy boots ad the like are rather incongruous choices to be discouraged.

CONDITION

The plant or plants should be in active growing state, not merely sitting in the pot, static, dull and miserable.

One of the greatest hazards of showing Succulents and Cacti in a Flower Show is the physical injury caused by carrying and placing, as the plant parts often trail and snap off easily. Such mechanical injury should not be penalized as heavily as injury caused by cultural malpractice.

Plants which are straggly and elongated (etiolated) or decolorized (bleached) due to lack of light should be penalized accordingly. Too much water in some species may lead to a rupturing of the skin through over-distention, leaving unsightly scars and a mess of dried sap over the lower parts of the plant. Hard water used to spray desert types may deposit saline salts which develop into white, yellow or brown spots and scars. Rot may be caused by too much water, too high temperatures during the resting season, too much nitrogenous fertilizer or stagnant moisture caused by a too-heavy soil and lack of drainage. A plant may actually suffocate from a caked, "close" soil.

Lack of flowering may be due to inadequate ventilation, insufficient sun or high temperatures during the resting period. Other examples of cultural malpractice and neglect may be evidenced by:

. abnormal, distorted growth	(over-use of fertilizer)
. general lack of thriftiness	(planted too deep, potbound, root and mealy bugs, aphids)
. small, scabby spots	(Red Spider)
. discoloring, dull or grey-white cast	(Thrips)

. small, brown punctures	(left after removal of Scale)
. crumbling dry, discolored pat-ches	(Dry Rot)
. transparency, internal tissue deterioration	(Fungus, Virus Diseases)

EDUCATIONAL VALUE

To have full educational value a plant should be grown to its peak of bloom or growth. Of course, the Judge has to take into consideration the fact that many plants never can be considered truly mature as pot plants, especially mature in view of their growth in their native habitats. Many plants never reach such size as potted plants and a good thing! But with controlled pot care, they can be grown to be satisfactorily mature as house plants.

The Judge must penalize any plant which is immature or an inadequate example of the type. The plant must be old enough to reflect the care which has been given it for a considerable period of time. A casual rule of thumb might be that a plant should be at least a year old before being exhibited. A carefully worded schedule can circumvent the exhibition of baby plants.

Educational value also includes consideration of trueness to type; is the plant typical in form, color, flowering, branching, spine and glochid formation?

The exhibit also has educational value if it is a new variety created by some hybridist and shown for the first time in the area; or if it is a new species which has just been discovered, or imported and propagated; or if some new or unorthodox growing or training method was used to create successful results, or examples of cultural experimentation, as for example, the grafting of a pendulous form (Rattail Cactus) on the top of a tall, erect stem (Cerus).

Rarity has been deleted from the judging scale of points because often the plants are termed "rare" when the Judge is simply not familiar with the plant. A plant that is common in New Mexico might be uncommon and have great educational value in Maine, but should this plant be given low points for rarity in New Mexico and high in Maine? There should be uniformity in judging throughout the nation. Due to classification and other progress; interest, regular flowering and fine condition have come to be more desirable than mere diversity or rarity.

NOMENCLATURE

The correct naming of any exhibit in a Show is of inestimable educational value, and especially as concerns the hundreds of Succulent and Cacti and the general tendency to use colloquial names which cause no end of confusion and dissention.

Good nursery catalogs specializing in Succulents and Cacti are a help in identifying and convincing. Name signs should be clean, proportionate to pot and plant, neatly written, and above all — correct, with the species name if at all possible as well as the common name.

SUMMARY

Interest 45 Points (divided between shape, textural and coloring interest. 15 each)

*unusual *unique *novel *high, natural 'sun coloring' *fruiting or flowering

-commonplace -mediocre -plain -scorched color

Staging

Pot Choice: *good drainage provided *complementary to plant in color,

10 Points -lacks drainage provision -pot cracked, unsightly -pot soiled -unharmonious color choice -texture incompatible -shape incongruous

Pot Size: *proportioned to plant size *size well chosen for plant type
10 Points -undersize -top heavy -inadequate -too large in proportion -over potted

Condition: *attractive *healthy *clean *vigorously growing *thrifty

10 Points -excessive shrinking or wrinkling due to severe lack of moisture -soil and dust residues -static state of growth -scarring -soil "close" (lacking in porosity) -scorched -etiolated -bleached -dried sap -wounds -abnormal -distorted -brown or white spots -areole spines or glochids missing or torn loose

Educational Value 15 Points

*typically mature for potted plant of the variety *new to the area *unusual training or handling

-immature -abnormal -not true to type

Nomenclature 10 Points

*neat *well sized *correct

-carelessly written card -over or under sized card -incorrect (remove all points)

DESERTARIUMS AND DISH GARDENS FEATURING SUCCULENTS AND CACTI

Desertariums are glass-enclosed, miniature deserts; and dish gardens are miniature desert scenes on trays or other type bases. Artistic ingenuity can be appreciated in the combining of rocks and plants to form realistic scenes.

The plants chosen to share the same soil in a container must be related as to cultural needs, and should not be a hodge-podge of ivy, ferns with succulents and cacti, nor even a mixture of desert and tropic Cacti. Overcrowding should be penalized and the small to minature types used, the use of baby plants of large types should be penalized.

The harmony of textures, and colors must also be considered. There should be no mold or excessive moisture in evidence. The use of coarse sand or gravel adds a realistic touch to the surface.

Flat dishes may be contrived from natural materials such as wood planks, shells, or of commercial materials such as pottery, plastic, metals and the like. Depth should be approximately 2-4" depending upon the varieties used. Drain holes should be provided and the container should have sufficient depth to allow proper root development and watering. Generally enough room should be allowed between the plants for three year's growth.

SUMMARY

*well spaced *well chosen as to similar habits and culture *compatible colors and textures *ingenuity evident in selections and/or placements *all plants presenting healthy appearance

-crowded -molding -excess moisture or condensation -poor selection as to habits, culture -improper container -too shallow -plants out of proportion to each other and setting or accessories

DISPLAYS OF SUCCULENTS AND CACTI

Displays are judged both on artistic and cultural basis and consideration includes the background, pot placements, appropriate pot selection, including size, shape and type. Staging can be artistically accomplished by the use of sand for ground cover, a taller plant in the background for atmosphere, or could be a background of a desert setting or table decorated with desert rocks on and around which the exhibits are displayed. Such ingenious displaying rates extra points.

Succulents

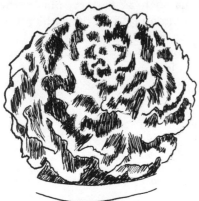

1. Echeveria, "CURLY LOCKS"

2. Zebra Haworthia fasciata

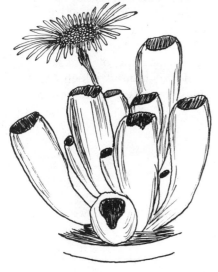

3. Window Mesembryanthemum

4. Cowhorn Euphorbia

5. Cobweb Sempervivum

Cacti

1. Orchid Cacti "CRIMSON GIANT"

2. Rattail Cacti

3. Opuntia microdasys albata
'ANGEL WINGS'

4. Crested Opuntia serpentina

5. Barrel Cacti, 'WHITE KNIGHT'

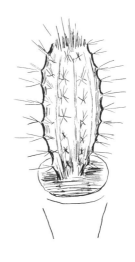

6. Sky Blue Cereus

Tulips

SUGGESTED CLASSES:

1. One stem, Type 1 through 12
2. Three stems, same variety, Types 1 through 12
3. Three stems, different types
4. Three stems, different varieties
5. Forced, one pot, specify size

In a show where many entries are expected, classes can be made for color sections within the types.

TULIP:

A group of true bulbs belonging to the Lily family, tulips develop several long, broad pointed leaves and a single scape (stem) bearing one (in common varieties) erect, cup-shape or bell-shape flower with three petals and three sepals in a wide color range.

The word Tulip means turban, which an inverted flower resembles. Tulips are divided into twelve types and listed according to time of bloom.

The three best known to gardeners being the Cottage, Darwin, and the Breeders, all of which flower at practically the same time, in the order of their listing. Lines of distinction in tulips are becoming indistinct through cross-breeding. There are several hundred named varieties of Tulips and more than 100 species have been described, several of the more well-known are listed here.

TYPE 1 SPECIES AND SPECIES HYBRIDS

A-Foseriana and Hybrids

- early bloom
- very large bloom (up to 9" when open)
- stems up to 18"
- superb substance
- whites, yellows and red predominate
- 'RED EMPEROR' is a fine example

B-T. kaufmanniana (Waterlily type)

- earliest of all hybrids
- short stems 6-12"
- striped, mottled or spotted foliage
- reds and yellows predominate
- large flowers, broad petals, wide open form
- self-seeding
- Example: 'GAITY'

C-T. clusiana (Candy Stick)

- dainty
- petals red and white, violet base
- 14" stem
- small flowers, long, sharply pointed

D-**T. greigii**
- short stems
- leaves grey-green, mottled with purple
- colors red and orange range
- Example; 'PANDOUR'

TYPE 2 SINGLE EARLY

- 18" tall
- less substance than others
- some are fragrant 'PRINCE OF AUSTRIA'
- wide color range
- slender, graceful stems
- flowers after the Species, 2-3 weeks before Darwins
- fine for forcing
- Example: 'BELLONA'

TYPE 3 DOUBLE EARLY

- bloom season similar to Singles but with superior substance
- large flowers, fully double, up to 5"
- short, strong stems 14"
- excellent for forcing
- Example: 'DANTE'

TYPE 4 MENDELS AND TRIUMPHS
- crosses of early with late bloomers
- large blooms, vigorous habit

- blooms between types 1, 2, 3, and types 5, 6, 7,
- strong, tall stems, approximately 25"
- wide color and color pattern range, including selfs, bicolors, edges, strips, flushes, etc.
- some are good forcers
- Example: Mendel 'HER GRACE' Triumph 'ADORNO'

TYPE 5 COTTAGE

- so named because were most found in old cottage gardens in Europe
- May flowering
- wide color range
- 16-20" tall, slender, flexible stems
- rounded or pointed petals, large bloom
- Example: 'ADVANCE'

TYPE 6 DARWIN

- May flowering favorite
- wide color range, usually in solid or selfs, white to black ('QUEEN OF NIGHT') often with contrasted centers.
- huge squarish form, up to 6" ('GLACIER')
- 'HOLLANDS GLORY' is a example of a Darwin-**T. fosteriana** cross

TULIPS

307

TYPE 7 BREEDERS

- May flowering
- so-called breeders because self-coloring makes them valuable as hybridizers

- pure-toned, no whites
- native color ranging from brown, bronze, orange, often with a "bloom."
- robust stems, relatively thick, heavy, 24-36"
- large flowers. Some scented ('JESSY')
- Example: 'LOUIS XIV'

TYPE 8 LATE DOUBLE-PEONY

- May flowering
- double, large flowers
- robust stems up to 24"
- wide color range
- Example: 'EROS'

TYPE 9 LILY

- officially listed with Cottage
- May flowering
- wide color range
- wiry, strong stems, 20-28"
- some scented 'LA MERVILLE'
- form-petals gracefully reflexed, pointed long hour-glass or bell-shape
- light, airy appearance
- Example: 'ARKADIA'

TYPE 10 PARROT

- May flowering
- sports of previous types

- form-ragged, variously shaped petals and sepals twisted, deeply cut
  -a few double forms 'DOUBLE FANTASY'
- multi-colored on individual flowers
- stems often too slender in relation to huge flower. Stem 22-36"
- Examples; 'CAPRICE' and 'FANTASY' which is a mutation from Darwin 'CLARA BUTT' and 'FIREBIRD' which is a sport of 'FANTASY'.

TYPE 11 MULTIFLORA

- bunch or bouquet inflorescence
- one strong main stem with 2-8 branches half way up the main stem, each carrying a bloom
- center bloom is often the largest
- gracefully spaced, medium size
- Example: 'BO PEEP'

TYPE 12 BROKEN, REMBRANDT, BIZARRE AND BYBLOEMEN

- some authorities regard these as a distinct type while others insist the sudden color change, though often permanent and hereditary but due to virus disease, precludes them from being typed
- colors are striped, flamed, variegated in the smooth petal form

- of Darwins, and should not be confused with the Parrots' lacinated form
- In nature, aphids spread the virus which causes the color "breaking". This can be done artificially by grafting an infected piece into a healthy bulb. Such color breaks are not as popular as they were years ago, when they instigated the famous "tulipomania" of Holland in the 1600's.
- Examples: Rembrandt 'AMERICAN FLAG' Bizarre 'INSULINDE' Bybloemen 'APPLE BLOSSOM'

The classified list obtained from the Nat. Tulip Society can be used to check proper classification of named varieties.

TULIP SCALE OF POINTS

Flower	75	Stem	15
. color perfection	20	. length and stiffness	
. size according to variety	20	**General Condition**	**10**
. substance and texture	20	. foliage . age	
. form perfection	15	. carriage . grooming	

COLOR

Tulip colors range the entire spectrum from pure white to some of the nearest-to-black flowers available to man. Many varieties even exhibit varying degrees of green coloring. If the designer (landscape or artistic) wants intensity and clarity, Tulips have it; if he prefers sombre shades or the most delicate tints, these, too are to be found.

Color patterns include:

a—bands, edges, margins
b—conspicuous centers
c—blotches, mottling
d—interior one color, exterior con-

trasting
e—petals one color, sepals another
f—streaks, stripes
g—flushes, blends, feathering, etc.

The color should be typical for type and variety. Some tulips must be open for several days before they attain a color which is typical. A Judge must guard against any prejudice concerning variegations and combinations, particularly in the green, brown and purple-brown colors such as are found in the dull-toned, so-called "art" shades of the Breeders.

Judgment should be on the clarity and purity of the colors. Combinations must be pleasing and attractive. Breeders carry the dull, art shades, with no whites; Cottage have a wide range, but particularly orange and yellow; Darwins are limited in the oranges and yellows.

Any non-varietal streaking, or spotting, or dulling will be considered a fault under color. White spots on colored flowers and brown spots on white flowers are symptoms of Tulip Fire (Botrytis) and must be ɪ.. 'ly penalized. Color changes, fading, bleaching or blueing are also faults to be penalized here.

SIZE

Growers generally agree that unless you can supply them with exceptionally good care and have a soil exactly to their liking, the flowers from tulips will be better the first spring after planting than they ever will be again.

Size variance between types ranges from the diminutive **Tulipa biflora** to the huge five and six inch blooms on 36" stems of the Darwins, and to the short stems, but immense blooms of the **T. fosterianas** which may reach 9" in diameter when open.

It is not possible to judge size in relation to stem in Tulips as the huge blooms of for instance, the Parrots, are typically oversize in comparison to the stem strength and diameter. Size, therefore, is very closely related to type. The size varies between varieties within a type, also. Tulips puny and small for the variety indicate poor culture, "running out" and are severely penalized.

SUBSTANCE AND TEXTURE

Substance

The heavy, crispness of the petals and sepals varies from type to type and variety to variety. Greater substance being found in the Triumphs, Mendels, Cottage, Breeder and Darwins than in the early or late bloomers, with the possible exception of the Fosterianas.

One of the valuable qualities of Tulips is their ability to hold up, due to the amount of material in the petal-sepal structure which supports them. A well-conditioned Tulip will last days when cut.

Thinning of the edges on any segment indicates a loss or lack of substance; a limp or flabby look is also very objectionable. The specimen should look fresh, crisp, with a thick appearance to each part, and be free from any sign of age.

FORM

The form or shape of Tulips varies even in the same type and cross-breeding between types is further blurring the accepted type outlines. For instance, Cottage 'MARJORIE BOVEN' is egg-shaped, long, elegant and tapered, while Cottage 'IVORY GEM' is blunt at both ends, squarish and globular.

Darwin 'GOLDEN SPIKE' is a long, slim classic form fitted to its name; Darwin 'SCOTCH LASSIE' is short, clubby and loosely formed; while Darwin 'FLORENCE NIGHTINGALE' is very blunt and squared off at both base and tip.

Cup, goblet, urn, globe, and vase are a few of the words used to describe tulip forms. Classic or ideal form for exhibition of the Single Early, Darwin, Cottage, Breeder, Triumph types of form may be described as egg-shaped with long petals tapering to an oval; the bloom proportions being longer than wide. Darwin 'ARABIAN NIGHTS' is an example.

Single Early, Triumph, Mendel, Cottage, Darwin, Breeder, Parrot and Lily types should be shown one-fourth to one-half open and the segments must not turn in at the tips, but stand upright and gently reflex according to type. The perianth of these tulips is composed of three sepals and three petals of about equal size and length and development, any variations here would be considered a fault. Any spreading or loosening at the segment bases is a sign of relaxation and age.

In the Doubles, the stamens have been transformed into petal-like structures called petaloids. Such varieties should be shown approximately three-fourths open.

T. kaufmanniana (Waterlily) type should be shown wide open.

Many people feel the size and striking center of a wide open **T. fosteriana** ('RED EMPEROR') cannot be appreciated unless shown wide open. A special class can be included in the schedule as is done in many Rose Society shows for such full-blown specimens if the Show Committee so wishes.

Lily Flowered types should have the typical hour-glass or bell shape with the petals characteristically pointed and reflexing.

STEM

The stem should hold the flower erect, rarely nodding (exception: Parrot) and the flower should be set squarely on the end of the stem.

Length

Length of stem varies with the type and varieties within the types.

up to approximately 10"	Approximately 10-20"	Approx. 20" and up
. miscellaneous species	. Fosteriana	. Mendels, Triumphs
. Kaufmanniana	. Greigii	. Cottage
	. Single Early	. Darwin
	. Multiflora	. Breeders
		. Peony
		. Lily
		. Parrot
		. Broken

Length should be in good proportion to the flower and typical for type and variety. Weak, crooked, overlong, pale, untypical stems are faults to be penalized. The stem should not be cut off so long that a blanched end remains. The stem should carry at least two leaves, but at least two leaves must be left on the plant to mature the bulb.

Stiffness

Stiffness and strength of the stem varies decidedly with the type:

slender, wiry	sturdy, rigid
. Single Early	. Double Early
. Cottage	. Mendels and Triumphs
. Lily	. Darwin
. Parrot	. Breeders
. Most Species	. Double late, Peony
	. Multiflora
	. Brokens
	. T. fosteriana

311

With the exception of the Parrot type, which is often typically unable to support the bloom, and where some crookedness is permitted, stems should be straight and strong enough to hold the flower without undue nodding or bending.

The stems of Peony Tulips may be weakened if grown in full sun. The variety of Lily called 'PHILEMON' droops typically.

Improper conditioning (not supporting the stems) will cause them to be crooked.

GENERAL CONDITION

Foliage

Tulip foliage is linear to very broad and is, in general dark green. Exceptions are **T. kaufmanniana** and **T. greigii** which have mottled, striped, gray-green foliage.

Tulip Fire (Botrytis) causes a shriveling and yellowing of the foliage tips, followed by spots at the edges which increase and run together. This condition must be penalized heavily.

Abnormally discolored, twisted and deformed foliage is often the result of aphid attacks. Unseemly weather sometimes affects the appearance. Damage done by disease or insects is to be penalized more heavily than that done by the elements.

Tulips should be exhibited with at least two healthy, normal-appearing leaves. To exhibit many large leaves shows poor cultural practices as the leaves are needed to mature the bulb for next season's growth. Overlarge, weak, succulent leaves should be penalized.

Carriage

The flower should be squarely placed on the stem, with graceful or majestic pose as is typical for the type.

Age

All Tulips but the doubles carry six stamens shorter than the petals and sepals which are fine indicators of age. Dropping pollen, and dried ends indicate a stage past maturity.

Grooming

Foliage, flower and stem must be cleaned of all soil and foreign materials and shown without scarring or damage of any sort.

POTTED SPECIMENS

Plants well-grown, exhibiting care and attention to cultural needs. Ample flowers typical of variety, with typical color and form. Flowers should be held above the foliage. Entire plant or plants should be healthy, clean; not leggy, weak or pale. Choice of variety and types should be those suitable for forcing.

SUMMARY

Color 20 Points

*typical for type and variety *pure *clear *whites clean *rich *combinations attractive and pleasing

-dull -lifeless -diluted -weak -spotted (water or disease) -faded -bleached -blueing

Size 20 Points

*typical for type and variety *above average

-small -puny -untypical -gross -ungainly

Substance and Texture 20 Points

Substance *fresh *crisp *thick *strong constitution *solid

-weak -thinning -limp -flabby

Texture *typical to type *smooth *satiny *silky

-ridged -crepey -uneven

Form 15 Points

*typical *classic *open properly for type

-loosening -collapsing ·squat -uneven petal length, width, development -too wide open for type -too tight (doubles)

Stem 15 Points

Stiffness *straight *strong *erect *typical *upright (Exception: Parrot — some curvature allowed)

-weak -nodding -bending -crooked

Length *proportioned to flower and type

-too short -overlong

General Condition 10 Points

Foliage *typical in color, size, substance and shape *two leaves shown

-shriveled -yellow -discolored -twisted -deformed -scarred -torn -overlarge -weak

Carriage *flower squarely on stem *graceful or majestic as to type *well posed

-off center -nontypical

Age *fresh appearance overall
-dropped pollen -general over-mature appearance -double immature

Grooming *clean *unmarred *pollen brushed off

-soiled -scars -tears -mechanical injury -dusty

313

DIVISION 3 SECTION 4
ARTISTIC QUALITIES
Design

... The composition of a picture is the greatest of all its parts.

... Da Vinci

"I know of no way of judging the future but by the past," said Patrick Henry. Not only our immediate past, but that past which stretches back to the dawn of man's awareness of certain aesthetic fundamentals which we call the principles of art.

In flora arrangement, a design is the arranging of the elements of fresh, dried organic and inorganic objects as requested or allowed by the Schedule and according to these age-old principles of art and composition. *Elements are the basic visual qualities of any art form.*

The **elements** are		The **principles** are	The **goal** is the creation of
. space	*. line*	. balance	
. form	*. color*	. proportion	. beauty
. pattern	*. texture*	. scale	. harmony
. size		. rhythm	. expression
. position and light are thought of as elements in abstract designing		. contrast	. simplicity
		. dominance	. order

A successful design is one in which every part aids expression, and conversely, is one which brings out the greatest possible expression of each of its parts.

A design must be a whole . . . without principles and without discernment, one never finds a successful design. No matter what type is exemplified, it must reveal to the Judge a clear understanding of design principles, and a fulfillment of individual expression through selection. Good taste and good sense, reinforced by the principles dictate the specially appropriate solution for each special problem.

The only right theory is that no theory is right. There should be no rules in present-day flora designing, only consideration of the principles of design used emphatically and knowingly to maintain the vigor of visual image while creating order. Too much uncontrolled freedom and disregard for the principles is apt to result in chaotic design . . . too much regimentation and intellectualizing produces static, inexpressive design. The successful designer who finds a happy medium balanced between the two extremes gains her Judge's approval.

No definite style of design should be cherished by the just Judge to the exclusion or minimization of all other.

To assess the impression of completeness and success in an arrangement . . . there will be some **repetition** to activate the eye, some **variety** to hold the interest, a bit of **contrast** for visual impact, a well-balanced dynamic **equilibrium** vertically, horizontally and in depth, **rhythm** to give vital movement and a **dominating element** to tie the spaces and solids together.

Principles of Design

BALANCE

There is no "rule" for achieving balance, because each piece of material, each container, each base chosen by the designer for a specific design exerts a different force and demands a different balance solution. Balance is stability secured through the proportion, scale and placement of the elements as well as their visual force.

Size, form, substance, color, space and texture are factors which exert visual weight and force and in combination, repetition or opposition satisfy our sense of visual balance.

Balance is closely allied to proportion which is the comparative relationship of the amounts or areas in a design. An element is said to have more or less visual weight, not by actual weight but as regards to visual force.

The principles of balance and rhythm are also closely allied; balance controls and stabilizes visual movement from shape to shape and along the lines, achieving unity. Balance does not mean repose in the sense of rest or lack of activity; it means that one visual force holds another in equilibrium.

Many qualities affect visual weight or force:
. the farther an object is from the imaginary central axis, the more visual weight it seems to have
. cut edges (serrated) appear lighter than smooth, complete margins
. unusual form carries more visual weight
. closed form (zinnia) has more weight than open forms (lily, iris)
. full chroma carries more weight than tints, tones
. warm colors carry more weight than cool (a small bit of red balances a larger amount of green)
. rough textures appear heavier than smooth (a small amount of highly textured material generally balances a larger smooth, dull surface)
. the size and importance of a space can balance a seeming, too-large container or too aggressive a color
. environment (juxtaposition) influences weight. For instance, space isolation increases impact. Some colors kill or liven others. (See Color — simultaneous contrast) Light and shadow change visual weight
. directional emphasis. A fist is a closed form, open one finger to point and the eye is directed outwards. Every design needs directional emphasis. This can be supplied even with round forms by grading of size, color and placement. Directional movement reduces "focal-hold" trouble which is where the eye is held in one interest area

SYMMETRICAL AND ASYMMETRICAL BALANCE

Balance is said to be symmetrical or asymmetrical. **Symmetrical** designs are most often associated with Period Occidental Designs. **Asymmetrical** are associated with Japanese Traditional and more recently, 20th Century Traditional, Modern and Abstracts.

SYMMETRICAL, visual stability is achieved through equal balance of weight on either side of an imaginary central axis. Symmetrical, formal balance involves the actual matching of a leaf or flower on each side of the design. Formal balance, then, means methodical or regular placement. The central axis is actually stressed.

Rhythmic vitality can be achieved in a symmetrical design by controlled timing or spacing of dramatic interest areas interspersed with interesting and working space areas. The design may be symmetrical, yet the balance of dynamic attention-getting elements **within** the outline keeps it from being monotonous and uninterestingly rigid and methodical. Such handling may also be called **balance by contrast.**

To illustrate this dynamic interest within a symmetrical outline we can use the human body which can be called symmetrical as it has a prescribed number of equal parts balanced around a central axis. How then is it that we do not all look alike? Because there are more or less slight or obvious **differences** within the symmetrical outline. Elongation, contrast, proportion and scale all work to bring about the ideal of interesting variety within satisfying unity. The result is informal balance of dynamic interest areas.

ASYMMETRICAL BALANCE (informal) is visual stability achieved by an equilibrium of visual weight on either side of the imaginary axis, though the elements used on each side are different. It is created by in-balance, out-of-balance placements of materials. Asymmetrical balance is natural, often found in Nature and may be (1) self-contained and depending upon structure alone for balance; or (2) balanced by placement and must be moved on its base to attain visual balance; or (3) balanced by the use of an accessory.

The main axis is seldom emphasized (Classic Japanese excepted) in self-contained, and seldom stressed in balance by placement. Asymmetrical balance, being more free and flexible, is favored in most modern and abstract designs. Balance is also referred to as static or dynamic.

Static Balance may be found in symmetrical or asymmetrical designs and is arrived at by actual or visual weight, each holding the other steady pulling in opposite directions and exerting equal force. Such easily detected balance is less appealing and because the eye needs stimulation to enjoy, a static design cannot hold the interest for long. When all objects have equal visual force on either side of an imagined axis they cancel each other out, resulting in a lack of motion, interest, life. Balance must be activated to inject vitality.

Dynamic Balance is activated by the fluctuating force of inner contradictions. The design may be symmetrical or asymmetrical, circular, triangular, or other but within that outline the arranger uses various types of contrast or opposition to create dynamic interest within the outline which may be conventional or commonplace. Such contrasts may include:

- opposing color values (light and darks)
- opposing spaces
- opposing textures
- opposing sizes
- opposing directions or positions of like materials
- opposing shapes

The visual forces work both **together** as well as **against** each other to create balance and movement. The Judge checks to see how the arranger has balanced:

- one color value against another
- one shape against another
- one texture against another
- one space against another
- a compressed space against an open-end space
- a closed form (round) against an open-form (lily)
- a pause against motion
- any one of these against any other

The combination possibilities are as endless as imagination. For example, dynamic balance can be achieved and the design given stability without having a balance of either actual or visual weight when enough motion is applied. A bike or a top are visually and actually balanced, but we know they will not stand alone simply because they are visually and actually balanced. But they both will balance upright when speed is applied, because the force of motion is greater than the pull of gravity. In an arrangement, the Judge can expect to find the rhythmic thrust of visual movement up and out equaling the pull of gravity, thus achieving dynamic balance. He credits such when it is well-handled.

BALANCE OF ATTRACTION

In much the same way the Judge mentally divides a show table (see Table Section) to determine balanced placements, the balance of interest in an upright design can be assessed for proper placement in space. If the frame of reference occupied by the design is mentally divided into thirds vertically and horizontally, there will be four intersections, any of which may serve as a natural place for interest emphasis. If the designer has used several intersections as attraction areas of decreasing or increasing interest, the eye is carried along effortlessly and the interest is balanced throughout the design.

The attraction may be a heavier massing, an emphatic space, light or shadow modulation, the end of a line, a change in color or texture, a change in direction or form, and may not be exactly on the intersection. Any element placed on the vertical axis acquires a visual impact and conspicuousness all out of proportion to its own size. Lightly penciled divisions on published pictures of arrangements and paintings will familiarize the Judge with this balancing principle which in theory sounds like scattering shot, but in practice tends to unify the whole.

COLOR BALANCE

Color balance is closely related to proportion; humans naturally are more comfortable with inequality in hue, intensity and value distribution. In checking color balance, the Judge asks if the law of areas has been considered. In abstract designs liberties are taken with this

317

law; the designer may use the shock effect of full chroma contrasts to create a scintillating push-and-pull tension in the design.

The Judge expects intelligent and balanced color harmony and handling in any design, even though the Schedule presents no specific color problem. He consciously attempts to detect interest areas of varying color dominance which force the eye to move about; this is possible and necessary even within the symmetrical design.

BALANCE OF DEPTH

The design must be balanced horizontally, vertically and in depth. Man naturally balances things to a vertical axis from left to right to prevent a "tipped" sensation. But if the horizontal balance has been neglected, the design will appear either top or bottom-heavy and must be penalized. The materials should be placed so that space works at lightening the heavy mass, and facilitates visual movement into the rest of the design.

Depth balance prevents a flattened appearance and is achieved through careful relationships of foreground, middleground and background. Light and shadow, directional shapes, overlapping, receding and advancing texture and color must be used adroitly, enabling the eye to move easily from front to back and front again as well as side to side and top to bottom. A too dominant foreground with no directional release will delay, or halt the eye completely, upsetting depth balance. Lack of depth flattens the design to two dimensions of height and width, which brings penalty.

There should be no consciousness of a focal **point** or bull's-eye in a successful design. Rather, there should be areas of more or less interest which direct attention onward. These will vary in position, size, direction, color, and texture. There should be pauses or rest from motion, balanced by activated areas.

The Judge must learn to see and **feel** the opposing forces with which the arranger has met or missed his goal. He must be able to state how, where and why the design is unbalanced; to do this he must be aware of the various ways balance is achieved and realize that the forces of visual motion, the balance and counter-balance of differences in elements is what gives life and zest to the design.

If the Judge senses the need to adjust or move a unit of the design, faulty balance is no doubt the culprit. The mental "removal" or actual coverage of an element will show if it is needed in the design. If the element is missed, if it plays any part, large or small in the life of the design, it is working!

Some containers are quite rigidly symmetrical, particularly those with an identical handle or similar repetitions on each side. An asymmetrical design in such a container would be risking unsuitability.

Only experience will develop visual skill needed to determine fairly:
if the container has the weight and stability to carry the design

. whether greater height is needed to balance the visual force of base and
container
. whether the accessory is placed at the correct distance to attain best balance
. whether the long line here is well-balanced by the large, round form there
. whether the various interest areas are balanced in accordance with the
type of design being judged (traditional or abstract)
. whether depth and color are balanced
. whether spaces have variety and interest which balance themselves and
the solids

Looking back at a design through the crook of the arm from a distance of a few feet or, again with the back to the design, looking at its
reflection in a mirror will make any faults of balance more readily
apparent.

Too often the Judge looks only at the outline to perceive balance.
The general outline is merely a boundary which gives little or no indication of the internal tensions set up by the visual forces which give
real life to the design.

The Judge must remember that in the hands of the modern artist
and with the new freedoms allowed, liberties are taken to create emphasis and still maintain balance in a specific structural outline. The
Judge's development in the study of balance must at least equal that of
the designer, or fair decisions cannot be reached.

SUMMARY

*interesting balance of dynamic areas *visually stabilized *satisfying balance
*balances well thought out

-balance impaired by insistent area -disjointed appearance -balance weak
-balances disturbed by loose construction -tilting backward, sideways -un-
stable

Proportion and Scale

Every Judge understands that **proportion** is the relative amounts of
one **area** to another as different from **scale** which is the relative size of
one **part** to another.

Proportion is the visual relationship of color, texture and form areas,
while scale deals in size alone, although it affects every other principle.

Scale deals with:

. size of one object to another
. size of an object compared to the
container
. size of the arrangement for its
niche or placement
. size of accessory to container, etc.

Proportion deals with:

. amount of light color area to dark
. amount of flora material to fruit,
etc.
. amount of rough texture to
smooth
. amount of plant material to
container
. amount of round forms to spike
. amount of occupied space to unoccupied space, etc.

When the Judge asks himself "has enough of this color or texture been used to balance the other areas" he is referring to proportion. When he asks "has too large a flower been used here" he is referring to scale.

The proportion of the light to dark areas, the proportion of solids to spaces that form the pattern or silhouette make the first impression — clear-cut, buxom or massed-line. This is seen and assessed before the many details are considered.

The proportion or amount of any one element establishes its relative importance in the design. If the design is characterized as one of dignity because straight lines are more evident than curved ones, these, because of their amounts or proportions, are dominant. There should be a proportionately less amount of curved lines and forms used merely to prevent boredom and monotony. Any equality in proportion usually divides interest and destroys unity.

Height

In judging proportion, consider the visual weight of the materials in evaluating height. Evaluate depth as well as width and height, and a pleasing relationship of one area to another within the design's shell.

While the ratio of one-third container to two-thirds plant material is generally pleasing, the Judge must maintain a flexible viewpoint. Visual weight adjusts the height proportion. The more light and airy the material, the higher the design may soar. The texture and color of the container may demand increased height for aesthetic proportion. The size and shape of each container demands a different height relationship depending on the materials used. These variations point out the fallacy of depending on a definite and unchangeable height ratio.

Interest Areas

The proportion of interest on one side must balance the other; the proportion of interest in the top must balance the bottom, otherwise the design will seem to tip or seem top or bottom-heavy. This illustrates how closely related are the principles of proportion and balance. The Judge decides whether the final unity of the whole is disturbed or strengthened by the balance of the proportions.

Container Proportion Adjusted

The Judge is aware that the spot where the upright design lines meet the horizontal line of the base often contributes to bottom heaviness, and will note the designer's handling of this problem area to make it an expressive part of the design by such "tricks of the trade" as supplying a break, a line change, interest variation or space to "lift" the design and keep it from seeming to be too firmly attached to the table, or heavy in the lower proportions. Many modern containers reduce container proportions by piercing space with holes completely through the container, which illustrates again the effect an area of space can have visually.

Color Proportions

Satisfying color proportions should have been attained by the use of unequal amounts of hue, value and chroma. Thirds or similar amounts are preferable and exact fifty-fifty divisions will usually draw penalty. The eye is satisfied by unequal proportion and this accords with the principle of dominance.

The careful handling and proportions of light and shadow is a tool wise arrangers use to strengthen the three-dimensional effect, and a good Judge will recognize this and give credit. The Judge must decide how adroitly the arranger has handled all the areas to distinguish the design.

SUMMARY

The Judge must also analyze the design to ascertain how the proportion affects all the other principles. The overall size of the arrangement is important only in relation to the space for which it is planned, as in a niche in the flower show. A small space (proportion) requires not only a small arrangement but a small container (scale) and small masses (proportion). Improper proportions are one of the most frequent errors of flora arrangers.

*satisfactory proportion *color areas well balanced *unequal interest areas

-container too tall for material -container too small for material area -too many round forms compared to spike -color areas too equally divided -too much occupied area (niche)

Rhythm

Rhythm is visual activity or movement throughout the design. It is the distribution of persistent interest which causes the eye to travel from one point to another, thus unifying the whole. Rhythm is closely allied to dynamic balance, one abetting the other in vitalizing the design. Basic rhythm usually falls into a simple line, then a space, then a counter line.

Repetition, gradation, radiation from a single point, transition, line direction and visual tensions all work to establish rhythm. Balance can be achieved through the use of twos but rhythm usually needs three or more solids and/or spaces to supply a flow of movement, except in the case of a solid line, which draws the eye over its surface and onward.

In traditional and modern design, formal rhythm is achieved when the eye sees a center of interest first and then moves smoothly outward to the secondary areas of interest. In this type there should be a gradual linking of the elements to provide an uninterrupted flow upward and outward. Too many such arrangements are made with good lines and a focal area with faulty, interrupted rhythm or no connecting rhythm to tie the two together. Unity is produced by dominance and dominance is produced by repetition. Repetition of a line, color, shape or space carries the eye easily through the design insuring unity. Some forms (spike) are releasing forms, allowing the eye to slide off their ends. Some forms are holding forms. Some, made up of small leaves or flowers are filler, transitional forms. Some colors, greys and cool are releasing; some, warm and white are holding; some, greens and violets are transitional. The Judge must decide if the arranger has carefully used these forms and colors to expedite movement or hold it, as the need may be for a successful design.

In abstract the rhythm is usually informal and achieved through inter-related units. There is unity of a different sort, as the placement of the units in space, their directions and balanced tensions supply movement through the design.

Repetition may be carried from the curve of a container line to the curve of a flower form to the curve of a directional line or space. Or the repetition may be in the proportions, as a round flower or round spaces repeating the rounded form of the container.

The emotional effects of repetition may be different, depending upon what and how the repetitions occur. The effect may be monotonous, irritating, exasperating, mysterious or stimulating depending on the sensitivity, taste and education of the viewer.

The repetition may be obvious or subtle; like balance — the less obvious and more subtle, usually the more distinctive the design will be. The repetition need not be exact, but merely related as an oval is related to a circle; or a rectangle to a triangle; or a straight line to angular. The same qualities may appear in different forms, placed at different intervals thus establishing the character of the design.

The repitition must not seem fixed or mechanical. Too much repetition without variety kills interest. Some variation is needed for dynamic quality. Some ways of attaining repetition with variations are:

. repetition of shape and object with variation of size and value or hue
. repetition of shape and object with variation of size
. repetition of shape with variation of object and size
. repetition of lines with variation of object
. repetition of lines with variation of size and value
. repetition of shape with gradation of size
. repetition of number with variation of object

There can be rhythm without repetition where the arrangement of lines and masses leads the eye easily from one line to another, one mass to another or from line to mass, or mass to line. The speed the eye moves over the design is established by the definiteness and closeness of the placement of the lines and masses. The eye races up a line made by closely spaced objects or a solid line, but is slowed by spaces. The movement generally is fast in an early Traditional design, slowed in Modern and much slower in Abstract as the eye starts; stops and backtracks over the whole design instead of taking a single path from focal to the outer boundaries.

Line Rhythm

Of all the principles rhythm is the most expressive and line carries rhythm as nothing else can. Lines have become universal symbols, expressive of emotions. (See Communication.) Rhythm may be gained through a series of lines (and shapes) pointing in the same direction; through a graded series of curves; through stress on lines rather than plane or points. This is not to say that all lines must move in the same directions, some contrast is always needed if only to point up the dominant direction.

Placement which leads the eye nowhere, or results in a static, motionless state is penalized. The designer should use line to lead the eye from one point of interest to the next in logical sequence.

The movement along easy, long curves is gentle and even. In Modern and Abstract crossing and changing directional lines speed the eye movement, and when used properly give vigor and sparkle to the design by creating strong spacial tensions. Such crossing is considered *a fault in judging early conventional design if rhythm is 'interrupted'.*

In Modern Transitional and Abstract design the eye is led by implied di-rection, drawn from one interest area to the next by allowing the viewer's imagination to bridge gaps between the units and using the need for balance of visual tension to supply the movement. This type of placement would be penalized as a break in rhythm when judging *an early 20th century Line, Mass Line or Mass design.*

Gradation of size from small to medium to large sets up rhythmic movement. The progressive increase in the size of space intervals (voids) provides rhythmic transition from solidity of mass to surrounding and supporting space by way of tapered line and reduced interest.

Color Rhythm

The gradual change in color from light to dark, dull to bright, value to value and hue to hue all add variety with movement. No matter how minor the change the result will be movement. The change is *orderly and gradual in Traditional/Conventional, but aggressive and* abrupt in the more modern styles. A center of interest which rivets the eye to one spot is to be penalized. Color rhythm used to strengthen line by following the same contours adds emphasis and dominance. Distinction may be increased when form design and color design work together.

In the Traditional/Conventional and some Modern Transitional colors form a definite pattern and flow together without an effect of interruption or scattering. The analagous and monochromatic harmonies are examples of close color rhythm. Contrasting colors require gradation of value and intensity and repetition for rhythm. If the color rhythm is interrupted or sandwiched as for instance with a solid area of yellow, then one of deep brown and back to yellow with no transition, penalty is expected. Handling of color in Abstract is much less closely graded. Refer to Color and to Abstract.

Space Rhythm

Space, its shape, direction and intervaling can control, activate or slow down the visual movement through a design. The designer who uses space wisely to increase rhythm and thus unity, is to be credited.

The shapes of the spaces, as well as the masses are considered and should be varied and interesting. Monotonous space intervals usually are found with sluggish, dull rhythm and deserve penalty.

Space movements differ in variety and speed. Some rhythms are sharp and staccato. Some are smooth and even. Some make us reach for balance, others have easy balance. The Judge must be aware of the differences and decide whether the exhibitor has used the right one for the particular design and type.

Depth Rhythm

Rhythmic direction is important in expressing roundness, front, back, sides — in other words, third dimension. The repetition of similarly shaped objects placed diagonally behind each other create an illusion of rhythmic depth. The wise designer will utilize the depths evident in natural lines. A spiral may be flat (two dimensional) as in an early fiddle head of ferns, or three dimensional as in the curling tendrils of climbing vines. A flat leaf can be given depth by bending or curling it while its companions are used in the natural plane; thus repetition is satisfied and depth and contrast added. Such perceptive use increases points for rhythm and interest as well as unity and often distinction.

Light and shadow modulation play a part in deepening depth movement by repetition of line and rounding of forms. While most show lighting is pure chance, the designer is usually not schedule-restricted in her use of artificial lighting to unify her design. The Judge will carefully assess her efforts in the use of light, adding points if the design is improved, deducting if not.

Rhythm in the Traditional Design

The Judge will penalize the design in which too many forms of similar size and importance tends to freeze the rhythm. Monotonous regularity of too many evenly spaced voids around the boundary brings penalty. Too many evenly sized and spaced forms (such as round Mums) around the boundary will also mean a point reduction. Any placement which divides the design, or seems to cut the visual picture in half is a fault. Unity is of paramount importance. If a smooth visual path is lacking between the main line and the dominant feature, points are reduced. If the rhythm is confused, leading the eye in too many directions with none dominant, penalty is taken. Sandwiching of form or color, either horizontally or vertically, so the eye is prevented from any movement except up or down, or sideways is to be penalized.

A smooth, uninterrupted rhythmic flow of interest is less apparent in the Modern design. This does not mean it does not occur, but simply that it is not considered a requisite as it is in the early designs. Lines may cross and rhythms be incomplete, supplied by imagination through the eye. Releasing forms and colors are used to supply movement rather than close placement and fillers.

Rhythm in the Abstract

Movement, visual pull between areas of tensional interest, is important to Abstract. Objects are placed apart in space rather than close as formerly done. Movement is not necessarily smooth and is seldom achieved through gradation or transition alone. Rhythm through repetition is apparent in similarities rather than exact duplication or delicate size relationships. Rather than one single path from focal to outer edges, the Abstract movement follows many paths.

SUMMARY

*repetitions varied *pleasing or exciting rhythmic action *subtle, interesting *achieved through line placement, form placement, tensional pull, etc.

-monotonous rhythm -lacks variety -rhythm lacks grace -needs more emphatic rhythm -too many colors or values and chromas give busy, unrhythmic effect -one overcrowded or over-dominant area overbalances the rhythmic movement -confused rhythm, leads nowhere -rhythm too strong or fast in one area

Contrast

It is apparent by now to every Judge that it is impossible to speak of one principle of design without relating it to the others. The interlocking of dominance to contrast, of rhythm to balance, dominance and proportion, and proportion to scale and each of these to all the elements *line, form, pattern, color, texture, space and light and position is a fundamental truth of design.*

Contrast is another way of saying "different" or "opposite". Contrast in flora arrangement means the placing of the elements and using the principles in such a way as to point out or emphasize the differences as opposed to dominance which is the emphasis of similarities.

The law of unity is major agreement — minor contrast! In other words, one dominant line, size, etc., with a bit of contrasting line, size, etc. There can be no dominance without something over which to dominate.

Contrast adds richness, spice and impact through contradiction. Contrast is needed in any design to save it from monotony and dullness. Any curved line looks more rich or sinuous when contrasted by a straight line; any rough texture looks rougher beside a smooth texture. Contrasts stop rhythm and dominance from going too far! An arrangement all repetition, without opposing elements is weakened. When everything is seen and understood at first glance the design fails to hold the viewer's interest and attention.

Contrasts may be:

. of line
. of form
. of stem length
. of line direction
. of space, shape and placement
. of hue, value, chroma
. of color intervals, color areas
. of receding and advancing color

. of light and shadow
. of texture
. of proportions and areas
. of greater and lesser interests
. of space and solids
. of solids and transparency
. of heights and widths

Man's eye appreciates repetition but is vitalized by contrast. Oddly, though they are opposites, both repetition and contrast are used to emphasize a quality; one by duplication, the other by drawing attention by supplying a difference from which to compare . . . in the same way that Jeff's shortness is more noticeable when contrasted by Mutt's tallness.

Too much contrast, however, can cancel out dominance and bring a judging penalty. If a design contains round and square forms, one or the other must dominate for all-important unity. One form, the contrasting one, must remain subordinate in its relationship to the dominant one. Controlled contrast emphasizes unity; uncontrolled, chaos and confusion results!

Rhythm and movement through the design depends on variety (which is gradual change) or contrast which is **forceful change.** Variety, similarity and repetition move the eye along easily, smoothly; contrast jolts the attention through a definite change and is most apparent in Abstract designing.

In Traditional design, the greatest amount of contrast from the rest of the design is found in the area of interest where the lines converge and the design's lines radiate out from the holder. The color values, massing and contrasts should diminish the farther they move away from the center of interest. In a Traditional design the container, base and background are subservient to the plant material; their colors, textures, and lines do not contrast sharply. In Abstract designs, contrast is important. Equality of units when carefully handled, gives importance to each without competition for dominance. The container may share equally with the foliage and flowers and yet unity and harmony are achieved through the placement, direction and tensional balance of the space and solids as well as the dominating idea.

Container, base and background may figure as separate parts of a color-harmony under the new freedoms allowed arrangers. Contrast in a background, however, should not be so over-powering that it tends to swallow up the design. The design is the thing . . . not the background alone.

In Modern and Abstract designs, the contrasts are often emphasized and have great impact due to the fact that little or no transitional material is used as common in the Traditional designs.

Contrast must be used with purpose . . . a planned part of the design. Careless contradiction to no specific end should be penalized. Contrast can upset balance, interrupt movement, dilute dominance and destroy unity and harmony if improperly and carelessly used.

Communication With Contrast

Interpretation plays a part in the approval or disapproval of contrast. The Judge should take into account the use of differences to point up theme requirements. With dominance of vertical line, depicting aspiration, an opposing contrast of line will intensify the mood of aspiration. If a gay mood is expressed with a dominance of warm colors, their warmness and brightness will be increased by a cool contrast.

To meet some thematic requirement, the designer may have wished to de-emphasize her container or background; in this case, the Judge must not expect contrast but harmonizing relationships.

Contrast in the Design

Light areas attract the eye more than dark areas and contrasts must be carefully controlled to insure depth and movement. Light and shadow supply contrast, increasing depth, but too much mottling or scattering of light and shadow can destroy form, cancel unity and upset balance.

The eye is less attracted to a comparatively dark foreground, allowing it to pass easily to the brighter or lighter portion beyond. Cool colors, because of their recessive qualities may appear as a "hole" when used as a focal area against warm hues.

When contrast in the focal area is too forceful and/or extensive, the rest of a Traditional design becomes mere background and must be penalized for lacking rhythm and unity.

Too much contrast in size as between Iris and Coral Bells confuses and disturbs rhythmic unity in traditional designs where transition or "passage" is used to bridge disassociations.

Curves need the steadying influences of a straight line here and there to avoid over-richness and monotony. The richer and fuller the curves, the more severe may be the straight lines that contrast and balance them. Of the two extremes, one tires less quickly of straight lines than of curves.

A design constructed of all warm colors will not look as interesting and scintillating as when a bit of cool, contrasting color has been added.

The designer who has overcome the problem of a shallow niche by employing depth through contrasting the middle ground with the fore and rearground and background, and thus forcing the eye to travel back in seeking repetition is to be rewarded. Placing darker-hued flowers and/or foliage in the rearground of the design which contrasts with a lighter foreground also increases depth illusion.

Depth and spacial illusion can be judged by considering the:
. contrasts of receding and advancing colors
. contrasts of directional movement

. contrasts of light and shadow (lightest values advance, blacks recede)
. contrasts of textures (rough textures advance, smooth, dull recede)
. contrasts of transparents with solids

All these are contrasting optical forces the Judge must recognize and appreciate when used as individual solutions to solve a specific problem.

SUMMARY

*interesting contrasts of spike and round forms *contrasts well controlled *contrasts add interest to dominance and rhythm *unity preserved through contrast adds interest *contrasts well used to increase depth *interpretation increased through contrast

-lacks contrasts -tiresome -boring -not enough change to maintain interest -too much contrast between sizes without transition (Traditional designs) -monotony of rounds -overpowering sameness -contrast without purpose -unplanned contradiction -excessive contrast cancelling out dominance

Dominance

To achieve unity and harmony, the designer must apply the principle of dominance where:

. one line
. one shape
. one direction
. one texture

. one color
. one characterization or
. one idea

plays the major or commanding role.

Maintaining dominance of the elements establishes order and character. Dominance is synonymous with emphasis and focus, and is based on unequals and infers subordination. When one element is emphasized, others must play a secondary role.

By making the less important details in the design subservient to one lone commander, they become supporting accents rather than competitors, thus unifying the whole. Though one element is the common denominator, they all are present in some degree and work together to establish unity, with variety and contrast for interest.

Dominance is most evident in the development of the focal area in the Traditional designs, the dominating boldness of Modern, and in Abstractions it is evident in the emphasis of a dominant expression or element.

A dominance of solids over voids is characteristic of traditional mass and massed-line designs. A dominance of voids over solids is characteristic of modern and abstract designing.

Dominance is most commonly achieved through repetition, by spacing and position, and through emphasis of texture, color, size, shape and direction.

Repetition and Similarity

Repetition and similarity are perhaps the most effective means of gaining dominance and through it, order and simplicity. A repeated line produces a dominant direction. One shape used throughout but of varying value, texture, scale, elongation, angle, solid or space makes for unity with variety. An echoed color determines the color key by increasing the area or chroma or both, and unity is achieved.

The Judge looks for lines of continuance which bind together the many separate movements of a design. A main dominant line of movement can unify. It may be a physical stem, or it may be a visual path created by repeated groupings of shapes, or it may be activated by the push and pull of attracting-opposing focal fields. The eye will leap from color to shape, along established lines and across space to another point, tracing a path which is forceful and unifying even if not actually visible in its entirety.

The eye is attracted to similarity as well as repetition. Although the elements may be otherwise unrelated, the eye enjoys finding similarities or "likes" — like lines, like directions and the like. The discerning Judge must train himself to peel away the surface differences, to see and appreciate the under-lying likenessess the designer has discovered and used to unify through dominance.

If there is enough repetition or similarity to establish a dominant element, area or idea, the arrangement can receive its share of the points under design for the quality. It is a unity of little things that make for great achievements.

As in balance and rhythm, subtlety rather than obviousness, will often make the design more distinctive. The Judge should not expect to see all the unifying factors in one glance. The process of discovery is the stimulating attraction of abstraction and should be found in the distinctive early 20th Century designs as well.

Simplicity

Simplicity, the hallmark of distinction, is often the offspring of dominance. In using fewer kinds and having one dominant, non-essentials are eliminated or subjugated. Any careless accumulation of unrelated items or haphazard selection of materials will be penalized. The fewer forms used the purer the art, the stronger the message.

Because of this emphasis, each must be all the more carefully chosen and placed. It is dominance which can be credited for the seemingly effortless **fitness** of a successful design. Without dominance, a design disintegrates into chaos and confusion.

Unequality

In determining pleasing proportions of elements or areas to one another, it becomes apparent that unequal rather than equal amounts are more interesting and stimulating. Equalization is death to dominance; a vertical arrangement in a horizontal container of equal proportion creates conflicting and divided interest and characterization and so destroys unity.

If the main line is vertical, the whole design should reflect a state-

DOMINANCE

ly character. Unity is the goal, however too much sameness is a serious fault. Contrasts applied without threatening the oneness of effect will be rewarded.

A design restricted to only one shape or line soon tires the eye and the interest; the Judge will be able to analyze the fault as a lack of "something over which to dominate" and take the proper deduction.

Single Theme

A single characteristic should be dominant and in keeping with the required theme, for instance, if the class suggests an elegant design, texture and colors should be compatible with that dominant characteristic. If a more rustic theme is to be communicated, the elements must bow to that dominating quality. Unity of line, texture and design of both container and plant material may be so compatible that dominance is achieved in a non-objective design; or the choice of elements (container, decorative wood, figurine, lines, colors) may be so compatible that the idea conjured up in the imagination is sufficient to meet the requirements of dominance. The Judge would be remiss in penalizing a design which might be lacking the common, **obvious** means of achieving dominance; a careful assessment is required before taking penalty.

The Judge must recognize the Modern or Abstract arranger's right to take liberties in the interest of expressing a particular sensation or mood. While dominance contributes to a feeling of harmony, it may be that this is at variance with the emotional turmoil or nervous tension the designer wished to communicate. His individualistic solution to the problem may be based on a struggle for dominance. There is seldom only one correct course of action. It is the Judge's willingness to keep an open mind that keeps flora art a lively, interesting part of flower show work.

Unity

From every view a successful design holds together in unity and interest. All sides will not carry equal emphasis, however. There will be varying areas of greater and lesser attraction, bound together by actual lines or directional emphasis to give the eye a way of entering and moving around in the space of the design from different angles.

Too many bold, varying forms, such as Clematis, Roses, Waterlilies, Iris, large figurine and a forceful piece of decorative wood all in the same design is an extreme example of the type of visual competition and haphazard selection which destroy unity through lack of a dominant form.

The size and structural strength of the container and the lines and colors of the early 20th Century arrangement should be sufficient to dominate the background. In Abstract and Modern the background and container often play a more forceful role.

Just to have a dominant element is not enough for successful designing; it must be related to its supporting subjects. A dominant color, spotted or scattered or poorly placed can interrupt eye movement or lead it nowhere, and though the arrangement has a dominant color, the design suffers penalty due to ill-use of the principle. To simply state then that a design has "dominance" is of little or no importance. It is the effect of that dominance as related to the other principles that is to be judged.

A design lacking in the cohesive unity . . . the oneness achieved through dominance, then must be penalized. Even Abstractions where interest is equated over the whole are unified through a dominating vertical thrust or timed and repeated space intervals, or undulating curves, or duplicated diagonals and angles, or subordination of details, or limited use of kinds and colors, or repetition or similarity of color, texture and directional shapes to lead the eye as well as unification through a dominant idea.

SUMMARY

*one dominant line, texture, color, direction, character, shape unifies whole *dominance in boldness of form establishes balance *dominance in power of a line controls movement *dominating color activates rhythm *dominating height stresses theme *unequality satisfies proportions *subordinate materials offer contrast, interest

-lacks dominance due to equality of material areas or container -lacks unity -lacks a dominating factor -no structural dominance -background dominating whole -spotting of dominant color -misplaced dominance which adversely affects another principle -haphazard selection

Color

COLOR SELECTION (according to Schedule requirements and harmonious relationships)

COLOR ORGANIZATION (according to the principles of design)

The Judge must have a knowledge of color in order to fairly judge any artistic exhibit. The Judge must put aside personal color prejudice. When he is working, no color can be ugly. His objections must be based entirely on color selection and placement.

Basically, a Judge's color vocabulary includes the following words and definitions.

COLOR is a visual sensation with three definite qualities or dimensions:

1. Hue: the name of the color family
2. Value: its lightness or darkness
   . pink is a light value (tint)
   . maroon is a dark value (shade)
   . Bright red is a middle value
3. Chroma: intensity, brilliance or dullness
   . said to be strong, moderate or weak. Texture affects chroma and value

COLOR HARMONY or SCHEME: various usable or pleasing combinations of colors

NEUTRALS: black, white, gray
TINT: white added
TONE: grayed through adding gray or the complement
SHADE: black added.

COLOR TEMPERATURE

. warm (advancing)   : red, yellow, orange range; also and less actively, red-violet and yellow-green

. cool (receding)   : green and violet mixtures, blue and less actively, blue-violet and blue-green

DOMINANT, HOLDING COLORS: warm, advancing hues and light values

RELEASING COLORS: cool, receding colors, grayed values

TRANSITIONAL COLOR, PASSIVE: violets, many greens. Colors that are neither light nor dark; strong nor weak; advancing nor receding

RELATED HARMONIES

1. Monochromatic: one hue only with all values and chromas
2. Analagous: adjoining, adjacent colors
   . no more than one-third the color wheel is ideal
   . no less than three colors is ideal

CONTRASTED HARMONIES

1. Direct Complement   : 2 hues: directly opposite
2. Split Complement   : 3 hues: one hue with one hue on each side of the omitted complement
3. Paired Complement   : 4 hues: two pairs of complements in a close X
4. Adjacent Complement   : 3 hues: one hue, its direct complement and either of the splits
5. Analagous Complement   : 4 hues: 3 adjacent with one direct complement of any of them
6. Near Complement   : 2 hues: one hue with either of the splits
7. Triad   : 3 hues: equidistant on the color wheel

COLOR CALISTHENICS

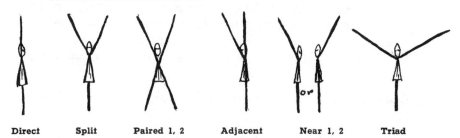

Direct   Split   Paired 1, 2   Adjacent   Near 1, 2   Triad

LAW OF COLOR AREAS: A small amount of strong color balances a large area of weak color

AFTER IMAGE: When forced to look too long at one color (e.g. red) the eye automatically switches to the complement (green), referred to as after-image

USES OF COLOR

. color is function
. color sways emotions, communicates
. color identifies form
. color helps achieve balance

. color has rhythm
. color aids depth illusion
. color minimizes faults
. color emphasizes and develops design
. color creates beauty

Four V's of Color Interest

. variety of hue
. variety of value
. variety of chroma through hue and texture
. variety of color intervals, variety of areas

Four C's of Color Excitement

. contrast of hue
. contrast of value
. contrast of chroma (hue, texture)
. contrast of color intervals

MAJOR CONSIDERATIONS WHICH INFLUENCE COLOR CHOICE

1. **decorative value,** appeal of accepted harmonies
2. **identification** (black coal; blood red: rainbow spectrum; sunrise, rosy, blue-grey) etc.
3. **expressive symbols** (red, danger; pink, femininity; purple, regal etc.)
4. **naturalistic effects** (atmospheric effect; greyed color, blue-violet, pale values indicate distance)
5. **dynamic pull** (ability, force of color to move the eye in and out, up and down, side to side and from one area to another. Favored in abstract designing)

ACTIVE
. warm colors seem to increase size : cool seem to decrease
. warm colors advance : cool recede
  light colors advance : darks recede
. lights have less visual movement : darks have more visual force
. lights move up : darks draw down
. lights seem larger : darks seem smaller

PASSIVE
. greens and violets move in proportion to the advancing or receding colors in their make-up. Pure green and violet stay in place visually

A combination of active opposites moves the eye more strongly than a combination of active and passive (e. g. orange and blue exert more tensional pull between them than do orange and green)

Equal strength of two complementary colors cause the eye to switch or fluctuate back and forth between the two . . . this force is used in abstract designing

6. **simultaneous contrast:** some colors "deaden" or liven others. A ring of the same grey color placed on a black square appears brighter than on a white square. A white ring will appear more luminous on black than on grey. A black ring appears blacker on white than on grey. A hue appears more **saturated** when placed on or near its complement. A hue appears more **brilliant** on or near black. A hue appears more **greyed** on white. Each hue appears to alter when placed near or on one of its analagous hues. The phenomenon is purely visual. It has nothing to do with any change in the surface or lighting or change in the colors. It concerns only the fact that colors seen in juxtaposition to other colors are altered. This is called the color principle of simultaneous contrast. Colors seem to advance or recede dependent on adjacent or underlying colors. A dark hue on a light background will advance more than a bright hue on that same background, regardless of temperature. Against a neutral ground **all** hues of **equal value** stand equally side by side.

Color Selection

. must comply with any scheduled requirement
. be correct for the style or period designated
. express the mood or theme stated
. must be made to serve a purpose in the design, not haphazardly chosen

Universally, certain colors are symbols of emotional expression. See Communication.

Strict color classes limit creativity and are not practical in competitive exhibiting. When such classes are judged, it is now acceptable to consider the container or background as one part of the color harmony. It is more difficult to achieve close harmony as in analagous and monochromatic classes when a visual step has to be made from the container or background to the plant material.

If the impact of any one color of a required scheme is so minor that it barely enters into the visual harmony, deduction is made.

If a class does call for a specific harmony, and a design does not conform, all points for color selection or conformance must be deducted. If the Scale provided does not divide the color points into color selection and color organization, the one-fourth of the total points are selection and color organization, then one-fourth of the total points are allotted to selection and given or deducted as it fits the requirements. Of course, additional points would also be removed under Interpretion and/or Distinction to keep such non-conforming entries from winning.

Color Characteristics

. black and dark colors carry the most visual weight
. white and medium value (full chroma) have the most force (e.g. a girl in bright red stands out, a girl in grey must depend upon form to attract attention)
. strong, intense color holds the attention
. weak, greyed colors release attention, are inobtrusive
. color qualities change in relation to our distance from them
. careless color choice can do violence to its neighbors and the design as a whole
. color is more compelling than shape, e.g. a grey ball will "stay" where it is; painted red, it will seem to balloon out from the center and move forward in space; painted blue, it will seem to draw in from the edges and move back in space
. black and white are opposing, contrasting
. a few colors can seem like many if they are well used
. unimaginative formularizing inhibits creativity with color
. texture is sometimes referred to as the 4th dimension or quality of color; rough textures darken color
. color qualities change through their placement and relationship to other colors (visual mixing and colored spot lights, see simultaneous contrast). Color may be altered, made to seem stronger, weaker, richer or less, alive or dead by mere contact or juxtaposition with another color. (e.g. pure yellow livens cold blue) Every color tends to cast a reflection of its **complement** on adjoining colors, thus no color has any definite or fixed existence all its own. It is changed and varied infinitely as its environment, surroundings, including light, change and vary.

Colors said to "not go well together" are generally not close enough on the color wheel for union and not far enough away for contrast. Red-violet and orange-red are at each end of the red interval, thus do not "go well" for most tastes.

In judging arrangements for color depth and balance, view them through a tube made by the half-closed hand held to the eye. Surroundings are shut out and colors permitted to show to their best, and the single eye receives an impression of perceptive depth greater than appears when using both eyes.

Judging Color Organization In The Design

COLOR BALANCE: is achieved by using small areas of stronger chroma and darker values to balance larger areas of weak chroma and lighter value.

. balance of color should be accomplished in all dimensions (side to side, width; top to bottom, height; front to back, depth)
. balance in depth achieved by careful placement of receding and advancing colors which bring forward and push back parts of the design. The eye unconsciously adjusts to each and a three-dimensional illusion is created
. an arrangement of advancing color in a container of receding hue will seem to separate, appear disjointed unless a transitional color is used to establish unity (Traditional designs)
. a design rearground of advancing color may advance right around a focal area of receding color making a visual "hole" unless the advancing color is greyed and the receding color is full chroma (Traditional design)
. a small unnoticed area can be brought into balance through the introduction of a color which strongly contrasts with its environment
. a small area of dark or black will balance a large area of light or white
. a small area of warm will balance a much larger area of cool color. See **Balance**

COLOR PROPORTION relates to the amounts of color used. Proportions according to "golden mean" are **least** of dominant colors, **more** of transitional colors, **most** of releasing colors for pleasant relationships. **Not** a rule. Abstracts except the "golden mean".

. the container and the background are considered under proportion
. unequality of hue, value, chroma satisfies the eye
. unequality of light and darks
. faults are: too much, too little, too weak. See Proportion

COLOR RHYTHM is the arrangement of color areas to carry the eye through the design by repetition and gradation of hues, values and chromas and tensional pull.

. the effect of a direct contrast is more pleasing if the chroma or value of one hue is different from its complement. e.g: a tint of red with a shade of green. Traditional designs
. greyed and cool colors merge with space, draw the eye back
. color repetition and gradation can draw the eye from side to side, up and down
. gradation is gradual change from light to dark value
                        from bright to dull chroma
                        from hue to hue (neighbors on the wheel)
. dark and greyed colors help reconcile colors less closely related
. white tends to divide and intensify differences
. color groups should flow easily together in Traditional design. See Rhythm

COLOR SCALE:

. *consideration of size of color areas*
. advancing colors and full chroma appear larger than receding colors and tints, tones, and shades. See Scale.

COLOR DOMINANCE: closely related to balance. One color and/or value dominates and others are subordinate.

. repetition and similarity effectively establish dominance
. dominant colors should be used in the center of interest in Traditional designs
. one color should predominate, exception, Abstracts
. color design which follows structural design adds emphasis to both
. too many colors, values, chromas destroys unity; divides interest; adds confusion
. an area that is dominant due to area, texture or position may be subdued through recessive color to bring it into balance with other areas
. with equality of color emphasis, the Traditional design lacks unity and cohesion, seems to divide, separate or fall apart
. over-dominant focal color is a fault in Traditional design. See Dominance

COLOR CONTRAST: enough variety to be interesting and not monotonous.

. color harmony does not mean everything matching, variations add interest, and contrasts add excitement
. contrast of color emphasizes the differences
. contrast is not gradual, but **definite** change
. check the contrast of hue (red flowers, green leaves)
         contrast of value (red flowers, black container)
         contrast of chroma (red flowers, greyed background)
         contrast of color spacing, timing
. contrast need not have shock effect
. contrast must be used with a design purpose
. the complementary hue placed next to intense color tends to subdue or neutralize
. color contrasts hold rhythm and dominance in check
. background contrasts must be carefully chosen
. a design of harmoniously related flowers and container, placed against contrasting background becomes a contrasting color harmony **by placement** See Contrast

Distinction (Aesthetic Appeal and Compatibility)

Distinction, while closely linked to communication, creativity and design has evolved in recent years to mean aesthetic appeal or compatibility achieved through skillfull execution and fitness to theme.

Distinction defines a design in which every detail helps the general aesthetic effect, but conversely is one which also brings out the highest beauty of each of its details. No detail is sacrificed to the whole, and because of that each attains a greater aesthetic rightness.

Aesthetic compatibility is a fitting phrase — aesthetics is the science of deducting **from nature** and taste the rules and principles of art. The result being a particular excellence, justness of composition, harmony and unity.

Distinction is the impact of **quality** upon the viewer. The public expects award winners to be something above the average but it should be made clear that the "elegant, rich, exotic" connotation of quality is not necessarily implied by the word "distinction" as used in Flora Show work. The materials used in a design need not be rare or expensive. This has been made abundantly clear in Modern and Abstract designs which have broken the barrier with the inclusion of discarded objects, both organic and inorganic, which when used with good taste, good sense and good design often achieve a certain aesthetic appeal. Aesthetic appeal is the sum total of a look of quality and excellence due to compatible character, craftsmanship and condition, and is **not** to be construed to mean the Judge's idea of what is "pretty" or its opposite "ugly", for which he mistakenly and automatically lops off points if his judging has not kept pace with the times.

Distinction goes beyond originality or creativity. Originality is imagination — distinction is craftsmanship in expressing what is imagined! Originality may be expressed in the choice of a curled wood shaving hung on a diagonal branch, but the finished arrangement has distinction only if the mechanical proficiency in fitting the pieces together has resulted in a design which satisfies all the principles. If not . . . the originality of choice will end in a bizarre monstrosity, rather than a design that has aesthetic appeal . . . distinction.

Simplicity is apparent in the design which has aesthetic rightness. Only enough plant material should be used as is necessary to communicate an impression of harmony and beauty. Lack of restraint has impaired the distinction and inherent good taste of many designs. Only enough should be used to tell the story, set the mood or complete the design.

A few shapes used well are worth more than many used without distinction. This does not mean to imply bleakness or starkness or scarcity but a satisfying **need** for everything used. There can be simplicity of line, but elegance of detail. Elegance (derived from the Latin eligere . . . to select) is a sort of harmony that resembles beauty, though beauty is a gift of nature and elegance is the result of art . . . the art of selection (see Selectivity). The suitability of all the elements and the execution and perfection of the organization contributes to the beauty of the whole.

Unity and dignity, as well as simplicity contribute to distinction. The use of a dominant color, character, texture unifies the design. Focusing attention on related or contrasted textures, colors, patterns in leaves, flowers, accessories, backgrounds or container achieves unity and dominance which leads to distinction.

The objects used must have compatible characteristics if the expression or interpretation is to be sincere. Good taste precludes overstatement. Over-emphasis, a too-positive note, too-repetitious use or the over-use of contrast can lessen the aesthetic appeal and distinction.

Deduction may be made here when the Schedule requests are ignored. If, for example, the Schedule requests a Modern expressive interpretation of an emotion and the designer offers a non-objective Abstract which communicates no emotion other than a reaction to the placements of the elements, penalty is taken.

Condition

Aesthetic appeal is also reduced by any lack of perfection. Soiled water, soiled container, cracked container (unless it contributes to the interpretation), obvious wiring, rusty mechanics, mechanics which detract from the design and less-than-perfect flower freshness and careless grooming, and pressing of fabrics are all reasons for deduction.

Construction   (Craftsmanship and Techniques)

Distinction is often the result of inspired and skillful techniques. Such proficiency draws on experiences, experimenting and training while communication and creativity draw on the resources of the inner self for inspiration.

While craftsmanship is important, it must be kept in mind that the goal of any creative expression is distinctive communication and not merely a display of technical skill. There should be, however, a sense of satisfaction and completeness in viewing a successful design; there should be no desire to change a line or a proportion or to reorganize a part.

Inventiveness is a tool of the award-winning designer. If the inspiration is strong enough a way will be found to express it. Distinction is gained by working out a difficult problem of balance or organization as is often required in Modern and Abstract design. The knowledgeable handling of space to adjust scale and proportion, establish balance, add movement and to contrast with solids is expected technique. Selection, relationship and integration are at fault if an element seems to lack purpose in the finished design.

Look for the arranger who has dared to do the unusual. The designer who has used light and shadow to gain distinction and unify the design at one and the same time is to be credited. The Judge should be conscious of the fact that light reflecting from smooth surfaces, container and plant material will unify even though the surfaces are of different colors. An accessory placed so the light flowing over its smooth contours, or penetrating through its pattern makes light as much an element as spaces and aids distinction.

Shadow (the lack of light) can make a group of small objects appear as one large area. The Judge must assess what he sees, counting this as one area, rather than thinking "it **looks** like one area . . . but I **know** it is made up of small-scaled things which **my** good sense says are too small!" Be fair . . . such knowledgeable handling deserves credit. Stand back and enjoy the effective techniques of the advanced designer.

The use of dynamic interest and balance within a commonplace outline can lift a design above the ordinary. Well placed accessories can strengthen depth illusion and if more than one surface is exposed the sculptural quality is strengthened. An accessory placed behind or to the back of a design lures one to "look back"; overlapping accessories or planes increase the three-dimensional illusion.

The harmonious integration of container, accessory and background contributes to the general aesthetic compatibility. These and many more ingenious, inventive and inspired techniques contribute to that elusive quality we call distinction. They deserve credit on the Judge's score card. **"Trifles make perfection . . . perfection is no trifle"** . . . Michelangelo.

SUMMARY

*well thought out interpretation *well handled contrasts *firmly put together *unfamiliar space organization *good taste apparent in restraint and simplicity *has smartness, style, finesse *well organized *clever techniques and mechanics *reflects designer's pride in his work *expressive of class *interesting silhouette *dynamic interests *angling, overlapping of foliage, other

-crowding -lacking artistry to same degree as design is faulted -cluttered -lacks simplicity -wilted material -indifferent organization -wrinkled fabrics -lacks grooming -dowdy -clay, mechanics detract -a general, unplanned appearance -unstable due to faulty construction

Conformity (Fitness To Theme, Class)

Fitness to theme or class requirements applies to conformity as to style, type, size, color, national influence, traditional, abstract, miniature, still life, etc.

Ideally, the Class Consultants will have worked out details with confused exhibitors unable to interpret the class correctly, or the Classification Committee will have disqualified non-conforming exhibits, making it unnecessary for the Judges to eliminate or mark down an exhibit on this score.

But ideal conditions do not always exist, minor infractions may have escaped the Classification Committee requiring deduction or complete elimination during the Judging process. There are **degrees** of conformity which the Classification Committee (not being Judges) hesitate to question and thus pass the decision on to the Judges' Panel.

If major deviations from the requested style are presented, the Judges may request a review with possible adjustment to another unjudged class. Failing this, the Judges must have some quality under which they can record the fault. In a scale which does not contain a specific reference to conformity or suitability, the Judge can deduct points under distinction or communication.

It is readily apparent that a design cannot be a **distinctive** abstract or a **distinctive** Rococo-influenced arrangement if it fails to meet the basic requirements of that particular type or style.

To simply state on the entry card "does not conform" is not an educational solution. The comment should explain how or why the design did not meet requirements.

The Judge may be confronted with the decision as to whether an item used is technically a fruit or vegetable. A vegetable (according to a Federal Court ruling) is one which is **normally** used with the main course.

Fitness To Class

The trend, long overdue and welcome, is to simply state a subject such as "Eruption" with no restrictions other than that either fresh-cut or dried plant material be included and excluding artificial flowers and foliage, thus assuring use of flora materials.

If the Schedule requests **"Modern Design Inspired By Fall"**, the Judge has at least one point to check for conformity to class. The design must be in the modern manner, which see. The elements of the design must be representational of the designer's conception of "fall" with attention to color, texture, spirit of bounty, harvest, etc.; these are considered under conformity if interpretation or communication are not listed in the scale being used.

Things get more complicated when the Schedule calls for **"An Abstract Expressing Rhythm in an Emphatic Manner in Both Line and Color. Staged in a Niche, No Dried Materials Allowed"**. Now the Judge must look for rhythm, must decide if the rhythm is emphatic or subtle, must check to see if the rhythm is emphatic in first line, then color, if in a niche and if all fresh-cut are used! As has been pointed out previously, when a Schedule defines a class in too much detail, making too many requests or restrictions, the task of both arrangers and Judges is immeasurably more difficult.

Simplified scheduling limits the possibility of dissention and misunderstandings. The day is not too far off when classes will not request Period, Traditional or non-objective, but leave the choice up to the designer to select the type as well as the interpretation she wishes. As each is judged against perfection of its kind the task will be no more difficult, but will require certain knowledge on the part of the Judge in determining ideals for each.

Communication

Personal Expression, Individual Intent, Interpretation of Class

Using the relationships of the elements and psychological communication symbols to express a mood or activate a memory requires imagination and research on the part of the artist, and from the Judge are required perception, contemplation, knowledge and emotional involvement.

Despite the Judge's need for objectivity, he must respond in some manner or communication has failed. The way of expression or personal reaction need not be that of the Judge, however; he must guard against the human tendency to see only those things which are familiar and which correspond to his own special interests, concepts and beliefs.

Each person responds according to his own knowledge, experience and external provocations. Because of this, the artist himself is never more than partially cognizant of what his work communicates.

In judging the other qualities of a design, such as organization, distinction and creativity a Judge can lay aside personal feeling, but is less able to do so in judging communication as one must exert one's own imagination to "receive the message".

Themes for the show and subjects for the class titles enable the public to better understand the designs, and often give the exhibitor a "hook" upon which to hang his idea. Exhibitors draw inspiration from many and varied sources and Judges must develop an awareness and readiness to read the messaged inspiration. The Judge must not let communication, however strong, unique or appropriate to sway him unduly . . . design is paramount. Communication is but one segment of the design. It makes the design understandable, gives it reason, but good design can exist for itself, as witness the non-objective designs which are planned purely for the relationships of the design elements. They have no story to tell, no impression to communicate, but are pure design with objects chosen and used only for what the organization of their color, direction, texture and visual impact contribute to the design, whereas in expressive abstract a message is communicated in keeping with the title or the artist's wishes.

Judges must guard against the opinion that abstract **must** be non-objective. Many abstract painters, such as Klee and Miro included detectable objects, and many Abstract designs are made to express an emotion or reaction.

The expression of a design may be motivated by "spirit", "feeling" of the subject (insight), or it can be from a surface or literal reality (sight) which is something which appears generally the same to everyone. There has recently been a shift of emphasis from naturalism or realism to inner man, deep emotions, abstracted impressions in these designs.

There is a rather general feeling that the designer who can express a class title without resorting to the reality of a realistic figurine is expressing more creativity. It takes more concentrated awareness and effort, and the exhibitors who enthusiastically search out the just-right materials should find their search rewarded.

Literal, Figurative

Rhythmic lines to express "dance" or elements which indicate the activity and pauses of the music take more effort to search out and arrange than do mere addition to a pastel design of a dancing figurine to carry the weight of the interpretation. Beginning arrangers and the public often fail to understand this fine point and therefore do not feel in accord with the awarding. Their judgment is still based on apparency and realism.

The interpretation may be a subtle one, based on just a fragment of the theme rather than the overall picture. This leaves something to the imagination of the viewer as he embarks on a trip of discovery through the design. The expression, when a realistic figure is used to tell a story or resurrect a scene, is literal. When the abstract feelings about the story are told, it is done figuratively, metaphorically. Literal interpretation is considered unimaginative, matter-of-fact, according to the letter. Figurative expression is emblematic, is resemblance rather than imitation, and requires imagination on part of both viewer and artist.

PSYCHOLOGICAL COMMUNICATION

The Judge must decide if the designer has strongly communicated the main idea, either literally or figuratively as is required by the class or his added explanation. He evaluates the depth of the emotional appeal. A design may have distinctive aesthetic appeal but if it fails to communicate it lacks emotional appeal. A weak statement is penalized. Lines, forms, colors, textures, spaces and their placement influence a dominant, clear expression when meaning and material merge.

In order to prepare himself to receive and judge the clarity of the statement, the Judge must be aware of certain reactions and impressions which are **generally** acceptable, though he must make allowances for personal impressions of the designer, as these often contribute to the originality and distinction of a memorable design.

Line Direction

Generally these lines give the following impressions:

- vertical — inspiration, stately, aloof
- sweeping — grace, gaiety
- drooping — sorrow, weary
- horizontal — restful, stable, man at rest
- zigzag — restless, indecision
- curves — feminine, gentle, waves, dance
- concentric curves — expansive
- bent, refracted — sharp, stacatto, urgent
- leaning — protective
- serpentine — evil, Satan
- spiral — growth, continuity
- diagonal — activity, motion, power, resistance, man against the wind
- jagged, scattered — disorder, fear, lightning, strife, battle

Line Character

- heavy, broad — bravery, pride, dignity
- fine, airy — feminine, graceful
- crossed — apprehension, fear

Shapes

- cube — weight, steady
- circle — completion, unity, smoothness, holds eye within circle making its design power passive
- cone, triangle — balance, precision
- horizontal oval — quiet, restful

342

. slanting oval — instability, balanced by placement, has more interest than
  a circle
. rectangle — strength, stability
. straight lines, angles — masculine
. curves — feminine

COLOR RESPONSE

Due to personal past experiences, people may be repelled or respond differently than is universally common. The Judges must be tolerant of such variations.

. warm colors — joy, gaiety
. cool colors — soothing, restful
. reduced intensity, light values — well being, comfort, contentment
. low key chroma, dark values — mystery, gloom
. intense, brilliant, full chroma — nervous tension, restlessness especially
  in warm colors
. tints — feminine, weak
. full chroma — masculine, strong
. shades — sombre
. tones — dignity
. strong contrasts — drama, excitement
. related colors — calming

Set By Occasion, Events, Animals

. red and green — Christmas
. white and green — Easter, also lavender
. red, white, blue — patriotic (American)
. green — St. Patrick's Day
. medley of full chroma — harvest
. orange and black — Halloween, witchery, tiger
. spectrum — rainbow
. pink, grey — elephant
. black — bat

Symbolic Color Communication

. white — youth, purity, innocence
. black — sorrow
. pink — gentleness, femininity. Hot pink festivity
. lavender and pastels — gentleness, femininity
. red — stimulating, exciting, aggressive, danger
. yellow — sunshine, cheer, energy, conviviality
. orange — caution, excitement, aggression
. blue — sadness, dignity, formality, truth
. green — eternity, safety, rebirth, abates excitement
. purple — dignity, royalty
. grey — humility, mousey, non-committal
. greyed purple — twilight, old age
. brown, dark values, low in design — earth, stability
  A slight shift in value makes a difference, certain yellows look cheap,
  sickly to some. Color affects the eye physically as well as emotionally,
  drawing the eye back and forth by the pull of changing value, temperature and chroma. See Color

SYMBOLISM

Symbolism began with the ancients, recorded history notes many examples, many of which, surprisingly enough are in date today. The Japanese attached symbolism to the actual design . . . each flower, leaf, space and combination meant something when placed in context in the design.

The Victorians had a language of flowers also but these were expressed by the flower itself, not in any particular combination.

Once again Americans, with their penchant for blending and mixing European Occidental and Oriental, have taken these two concepts and now design in the modern manner using both ideologies in their interpretations with new applications of the age-old principles.

With the subtlety inherent in successful interpretation, the Japanese did not use a realistic figure to represent Man, nor a rock to illustrate Earth. In the same manner, Judges must be aware of the hidden nuances of modern interpretation. Obvious or realistic portrayal places the design in the Traditional, realistic style. The act of discovering the interpretation is a part of the modern concept.

Interpretation may be based on, strengthened or hinted at by the use of appropriately named or formed plants:

. tiger lily	. snapdragon	. baby tears
. rattail cacti	. pussy willow	. bluebonnet
. cattail	. violet (shrinking,	. gladiolus, sword
. daylily, fleeting moments	tender)	. etc.

Variety Names Communicate

. 'Peace' 'Nocturne' 'Northern Lights, 'Green Lights' 'Queen Elizabeth'

Textures, too, carry characterization, as does fragrance and taste.

. waxy . tweed . satin . velvet . weathered . thorny (barbed wire)

Localities Carry Connotations

. marigolds	Mexico	. magnolias	South
. cactus	Pacific Southwest	. evergreen	West, Pac. Northwest
. sage	West	. palm	tropics
. state trees and flowers		. etc.	

Characteristics of the Famous

. cigar	Churchill	. nose	Durante
		. cherry	George Washington

Functional Articles of an Industry or Area

. ax, bark	lumberman	. burlap	rural area etc.

ACCESSORIES

The lists are endless and it should be abundantly apparent to the Judge that the extensive use of **realistic figurines** is not needed to express a given interpretation.

This does not mean that accessories do not have their place; many designs incorporating accessories richly deserve their high awards. Many are so expressive only a minimum amount of plant material is needed to communicate the idea. Decorative wood, too, is a powerful, often abstract factor in the creation of mood designs. The Judge, however, should guard against any tendency to allow an outstanding accessory piece to influence his decision.

With the great freedom allowed moderns, the container, base and background can and often does figure in the impression communicated. Accessories, if used, are apt to be non-realistic, distorted, elongated, abstract, unique, barely recognizable, often with little or no surface detailing.

Whatever its type, the accessory alone should not carry the interpretation. The Judge expects it to merely be a **part** of the total. The remainder of the elements must also enter into the expression, being compatible, in harmony with it, and all telling the same "story". Special lighting can be used also, to increase emotional intensity.

Judging The Mood Setting

Strong moods often seek expression in violent physical activity and the Judge should look for expression of this in thrusting, vital lines when the theme demands. In a class to depict anger, a Judge would expect to find thorny, refracting lines, prickly texture, serrated edges, rather than smoothness, rhythmic lines and close harmonies. Harmony, serenity, dignity and restraint should prevail in most religious interpretations.

Lines are strongly interpretive. Circular shapes attract and hold the eye and are apt to demand too much attention in some interpretations. If the design is one to communicate vertical movement and an over-abundance of round lines and shapes were used, the movement would not be in accord with the class, generally.

The greater the variety of contrasts, the more excitement the design will communicate. If a less dramatic, more restful effect is called for, the dominant feature should be echoed with a minimum of strong contrast.

Space

The Judge must not ignore the designer's use of space to solidify the impression. Space in the design frees the viewer to use his imagination to supply the details. Spaces within the structure, as well as surrounding it, can suggest abstract ideas and emotions; solids give an impression of heaviness; open, airy patterns contribute a freer feeling.

INDIVIDUAL INTENT, PERSONAL EXPRESSION

The Artist Speaks

There is no way in which a person reveals himself so completely as he does through his choice of things . . . clothes, cars, jewelry and his created objects. He is electing them to speak for him; to speak of his deepest emotions, either tortured or normal. The choice and often the use is a matter of temperament and should show his personality in the most interesting and aesthetic manner possible, rather than mere copying of a set formula.

Sometimes, however, clarification is needed. Unless a Judge is also an Iris enthusiast, he could hardly be expected to know that the Iris used to depict a fabric in a class "FABRICS ARE FABULOUS" was

'BLACK TAFFETA' or 'FINE LACE'. It is even possible that a Judge would not recognize the rose 'PEACE' as that symbol.

The Judge must be a design-reader, but he should not have to be a mindreader, as well. Many times Judges are criticized, and often feel very inept, when an interpretation is **pointed out** and then it **stands out!** The key here is to point out! A neatly typed, unobtrusive card signifying the arranger's individual intent or personal expression or interest facts may accompany an exhibit. Such notes are helpful, even educational for both Judge and public.

For instance, a design of a truck spring and a bicycle fender is so **used with plant material as to express futuristic architecture. The** Schedule class given is "ESCAPEE FROM A JUNK YARD" . . . the individual expression was "ESCAPE TO THE CITY OF TOMORROW".

To one designer the class "WIND" might mean a March wind when kites ride high and geese go north, while a swirling mass of bulging lines may be another's impression symbolic of his feelings about the swelling, bursting energy of a hurricane. Used with his own choice of colors, and individual application of the principles, the emotional impact communicated by each becomes a symbol of the designers own personal feelings about wind.

The designer has applied the principles not only in relation to the design, but her own feelings as well which results in a personal revelation of exactly how she feels about the subject, or what about the subject impressed her most, or is a reminder for her. Her feelings may be entirely different from the Judge's. The fact that she has communicated according to the stated title **is** important, not that what she has communicated does not parallel what the Judge expected or would have expressed himself. Only if there are weak or conflicting impressions, or lack of adequate design organization should deduction be made here.

When a design fails to communicate anything, leaves a feeling of indifference, "so-whatishness" or confusion, points can justly be deducted in classes intended to be expressive.

The Judge will find it easier to first "stand still and enjoy". Let the communicated expression come through to him and then proceed to the analysis of the organization of the whole.

SUMMARY

*one dominant story, idea characterization *all parts contribute to the expression *unexpected implication *readily apparent *expression fits the stated title

-weak statement -indifferent interpretation -lacks clarity -gives confused impression -conflicting impressions -not in accord with stated title

Overall Relationships (Suitability, Selectivity)

Suitability (compatibility) of relationships is a quality often listed in the scales of points and may be considered under two headings:

1. Fitness to purpose (relationships, elements used, according to the principles. Achieved by harmony or contrast. Fairly contant standards).

2. Fitness to Character, Spirit (Subject to change. Overlaps Communication but suitability of character is seen, and communication of idea, emotion is sensed).

Suitability and appropriateness are synonymous with fitness and harmony and are closely linked to distinction. Harmony is the goal of the successful design. Harmony is that quality of inter-relatedness with the selection according to psychological effect of materials, their associational values, shape, color, texture, so arranged that a harmonious whole is achieved. The Judge must understand that harmony does not mean everything matching, but rather everything compatible, and organized to achieve unity even with variety and contrast.

Texture, Character

The underlying relationships of all the elements have been discussed under the principles of design with the exception of texture. Texture often governs the choices and establishes the character . . . the finer and smoother the texture, the greater the degree of refinement, and formality. While there should be some variety or contrast of texture, one, either rough, fine, woolly, sleek, etc., must be predominant.

Judges must learn to designate between character and texture which are often confused.

1. **Texture** is surface quality

2. **Character** or spirit is the degree of refinement or elegance of the materials and involves a "feeling" or impression of robustness, rustic, cool, friendly, etc.

Texture can and often is contrasted with ease.

Character is difficult and often impossible to contrast. Distinction is often adversely affected . . . the lines of communication are "jammed". One character or spirit must be dominant.

To illustrate, a bi-colored miniature rose would hardly be a suitable selection to be used with 'PEACE' in the average design. The textures are the same, the colors are the same, the form is the same **but** the sturdy, robust **character** of 'PEACE' would be extremely difficult to bring into compatible relationship with the tiny, delicate miniature. In the same way a pansy and an iris, a calla and a sunflower, iceland poppy and giant-flowered tuberous begonia are of contrasting character. This is not to say it cannot or **never** should be done, however.

Abstract designers use form, color and texture for what they contribute to the balance-counterbalance of the design, often with complete disregard for "character", and many do fall short on harmonious relationships, though unified through a dominance of line, texture or form.

Fitness to Purpose

In classes which set problems of Period, National or geographical designs, as well as tables, the relationships of **all** the elements, plus the correctness to style (interpretation) must be considered.

The relationship of container, base and background need not be subordinate in the abstract design. These often take their place as an integral, even forceful part of the whole. Thus the Abstract designer is given much more leeway in selection and use of contrasts. Equality of units when carefully handled, gives importance to each without competition.

Harmonious Patterns

The same radiating pattern is found in a spider web and the underside of a mushroom and a starfish; found in the basic harmony of swelling shape of the King gourd and the rose gall; in the tubular shape of some palm spathes and the calla lily. These and many more have a marked similarity of pattern and may serve as unifying factors though they may be unrelated in other ways. The related harmony of shape and texture in container and flora material also shows imaginative selection. Many designers (and Judges, more's the pity) see only the obvious relationship of color, and miss the joy of discovery in more subtle relationships.

The exhibitor who has discovered and exploits the design relationships found in nature, who mates them with design principles and brings theme into focus for the viewer, is using relationships to achieve dominance, unity and distinction worthy of notice and award. The Judge must train himself to watch for these subtle nuances of repeated form, shapes, textures as well as the more obvious color.

Depth

Arrangers use contrasting textural relationships to increase depth perception. Heavily textured objects come forward to meet the eye and a smooth dull surface seems to recede. See Color for its relationship to depth illusion. See Balance.

Rhythm is aided by textural relationships . . . the eye moves quickly over smooth and glossy surfaces and more slowly over rough.

Condition is also related to suitability. No material is suitable if it collapses before the design is even judged. Material chosen with complete knowledge of its lasting qualities can be considered under suitability.

The Judge asks himself if the designer has made the most of the materials and relationships as factors in the design and interpretation, and if the relationships heighten the interest and clarify the expression.

Fitness to Character, Spirit

The materials chosen must belong together in spirit, character (less binding in abstract). The "fitness" and distinction of the design calls for a dominant character.

The theme is also strengthened through the careful selection of materials which aptly express it. Exhibitors who enthusiastically search out the just-right flora materials will find their search rewarded by the Judges if what they select freely communicates the spirit or character intended. However, the Judges must stay alert to and penalize any hidden subtleties which are at variance with the character and theme.

Dominance is one of the principles which is very important here . . . as an unsuitable selection will stand out and adversely fix attention all out of proportion to its actual importance.

Changes Affect Relationships

An open mind must be maintained as relationships which were considered inappropriate, even incongruous a few years ago are now perfectly acceptable. Roses, only a few years ago, were used only in refined vases, now we realize that roses themselves are different; some are robust, even coarse; color range has widened to include thousands beyond the traditional pink, red and white which **do** look so appropriate in silver and crystal.

The coarse-colored orange and harsh yellow marigold has ballooned out like a giant powder-puff and spreads its colors over a range of the most delicate lemons and limes more suitable to finer textured companions than the marigold of old!

The Judge must be careful in penalizing an unorthodox selection in Modern and Abstracts. This is personal expression at work! His job is to assess the selections for what they contribute to the design and the interpretation as a whole. As times, ideas and advances in both flora art and horticulture bring changes, adjustments must be made in assessments of what is or is not suitable and appropriate.

Familiarity should not lead the Judge into allowing commonness, prejudice or some other quality to influence reduction of points under suitability, such as the classic case of the Judge who wouldn't place a ribbon on an arrangement of calla lilies because "they are so common here". He can fairly object to a lack of distinction in the use of the flower, but it is unfair to call the flower itself unsuitable. It is just such mistaken application which infuriates the exhibitor and blights the name of the Judge.

Textural Relationship

A close relationship of spirit may be the outgrowth of textural unity as for instance, a gnarled piece of wood which repeats the aging twisted form and rustic, weathered texture of an old-man figure. Repetition of the dominant texture strengthens the characterization communicated to the viewer . . . that of having lived long and weathered many storms.

Personality

Aside from the universal messages (see Communication) all individual flowers, leaves, branches, decorative wood have a personality. They may express ponderous masculinity or boldness, or power, or may appear delicate, retiring, feminine, or weak.

Each projects its particular inherent character, not because it looks like or is concretely or literally representative of something but because of its abstract feeling.

Schedule Requirements

Suitability of choice to fulfill the Schedule requirements or theme is considered here and/or under distinction if the scale has no points listed to interpretation, personal expression or other related quality. If the Schedule calls for all fresh cut material and the designer includes some dried material, points must be deducted for lack of suitability to the theme or class. The Schedule is the law of the show and its requirements must be heeded by both the Judge and the exhibitor.

Occasionally, the Judge may find that a scale lists both suitability and Interpretation and as well as Distinction. If he finds faults which are applicable to either, he deducts from the one quality most affected by the fault, **or** he may deduct from all qualities to a total of the number of points he has decided should be attributed to the fault. This same adjustment can be made in judging the relationships which also affect design.

SUMMARY
Suitability of Purpose

*has fitness *harmonious *fits schedule and interpretation *point up subtle and similar relationships

-unsuitable choice as to substance, lasting quality -choice of form, texture, color does not fit interpretation

Suitability of Character

*harmonious *just-right character, spirit for interpretation *textural harmony

-conflicting character -weak "statement" -spirit not in accordance with interpretation

Creativity (Freshness of Concept)

. . . The execution of an art is never as difficult as the devising.
. . . Da Vinci

Creativity is imagination made visible. Creativity is never dated because it comes from the mind, heart and hands of a person living **today** . . . a person attuned to today.

Abstract designs put emphasis on fresh applications of the age-old principles, emphasis on novel organization of the elements of line, form, pattern, color and texture, plus space, light, angle and tension. They are saying the same things, expressing the same emotions often with the same types of materials, but saying it in a unique and individual way. The creative arranger does not imitate, she originates. She treads virgin ground and brings us a harvest of over-looked, unaware beauty to be judged.

To be creative or original does not consist only of doing or saying what has never been done or said before . . . any madman can do this; it consists, rather in the ability to rearrange thoughts and ways in such a manner that they never again can be viewed only in the old dimensions. Creativity is a certain something which "red mittens" the attention, that either subtly or emphatically says "hey — you haven't seen ME before".

Creativity is not a matter of cost. A dozen orchids done in an ordinary way will rate fewer points than a design using marigolds handled with a fresh approach. Creativity is what distinguishes an art from a craft. A technique can be taught but imagination cannot. Imagination can be encouraged, however, and here Judges can help through their choices in the Shows; choices governed by an appreciation of creativity, expressed according to the principles, rather than an application of man-made rules.

Some arrangers have great imagination and skill, but fail to express it for fear of ridicule for "having broken a rule". They fear people will think they didn't know the rule! Judges, by their choices in Modern and Abstract classes can show there are no rules . . . just the principles and good taste plus a fresh individual approach.

Individuality is a suitable synonym for creativity which means that quality of a design which makes it seem different from other designs . . . freed from precedent and regulations. It may be a different way of putting in a line, or an unusual combination of materials, unexpected viewpoint, unexpected balance, a more interesting interpretation, unique accessory placement, it may be the use of space where we used to have the focal area . . . whatever it is . . . it makes the design "one of a kind" . . . something special.

Copies

Originality is also a synonym which has appeared in Point Scales for years and often leads to controversy when starkly stated. There is really little new or original under the sun. To state flatly that something is or is not original is to imply **complete,** all-enveloping knowledge! Everything once heard, seen or experienced is buried in the subconscious and filters through to fill a need even though the thinker may not be aware of any pre-use. She distills what is remembered, mixes it with her own personal creativity and what she has on hand to use and the result is a freshness of concept which is more fairly assessed and yet cannot be called a "copy". It is said that anything which contains a mere three percent of one's own expression or words can be considered original . . . if true there is much more leeway than many Judges allow when confronted with the word "originality" in a Point *Scale. Quality of creative adaptations must be considered.*

A design might not be exactly a copy, but still not rate high for creativity because of the commonness of the choices and handling. To illustrate, pine and roses are frequent companions in an asymmetrical triangular design. They are lovely together and in the traditional class, not competing under a point scale which gives a large number of points to creativity or originality, they still win awards.

The judging and stressing of freshness of concept is not new as such, it was expressed thusly by a designer in response to an early 50's class on a harvest theme. The universally accepted symbols of harvest are cornucopias and abundance. Knowing that pottery, reed and wire horns-of-plenty lying on their sides spilling out the produce has become a "cliche" of harvest, she presented a fresh application by using actual cowhorns mounted gracefully upright and a vertical treatment of the usually horizontal fruits and vegetables. Less traditional concepts are to be expected in Modern design.

Triteness

Inspired, or unusual handling, clipping, bending of plant material is effective the first few times used, but an outstanding handling is often repeated and repeated to the point of triteness. This has happened with clipped palm, some refractory lines, knotted reeds, triangled canes, upside down multiple-twigged branches and many others. Their very popularity put them beyond the pale of fresh approach in all but the most remote area, or in combinations even more unique. This is why that plant material **accidentally** contorted by nature and used by the person who truly understands the principles and Modern concepts of design achieves a distinctive freshness not possible when following another's lead.

Nature's Designing

The free-form patterns of branches, vines and roots found in nature are all unique as nature never duplicates herself, such lines are often a short-cut to creativity and distinction. Each arrangement in which Nature dictates the design will be a fresh new experience . . . vital and interesting.

The Judge should feel that he is looking at something new in concept, even though the subject has been interpreted many times before. This creative state of affairs is brought about by the arranger's deeper-than-surface contemplation. Self-expression sparks originality, but sometimes the interpretation may be too remote to communicate without the brief explanation supplied by the arranger. Her efforts to develop something new should be matched by the Judge's effort to understand. Such designs must be studied . . . they cannot be evaluated at a glance.

"Found" Versus Flora

Creativity should not be judged only on what is used; that is originality of choice. Too often localities and prejudices govern the concept of what is unusual. What is a common plant in one area may be anything but commonplace or ordinary in another. Creativity should mean that the designer has given the design her personal touch despite, rather than because, of the material used.

The rush to the junk-yard for "found" items was no doubt touched off by the emphasis on originality of choice. Misguided or not, it woke many from the sleep of boredom. But it must be remembered that the emphasis in Flora Shows should remain on plant material. The Judges can guide and direct again through their choices. The plant world is our medium and while unrelated items often add a certain something to a design, the balance in their favor should not tilt so drastically that a Flora Show becomes anything less than that.

The original and abiding objective of a Flora Show is to first show how culturally perfect a specimen can be garden-grown, and second to show how that garden-grown material can be used artistically. Judges are remiss in their judgment if their attention is unduly diverted by unusual containers, rare and exotic flowers and industrial materials used as an easy-out substitute for plant materials. Creativity is of a high order when the exhibitor sees a new line or form in an inorganic material and searches until she finds a duplicate in plant materials, or in some other natural objects, such as rock, shell and the like. Accidental shapes of natural objects are often much more exciting than man-made. This is not to mean we should restrict man-made to container and accessories . . . remember . . . no rules! But their use as substitutes for natural objects should be kept to a minimum if the concept of Flower Shows is to be maintained, and Judges bear the brunt of influence through their choices. The Judges who present ribbons indiscriminately, without regard for the Flower Show objectives are lending approval to a trend away from our medium of plant materials.

In summary, a Judge remembers that an arrangement may rate high for creativity and yet fail to have aesthetic appeal or distinction or good taste or fail to communicate the stated title and so will risk penalty. On the other hand a design may lack creativity and originality and yet have distinction and aesthetic appeal through faultless execution and fitness. When the Judge finds one which has creativity plus all the other attributes he feels justified for all the mediocre designs he ever faced.

*fresh application *courageous self expression *novel organization *special *individual *unexpected balance, viewpoint, interpretation, etc. *creativity plus distinction and good taste and design *card accompanying interpretives

-common -ordinary -often seen -trite -traditional -conventional

SECTION 5 ARTISTIC CATEGORIES

History of Flower Arrangement

MAJOR PERIODS OF FLOWER ARRANGEMENT	LESS INFLUENTIAL OR WELL-KNOWN PERIODS	
	. Egypt	2900 to 28 BC
	. Greece	600 to 146 BC
	. Rome	28 to 325 AD
	. Byzantine	325 to 600 AD
Japan 586 AD to present		
	. Persia	1300 to 1700
	. Renaissance	1400 to 1600
	. China	1368 to 1912
Dutch-Flemish 1600 to 1700		
	. European Baroque	1600 to 1700
French Rococo 1715 to 1774		
	. Early American	1620 to 1830
	. Classic or Neo-Classic	English Regency 1760 to 1830 French Directoire 1795 to 1799 French Empire 1804 to 1814 American Federal 1789 to 1830
English Georgian 1714 to 1820	. Geo. I	*1714 to 1727*
	. Geo. II	*1727 to 1760*
	. Geo. III	*1760 to 1820*
English Victorian 1830 to 1890 (Romantic Era)	. American Colonial Williamsburg	1700 to 1800
	. European Art Nouveau	1830 to 1910

Twentieth Century

Traditional (often called Conventional)
A. Realistic   B. Decorative — Approximately 1910—
Line, Massed-Line, Mass
Hogarth, Crescent, Vertical,
Horizontal, Triangle, Circle, Oval

Modern Interpretive, Expressive
(includes modern "isms"   Approximately 1925 —

Creative Modern, Transitional, Free'd Styles, etc.
Approximately late 1950's to —

Creative Abstract, Assemblages, Constructions, Extra-Sensory, Avant-Garde, Kinetic, etc.
Approximately late 1950's to —

Oriental (Japanese) Traditional

SUGGESTED CLASSES:

1. In the Manner of Classic (Ikenobo, Seika, Shokwa)
A: Formal (Shin) B: Semi-Formal (Gyo) C: Informal (So)

2. In the Manner of Nageire (Vase)
A: Upright B: Inclining or Slanting C: Cascade

3. In the Manner of Moribana (Low Container)
A: Simple B: Naturalistic scene C: Divided Form
D: Morimono (fruit, etc.) E: Water Viewing F: Water Reflecting

4. Free Style
Other classes, such as Heika, Koryu, Kakebana (Hanging), etc. may be added to meet the capabilities of the exhibitors. If a specific style is not listed in the schedule, the Exhibitor should include information of the style on his entry card. Failing this, the Judge should penalize under Design and Suitable Container.

JAPANESE INFLUENCE ON FLOWER ARRANGEMENT

Ikebana is the Japanese word for flower arrangement. The Judge keeps in mind that while there are many schools, these differ mostly in details of stem length and placement. Various spellings add to the confusion, but the fundamental principles are the same, though the varied stem lengths, placements and containers make them appear different. Adaptations may be a composite of basic principles of several schools.

The ultimate purpose is to arrange flowers and branches according to nature's irregular graces; to use such spacings and curvatures that no stem, branch or flower is obscured, each standing forth in individual beauty; to accentuate and idealize the individuality of each plant, its stems, leaves and flowers. The exhibitor's task is to present the essence of nature, never overlavishly, but with exquisite selectivity.

While most shows request classes "in the Oriental manner" or "showing the influence of," still the Judge must have a fundamental knowledge of the classic traditions, symbolisms and rules. Once these are understood, adaptations will be more easily and fairly judged. Purists will consider the remarks here as oversimplified, but this chapter makes no attempt to instruct on the detailed differences of each school, but rather to serve as a refresher for the Judge who has availed himself of knowledge through practice and guidance from the many fine books and lecturers on this complicated subject.

A number of different schools have evolved, the oldest being the Ikenobo, its first arrangement form was known as the Rikkwa. Another development of Ikenobo is called the Enshui School and a product of Enshui is a method called Koriu, both of which incorporate a greater manipulation of curves.

Ikenobo also fathered the Shoka (also spelled Shokwa and Seika) style. Misho originated the combined Ikenobo and Saga teachings. Sho-fu, Ohara and Sogetsu are 20th century schools, the latter having been founded in 1926. The Ohara School originated the Moribana style of arrangement in which natural growth is treated informally. Heika is a term designating a vase design of the Misho and Ohara Schools.

Nyu-Ike or Double Shokwa is two arrangements composed in a single double-tiered **vase-type** container. The styles of formal, semi-formal and informal may be combined in the composition.

Kakibana are hanging designs which incorporate the Heaven, Man and Earth lines and may follow classic or Nageire styles, particularly the Cascade Nageire. Shallow containers, often boat-like, are used.

The Japanese were and are masters of expressive lines, composition and the subtle use of color, and the modern trends can never erase the sensitivity of the truths learned in the classical past. Faultless balance, rhythm and depth exist in all traditional Japanese floral designs regardless of the School or style and must be present in **adaptations** as well.

While modifications, **adaptations,** designs "in the manner of . . . " may not follow the strict patterns set down by the traditionalists, yet if the rules they clarified relative to the asymmetrical triangle, tri-dimensional placement of Heaven, Man and Earth lines are followed, these adaptations will possess the vitality and life characteristic of the classics. While some Schools stress certain length proportions, these are actually set by the length of the Heaven line in relation to the type, dimensions and visual weight of the container, and base, if one is used.

An arrangement in the Japanese manner should meet the basic requirements of the style as given by the Japanese. The line between a modified Japanese and a contemporary line arrangement is very fine. The design which goes too far afield from the basic characteristics of linear emphasis, triangle pattern based on Heaven, Man and Earth placements, restrained simplicity and traditional-type container form is no longer an adaptation of the Japanese.

Three major style categories are the:
1. **Classic Ikenobo** whose main identifying quality is the nemoto (trunk)
2. **Nageire** or vase-type design
3. **Moribana** which is the low container style, often scenic

The main characteristics of all styles are:
1. Dynamic linear quality emphasized, and color subordinate
2. Asymmetrically balanced triangle based on three lines of related length
3. Simplicity and restraint
4. Flower identity kept intact
5. Symbolism, vitality ("as in nature")

Linear quality is emphasized. The silhouette is important. The designs must have all three dimensions of **height, width** and **depth.** Generally, the position of the Heaven lines gives height, Man gives width and Earth gives depth. The positions of Heaven and Earth vary with different styles, but all achieve the three-dimensional form with motion and expression.

Though the three major groupings of Heaven, Man and Earth are mandatory, holding to a rule of unevens throughout, including the supplementary lines is not mandatory in **adaptations.** However, asymmetrical balance and the triangular linear pattern is more easily made and maintained with uneven numbers. No supplementary line may extend beyond the limits set by the Heaven, Man and Earth lines.

A hint of the Hogarth Curve is often discernible in Oriental designs as this curve appears in nature frequently. As in a painting, the designs are intended to be looked at directly from the front; but the effects from the sides should also be considered.

Asymmetrical balance and the triangular form are created by the symbolic unity of Heaven (Shin) Man (Soe) and Earth (Tai). The triangle can have its widest spread vertically, horizontally or at a slant. The tips of the main branches indicate the triangle.

While as many supporting lines may be added as needed, they should not be used to excess as the goal is restraint and simplicity. Adaptations of Japanese flower arrangements should retain the delicate and expressive linear charm featuring the three main lines which is their main characteristic.

This linear pattern should be so well planned and executed as to be perceptible at first glance, though in Free Style Modern (which see) it may be hidden. If the triangular pattern is not visible in traditional adaptations deduction of points must be made under correctness, design and distinction to total the degree of fault.

Symbolism is expressed by copying natural growth. Plants which grow together in the same environment and at the same time were used together to create the impression of living plants. Relative positions of growth were copied, the tall-growing willow placed higher than the low-growing daffodil, the daffodil placed higher than the earth-hugging crocus. Flowers past their prime or season were called "dead" and were unacceptable. Most designs contained some green to signify continued life, and seed pods were used to indicate the promise of life.

Selections also indicated the passage of time, as for example, iris in the spring, tall leaf, low bud; summer, full flower, low leaf; winter, dry leaf, seed pod. A single flower or branch low on the nemoto was sometimes included to suggest growth springing from the root.

Emotion, physical characteristics, weather conditions, time, season and place were all subtly indicated by material selection, line direction and angles formed by the material in the authentic, traditional Japanese Flower Arrangement. Though most of us can neither "read" nor "write" the floral messages, yet we can appreciate the clarity, simplicity and techniques in adaptations influenced by the Oriental.

Style correctness as requested by the Schedule	25	Suitability of materials, container, base	15
Design according to School or Style	40	Distinction	10
		Condition	10

CLASSIC

Style Correctness

The basic teachings of the Classic Schools of Ikenobo and Enshui and of Koriu are close in concept. Their three basic forms of classical arrangement — the formal, semi-formal and the informal, along with the Nageire and Moribana form the majority of designs showing Oriental influence exhibited in Flower Shows and Fairs.

The principal characteristics of Classic, adapted from these teachings are:

1. Nemoto Placing
   all lines held together at the base for two to six inches above the water line
2. Triangular Outline
   Formed by Heaven, Man and Earth lines. Supplementary lines may be used within the pattern set by the three major lines
3. Asymmetrical Balance
4. Tip of center line must be directly over the point of emergence from container
5. All tips turn up
6. No two lines the same length
7. Restrained simplicity (1-2 kinds of material, 2-3 colors)
8. Uneven numbers

The angles and spread of the lines, plus the container choice designate the Formal, Semiformal and Informal designs.

1. Formal (Shin)

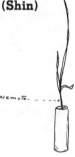

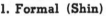

- vertical upright vases, one opening

- erect, very slightly curved (similar to standing man)

- does not extend beyond the vase limits

- no dried materials (traditional)

2. Semiformal (Gyo)

- usabata containers, boat shapes, low metal bowls

- tips of Earth and Man extend beyond vase limits

- suggestion of man walking

- weathered wood (boku) may be included

3. Informal (So)

- the more the Heaven line curves the less formal the design

- widest width and curvature of all lines

- freedom of running man

- wide assortment of low dishes, shapes vary; includes "windowed" or tiered bamboo tubes

CLASSIC DESIGN CORRECTNESS

Japanese flower arrangements are built around three principal groups, called Heaven, Man and Earth by Westerners. In Classic Ikenobo, the first or center group represents the main trunk and should dominate the design.

The second is the Man group, representing supporting lines found in natural growth. It adds strength and width to the Heaven grouping.

The third is the Earth group. It is the lowest group and gives balance, weight and contrast to the Man group. It is the stabilizing and strengthening line for the Heaven group. It should add depth and dimension to the design.

A great deal has been written about the "formulas" of proportion and stem length. Suffice it to say that the Japanese never, in a Classic arrangement, allow the Heaven line to be **less** than one and one-half times the container height with a generous allowance for tip. The height is governed by visual weight of the container and the material. The measurement of Heaven (the tallest placement) should be **at least** one and one-half times the height or width of the container in an **adaptation.** It may be much taller. The height of the Man line is two-thirds the height of Heaven and the height of the Earth line is one-third the height of Heaven.

The lines (including any attributes, or supporting lines) should bal-*ance around the principal (Heaven) line. All lines must be vibrant and* rhythmic to give the illusion of vital growth. All supporting lines must be subordinate to, shorter than and less important visually than the major Heaven, Man and Earth lines.

The placement should create depth. The tops of Heaven and Man should lie diagonally across the container, from back to front, with Earth pointing over the viewer's right or left shoulder. A flat, left-to-right design is severely penalized. The voids are important to the design, contributing to a sense of balance.

The lines never jut out directly backward, forward, to the left or right, but are carefully placed to emerge at an angle. Deduction is made for misplaced lines.

The Heaven line should stand firmly in the design's center. If necessary to balance the forward movement of the Earth line, Heaven may lean a little toward the back of the container. If the tip of Heaven ends at a point other than directly over the spot of emergence from the container, the design cannot attain self-contained, asymmetrical balance. The control of balance is with the center line.

Flowers, foliage and supporting lines should lie along the **UPPER** sides of the Man and Earth placements, with little drooping material to mar the clear outlines of the undersides. While the Japanese seldom used flowers in or for the Man line, such liberties are taken in **adaptations.**

The Nemoto is an important characteristic and the identifying quality of the Classic design. This emergence of the three main structural lines from a seen and known point or 'trunk' is the secret of expressed vitality inherent in living plants and stressed in the nemoto placement.

The stems should be held so closely and tightly together as to give the appearance of a single stalk. Spreading or separated emergence lines are the ruination of a Classic arrangement and must be penalized severely.

The nemoto must be free of all leaves, flowers or small branches for two-six inches above the water level or container lip. The exception is when, symbolically, a flower or small branch is placed low on the nemoto to suggest root growth. The nemoto is actually an all-important subtle interest area, so understated that it does not compete with the linear pattern.

A 'nejime' or root hider placement of flowers may replace the Earth group. This is often used when branches are used for Heaven and Man almost as a Contemporary focal area is used, BUT the nejime's parts must follow the angle that Earth takes, and its parts must not droop down and obscure the unity and strength of the nemoto, otherwise severe penalty is taken.

Because of the length of the nemoto, plant materials never approach or touch the rim of the container in Classic designs, and almost one-half of the container opening should be clear of plant material.

Simplicity and Restraint

Classical arrangements should be very simple and restrained, both in the amounts of materials used and the number of different kinds included, as well as the number of colors. A general rule is that more than one to two different kinds should bring a penalty, though three kinds are acceptable in double designs made in a single double-opening container in the Informal style.

Each branch or flower stem should have been carefully pruned to remove crossing twigs, dense or bruised leaves, superfluous blooms and all other unrelated, non-essential parts. The result should be a **CLEAR-CUT** outline which is typical of the Japanese influence.

Simplicity and restraint are achieved through the use of only enough plant material as is necessary to create beauty by carrying the linear pattern to completion. The one perfect bud, elegant line of bare stem, the single leaf giving the expression to continued growth and vitality of line as in Nature.

The Japanese are masters of the subtle and restrained use of color, but **adaptations** often offer strong contrasts, even in Formal Classic, such as the strong green leaves and the bright red berries of the Japanese Rhodea. But always lines must dominate over color. Traditionally no more than 2-3 contrasting colors in addition to green of the foliage and stems were used.

Balance is achieved through the relationship of fluid lines and swelling curves. The control of balance is with the center or Heaven line, which tip must be directly over the center of the point of emergence. This is a point of great difference from Contemporary designs in which balance is achieved through symmetrically spaced area relationships and geometric patterns.

The intriguing charm of the Japanese upright arrangements lie in the depth achieved with the use of only one, two or three branches and a very few flowers. Plant material, container and base (if used) are considered as a single unit.

In judging Kakemono, which is a grouping containing a scroll of painting or calligraphy, check the balance which must be maintained between size, color and subject matter. The subject of a painting is not duplicated in the arrangement, such obvious matching creates monotony and lessens distinction. An all-green design can complement a colorful painting.

In a Kakemono with a painting of a waterfall, plants that grow in or near water are suitable with a sculptured water bird placed to balance the group. Accessories used with designs made to show Japanese influence should be subordinate to the design of plant materials, strengthening line interest rather than dividing it. Traditionally, accessories where not used **IN** a design, but placed outside it, and often some distance away to balance the scroll or design.

In judging a grouping in the manner of Japanese tokonama (alcove, niche), at least one-third of the space should remain unoccupied. Crowding should be penalized.

CLASSIC

Suitability of Container, Plant Material, Bases

All **flowers,** grasses or tree branches are acceptable in modified Japanese design and the greater use of foliage and greens than blossoms, traditional to Classic flower arrangements, is not so closely observed in **adaptations.** Oriental species of plants are especially suitable, but not necessary for **adaptations.**

Classical arrangements were noted for simplicity and restraint, both in the amounts of materials used and the number of different materials included. More than three different kinds or colors should bring a penalty, for not being typical.

The Heaven and Man groups are often made with one kind of flower or flowering branch or evergreen and the Earth group is made with another different kind or color.

Containers for **adaptations** may be modernized versions and materials but should follow the general outlines of:

Formal:	vertical upright
Semiformal:	usabatas, boat shapes, low bowls
Informal:	wide assortment of low dishes, shapes varying, including 'windowed' or tiered bamboo tubes

Colors of containers were subdued or neutral. The design of the container should be simple and not highly decorated. Colors for **adaptations** have more leeway but the design should follow the traditional for simplicity and decoration.

Bases Tall slender tables and elegant low stands were used under Formal Classic; finely finished flat bases may be used in **adaptations.** Any type base, including burl and the like, may be used under the Semiformal and Informal. A base or container may be used one upon the other in the Informal. A base should not be used unless it contributes something to the design by stabilizing balance, increasing height or adding interest.

Accessories were used with restraint in Japanese arrangements and were not placed in the design but used to attain spatial balance through placement outside the container. An exception was the use of the fan, the lower parts of which were used in such a way that the nemoto emerged from between them. On certain holidays a raffia bow was tied to the nemoto. Other than these, hanging scrolls, depicting either paintings or calligraphy and perhaps one other art object were often combined to create a related grouping. The **ideal** Classic **adaptation** will observe this characteristic of the traditional.

NAGEIRE
Correctness of Style

Nageire is called the vase form because traditionally an upright container was used. It is referred to as "thrown in" or "over the cliff" because of the studied casualness, planned simplicity and stress on naturalism which are characteristic qualities.

It may be done in three forms with variations of each:

| **Upright** | **Incline or Slanting** | **Cascade** |

Nageire retains the three groups of Heaven, Man and Earth; Nageire retains the triangular form and asymmetrical balance; Nageire does not stress the nemoto placement of stems.

Seasons of the year were indicated by the quantity of material used. Spring is moderately full, Summer is more full with abundant flowers. Fall, moderately full with less perfect flowers, includes dry branches and seed pods and the one-flower design. Winter is sparse, evergreen branches used. **Adaptations** may reflect any of these qualities or materials and combinations.

Design According to Nageire Style

The familiar triangular form is created by the tips of the three main lines. The design should have a well-established central axis and the Heaven line should be the basis for this axis with all other lines centering around it. This Heaven line may be lower than the Man line but it still remains the pivot of balance.

Balance is subtle, often the imaginary vertical axis is found on the outside of the container. Better balance is achieved if, when the Cascade is made, the longest lines do not extend more than two-thirds the distance from container lip to the floor.

There must be compatible relationships between container size and height and the amount and height of materials used. The eye must judge the proportion and the overall relationships. Specific measurements tend to confine the imagination and scope of arrangements in the manner of Nageire. They often have more width than height.

While the stems should lead out of the container together, the stems are not forced into a prominent nemoto as in the Classic Ikenobo. The predominance of material is toward one side of the container.

Although a lone tree form can still be interpreted, flowers now may predominate and flowers and foliage may extend over the container rim. Bushy or leafy branches are acceptable and need not be so severely stripped down. Greater freedom is allowed in flower numbers and odd numbers are not mandatory. Half the mouth of the container is free of flowers in traditional designs. A nijime or root-hider of flowers serves as the Earth group, particularly in slanting designs. Nageire arrangements often have Heaven and Man groups made of one kind of flower and Earth in another color or entirely different type of bloom. The arrangement is penalized for a lack of depth or if it appears to topple forward.

Adaptations on the one-flower designs may put the flower form as the highest, using it as Heaven, or as Man or as Earth, but it must be balanced by the other elements wherever it is placed. In the one-flower-bloom designs (Chabana) all correctness-of-style and design points apply. Even one-bloom designs should give a feeling of vitality and growth. A round flower is more suitable than one of irregular shape, and it should be fresh, crisp and perfect. Any of the styles, Classic, Nageire or Moribana can be used for such designs. The schedule must make clear whether **one-bloom** or **one-flower** is intended. One flower might mean **only** petunias, one-bloom means strictly **ONE BLOOM**. Multiple-flower spikes or clusters are not eligible as one-bloom.

Nageire adaptations often appear quite contemporary or modern with dried stark branches of interesting form supplemented by lip-groupings of contrasting color and form.

When two or more containers are used, there must be a close relationship in texture, size, shape and color as well as proper spacing, position and height and compatible association of plant materials. The designs may be different styles, as a Nageire in one and a Moribana in the other, but the whole must achieve a harmonious relationship.

Suitability of Plant Materials, Container and Base

Since Nageire is traditionally the 'vase' style, containers for **"showing the influence of"** should be tall, cylindrical types. They may be of metal, pottery, driftwood or reed and are less formal and expensive than originally used in the Classic Seika.

The shape is usually simple, and conventional though variations on modern lines occur; the colors were subdued or neutral in the traditional, but have become brighter in the **adaptations.** Glass or transparent containers increase the problems of aesthetic stem handling and no record was found of their being used in the original designs.

Materials

Dried materials, bare branches and weathered wood or driftwood (boku) may be included in adaptations. An uneven number of flowers or branches are not mandatory.

Unlike the Classic, in Nageire the flower beauty may be emphasized, or the design may be made entirely of flowers, such as petunias or lilies. Any branches, whether bare, with leaves, flowers, fruits or berries and grasses are acceptable as long as the combinations are harmonious and compatible. More freedom is allowed in Nageire in which there is more abundant color, more material and more different kinds of materials, though the major characteristics of the type must be met, including restraint and simplicity. **Bases,** stands and tables may be used when needed for balance, height, rhythm, etc. **Accessories.** While Morimono is the only style which traditionally used accessories, these are acceptable in **adaptations** if the basic characteristics of the style are expressed, but the **ideal** design would not include them.

MORIBANA (Shallow Container Style)

Correctness of Style

Moribana designs are more informal. The meaning is interpreted as "heaped up" or profuse, but this is actually rather misleading since the Moribana should not approach anything like a mass design. The word was used by the Japanese because it was such a marked change from the austerity of the Classic Ikenobo.

364

The designs were based on natural growth, seasonal change, unfettered by slavish rules and exacting techniques. There was little manipulation of stems. As in the Classic and Nageire, the tri-dimensional outline of height and width, plus depth must be observed. The triangle is also used, and despite the name, simplicity and restraint prevail. In Moribana variations the balance is by placement.

Variations are:

Simple Moribana

- means heaped up
- use of flowers, foliage, etc.
- triangular outline
- may emphasize color
- **adaptations** may incorporate logical figures though not ideally
- may be scenes
- free standing
- flat, low containers of pottery, wood, etc.

Morimono

- uses fruits, vegetables, seed pods, flowers, bare, foliaged or flowering branches, stones, long-lasting materials, figures
- triangle shape maintained
- elements may be combined in any way desired

Water Reflecting. Water Viewing

- scenes of sea, shore, woodland pools
- triangular design
- free standing
- rocks, flower petals may be in the water
- adaptations incorporate logical figurines though not ideally
- water is an important element

DESIGN ACCORDING TO MORIBANA STYLE: ALL VARIATIONS; SIMPLE, MORIMONO, WATER VIEWING

As in all Japanese flower arrangements and despite the title "heaped up", Moribana perfection is attained with as little material as possible, and a cluttered effect is penalized.

As in the other Japanese designs, the triangle is formed by the tips of Heaven, Man and Earth and all supporting stems are arranged within its limits. Plant material does not fill the entire space — voids are necessary to the design. Supporting stems may be of the same material as Heaven, Man and Earth, but must vary in length.

The union of stem and holder may be concealed by low groupings of leaves, moss, or other such items. Unlike the Classical designs, some supporting lines may be placed lower than the main Earth and Man lines if such placement makes the design look more natural which is the aim of the Moribana. What the Classic suggests symbolically, the Moribana achieves realistically.

The placement of the design may be off-center in the container. Balance may be achieved by placement on the base, etc.

A grouping of three separate containers, each with its own design, which when associated, form a compatible relationship, may be placed so as to form a scalene triangle and used either with or without a base.

Although Moribana designs often include two or more groupings in one container, approximately one-half to two-thirds of the water or container bottom is left free of materials. Any combination of plants is acceptable; it is more authentic if they are arranged according to growth habit, i.e. trees over low growers, etc., but **adaptations** should not be penalized on this account if the "spirit" of the Moribana is portrayed.

Although Classic and Nageire designs give a satisfying feeling of depth when viewed from the front, Moribana present actual three-dimensional quality from any side, making them completely free standing, otherwise penalty is taken.

Several holders may be used. Although a holder containing the Heaven line may be placed almost anywhere in the container, the visual weight should not be concentrated too near the center or crowded against a side of the container.

DESIGN CORRECTNESS VARIATIONS

Simple

Placement "as the plant grows" in nature is ignored in many **adaptations** and flowers are used for the usefulness of color and scale.

Proportions of the stem lengths are set by visual weight of the container and materials used. Balance is by placement, there is little curve manipulation of stems; those naturally curved by nature being enough to satisfy rhythm requirements.

Contrast achieved by placing the delicate beauty of a flowering branch with a rough wooden bucket and base can heighten the characteristics of each, but one texture must remain dominant to achieve harmony.

In a natural-scenery design, using materials from the roadside where they are subjected to high winds, it is permissible to allow a broken or bent stem of frail grass to horizontally cross through the design, about one-third of the way up, or where balance is satisfied.

The material used to simulate a tree in a scene should show a well-developed nemoto or trunk, while small branches, flowers, etc., added at the base indicate natural growth habit of a bush at the foot of the tree, but they should not be so heavily grouped as to hide the trunk, and should appear as naturally as possible.

Morimono Design Correctness   (Fruit, etc.)

The arrangement should be dominated by one plant form and all other elements are related subordinately to the featured form.

The **strongest** characteristic of the stem, flower, leaf or root used should be emphasized.

The items may be combined in any manner, but the triangular form is retained. If the triangle cannot be found, points are deducted.

Like the water area of a Moribana design, approximately two-thirds of the tray or mat should be left free of material.

Since the materials are used directly on the base or container, texture and color of both are very important and must be compatible.

The effect should be uncrowded and the featured object or group should stand out clearly.

Water Viewing and Reflecting Correctness of Design

In the Water-Viewing form, a wide expanse of water must be visible. The base of the stems need not emerge as one tight unit, and the needleholder may be covered over with moss or stones. Strict adherence to uneven numbers is not mandatory in any Moribana.

Water-Reflecting designs are especially made to make the beauty of a simulated tree or branch doubly apparent by the reflection in the clear open water. A blossom from a flowering branch may be floating on its surface. Rock outlines add to the reflection.

Divided Form

Divided-form Moribanas made by placing Heaven and Man on one holder and Earth on another; or Heaven on one and Man and Earth on another, or three groupings on three separate holders, should be judged as a complete design. These may be Water-viewing or dry-bottom scenes. The holders should be diagonally opposite each other.

In Water-viewing, the holders should be arranged to accent the surface of the water and to emphasize the width of the arrangement. In all, the eye must move easily between the groups, unified by color, stem length and placement. The main lines must turn toward each other.

One group should be dominant, one intermediate, one subordinate. Moss, sand and pebbles may be built around the bases of the holders to simulate a bank or shoreline; an unplanned pile which lacks this effect will lose a point or two.

SUITABILITY OF MATERIALS, CONTAINERS, BASE FOR MORIBANA SIMPLE

Materials

The choice of flowers and colors is wide and almost unlimited since the rules are relaxed. As in other styles, two of a single kind of material can be used to express life's beginning, but odd numbers result in a more asymmetrical plan and facilitates the making of the triangles. Often more than one triangle may be found in designs made up of odd numbers. Four of anything was avoided as signifying death. Dried materials may be used to form permanent outlines.

Containers

Flat containers, bowls, trays, boards and the like are appropriate. Container and floral material must be harmonious in color, texture, proportion and spirit. A woodland scene requires a container of rustic appearance. Containers which are fine and delicate should be paired with flowers of a more fragile nature, though careful use of contrast can enhance and point up their fragility.

Stylized or traditional forms are acceptable containers. The colors are those from nature's scenic background; earth, sky, water and rock colors in muted, subdued hues.

Base and Accessories

The bases may be any type which is compatible with the overall texture of the design. Many times bases are used even when container or design does not require such, penalty should be taken for any non-essential materials or items used. Accessories traditionally were used in the Morimono (fruit, etc.) design only, though a lid of a container sometimes appeared in other variations. **Adaptations** often include logical and appropriate accessories and decorative wood pieces. These should not be penalized unless their addition affects the design adversely. Their texture, color and spirit must be related to the other materials, container, and base, and their position must contribute to the balance overall.

SUITABILITY OF MATERIALS, CONTAINER AND BASE FOR MORIMONO

Suitable elements for Morimono must include fruits, and vegetables; flowers, branches and seedpods may be added for color and textural interest. The sprouting tops of vegetables and carefully cleaned roots may be included and often add distinction. Branches, stones, items from the sea and other areas can also be included.

Morimono is the only Japanese flower arrangement which traditionally used accessories such as bronze figurines, scrolls and even tiny growing plants. Appropriate figures can be used in adaptations.

A pair of Morimono designs, treated as a unit, may be staged on different levels. The base, tray, raft, board or leaf upon which the design is made should not be decorated, and should be harmoniously textured and colored.

SUITABILITY OF MATERIALS, CONTAINER AND ACCESSORIES FOR WATER VIEWING

Plant materials which grow upright in nature and preferably that which grows in or near water such as reeds, cattails, water lilies and the like rate high for suitability. Designs using only one kind of plant material may be judged as suitable as those containing more. There are no restrictions on the number of kinds in either flowers or branches in traditional Water-Viewing designs.

Water is an integral or important element, at least one-half of its surface should be exposed. A branch of the design may dip into and out of the water, simulating a branch over an actual pool.

The reflection is considered as an important part of the Water-Reflecting design, and if balance or aesthetic appeal is lessened by the reflections, points must be removed.

Gnarled, weathered or driftwood may be combined with fresh material to symbolize "new life from old". Containers may be oval, round, rectangular or free-form and may have a blue lining symbolizing water.

DISTINCTION (as applied to all styles)

Because of the diversity and interest of Nature's handiwork, no two arrangements are ever identical. Though the underlying framework or basic principles are repeated, distinction can be "built in" through careful techniques and superior construction and a good eye for proportion and rhythmic movement.

The emphasis is always on the individual beauty and interest of the plant featured. Distinction is reduced if a bunch of iris blooms form little more than a mass of color.

Clarity of line and contrast of just one bloom against its own lance-like leaf makes the iris stand out distinctively in sharp relief. This clarity of design is the hallmark of Japanese flower arranging.

Careful color relationships is another distinguishing characteristic typical of Japanese designs. Attention to textural contrasts and repetition also adds to distinction.

In showing the influence of Japanese arrangements, emphasis is seldom placed on containers or base. When a unique or prized possession is used, the floral design should be very simple. The right stand, or base — right in texture, shape, style and size often gives the finishing touch that an arrangement needs to achieve distinction as well as balance and proportion. However a base which does not contribute to the design should be penalized under design and distinction to a total of the fault.

The spirit of the Japanese flower arrangement which makes it distinctive is a strong impression that the plant material is the **most** important thing. Its identity should be easily recognizable through the restraint and simplicity with which the triangular design is constructed. If confusing details, too many colors, forms and materials mitigates this impression, penalty is taken.

Extreme simplicity and clarity of line marks the distinctive **Classic** design. Material should be stripped of all unrelated parts to allow the eye to enjoy the curve of stem and individuality of form. Heavy overlapping leaves that hide the graceful lines of Heaven, Man or Earth of a Classic design should have been trimmed away and must be penalized.

The kubari (stick holder) used in a Classic design may be teamed with a pin holder. They should hold the nemoto neatly and firmly together for the required distance. The pin holder may be concealed only with pebbles or stones, never with a collar of leaves as one of the distinctive qualities of the Classic is a clearly outlined nemoto or trunk and anything less must be deducted.

Uncluttered, pleasing **Nageire** designs usually have one-half to two-thirds of the mouth of the container free of plant material. Though the title means "thrown in", a careless appearance will be penalized.

As in all Japanese flower arranging, perfection and distinction is attained with as little material as possible and though the title of **Moribana** means profuse or "heaped up", lack of design and care in placing the materials according to correctness of style means less distinction, therefore a deduction.

Discrimination in the combinations of plant materials is important for the finished **Simple or Water-Viewing** Moribana should appear to be a group of amicable, growing plants.

Materials used to cover the pinholder in the Moribana should not droop listlessly on the water, nor form a stiff or unnatural mound or collar, but should appear to be actually growing. Pebbles should not be heaped in a meaningless mound, but grouped to appear as if they had been washed up on the shore, otherwise deduction must be made under both design correctness and distinction to a total of the fault.

Rocks must be carefully used if they are to contribute to distinction of the Moribana design. They may balance heavy lines, add dignity and strength to slender lines, emphasize the beauty of a delicate flower and indicate a particular setting. If they do none of these things, their presence is superfluous and deductible.

CONDITION

Condition in the Japanese design applies more to wilting and cleanliness than to perfection. A furled leaf, torn tip or insect-chewn petal may be included to express a natural state of affairs. Of course, only one of any one of these is needed to carry the impression and more would surely bring a reduction of points.

The water should be absolutely clean; free of debris but a fallen leaf or petal may be afloat on the surface of a Moribana to simulate this natural occurence.

Freshness, crispness, a general lack of wilting is necessary with the minimum use of material. When attention is spotlighted on the beauty of each individual stem, leaf and flower, it becomes of extreme importance that the materials used be crisp, clean and fresh.

Trimming and pruning is an essential part of the construction. The light inner layers exposed on branches by the removal of twigs should be darkened to blend into the remaining bark or bear a reduction of points. The fruit, vegetables and all other materials used in a Morimono design must be free of soil, insect spray and signs of overmaturity.

SUMMARY

Style Correctness 25 Points

*triangular outline apparent *dynamic linear quality *asymmetrical balance *simplicity and restraint *material used easily identified *gives impression of natural growth, life

-symmetrically balanced -"spirit" of natural growth lacking -triangular requirement ignored -linear outline blurred by excess material -Morimono lacks either fruit or vegetables -Classic lacks nemoto

Design Correctness According to Style 40 Points

*three major groupings *stems of varying heights *contrasts relieve monotony *½ to ⅔ of container mouth, tray or water unoccupied *tips upturning (Classic) *tight, neat nemoto (Classic) *nemoto 2-6" *tip of Heaven directly over point of emergence *diagonal placements *one form dominating Morimono *Moribana balanced by placement *eye moves easily over design *materials, container in scale

-drooping flowers, twigs obscure lines and angles of three major groupings -one sided -lacks depth -design too low -container too large for material -plant material fills too much of space -the stems same height -main design too near center or sides (Moribana) -container too large for design -unnatural placements -flat appearance -nemoto separated (Classic) -crowded, cluttered -too many points of interest -lacks unity -one branch or flower hiding another -lines jutting out directly front, left, right

Suitability of Materials, Container, Base, Accessories 15 Points

*texture, color and spirit harmonious *characteristic container of style *accessories (if used in Moribana) logical to scene *water incorporated in water-viewing design *reflection aesthetic in water-reflecting *container and materials as formal as the style portrayed

-inappropriate combinations of textures, colors -not typical of style -illogical accessories -Morimono tray overly decorated -unattractive reflection -dryland or 'desert-type' plants in water viewing design

Distinction 10 Points

*careful techniques *well proportioned *identity of plants preserved *harmonious relationships of all elements *absolute fitness *Moribana scene appears natural *has life

-crowded -careless construction -lacks spirit of style -pinholder poorly handled -Nageire container mouth stuffed -container or base supersedes design -characteristics typical of style absent

Condition 10 Points

*a torn or damaged leaf may be included to reflect natural accidents *water clean (though a leaf or flower may float upon it) (Moribana) *crisp *clean

-wilting material -dirt, dust -spray-marked fruits, vegetables -trimming scars -soiled water -excessive use of torn or damaged leaves

Traditional Occidental Period Designs

SUGGESTED CLASSES:

1. Suggesting Greek Culture
2. Showing Eygptian Influence
3. In the Manner of the Dutch-Flemish Era
4. Indicative of Early American
5. Adapted from American Colonial Williamsburg
6. Showing French Rococo Influence
7. In the Spirit of the English Georgian Era
8. Inspired by Victorian England
9. Period Interpretive

OCCIDENTAL PERIOD

Since there were no formal schools, no rules for flower arrangement were formed in the Occidental Era until the Contemporary Period. Judging is done in the "spirit or image" expressed and more leeway is allowed than in judging the Japanese designs.

Authentic designs of both Oriental and Occidental Periods are made for educational exhibits and are not judged easily because few are qualified. Adaptations are used as authentic fabrics, containers and plant materials are often unobtainable.

Arrangements to show the influence of a certain period in history should be made of flowers and foliage available in that century or of other more modern plant materials which seem to express the spirit of that time. Recognizable hybrids (the Hybrid Tea Rose came into being in 1867), products of the 20th Century, lessen the authenticity but the Judge should not quibble over the kind of flowers used in a design to show influence, if the general spirit and style is expressed by those chosen. Species plants are grown less and less and actually the records are incomplete in some cases. Some flower may have been grown at the time, but was not in bloom, was disliked by the painter (from whom most records are taken) or for some other reason did not appear in the pictures painted or the tapestries woven during that era.

The container should be a good reproduction, if not authentic. Accessories and fabrics should reflect the period; colors should be typical of the period and the design should be of characteristic pattern. Early Occidental designs stressed masses of color; there was little distinguishing line to identify them clearly as in the Japanese, but slight variances do occur which are pointed out. Descriptions of both major and minor periods of Occidental flower arrangement evolution are necessarily brief. The Judge, informed of an opportunity to officiate in such classes, is urged to delve into details in the many flower arranging history books.

Most of the early Period arrangements were free-standing — to be viewed from all sides. The use of flowers in containers as decorative units on tables where food is served was of European origin. Accessories were never used in the designs with the exception of the Dutch-Flemish when it is permissible to set a butterfly or insect on a flower. In other designs the items were laid beside the designs or in front, but with none of the attention to spatial balance employed by the Japanese.

A Judge may be confronted with a design which presumes to be influenced by the French Rococo, for example, which is delicate and pastel but the characteristic mass has been reduced to the point of being a massed line, thus it becomes a Contemporary design, and points are deducted as lacking typical characteristics of the period relative to "massed design".

Classes calling for an antique container should not be confused with those to show influence of a specific historical period. For instance, Early Americans would not have used a lamp as a container but for the purpose it was made — to give light! Arrangements depicting a period should be in containers typical of that period, that is, containers **used** during that period for flower arrangement.

In the same sense, an accessory of a Japanese or Chinese man would not "make" a Japanese arrangement showing the influence of that country without the other typical characteristics of their designing.

The main object is to determine if the arrangement expresses the **spirit** which dominated during that particular period in history.

The Schedule can, of course, call for PERIOD INTERPRETIVE DESIGNS which attempt to express the spirit of a period in history through the use of figures, form or line rather than adapting what is available in containers, color and materials to make similar designs. Interpretive Period Designs reflecting a particular era can be made by simulating a tapestry, decoration, item or character of that Period. Such an interpretation of France's gayest era could be a design expressing the minuet in freely flowing, delicately rhythmic curves and pastel hues, but the design would be a line or massed line rather than the oval mass design of the period. Busts and figures of Aphrodite supplement Greek Interpretives, as well as sculpture representing Venus, Diana, Juno and other gods and goddesses. Such use would not be a "typical design of the period" **but** rather "an interpretation of the life, people or ideology of the period".

The bee, Napoleon's personal emblem, its colors or habitat expressed in modern lines or its stinger in Abstract would conform to Period Interpretive, as would a flower arrangement copying the colors of a Van Gogh or the Art Nouveau of Toulouse-Lautrec if Modern or Abstract designs were used.

SUGGESTED SCALE OF POINTS

Period Correctness, according to Schedule requirements	25	Color Suitability	20
. characteristics		Appropriate Materials and Container	20
. spirit		Condition	10
Design Correctness	25		

DUTCH-FLEMISH PERIOD

Period Characteristics

- symmetrical, massed oval
- flowers in profile, face out or showing backs
- profuse, ponderous
- S-curve appeared in some Dutch
- large top flower (Flemish)
- rich, varied colors
- many accessories
  SPIRIT: rich, weighty, vital, ponderous

Design Correctness

The designs were typically early "flower pieces" or still-life group-ings of plant materials and other objects with the plant materials play-ing a dominant role. The design outline was a massed oval, but each flower appeared at its best, indicative of the early nursery "catalog paintings" of the era.

The Flemish showed a strict adherence to symmetry and details were equally as important as the flowers. The Flemish were the first to combine flowers and fruits in an upright design, with grapes being their favorite choice. Their designs always used a "noble" flower at the top, coinciding with the tip of an imaginary central axis. The Dutch softened the design with an S-curve and used a diagonal line at times.

Textures were varied, from the harshness of metal jewelry to the softness of feathers, fur, fabrics and flower petals.

Both the Flemish and the Dutch showed the backs of flowers, flowers in profile and facing out. Few spike forms, other than foxglove, hollyhock and lupine should be included as round forms seemed to be a favorite choice.

The size of the bouquet should overpower that of the vase with the floral material being two to three times the container height.

Arching lines are bold with a controlled confusion of movement and the flowers placed rather casually. A triangle pattern often appear-ed, formed by the placement of the conspicuous flowers within the oval outline, but never a definite focal area.

There should be no quiet spots, the eye moves consistently from arching stem, to nodding flower to curling leaf; from red to white to yellow; from flower to container to accessory and back. The result should be one, not static or packed, but voluptuous and opulent. The spirit to be depicted is one of a rich, energetic and vital era.

Color Suitability

Mainly the general effect should be warm and glowing. To achieve this, the colors should be strong and vibrant in medium to dark values, highlighted with some white and pink.

APPROPRIATE MATERIALS AND CONTAINER

Spring flowers predominated in the painted flower arrangements from which our information of this period is obtained. The painter reputedly portrayed certain varieties as they bloomed and often took several years to complete a painting. At least one tulip appeared in each, as this was the era when "tulipomania" swept the continent. Large, spectacular, conspicuously marked flowers were preferred.

Since it would be impossible to have a tulip in an **adaptation** made in another season of the year, other large spectactular, boldly patterned flowers can be substituted and should be used. Deformed fruit and leaves were sometimes included and grapes were popular.

Containers of stone and alabaster urns, pewter jars, heavy amber and green glass, baskets, bronze ewers, silver and pottery bowls are suitable choices but shiny brass or other metals are inappropriate.

Foliage is incidental, mainly that which would, by nature, be attached to the long stems used. Castor bean, coleus, poppy and lily foliage was often portrayed, showing a liking for distinct and conspicuous contrasts of form and color. Every kind of flower available at that time was used.

It was during this era that the pineapple replaced the melon as "king" of fruits. It was so choice that the pineapple became a symbol of hospitality, and was often used as an accessory along with other unrelated items such as watches, gold-fringed velvet and brocade fabrics, flowers, fruits, insects, parrots, birds' nests and eggs, sea shells, butterflies, nuts and skulls (always minus the lower jaw).

FRENCH

The French periods of flower arranging were influenced by four specific economic situations and political personages, the most distinctively French is the second which has come to be known as the Rococo Period. The first was the Baroque, a heavy, rich appearing design followed by the sprightly Rococo; then in the latter 18th Century by the Directoire Period when styles were influenced by Louis XVI and Antoinette whose favorite color, turquoise, was used along with slightly deeper and more grayed shades of those popular in the Rococo Period. A greater change came in the 19th Century when Napoleon's influence brought about a definite masculine appearance in the Neo-Classic or Classic Revival years which was called the Empire.

FRENCH ROCOCO   (Louis XV)
Period Characteristics

- airy grace, delicately elegant
- design taller than wide
- not quite symmetrical
- no focal area
- curves, shell-like spirals, scrolls, tendrils and garlands
- colors varied but delicate, subtle analagous or monochromatic harmonies used
- one color dominating
  SPIRIT: Youthful vigor, gaiety, charm, sprightly grace

Design Correctness

The lines of the airy designs followed graceful, lightly-bending arcs and ovals. Variations used during the Rococo period included symmetrical pyramids of fruit for banquet tables, Easter "pineapples" constructed of daffodil heads and leaves; vases holding only foliage and garlands for terrace decoration.

Fewer flowers are used than in previous periods and these are placed loosely. Little thought is given to design and it should not be strictly symmetrical lest this reduce the gay liveliness to be expressed. There should be no hint of a focal area.

A few large flowers such as peonies, poppies, large tulips and full-blown roses are used but their effect should be lightened by the addition of smaller flowers plus sprays of lilac, tendrils of honeysuckle, fern fronds and the like.

Proportions of material to container may follow two patterns according to container style. First, the height of the flowers in bowls and baskets may be less or the same as the container height. Second, in a tall stately vase, the material should be of graceful stems at least twice the height of the container and the design should be taller than wide.

Through scale, lines and color, **adaptations** can express the spirited, gay mood typical of the Rococo Period. Designs may be small and curving or very tall, slim and willowy. The stems of the flowers should show clearly; the flower heads stand out, giving the grouping a light, airy, open look. Any appearance of crowding or massing so the flower stems are hidden should be penalized.

Suitable Colors

Light, gay, pastel hues in harmonious analogous or monochromatic sequence, with one color dominating are typical. Characteristic colors of the Rococo Period are soft and pale orange and buff, yellow, pinks, greens and blues. Minor contrast is supplied through additions of touches of dark blue, violet, red and black.

Appropriate Materials and Container

Container shapes include wall pockets, vases, urns (often with handles) five-finger vases, bowls and basket shapes, both tall and low. Containers should be made of fine ceramic, porcelain, glass, metal, Delftware and crystal.

Dolphins holding shells aloft and cupids, shepherds and goddesses serve as stems. Epergnes are used on tables; shapely, elegant urns for the more formal designs may be ornamented with painted, carved or bas relief scenes, figures, shells and garlanded forms.

Appropriate accessories (if typically French looking) are lace fans, delicate figurines, eye-masks, small finely-bound books and flowers as well as candles and embroidery frames and other needlework items.

Backgrounds for adaptations may be typically carved wood panels or fabrics of satin, silk, velvet or rural scenic wallpaper.

Flowers should be delicate, scented and spike forms used as well as round. A fresh, delicate yet crisp appearance should have been achieved through the use of flowers with papery textures such as bachelor-buttons or the silky petals such as poppies, and through the use of perfectly conditioned, fresh plant materials.

GEORGIAN ENGLISH   (Early and Late)

Period Characteristics of Early Georgian

- dignified handling of horticulturally perfect flowers
- in symmetrical balance, triangular form
- rather heavy mass

- influenced by Italy and China
- warm colors (full chroma) and cool colors (deep values)
- heavy vases of metal, marble
  SPIRIT: Formal grandeur, elegant restraint, stability

Period Characteristics of Late Georgian

- rich, dignified, less ponderous than Early Georgian
- shows some French influence
- formal balance, triangular outline
- use of horticulturally perfect plant materials
- one kind of flower often used, often all-white designs made
- velvety textures of flowers and silver containers popular
  SPIRIT: Less dignified than Early Georgian, but still formal stateliness

377

DESIGN CORRECTNESS
Early Georgian

Designs were influenced by the continent and China, taking artifacts and characteristics from both. Swags were popular decorations. Flowers spill over the container rim, but without forming a focal area. The design may have a strong central axis of delphinium or iris. Large flowers are casually placed throughout and at the outer edge of the design. Proportions should not be over two times the container height. Both design and container should give an impression of stocky sturdiness and moderately massive stateliness.

Late Georgian

In reflecting the influence of French Rococo, designs are more open with more arching lines, but never achieving the airy crispness of its French predecessor. Blossoms fall loosely over the vase rims, forming no specific focal area.

Color Suitability

Low color key; deep tonalities of purple, blue and greens highlighted with scarlet, yellow, white and pink. An all-white or one-kind-of-flower arrangement may be reflected in the Late Georgian period.

Appropriate Materials and Container

Both fresh and dried flowers used according to season. Pride in horticultural perfection should be expressed in the choice of plant materials.

Ceramic wall pockets with molded decorations of faces or scenes, footed vases, wide-mouth bowls, chalices, goblets, tureen shapes in ceramic, Lowestoft, Delftware, silver, glass and reed baskets are acceptable. Turned wood, highly lacquered were interesting vases of the period.

Accessories included flowers laid on the tables beside the designs as well as figures of men and birds, rose jars and the like from France, Italy and China.

Backgrounds of brocade, velvet, wallpaper, glass and wood are suitable. The arched niche is particularly appropriate.

VICTORIAN   (Romantic Era)
Period Characteristics

- compact, handsome but heavy and billowing designs
- wider than high
- no center of interest
- in the "language of flowers" many emotions were expressed
- frilled, striped, full-blown flowers
- ornate, gilded containers
- draped, puffed fabrics
  SPIRIT: Romantic and nostalgic but substantial. Complacent but with warmth and tenderness

378

Design Correctness

Early Victorians were still French-influenced and liked open designs of light color and white. Late Victorians preferred large overflowing bouquets, the pattern of which was varied with an occasional trailing or curving line.

Proportion of flowers to the container should be approximately equal. A spotty effect, resulting from the casual placement of conspicuously-marked flowers is typical of the period. A straight line of yellow flowers or a grouping of red, etc., should be penalized as nontypical.

There should be contrasts of size and shapes but used without plan. Weeping, trailing fuchsia and bleeding hearts express the languid, fainting attitudes of the ladies of the era, these were combined within the general mass, or allowed to droop beyond the general outline, but should never be so prominent or abundant as to have lightened the heavy massiveness which is typical. Tussie-Mussies, made in concentric rings, are acceptable designs of this period.

Color Suitability

Heavy browns, dark purple, lavender, orange, yellow, red and white were favorite colors and the total effect should be one of romantic richness with no set color patterns or harmonies.

Appropriate Materials and Container

Artificial plant materials were used in flower arranging for the first time. Flowers of wax and shells and beads on velvet were painstakingly made. Despite the fact that such were typical of the Period, the use of artificial plant materials is restricted in Standard Shows and consultation with the Flower Show Committee would be in order if such a design were displayed.

Magnolia and fern leaves were skeletonized and may be included as long as their addition does not lighten the typical mass effect. The textures mainly should be rich, heavy, lush in both flowers and fabrics.

As in the Japanese Schools and Renaissance Period, the language of flowers was important. To the Victorians flowers had such emotional meaning as love, flirtation, rejection and similar emotional connotations.

Containers of glass, cast-iron, trumpet epergnes, open-work compotes and vases with round, bulging bodies and fanciful scrolling suit the period. Accessories including what-nots, ornately-bound books, pictures, paperweights and embroidered samplers reflect Victorian tastes.

Condition   (applies to all Periods)

Materials, accessories and container must be spotless, dustless and in condition worthy of exhibition.

A glaring chip out of a container or accessory should be penalized; however lines left by repaired cracks should not be deducted unless the patch-work is exceedingly unsightly.

Cards giving supplemental data relative to the historical interest of a container or accessory should be small, neatly printed and in good taste.

While plant material in all designs should be in a non-wilted state and be prime examples, this is particularly true of those designs typical of the French Rococo in which a crisp freshness is a vital characteristic and in Georgian when horticultural perfection was of extreme importance. Wilting or other damage should be deducted under both Period Correctness and Condition to a total of the degree of fault.

Deformed fruit and leaves were sometimes used in the Dutch-Flemish Period and this characteristic should be taken into consideration when judging and not penalized unless carried to excess.

SUMMARY

Dutch-Flemish Period Characteristics 25 Points

*massed oval *accessories included *numerous bright-to-dark colors *opulent *each flower stands out *symmetrical *large top flower (Flemish) *flowers almost conceal container *S-curve in some designs (Dutch)

-triangular outline -too open -too many voids -pastel colors -lacks accessories -container too obvious, not covered enough

Design Correctness for Dutch-Flemish 25 Points

*design two-three times taller than container *symmetrical *flower placed in profile or back or frontwards *much contrast in texture and colors -container too prominent -off balance -all flowers facing out -quiet spots in the design -static -lacks contrast -one color dominating

Color Suitability 20 Points

*warm *advancing *vibrant *varied

-pastels -one color dominating -focal grouping

Appropriate Materials and Container 20 Points

*round forms predominating *large, spectacular flowers *tulips and grapes *bold foliage forms *appropriate accessories

-shiny, modern appearing container -too many spiked or curving lines

Condition 10 Points

*a piece of torn or deformed foliage or fruit may be included

Rococo Period Correctness 25 Points

*airy *graceful *height greater than width *fresh *crisp *curves, tendrils

-weighty -robust -rigid -lacks curves

Design Correctness 25 Points

*balanced but not rigidly symmetrical *open, airy design *tips curving *design taller than wide *no focal area *many flower stems showing *flowers have "nodding" room

-too many heavy forms used -top heavy -focal area grouping -massed too tightly -flower stems all hidden -accessory scale too heavy

Color Suitability 20 Points

*delicate *pastel *varied *no color grouping *analagous or monochromatic harmonies *minor contrast in dark or bright TOUCHES

-too many vivid or dark colors -too much vivid or dark color -needed more color variety -one color in a straight, diagonal or lazy S-line -lacks a dominant color

Appropriateness of Materials, Container 20 Points

*appropriately delicate vase (handles or cupid stem allowed) *tendrils and curves in plant material about equal to amount of round forms *accessory (if used) finely scaled and in keeping with design spirit

-appears too modern -container lines too formal, straight -container too shiny -too many round forms -too stiff appearing -lacks curves

Condition 10 Points

*particular attention to fresh, crisp appearance

Georgian Period Correctness 25 Points

*mass design *symmetrical balance *triangular outline *formal *horticulturally perfect materials

-oval rather than triangular outline -too open and light -mediocre plant materials -too casual appearing

Design Correctness 25 Points

*no focal area *flowers fall loosely over vase rim *plant material approximately twice container height *Early Georgian moderately massive *Late Georgian more open, with more curving lines *one color or kind of material predominating (typical of some Late Georgian designs)

-conscious grouping in focal area -container lip too dominant -one sided -materials too finely scaled -too many curves -one color or kind predominating in Early Georgian

Color Suitability 20 Points

*warm, advancing colors set off by darker cool colors *rich elegance

-too many pastels -colors too predominantly warm or cool

Appropriateness of Materials and Container 20 Points

*appropriate, similar-to-period container *container decorated *accessories typical of France, Italy or China (if used)

-container too plain -plant materials wilting, second-rate

Condition 10 Points

*all plant material used must be prime examples as horticultural perfection was an important characteristic of the period

Victorian Period Correctness 25 Points

*heavy *overflowing *ornate container *conspicuous flowers *flamboyant *wider than high

-slim -taller than wide -willowy -airy -too quiet

Design Correctness 25 Points

*compact *round *design varied with trailing line *symmetrical *contrasts of size and shape *proportion of flowers to container about equal

-triangular -off center -container too large -plant materials too tall -rhythmic pattern of sizes -too many voids -appearance of falling apart at center

Color Suitability 20 Points

*spotty effect *colors heavy, rich *no set patterns or harmonies

-one color dominating -color grouped -center of interest -pastels dominating -colors graded from dark to light

Appropriate Materials and Container 25 Points

*conspicuously marked flowers *container ornate, full-blown *flowers fully open

-straight-sided, plain container -container too modern appearing -too many buds and small flowers -too many tendrils or spike forms -accessories too delicate or French appearing -not enough varying materials -one plant or color dominating

Condition   (all Periods)   10 Points

*fresh *unwilted *crisp *prime *clean

-wilted -dirty -dust -chipped container or accessory -damaged or deformed (particularly Georgian, is allowed in Dutch-Flemish)

CHARACTERISTICS OF MINOR PERIODS IN FLOWER ARRANGING

Egypt

. clarity of outline in container, materials and design
. colors bright and strong; brilliant harmonies
. limited to two or three colors
. Lotus, Papyrus, Lily and the Phoenix Bird had special significance
SPIRIT: Exotic, Dignified. Orderly Simplicity

Greece-Rome

. garlands, swags, wreaths of symmetrical design
. little record of flowers used in containers for decorative purposes
. ivy, laurel and grains were favored plants
. symmetry and beauty of form
. bright clear colors, fragrance important
. tightly grouped fruits in cornucopias or pottery baskets or trays (Greece)
. flowers arranged loosely in baskets with voids between branches (Rome)
SPIRIT: Emphasis on beauty of form (particularly the human). Simplicity (Greek) More lavish and ornate (Roman)

Byzantine

. major contribution was an awareness of the cone and the spiral
. tight stylized designs taken from mosaic patterns
. their designs are reflected in our "topiary" fruit, flower and leaf cones
. color harmonies were knowledgeably handled, vivid and scintillating as jewels
SPIRIT: Exotic richness. Oriental dignity

Persia

. pyramidal outline
. vivid analagous, monochromatic and complementary harmonies are determining factors
. advancing colors predominate with accents of receding tones
. tulips, narcissus and fruits favored
. tapestries and rugs afford design ideas
. containers simple; of pottery, terra cotta, tile
SPIRIT: Rich, exotic medley of colors

Renaissance

. floral meanings such as poppy for sleep, narcissus for beauty, etc.
. symmetrical, unstudied designs, open, almost airy appearance, though some were tightly bunched
. container and flowers same proportion OR flowers up to two times taller than container
. pattern outlines included the arc, ellipse and triangle
. small flowers preferred
. cucumber appeared in decoration and display, as well as melons, figs olives, grapes and peaches
. dried materials in della Robbia handling and fruits and vegetables were generously but casually laid on round trays or in baskets
. colors, bright, vivid, no specific harmony between color of flowers and container
. elaborately decorated containers
. tulips and peonies were not used
. spirals of metal or twisted candles rose from some designs
SPIRIT: Unstudied, not dramatic. Slow awakening to sensitivity to form, floral beauty and rich textures

China
. plants had deep symbolic meaning
. rhythm and movement unrestrained
. scale, dominance, rhythm and unity are principles employed
. mass design dominated by one major line with several subordinate ones
. one line, one idea, one flower dominates
. floral material and container about same height, giving design a square, low, broad effect
. bright, showy flowers, analogous harmonies were favored
. vases round or four-sided of pottery or porcelain or bronze; plain or decorated with birds, dragons or plants such as the willow
. a tall vase of flowers and a low basket of flowers, fruits or plants often combined in a single composition. Fungus and rocks included
. bases used under footless containers
. accessories never included Chinese figures, birds or Buddha in authentic designs. Books, scrolls, incense burners, fruits, real or sculptured were used **WITH** not **IN** the designs.

Baroque
. reflected in Flemish-Dutch, French and Italian Baroque Periods
. symmetrical design, more height than width
. large flowers often used at outer edges, no focal area
. the Hogarth 'lazy S' often outlined or appeared within oval or elliptical designs
. colors were dark or vivid rather than pastel
. flowers massive, conspicuous
. urns, tall vases, low baskets
. a variety of accessories, including fruits, figures, jewelry, shells
. French Baroque was lighter and more graceful than Italian or Dutch-Flemish
SPIRIT: ponderous richness, robust, masculine

Early American
. primitive simplicity, mixed bouquet
. dooryard flowers, herbs, grasses, geraniums
. no studied color harmonies
. rustic textures
. commonplace, functional containers of earthenware, wood, common metals
. baseless jugs, gourds, basket forms
. backgrounds of pine or wallpaper; hangings of homespun or dimity
SPIRIT: Sturdy, functional pioneer, cheerful, frugal

Neo-Classic   (Classic Revival)
. rigorous, symmetry and straight lines replaced the sprightly Rococo swirls
. colors limited to two to four, wheat, ivy and laurel popular
. includes Regency, Directoire, Empire and Federal Periods

English Regency
. elegant distinction, straight-sided urns, swags

French Directoire
. not completely symmetrical, no focal area
. scale smaller than Empire
. extremes in height and slenderness; in balance and fineness of materials
. colors of turquoise, sage green; greyed cool colors plus ash rose, lime, light yellow

French Empire
. triangular and more compact than Rococo and Directoire, but less massive than French Baroque

. roses were favorites, combined round and spike forms
. no focal area
. metal urn with columnar base, also porcelain, alabaster, bisque
. Roman and Egyptian motifs (lions heads, sphinx, winged griffin) portrayed Napoleon's campaigns
. fruit and flower accessories also used
. colors, red, green, white, gold, royal purple and black plus greyed values of earlier French Periods

Federal American

. symmetrical, massed designs, but rather open
. flowers over container lip with minor Rococo curves
. designs may be low mounds simulating carved mantel decoration of the Period arranged in low containers OR arranged in tall classic vases, epergnes or compound vases
. native and cultivated fruits and flowers, colors varied
. velour textured wallpaper, also narrow striped and rosetted wallpaper backgrounds
. eagle and symbols depicting the thirteen states
SPIRIT: Stability and patriotic pride

American Williamsburg

. showing French influence but less sophisticated, and
. Georgian influence but less formal
. flowers lightly grouped at the top, more tightly grouped at container rim
. proportion of height to container from one to four-five times container
. fan shape, rectangular or triangular
. flowers often low over the container rim, often almost concealing container
. containers include classic urns, epergnes, cornucopias, five-finger Posy holders of silver, glass, Spode, Lustre
. a few sprigs of wheat and barley may be combined with fresh flowers OR
. all dried flowers may be used
. materials of fine quality
. fruit and flowers used as accessories
SPIRIT: Stately dignity

Art Nouveau

. birth of arts and crafts for the common man
. open, unaffected designs
. branches often used in a manner similar to Japanese or round and elliptical designs
. containers often taller than material they contain
. colors muted, dusty rose, mauve, buff (bright intense color penalized)
. lacy, fernlike foliage and baby's breath in bouquets of flowers
. vases more simple, lightly decorated

Spain

. low color keying, rich dignified, dark, plus golds and rich greens, iron
. showing Persian influence

Mexico

. reflecting both Spanish and Indian heritage
. bold clear colors, particularly orange and blue
. semi-tropic foliages and flowers
. religious connotations

Pacific Islands

. exotic, tropical materials
. bold, clear colors
. free, open designs

Contemporary Flora Design Categories and Styles

The major divisions of 20th Century flora artistry fall easily into two categories based on **construction.**

Radial Structure
(Older Style)
Based on the radial structure with an area of interest (subtle or strong) at or near the single point of emergence, with interest tapered to the outer edges. *Includes Period Traditional, Modern Conventional Line, Mass, Mass-Line, also many Free'd types, Transitionals and 'Isms so constructed.*

Interest Equated
Newer Style
Emphasis equated over the whole and no single point of emergence required or focal area emphasized. Includes Creative Abstracts, Assemblages, Avant Garde, Constructions, Extra-Sensory, Free'd types, Kinetics and 'Isms, etc. so constructed.

Various "styles" borrowed from the field of painting have created a great deal of confusion in scheduling, classifying and judging. They are defined here briefly to help the Judges avoid slipping on these semantic "banana peels" and in spite of the obvious danger of over- simplification, and the realization that art is not static but in a state of ferment and constant redefinition.

These quicksands of terminology and interpretation become a matter of concern lest through applying outdated critera, we exclude some activity that has become operable through further shifts in space, substance, identity and meaning.

We need a less binding interpretation to be applied to that design which is neither clearly collage, assemblage or avant-garde, but an amalgamation of all three or even some as yet unrevealed technique or choice, *or even an untouched possibility. Could we call these "Extensions", "Transitions", "Released", "Adaptations"? Names come and go, Free Style, Free Form served for a time to define a floral transition period.*

The acceptance of a new standard, broader and related to new space concepts would ease the task of classifying and judging these bewildering hybrids now coming into existence.

It is well to remember that these present types overlap and that flora arranging is an art and strict classification is neither desirable nor possible due to the fact that most definitions are arbitrary, and may apply only if the designer's intent is known. The dominant feature of any type is the criteria for classification and the Judges must know what to expect when faced with these in a Flower Show Schedule.

It is suggested that more creativity is allowed if the Schedule simply supplies a title and lets the 'type', 'style', 'structure' be designer's choice.

CONTEMPORARY STYLES

Interpretive, Impressionism, Expressionism

(The three terms have come to generally be used interchangeably to reduce confusion)

These are designs which use the elements in such a way as to require emotional and visual response. They are visual echos of an inner thought, impression or emotion.

Impressionism

communication of inner feelings as produced by SEEING a place, person or object. Objective impressionism is a result of the arranger's impression of an object previously seen (i.e. sunset, bullfight). Represents vision into form.

Expressionism

produced as a result of a thought, idea, or sensation. Subjective expressionism is the expression of a feeling (anger, humility). Represents feeling into form. More private, personal. Most truly modern.

Fauvism

is a particular type of interpretation in which intense, bold colors and **distorted** shapes are emphasized.

Surrealism

attempts to portray dreams, nightmares. Depicts contexts and juxtapositions impossible in Nature. Fantastic, weird, haunted, often sinister. Interpretive.

Cubism

based on the fact that an object changes shape as it is looked at from different angles, different planes. Varying angles and planes are blended into one. Picasso's vase painting showing a vase top, sides, inside, and bottom all blended into one illustrates.

Futurism

overlapping planes in sequence represents motion — based on the concept that no object, whether moving or stationary is seen in isolation. Duchamp's "NUDE DESCENDING THE STAIRCASE" illustrates.

Purism

construction of a design generally using plant materials and objects purely as straight lines, circles, triangles, cubes, cones. Objects are seen and used as pure form. An orange is used for its circular form, clipped palm for triangular and a straight branch for line. Usually non-objective rather than interpretive.

Creative Modern, Transitional, Extension, Release, Free'd Styles

A stage in the progress of floral design. Combined features of both passing and coming style, released from confining traditional, conventional rules and use of principles. Irregular, fluid, forceful boundaries marked the dividing line between old and new ... between past radial, as-grown construction and coming interest-equated, abstract styles. Increasing use of eclectic and non-art materials drawn from various sources. Extending beyond the basic, established geometric patterns of the past (i.e. circle, triangle, etc.), of no pre-determined outline. Uses Nature's infinite variations of form to dictate design pattern with directions difficult to match through manipulation by human hand. Curvilinear, sweeping shapes often accidentally distorted. May have more than one area of interest, or a lifted or subtle focal area. Balance increasingly asymmetrical. Materials may be other than naturally grown (i.e. rolled, knotted leaves). Spontaneity, position, space emerging. Free'd style using free forms exampled by pulling a rubber band into rhythmic, continuously flowing lines. Use of form, color, space, lighting at designer's discretion. Includes any design that is not totally traditional, conventional, forerunner of abstract designs. Extremely popular.

The above types overlap, and may be conventional (radial) or creative abstract in concept and/or construction.

Assemblage

abstract designs using flora combined with unrelated, non-art and art objects fitted together in a pleasingly aesthetic manner to create a cohesive unified whole which evolves from the accumulation of eclectic components. Since its source is often obsolescence, the finished works may closely depict everyday life because the components contain and gain connotations that unmarked materials lack. Wordlessly associative, they add a vernacular realism heightened by the process and concept of abstraction.

Non-art includes "throw-aways", artifacts, "found" bits and fragments with "history" . . . rusted refuse, machinery scrap, wood, stone and possessions enriched by use, deterioration and fragmentation. The disparate selections are generally unusual, not often found in combination, thus differing from Still Life designs which combine related, more common, actual-size objects true to their function in every day life and events. (p. 511)

In assemblage, each element need not be 'abstracted'. Abstract concepts can predominate even if some plant materials emerge head-up as grown. An arrangement with accessory is not considered an assemblage. The parts may or may not be physically fastened together, and may adhere to the background. Schedules govern staging in niche, on pedestal, free standing, with or without background panel or triptych. In any case, Judges assess color, textural unity, proportions, sizes and positioning relative to space within and alloted, and the visual and emotional appeal and reaction as fits the scheduled requirements. Review Abstract, Niche, Still Life.

The creative method of Assemblage is that of juxtaposition . . . "setting a thing beside another without connective" as differentiated from radial construction which uses form and color transition or "passage" to soften the shock of discontinuity, and to bridge disassociation of image. It has been noted that a quite mysterious prehension, envelopment and involvement takes place when the 'right' combination has been achieved. Each element is altered and enriched by its participation in the gestalt of the assembled unit, taking on a new identity and aesthetic harmony. Judges must realize this harmony of total expression is of utmost importance. Without it, the Assemblage is merely flora and refuse masquerading as art.

Collage

abstract assemblage mounted in wall-hung panel or frame, secured by gluing a combination of diverse low-relief plant materials and usually non-art objects to a plain, painted or textured surface to emphasize texture and 3-D effects. Objects are organized in bas-relief projecting from the background. Comes from **collé** (Fr.) meaning "to paste or glue", so must have this characteristic to apply. Valentines and folk art using butterfly wings, feathers, arrowheads, pebbles preceded today's creative collages. Differs from plaque which consist of conventional organization, radial focal, flora as-grown, and similar, related objects and dried flora. (p. 542)

Constructions

"putting together" by ingenious organization to form a complex structure from a number of simpler forms. Copies Assemblage, may masquerade as stabiles, stamobiles*, other. Time and space treated as material components. Dynamic linear tensions, bold forms flow together to form harmonious construct. Contrived construction materials might be single dried hydrangea florets glued to cattails angled for dynamic depth in three dimensions. Major characteristic is 4-D, architectural, clarified, sculptural effects.

*coined by author, 1966

Extra-Sensory, Kinetics, Mobiles, Vibratiles, Other

those designs which involve senses other than seeing and scent. Employ sound, actual or implied movement. Action and space stressed. Amplify communication between viewer and design, actively and subliminally exploits subjective sensations. Contrived of all manner objects. Refer to 424, 431.

Avant-Garde, Progressives, Liberated, Other

freed, creative use of imaginative, unorthodox, unconventional design ideas, containers, backgrounds, materials, techniques. Respects flora and aesthetic effects. Departure from norm rather than mere boldness. Liberated . . . taking liberties with principles through exaggeration, angle, positions, creative adaptations (individual take-offs from original). Space, contrived forms, positions, movement, light, sound expected. Takes off on very newest, latest trends in art, architecture, psychology, other fields. Little evidence of past trends, styles. Epitome of "doing it my way". Backgrounds, containers may be featured, play decisive role. Flora included or design becomes foreign to our medium.

New design names often prove faddy, short lived; definitions should not be allowed to stifle creative, new directions; use to point out a component's activity, diversify use of an element, or to illustrate variation of a principle. Names understood by all do make schedule writing more specific, enabling attention to be drawn to combinations, transparencies, reflections, projections, sound. In line with this, Schedules may specify **"Projectiles"** (some part seems to be hurtling outward); **"Eclectics"** (combination of diverse materials, ideas from various periods, sources) Eclectics may also classify as **"Transitionals"** in being a freer style than Conventionals. Judges must be prepared to judge vanguard, challenging, thought-provoking, new-century aspects. Refer to Abstract (405), Extra-Sensory (431) Assemblage (387)

It is interesting to note that a design may fall into one of these types only after completion (with exception of collage and mobile), and with the artist not knowing, planning or even caring which type it will be (or be something totally new), by merely following her creative urges.

All creative designers require understanding of **plastic organization** which involves spacial positioning in such a way as to make entire space occupied by the design and all its parts cooperate in all three dimensions of height, width and depth. A plastically organized unit has no detectable front, sides or back . . . it is integrated in all dimensions.

Because of their actual and/or visually fitted-together structure, and strategically placed interest areas, Assemblages, Constructions, Avant, etc. require appreciation of plastic organization used to create and manipulate space and physical components in such a way as to vitalize movement. Disparate elements are experienced according to their position in relation to their surroundings, to each other and to the design principles. The eclectic parts, without losing their own character, take on an expanded identity, vitalize space, interact with each other giving the design and space which contains it a cohesive living and aesthetic quality with no one part more arresting than any other. Each area of disparate and tensional interest has its own power to impact viewer attention . . . yet are seen as an integrated whole, thus a new entity of memorable distinction is created through visual and subliminal interaction.

The Judge must evaluate how knowledgeably the designer manipulated force of form, textures, positions and lines which give each its dynamic quality. Though relatively isolated, when plastically organized, all elements unified by color, purpose, space, repetition and position vitalizes Einstein's fourth dimension . . . time . . . taken to observe the entire complex composition. Plastic relations produce changes. It is to clearly understood and appreciated that relationships never leave related things untouched.

It is suggested that to give creativity full rein, and to allow emergence of still undefined methods, classes state:

A: Style (i.e. Assemblage, Avant, etc.): Abstract.

B (i.e. Assemblage, Avant, etc.): Other (may be something just over horizon)

SUGGESTED SCALE FOR CREATIVE TRANSITIONAL, OTHER

Design: principles applied	30	Creativity, Individuality, Spontaneity	25
Suitability of Relationships	30	. departure from conventional	
. colors, textures, aesthetic appeal,		Distinction	15
character, etc.		. condition . construction . conformity	
		. superiority	

SUGGESTED SCALE FOR CREATIVE ASSEMBLAGE, AVANT GARDE, OTHER

Design: plastically org.	30	Creativity, Individuality	25
. effective combinations		. perceptive, courageous, singular	
. interest equated . 4-D		. choices, positions, space use	
Distinction	20	. emotional communication	
. conformity to type, schedule		Dramatic Impact	25
. aesthetic rightness		. unexpected, high styled, tensional	
. execution, techniques, condi.		. departure from precedent	
		. rememberability	

388

20th Century Traditional/Conventional Design

Early in the 20th Century a style developed which used the best of Oriental line softened with Occidental mass and color and which spoke a literal message. Accessories were used to express a theme . . . a complete break from the past and Distinction appeared in the judging scales of points.

20th Century Traditional separates easily into two categories (1) Imitative of Nature (Realistic or Naturalistic) and (2) Imitative of the Past (Decorative).

20th Century Traditional has evolved into Conventional in which there are still the same main types of Mass, Mass-Line and Line. Mass are usually decorative; Mass-Line and Line mainly in the Imitative or Realistic category, and with Mass-Line being favored.

Designs were based on geometric forms . . . the cube, the sphere and the cone from which were derived the oval, triangular, vertical, horizontal and also the Crescent and Hogarth lines. Most designs entered in classes requesting specific-line arrangements are essentially decorative rather than expressive or interpretive. They are often designated for some specific spot in the home, e.g. mantle, hall table, etc.

Realistic

The Realistic category is a photographic attempt to closely approximate scenes in nature, they are copies of a subject, a literal picture. For instance a triangular design using pussy willow, daffodils, dead or dormant branches and a bird figurine graphically depicts a spring scene. The type differed from the Oriental in that the interpretations were more individual, whereas in the Oriental, it is set by tradition in the materials themselves and the placements. Realistic accessory objects were used to bolster and clarify the theme.

Natural growth habits were copied in that all lines sprang in orderly movement from a central growth point and a sense of depth was achieved through the use of turning flowers in profile and the natural vanishing point perspective . . . small items high and in back accords with the natural fact that the farther away an object is . . . the smaller it appears. Atmospheric haze was copied by the use of low intensity hues in the back and sides of a design simulating the natural fact that the farther away an object is the less brilliant, paler it appears. The natural growth was copied by the use of a well-defined focal area which gradually, through gradation of size and inclusions of voids, was broken up as the eye was moved toward the outer edges; this copied the spreading growth of a bare tree from main trunk dividing and redividing into progressively smaller segments interspersed with widening triangles of space.

Nature was again represented in the fact that balance was more often asymmetrical than symmetrcal, in the favoring of simple, natural containers and the grouping of kinds and colors; there is continuity in a natural landscape, seldom does one plant grow alone naturally but is accompanied by a group or grove of others of similar form and color.

Decorative

The Decorative category placed emphasis on mass and color. Flowers were used for flower's sake, not to express any particular mood or geographical location. The intent was purely ornamental, based on sensory appeal, pleasing to the eye, calming, pretty, often romantic rather than nostalgic and requiring nothing of the viewer except placid enjoyment. They are equally at home in casual or formal decor depending upon the character or degree of refinement.

Characteristics

It should be noted that the characteristics of 20th Century Tra-ditional/Conventional shared by both categories are:
- well-defined focal area, stressing orderly growth movement
- depth achieved through gradation of size and color
- all lines arising from a common point
- simple container
- grouping of kinds and colors with transitionary shapes and values
- asymmetrical balance or balance by placement preferred, but symmetrical used

- patterns of design follow the cube, sphere, cone
- consciousness of color harmonies, e.g. analagous, contrasting and an awakening realization of color's effect on balance, proportion, rhythm and dominance
- dried and fresh plant materials used
- realistic accessories often used to portray theme, placed IN, or on the edge of the container as well as beside
- miniatures became popular

Adaptations of 20th Century designs (refer to p. 386, Creative Modern) appear in which the characteristics are employed but with a more free and natural manner, with little or no attention to the "rules" which caged the earlier designers. These are judged accordingly with new relaxations. The rules are mentioned herein to point up where changes have occurred.

SUGGESTED SCALE OF POINTS FOR CONVENTIONAL DESIGN

Design	30	Color 25
. according to the principles		. according to the principles
Appropriate to type	25	. according to schedule
. focal area		Distinction 20
. geometric pattern		. aesthetic appeal
. color grouping and rigid harmonies		. compatibility of character
. vanishing point gradations		. craftsmanship
		. condition

Design

At the beginning of the 20th Century a merry war was declared between the flower arrangers and the horticulturists who shuddered at the cutting of a long and perfect stem, at the use of less-than-perfect-sized flowers, crooked stems and bare branches.

But the arrangers were not diverted from their use, particularly *in the Mass-Line and Line designs. The linear pattern is stressed and* even in mass designs there is a sincere attempt to show off each individual flower. Designers began manipulating their material to a great extent to force it to follow the dictates of the prescribed geometric pattern. Rolled leaves and the like were devised to hide the offending "prickett holders" now known as needlepoints.

All the principles must be considered in judging these designs which still appear in great abundance in flower shows and fairs. Too often the designer becomes so involved in story-telling that the design qualities are neglected or play a secondary role, such a situation must be penalized.

Dominance

Even though it may be the smallest area, the most dominant part of this type is a well-defined focal area which needs only enough power to catch the interest and direct it on its rhythmic way through the design. The focal area is placed just above the lip of the container or the point of emergence of the stems. If emphasis is not fully achieved due to a breadth of color or looseness of construction, penalty is taken since both rhythm and dominance suffer.

A focal which is too high and unrelated to the container rim or point of line emergence is to be faulted. An overly assertive focal with no transition colors, sizes or forms to lead the eye on is to be deducted. The focal should not be split by differences in size or color of blooms.

The purpose of the focal is to attract the eye and not to halt it completely. *A too arresting focal is called a bull's eye and is deducted. There must be only one dominating focal area in the design; another or several equally dominant areas brings penalty.*

*Focals usually achieved through use of massing, brighter color, un-*usual shape or differing texture. A focal may be of a light value if the rest of the design is even more subdued. An arrangement of red salvia for the spiky material with a focal of grey-lavender mums would be penalized for a weak focal.

Spike forms are releasing forms, bright colors are dominating. *Target forms are holding or dominant form, and greyed values are releasing* A red spike form (salvia) used with small greyed mums which are holding in form but releasing in color would show a lack of understanding of the function of form and color in a design, would result in an inadequate focal and subsequent penalty.

20th Century Traditional/Conventional requires use of 'filler' material as transition to carry the eye from the focal to the outer limits of the design. While this focal area is admittedly the most prominent part of the design, it must appear as a **part** of the whole and not seem separate; the gradation and transition of sizes and colors helps to integrate it into the design.

Balance

Balance is achieved in any manner with asymmetrical or balance by placement being favored, but not required. The visual weight must be balanced on both sides of the imaginary axis. For instance, a balance by placement crescent would be penalized if the top part of the curve was weak, thin and short in proportion to the bottom part. Any visual "tipping" is to be deducted. It should appear stable, and neither top nor bottom heavy. If visual weight is divided in the focal area deduction is made. Balance is also achieved by keeping large and dark flowers low and a dark container and base may have a comparable effect, but must be balanced by a much larger proportion of light value material in the upper part of the design.

Proportion

The voids should be well-shaped and a variation in their sizes is necessary for contrast and interest. But no one void should be so wide as to seem to split the design. There must be variation in the length of stems as well as in their placements. One frequent fault is a lack of adequate plant material in proportion to the container area. Points are forfeited when the design needs more height or width to balance the visual weight of the container. A guide for pleasing proportion in this type is:

. arrangement to container: material 2/3. Container 1/3
. arrangement to accessory: arrangement 2/3. Accessory not exceeding 1/3

Note this is a **Guide** and must by no means be taken as the only aesthetic proportion possible.

However, it is characteristic that within the design itself proportions are:

Mass   :solids exceed the voids
Massed-Line :voids equal the solids
Line   :voids exceed the solids, otherwise deduction is
            made

Scale

While scale is important in any design, it is particularly necessary that objects be the right size in relation to each other when they are so closely grouped and particularly in those designs using accessories in the realistic category. Flowers which are too small in relation to the container will make it appear even more heavy and oversize. There should be effective transition from larger to medium to small-scale materials progressing from the focal area on out.

Rhythm

Rhythm is an important principle since the eye movement in massed line and line depends upon the knowledgeable handling of color, form and texture to carry the eye along in a smooth and orderly manner. Crossing stems divert the eye and "holes" interrupt the rhythm and are penalized in this type. There is to be an easy gradation from the massing at the focal area to the voids and lesser solids at the outer edges.

The flow of movement should relate to the container. A too heavy, compact or dominating focal area will impede rhythmic movement and make the design seem bottom heavy. A large bloom placed in the outer edge may be penalized. Similarly sized round forms grouped too evenly equalize interest and halt visual movement. If the rhythmic structure has been interrupted by the split direction of two parts (such as two large leaves) penalty is taken.

A straight obvious horizontal, vertical or diagonal line of blooms, forms or color may seem to split the design or disrupt the rhythm and are to be deducted. An accessory is placed close to the design, in front or to the side, so the eye does not jump distractingly from one to the other, or else it must be placed so the curving or pointing lines of material draw attention to it, and it in turn directs the eye back, thus making it a working part of the design. If the accessory seems to stand alone, with no part in the design, it draws penalty. A figure is not generally used outside a Crescent, but behind the focal so it forms an actually visual axis with the curves of the crescent balancing on either side.

Contrast

Designers were just becoming aware of flowers as forms. Of the tulip as a cylinder, pom mum as a sphere, a rolled leaf as a cone. But when too many such forms are used interest is divided and there is confusion as to where to look next. One form, color or line should be-dominant but it needs some small contrasts for interest. If a designer used all round forms in a round outline, in a round-bodied container then dominance is achieved, but the design will lack interest, be monotonous, needing contrast or variety in all its unity.

A design should not present a solid, heavy texture overall; smooth, glossy texture carefully used with the dull, gives a design a certain sparkle and gaiety more subtle but just as effective as that of color.

Appropriateness to Type   (Background, Base, Container)

Backgrounds in the Traditional are expected to stay in their place . . . subordinate to the design and of a color just different enough so the design is not lost against it. Any background pattern is limited to that such as found in muted home wallpaper.

A base, like the background and container, should not be so outstanding, ornate or prominent as to call attention to itself. Queerly formed, intricate or twisted receptacles "detract from good design ˋas the eye cannot help exploring their unpleasing contortions". (How times **have** changed!) Containers must be simple, understated.

The plant material is expected to dominate over the container, background and accessory. A "rule" of the type was that the container rimline must be broken with a piece of material drooping over to achieve unity between the two. Another "rule" was that "a pitcher must pour" so the design was to be constructed as to seem to flow out of the spout with the focal at or near the handle. Leniency is allowed in judging such designs in today's show, the "rules" are mentioned so they may be modified.

If the Schedule specifically calls for a Crescent design and a Vertical Line is **exhibited,** or if the Schedule prohibits accessories and one is used, enough points must be deducted so the exhibit cannot place. The points can be pro-rated among the qualities of design, distinction, and appropriateness. Such blatant disregard of the Schedule deserves a more severe penalty than a slip-up over lack of a well-defined focal or some other expected characteristic of the type.

Suitability

The category of depicting a realistic theme is often misunderstood by the novice who may attempt to enter a tray garden or the like. Such would be disqualified by the Classification Committee or eliminated by the Judges for lacking conformity to the concept of flora design which involves the use of a container, mechanics and plant materials arranged according to the principles of design.

Much attention was originally paid to what was suitable, what went with what! Roses only in fine vases; roses with calendulas . . . satin and seersucker . . . was frowned upon. Judging of Traditional today should be more lenient in these respects.

Horizontal

Horizontal designs are usually symmetrical, free-standing and a favorite for table classes. The design may be 1½ to 4 times the container's longest diameter, depending on the visual weight of the material.

The center should not be depressed or overly compact, it should blend smoothly due to reducing mass, into the outer ends of the design. A separation or break in rhythm from the focal to the longest primary lines is penalized. The bare stems of the primaries must be covered by the filler or focal area materials. The focal is achieved and transition obtained in the same manner as in the upright designs.

The pattern of the design when viewed from above or in profile must be interesting with well-placed voids and solids. A rigid, stiff effect should be penalized. A "rule" of the time was that plant material was not to hang down and touch the tabletop. If intended for a table, guests should not be treated to a view of too much bare container, the Judge takes the position of the guest to ascertain this.

If a clear glass container is used the stem pattern within the glass is considered and deductible if not orderly. If a holder is used in clear glass, it must be disguised or hidden.

COLOR

Harmonies

The trend was to the use of very definite color harmonies such as complementary, analagous and the like. While modern Schedules seldom require classes based on a specific harmony, they might wish to do so to recall this particular period or as an instructive device to suit a scheduled purpose.

In judging, any deviation (other than incidental colors e.g. bracts, centers, etc.) is to be penalized. If the class specifies a particular harmony, the Judge deducts one-fourth the total color points for lack of conformity. At first, in Traditional, the "rule" was that the color of the container had to be a part of the harmony, later relaxation allowed the container, or background to form one part of say, an analagous harmony and this practice is now followed though it is more difficult to achieve smooth movement in related harmonies.

Grouping

Colors in the design are to be grouped carefully in an orderly progression from darkest or most brilliant in the focal area to progressively less assertive values in the outer periphery. The use can be reversed but only if great care is exercised. That is, if a light colored focal area is used, the dark or bright colored flowers used in the outer boundaries must be smaller, and much finer in order not to steal the show from the true focal area. There must be variety in color spacing and shadings, but a spotty, scattered effect is to be penalized.

Color is often distinctively used to outline and strengthen the design form. To illustrate, a Hogarth curve is first established with dormant branches and then yellow daffodils used following the outline. A large "skip" which leaves a "hole" rather than a smooth progression of color, disrupts rhythm, and might affect other principles. This is not to say that the color must be tightly packed or compact . . . rather the flowers may be loosely placed, but touching or pointing to the next one so the eye shifts smoothly and easily up the design.

Darker values low in the design should be balanced by lighter values at the outer edges. One hue or value should be dominant. There should be some contrast of color, value or chroma for interest and variety, even in a one-color monochromatic harmony.

The proportion of dark areas should balance the light. Pleasing proportion is gained if there is one part bright color, two parts medium color and three parts light color. A small area of bright color should be used to balance a much larger area of light color or low value. A vice-versa situation is penalized.

Color sandwiching is a fault in this type. For example, a layer of red, a layer of yellow, topped by a layer of white is an extreme example of sandwiching which halts the rhythmic movement. Cool colors are usually placed above the warm colors and light colors above the dark.

A sequence of color or a modifier smooths the rhythmic flow, e.g. lavender between pink and blue; green between red and yellow, although too much green can be a detrimental factor in a colorful design.

Distinction

Distinction in this type of design is usually achieved through the aesthetic appeal, general quality or superiority of the whole evidenced by a complete correctness in the use of the principles. Mechanics must be completely covered or disguised so they do not show or penalty is taken under distinction. However, the appearance of a collar or ring of foliage around the bottom is an inept handling to be deducted. If a cup holder is used, the needles should not be evident.

Overcrowding is a common fault and reduces the score. Simplicity, meaning restraint in the amounts and colors and kinds, is ever distinctive.

Distinction cannot be present when the Schedule requirements are ignored. If the Schedule requests a Line arrangement stressing rhythm and the exhibit is well-done, but is a Massed Line, it cannot be given full points as a **DISTINCTIVE LINE** if it **isn't** a Line design.

The textures of all items used should be compatible, with sturdy coarse blooms in heavy containers and delicate flowers in finer vases.

Condition is considered under distinction in this scale of points. Plant material must be clean, fresh and turgid. Wilting or damage is penalized. Condition is not to be confused with malformed branches, non-typical colors, or contorted stems which often serve the arranger by supplying materials to form the design pattern. The lack of proper conditioning and soiled materials indicate a lack of attention to detail in the preparation and execution of the design.

SUMMARY

Design 30 Points

*well handled focal *dark flowers low *visually stable *rhythm smooth, easy *accessory contributes to rhythm in color, line, placement *enough contrast for interest

-weak, loose focal, divided focal -too dominant focal -seems to tip, bottom or top heavy -lacks transition of color, size -rhythm interrupted, rough -sandwiched colors -design too short or tall for container

Appropriateness 25 Points

*has well-defined focal *colors grouped *pattern follows geometric form (circle, etc.) *simple container *container and background subordinate to design *container rim broken by leaf, etc.

-too many interest centers -too free form -too much mass to be a line, etc. -elaborate container -container or background too dominant

Color 25 Points

*scheduled harmony complete *colors grouped *color handled in orderly progression from dark to light *color follows design form

-receding color in focal leaves a "hole" -too much bright color high in design -lacks color contrast -color sandwiched

Distinction 20 Points

*simplicity of number of kinds, colors, etc. *according to Schedule *fresh *compatible relationships *well constructed

-mechanics show -lacks schedule conformity -poorly built -wilting -too many conflicting textures, colors

Modern Creative

Almost simultaneously with the progress of the 20th Century Conventional both decorative and realistic designs, we find a maverick group of designers searching for creative release from the prevailing tedium of the medium; rebelling against the set "rules," "pretty" designs, geometric patterns and copies of naturalistic scenes.

They came to feel that the copying of a scene or a set geometric pattern was nothing more than a display of mechanical skill; a craft, *rather than a creative achievement. The word "originality" entered the* flower show vocabulary, a word later to be more or less replaced by "creativity" and "personal expression."

*In direct contrasts to the Traditional/Conventional realism with its preoccupation with the imitation of nature (sight), the modernists swung to non-imi-*tative, with emphasis on the dramatization of the inner self, inner feelings, emotions and ideas (insight), executed with combinations of organic and inorganic materials but still inseparable from the principles of design and a common point of radiating emergence. Natural scenes were still depicted but with greater imagination and freedom of inter-*pretation, not so realistically or literally; the Creative Class was born, its popularity continues.*

As the trend gained momentum, words such as "impressionism", "expressionism", and "interpretive", "objective", "subjective", "Fauvism", "Cubism" and "Surrealism" were borrowed from the painter's *vocabulary. Such "ives" and "isms" may be either transitional or pure abstract in concept and construction.*

The characteristics of Modern Creative Designs are:

Modern Creative Concept
. *bold, commanding, tall designs or wide, fluid, forceful*
. *simplicity (selections often limited to 2–3)*
. *communicative, eclectic, unconventional*
. dramatic impact, high style, daring, often long lasting
. perceptive selectivity, unusual combinations of materials
. *complete freedom of flora, colors, positions, mechanics*
. *flora usually used as it grows, though some abstraction occurs (See Design)*
. *combinations of non-art objects, flora (Refer to p. 386)*
. some distortion, but objects usually recognizable (e.g., curling of leaves, knotting, clipping, etc.)

Modern Creative Construction
. *radial placement, lines from common point, or interest equated*
. *strong or subtle interest area at or near the point of common emergence*
. *space integrated, open silhouette, no pre-determined pattern*
. *may be restrained mass, massed line, pure line*
. *knotted leaves, folded back tulip petals were departures from traditional handling, natural forms*

. disciplined construction, structural clarity, the tailored look
. all design principles adhered to
. contrasts emphasized
. interesting from any angle
. little or no transition materials, no filler materials as such
. interesting silhouette, sharp contrasts in line direction, diagonal line a favorite
. greater height and width than formerly
. material dictates the pattern
. closely related or neutral colors OR maximum contrasts favored
. balance may be symmetrical, asymmetrical, always dynamic

Not every modern design will have all these attributes; these are, however, indicative of the type. The dominant classification character-istic is boldness with space integrated into the design. The Judge, faced with a class requesting modern design should compare the exhibits to the charac-teristics and deduct deviations accordingly which reflect too much tradition. Not all contemporary designs are modern for they follow old restrictive geometric patterns and rules without the spark of any degree of creative origi-nally or freshened concepts of elements and techniques characteristic of what is understood to be creative transitional designing.

SUGGESTED SCALE OF POINTS

Modern Creative

Communication   35
. expression of theme given
. clarity of exhibitor's message, personal ex-pression (not the Judge's reaction)
. perceptive selectivity of flora, container, etc., compatible with theme

Creativity   20
. dramatic impact
. high style, daring, individual
. material allowed to dic-tate pattern

Design and Transitional Character   30
. principles adhered to
. color design
. radial placement, inter-est area
. space, depth, movement
. disciplined construction
. silhouette interest
. bold

Distinction   15
. aesthetic appeal
. compatibility, simplicity
. craftsmanship
. condition

COMMUNICATION
Beauty and the Beholder

Judging interpretive designs should be an appreciative, receptive activity, not a ritual according to formula. Interpretive judging requires a high degree of perceptive power, but this must be undiluted with per-sonal prejudice or preference. It must be a fair, unbiased attempt to see as the designer saw in the objective realistic design and to feel as the designer feels in the subjective design.

Many Period and Conventional designs are retinal, they do not go be-yond the eye, they evoke a passive "isn't that pretty" response and are easier to judge. The realistic design **informs** the viewer of a scene once seen; a subjective design touches us in a more personal way, evokes a responsive feeling. Sometimes the response is subtle, almost unconscious, twinging an ache of reminder in the viewer's memory and imagination of remembered also-encountered emotions and feelings; at other times the response is clear, even violent.

Character

The Judge must be cognizant of the fact that each chosen piece in the design, organic or inorganic, has an individuality, a character of its own and must have been used in such a way that this individuality is expressed in keeping with the main idea being communicated. The expressive quality of an object is created by its form, texture, line and color and the reflective light upon it. "Antiquity" can be modern in character. Modern-appearing containers have been dug from archeological ruins, found in attics, unearthed from forest and beach. The Judge judges on the overall "spirit" communicated by the selection.

Character of texture

The modern designer points out to the Judge and the public, the unusual about the familiar, the hidden similarities, the texture below the color of the croton leaf, the expressive gesture of the reaching branch, the negative space which has taken a positive place in the interplay of match mix-match, balance counter-balance. These things communicate to the viewer even if the design is basically decorative rather than interpretive. Communication is more direct in the interpretive designs which express emotion, places, people, with or without accessories.

While texture is a design tool also valuable in the creation of harmony and interest, its greatest contribution is its expressiveness of character. The Judge must evaluate the effectiveness of its use in establishing the idea or emotion being communicated.

Character of Line

Lines are exceedingly expressive. The symbols of the modern era are space and speed and modern designs often express these, thus the diagonal thrust which represents a bird or a plane fleeing terra firma and the parabola with its ends extending to infinity are favorites.

The freedom to express any feeling or story led to the loosening of former restrictions regarding crossing lines; in Modern designs crossed vertical or horizontal lines may be used to stabilize, or diagonally, they contribute to confusion which may have been the designer's **IN-TENT**. The Judge must consider communication as well as design as he was taught it.

Character of Color

Color in Modern design is used with the realization of its psychological qualities and also as a practical design factor affecting balance, proportion and rhythm, in contrast to its earlier role mainly to "pret tify" the design.

Color harmonies may be closely related or of maximum contrasts. While dramatic impact, excitement and daring use of contrasting or strong, rich colors are characteristic of Modern design, the Judge should realize that an arrangement does not have to rely entirely on intense color to achieve force and boldness. Deep emotions can be communicated by greyed or hazy effects and subtle nuances of neutral monochromes; the Judge should train himself to credit well-handled light-valued effects.

Fewer colors should have been selected and used carefully to create depth and movement. Contrasts of value and temperature should have been employed to emphasize depth through separation of planes.

Communication is often stabliized through the display of a small neatly typed card briefly describing the inspiration.

Design

Variations of the cube, the sphere and the cone were briefly and nearly eclipsed by the parabola. While the popularity of traditional geometric lines such as the crescent and the hogarth descended, the parabola was hailed as the "most expressive line of contemporary living" probably because of its abstract quality of "into infinity", and freedom of expression. The streamlined form of dolphins, airplanes and eggs exhibit the tense, swift, graceful movement of parabolic lines, which when applied to flora art, are open at both ends and cannot be joined no matter how far extended, and thus differed from its close relative, *the crescent. The parabola, after brief glory, gave way to evolving concepts which also spelled the demise of two later briefly popular, often confused, confusing classes: Free Style, a transitional between Conventional to Creative delineated by geometric boundaries, and Free Form, of no predetermined boundary . . . an outgrowth of the art term which defines objects of irregular flowing contours (i.e. clouds).*

Line, in Modern design, appears independent of color and is used to create rhythmic vibrations and fluctuations — as a dynamic design *force rather than merely to outline form as in the Conventional Decorative.*

The realization of the effects of areas of light and dark mark the Modern creative design as well as the motion created by alternating planes of warm and cool hues, weak and strong chroma and rough and smooth textures.

There may be a certain degree of abstraction, lack of detailing in the expression of Modern design; leaves are rolled (thus altered from the natural), objects used in unexpected ways, often unrecognized and tend*ing to lose identity, but the classification factor in conformity to a Show-scheduled class is based on integration of space and depth and the boldness of form, force of color and strength of line. Refer to Abstract for Space and Depth Design.*

Balance

The balance of Modern design may be symmetrical or asymmetrical, self-contained, by placement, or by accessory. Contrary to some opinion, a symmetrical design can meet the concept of boldness and dramatic impact if the dynamic balance of interest areas within the outline are emphatic and meaningful. It must not be static, the interest areas should draw the eye about within the pattern.

Regardless of the subject, the eye demands balance and in this type, the spaces are considered as vital to visual stability as the solids. Opposing areas of space and solids on either side of the imaginary axis create a feeling of balance as well as interesting contrasts.

The balance principle must be applied, not only to height and width, but to depth perspective as well. This is judged on how adeptly the designer placed foreground, middleground and rearground materials to achieve depth equilibrium. A too-dominant foreground will hold the eye, thus upsetting depth balance. Various and varying areas of interest in the fore, middle and reargrounds should be balanced visually. The Judge must look not only at the outline for balance appraisal, but **within** the design as well. New trends demand dynamic equilibrium in preference to static repose. See Chapter on Balance

Proportion

Satisfying proportions of container, accessory's and flora design are expected. The added problem of assessing the proportion of space to solids confronts the Judge. Space within or surrounding an object allows it to appear lighter. Space injected under a heavy container or in its body (interpenetration) is often used to adjust proportion. The proportion of the focal area to the rest of the design may be adjusted in the same manner. Refer to Chapter on Proportion.

Scale

The size of the objects stand "on their own" in Modern design — less transitionary gradation is used, thus there is often greater contrast of size within the design's body and of container and accessory's as well.

The Judge must be conscious of how both space and light affect size, and either credit or penalize the designer's handling of these elements to adjust scale.

Rhythm

The concept of rhythm changed to accept the fact that continuity of form is not imperative ... that the eye, activated by the imagination, will leap a space to complete a line. A Judge faults a Modern design for lack of continuity **only** when the eye is led nowhere. The objects must have sufficient force to move the eye along the directed path or penalty may be taken. It is the balance of these forces which unifies.

The Judge must understand the designer's use of the function of color and form in achieving rhythmic movement. In Modern design releasing forms in the focal area and releasing colors are less closely spaced than formerly.

Space, as well as solids, plays its part in directing the eye. Repetition of space areas and shapes can be as effective as of solids.

Gradation of size to achieve movement is less characteristic of *Creatives than of Conventionals. The Judge expects the modern designer* to use more sophisticated methods to instill activity. See Chapter on Rhythm.

Contrasts

Textural interest, both contrasting and similar, are used with much *more variety. Contrast works hard in creative design pointing out the* differences between space and solids and relating these to the principles. The contrasts of lights and darks, rough and smooth textures, warm and cool colors contribute to depth illusion (see Depth). However, careless, unplanned contradiction which upsets balance, interrupts movement, destroys unity and dilutes dominance is to be penalized.

Contrasts between the forms, colors and textures of the arrangement elements of container, background and plant materials are more evident in Modern design, but must not be completely unrelated, thus risking lack of unity. While less transitional material is used, the focal area should not be so forceful or contrasting as to make the rest of the design mere background. See Chapter on Contrast.

Dominance

With boldness of all elements the keynote characteristic, the designer must have taken care to assure the dominance of one. The exotic and interesting forms used to establish boldness often also double as dominating factors.

One dominant (either strong or subtle) center of interest at or near *the point of emergence is expected in radial types. Releasing forms and colors as well as gradations blend this area into the rest of the design. While a line in the outer periphery may terminate in a bold form, it still is subordinate to the accepted area of main interest in a Modern design.*

Dominance of space results in a Line design, dominance of mass results in a Massed design. In the Modern Line, the center of interest should be subordinate to the line and is usually of pointed or directional material so as to not hold the eye. "Filler" or fine transitional material weakens the effect of boldness.

Creativity

By standing across the room and getting a full-scale picture of a whole class, the Judge will be struck by the similarity of design patterns, materials and containers in most Traditional classes. This effect should be lessened considerably in classes requesting examples of the

Modern. The most creative interpretations will speak clearly even from a distance.

Because it is much more difficult to conceive and execute an interpretive design than to copy a realistic scene or a Period decorative, more consideration is generally given to the expressive motif.

The designer is allowed full scope in her selection of design silhouette; it may be exaggerated, angular, unconventional, free-form, but should be interesting with varying spaces and solids within the design adding to the variety.

In creative designing the material should dictate the line rather than seeming to be forced into a geometric mold. The Judge should credit the arranger who, with perceptive awareness "sees" an emotional gesture in a piece of flora and strengthens the impression with judicious pruning and placements.

The Modern design is characterized by a masculine, bold, forceful, commanding appearance as contrasted to the predominantly pretty, feminine appearing designs of past eras.

The whole design should project a vividly alive, exciting or dramatic impact upon the viewer even before he is aware of any communicated message.

Creativity must be tied to communication and based on the principles; to merely have done something different should draw a penalty if the action has no meaning to the design.

Avoidance of the obvious choice, the usual color harmony, the conventional silhouette, the trite technique marks the creative design.

With all this creativity, a Judge must develop critical ability . . . some new ways **are** undesirable, some old ways will always serve a purpose. The judgment of each arrangement must be made on its own merits, not on what was or is the current fad.

DISTINCTION
Compatibility, Aesthetic Rightness

Careful selectivity is important because with fewer kinds, colors and textures used, those selected must be compatible, each depends greatly upon the other for effectiveness.

Simplicity and unity contribute to distinction and aesthetic appeal. Simplicity is not necessarily plainness, nor freedom from elaborateness, but freedom from too many unessential parts. Too often there is a tendency to say too much, to over-detail, to over-crowd. These faults are to be penalized particularly in Modern design.

Modern designers limit themselves to two or three colors, textures and kinds, always with one dominating; this simplicity reinforces the bold effect which is characteristic of Modern.

The choice of materials includes inorganic as well as organic. Dried or dormant branches may be used to form permanent design patterns to which fresh materials are added. The addition of metals, plastic, glass and the like is acceptable unless restricted by the schedule or unsuitable in character to the rest of the materials, then penalty is taken.

All manner of altered, treated, sparkle-decorated material is used if compatible with theme and schedule. Because ours is a flora medium, plant materials should predominate or make up the major areas of the design.

Containers may be free-form, fanciful or more conventional and of any texture, color and material that is compatible. Backgrounds may be integrated through color, texture, non-objectively patterned or even carry representational sketching to further the theme.

The Judge must not remove points for a design's lacking what he describes as "beauty" or "prettiness" and mistakenly attributes to aesthetic appeal. Modern designs are not pretty as such, their aesthetic appeal lies in the effect of quality achieved through perceptive selection, careful construction and well-groomed, clearly defined, clean materials.

Craftsmanship

The container rim (hidden since Japanese Classical) emerged in Modern design, and the frenzied covering of mechanics disappeared. However, if the mechanics detract from the design or are in poor condition they will be penalized. The out-of-date attempts to cut the container rim or camouflage the holder often leads to bottom-heaviness or to a too-dominant focal which is to be deducted.

The elements are used in a more or less logical, practical and expected manner. A winner requires perfect placement of a few well-chosen parts in an integrated whole.

The structure is disciplined, clear cut, sculptured-appearing with no non-essential parts clouding or flawing the force of the main lines.

The Judge should appreciate the effort to "lift" the design or minimize the impact of a too-heavy container through the use of space near or in the focal area, space under the container, or the placement of strong interest (brighter color, larger size, distance from imaginary axis) higher up in the design.

Condition

The boldness, simplicity and clarity of construction gives Modern design a neat, orderly appearance. Because of this clarity, all flora used must be clean, crisp, unwilted.

SUMMARY

Communication 35 Points

*interpretation has clarity *lines, pattern express theme *materials, including container, fit theme *small neat card of explanation

-weak statement -conflicting character spirit

Design and Modern Character 30 Points

*space, depth emphasized *radial placement well handled *disciplined construction *focal area well done *bold *silhouette interesting *less "filler" materials *dynamic balance unifies whole *objects placed farther apart in space

-focal area overly dominant -too "pretty", lacks boldness -cluttered -too much material used -lines look forced -"filler" material weakens bold effect -flat appearance, lacks either actual or illusionary depth

Creativity 20 Points

*unusual space effects *space, light, angles add new look *high style *points out something new about the familiar *space used with purpose *unusual selection, preparation or placement

-common -often seen -trite geometric pattern -conventional silhouette

Distinction 15 Points

*simplicity reinforces bold effect *has a look of quality, rightness

-haphazard construction -rusty mechanics -wilting material -design faults affect rightness

Abstract

"Filling our ears with all we have learned to say, we must not be deaf to what we have not yet learned. . . . Wendall Johnson

The Abstract design broke the last bonds of the tyranny of tradition, creating a climate for creativity unparalleled in flora arranging history. The space age is a world where change is normal, a world which moved rapidly from the wire to the wireless, the track to the trackless, the visible to the invisible where more and more can be expressd with less and less and flora art moved with it. The principles of art remain constant but form, emphasis and expression changes to fit the age in which it is produced.

Today we live in a world in which a million differing realistics collide, far too many to digest. Sheer quantity, diversity and contradiction make carefully partitioned impressions impossible, so we achieve an impression of reality in abstracted fragments from which the truth may arise.

Formerly plant material and color were over-organized and made to conform to a set pattern; any communication was engendered by the symbolism of the material within that set pattern. In Abstract the material finds its own place in space; the lines, forms, colors and textures are appreciated for their own value. The designers are guided by the principles of design, not bound by rules; they are a pathway — not a rut!

Basically, Abstract designing is the unification and organization of all elements restricted to the simplest form and emphasizing space, movement and creativity and the elimination of detail. It is a happy mean between mathematical rigidity and irrational irregularity.

These designers have not abandoned nature in their interpretive concepts, rather they abstract and condense from nature, often thus emphasizing natural reality. Abstracts do not **tell** the whole story of Nature, but they bear her **signature.**

Nor has Nature been abandoned in construction . . . we find tensional pull, equalized forces, crossing lines, distortion, mutation, contrasts, space emphasis, mystery, decay and beauty in Nature's designs. Designers have simply moved on from one way of approaching designing to another that fits the era.

SUGGESTED SCALE OF POINTS
Abstract Expressive — Scale 1

Abstract Character   40

Abstract Concept   20
. essence of a subject
. suggestion rather than fact
. flora used creatively

Abstract Construction   20
. plastic organization (new ways of creating form incorporating space, relating all parts to each other and to space, so entire design is seen at once)
. interest equated over entire design
. no focal
. structural clarity
. controlled interest
. departure from n a t u r a l growth, tradition
. emphasis on eye movement throughout

Design   25
. includes both principles and color design

Communication   25
. clarity of exhibitor's message (not Judge's own reaction)
. perceptive selectivity of flora, container, other units to carry theme.

Distinction   10
. quality, simplicity, aesthetic compatibility
. craftsmanship
. condition

Scale 2.

Plastic Organization   30

Personal Expression   20
(in projecting fresh concepts)

Perceptive Selectivity   20

Interpretation   20

Distinction   10

Abstract Non Objective

Abstract Character   40

Abstract Concept   20
. inspired by nothing other than composition
. objects used purely as line, form, color, texture
. reveals designer's awareness, personal expression

Abstract Construction   20
. interest equated
. *several focus areas strategically placed*
. space integrated, dynamic balances
. structural clarity
. *plastically organized (p. 382)*

Design   25
. principles
. color according to principles

Freshness of Concept   25
. perceptive selectivity of design elements to satisfy composition
. has impact, individuality

Distinction   10
. quality, success, aesthetic compatibility
. craftsmanship, unique techniques
. condition

Abstracts fall easily into two categories based on designer's intent . . . Expressive and Non-Objective. Abstract Character falls easily into concept and construction.

CONCEPT (Expressive)

In Abstract Expressive classes the title supplies a subject theme to be interpreted in abstract concept and construction. Understanding and ability to abstract takes time and concentration. It is the first awareness of the crib scene which gives the child his first hint that Christmas means more than tinsel and toys. He solemnly stares and asks about the Baby, about the mommy and the daddy and is told the simple story of Jesus' birth. As he grows in awareness, he learns the true significance. It is always hard to understand anything in abstract. Many people, like the child, can only understand what they can see before them and **that** only in the light of their own experiences. To strip something down to its very essence and make that essence **visable** is the task of the artist and such abstraction is resisted by many because their awareness is limited like the child's to realism and apparency. But, like the child, bit by bit, as their understanding grows, the ability to abstract and to appreciate abstraction becomes theirs.

Abstract-expressive only **implies** . . . it does not represent or depict any realistically recognizable object as say male or female, or place as beach or forest, but presents the artist's **feelings** about these things.

The farther the designer departs from the natural and traditional the more abstract his design will be. The farther away from the original or true shape . . . the purer is the abstraction. The degree to which a design approaches pure abstraction depends somewhat on the beholder . . . his training, background, personality and emotional development . . . for the eye can see only what the mind and emotion comprehend.

Realism is a bird with feathers, tail, eyes and is seen with the mind. Semi-abstraction is a bird form without details of feathers, eyes; only a resemblance to body and wings and is "seen" with the mind and the memory. Pure abstraction is an impression, the essence of bird . . . the thrust or plummet of its flight and is "seen" with pure feeling.

A hard line painted around an airplane does not express movement . . . only when the line is blurred do we "feel" the rush of movement in what is seen. The expression of motion depends quite as much on what is left out as what is put in! It's a case of the shadow being more expressive and interesting than the object which fathered the shadow.

This kind of designing loses its sense of reality in its effort to make a feeling or thought visible. Rather than mere symbolism, it uses the pyschological reaction to the force and power of color, form, lines and textures to express emotion. It leaves to the photographer the reproduction of things as they are seen . . . it expresses what the photographer can never reproduce . . . things as they **seem!**

One definition of Abstract is "to separate **one** element or characteristic . . . view it alone", which results in an intensified awareness of a natural phenomena. To take the spiral of a seashell, duplicate it in the spiral petal structure of a rose bud (chosen for its structure, not because it is a rose), duplicate it again in the curling twist of a vine is to abstract one thing the designer found beautiful and which expressed his feeling about life's continuance; and through placement and selection draw attention to and communicate this enjoyment and feeling to the viewer. Thus abstraction helps one to see something, however common, with new eyes . . . new awareness. The Abstractionist's reward is to have someone say "I never noticed **that** before"!

CONCEPT   (Non Objective)

Composition is the subject of Abstract Non-Objective design. Emphasis on shape, color and texture creates an awareness of these . . . an awareness of color and texture with purpose and form with function. The Schedule title should be no more than a distinguishing label, carefully chosen so the designer need not fit his work into an interpretation of a theme.

Abstract Non-Objective communicates the designer's awareness of material as circular shape (not as a chrysanthemum, etc.), color as a design force (not simply as a reminder of fire, etc.), and texture as a design force (not its similarity to a fabric, etc.). All are judged on the ability of their form and content to aid in the spatial illusion and design fitness.

What the viewer gets from the Non-Objective design depends upon his sensitivity to texture, color, shapes and forms. It could be said that Abstract Non-Objective has come a full circle from Traditional Decorative, but on a different course. It, too, can be used to decorate a specific spot as its sole purpose, while its communication is based on the satisfaction found in the relationships within it and to its setting.

The Judge will no doubt find "borderline" designs which can accurately be called Transitional . . . designs which are Abstract in that they use Abstract-Modern construction and are Abstract in concept, often with interest equated over the whole including an interest area at the point of emergence (focal) and with materials used in ways other-than-botanically normal. The Judge will have to decide which are the dominant characteristics and judge accordingly. The flower show Schedule should be explicit as to the category of abstraction required.

Assemblages and Collages are Abstract in concept and construction as is Avant Garde or progressive art. To hear some pronounce the words Avant Garde Abstractionist is to be left with the impression that the speaker is not only using a foreign language but it is the language of a country with which we are at war! Someone has said "a stranger is the ancient enemy of communities". Abstract and its relatives the "isms" and the maverick Avant Garde are strangers in the "community" of the Conventional. Judges by their choices and their constructive comments which point out that these are not made with reckless abandon, but knowledgeable control of the principles, can further the acceptance, understanding and eventual enjoyment of Abstract Art.

CHARACTERISTICS WHICH MARK THE ABSTRACT EXPRESSIVE AND NON-OBJECTIVE DESIGN AS TO CONCEPT AND CONSTRUCTION ARE:

Expressive Concept
. arrangement inspired by personal interpretation of a theme, subject
. distilled to the essence
. no surface likeness, detailing smoothed away
. distorted, abnormal shapes represent actuality
. emphasis shifted from the visible to the invisible
. implies rather than represents, suggestion rather than straight fact
. vestiges of recognizable figures are detectable occasionally
. truth not literal representation
. unpredictable, powerfully individual, private, instinctive designing

Non-Objective (decorative) Concept
. no subject but its own design
. no reference to natural appearance in either conception or construction
. exalting material for material's sake
. **is** something rather than **about** something
. communication present only in the viewer's awareness and reaction to placement, color, texture
. makes others aware of beauty or uniqueness of an object
. teaches awareness and appreciation of plant material as pure form, color, texture
. disturbing, unexpected

General Abstract Concept
(Applicable to Abstract, Expressive, Abstract Non-Objective **and** some *Transitional which may be abstract in concept but conventional in construction having focal area, etc.)*
. non-conformity (departure from tradition)
. deification of space (space integrated, space enclosed)
. awareness stressed; emphasis on shape, color, texture
. exotic, overlooked or "found" materials, organic and inorganic
. flora used other than as grown (head down, roots up), tending to lose identity (stripped to the veins, clipped, fragmented)
. items chosen not for identity but for design purpose and function
. dramatic impact, high style, daring, often durable
. *bold, often big . positioning used with design intent*

Abstract Construction
(Applies to both Abstract Expressive, Non-Objective Assemblages, etc.)
. *interest equated over entire design . eye bounces from point to point*
. no specific focal or center of interest
. *multiple emergence points and multiple opening containers favorites, but not required . plastically manipulated for impact, depth*
. *all design principles observed . position, light, space impact*
. emphasis on spatial relationships, interpenetration, space enclosed
. emphasis on depth, emphasis on movement, emphasis on dynamic balance (tension areas)
. emphasis on creativity
. disciplined construction, simplicity, severe, austere
. separates clarity from confusion, the important from the unimportant
. **complete freedom** from pinholders, set rules, geometric outlines, single emergence, and the rule of 3s

- lines may end in forceful forms, odd as well as even numbers of identical objects
- no attempt to aid transition through graded size or color
- ingenious techniques, craftsmanship
- interesting from any or many angles
- perceptive selectivity, unusual, unexpected combinations
- material dictates pattern
- any balance or outline pattern, free form
- departure from visual fact
- departure from "as in nature", natural growth, radiation ignored, also diminishing size, distance-lightened hues, etc.
- complete disregard of the "rule" of grouping kinds and colors, except as fits a specific need

DESIGN

While the principles of art are the guiding lines for Abstract designing and judging, four of the six bear the structural load. These are contrast, movement (rhythm) and emphasis (dominance) which all contribute to the fourth . . . dynamic balance. Proportion and scale depart quite radically from the concept of the "golden mean". The elements of design most involved are line, form, space, color, light and shadow (chiaroscuro), angle and texture.

While the lack of physical focal area, with interest equated over the whole design would seem to result in a bizarre or weird arrangement, the use of the principles restrains disorder and disunity, otherwise penalty is taken.

The Judge looks for and rewards the design with individuality developed through proper placement of tension points, perceptive and restrained flora selections, color in balanced areas of interest, with areas and forms of space as vital as the solids, which either suggests an abstracted impression or has pure composition as its subject. He expects to find placements farther apart in space and the elements less closely linked in texture, color, form and size. The design takes any form or pattern from ovoid to free-form.

He expects to find flora materials used in other-than-botanically-normal ways because designers have found that a flower, leaf or line in a different stance or pose is capable of different directional and spatial influences. This increases the design potentiality as well as the Abstract quality of their material.

Color is used with restraint and an understanding of its dynamic force in the design. Monotones and muted neutrals are as popular as strong contrasts but when they are used, form and texture are featured to supply dynamic force. Often the color is bold, scintillating, full chroma and completely contrasted. See Color chapter for color organization applicable to Abstract judging.

A good practice for Judges is to lightly pencil lines on pictures of designs to train the eye to see related shapes of both solids and space and combinations of contrasting shapes in the same design (circle, square, triangles). Outlining areas of dynamic interest will train the

Judge to see proportionate areas and balance as **absolutes,** a positive in the design, not as a vague principle.

SPACE DESIGN

The modern preoccupation with space could be described as "emphasis on the importance of nothing". Painting is art **on space** (the canvas) while flora Abstract is art **in space.** The use of space differs from Traditional in that circles, triangles and free-form shapes of space enclosed within the design silhouette are considered as important as the solids, whereas in the Traditional, the voids were limited to the outer boundaries of the design. One looks **at** the Traditional design . . . but looks through the Abstract. The Abstract absorbs space as it contributes to it. Space exists in all dimensions. Space carries and is carried by the design elements.

Objects are placed apart to show the beauty of space between the solids. Space interpenetrations, the ability to look through the design and even the container is characteristic of Abstracts.

The Judge considers how carefully the designer used space "forms" to balance, to adjust proportion, to create an illusion of depth, to activate visual movement, to add interest through contrasts and to establish dominance through line emphasis.

Space shapes can be the most dominant feature of the design, they are no longer empty, but charged with interest through form and direction and their message often over-powers that of the solids. A spiral of vine is not only a solid line, but a solid line twining around **space!**

The surface of a leaf has length and width, when bent it encloses space. This enclosed area becomes a new design form. Properly used, it supplies rhythm and movement, contrast and balance through its invisible **visible force.** Improperly used, it can give a spotty effect and halt or divert direction as completely as can a solid object or a color.

The precocious designer does not leave the distribution of space to chance, but uses it knowingly, not negatively but **positively.** The Judge must train himself to be conscious of the spaces, not just the solids, to analyze how and where space is working in the design. Without the variety, contrast and organization of directional movement of spaces and solids, advancing and receding colors, and textures a design is lifeless.

The Judge will recognize the several ways the designer utilized space (1) by enclosing space within the design's structure (2) by absorbing space into the design's outline (3) by having some part of the design displace space — thrust in to it! The Judge must penalize the emphasis of space without purpose and the sacrifice of beauty and distinction to the inclusion of space.

Pedestal Placements

There is no specific proportion of height of design to height of pedestal. The limits of these free-standing designs (as with sculptures) may extend beyond the actual dimensions of the pedestal surface. The design's outer periphery creates the visual column of space within which the designer balances her elements.

DESIGN DEPTH

Depth is stressed in Modern design as well as Abstract and the Judge must be cognizant of the various ways of achieving its illusion or actuality as direction back into the third dimension. Designers now realized that a sphere is a circle, a cone is a triangle and a cube is a square no matter how you look at it and through stem placement, color, textures, overlapping they use illusion to gain depth.

Placements of a line may overlap a form in contradiction of earlier restrictions which did not allow a stem to cross a flower's face . . . now a preoccupation with depth and communication loosened the bonds of the "rule". The advanced Judge will judge only on the contribution made to the design or the interpretation.

The container, base/s, background and accessory/s, as well as the design materials should have been selected and placed to further the illusion of depth. Objects used should be interesting in all dimensions and there should be enough turnings and profiling to give the effect of a third dimension when viewed from the front. Despite minimum material used, flatness does not result if every part carries some direction into depth.

Depth in the Abstract design, however, is not established by objects arranged to direct the eye from foreground to middle to rearground as in the Traditional. Such would be an imitation (rather than a deviation) from natural perspective and so is not abstract and deserves penalty. The Abstractionist achieves depth through varying tension in contrasting areas. Instead of interest leaking off into space by gradation to successively smaller sizes and progressively lighter colors, each part of an Abstract advances and recedes, carrying the eye back and forth.

The Judge should recognize that depth, dynamic movement and spatial illusion may be achieved through:
- contrasts of receding (cool) and advancing (warm) colors
- *directional movement (horizontal and vertical lines advance, diagonals may recede due to line direction*
- variations in light and shadow (darks recede and push down; lights advance and rise). Overlapping
- changes in texture (rough textures come forward, smooth dull textures recede)
- contradictions of transparents with solids draw the eye back
- contrasts of dynamics and statics

PRINCIPLES APPLIED TO ABSTRACT

The Judge is also referred to the chapters on the Principles of Design.

Balance

The Judge checks balance in all dimensions of width (lop-sided), height (top or bottom heavy) and depth (interest held in fore, middle or rearground.

Dynamic balance creates visual stability through the attraction of opposites and likes. No part should have so much attraction force that it overbalances any other. The balance in Abstract is always dynamic, never static, nor the equalized left-to-right see-sawing on each side of a traditional imaginary axis.

Abstract speaks emphatically, with the balance in the division of interest between areas and consistent details unifying the separate centers of interest. Balance is controlled by proper relationships of sizes, directional shapes, forces of color and texture, subtle repetition and timing (spacing) of spaces and solids. Balance becomes even more intimately involved with the other elements and principles when there is no single center of interest.

A relatively small object in an otherwise empty space may, through isolation, attract attention and work as a balance factor in the design all out of proportion to its size and presumed importance. A small amount of highly-textured surface generally balances a much larger smooth, dull surface.

Areas of light and dark (chiaroscuro) must be balanced in all three dimensions. The Judge can more easily evaluate this by tilting his head to one side.

A large form may be placed anywhere but there must be a corresponding area of interest to balance it. While the objects are placed apart from each other, the force exerted on the eye is balanced so interest is equated over the **plastic whole.** In other words, the elements are placed so that their relationships mold into a total unit — hence **plastic** organization!

The balance of an Abstract is never formal, exact, perfect . . . it should be varied. It interests, surprises, gratifies, even disappoints, but it is everchanging of the "stitch", as it were.

An arrangement designed to use dynamic balance (the geometry of visual energy) as its basic structural principle is infinitely more interesting, craftsmanlike and vital than former staticism and inertia.

Proportion

Solids must be proportioned to those of the spaces, and may be used to strengthen the three-dimensional effect. The measure of successful proportion also involves satisfying proportion of container, accessory/s, background and flora design. The Judge must also consider the proportion of lights to darks, proportion of smooth texture to rough and the proportions of color values and chromas.

Scale

Scale often seems exaggerated in Abstract, but accords with the concept of equality of units and also with styles such as Surrealism where distortion is necessary to project the fantastic, unlikely impressions.

Depth achieved through the traditional handling of scale (gradation) or the vanishing point perspective is not characteristic of Abstract.

Lines often terminate in forceful forms in accord with the concept of equating interest all over the design rather than a gradual tapering off into space.

The size of the component parts is adjusted to meet the requirements. The Abstractionist and his Judge fully understand that color and texture affect the apparent size of an object. Rough textured objects seem larger than smooth. Warm-colored objects seem larger than cool. This is relative, of course, to the environment of each. A yellow form placed near an orange form has less emphasis visually than when placed alone in space. The Judge must evaluate with a new freedom.

Contrast

The Judge must be prepared to evaluate the designer's use of the contrasts of color, form, space and texture as an aid to increasing depth and activating visual movement. See depth, this chapter.

The designer is free to use any combination necessary, the evaluation is not done on the basis of suitability but on the effectiveness of the combination in achieving the desired effect.

The characteristic of simplicity and boldness puts a brake on the number of contrasts found in a successful Abstract. Seldom do more than two or three kinds, colors and textures appear. But the contrasts of these are definite, not mere variety, but forceful change which keeps the eye alert and the interest active.

Rhythm

Movement is an essential of design, there is great freedom of movement in the Abstract as the eye has many paths to follow, and is not limited to one beginning at the traditional focal and leaking off into space. Each line, plane, color and texture has a double function of establishing an object and creating a sense of motion beyond it.

Visual activity within the Abstract design is not necessarily rhythmically smooth and easy as when achieved through Traditional gradation. Rather, it may be and often is interrupted and staccato because the designer wishes more vigorous visual action.

There is enjoyment for the eye in stopping momentarily and starting again on its way through the design. In traditional work, the eye is forced to begin at the focal and tends to move quickly due to the closeness of the placements and size gradations.

Movement is created by tensional interest and there may be an endless variety in patterns of movement. Solids should be positioned to move the eye along at various speeds, slower here (as space intervenes) faster there (where units are closer together) thus establishing action and unity simultaneously.

Dominance

The Abstractionist rejects the notion that designs must have visual climax that smacks the eye such as a Mona Lisa in the midst of a landscape; instead every square inch of space and solids should bear up under an equal pressure of interest.

The Judge must realize the eye may be attracted first to any part of the Abstract . . . to plant material, container, high or on one side of the design. All details are seen simultaneously and while the eye moves over the design, the viewer remains conscious of what has just been seen.

Even though interest is equated over the whole, dominance prevents conflict. The design should be unified through either dominating vertical thrust, timed and repeated space intervals, duplicated diagonals, curves, angles, simplicity and clarity of construction, emphasis on one dominant line or other ways. The result should be a creative, distinctive design in which areas are related through the combined effort of the principles to achieve oneness of design which is physical, as well as of the spirit, which is psychological unity.

Rather than the dominating physical focal area achieved through flora interest in the Traditional and Modern, the focal "area" of an Abstract may be **space.** This lack of a physical focal area is the greatest variance from former constructions and a main distinguishing feature of an Abstract.

CREATIVITY IN ABSTRACT

The whole concept of Abstraction is rebellion against rubber-stamp copies. The realization that to continually copy past periods and opinions leads, like too many modern possessions, to standardization, uninspired assembly-line perfection and uninteresting prefabrication. The Judge of Abstracts should be able to find something special, provocative, individual in each design . . . the designs should not appear identical, interchangeable, prefabricated, or points are deducted.

Creativity is the touchstone! The reason this type will endure is because creativity is never dated. There are no cliches in creative work. The modern designer differs from the architect and the oil artist in that he must **build,** assemble to make obvious and to communicate what he feels.

Imagination is the ability to create mental images; creativity is the ability to transform these mental images into visual actuality; individuality means something new, different, a change from the expected. These qualities applied to the projection of fresh concepts and plastic organization contribute to designs of great distinctiveness.

The same geometric shapes are used, but **not** as a formal outline as in Traditional design. The triangles, circles, etc., are found within a non-stylized outline. Neither formula nor rule can be given for development or judgment.

The only conformity Abstracts adhere to is the guidance of the principles of art which results in disciplined, controlled creativity rather than chaos. **"We are free in the degree in which we act, knowing what we are about".** — J. Dewey.

While generally, unity is enhanced when an easily identified figure is used in a natural setting (emergence from a single radiating point, etc.), this should not be considered a rule. Identifiable objects are found in the works of Abstractionists such as Klee, Miro and others. Abstraction is not necessarily complication . . . rather, it is simplification! If the designer used elements (figures included) as symbols to convey her feelings about a subject, rather than as mere setting, the concept is abstract, therefore acceptable. However, if the Abstract design is too literal and natural in either concept or construction, it is to be penalized.

Using or allowing flora material to dictate the design results in a high degree of instinctive spontaneity in the designing; if the design pattern also happens to be vertical or circular, or some other such form, it is of no concern to the designer or his Judge.

Flora materials which in the past were discarded or overlooked . . . dried, distorted branches, grotesque seed heads, dried fungi, mushrooms, galls, bark strips and the like are used in such a way as to prove that some waste has taste. The creative Abstractionist can make the ordinary seem extraordinary. The Judge must accept and evaluate the result . . . not the path to the result! Because of its bold clarity, the Abstract design does not allow for mistakes and these are penalized.

Abstract creativity indicates and often develops the exotic in the commonplace by breaking nature's forms into expressive fragments, then inventively and subtly weaving form and feeling into deceptively simple structures which basically satisfy the principles of art. To object to responsible manipulation violates one of the freedoms of contemporary designing.

Special lighting effects are often attempted to stress an emotional effect, emphasizing an area or to integrate the background through shadow of design parts. The Abstractionist recognizes the fact that light and shadow change the visual shape of an object. The Judge should be prepared to consider its success as a stimulating and meaningful design device.

Creativity is the determining factor when confronted with competing early Traditional and Abstract. Because the Abstract is creative in concept and interpretation as well as construction, it rates considerably higher than the most original of Traditional designs.

The Judge must understand that the lack of restrictions and defiance of tradition often results in Abstract distinction and individual and personal expression. Only by understanding is he able to analyze and evaluate. The Judge himself must be familiar with the special code which governs choice, manipulation and placement of the units.

Personal Expression, Expressive Communication

The creative design is a personal expression of the designer's courage in deviating from traditional ways, her friendliness and warmth, her own feelings are expressed in the choices of color, texture, form, and their placement in the design. See Chapter on Communication.

Judges must develop receptive attitudes to credit those creative arrangers who compose within the guidance of the established principles but are not intimidated by the rules. General knowledge of artistic design has progressed to the point where many shows have a creative audience which demands equal knowledge in the Judges.

There are usually three things present in the creative designer and her design:

1. a sense of confidence based on knowledge and use of the principles
2. a sense of freedom in perceptive choice of the elements
3. a spirit of audacity, adventure in the inventive handling of the elements.

These are present in both because the design is the designer . . . a reflection of her way of life and her way of looking at life. The creative design is done not so much with the hands and intellect as with the interests, enthusiasms, hatreds, fondnesses, and fears of the designer. It is exciting for the experienced Judge to find the occasional piece which shows the inner fire . . . the creativity and impact which transcends mere competence!

COMMUNICATION
Sincerity of Communication

In Traditional designs a fact is simply that . . . a fact! But the suggestion of an Abstract may be a dozen facts, depending upon the designer and the viewer. It is often the fact unexpressed or partly expressed that is the most expressive and impressive . . . which accords with the phenomena that what we overhear is more exciting than what we hear!

The most sincere and most powerful impression is made when as many details as possible are sacrificed. All the pretty and many-detailed landscapes and portraits fade in memory beside that of a seemingly solid black abstract painting with a band of black-red at its top; simplification in the extreme, but provokingly memorable because of that; and with a statement dissimilar for each who studied it! The provocative incompleteness of an abstracted thought, a figure without detail . . . like the unfinished sentence . . . spurs the interest and unbridles the imagination.

Simplicity then not only leads to design clarity but aids sincerity of abstract interpretation. Trying to say too much with too many forms, too many textures and colors blurs that realization of the definition of Abstract as viewing **one element alone . . . apart from all others!**

Awareness, Perceptive Selectivity

Even without the dictum that plant material be stressed in a flower show, it is worth recalling the mythical giant Antaeus who was invincible in wrestling as long as he remained in contact with the earth and nature.

The mediums of paint and plaster lack expression until transformed by the artist. The flora medium, however, already possesses form, shape, color, texture, even symbolism, all complete in themselves and needing the artist only to indicate and emphasize that expression through added relationships. Careful consideration is given to how effectively the units enclose or cut into space and yet serve to unify while equating interest over the design.

Normal and accidentally distorted and manipulated natural materials should be the main factor or at least of equal emphasis with container and accessory/s and inorganic materials in any style Flower Show design (see chapter on Creativity). Flora can be found or flexed to follow the lines of aluminum rods, twisted plastic and rusty cables without the coldness and impersonaiity of the latter, which should be used only to bring out some desired design quality rather than making up the whole.

The perceptive nature student knows that trees and plants have gestures of expression; some seem to dance, some curtsy, some reach, some stand at attention, while others sulk . . . some have a lyric line, others a regimental silhouette, others a comical stance. To abstract these qualities . . . to put on view one characteristic alone is the job of the designer; to perceive and to evaluate these qualities in the resultant design is the job of the Judge.

The interpretation in an abstract may be a subtle one, based on the selection of just a fragment of the theme rather than the overall picture, thus leaving something to the imagination of the viewer as he embarks on a trip of discovery through the design. The aim is to catch and pin down the essence of that aspect of reality which moves one . . . to fix and mark out the **shape** of one's sensations. This may be done through exaggeration, as well as elimination; emphasis through distortion is the designer's privilege as long as it serves a design purpose.

The Judge evaluates the designer's ability to distill the spirit of the subject without actual representation. He asks if the material used is adaptable to the impression to be given as well as if it is adaptable to the design itself. The successful arranger will have searched and not settled for anything less. The Judge should expect the same. The character of abstraction is the result of such discovery, search and research and the designer's ability to convey the inspiration or reason for the selection.

Art is said to be ninety-nine percent communication and the Judge whose mind is bound about by convention and tradition, restricted by his own prejudices and preferences is not perceptive enough to be able to discover and evaluate the abstract expression which is much deeper than that which is only visually apparent. The Judge must attempt to sense the vigor, the aptness, the communicated feeling of the interpretation. Because viewer responses do differ, a small, neat card should accompany interpretive designs; without it, the intent may be incomprehensible.

FRESH CONCEPTS

Judges will expect to find a fresh approach, fresh concepts readily apparent in the Abstract design. Among the more important ones are:

. space used as an active compelling factor
. space and form as equivalents of design
. extreme counter movements, dynamic balance
. controlled interest
. space enclosed
. eye pulled strongly from one point to next
. no single unit more important than another
. all units visualized as essential parts of each other
. concern with tactilism (use of items which appeal to sense of touch)

. background an active design factor
. departure from natural growth, tradition
. distortioh if contributes to design
. light, shadow as design factors
. container and/or base may dictate design
. meaningfully empty space
. lines stemming from more than one emergence point
. color used dynamically without consideration for set harmonies
. the right to use any means towards a logical and desired result

DISTINCTION
Aesthetic Compatibility

Abstract is a design which excludes no material (other than schedule-restricted) as long as it is of use as form, color, texture or has a power of suggestion. Objects are chosen to invoke or provoke response or to serve a specific purpose in the structure. No attention is paid to what "goes" with what. An object is chosen because it has a rough texture, a warm, advancing hue and a round form . . . if it also happens to be a chrysanthemum . . . fine! A line is used because it is the right diameter, the right height, the right color and ends in a forceful thrust . . . if it also happens to be a cattail, that fact is of secondary import.

Abstract (and Modern designers) have gained a fresh sense of line and space . . . the courage and ability to say large things with an economy and clarity Traditionalists were never able to achieve. Simplicity is essential to the structural stability and clarity and the refinement of line expected in Abstract.

The easiest way to assess simplicity is to check the numbers of kinds, colors, textures used. The most successfully simple design seldom has more than three variations. The Abstract is free of irrelevant inconsequential parts . . . overcrowding and overdetailing are severely penalized. The Judge will expect the old "rule" of threes and uneven numbers to be passe' . . . though threes are used, the design is often achieved through unique handling of one, two, four objects, or any other number. Flowers may be grouped to increase color or textural impact.

Simplicity is arrived at in approaching the real essence of a thing. Peeling away superficial detailing as the cartoonists have been doing for years and centuries earlier when the motto of the Greek sculptors was "nothing to excess." Even their wrestling and running figures give no hint of overstrain or violent action. This motto applied to Abstract flora design creates the effect of ingenious neatness which is essential to distinction.

The Judge will expect the use of durable, long-lasting flora materials because the pattern often restricts the opportunity to place plants in water.

The abstract quality of flora material may be increased by alteration of color or texture (painting and glitter), by rolling, clipping, using parts (leaf veins, flower centers, or only the stem) and by taking them out of context, using material upside down (heads down, roots up). Again, the Judge must accept this as characteristic of the trend to use flora as pure **form** rather than how it grew naturally. The privilege must not be abused or used only for the sake of novelty but must always be judged on its **contribution** to the design and the interpretation.

In the final check of aesthetic compatibility, the Judge asks if the choice of materials, the space intervals, the tensional movement, the balance of light and dark, the color vibrations and connotations, the textural and spiritual relationships is most suited for the scheduled interpretation.

It is the unexpected and unsuspected viewpoints and relationships of many Abstracts which gives them their beauty and distinction. The Judge must understand what pains as well as what pleases; his failure to understand is often what makes Abstracts disturbing. Abstracts cannot be viewed casually. The viewer must make the effort to participate with the designer in the discovery. If he does not participate he turns away without understanding and deems the design unsuccessful when he himself is at fault! It is the ability to determine **consciously** and logically what it is that interests him and why, and its effect upon the whole that differentiates the trained and perceptive Judge from the viewer-Judge. Whether the Judge understands what is said (regardless of whether he likes the "language") is the important consideration.

Construction

Because of their structural clarity, Abstracts, like Modern design, must have real technical perfection . . . a meticulous neatness that condemns carelessness. The disciplined, yet often unexpected organization depends upon ingenious techniques and clever mechanics which may themselves play a part in the design.

Containers, Bases, Backgrounds

When it is said that a container should be "in harmony", this does not necessarily mean it must blend in or be subordinate. It means the container must be a part of the total, carry its share in the proper proportion, scale, balance, dominance, rhythm and contrast of the design.

Containers, bases and backgrounds play a flexible, rather than a subordinate role in the Abstract, their selection must reflect the designer's awareness again of texture and form. Multiple opening containers are popular, resulting in a distinguishing characteristic of Abstract . . . several points of emergence. While such "parallelism" was considered a serious fault in Traditional, it is a wholly acceptable device in Abstract. Many containers have openings allowing light and space to penetrate, thereby creating a third dimensional quality. Containers best suited to Abstracts usually bear little resemblance to the commonly accepted concept of a "vase".

The Judge worries not over the container rim or mechanics. The lip may be free and distinct or completely covered as is needed by the design. The mechanics are often clever and individual, tailor-made for the specific design problem. There may be several pinholders used to achieve multiple placements.

The background often exerts a force in the design by reason of its effect on depth, space and movement. Its color, texture and lighting may be an abstract part of the whole. Background texture and color seen through the design spaces add interest and distinction.

Condition

Simplicity tends to exaggerate faults, everything used must be neat, clean, turgid.

SUMMARY

Abstract Concept 20 Points

*essence of a feeling or pure design as the subject *brings new awareness *flora used in abstract ways (other than expected) *bold *dramatic *deliberately exciting

-too literal -too realistic a figure used -too conventional -weakly pretty -trite interpretation

Abstract Construction 20 Points

*interest equated *placements farther apart in space *clean cut *see "through" *space, movement, lighting and shadow integrated, well used *textures, colors, form have design force, not merely symbolic *consistent dynamic relationships *space enclosed

-focal area too evident -interest held in one spot -cluttered -ungainly -conventional placements -conventional use of flora -too solid -balance too static for Abstract -too traditional groupings -natural perspective used to achieve depth

Design 25 Points

*all principles adhered to *balanced tensions create movement *unified *space working *illusionary or actual depth *space adjusting size *definite contrasts keep eye active *eye follows many paths *vigorous visual movement *dominance achieved in line etc. *interesting from any angle *visual pauses create interesting imbalances

-principles ignored -disorderly -lacks unity -lacks depth -too many contrasts -space used without purpose -conflicting purposes -awkward -static -line ending in large form lacks equalizing balance -lacks a dominant quality -rhythm too smooth and traditional -space and spatial relationships used indifferently -soft, gentle, related color harmony not characteristic

Creativity, Freshness of Concept 25 Points

*special *provocative *individual *points up beauty in the "overlooked" *special lighting brings it above ordinary *shows courage *unexpected organization *not intimidated by "rules"

-standardized -lacks spark -ordinary -often encountered -hackneyed

Communication 25 Points

*"feeling" comes through *extraordinarily communicative *sincere interpretation *plant "expression" matches theme *exaggeration, simplicity used to strengthen theme *small card clarifies

-theme vague -weak statement -conflicting message -communicated theme lacks force -material chosen lacks power of suggestion applicable to stated theme

Distinction 10 Points

*follows schedule requirements *lighting effects meaningful *simple *clean-cut, disciplined construction *well executed *neat *ingenious techniques, placements *harmonious

-overcrowded -too much detailing -ill contrived -unstable -inadequate construction -mechanics detract -lacks unity overall -weak, fussy material not characteristic -carelessness in preparation, conditioning, selection -wilted material -traditional type vase inappropriate to type -violates schedule requirements

Japanese Free Style, Modern, Other

Sho-fu, Ohara and Sogetsu Styles are the well-known 20th Century forms; Sogetsu being the most uninhibited of the modern Japanese schools. Its founder felt that strict adherence to prescribed rules previously stressed made for mere craftsmanship and the creation of new, fresh and animated styles are urged. Perhaps the relaxation of rules in the adaptations of Oriental flower arrangement in American flower shows had a small part in this thinking. Japanese Free Style is the all-inclusive name for modern Ikabana which does not follow stated rules or established design.

Most designs are non-objective, having pure design as their only subject, some are expressive and a few are fairly realistic in concept such as Moribana or Morimono with new freedoms. Construction may be as in our Modern or Abstracts. Improvisation and ingenuity are encouraged. Almost everything said about abstract is applicable to Japanese Free Style. In fact, unless the designer so states, they are often interchangeable.

Free Style abandons traditional rules, measured lines, precise placement and numbers. Unconventional containers are used, and colors are not limited to those from Nature's background; in fact, one of the biggest changes is apparent in the brilliance of the container colors. Natural growth and seasonal change are ignored . . . daffodils may be used with headed wheat simply to express interesting contrasts of texture and form. As in our modern design, space and depth are emphasized.

Free Style retains and makes use of the definite principles which guide and assist but are not so restrictive as to inhibit creativity. The triangle may not be evident in height, that is, it may not be a vertical triangle, but visible when the design is looked down upon or into.

Dynamic linear quality is also still present, though it may take unconventional turns and set up unusual rhythms. The designs are no longer limited to the asymmetrical triangular form as in traditional Ikabana; circles, ovals, squares and rectangles and free-form are freely applied. Rather than having one pattern in the outline of the overall design, there may be a definite scalene triangle of material, a circular mass of material and an isosceles triangular vase used in the same design.

Simplicity and restraint are still inherent in the ideal though no restrictions on the use of numbers of plant materials are made; limits of combinations to no more than three result in better designs and more typically clear-cut characteristics. The design should have characteristic depth, is never flat across the back.

Modern Japanese Ikabana tends to express individuality. There are no rigid rules for the interrelationships of Heaven, Man and Earth. There is unlimited latitude in the choice of containers, bases, controls and materials. No accessories are used in Japanese Free Style except in special styles of a few schools. A figurine, interpretive or realistic sculpture may be used as a Heaven, Man or Earth placement.

Form, texture and color are dramatized. Naturalness or "as in Nature" is not portrayed except in a few realistic Moribanas. The Heaven, Man and Earth lines may be prominent, disguised or non-existent. The lines, as in the Heavenly Sogetsu may be completely straight, utterly devoid of curves in direct opposition to former concepts that in Nature straight lines are rare indeed. Or the materials may be so closely grouped that Heaven, Man and Earth are interpreted as mere **levels** of different colors, species or textures, reminiscent of our early 20th Century styles.

A single composition may combine a Nageire Heaven and Man in a tall vase and a Moribana Earth line in a low container. The containers may be of different colors and the color scheme may not be traditional, but it must be harmonious.

When multiple containers are used, they usually are staggered for depth and are visually tied together by related spaces or lines reaching out enabling both designs to share the same spatial environment. Glass containers are popular, not necessarily fragile, but the heavy modern types.

If the material is used in the focal area or at the container lip, it may be contoured to the shape of the lip line rather than simply massed there. The focal, if present, may be anywhere in the design, and is often higher than in the Traditional.

The Judge should expect to find all manner of freedoms . . . a piece of wood may lie across the container with both ends serving as parts of the design. There may be a careful matching of twos in defiance of the traditional rule of threes. Materials may be used in unconventional ways, upside down "so it will forget how it grew".

Wood, metal, plastic, roots and the like are arranged with flowers for original and unusual effects. New Formation and Objet designing use other than flora material as the dominant part. In the flat type floating design, if two flowers are used, they may be placed separately with the larger one to the back. Deduction should be made for confusion, clutter and designing which ignores the principles of art. Simplicity and a clear-cut disciplined arrangement are still key characteristics, though mass designs are finding some favor in Japanese Abstracts.

As can be seen, the range of modern Japanese Free Style is wide and varied. However, in Judging, some of the characteristics of the Traditional should be apparent, else the design reflects only American Modern and Abstract trends without any reflections of the Orient. The *scales of points suggested for Conventional, Abstract, or Assemblage are applicable.*

Mobiles, Stabiles and Hanging Designs

SUGGESTED ENTRY:
1. MOBILE, suspended, with moving parts
    A: featuring plant materials (treated, dry, fresh in any combination)
    B: no restrictions as to materials used
2. STABILE, a table top design expressing arrested or imminent motion or **seeming** to move. Any combination of treated, dry, fresh plant materials. Accessories permitted.
3. STAMOBILE, a table-top stabile with one or more moving parts. Any combination of treated, dry, fresh plant materials. Accessories permitted.
4. HANGING DESIGN. Any combination of treated, dry, fresh plant materials. Accessories permitted.

DEFINITIONS:
Mobile: mobile means moving easily and freely. Defined, an artistic mobile is an art form of moving sculpture . . . a composition of balanced moving parts suspended from above. The motion of a mobile can be likened to a music of vision — a tune of pure silence, its tones are varied forms, its rhythm and melody is change, its cadence is measured on the wind.

Much of the charm and attraction of a mobile lies in this beauty of motion which is sometimes referred to as the fourth "dimension". The motion is usually silent, though some do incorporate sound — light and airy tinklings in tune with the design. Sound is sometimes referred to as the fifth "dimension".

The evolution of the mobile inspiration has come full circle. In the 1930s Alexander Calder, an American artist, used nature as his inspiration for metal mobiles . . . now we use nature's own materials as both inspiration and elements.

Stabile: defined in Hagger's Dictionary of Art Forms as "a sculpture which remains motionless and still". Note that the word "sculpture" appears in each definition. Literally, sculpture means "carved work in metal, stone, wood, etc.", the "etc" can include plant material. Interpreted in floral design stabile means an arrangement which has stability although it should not be static but look as if it or its parts could walk, take off in flight, or move in some direction at any moment. It is a composition portraying arrested or imminent or implied motion and is not new to flower arrangers.

This implied movement gives vitality and zest to the design. In a stabile flower design, the base, stem or pedestal is a definite part of the design and can be the dominant element. The container and/or accessory sometimes forms the dominant feature and carries the interpretation. Accessories are often wind-sand-sea sculptured pieces of wood which carry an abstract resemblance to animals, birds, etc. The design may be free-standing or three-sided, and must have depth.

Stamobile: (a contraction of stabile and mobile) a design to which has been added an extension which actually moves or has attachments which move. In other words, it is a stabile arrangement with a mobile included which increases the interest. The mobile may be actually attached to the stabile's base or it may hang from the ceiling above or the wall or niche behind the stabile, but it must join the stabile in forming a related and rhythmical unit.

Hanging Designs are of two kinds: 1. contained in an object and hanging on a wall, door, etc.

2. pendant, hung from ceiling, door, wall, etc. and rotatable as a single unit about a vertical axis.

Most mobiles and stabiles are suitable only for modern interiors while hanging arrangements may suit earlier periods, provided container and designs are compatible with the style, period and color of the intended placement.

The Schedule can specify placement such as stairways, child's room, doors, etc. The design can be of casual character or more formal in feeling to fit the placement.

SCALE OF POINTS
Mobile and Stamobile

Design	30	Relationships	30
. rhythmic movements, visual and actual	10	. color, texture, form	10
. balance, visual and actual	10	. suitability of combinations	10
. other principles	10	. space relationships	10
Distinction and technique	20	Individuality	20

Stabile

Design	30	Relationships	30
. visual movement (illusion of)	10	. color, texture, form	10
. visual balance (stability)	10	. space relationships	10
. other principles	10	. suitability of combinations	10
Individuality	20	Distinction and technique	20

SCALE OF POINTS
Hanging Designs

Relationships of	30	Design (all principles)	30
. color, texture, character, etc.	10	Distinction	20
. suitability of combinations	10	Individuality	20
. suitability to placement	10		

Since there is a great difference both in construction and mechanics between the several types, it is unjust to judge all by the same scale. The Schedule should define the type or types to be exhibited.

DESIGN PRINCIPLES
Rhythmic Movement, visual and actual (physical)

Rhythmical movement and balance are the keynote ingredients in mobiles, stabiles and stamobiles.

The movement is not only physical and actual but visual in mobiles and stamobiles. The principle of rhythm is even more important to this type of design than it is to the static where we first expressed it. Visual motion is attained through gradation, repetition and line direction.

Therefore, the Judge checks not only to see if the moving parts of a mobile or stamobile revolve freely, gracefully and smoothly in each little air current but that the eye is satisfied by finding repeated colors, repeated textures, repeated forms and repeated space shapes. He checks to see if movement is expressed by gradation of size from small to larger; of color from dark to light, bright to muted; and of textures from rough to smooth with satisfactory transitions to carry the eye along.

The Judge checks the movement of line direction — a curve here carrying on and continuing a curve there. A shell form here abstractly expressed in a grouping there; a straight line here strengthened by a companion line there.

All these things, if well thought out, blend into the fine relationship of component parts, including space and the suitability of combination which is demanded of a distinctive design.

The type of balance employed has an effect on the visual rhythm. Symmetrical balance is self-contained and has a tendency to halt motion, the equal forces tend to hold the design static and so a purely symmetrical design will probably garner less points for movement and rhythm than an asymmetrical one which has an alive, active, fluid grace in which interest flows easily from one shape, color or space to the next.

The actual or physical rhythm should be balanced and smooth, not awkward and jerky. The parts of a mobile or stamobile should seem to glide when in motion and float when motionless, rather than just **hanging** in space.

Balance

Both physical (actual) and visual balance is an essential ingredient. The physical balance may be symmetrical with objects of equal weight equidistant from the center. Or the balance may be asymmetrical with heavier weight closer to the center and lighter weight farther out. The asymmetrical is more difficult and more interesting. If properly constructed, mobiles and stamobiles will keep their balance, with the moving parts hanging level and equal, except when in motion.

Visual balance is based on the fact that we react to things as they appear to be; not as they actually are. A dark red flower is the same physical weight as a light pink flower but the visual weight or force of the red is much heavier, the visual impact is greater. The Judge takes this fact into account as he weighs the visual stability of the design. A light texture where a heavy texture should have been used for visual stability is a fault to be demerited also. An object with a regular outline appears heavier than an object with a jagged or serrated edge; too many regular outline objects may create a density which belies the mobile aspect and will result in a penalty.

The visual balance overall should be equalized around an imaginary central axis with equal interest on both sides. A small moving area will balance a much larger static area. Also, the design should not appear either bottom or top-heavy, but with visual interest interestingly distributed.

If the Judge has an urge to move any object nearer or farther from the central axis or another form, the security and stability is at fault. The lightness and delicacy of the balance has an influence, too, on the ease of movement.

In hanging designs, the balance is mainly visual and is judged the same as for regular table-top designs.

Other Principles

The size of all parts used should be in scale and the areas of the design should be in proportion to the items used and the space it occupies. To achieve proper proportion the forms should be suspended a reasonable distance from the frame of the defined space in mobiles and stamobiles. Spottiness caused by having too many forms or areas the same size and interest is a fault. A Hanging design which is too large or small for the door, etc. is penalized here.

A Mobile design should be a nice balance of areas both horizontally and vertically; if it is too wide, it will look awkward. If the wires or strings are too short and close so it looks crowded, closed in and lacking that airy look demanded, penalty is taken.

The parts of a stamobile should be in scale. Usually it is best that the lower or static part be the most dominant and largest in area and in visual impact. Accessories and bases of stamobiles and stabiles must be in proportion and scale to the other parts.

Dominance or emphasis is achieved by featuring one form, or color and is established by the force and repetition of the color, the size or shape of the part. Too many items all one shape, texture, etc. will cause monotony, however. There must be some accent or contrast to add and heighten interest.

Relationships

The consistent use of materials gives an overall unity and harmony and a sensitive blending of patterns and textures increases the suitability of the relationships. The Judge asks himself if the parts of a stamobile and mobile are interesting at every turn as they rotate in the formation of different patterns and space relationships. The staging should be such that the mobile hangs near a side wall rather than the middle of the room. The incorporation of shadows moving silently on a plain, pale background intensifies the floating-in-air character which makes these so appealing, moving shadows are a charming element not found in other designs.

The Judge awards extra points to the designer whose mobile or stamobile throws ever changing, flickering shadow patterns on wall, ceiling or floor. Shadows' muted values contrast the color of their creators and their gliding echoing movement are a silent foil to any sound supplied by their material counterparts. It is the unpredictability and the interlocking and parting movements that gives the illusion of life to these relationships.

It is more difficult to use fresh plant material in a mobile than in the other designs herein discussed and the Judge is justified in allowing extra points to the designer who manages this and still maintains the balance and airiness. Transparencey of at least some of the items in mobiles and stamobiles increases the weightless effect as do forms suggested simply by wire or straw outlines. Bits of shiny metal, mirror, etc., may introduce a luminous reflective quality but must be appropriate and related to the other parts.

The area of the spaces around the forms and the adjoining items increases or decreases the power of attraction. A yellow form placed near an orange form has less emphasis than when hung alone in space. Contrasts are important in creating rhythmical interest. A warm color contrasted by a cool, a dark color against a light can change and intensify the visual movement; the intervals of space between the parts which slows or speeds the visual movement through the design are techniques of space relationships to be appreciated.

Space is considered in two ways, first the volume or space required for staging, particularly the mobile and whether it is hung at ceiling, eye-level or lower. Second, the space provided within the design which gives it the airy floating impression. Any feeling of ponderous heaviness should be penalized.

There should be some diversity of speed in the actual movements in the mobile or stamobile. The centers of interest shift and the one which is moving fastest or the one nearest the eye will have the greatest attraction, albeit momentarily.

The design of many Hanging arrangements must necessarily continue the basic line below the container in order to relate the arrangement to the surroundings and bring it down to eye level. The *Judge will note this particularly in Judging Hanging designs in Home Shows.*

Objects used to furnish the rhythmic movements must be inanimate objects, not living things. The inclusion of a living tethered butterfly or a live bird in a cage is reason for elimination from competition.

Distinction

The illusion of spaciousness and light, weightless, free and easy movement are the qualities to be found in an award-winning Mobile and to a certain extent in the Stamobile. The illusion of arrested or imminent motion must be easily apparent in the Stabile.

Distinction involves the craftsmanship, the execution, the technique required to produce a superior design and these require greater mastery than in the usual static floral design.

Dried or extremely long-lasting plant materials such as berries, mums, succulents, everlastings, etc., should be used. Any wilting down or ineptness in supplying moisture through proper mechanics is a heavy mark against distinction.

All materials should be handled with engineered precision; simplicity of form and clarity of contour are a natural outgrowth because clutter and excess will visually or actually over-balance a Mobile or Stamobile.

A designer's mind conceives the imaginative design, but to be able to put forth the idea, he must have a command of techniques and mechanics of construction. All strings, wire, etc. should be clean, neat, without long or frayed ends, neatly tied and/or attached, and of a proper length to allow all parts to move freely. Easy moving joints fashioned on fishing swivels, metal eyes, etc. should be noted.

Asymmetrical balance in Mobiles and Stamobiles is more difficult, more interesting and distinctive and requires a great degree of technique to achieve the required free and balanced movement. The successful asymmetrically balanced design warrants extra points.

If a class calls for a Mobile and the designer has not understood the demands of the definition in that he submits a Stabile or a Hanging design, points will be deducted under distinction and design. A design cannot be a distinctive Mobile if it **isn't** a Mobile in which the design principles of balance, scale, etc. are applied differently. Such non-conformity should be severely penalized, if the design was not disqualified by an alert Classification Committee.

Individuality

Because each exhibitor collects and assembles in a different way, each such design will have at least some measure of individuality. The idea itself is not original, but appears frequently in nature's hanging moving leaves, fruits, flowers and seed pods; the moving mane of a horse, the plume on a bird's head, a leaf caught on the antlers of a deer. To be more than simply repetitions of nature, an artistic Mobile or Stamobile must have behind its successful execution, the individuality of an interesting, imaginative idea or theme carried out in a related and balanced rhythm.

Themes can be based on a related scene such as things collected from the desert, sea, or forest; a related subject such as religion, abstract forms, birds, butterflies, etc.; or related through materials such as glass, reed, grains, pods, or related through colors, textures, forms both abstract and realistic. The individuality apparent in collecting and combining the materials, and how well the designer has expressed his theme through the selections and relationships of the materials are the evaluator's concern, and not whether it is "better" to have a theme on birds rather than one of abstract forms. What is used can influence the mood expressed — dark sombre solids may impart a heaviness not compatible with the airy mobile concept and will suffer point penalization as a result. While it is possible to construct a Stamobile or a Stabile and attain the visual movement with a manufactured figure, more individuality is apparent in the design which achieves the aim of arrested or imminent motion with plant materials only plus dried items and decorative wood, etc. Originality expressed in choice of container or selection of materials in Hanging designs rates extra points. Imagination makes these designs come to life.

It is the Judge's duty to reward those designers who are able to resist conformity by presenting new forms and ideas and designs. The concept may be realistic or abstract. Experiments with different materials increase our knowledge of this artistic expression whether the design is entirely successful or not and the Judge should recognize the perceptive thought, untiring investigation and discriminating selection required to present a new approach.

SUMMARY
Rhythmic Movement, visual and actual 10 Points

> *moves freely *smooth movements *visual movement through gradation, repetition, line direction *glides *floats

> -static -awkward -jerky -uneven visual rhythm -visual movement halted by gaps, too strong contrasts, etc.

Balance, visual and actual 10 Points

*physically well balanced *visually well balanced *no urge to move any item

-off balance -top heavy appearance -bottom heavy

Other Principles 10 Points

*parts well scaled to each other and to area *design proportioned to area *dominance principle satisfied *interesting contrasts

-spotty placements -too large or small for defined frame -awkward -crowded -closed in appearance -monotonous -needs contrasts -ungainly

Relationships 20 Points

*selections harmonious in character *interesting from any angle *shadow interest *difficult fresh materials well used *forms well related to space *movement achieved solely by inanimate objects

-background overpowers design -ponderous -heavy -objects lack unity, harmony, continuity -movement supplied by living objects (mobile) -choices too sombre

Distinction 20 Points

*Mobile airy, spacious *meets definition *free moving *neat construction *Stabile movement implied *meets definition *clean cut

-not as defined -wilted materials -inefficient techniques -inadequate mechanics -strings, etc. soiled -frayed ends

Individuality 20 Points

*different *imaginative *unexpected viewpoint

-copied -seen before -ordinary -materials too sombre for airy mobile

EXTRA-SENSORY DESIGNS

Our other senses can be exploited when scent and vision are teamed with sound, touch and illusion in floral design. Color, which is tied to visual sensations and emotions, contributes to the effect. Synesthesia, where sound produces a mental color image or vice versa is a seldom-exploited sensory phenomena. Extra-sensory designs include op-art, psychedelics, mobiles, stamobiles (table-top mobiles named, defined by author, 1966), vibratiles (sound producing vibrations) and others which come under the heading "kinetic". Kinetics are a branch of dynamics which deals with matter in motion as opposed to visually stationary or static objects. Designs may be abstract, actual-action with moving parts, or rely on visual effects only, or combination. In the 1960's an innovative artist added vibrations to a sculpture, soon others followed with variations activated by various means, including viewer touch. Movement plus sound are the hallmark of the vibratile. "Illusionary sensation" can be produced, for example, by fixing pieces of glass upright in slotted base, giving the illusion of rising without support, or a basket appearing to float by mounting on black base against black background.

"Reflectives" are subtle kinetics in which some part reflects viewer motions, expressions or apparel colors as accessory or feature.

Op-art and psychedelics involve strong illusions and tricks of perception where various parts seem to vibrate visually due to tensional pull between elements. Lighting effects are employed with distortion and violent visual action. Staccato, pulsating lights, alternating at mind-blowing speed are endemic of the types. The appearance of pulsating movement is a dominant feature. The earlier category of dream inspired, weird, haunted Surrealistic designs is similar in concept. These designs bring into play extra-sensory perception.

Actual-action designs with moving or movable parts may be activated by motors, air currents, or manual manipulation by viewer involvement. Judging involves assessing stability, often endangered by zealous appreciators. Sound-makers must be secure as well as visually coordinated with other components. The kind of sound (melodious, intermittent, persistent, etc.) should be in keeping with class title. Designs may, as with pedestals, extend over their bases. The Schedule must be carefully structured as to staging, and to control or allow public involvement. Sound and movement, actual or imagined, is integral part of making and judging of extra-sensory designs, and must not appear as afterthoughts. Review text on Mobiles, (p. 424) Abstract, (405) Avant (388) for adaptation, judging, point breakdown. Increase emphasis in scales for motion, sound, or other means of extra-sensory impact. Creativity should not be hampered by conventional rules. It is best to print scales in Schedules to assure full understanding by Judges, designers and public as to criteria used. It is suggested that Schedule writers develop two classes: A: Extra-Sensory: Abstract and B: Extra-Sensory: Other (thus allowing for some other or emerging creative concepts).

DIVISION 4 — MISCELLANEOUS

Accessories

Accessory is defined as "a thing which aids or contributes subordinately . . . an attendant or helper". But actually the word has come to mean an object in flora arrangement terminology, since grammatically it is often mis-used in such classes which request exhibitors to "feature an accessory". Any object may be featured, but since it then dominates the design it ceases merely to be an "accessory" to the design.

Accessories may be any component of a design, i.e. fungi, shells, art, non-art objects, minerals, figurines, decorative wood, plant materials (fresh or dried), other objects and props. These may be combined as Schedule requests or permits. REFER to Minimum p. 434.

The accessory may be placed in the container, on the lip of the container, apart from the container, but wherever it is placed it must be needed to complete the design.

If the accessory does the following (all or in part) it is working in the design —

1. contribute to the design by
    - a: giving visual weight and balance where needed
    - b: stressing rhythmic movement by repetition of color, texture, line direction or dynamic force for added emphasis and interest
    - c: continuing or stopping a line
    - d: lessening the force of exaggerated line
    - e: serving as a center of interest or as one of 3 major lines in modern Japanese
2. helping communicate the spirit or theme of the class
3. aiding aesthetically rather than distracting

If the accessory is not in
1. harmony as to color, texture, character
2. scale and proportion
3. unity with container, plant material and background, then it has failed its purpose and its presence is penalized.

In general an accessory which is too large or small for the design must be penalized, but there are always exceptions as for instance when the exhibitor has attempted to communicate man's insignificance in the presence of God's great outdoors, or a Surrealistic interpretation.

Figures such as fish, fawns, water birds and animals or barefoot humans are at home standing directly in the water, but some figures such as the Madonna, should be elevated.

The repetition of a figure's movement repeated in the lines of the plant material increases distinction and interest. In a Traditional realistic design, realistic figures which are looking, running, walking or flying may be placed to view, approach, enjoy or participate in the "scene" created by the flora design. When realistic figures are placed so the direction of their "eyes" encompasses the design, the viewer is drawn into the design, creating a unity of communication.

Figures placed to move the eye out of the design reduce design emphasis. For instance, a Madonna staring down at flowers at her feet is more united with the design than one in which the "eyes" stare directly to the front.

Of course, the story may be strengthened by having the figure "leave" the scene, the Judge should be aware of the intent of the placement before criticizing. Ordinarily the more realistic the figure, the more traditional and natural the setting; the more Abstract the design, the less detailed or more Abstract the figure to achieve unity and compatibility of spirit or character of the overall design. Wise exhibitors are credited when they use the accessory piece to strengthen the story or mood suggested.

Every element added to a design makes it more difficult to achieve perfection, most designs incorporating an accessory are more successful if they are kept simple, with limited numbers of colors and types of plant material. An overstuffed, disjointed appearance is to be penalized.

If the Traditional design, in which an accessory is used in the focal area, appears divided into two vertical sections, deduction is made.

If neither the accessory nor the plant material is dominant, the design will suffer under the disregard of this principle.

A realistic accessory (one which is easily identified) carries more interest impact than one which is more abstract. In other words, a five-inch bird with beak, wings, tail, feet and feather markings carries more visual weight through virtue of recognition than a five-inch piece of wood that "looks" like a bird. By the same token, a piece of wood that "looks" like a bird will command more attention than the leaves and flower forms with which it is used.

The use of too many accessories with a single Traditional design usually results in competition for attention and should be penalized if this is the result.

Frequently a carelessly placed accessory will throw completely out of balance an otherwise well-adjusted design, indicating beyond doubt that the object was not needed or was poorly handled.

In most instances the design will be more unified if accessory/s and arrangement share the same base, however, separate bases may be carefully used to emphasize the importance of an accessory object. A small-scale object isolated or placed apart from the design may gain sufficient importance to equalize the visual force of the plant material, whereas if the same figure is placed conventionally near it would draw penalty under scale. Before the Judge criticizes a designer for using an accessory in an unusual position, consider well. Was the placement done to emphasize some point? Does the accessory, because of its visual impact or theme-carrying properties deserve the space and attention given it?

Artificial and Altered Plant Materials

The basic fundamental principle underlying the concept of a flower show or floriculture department in a Fair is to educate the public by showing how beautifully and perfectly plants can be grown in the area and to show how the flowers and foliage of these same beautiful plants can be combined, trimmed and manipulated into satisfying examples of creative art.

The static artificial forms, unchanged by natural opening and closing, the colors unvaried in minute details or cultural accident, the unnatural compliancy of the stem directions; the sleek sameness of the textures all belie the **life** present in natural (even natural-dried) flora materials which no matter how perfectly formed (or perhaps because of this perfection) can never be imitated.

The aim of flower arranging is not only in the combining of line, form, color and texture, but in the bending of capricious and often strong-willed plants to meet one's needs to complete a design. If one uses artificial flowers (even in the "shape" of flowers) one cannot call this **Flower** arranging; the result belongs in a field other than flora artistry.

Flower arranging defined is the use of plant material, container, accessories and base (if used) and thus must contain the element of plant material or it cannot fill the description.

Flower arranging implies skill and a knowledge of how plants may be used, how much they can be manipulated, which plants are suitable as to substance and longlasting qualities; it implies an eye for spiritual, color and textural harmonies and contrasts. Little horticultural knowhow is needed nor expressed in the use of artificial flowers and foliage and this intimate knowledge of plant **life** is lacking (and missed). When artificial flowers and foliage are used the result is as artificial and devoid of life as the element.

Judges and exhibitors must have full, complete and mutual understanding of the terms here applied.

Artificial is defined as "not real, not natural; in imitation of natural or real". Any plant material assembled or constructed of material other than flora, intended to imitate the real thing must be termed artificial. This includes polyethylene, plastic, wood fibre, yarn, silk, paper, macaroni, feathers, other. Schedules may allow a **minimum** amount of artificial grapes, fruits, branches or other items not recognizable as flora.

Minimum means the least amount assignable, giving other components predominance. Opposite of 'featured'. Flower Show intent is to "show-off" fresh flora, thus classes allowing **all** altered or treated flora are limited to 1: "a minimum number in the Show" or 2: Schedule states "fresh flora required in all classes unless otherwise specified". In such exceptions, class title or sub-statements control and clarify.

Contrived Plant Materials, *coined and defined by author, 1966. "Contrived" are flowers, foliage and fantasy forms made from reassembled, recognizable fresh or dried plant parts. Materials used and resultant product must be recognizable as* **unprocessed** *plant parts. Dried, altered, treated, fresh or glycerined, etc. leaves, flowers, husks, seeds, nuts, petals, cone slices, bark, mushrooms, fungi and the like, qualify. Wood fibre, rope, feathers, silk, other not acceptable (see Artificial). For ideas, refer to author's "CREATIVE DESIGN WITH DRIED & CONTRIVED FLOWERS" . . . chapter on "CONTRIVED . . ." Simon & Schuster, N.Y.*

Treated Plant Parts *(used only when scheduled.) Dried flora which have been dyed, painted, varnished, bleached, waxed, glycerined or otherwise treated to alter its natural color or texture are considered ornamented, embellished or treated. Holiday Schedules may allow minor ornamentation of fresh evergreens with 'snow', 'glitter'. Does not include peeled, trimmed, bent, etc. Clerks should not be asked by Judges to determine fresh or dried condition. Judging is done from 3' distance. If apparent that fresh flora was treated, points are deducted under conformance or distinction.*

Featured *means to focus strong visual impact, to isolate by volume, visual, subjective effect. Opposite of 'minimum'. Any component or element may be featured, thus be dominant (p. 328). May be plant material, container, background, color, texture, space, unusual positions, etc. as Schedule directs or allows.*

ARTIFICIAL

A base should contribute more than simply serving to separate the design from the table covering! A prize-winning design needs no such support. Nor should a base be criticized because "they aren't being used *today*"!

A base becomes a part of the overall design, considered in one with the container in evaluating proportion, and its use only as a separator may throw the whole design out of proportion, scale and balance, especially if placed after the design is constructed.

Bases are used to:
- balance
- may serve as 'container', supporting holder, etc.
- coordinate accessory and design
- add rhythm
- adjust proportion
- reduce bottom heaviness (though if incorrectly chosen, can increase it)
- strengthen the dominance of a color, texture, line or character
- give visual stability

If a base does not do any of these things, it is superfluous to the design.

Open-frame bases are used to give a weightless feeling, a feeling of lifting the design off the tabletop, to compensate for visual heaviness. By allowing space to move in and under the design, bottom heaviness is reduced by the knowing exhibitor and should be credited.

There should be no hard and fast rules, such as the one which states that a base should never be used under a footed or stemmed container. The usabata is a footed container often used successfully with a base . . . it all depends upon the needs of the individual design. Despite their frequent appearances, bamboo mats and Japanese scroll bases are incorrect with many designs. Some Modern and Abstract designs are using groupings of colored sand or pebbles right on the tabletop for a base. If a base is too large and overpowering, or too fragile-appearing to support its burden, or too formal for its design partners penalty is taken. If the base is in keeping in texture, character and color besides fulfilling a purpose as above, it adds to the distinction of a design.

435

Corsages

SUGGESTED CLASSES

1. Corsage, open class, no specified occasion or costume
2. Corsage, fresh cut plant material predominating
   A. tailored
   B. informal (afternoon)
   C. formal (evening)
3. Corsage, dried material predominating
4. Floral Accessories (wristlets, hats, necklaces, etc.)

More elaborate classes can be listed in the Schedule for Advanced Shows. For instance a theme "Girl Friday", with classes that follow a secretary to meet a plane (tailored corsage); to a luncheon (informal corsage); to a dinner dance (formal corsage).

Since appropriate corsages can be made from almost any flower, these classes are equally adaptable for specialized shows of Glads, Daffodils, Roses, Iris, Orchids, even Succulents, etc.

Schedules should state clearly if any special background or display media will be provided and if display in boxes or plastic will be acceptable. Reflections tend to hide and distort the beauty of a corsage. Placement is ideal if the corsage can be exhibited and judged at the level at which they will be worn. Placement should be such that the Judges can carefully examine the exhibits for technique.

CORSAGES

Corsages are fashion accessories made to enhance daytime and evening ensembles for every occasion. Corsages are really small scale flower arrangements and their designing, like that of flower arranging, is the art of organizing the elements (flowers, foliage, ribbons and other items) in such a way that an impression of beauty is achieved through harmonious and simple placement.

SUGGESTED SCALES OF POINTS
Fresh Cut Materials Predominating

Open Class		Advanced Show (Specified Classes)	
Design	25	Design, including color	30
Distinction and Imagination	20	Distinction and Imagination	20
Technique	15	Technique	15
Color	15	Suitable Combinations	15
Suitable Combinations	15	Schedule Interpretation	10
Condition	10	Condition	10

Dried Materials Predominating

Design	30	Individuality	15
Combination	20	Color	10
Distinction	15	Technique	10

436

Design

A corsage is judged according to the same elements and principles of design as are applied to all other arts. The elements are line, form, pattern, color, and texture. The principles are balance, proportion, scale, rhythm, contrast and dominance.

The Judge must ask how well the corsage creator has met the challenge of controlling the elements by her use of the principles in the organization of the corsage design. The function of line, the first element, is to lead the eye through the design from the focal area on to the outer periphery and back again. Rhythm plays a large part in leading the eye smoothly. This is achieved by (1) gradation, (2) repetition and (3) line direction.

The direction of all the lines should lead into the focal area of the corsage. These lines may be curved or straight but their main function is to lead the eye to the focal.

The gradual gradation of size from larger forms in the focal area and by easy transition to medium size and then on to smaller sizes at the outer edges should be checked by the Judge. A corsage constructed so the largest, most eye-catching forms are on the outer limits would be pointed down because of breaks in the rhythm. Gradation of color is also an aid to the movement throughout the corsage. Shading from deep pink, to light pink, to lighter pink or white draws the eye along.

Gradual changes in texture from coarse to fine, and changes in visual weight, from light to heavy, move the attention along smoothly. This should be done subtly so that the focal area remains the most important part of the design.

The human eye searches for similarity, and repetition of colors and forms satisfies this need. However, too exact or orderly repetition gives a monotonous impression that lessens the beauty. Such lack of contrast is to be considered a design fault.

The form and pattern are the shape and silhouette of the finished corsage. The most graceful shoulder shapes are the oval, the Hogarth line (lazy S) and the crescent, all of which are derived from the circle. The triangle is also very successful. Other forms are the straight lines, squares and rectangles, which are more difficult to use successfully.

To have an interesting silhouette there should be some voids (spaces) between the solid materials in the outline of the corsage, but if the voids appear **within** the form, they are called "holes" and are penalized.

Proper scale and proportion are necessary to achieve good corsage design. These two principles are very often confused. Scale means the size of the aster to the babysbreath; the size of the rose to the width of the ribbon; the size of the leaf to the size of the flower. In other words, scale is the size relationship of each item to the other. A ribbon too narrow for the rose, babysbreath too tiny for the aster, the leaf too large for the flower are all faults to be deducted.

Proportion means the **amount** of leaves for the amount of flowers, the amount of ribbon for the amount of leaves, the amount of taped stems showing for the amount of leaves and flowers. In other words, proportion means the size relationships of the **areas,** one to the other. A corsage where the amount of ribbon dominates the flowers, or the amount of leaves overpowers the flowers is incorrectly designed, and points are levied against it commensurate with the degree of damage done to the design.

In general, the dominant flower should face front. The corsage should appear to have depth, rather than present a flattened appearance. The form should taper gently at both ends with the addition of properly sized foliage, buds or small flowers. A blunt end is less graceful and may make the corsage look squat and dumpy. The materials should not be grouped so tightly together, that the beauty of their individual forms cannot be appreciated.

The focal area should be well defined and placed at approximately the halfway point, except in the triangle forms where it will appear at, or near the bottom. A focal area too high in the design will result in a top-heavy look. A strong focal area is attained by the proper placement there of larger blooms, deeper colors, interesting forms or special textural contrast. Small flowers can be used to form a focal if they are grouped closer together than they are at the outer edges.

Wired and taped stems may be cut off neatly at the back, or they may be brought out and utilized in the design. The stem endings which are left to show must form a part of the overall design, following the line direction and harmoniously related in color. If the stem endings dominate or alter the design, penalties must be levied against them.

Distinction and Individuality

A corsage gains distinction through skillfull and creative handling of the materials selected.

Two designers may select the same waxy, yellow lilies and frilly, brown-centered calendulas. Designer Number One wires and tapes her materials in the usual manner. Designer Number Two takes the stamens out of the center of the lily and inserts the yellow calendulas in their place. The results: Distinction and Individuality! The use of common materials in an uncommon manner!

Designer Number Two has taken the same materials as Number One, but handled them with a creative approach that added a superior quality to her design, making it stand out from others, and making the work of Number One seem mediocre even if the technique and design were equally as well done.

Distinction is strengthened by simplicity! The use of too many colors or too many textures, or too many forms is against the design principle of dominance. Such handling creates a busy, confused appearance which considerably reduces the score for distinction.

The Judge should reward the skilled designer who avoids combining so many small and dainty dried or fresh materials that the design has a "weedy" look.

The grouping of small flowers, pussy-willow tips, dried grasses, etc., on a common stem reduces the number of stems showing in the finished corsage. This gives the more natural effect of several normal-sized stems instead of a great cluster of tiny stems that simply look like green wires. A distinctive touch can be added in further covering taped stems with a related or contrasting net or ribbon.

There is nothing particularly original about the use of holly leaves in a design, but trimming away the sharp points is skillful handling, therefore a bit of distinction is added.

Unique handling by tying knots in the ends of day-lily foliage; by feathering to reduce bulk; the stripping away of petals to use the calyx; the turning of mum petals to take advantage of the delicate, green bases of the petals to make interesting green tips; the use of two rose petals placed back to back to form a "sweet pea"; the making of Calla-glads by rolling one petal and placing it in another; the manufacturing of "flowers" from pine cone segments, leaves and other materials, all are distinctive handling of common materials. A rare orchid would not rate any higher than a clover blossom, all other qualities of the design being equal. Price is not considered; rather the ability to "see" beauty in a common object and put it in a setting which allows others to appreciate it rates the highest.

Green cones, clover blossoms, flower calyxs, unique ribbon, houseplant flowers and foliage, herbs, succulents, pods, nuts, grains, grasses, fruits, berries, tree fungi, twigs, mushrooms, fruit blossoms, all these and many more contribute to individuality.

Often distinction and individuality cannot be separated. For instance, the use of brown floral tape cut in the shape of a slender leaf may be an individual approach, to press some yellow net over the tape gives it an interesting two-tone effect which adds distinction, as well.

Technique

Technique means the ability of the designer to use tape and wire in such a way that bulk is reduced and the design is flexible yet firm with no flowers falling overboard.

It goes without saying that a Judge must be allowed to handle the exhibits, albeit very carefully, in order to determine skill and control, or lack of it. If a Judge is not allowed this privilege, she is justified in deducting most or even all points for technique. While the technique involved in tying the ribbon and attaching it, as well as some taping may be observed from the front, the "underpinnings" upon which the wearability and beauty of the corsage depends must be observed from the back. The back of the exhibit should present a neat, airy appearance with all lines leading to the focal area. The grouping of the stems of little flowers on a common stem makes the "waist" of the corsage smaller, lighter in weight and easier to pin on and wear.

Wire is used as a substitute for the stems to reduce weight and bulk, and to increase control and flexibility. The proper weight wire for the material being used should be selected. The Judge should examine the handling of attachment of wire to the material, bridled wires in the calyx should be covered securely by tape so as the material shrinks and wilts it will not fall over. Hook tips placed in the top of ball forms such as mums, must be well hidden in the florets. No wires should show either at the base of the flower, anywhere on the stem's length, or at its end. Exposed wires may rust onto, or tear fabric, or wound the wearer and such careless technique should be severely penalized.

A great knot of twisted wire at the back indicates improper technique, for the stems of many small materials should have been combined into one common stem. Each wire stem to be used must be taped, and no natural or wire stems should show.

Tape may be decorative, but its main purpose is utilitarian. It gives greater control and also helps reduce wilting by sealing off stems and stem ends. The tape should appear skintight, firmly spiraled over the wire and calyx and pulled down over any cut ends in a thin, smooth layer. The ends of the wires should have been cut off squarely to avoid a needle-sharp point. Any loosening or gaps in the tape will be reason for deductions.

Because a corsage is nearly unuseable without at least two corsage pins, these should be displayed as a part of the exhibit, and their lack penalized slightly. The pin tops should harmonize with the other colors in the corsage. They may be tucked into the back, or used to close the bag which contains the corsage.

Color

While color is one of the design elements, discussion and points are listed separately in the open class scale.

Because of the small scale of a corsage, the simple color harmonies, such as the complementary (example: red and green), analogous (example: yellow, yellow-green, green) and monochromatic (one color, from light to dark) should be used. The use of too many different colors gives a corsage a busy, unrelated look.

A balance of color is important in corsage work; too much red on one side of an imaginary central axis must be balanced by some color or form equally interesting on the other side. This is asymmetrical balance. Symmetrical balance is when the same amount of color or other elements are found on both sides of the imaginary central axis.

One color should dominate the corsage, with any other colors subordinate to it and added only to contrast and give accent and "zing" to the design. When equal amounts of two colors of the same value and intensity are used, the eye is pulled between them equally, causing each to be neutralized rather than harmonize.

Suitable Combination and Schedule Interpretation

The same good taste in combinations used in dress and interior decoration applies to the choice of corsage materials. Sneakers and a silk suit are not suitably combined, neither would the use of orchids with wood roses result in a suitable combination. This is not to mean that there is any rule against using fresh with dried, rather that the forms and textures of these two are poles apart and the area of a corsage is too limited to include enough of the transitional materials necessary to draw them together.

Suitable combinations are judged on the basis of color harmonies (see Color) and textural and size relationships (see Design) of the assembled plant materials and the ribbon, if used, as well as their suitability for the costume and occasion for which the corsage was designed. Judges must note the Schedule class and evaluate suitability and schedule interpretation with its requirements in mind.

Texture is often the turning point in making a corsage a prize winner. The texture or surface roughness or smoothness of the flowers, the ribbon, the leaves must be harmonious. Not only must the actual items that go to make up the corsage be texturally compatible, but the occasion and the fabric of the costume must be considered. A corsage of common marigolds would be more suitable on a wool suit than on a satin evening dress. The demands of the class must be satisfied as perfectly as possible, or else points must be deducted.

Textural relationships can add interest to a corsage. Flower petals may be rough, glossy, woolly, etc. Berries are shiny, dull, rough. Leaves are waxy, crinkled, and smooth. Ribbon is dull, glossy, coarse and fine.

Delicate net and baby blue ribbon, narrow and fine, would be texturally unsuited with pine needles or hen and chicken succulents. If ribbon is used, it must be suitable in color, texture and width, and always subordinate to the plant materials. Daytime corsages are often more chic if ribbon is omitted. Sparkle, glitter and fancy ribbon are unsuited to daytime corsages.

Corsages entered in classes for evening use should be made of colors which do not lose their effectiveness under artificial light. Blues, dark purples and orchid tints are unreliable in this respect, and often "grey-out" especially in dim lighting. Yellow loses its identity at night. White, pink and rose are at their best while deep red turns black in dim rooms.

Any great gulf between sizes and form reflects on the suitability of the combinations. Check to see if some transitional material has been used to bridge the span.

Not every corsage needs foliage, but the suitable and appropriate selection of foliage can be the doing or undoing of a corsage. The Judge must evaluate the foliage not merely as a filler, but as an integral part of the design.

Smooth textured leaves may relieve the fussiness of fine flower forms. Foliage can make the corsage stand out from a dress in which the color of the fabric is too similar to that of the flowers. Foliage added at the focal area may give needed color or weight there and foliage can serve as accents, taking the place of ribbon through looping and tying. Entire corsages made of foliage are very suitable and conform to Schedule requirements for tailored corsages. Foliage textures must not be too coarse or too fine for the flowers, nor its size be too large or small.

The wise selection of materials that are fragrant, but not odorous should be considered here. Some plants are so overpowering they are objectionable as corsage subjects and points can reasonably be deducted under suitability.

Condition

The Judge must be prepared to reward the exhibitor who understands her plant materials so well that she selects and uses those which will hold up, without wilting, during the show period.

Even common corsage flowers such as roses, daisies, asters and carnations will suffer more bruising from the necessary manipulation during construction if their tissues are starved for water. Hardening the plants and foliages will assure a state of turgidity necessary to take this abuse.

However, even the most careful hardening will not materially lengthen the life of flowers and foliage that are thin-walled and lacking in native substance such as alyssum, clematis, cosmos, poppies, etc. These have a corsage life of barely one day, and all things being equal a Judge is justified in deducting points, either under suitability if still holding, or under condition if wilt has set in.

Wilting of any parts in a corsage (including the ribbon) must be penalized and excessive wilting will eliminate the exhibit from any award as all the qualities on the scale are affected.

Because corsages, like dinner table designs, are placed in a position where they are closely observed, all parts must present a fresh, crisp and particularly, a **clean** appearance. Any limpness, blemishes, insect or disease damage, soil and tears must be penalized.

The ribbon must present a perky, freshly-tied appearance with the ends neatly clipped. Any evidence of having been retied, mussed or twisted is to be considered a fault.

Check the taped stems. Pastel tape, because of its sticky surface, often exhibits a soiled appearance which must be penalized. Usually the Judge will find that the exhibitor who is careless of the appearance of his finished work, also is careless in his color choice, suitable relationships and in his design.

SUMMARY

Design 25 to 30 Points

*eye moves easily over the design *well-handled repetition *contrasting forms add interest *lines all leading into the focal area *interesting silhouette with voids *flowers well scaled to each other and to foliage and ribbon *exposed taped stems add to design *design has depth *well-defined focal area

-lacks rhythm -movement halted by incorrect placements of forms, colors, textures -monotonous -"hole" in design -aster too large for babysbreath (scale) -squat -too much ribbon (proportion) -corsage appears flat -exposed taped stems confuse design -top heavy

Distinction, Imagination, Individuality 20 Points

*unique handling of common materials *refreshing approach *unusual materials *simplicity prevails *tiny flowers wired to common stem

-appears busy -mediocre selection and handling

Technique 15 Points

*wires all taped *bow (if used) neatly tied and neatly attached *tape pulled tight *no exposed wire *no stems untaped or unwired

-wire too fine, material nodding -exposed wires -tape loosening -some stems not wired and taped -tape messily or carelessly handled -tape bunched

Color 15 Points

*colors harmonious *color repetition in tape, materials *color limited *design visually balanced, color wise *one color dominant

-color balance destroyed by poor placement -no dominant color -too many colors -colors not suitable for occasion -complicated color harmony

Suitable Combination 15 Points

*good taste in choices *choices suitably related or contrasted in form, texture, color *fragrant *foliage (if used) serving more than just filler *textures suitable for occasion and costume

-incompatible textures -unsuited to occasions, use or costume -unsuitable color choices for evening (blue, purple, etc.) -foliage not serving in design -foliage texture too coarse for flowers

Condition 10 Points

*ribbon perky *materials clean *fresh plant material crisp, turgid

-ribbon mussed -wilted materials -dirt -soil -insect or disease damage -frayed ribbon ends

Home Christmas Decoration Contests

SUGGESTED CLASSES

. Daytime Appeal
. Nighttime Appeal
. Combination Day/night Appeal
. Door
    A: wreaths   B: swags
    C: other
        1. plant materials predominating
        2. other materials predominating

. Traditional
. Modern
. Religious
. Humorous
. Novelty (Toy Parade, etc.)
. Entire Block
. Expense Limitations (under $10, etc.)
. Commercial Figures, etc., used
. Entirely Do-It-Yourself

. Window
. Child Appeal
. Lawn
. Yard
. Rooftop

. Combination Commercial, Home-
made
. Tree
A: Lighted   B: other

SUGGESTED SCALE NO. 1 GENERAL

Artistic Effect   50
. easily seen from a stated
distance (e.g. 15' or from
nearest thoroughfare)
. according to class requirements
. design composition
. techniques
. color usage

Communication of the
Christmas Spirit   20

Ingenuity   15
. utilizing surroundings,
house structure to best
advantage
. in use of materials, including lights, etc.

Integration and Com-
patibility   15
. with surroundings
. adjoining or adjacent
buildings, other perman-
ent features
. functionalism maintain-
ed where applicable

SUGGESTED SCALE NO. 2 EMPHASIS ON LIGHTING

Artistic Merit   35
. composition
. color usage
. effective use of materials
. suitability

Lighting Effectiveness   25
. from a stated distance
(e.g. 15')

Creativity   20
. newness of idea
. new use of materials
. techniques

Communication of the
Christmas Spirit   20

Artistic Effect

● balanced within the composition, balanced as to house or yard.
All interest concentrated on left or right side of house front or
yard is deductible.
● proportion. Areas of decoration to house or yard area. Must
not appear skimpy.
● scale. Size of objects in relation to house size, to door, window,
yard.
● rhythm. Continuity of interest areas, not spotty.
● dominance. One idea portrayed, e.g. Nativity scenes not mixed
with toys.

The artistic effect would be lessened by careless techniques, wrinkled fabric used as a door cover, etc. Neatness is stressed. Balanced simplicity results in a more effective design.

The design which is held to two or three major colors and large,
well placed scenes or figures rates higher than a scattered hit or miss
collection of numerous small objects.

As in any composition some area, theme, color should carry the
dominant role. The materials used should be of such construction and
materials that they are durable for the entire holiday season. Any
color streaking or disintegration is to be penalized.

444

The decorations of doorways and windows particularly should be effective from a distance stated in the Schedule or from six to fifteen feet at least. The Judges should judge the decorations from the distance stated in the Schedule or from reasonable vantage points, getting out of the cars if necessary to perform the task.

The Judge/s should consider the door or window frame in such classes as the boundary of the design and consider the proportion, balance, scale within that specified area, rather in the same manner as a niche.

The total effect should not be amateurish even if it is a do-it-yourself project.

Creativity

New lighting ideas and effects, new ways of using commonplace ideas, new handling of roof, eaves, fences, sills, frames, etc.

Communication of Christmas Spirit

All decorations should conform to the same theme. There should be continuity of design. A religious window with a Santa Claus on the rooftop is an example of such variation which should be deductible. Should be either gay enough to say "Merry Christmas" or reverent enough to express the **true** spirit of the season.

Lighting Effectiveness

Adequate candlepower, evenly distributed, should be used to show the design off in its entirety; deep shadows thrown by ill-placed lights can make the theme vague.

The mechanics of lighting should be concealed by snowbanks, shrubbery or a part of the decorations in such a way that the source of the light is not a detracting factor. There should be no distracting bulb rim brightness.

A single feature may be spotlighted, such as a tree, door, chimney, yard scene or a combination of several into an eye-appealing overall scheme, rather than strings or groups of lights hung haphazardly from gate to rooftop.

It should be remembered that light **is** decoration and over-use can be as detrimental to good design as too little. Too much light concentrated in one spot can wash out details and give a harsh effect. There should never be too many lights or too many colors of lights which give a gaudy effect.

The use of strings of lights alone around a door or window is too skimpy and cannot be considered as a complete unit or exhibit.

If the outdoor tree looks spotty, it is because too few lights are used and those are poorly placed. A "formula" which makes for an ample number of lights is:

Height of Tree (Feet)	Number of Tree Lights
4	35
5	56
6	77
7	102
8	140
10	210

A misshapen tree can be given visual symmetry if the lights are run vertically in "teepee" fashion from the top of the tree down to stakes in the ground around the outer branches. This ruse is particularly effective for night appeal classes, but the Judges may feel that day appeal should be penalized a point or two.

The total effect of the whole scene should be one of a well-designed Christmas Card to the whole Community.

Decorative Wood, Driftwood, etc.

SUGGESTED CLASSES

1. Theme optional: Featuring Decorative Wood combined with fresh-cut plant material. No accessory permitted.
2. Theme optional: Featuring Decorative Wood. Natural Finish. Must contain some fresh-cut material. Accessory/s permitted.
3. Theme optional: A design featuring decorative wood. No restrictions on finish, materials or accessory.

DRIFTWOOD

Much controversy has been created over various names given wood used in arrangements. These names often describe the species of wood, the location of discovery, the surface texture, or a combination of some or all of these.

Weathered wood is defined as any wood that has been treated by wind, sun, rain, frost action; often having altered its shape, texture, color. Found in woods, canyons, roadsides, construction areas. Called ghostwood when found in the desert.

Driftwood is any wood which has been washed and worked over by the action of water. Often color, shape and texture are altered. Found on shores of lakes, ponds, oceans.

Cypress Knees are neither or both. They do not commonly drift, but after heavy storms, have been known to . They are weathered by sun, wind and water. Cut or found in low marshes, swamps, river banks.

Natural Finish, Untreated. No stain or artificial color applied. Water, bleach and a brush, gouge or sand blaster may be used to clean off rotted bark and imbedded soil. A thin layer of colorless wax may be applied.

Treated or Finished. Any wood which surface color and texture has been artifically altered through the application of a finish. Includes paint, chalk, stain, dye, varnish, glue and glitter, other.

And then some purist asks — where do we classify roots, bark, branches or a palm spathe washed up on the beach? It is even possible that a Garden Clubber tiring of a piece of driftwood, tosses it out beside the road many miles from the ocean where she found it. Another sees it, and uses it in a class calling for weathered wood. Confusion multiplied!

Driftwood "experts" can be fooled, too, because the wood species, plus environmental variations during the process of drying or weathering alter cases. Very often it is difficult to determine if the piece has a *natural color or is bleached, waxed or otherwise altered. Bleach and waxing are included in the definition of treated wood. Refer to* **Treated** *p. 435.*

When any of the three first named woods above are used by name, the following problems are apt to occur in a less-than-specific Schedule, with an inexperienced Classification Committee.

1. Class calls for weathered wood. Cypress and drift are used and passed by Classification Committee.
2. Class calls for weathered wood, driftwood permitted. A Cypress Knee is entered and passed.
3. Class calls for weathered wood, driftwood and cypress permitted. No mention of finish. Painted or varnished pieces are entered and passed.

As noted, the definitions overlap, the borderlines are indistinct and very often misunderstood by exhibitors and Classification Committees when used in the schedules without definition. Extensive definitions increase size and cost of schedules. The following solutions are suggested:

That either the general term "driftwood" be applied to all. **Or,** that the use of a common word, such as decorative wood, be inserted into the Flower Show vocabulary.

Decorative Wood: includes any drift or weathered wood, as well as cypress knees, roots, other.

The use of this term would allow leeway without contention and is in the interest of giving creativity full reign by letting the choice be up to the exhibitor. If wished, the Schedule Committee can restrict artificial finishes.

SUGGESTED SCALE OF POINTS

Interpretation	25	Individuality	20
. of scheduled requirements		. personal expression	
. of class title, theme		Technique	10
Design	25	. condition	
. principles		. scars	
Relationships	20	. cleanliness	
. color		. gluing	
. forms		. finish	
. textures		. mechanics	
. space		. support	

INTERPRETATION
Scheduled Requirements

The Schedule, the law of the Show, must be specific and very carefully worded in classes notorious for their controversiality, such as *driftwood and its relations. Decorative wood can be classed as accessory when it is subordinant, or featured if it predominates.*

If the Schedule simply requests decorative wood, the Classification Committee and the Judges must accept any and all degrees of treatment; unfinished, varnished, painted, and the like. **And** must accept any and all woods, cypress, juniper, drift, weathered and others.

If only treated wood is wanted, the Schedule must so state.

If only untreated wood is wanted, the Schedule must so state, otherwise any finish is acceptable. If the Schedule requests only natural *finish, and a finished piece is entered, Judges will remove points under misinterpretation, distinction or lack of conformity.*

If the Schedule makes no reference for or against finish or treatment, then all are acceptable and the finish must be considered and judged only as it affects the design, textural relationships and theme.

Decorative Wood Featured

If the Schedule Committee wishes the wood to be the dominant, featured or main interest in the design, the Schedule must state so very clearly.

If the Schedule merely states "A Design **using** Decorative Wood" *then either **wood** or other **plant materials** or components may be dominant.*

Even if the Schedule does not request that the wood predominate, since it is a decorative wood class, enough of the wood should be shown to influence and enhance the design. A timid, little piece laid on the base or poked in as an afterthought should be severely penalized, under interpretation and/or design.

If the Judges find a design which does not fit the class, they may ask the Classification Committee to reclassify to a more fitting one. If *there is no other class, or the request is refused, Judges may remove enough points so the exhibit cannot win an award, which it would probably not deserve because of lack of conformity or misinterpretation.*

Theme Interpretation

All materials used must be wisely and perceptively chosen to intensify the theme, feeling or spirit. The latent strength and rhythm of the contours *of decorative wood can be used to express many themes. A descriptive card relative to designer's intent may be placed if Schedule allows.*

Design

The decorative wood is not considered separately for its own form, size, beauty or texture, but as these qualities affect the overall design. When the wood is to dominate or be featured, it must be so integrated that its removal would destroy the design.

Consider the piece as a branch, should it have been pruned, trimmed or placed to better advantage of line interest as affects the overall design.

Rhythm, balance and proportion upset by untrimmed nubs or protuberances should be penalized.

Simple proportion and a clean, uncluttered look complements the natural, often sculptural lines of the decorative wood. The main lines of the wood may be rhythmic, giving an effect of motion or charm; may be zig-zagged, seeming to express strife and tension; or may be mainly vertical, giving a dignified impression. Only enough plant material should have been used to strengthen and point out these dominant lines. To crowd out their effect with abundant material lessens the emphasis and impact of the design expression inherent in the natural contours.

Because of its visual weight and interest, decorative wood easily overpowers the design or makes it appear top or bottom heavy. Its proportion should have been controlled by properly selected amounts of auxiliary material. Bright colors or unusual forms used to balance the visual power of the wood piece are examples of expertise worthy of upscoring.

Some contrast is, of course, needed for interest, but a design in which the dominant amount of plant material goes one way and the principle lines of the wood go another deserves its sure deduction for divided interest.

Dominance takes a special place in appraisement of a design including decorative wood. Either the plant forms or the driftwood must be dominant according to the Schedule. If both are equally arresting an unpleasant division may result which destroys the unity overall.

Balance is almost invariably asymmetrical because Nature rarely fashions a symmetrical piece. The placement of the plant material in relation to the driftwood must be visually stabilized. If a base or further trimming or adjustment of visual weight is needed to make the design balance, points must be removed. Color and texture must also be balanced throughout the design.

Space adds another dimension. Many wood pieces have natural spaces, or gaps which allow the eye to move in and out of the design. Plant material should have been placed to take advantage of shapes of space afforded by such voids. If the additions of plant materials are used carelessly or with disregard for the advantages of the natural spaces, penalty may be taken.

The size of the leaves, flowers and accessories, plus the base used should be scaled to the wood. A huge, fully-open six-inch rose with a finely scaled piece is as out of proportion as a delicately tiny miniature rose would be placed beside a massive, cliff-like chunk. Less extreme examples need varying degrees of deduction.

Relationships

Natural dried material relates perfectly to wood since it is also dried plant material. Stone, lichen, fungi, moss, mushrooms, needle evergreen and native foliages have a natural affinity to the natural finish of decorative wood. But delicate flowers, cultivated and wildling, and fruits of varied textures do not suffer by the contrast. Such contrasting shapes and textures, if well planned, add interest and variety, contributing to the character of the design.

In the use of treated wood (varnished, painted, etc.) color and textural relationships must be compatible. A highly glossed piece of wood has had its native "personality" altered by the unnatural finish. Its placement on a rustic slab is an example of inharmonious texture and character for which scores would be reduced.

The base is often a definite part of the design and may serve as the "container" or holder. Its texture, color and general contours should be matched or blended with those of the wood.

Dried or fresh material may be used with decorative wood, according to Schedule requirements, but there must be unity rather than discord . . . a feeling of fitness in the choices.

The use of related forms, related lines, and dried materials copying the twists and turns of the wood brings unity and distinction to the design.

Any accessory used must be related to the other items and the theme and be an integral part of the design and interpretation. The dominating character of the wood often demands strong character in accessories which must be met to avoid penalty for lack of balance and inappropriate relationships in color and texture as well as scale.

To state dogmatically that rustic wood and roses should be penalized is unrealistic. Wild roses and weathered wood are natural companions. Both interpretation and relationships must be weighed in the decision. Does the interpretation call for a contrast of texture such as "Beauty and the Beast"? If so, finely textured roses and a gnarled, grotesque piece of wood may be just what the Schedule ordered.

To say roses are too fine for wood is passe. The shoe **could** conceivably be on the other foot. The "spirit" of wild roses may be too roguish for the sophisticated curves of a rhythmic piece of finely finished wood.

Roses have changed a great deal from the delicate, lightly tinted few grown when that rule was wrought! Sizes have increased to the point where a rose such a 'MISTER LINCOLN' can hold its own with almost any piece of decorative wood. The development of a wide range of strong, vibrant colors, the heavily textured petals, the robust, sturdy appearance and the vigorous growth results in roses which are superbly right with decorative wood. Outdated opinionated rulings should not be allowed to interfere with fair judgment. The relationships and the theme expressed in the specific design being judged **at the moment** are what are important.

The same applies to the combination of decorative wood and candles. It cannot be flatly stated that "they do not go together". The "togetherness" is judged according to theme requirements and the textural finish and color of the individuals and the combinations.

Individuality

Individuality is built into every piece of decorative wood. Nature has made each different in form, grain and surface patterns, and it needs only a perceiving designer to find and combine it to give visual life to a scheduled theme, portray a story or illustrate a mood.

Individuality can be expressed through an unusual combination of materials, unexpected balance, unique accessory placement or a particularly appropriate method of featuring the distinctive lines of the wood.

When the designer has been perceptive enough to note the individual form, striations and grain whorls of the wood and methodical enough to search for flowers, fruit and figurines which repeat the patterns, her individual approach should be well rewarded.

Taking advantage of holes or spaces in the wood and utilization of the wood's personality as suggested by the sweep of its lines, makes for individuality with a difference.

Placement and lighting so the dark shadows caught in the cavities and depressions contrast with the natural, light silver-grey patina can be counted as individuality and upscored.

Technique

Proper technique includes the knowledge and ability to select long-lasting plant materials, condition them and invent ways of continuing the needed water supply. Wilting, drooping fresh plant materials indicate a lack of technique and should be severely penalized.

Dirt and rotten wood should have been dug out, brushed or wiped away from wood, plant materials and accessory pieces.

Whether two pieces have been glued or screwed together should be the exhibitor's secret; unless juncture, shakiness or lines offend good design no penalty is taken. Pruning, sawing and joining scars should have been treated to blend with the rest of the wood.

Stability is essential, but the props to achieve it should be unnoticeable in finished design. They need not be hidden, but must appear natural and integrated.

If the wood has been chalked to highlight or alter its color, the blending should have been evenly and subtly applied. Heavy, inaccurate streaking should be penalized unless it is needed somehow in the interpretation. Any finish must have been applied carefully.

SUMMARY

Interpretation 25 Points

According to Schedule *conforms on all counts

-fails to conform as to: -featuring wood -regarding finish -fresh cut material requirement -accessory restriction -decorative wood too insignificant

Theme Interpretation   *decorative wood and plant materials express theme *well chosen accessory strengthens theme

-theme ignored -interpretation indistinct -lines and material at variance with theme

Design 25 Points

*wood well integrated in the design *well scaled *proportion of plant material and wood well balanced *either wood or plant material dominates *eye moves easily over the design *plant material well placed to point up wood lines, spaces

-wood seems added as an afterthought -balance, rhythm or proportion upset by untrimmed nubs, branches -plant material obscuring wood -crowded -cluttered -off balance -materials out of scale -plant material placement ignores wood lines

Relationships 20 Points

*textural contrasts well planned, pleasing *has fitness *harmonious textures, color, mood *unified thru related shapes, lines *well chosen accessory strengthens design and theme

-inharmonious textures -incompatible "spirit" -discordant -inappropriate base -lacks color harmony

Individuality 20 Points

*unusual combination of material *unexpected treatment of balance *unique accessory placement *spaces well utilized *perceptive repetition in form, texture, color *placement and lighting highlight contrasts

-nothing unusual -lacks "punch", impact -commonplace

Technique 10 Points

*firmly supported *materials fresh, well conditioned *finish expertly applied

-unstable -props detract -pruning scars -joint cracks -dirt and rotten wood clinging -carelessly finished

Floats

The noun "float" has many meanings such as fishing bobbers, a bouyant dock, a rock "sled", a plasterer's tool, but it also has come to mean "a flat-topped vehicle without sides for carrying displayed objects or exhibits in a procession; also such a vehicle with its displayed exhibits or objects".

Large parades of long standing experience often publish a manual of rules, regulations and requests to guide exhibitors and Judges. These often outline dimensions, define "float" and list the competitive classes and awards.

Size limitations are often stated in the rules and usually are arbitrarily limited by roadway widths, parade route turns and overhead barriers, such as bridges and overhead wiring.

It is hoped that several categories for judging are planned. Examples are 1. Most effective theme representation. 2. Most beautiful. 3. Best amateur-built float. 4. Most effective use of plant materials. 5. Most beautiful out-of-town or state or country entry. 6. Best display of originality. 7. Most humorous entry. 8. Float which best characterizes local color and so on.

Other classes for Civic, Religious, Fraternal, Educational and Business entries can be added to fit individual parade situations. Special awards other than those listed, if suggested by the Judges, may be awarded at the discretion of the Parade Officials.

The following scale of points is for general classes. If some quality is to be stressed, such as originality, humor or local color, the points for the quality to be featured can be increased by reducing the points for other qualities.

SUGGESTED SCALE OF POINTS

Design Excellence	35	General Overall Beauty and Interest	35

Design Excellence — 35
- consider design principles of balance, proportion, contrast, dominance and particularly scale
- appropriateness and execution of theme
- floating illusion
- silhouette from all angles
- neatness, including condition and suitability of materials used

General Overall Beauty and Interest — 35
- general appeal
- good taste, etc.

Originality — 20
- of theme or idea
- of design, color harmony, etc.

Color Harmony — 10

SUGGESTED POINT SCALE FOR NIGHT PARADES

Floating Illusion	30	Design	20
Lighting	25		
Originality	15		
Color	10		

Design — 20
- silhouette
- execution of theme
- principles

NOTE: Lighting and floating illusion are very important factors in night show or torchlight parades, therefore emphasis is placed on these qualities in the above scale.

GENERAL OVERALL BEAUTY AND INTEREST

Imagination plus mechanical know-how are the basis for beautiful and exciting floats. Total viewing time is short indeed, and there are different angles of spectator view — the child looks up, the roof and window percher looks down and others view the float from one side only, so it is necessary that the theme be portrayed and the story told clearly and understood quickly from any point of view.

No one has time to debate alternate meanings or to savor intricate detailing. Most floats are viewed so briefly at a minimum distance of fifteen feet, that miniature or too fine detailing is lost on the viewer. Effects should be broad, features prominent, lines bold, and the sizes of flowers, fruits, animals, cornucopias, swans and the like made larger-than-life size.

Any size less than eight to ten feet is ineffective and should be penalized under general beauty with the exception of children's classes. The maximum dimensions should not exceed 17' in height, 20' in width and 40' in length in order to allow for turning and other travel problems.

Clarity of meaning is also achieved by avoidance of clutter and confusion. One feature should be dominant, and should carry the theme. For instance, at first glance the dinosaur on a prehistoric-themed float is seen; at second glance the cave men, apes and other items are seen, but these secondary features give interest without confusing the primary picture.

The proven techniques of material selection and attachment, gluing, stapling, nailing and joining should have been utilized and appropriate materials used in carrying out the design to achieve unified overall beauty and distinction.

Formerly many floats were covered with loud placards and some even carried merchandise and prices. These have largely been replaced by productions of taste and ingenuity. The direct commercial pitch is passe' in today's parades. The advertising message, if any, should be subtle and tasteful. The sponsor's signature has become more discreet as more was learned about sight emphasis.

Observation reveals that the crowd does not look at the float directly opposite, but at the next one in line. Lettering in small size low in the front or on each side near the front is effective without being too obvious. The front view carries great impact and should be designed as an introduction to the float.

The float theme can be related to a business with taste and discreetness. A segment of the business operation such as a mining firm displaying a miniature dragline carries no direct sales appeal because few viewers will be in the market for ore. A scuba diver outfitter can show off his product is a reproduction of a local aquatic setting and a butcher can exhibit pride in his community's cattle or turkey production without transgressing good taste. A parade is an expression of pride in the general area, not in private possessions or products. Humor and imagination make the deepest impression. Civic, fraternal and religious organizations very often sponsor floats with general appeal as a simple matter of good will.

Animation holds the onlooker's attention longer than a float equally spectacular, but without moving figures. Animation must be used with care. Too many moving objects on one float, plus the float's forward movement confuses the eye, even while holding it. Judging should be done on the parade route as well as stationary to assess the effects of animation and its visibility.

In assessing the overall beauty and interest, the Judges will take into consideration the freshness of the materials, the coordination of the costumes of the participants, drivers and escorts (if used), the workmanship and attention given to minor details and the **finished** appearance of the aprons and rear of the float. Grab braces for live passengers should be rigidly but unobstrusively built into the design. If the float is not self propelled, the towing vehicle should be decorated in keeping with the float theme.

Novelties

Floats that dispense novelties attract a great deal of attention. These often entail the tossing of light souvenir objects at the audience. No article intended for such distribution must cause injury — crowd safety is paramount. The Judges should check the rules carefully, as some parades restrict such activities or disqualify the float from competition.

The use of fireworks should also have been cleared with the Parade Officials as special permission or restrictions may be involved. Fireworks, if allowed, should not be used only for the benefit of those near the Judge's reviewing stand, but at intervals along the entire parade route.

The decorative parade personnel are expected to put up the best possible appearance despite cold, rain or a long route. A huddled, bedraggled, non-smiling, rigid float model is a detraction rather than an asset to any production. Graceful, smiling, waving models do much to generate parade excitement and spirit.

Balanced placement of the humans is as important as that of the other float features. They should not be too heavily grouped in one spot. They may simply ride and wave and smile, or they may have a natural purpose such as driving a sleigh, riding a camel or depicting a sport; unnatural positions such as huddling under a bunny's feet usually detract from the overall effectiveness.

Floats which develop mechanical trouble **after** passing the Judges reviewing stand should not be penalized by hearsay.

DESIGN EXCELLENCE
Principles

Imaginative and colorful top structure should conceal the practical outlines of the basic vehicle. A float should look like anything but a flat box or a poorly disguised truck. Too often the effect of a float is spoiled because it sticks too closely to the functional outlines of the vehicle upon which it was built. The aim should be to mask the undercarriage completely with curves and swirls developing an imaginative topside form.

The float should be symmetrical and visually balanced, one side the same as the other. The Judge must remember that the sidewalk-bound viewer has no chance to see the beauties of the opposite side.

Rhythm and contrasts achieved through combinations of straight lines and sweeping curves with familiar forms, human, fowl and animal, both live or modeled add to the effectiveness of the design.

Bunting is used less and less as it is more difficult to shape and control that the materials which have largely replaced it, and it has a flimsy look when worked in with opaque finishes. A float generally represents a solid shape and transparent or translucent materials must be carefully incorporated, if used at all. Actually all floats are much lighter than their appearance implies, otherwise no pavement would be strong enough to support them.

Almost every float has a climactic or dominant point — the place where the pretty girl rides, or the massive emblem is mounted, or the animated figure goes through its routine. The upper structure should be shaped and decorated to lead the eye easily to this point.

The relative size of each part in relation to the others (scale) is important, though a flower can be overly large for the human seated within it, it must be properly sized for the float. Features that are too large for the vehicle give an unwieldy, top-heavy appearance which is penalized.

Theme

Themes can be based on a local crop or product, a natural feature, mineral resource, tourist attraction, or historic incident. They may be educational, carrying a message such as getting out the vote or cleaning up litter or they may simply be beautiful for beauty's sake. They are often plentifully garnished with feminine beauty.

The skillful use of perspective to achieve great depth with but minor contour variations can illustrate certain scenes such as the Grand Canyon. However, a near miss spells failure to be deducted.

Waterfalls and fountains are often difficult to handle; water is heavy, shifts in its containers and is blown about by the wind.

Illusions with paint to simulate columns for royal courts, houses, schools, rural landscapes, jungles and space scenes can be combined with animal or human figures — live or modeled, but the transition should be smoothly done.

A theme based on a direct advertising idea is less effective and aesthetic than a float whose message is universal. A float should be visual entertainment, a "thank you" to the public by the sponsor, or a source of public motivation, i.e. to vote, etc. The most popular floats are those which are themed around a story or develop a symbolism. If they advertise anything, they extoll the local products, scenic splendors and sports in general fashion. They concentrate on entertainment or an educational or inspirational message rather than persuasion. They show humor and imagination rather than heavy-handed commercialism.

Floating Illusion

A float should be designed to give one impression . . . that of floating or being suspended on air. This illusion is achieved through special construction and its embellishments, including the all-important fringe which hides the functional wheels and gives the float a look of gliding along without support.

The fringe goes around the bottom of the vehicle to hide the running gear. A float upon which a 15" fringe is used, should have been built 15" from the pavement, with a 1" lap of fringe for stapling; this allows 1" clearance, just right to create an illusion of floating. The springs should have been blocked and the tires uniformly inflated to maintain even fringe clearance.

An illusion of gliding unsupported is also achieved by properly scaled overhang. Six or seven feet in the rear with two feet or less at the front enhances the floating impression.

Lightness of construction, rigid but correctly braced and securely fastened is indispensable to an illusion of floating. A float that is too heavy appears to plod rather than glide and should be penalized.

Silhouette

The silhouette should be interesting and unified with varying height and interest levels and sweeping rhythmic lines from front to back. Height is restricted by overhead barriers, but clever designers can defeat a depressing flatness or boxiness by achieving an illusion of silhouette interest and height through gradual, billowing rises to the float's climactic point or the use of space under an object (airplane, bird, etc.) which is mounted on slender, camouflaged braces.

Neatness

The fringe should be an even length and clear the pavement by an even amount. One inch is the proper distance; the fringe should not look skimpy nor drag on the ground.

Neatness in lettering is an important factor in judging. No one has time to decipher wobbly lettering. If the lettering is done in floral material, it must have been well-chosen. Closing flowers and opening buds often make letters illegible.

Naturally no float entrant can anticipate the weather, but the Judge must judge "as is", not as the float may have appeared before the shower or whirlwind hit it. Sturdy, decorative materials impervious to unpredictable elements often make the best showing in off-season parades.

Originality

Individuality can be injected through color harmony, theme uniqueness and design effectiveness. Limited and conventional color schemes such as complementary red and green or white and green show lack of originality.

The attempt to achieve originality should not break the thin line into carnival-showmanship. Fire-eaters, snake charmers, freaks, oddities and the like are too garish for parade routes and belong properly in circus tents. Penalty should be exacted against such exhibits.

Local color or local stunts may be effectively incorporated in floats. For example, log-rolling done on a float by a birler equipped with hobnail boots whirling a barked log mounted on axles would rate high for local color and interest.

Originality can be achieved without an expensive extravaganza of form and costume as an intriguing concept, an imaginative use of commonplace materials can have a beauty and effectiveness far surpassing mere cost. At times it seems that unlimited funds are originality's greatest threat, permitting the purchase of professional "package productions" at the expense of individuality and an original approach.

Color Harmony

Few colors will clash on floats, either of the participants' gowns or the decorations. The materials are brilliant and more likely to accent the hues of other materials than to cause discord. Pastels are used more and more frequently, mainly to set off strong colors and it is in pastels that conflict is more likely to arise.

Some of the new metallic materials and plastics make color selection unnecessary.   The show and glitter of gold and silver add scintillating highlights. The color scheme may be in the theme of the parade such as patriotic red, white and blue or the colors of the flags of nationality groups, or may be arrived at from the idea of the individual float theme itself.

While colors seldom clash, the number should be limited. Generally, two or three colors are sufficient. These are a light background color to pick up and reflect light rays, a matching hue in a deeper value to set off the float's dominant decorative feature and a contrasting color for accent.

Floats of many colors and the repetitious figures of plaids and checks which look so attractive in fabrics are generally unsuited and may ruin the whole color plan. Stripes and running lines often enhance a design which aims at size and grandeur and are often used to carry the eye to the main or dominant feature on the float.

Lighting

A float which is dazzling in the daytime may be dull at night due to poor color and material selection which fail to reflect and make the most of artificial lights.

Effective illumination may be achieved simply by the use of colored lights creating changing patterns on a basically silver or gold float. Colored bulbs or filters may set off and point up the color scheme of the float, such tie-ins rate extra points.

Clear-glass bulbs with their filaments showing, used with on-and-off condensers or alone give a twinkling starry effect when used to outline the design as well as providing illumination and are effective night showmanship.

Concealed lights that shine through the float shell or the dominant object call for careful construction and special materials to assure emittance of enough light to put up a bright appearance, yet the bare bones must not show through. If such is the case, of course, penalty is taken.

Any lighting arrangement on the float that throws strong beams into the audience's eyes should be penalized. The flow of light should be directed at the decorative sheathing, highlighting the curves and dimensions of the float form. The less light shed on the pavement, audience or another float, the better.

Attention must be paid to the balancing of the illumination. The light should be evenly spread with the dominant feature well lighted or outlined. Any figures, live or animated, should be specially and carefully spotlighted. A single misdirected or over-powerful spotlight may wash out the other lights and colors and should be severely penalized.

The float outlines should be easily apparent; a vaguely-lighted shape that cannot be identified without eyestrain deserves its sure point reduction.

SUMMARY
General Overall Beauty and Interest 35 Points
*story clearly portrayed *story quickly understood *one dominant feature *unified design *advertising (if any) subtle *coordinated costuming *sponsor's name in small lettering *front view interesting *superior workmanship *of general local interest *aprons and float rear present **finished** appearance *graceful, smiling, waving personnel *human placement balanced

-meaning obscure -appointments too small -cluttered -disjointed appearing -ineffective size (less than 8-10', except children's class) -too much animation -too obviously advertising -decoration of tow not related to float -rear and aprons carelessly finished -humans too heavily grouped -fireworks or souvenir throwing restricted -rigid, bedraggled personnel

Design Effectiveness 35 Points
*basic vehicle lines well masked *symmetrical *shows humor or imagination *curves plus straight lines for rhythm and contrast *upper structure shaped and decorated to lead eye to dominant point *transition smooth from human figures to painted scenes *silhouette presents varying height and interest levels *appears to float *fringe clears pavement evenly *clear lettering *neat *fresh appearing

-vehicle poorly disguised -bunting and trimming have flimsy look -water poorly handled in fountain or falls -impractical theme choice -fringe dragging -too heavy appearing; plods rather than floats -fringe skimpy -flat, boxy appearance -wobbly lettering -tattered -scuffed -top heavy -out of scale

Originality 20 Points
*unusual color harmony *unique theme *imaginative design

-garish -lacks punch -commonplace -conventional

Color Harmony 10 Points
*interesting color choices *limited to two-three colors *stripes or running lines point up dominant features

-conventional colors used -too many colors used -colors unrelated

Lighting 25 Points
*outlines easily apparent *figures carefully spotlighted *color tie-in with materials and lights *flow of light directed on float *illumination well spread *balanced illumination

-colors or materials unsuitable under artificial lights -too vaguely lighted -strong light in audience eyes -"bare bones" showing -strong light wasted on pavement, other floats

Miniatures and Small Designs

SUGGESTED ENTRY:

1. MINIATURE: fresh cut plant material predominating, not to exceed five inches in any dimension.

2. *SMALL   dried materials predominating, not to exceed eight in-
   DESIGN   ches in any dimension, including background, mat, etc.*

Classes to fit the show theme can be added to fit specific spots in rooms or specific occasions.

MINIATURE FLOWER ARRANGEMENT

Miniature or small arrangements are small-scale designs in which *the dimensions have been arbitrarily set as not to exceed 5" and 8" respectively in any direction, including container, base, accessories. Many* Schedules limit classes to three inches; these are more difficult to stage and judge, and the construction of these tinier jewels is really a specialized field requiring great skill and understanding of design principles which is even greater than is needed to make five inch designs. *This is a matter to be settled by the local committee and made clear in the Schedule which should also state allotted space and staging, i.e., niche, shelf, other.*

SUGGESTED POINT SCALE

Scale	40	Individuality	10
Design (other principles)	25	Condition and Suitability	10
Color	15		

Scale

The Judge should allow the exhibitor to take no liberties with scale. Scale is defined as the size relationship of each part to the other and this involves the size of the flowers to each other, the size of each flower to the container, the size of any accessory or base to the container and the design, and the size of the whole to its placement (such as in a niche) or its intended placement (such as on a desk or bed tray). *A Small Design for a small desk would probably require less than the full 8", and a Miniature for small bed tray perhaps only 3".*

The design should fit the dimension of the niche if such has been provided for staging, leaving space on all sides. But the space should be equalized. For instance, if the niche is taller than wide, the design should be also, and not a horizontal one which leaves excess space between the top of the design and the top of the niche. If the space occupied is horizontal, the design therein should also be horizontal. Rectangular or circular lines of the staging niche frame the design with a hard line which is best considered in the design of a Miniature, i.e. curving or round arrangements in the circular niche, etc.

Size is Relative

The Judge knows that size is relative and that the secret of true scale is when each element assumes the size we expect it to be in a certain set of circumstances. When a thing does not fit this expectation, we say it is too large or too small. Size is relative — we think of a dwarf marigold as tiny when placed in a full-scale design, but it can appear enormous when placed in a miniature arrangement. Where a number of such small flowers might be mere filler material in a normal-size conventional design, a single one may be an over-powering focal area in a miniature design. The Judge would be compelled to reduce points under scale in such an event. Because of the reduced size and limited amounts, each item in a Miniature assumes great importance and each deviation from true scale is painfully obvious.

Selection of Materials

The success of a Miniature arrangement depends upon the careful selection of small items and while it is almost impossible to state a definite size, a rule of thumb often used is that the largest bloom should not exceed more than one-third the size of the **container;** or that no flower or leaf in a five inch design should exceed approximately one-half to three-fourths of an inch; or that one inch of container to two inches of plant material is a pleasing proportion for a three inch design; or that roughly, the container should be at least one and one-half times less than the materials used. Of course, these so-called rules of thumb are relative and vary with the fineness or visual weight of both the container and the materials used in it. The container may be a bit larger than this two to one ratio if the design cascades over the rim or if the whole design is within the container dimensions as in a Japanese Moribana water-viewing type. Usually the plant material proportion will be pleasing if no more than 3" in height or width in a 5" design. The Judge must develop an "eye" for pleasing measurements which can be applied to each individual design and its elements.

The combination of fine mosses, tiny berries, ferns, sweet alyssum, ageratum, miniature roses, and grasses must be done with an eye to variation or contrast of form to achieve interest without violating the principle of scale. While plant materials should by their natures be small in scale, some large bloom heads, composed of many small flowers, such as lilacs, goldenrod, sweet william, annual phlox, candytuft, hawthorne and others can be separated into small parts, revealing minute flowers of delicate charm and unexpected beauty often overlooked en masse.

Exhibitors often take for granted that all miniature flowers are like some wee roses . . . perfectly proportioned in leaf, bud and flower, but this is not always consistent; or he looks **only** at the size of the flower, neglecting to notice that often the bloom may be properly scaled to his needs, but that the leaves attached to the stem are rather large and should have been scissored away. Creeping Forget-me-not is a case in point. The foliage of miniature roses, grasses and mosses is ac-

461

ceptable as a substitute for natural foliage of less pleasing proportion.

The trick of dropping a bloom or leaf over the container rim to reduce the visual weight of the container is often employed by wise arrangers to bring the container into apparent scale, and the Judge should appraise fairly. If the ruse has proved effective even though the Judge **knows** the container **is** larger than it appears, give credit where due and refrain from hair-splitting.

Design

The Judge is justified in expecting the Exhibitor to use all the elements of line, form, pattern, color and texture according to the principles of balance, proportion, scale, rhythm, contrast and dominance to achieve a beautiful, harmonious design even though on a scale much tinier than most arrangements. Because the size relationship of the parts are so important, scale is the one principle which is discussed, judged and pointed separately.

As with full scale designs, the Miniature can vary in style and design from Period, including Japanese influence, to very modern designs. Line and Massed Lines are most neglected in the making of Miniatures, mass designs predominate in most shows, probably because they are easier to make. Line designs require more thought, effort and discriminating selection on the part of the exhibitor and the Judge should reward this effect, as well as imaginative theme conformance.

Rhythm

Transition of form should have been attained through the use of twigs and buds in conjunction with tiny mature blooms and foliage. No two stems should have the same length and blooms should face in slightly different directions to give depth to the design. A painfully flat appearance should be penalized. The subtle illusion of depth created through the placement of diagonal lines leading back and of a finer scale than similar materials in the foreground should be recognized and up-graded.

A common fault in many Miniature designs is over-stuffing, crowding in too much material so the small flowers become mere blobs of varied color, rather than revealing and enhancing the charm and diversity of small forms when viewed at close hand.

Stems support the wee flowers in individual ways — erect, weeping, forked, gracefully curved, thus adding a piquant charm if allowed to show naturally rather than being completely obscured by massing and the stem colors often add pleasing but natural color contrasts.

The Judge should penalize a congested effect in arrangements of tiny dried materials, too. Often the colors of these are muted and the emphasis should be on the simple, clean-cut pattern and the delicate but individual forms of the pods, grasses, seed heads and sprays. The goal of the designer should have been to call attention to the beauty of these tiny things which is so often overlooked. To jam a great number into a tiny container does nothing to achieve this goal.

Presentation, Staging

If the Staging Committee plans the use of mirrors in any manner, this fact should be noted in the schedule. If mirrors are used for staging and not schedule-listed, the Judge may either ignore the reflections or ask that the exhibits be placed off the mirrors, at least during the judging. The reflection of the back of a design or the bottom is seldom attractive unless made so specifically by the designer and it is unfair to stage thusly without his knowledge. However, if the designer himself used a mirror, its size must be included in the overall measurements and the reflected design, either the back or bottom is taken into consideration and penalized if found lacking in finish and attractiveness.

Suitable Textures

The wrong textures can be as distracting in a tiny design as in a full-scale one. Coarse flowers such as marigolds need a rough textured, plain, pottery-type container and penalty will usually be justified if these appear in a highly glazed, delicate porcelain urn. Textures can be contrasted, it is true, but the **character** should never be contrasted or an unharmonious note is injected.

Many times in the attempt to find tiny items, the designer becomes blinded to the need for harmony; mixing colors and characteristics with a complete abandon that results in arrangements which may be finely scaled but lacking in design, harmony and appeal.

Container

The container is a very important part of a Miniature. The Judge should consider its proportion in relation to the amount of plant materials used. Very often the Judge finds that the container is too large, or it is so compelling that it dominates the whole design. The container may invite but not hold the viewer's interest. The texture of the container should be such that it is harmonious with the materials used. For instance, a rough, pebbley surface is at variance with tiny delicate Forget--me-nots and deserves a point reduction. The Judge should check carefully to make sure an ornate, over-large conspicuous container does not overwhelm the tiny plant materials.

Color

It is **usually** best that few colors be combined because the small area does not allow space for extensive transition. One color should dominate the whole design with consideration of container, accessory and base if used. Splitting a minute design through the use of too much color contrast destroys its unified appearance, and while possible in a large design may be fatal to a Miniature.

The brighter the color, the better the pattern of the tiny design can be seen and appreciated. The small areas of color keep full chroma from being overpowering, and therefore brilliant color usually can be used without restraint if properly balanced.

Also, since the tiny flowers most often used are of natural species, rather than hybrids, there is less possibility of striking discordant notes as while the colors may be brilliant and vivid, they are never harsh; and with the green of stems and foliage to quieten the contrasts, sweeping color liberty is more acceptable than in large-scale arrangements.

However, color rhythm through repetition, line direction and gradation are important procedures not to be neglected, particularly in such a small area. The color of the container should be repeated somewhere in the plant material. The scale of the container can be visually minimized in this way. Points should be deducted for breaks in rhythm, due to spotty color placements.

If the designer has repeated a curve of a pink container in the curve of a pink-flowered branch to give color rhythm through line direction, her effort should be noted and rewarded. There should, however, even in this small design be some slight contrast of direction in other materials to relieve monotony.

If the designer has managed, even in this small area to achieve color rhythm through gradation by using analagous or monochromatic color harmonies, she deserves recognition through extra points.

Since the scope of the work is so limited, it takes an especially skilled arranger to use color to give an illusion of depth. If she has established depth through the placing of a receding hue behind an advancing one, or a dark value behind a lighter one, drawing the eye back and forth to give the design substance and the third dimension of depth, she deserves extra credit.

Even in such minute quantities, some colors exert greater visual attraction and must be balanced with larger areas of low-key color. For instance, if the lower one-half of the design is all brilliant color and the upper half is quiet color the lower half would over-throw the color balance. An equal part of full chroma will always over-balance an equal sized area of low-value color and requires a deduction of points.

Individuality

Individuality is anything which makes the Miniature different, unique and memorable for all its tininess. It can be achieved through the use of graceful twig lines such as broom, curled wild onion tips, grapevine and wisteria tendrils with strong rhythmic patterns; lichens, dill, fine grasses, branchlets of deciduous shrubs and trees and house plants such as wax Begonias. Gray foliage adds a delicate air in keeping with the tiny scale and is too seldom utilized.

Mechanics are particularly difficult in Miniatures and here, too, the Judge can reward the exhibitor who has an individual, different approach to the problem of maintaining stability. Penalty is taken under design for ineffective mechanics which allow the design to separate or tilt or otherwise appear unstable.

Accessories can add a needed note of difference, but the Judge must not be swayed to the point of overlooking a lack of harmony or scale, and deducting under those qualities if necessary while still giving a few points for individuality. When an accessory is used, the overall design unit is usually unified and improved by placing both container containing the design and the accessory on a single base. The Judge may take penalty here if a base seems to be needed to unify the design.

Clear glass presents problems and the Judge can give extra credit to the exhibitor who has found an individual way of utilizing a glass container to best advantage. Colored water and vermiculite are "old hat" but effective. A particularly pleasing stem design showing through the clear glass can add stability and continuity when well done, which is rare. An uninteresting mass of stems adds nothing and deserves point reduction.

Since these small designs are viewed at close range on desks, bedside tables, trays and other such places, the extra touch of fragrance through the use of aromatic herbs, roses and violets could be the turning point of a decision. The Judge should appreciate the use of interesting curves, interesting voids and lines and unusual containers such as those hand carved, those utilized from natural material such as driftwood, seashore items, seed pods and those borrowed from kitchen, medicine cabinet, dressing table and other common-place spots, as well as handmade forms, tiny egg shells, etc.

All to often the exhibitor is so involved with the problems of scale, he forgets that the end result should be one of distinctive beauty, however minute; containers should have been selected entirely for compatibility to the design and flowers chosen, either for unobtrusive balance or for added beauty of lines and color. Points should not be given for a different type of container alone, but for the integrated design **including** the container . . . a completed design which has that quality of difference.

Elegance, dignity and excellent design can be present even on such a small scale and the Judge should recognize and reward its appearance in a class too often filled with the robust whimsy of coarse over-sized flowers in the backs of miniature donkeys and dogs and the tops of miniature shoes and hats.

Condition and Suitability

Because the container's capacity for water is severely limited the need for wise selection of plant material is paramount. Proper conditioning or hardening off procedures are vitally necessary in order to help the materials hold up without wilting. Since the amount of materials used are so limited each plays a very important part in the design and each one must remain alert and working in the design.

The Judge will recognize the work of the experienced designer who selects fresh flowers which are not only in scale but are capable of remaining fresh in the minimum of water available. Lobelia, Heather, dwarf marigolds and mums, dock, yarrow, bluets, pinks, rock and alpine plants, succulents and fine-needled evergreens are very accommodating in this respect. While most miniature roses last well when cut, the experienced Judge knows that "Sweet Fairy" is one which does not, fading very quickly and deserving the sure penalty it gets when exhibiting this fault. Miniature Roses also have a very unsettling way of going from bud to full-bloom in a matter of minutes, thus upsetting scale. A Judge judges "as is", however. Dried materials must be dust-free and fresh appearing.

A Judge considers not only the suitability of the materials used, but the suitability of the design for its scheduled-stated use. A maximum-size miniature in a tippy container would be justifiably be considered unsuitable for the average in-bed tray.

SUMMARY

Scale 40 Points

*flowers in scale with each other and container *accessory well scaled to other parts

-each flower too large for container -some flowers too large in relation to others -accessory out of scale -container too large -too small -too tall -too wide -too low -design out of scale for niche or placement -overlarge foliage used -container size too insistent

Design 30 Points

*interesting pattern *easy transition through size gradation *all principles considered *depth attained through profile placement, diminishing sizes, etc. *open silhouette allows individual forms to be appreciated

-plant material should be taller to balance container -focal area too heavy -design too flat, lacks depth -congested -overstuffed -rhythm confused, leads eye in too many directions -incompatible textures -mirrored back or bottom reflection lacks finish and attractiveness -container dominates design -design mechanics inefficient -design tilting, separating -design top heavy -bottom heavy -visual balance heavier on one side -a monotony of round forms, needs contrast

Color 15 Points

*one color dominant *color areas of light and dark values well balanced *container color repeated in plant materials *color rhythm created by gradation, line direction, repetition *depth through color placement

-too many colors -spotty color placement -lacks color rhythm -lacks unity -equal parts full chroma and low values

Individuality 10 Points

*different *unique *memorable *unusual mechanics (if apparent) *interesting silhouette *perceptive use of material *well integrated acessory *fragrant *enchanting

-inappropriate container -uninteresting -commonplace -often seen

Condition, Suitability 5 Points

*size and design appropriate for schedule requirements *clean *fresh *unwilted *well hardened *materials wisely selected

-drooping -dried materials dusty -unsuitable materials -inappropriate design for the class -water soiled

Niches, Shadow Boxes and Framed Designs

NICHES

Niches are defined as boxlike recessed spaces, generally 40" high, 36" wide, 18" deep, 42-45" from the floor, however, any size is acceptable, but must be listed in Schedule. Triptychs (background with hinged sides) *and flat panels provide popular framing variations. Schedule should allow creative freedom in selection, placement and securing of components.*

In evaluating for a well-composed niche, consider the proportion and scale of the relationships of space to the solids. The knowledgeable use of space is of paramount importance.

All principles applying to design and accessory/s must be evaluated. Balance may be symmetrical or asymmetrical but visually stabilized within the space of the niche.

The principle of proportion involving the space occupied and unoccupied must be aesthetically pleasing and interesting. Generally if there is one-third occupied by the main design, one-third empty and one-third occupied by incidentals and space, the proportion is pleasing. The areas are occupied with different contributions so placed that the eye is carried around and back into the design without crowd*ing. If something beyond tensional balance, it upsets the form and function of balanced visual gravity. Conformity and proportion are minused when items extend beyond niche boundaries.*

In considering proportion and scale the Judge asks "has a large enough design been used; has a large enough accessory been used; is the design or accessory too large for the area". The material must never touch the top or sides of the niche or emerge at the front and there must be space at the back, otherwise a flattened effect results which is penalized. A too-low design is considerably less aesthetic (more clumsy appearing) than a too high one and probably will draw a greater penalty.

In a **general** way we can say that:

. . . a margin of at least 3⅓" between the top of the design and the top of a 40" niche

. . . a margin of 3" from sides of a 36" niche to the sides of the design, at least. (Both figured at 1/12 the height or width of the niche)

. . . container approximately one-third the height or width of the niche or approximately 12 to 14" in a 36x40" niche

. . . accessory one-third the height of the design.

Since contemporary handling of space and visual weight influenced by form, color and texture alters cases, no hard and fast rules should be made. These are listed merely to serve as a **general** guide for aesthetic proportion and scale, but are by no means the only proportions which are pleasing.

The actual depth is controlled by the actual dimensions of the box (generally 18") but the Judge rewards the designer who has achieved greater depth through the use of spatial illusion. Points to check for increased depth are:

. diagonal lines   . directional movement

. tensional attraction between:
 . receding (cool) and advancing (warm) color
 . receding (dark) values, advancing (light) values
 . receding (smooth) texture, advancing (rough) texture
. transparent or overlapping planes
. accessory placement (angled or placed deeper in the niche)
. vanishing point perspective (large forms advance, small recede, can be applied to figurines as well)
. space, voids accelerating visual movement
. background in its place, tho may play a part in Modern and Abstract

Distinction is evident in the design which draws one back to discover new areas and techniques to explore. Unusual handling of space, depth and materials; outstanding materials, elevations, unique forms and lines and perceptive combinations increase the score.

A background should be either unobtrusive or intimately related to the design. The texture, color and every fold or line should be expressive of some quality or complete some line or form. Background fabrics may be draped or folded without penalty if handled with thought and purpose. An ornate or demanding background complements a one-hue design without devouring it. Satin fabrics are usually a detriment to spatial illusion. Creases or wrinkles in the background, wilting material, distracting mechanics reduce the score.

SUMMARY

*space knowledgeably and distinctively used *space working *depth achieved *scale and proportion aesthetic *unoccupied space balances occupied *outstanding *interesting interpretation *design principles well handled

-design too narrow for niche -container too small -material protruding from the front -touching niche top, sides -top of niche area inadequately filled -design principles ignored -creased -wilting material -too much unused space -accessory too large, small -commonplace -lacks impact

SUGGESTED SCALE FOR NICHE DESIGNS

Proportion and Scale	25	Distinction	20
. to space		Color	15
. to each other		Suitability	15
Design	25	. of relationships, textures,
. balance . depth . line		forms, spirit
. rhythm . emphasis		. to theme

SHADOW BOXES

Shadows as an element of design make up two Flower Show categories. Lighting technique is of great importance in the distinctive handling of both types.

1. Shadows projected on the background
2. Shadows silhouetted on a transluscent foreground

In Type 1, the objects themselves making up the design, plus the shadow on the background must be blended into a unified design. The shadow is used to strengthen, unify, balance and add depth and interest.

Staging is usually in a niche and ingenuity in lighting effects and design distinction result in outstanding and interesting exhibits. In this type, the handling of all the elements and principles must be evaluated as they would be in a regular niche design. The position of the light or lights determines where the shadows will fall, their lightness or darkness and their influence on the design.

SUGGESTED SCALE FOR TYPE 1 SHADOW BOX

Design	25	Distinction	20
. emphasis on shadow influence		Color	15
. line . rhythm		Suitability	15
Proportion and Scale	25	. of relationships, textures, form, spirit	
. related to space		. to theme	
. to each other			

In Shadow Box Type 2, clarity of design silhouette and simplicity of execution are necessary to achieve prize-worthy results.

Color, texture and condition of material are of little import. Emphasis is on proportion, scale and balance of the lines, forms and pattern. The light or lights should be intense enough to cast a strong shadow of the design and be placed to best advantage. The lights themselves must be so placed that no glare or beams are apparent to the viewer, he should be conscious only of the design. These designs are best viewed at or near eye level.

SUGGESTED SCALE FOR TYPE 2 SHADOW BOX

Proportion, Scale, Balance	35	Distinction	20
Clarity of Design Silhouette	30	Interpretation	15
		. schedule requirements	
		. theme	

FRAME DESIGN

A design in which a frame is included presents a slightly different problem of design and judging than a niche as the frame serves more as an accessory than as a "container" for the design.

The width of the frame is considered in evaluating the principles of proportion and scale. Any carving is considered under textural relationships. The finish (gilt, varnish, paint, etc.) is considered in relationship to the texture and color. The spirit or mood inherent in the type of frame (modern, old-fashioned, dainty, massive) should be reflected in the design and flowers or other materials chosen. The outline of the design should be compatible with that of the frame which may be round, oval, rectangular or other.

The position of the frame varies; it may be in back of the design, in front of the design or the arrangement may come through the frame. The background (fabric or other), if used, may be staged behind both frame and design or it may be taut within the frame with the arrangement in front; or a regular wall, etc., may serve as the background.

When a frame is used, in any way, the whole composition is analyzed as a unit according to an artistic scale other than the Niche

Scale because these involve a space and area relationship within a set enclosure, whereas using a frame does not mean an enclosure in the same sense as that of the Niche.

SUGGESTED SCALE FOR FRAME DESIGN

Design	30	Creativity	15
Relationships	25	Condition	10
Distinction	20		

Home and Gardens Shows

The wish to use flowers for home decoration is one main reason for the popularity of Home and Gardens Shows.

The wish to see how flowers can be used in the home is another main reason. Living plant material contributes color, creates interest and emphasizes the character of its placement. Like a basic dress, a home must be enhanced by accessories to establish a personality.

Home and Gardens Shows are of three types:

1. Home Show (one home involved, cut specimens of horticulture in adjoining garage). Design staging must be actual, not improvised.

2. House to House Show (several homes involved with cut horticulture specimens staged in adjoining garage at one home)

3. Home and Gardens Show (two or more homes and gardens; designs and cut specimens staged in appropriate places, supplemented with outdoor, patio and landscape plantings (p. 537, 538). Cut horticulture may be in a public area.

The selections of the home/s based on location and characteristics is very important. Homes that vary in period, style and architecture will challenge the exhibitor to explore the possibilities of homes' individual locations suitable for the placement of a design, and inspire the viewers to see such possibilities in their own homes.

If multiple locations are used, the proximity of the homes and/or gardens must be considered. Houses separated by super highways complicated by cloverleaves or railroad tracks where traffic is periodically held up are poor choices for companions in a Home and Gardens Show. A clear, concise map of the home or homes, with addresses should be available for exhibitors, Judges and viewers. The hours the homes are open to the public must be clearly stated in the Schedule and on the map.

There must be available parking and space to facilitate easy movement of the crowds and easy accessibility for viewing. The exhibits and homes should be well lighted if open in the evening.

Safety is an important factor; walks well lighted and repaired; exits plainly marked and any lighted candles or decorations which might be fire hazards carefully used.

Because the exhibits must be planned and designed to complement the home and for a specific location (mantel, powder room, etc.), with specific and limiting adjacent factors (pictures, wallpaper, accessories, mirrors, architectural features, draperies, etc.), the exhibitors should be allotted a definite hour at which they may check the home and location in the home for the finished design. This insures higher quality designs that are harmonious in color, suitable in texture, correctly scaled and generally acceptable for the designated place and the style, character and type of room and home.

Advanced registrations will assure the required number of exhibits. Staging a show in two or more homes increases the number of exhibits, and increases the interest. By staging in two or more homes the Schedule can allow for four corresponding placements to make up the class or each room may be considered a class. Too many placements produce a cluttered look. The goal is to select placements and limit the number of designs so the room will be decorated in good taste as if the hostess were entertaining friends. If a class is staged in **more** than one room or home — it will be necessary to point score each exhibit. Emphasis in a Placement Show is placed on fresh-cut plant material which must be the dominant source of interest in the designs. The matter of fresh-cut material being the dominant source of interest can be applied to the individual designs . . . or there also can be a minimum of design classes made of anything other than fresh-cut plant material.

The problem of determining dominance has always been a knotty one. Predominance, according to Webster and other authorities, means "to have the greatest effect upon; to give specific character to". Test for dominance by turning away from the design and then back . . . quickly then . . . what did you see first upon turning back to the design? To predominate does not mean the **most,** but that which is **most eye-catching.** Not the most dominant in area, but the most dominant in interest.

The Schedule should list the scales of points to be used in the Artistic Division and in major Horticultural Classes. Accessories such as shells, figurines, dried, treated, weathered materials and other objects or properties, may be allowed and specified in the Schedule.

Locations are varied and numerous throughout the home/s and may be selected from such as:

1. Entrance hall: chest, mobiles, recesses, hanging designs.

2. Living room: piano, TV, stereo or hi-fi, mantel, occasional and coffee tables, chests, bookcases, floor designs, window, mobiles, etc.

3. Dining room: table, buffet, mantel, hanging, recesses (shelves, niches), window, mobiles.

4. Den, Recreation and Rumpus Rooms: desk, bookcases, game tables, coffee tables, TV, music equipment, chests, counters.

5. Bedrooms: dressing tables, chests, bureaus, bedside tables, bed

trays, TV, desk, valance boards, window treatment, plaques (bedroom classes may be divided into adult, child, teen).

6. Powder rooms: counter ,hanging, mobiles, etc.

7. Kitchen: plaques, hanging, shelf, islands, counters, cabinets, mobiles, breakfast nooks.

8. Patios, Porches, Breezeways, Poolsides.

9. Miscellaneous architectural locations: stairways, skylights, glass wall partitions, etc.

HORTICULTURAL DIVISION

It is advisable to confine the Horticultural Division to a single area if only cut specimens and house plants are to be included. Each section of Horticulture should be complete in a home or area to facilitate judging.

If the Show is a Home and Gardens (Type 3) with several homes and gardens included, special garden features may be included, and judged by competent Judges. These might be overall landscape designs, border plantings (annual and perennial), patios, pools, garden structures (houses, fountains, statuary), or bird feeding sites. Emphasis might be placed on a specialty plant, such as roses, iris, peonies, etc., thus giving the public a chance to see the plants in use on the grounds and the flowers in use in the homes. Classes can be made for both growing and cut material thus assuring at least or more than fifty percent devoted to horticulture. Special Garden Club and Society awards may be offered and presented provided all requirements for these are met.

Cut exhibits of horticulture may be displayed in a single home's spacious den, patio, garden, room, porch, garage, recreation room, tent, etc. Potted plants may be scheduled to show their decorative value. Advanced entries will control the numbers entered. The Schedule will control their locations. The quality and number of specimens, correct and legible labeling, percentage of club participating are wholly as important in a Home and Gardens Show as in a regular Standard Show. The staging of the cut specimens must be as carefully planned with consideration given to spacious placement, sufficient lighting, neat, uniform containers and placards. A general feeling of order and balance should prevail. Each section and each division should be complete in one home or area; entries are individually pointscored if in different rooms.

Advised sections including educational exhibits relative to the theme of the Show and designed to instruct; exhibits by sponsored groups such as Juniors, High School, Institutions and other patronized organizations and miscellaneous exhibits concerning birds, conservation, etc., can be included and staged in appropriate areas.

ARTISTIC DIVISION

Each exhibit in the Artistic Division is scored against perfection for its type. For instance, judging of dining tables is done according to an appropriate scale and standards of perfection; Mobiles according to an appropriate scale and standards of perfection; Occidental, Oriental, Contemporary, Modern, Abstract designs judged according to appropriate scales and standards, which see. In making up scales *consideration must be given to "suitability of placement" and a considerable number of points given, usually twenty-five.*

Because of the diversity of the class placements and the possible point-scoring effort involved, Home and Gardens Shows require the services of the most experienced and able Judges available.

SUGGESTED SCALE OF POINTS
Design with Accessories

Design (all principles)	30	Suitable relationships	20
Appropriateness to placement	25	Distinction	25

DESIGN

Design implies a proper order in detail, form and color, according to the basic principles of balance, proportion, scale, rhythm, contrast, and dominance. Only the arrangement unit (including accessories) is considered under design. Adjacent features and their effects upon the arrangement are judged under appropriate relationships, but of course, some overlapping is to be expected. The design could be perfect in itself but inappropriate to its placement, or with the other items near it. The design within itself must have balance, be scaled and proportioned correctly, with contrast and dominance as needed to produce a vital, yet unified design.

Appropriateness To Placement

The frame or setting governs the size and the proportion of the design. The room area, the ceiling height, the piece of furniture upon which the design is placed, dictates the height, width, and depth of the design. Hanging and Mobile designs must be correctly scaled to the room. A large arrangement overpowers a small room; a small design looks insignificant and "dinky" on a piano in a large room. This is the same principle we observed in controlling the size of a corsage to the woman. The choice of container, the materials in the design, their size, height and dominance are considered under placement appropriateness. A tall, tippy design is unsuitable on a bed tray, or for a patio table where a vagrant breeze or a sudden movement could be disastrous. Extremes are always disturbing, therefore less appropriate.

Suitable Relationships

Coordination and harmony of the design and the nearby adjacent factors with the period, architectural style, spirit and character of the room as a whole are considered here.

473

The number of materials one can use successfully depends upon the skill with which the designer relates textures, colors, spirit, and the problem is further complicated in a Home Show because so many things must be considered in addition to the selection of the materials that go into the design itself.

Mirrors, pictures (hanging and tabletop), wall surfaces, draperies and accessories (lamps, ashtrays, etc.) and architectural features in the immediate vicinity of the design dictate its lines, colors, texture and character. All must form a harmonious unit including the arrangement. Texture is the surface quality, character is the degree of refinement, elegance or casualness and while textures can be successfully contrasted to relieve monotony, it is risky to contrast character both within the design and as the design is related to the room.

The period, style and spirit of the room as a whole exerts an influence. An Avant Garde Assemblage in a French Provincial room is unsuitable. A casual, informal room is enhanced by a design of easy curves, homey materials; a formal stylized period room calls for symmetrical, decorative motifs. A modern type Mobile belongs only in a modern house. Hanging type arrangements may be suitable for earlier periods.

The color, texture, period and character of the furnishings in the entire room must be considered. A rustic design of cattails and burlap would be unsuitable in a delicately appointed teen-girl bedroom, but would be suitable in texture and spirit to the patio. But with reservations! A heavy, rustic container placed on a glass-topped, delicate wrought iron patio table is also unsuitably related. Cheerful colors and a more casual handling are more suitably related to a breakfast nook than a formal, symmetrical design of pastel or moody, greyed purple hues.

Colors that blend into oblivion with the background wall coverings; colors that "clash"; character and texture that are incompatible are faults. Dominant forms (round, cubic, triangular) must bear relationship to the surroundings. Design principles of balance, rhythm, contrast and dominance are applied to assess the overall suitability of the relationships. For instance, the pattern and lines of a design must include, not obscure a large hanging picture; repetition of lines or colors in both picture and design should create rhythmic movement. Such harmonious and compatible relationships would contribute to suitability.

Distinction

Distinction is a rightness for the setting achieved through perceptive, flawless craftsmanship and mechanical efficiency. Simplicity (the elimination of all unnecessary details) is one means of achieving distinction, using only enough materials to set the mood or complete the picture. Any unusual coordination between the design and the setting contributes to distinction.

Often it is the small things that make the difference; soiled, less than perfect materials; careless mechanics, a mirror reflecting the unfinished reverse side of a design are all faults which lessen distinction and must be penalized. Any faults of design, suitability to placement and relationship reflect on the ultimate distinction.

SUMMARY
Design 30 Points
*has visual stability *areas of container, color areas, accessories, base, plant materials correctly proportioned *accessories, plant materials in scale *one line, color, etc. dominant *eye moves rhythmically through design *enough contrast to relieve monotony

-lopsided -unbalanced -accessory too large, small -needs color, textural contrast -equal color values (no dominant one) -container too small for amount of plant material in it

Appropriateness To Placement 25 Points
*large as needed for room height and size *correct scale for placement *design form and pattern well chosen for placement and use

-too small, large for placement -poor design form and pattern choice for placement and use -tippy -squat

Suitable Relationships 20 Points
*harmonious with style, character of room *colors well selected for use and placement *harmonious with nearby items (lamps, pictures, etc.)

-too casual for room style and character -too modern (or traditional) for room style -colors ill chosen for location -colors clash -colors fade into background -design fights with, rather than integrates nearby objects (pictures, mirror, etc.)

Distinction 25 Points
*flawlessly crafted *simplicity achieved *unusual coordination between design and setting

-soiled, less than perfect materials -careless mechanics -general unplanned appearance -unfinished reflection etc.

Planters

SUGGESTED CLASSES
    A. Portable Planter   (size and minimum number and types of plants to be specified in Schedule)
    B. Interior Stationary
    C. Window Boxes, Exterior Planters

Planters and/or plants must have been in the exhibitor's possession at least three months. Home Show classes for Interior Planters can include built-ins (furniture tops, walls, etc.), portable or hanging types in baths, kitchens, halls, entrances, living areas, bedrooms, dens).

PLANTER
The term "planter" normally means a number of different plants artistically grouped in a single container. The container with only one type of plant is usually not an acceptable exhibit and should be entered in the flowering or foliage houseplant classes.

Design Effectiveness (arrangement of plants) . proportion, balance, scale . flexibility . distinction	30	Cultural Perfection . includes age, grooming, condition	20
Suitable Relationships . to other plants . to container . to location	25	Plant Selection	15
		Container Suitability	10

DESIGN

A well designed composition is the ideal a Judge looks for; including the right plants, the right container and the right location. The arrangement of the plants should have been at least as carefully planned as in a floral design considering the permanency of the arrangement. The same principles apply, and the effect is judged in a similar manner.

The stark horizontal and vertical lines of modern homes need plant's eye-easing curves and color to contrast and balance the decorating scheme, both inside and out. Planters are not limited to homes of contemporary design, but their types must complement the general style of the house.

Planters may be of any size and shape, but they must be judged on how well they are proportioned to the materials they contain, and their placement or intended placement.

Rectangular, triangular and hexagonal boxes arranged in geometric designs or with some boxes planted to permanent, slow-growing shrubs with alternate boxes planted for seasonal color; or tiers with the top box filled with dwarf material and attention paid to foliage, stem and berry color as well as flowers does much to enliven the design. A small trellis for vining plants adds an interesting elevated pattern, but such an addition must be in proportion to the box and the location. Dramatic lighting can also highlight a planter and add distinction.

Drift or other wood is sometimes utilized in planters and the Judge must decide if the piece adds to the general interest and beauty of the composition. If it is in scale and balance, the contrast with living plants may be a welcome note. However, little ceramic accessories usually do nothing but confuse the composition and unless really outstanding, should not be encouraged.

If both large and small foliage plants have been used, there should be some middle-sized foliage for easy transition from small to large forms. Variations in height add interest to the arrangement, plants all the same height create a monotonous effect.

Grouping should be well balanced, a slim vertical plant on one side either asymmetrically balanced by a low growing mass on the other side; or symmetrically balanced with another slim plant opposite. The plants should be scaled to each other and to the container.

A large grouping of plants in a small, cramped planter should be penalized for a violation of the principles of proportion.

Planters in Home Show entries should be considered from the standpoint of their "fit" to the room. A planter may be too short for the window or wall length for a pleasingly proportioned arrangement. Or its placement may be too high or ungainly to look well when viewed from the inside or the outside. Or it may be too wide, thus creating a hazard or nuisance by cramping the living area. Foliage which extends out excessively can unbalance the design of the planting.

Differing growth habits provide a point of contrast; a unified, harmonious, but different effect achieved through the selection of tall, vining and rosette types of Philodendron or upright, rosette and vining succulents is worthy of up-grading because of the harmony of relationship, plus the interest of contrasts which relieves monotony.

A small, portable planter of the type usually brought to a Standard Show should have been planted according to height; the lowest plants at the front, medium high plants to mask the bare "legs" of the tallest members of the group.

Or the basic pattern can be varied by placing the tallest members at the sides with medium and low plants at the front and middle. In either portable or permanent types a hodge-podge of heights with no apparent plan is to be penalized as is the other extreme of all one height, resembling a counter of plants for sale.

Spacing should have been done in alternate rows to give a more naturalistic look; regular even spacing is a design fault. A "busy" appearance, the result of too many varieties, heights and variegations should be down-scored.

Deadlocked decisions, all things being equal, might be settled by the flexibility of the design allowed by pots set in moss or vermiculite, rather than all plants sharing the same soil. Not only can the plants be easily changed when color is gone or shape and size alters the design, but culturally, root control, maintenance and regular quarter-turning for well-shaped plants is easier. The rims of individual pots should not jut above the edge of the common container, but should be recessed about one inch.

Suitable Relationships

Relationship to companion plant colors and textures and those of the room, house and garden are important considerations. Repetition of the wall color or fabric colors in flowers or foliage unifies the composition. A combination of violent colors such as those found in the croton and the coleus should deserve its sure penalty when used as companions in portable and permanent planters. Variegated foliage adds interesting color variations, but can easily be over-done to the point of penalty.

An all-green composition would be monotonous if the textures, shapes and sizes were too similar. The Judge will access the balance and proportion of glossy to dull, finely cut to entire leaf edges, and sizes from small to medium to large.

Shape relationships must be harmonious; too many round forms, too many verticals make for a monotonous design. Textures, color and style of plants should be compatible, also. Gardenias are too refined to be placed in a rope-wrapped container; cacti are too rough to be placed in a highly finished planter. The "personalities" of the plants should be considered, geraniums or cacti growing next to camellias violates a sense of "rightness".

Many planter plants grow tall and it is often necessary to provide supports. The stakes should be related in color, usually green; should not protrude above the flower head or foliage and should not be too heavy. The ties should have been carefully applied, leaving no scars. Shiny metal paper clips, white rags and the like are neither decorative nor suitable. If the Judge is conscious of artificial supports or ties, points are to be deducted. The shape of the plant should not appear restrained; even though staked and tied, it should retain a natural-looking form. The ties should be regularly interspersed along the stem and not simply a lone one at the top, giving the impression of the plant "hanging by its teeth" to the stake.

The planters are an integral part of the decorative scheme, both indoors and out. The relationships to use and location must be considered. Functional plant boxes serving as buffers for cars on parking areas, or traffic directors pointing the way to doorways should be sturdy, strong, made of appropriate materials, and planted to interestingly textured plants such as mugho pine, juniper, etc. Color should be carefully considered as well as the use of the plantings to soften architectural lines on terraces, porches, patios, along walks and near entrances.

Inside, the Judge considers the suitability of the planter as room dividers, traffic directors, built-in screens, as screening for structural defects, and as decorative conversation pieces. He asks himself if the plants and container used balance the furniture groupings and serve as more than mere specimens. A bronze planter on a teak base planted to Chinese evergreen, aspidistra and 'mums harmonizes with the spirit of a home decorated in an Oriental manner. An old washstand holding Ivy and different species of geranium complements a Colonial style. A Judge rates such happy blendings of planter, plants and decor very high, all other things being equal.

Points should be deducted here for the general appearance of the planters, peeling surfaces, poor quality materials, disrepair. Planters needing refinishing or renailing should be penalized. Disfiguring stains on the house wall or window sill are also faults.

Cultural Perfection

Since many planters are filled with individual pots, packed around with moss, the Judge should not criticize the proximity of a plant which requires an acid soil with one that requires an alkaline soil unless he is assured they are sharing the same soil, and either is showing ill effects. However, even plants in separate pots should have been selected for similar requirements as to light, temperature and humidity.

The form of each plant should be well-branched, and symmetrically balanced, having been kept compact with regular pinching and training of straggly growth.

The number of plants used depends, of course, on the size of the planter and the varieties used. Penalty must be taken for over-crowding which results in a lack of thrift in the plants. The plants should appear to be well established, in an active state of growth and are **not** juvenile plants. They should be of a size which shows growth over a period of time. Juvenile plants are usually delinquent in substance and size, slender-stemmed and thin foliaged.

Proper drainage is necessary if the box is not to become a coffin for the plants. An inch or more of headroom should have been provided for watering. Plants moved abruptly from high-humidity greenhouse or garden to a dry-air heated room show their discomfort by curling their leaves and dropping their flower buds. Drafts and sudden chill will have a similar effect.

The Judge knows the key to successful planter gardening is the wise selection of plants to suit the exposure. Plants placed too far from the light will reach out for it and become straggly. Regardless of what a plant requires in the way of light, it must be given a quarter-turn regularly to prevent the lopsided appearance which a Judge penalizes.

Both excessive heat and excessive cold have visual effects on plants. Low temperatures curtail growth and often cause the foliage to turn yellow and drop, beginning with the lower leaves. Plants which are spindly and weak, their stems lengthened unduly and their leaves spaced too far apart on the stem (often caused by excessive heat accompanied by a lack of light), lack the cultural perfection required for a full score.

Placement in full sun scorches the leaves and while flowering plants usually require at least three hours of sun daily, the Judge knows that direct sunlight will discolor the leaves of coleus, caladiums and other tender tropical foliaged plants. Chinese evergreen, Philodendron micans (Velvet Leaf) thrive in darker corners; Dieffenbachias and Dracaenas enjoy intermediate light as a rule. The Judge should be aware of these requirements especially when judging permanent planters.

Too high temperature or lack of water may turn leaf tips and edges brown. If left on the plant, these should be penalized, but careful trimming is allowed if the character of the leaf has not been altered. Completely dead or dried leaves and stems should have been groomed away completely, leaving no stub. The foliage should be **naturally** glossy, clean and vital-appearing. Plants that have been oiled or "dressed" should have points deducted under grooming and cultural condition as not being typical of the variety.

Judges have to be suspicious and nosey, peering under and around all the plants for disease or insects. Curled leaves, shrunken stems and any irregularities should be pointed down. If the leaves are abnormally small and the plant stunted with repeated branching, the damage may be gas poisoning. Slugs and snails love the humidity and darkness of a planter, their slimy trails and ragged holes disfigure the plants and bring deserved penalties.

A forlorn grouping of gangling, ragged plants and dried flowers and foliage is a depressing sight requiring sure elimination. The soil surface should be free of debris or litter of dried petals, leaves, match sticks, etc. All the plants should be shapely, with the size controlled and weak and crowded shoots removed through pinching and pruning. The entire aspect should be one of well-chosen, well-tended, thriving plants.

Plant Selection

Some plants, because of their growth characteristics are more adaptable for planter use than others, therefore it is important for the Judge to know a plant's cultural requirements.

The Judge must not unjustly penalize a permanent planter placement unless he is sure no artificial lighting is provided or that the plants do require full light. If a plant is silhouetted against the light coming through a window, the plant selected should have a shapely or interesting pattern.

While marigolds, petunias, coleus and geraniums are commonly used in planters and the Judge will give credit for their cultural perfection, a few extra points can justifiably be given for a more imaginative selection of plants which are more unusual such as grasses, strawberries, asparagus springeri and vegetables such as rhubarb, lettuce, rhubarb chard and herbs. Annuals, both bush types and climbers such as Morning Glory make effective interior plants. Of course, mere difference is not enough, the selection must be suitable to pot culture and harmonious with the other plants used.

Philodendron is probably the most commonly used and most suitable plant for interior planter use, and the variety in size, shape and growing habit (vining, tree and rosette) of the approximately 200 species makes it possible to achieve distinction in a planter through the use of only Philodendron.

Vines and groundcovers used to fill the bare spaces between pots and soften the planter rim should have been selected with an eye to training and pinching during their active growing season to control rank and rampant growth. Small-leaf vines such as Vinca Minor and Ivy are generally well suited in scale to most planters. If the vining plant has been allowed to become too matted, points must be deducted.

Those plants with tough, leathery leaves and stems are most tolerant to adverse conditions. For example, sturdy foliage plants as peperomias, sansevierias, dracaenas and dieffenbachias are able to withstand unfavorable conditions.

Suitable plants for exterior use are almost endless, the Judge's main concern is that plants which require sun or shade are used with knowledge of the appropriate location. However, Nature can be circumvented by bringing plants into bloom in the sun and putting the pots in shady locations in which the blooms last longer, so the Judge should be careful and fair in evaluating a north-facing planting accented with blooming chrysanthemums.

The color of the house should be considered as was the color of the room for interior plants. Intense blue petunias, red geraniums or zinnias clashing with a red brick house should be penalized. Light, bright hues are harmonious with stone. Repitition of some plants or dwarf species of the same plants as are in nearby foundation or border plantings will unify the overall design.

Container Suitability

The container should be of a simple, uncluttered shape **at least** three inches deep, in a color and material (pottery, wood, metal, etc.), that is harmonious with the plants used and its location. The general shape of the plant at maturity should have determined the shape of the container. Plants with a globe of foliage on a straight stem look particularly well in low planters; squat bushy plants look best in a low, square container; plants with tapering forms belong in taller units.

The size, of course, varies widely, but it must be deep enough to allow proper root growth for the plants planted therein. The minimum depth is approximately three inches, the average depth is 8-12". Shrubs such as azaleas, lantanas and the like, usually need a container 12-24" and "walkers" (wheeled platforms) make these portable. Window boxes should be at least 10x10" to allow ample root depth and sufficient room for making an attractive plant arrangement.

Planters decorative in themselves should complement the room decor and the plant textures. Rough surfaced planters such as those twine or rope-decorated or of flue tiles should be filled with correspondingly coarse textured plants and used in informal rooms. Boxes stained to match room or house color with highly polished surfaces or metal containers should be planted to finer textured plants. Containers finished in modern tiles and finishes complement modern style homes.

Interesting effects achieved through sophisticated display add distinction. For example, some Bromeliads are epiphytic (grown in trees) and some are terrestrial (grow on the ground or in pots). "Bromeliad tree" planters made by planting a large form at the base and smaller species in the crotches of the branches should be judged with particular attention to plant suitability. Mobiles, made of balanced segments of dried branches with plants attached may be judged according to the Mobile scale, but with the added quality of cultural perfection considered.

SUMMARY

Design 30 Points

*overall style complementary to placement *distinctive or original (tiers, alternates, lighting effects, trellis, etc.) *color not limited to flowers *transition achieved through size of leaf gradations *balance achieved through symmetrical or asymmetrical placement of plant forms *pleasing height variations *flexible design

-accessories ill chosen -driftwood addition upsets balance -crowded -small leaves next to over-large leaves, lacks transition -all same height, needs contrast -too many plants for container size -large plant on one side upsets balance -plants out of scale -container too large for amount of plants -not complementary to location -busy, too many sizes, shapes, variegations -individual pot tops visible

Suitable Relationships 25 Points

*color rhythm unifies composition *character well suited to location *textures well balanced (glossy to dull) *sizes contrasted effectively *balances furniture groupings *stakes inconspicuous *plant staked but looks normal

-colors clashing -variegations overdone -monotonous -supports conspicuous -too many round or vertical forms -incompatible textures in both companion plants and container -ties conspicuous -plants too restrained by tying, look unnatural -planter needs refinishing

Cultural Perfection 20 Points

*individually potted *all plants have similar light, temperature, humidity needs *all plants symmetrically shaped *well branched *compact *shapely *clean *well established *active state of growth *reasonably mature *aerial roots neatly controlled (Philodendron) *foliage **naturally** glossy

-alkaline and acid loving plants sharing same soil and showing ill effects -plant straggly -lack thrift due to over crowding -juvenile plants -lack substance -thin foliaged -weak stemmed -curling leaves -lop sided -drooping, yellowing foliage or flower buds -stunted -leaf nodes elongated -leaves discolored -leaf tips browned -shrunken stems -insect, disease damage -abnormal branching -weak, crowded growth -gangling -soil surface debris

Plant Selection 15 Points

*unusual choices *suitable to pot culture *harmonious to each other, planter, location *ground cover vines suitable and controlled *unity achieved through repetition of nearby textures, colors

-plants requiring light (or shade) wrongly placed -vines matted -plants ill chosen as to harmony of leaf size, color, location

Container Suitability 10 Points

*simple *uncluttered *harmonious with plants, locations *shape complementary to plant form *depth adequate (minimum 3". average 6-12". Shrubs 12-24". Window Boxes 10x10")

-too shallow -tall formal plant in squat container -too big -surface inharmonious with plants and location

Potted Foliage Plants

SUGGESTED CLASSES

1. Foliage Plant, pot size under 7"

2. Foliage Plant, pot size 7-15"

Sub classes might be provided for A. Erect, B. Spreading, C. Vining or for different leaf interests as A. Colored, B. Foliage Pattern, or for plants by name such as Fern, Coleus, Croton, Ficus, Fatsia, etc.

The Schedule should specify that the plant has been in the exhibitor's possession at least three months.

FOLIAGE PLANTS

The term "houseplant" refers to such plants as can be grown in the ordinary rooms of dwellings rather than as subjects requiring greenhouse conditions and expert care. A foliage plant is a plant grown primarily for the attractiveness and interest of the leaves.

Plants grown primarily for their foliage effect should not be judged in the same class as those grown for flowers because the qualities on the respective scales are different; foliage plants are usually considered easier to grow than most flowering plants as they tolerate rather wide extremes of temperature and humidity and make good growth in the limited light often resident in homes.

Foliage plants may have flowers at the time of judging but having flowers does not put them in the flowering class as their blooms are not the main reason for using them for decorative purposes. Foliage plants usually have flowers that are inconspicuous, small and unattractive or are hidden in the foliage and thus are incidental to the scoring as for example coleus, caladiums, some begonias, sansevieria, ferns, etc. Some Judges may like to give an extra point as the bloom indicates to them that some plants have had proper care for an extended period of time, as in the case of Monstera deliciosa, however the blooms on plants such as coleus shoud be pinched in order to maintain active growth. A deduction can justifiably be made in such cases.

The question of whether the same plant may win in several shows or in consecutive years is a matter to be settled in the Schedule or by the Classification Committee, as the Judge of course, does not know if an exhibit has won before. However, a well-grown plant is an asset to a show — the goal is to reward the exhibitor who is able to develop a top quality plant and keep it at peak cultural perfection; such a grower and his plant should not be honored in one show and penalized in the next.

If a potted plant is that of a recognized Plant Society, such as Succulents, Cacti and Begonias, refer to that plant for judging standards.

The fruit, flowers and foliage of **Bromeliads** are all so striking that it is difficult to place them in either flowering or foliage classes and if sufficient numbers are expected, a separate class for Bromeliads is **advised.**

Unless the Schedule specifically allows plants to be shown in water, which is a rare occurrence sometimes seen in Junior Horticulture classes, plants growing only in water will be eliminated for deduction under form, size and grooming. All house plants must be fastidiously clean and the leaves deteriorate quickly underwater. Size and form together equal 40 points and neither of these qualities would ordinarily be near perfection if the plant is grown only in water.

SCALE OF POINTS

Form or Symmetry according to variety	25	Freedom from Blemish	20
Foliage	20	Plant Size	15
. uniformity of shape, color, size		Grooming	15
		Correct Label	5

FORM

Form refers to the shape and proportions of the plant and must be that which is typical of the species or variety. Foliage plants fall easily into three groups according to characteristic form:

A. Erect

B. Spreading

C. Vining, pendant, hanging and trailing

Vining forms can always be pruned to control growth but they often have one bad side. Self-heading forms often present problems of controlling size, as many do not lend themselves to pinching and must be started from cuttings when the original plant becomes leggy. Self-heading forms are best for free-standing locations since their form is symmetrical and should give a pleasing appearance from all sides in such as **Dracaenas, Bromeliads, Ferns, Geraniums, etc.**

Coleus sometimes gives the impression of weediness, the plant should be well-clothed in foliage and symmetrical. **Ficus, Rubber Plant** is often leggy. **Pandanus, Screw Pine** is often allowed to become a forest of suckers, though young plants have a graceful, fountain form.

Tolmiea menziesi, Picka-Back Plant begins to take on a straggly, moth-eaten look with age.

After blooming, off-sets or "pups" appear at the base of **Bromeliads,** these pups are often left attached to form a group; the old rosette is useless after flowering and the young plants can be potted up separately to carry on for blooms. The erect, sculptured form is modern in appearance in the same general pattern as a pineapple top, a rosette of leaves in a graceful whorl.

Dracaena fragrens loses its symmetry after being allowed to bloom. **Dracaena** and **Hawaiian Ti,** botanically **cordyline,** have erect, single stem plant forms which make them very fitting for modern home use.

Sansevieria, Snake Plant should not be allowed to become overcrowded and **Dieffenbachia** has a habit of becoming leggy and top-heavy. **Wandering Jew** or **Inch Plant** should be penalized for extra-long internodes which is their particular fault. **Philodendrons** and others should be penalized if they are lopping over at the top of a too-short support.

The stem or stems of all foliage plants should be strong and proportionate to the foliage and able to support the foliage at a characteristic angle. Vines should be trained to a suitable support.

The stem internodes should be short, a lack of light makes them elongated. The stems should be fairly well covered with foliage. Unless otherwise specified, there should be only one well-centered plant per pot. The plants should be well-balanced, and symmetrical, indicating they have been turned frequently.

Foliage

Since the leaves in general are the most effective part of the plant reflecting both the culture and characteristic interest, they must be given considerable attention and "weight".

Foliage interest can be divided into two sections:

A. Colored Foliage (croton, caladium, coleus, etc.)
B. Leaf form of striking patterns (**Ferns**, sword-shaped **Sansevieria, Screw Pine, Phoenix roebelini,** machete-shaped **Birdsnest Fern** and contorted **Hoya carnosa compacta**)

There is a vast difference between juvenile and adult appearance of many **Philodendrons** in leaf size. **P. cordatum** usually seen with 3" leaves in a 4" pot may have leaves up to 16" when grown in ample rich soil in the greenhouse. **Fern** foliage varies from the many-divided fronds of **Boston Fern** to the glossy, wavy margined blades of the **Birdsnest Fern. Staghorn Ferns** have fronds of two kinds — a clasping type which is broad and succulent when fresh, and typically dry when mature, and the others are in the shape of antlers of the European deer giving the plant its name.

Most **Palms** are unattractive in the young state with some leaves undivided.

When **Monstera deliciosa** (usually incorrectly referred to as **Philodendron Pertusum** or **Split Leaf Philodrendron**) have leaves which have stopped splitting, the fault usually lies with a lack of light, soggy soil or a lack of fertilizer. Immature leaves are frequently solid also. The plant should carry an abundance of fine, large, heavily cut mature leaves.

The foliage of all plants should be abundant; the size and number of leaves should be according to variety, but sufficient to fully clothe the plant, well-spaced and in proportion to the main "trunk" or branch and appear healthy and thriving. Curling foliage should be suspected of harboring plant lice. Leaf color must be clear, true and bright and the margins, spots and other markings (if present) should be well defined. The color of green foliage should be regularly spread over the entire leaf and uniform over the entire plant.

All the mature leaves on a plant should be of uniform size, shape and texture. The Judge can penalize severely under typical texture if the foliage has been oiled or unnaturally prepared. The Judge should be reasonably familiar with those plants which typically have foliage which has a highly varnished texture such as **Synegonium auritum** and glossy as in the **Aspidistra.**

The foliage should be turgid and of a substance which is characteristic. For instance, comparatively, **Coleus** substance is much less than in **Rubber Plant,** but **Coleus** foliage must be turgid, firm and not limp; **Rubber Plant** must not appear shriveled or wrinkled.

Freedom from Blemish

Damage caused by insects and disease is more severely penalized than mechanical damage such as tears, water spots and the like. Scars caused by careless removal of scale should be penalized.

The foliage of **Coleus** is particularly sensitive to insecticides of sufficient strength to kill its worst enemy, the mealy bug.

The Judge is often requested to diagnose various plant ills. Malpractice in houseplant care includes:

Dying foliage from the base upwards:
- lack of light
- improper watering
- high temperatures
- gas poisoning

Browning leaf tips:
- improper water (over or underwatering)
- exposure to drafts
- insect attacks
- touching cold or sun-heated glass surface
- dry air

Browning, drying edges and spots:
- soil salts
- soil worms
- improper feeding program

Limp, lifeless foliage, plant looks as if it needs water, but is sufficiently moist:
- plant rot
- root damage
- "sunstroke"

Yellowing foliage
- too little or too much feeding
- overwatering
- poor light or
- excessive light (Ferns, Af. Violets)

Loss of normal foliage color
- overwatering
- lack of plant food
- sun faded
- insect attack, mealy bug, scale, spider mite

Size

Size is a relative matter, since some specimens growing in their native habitat may reach one hundred feet (**Ficus elastica**). Size is according to variety and varies considerably within species. Size should be judged on what is appropriate for the average home; not too small to make an educational and decorative showing of typical characteristics of form, leaf color, size and shape, and yet not so large as to be inconvenient. A large plant is not necessarily a well-grown plant.

Hybridizers are continually at work altering standards as for example the dwarf varieties of **Caladium,** so care must be taken to arrive at a fair decision on size. Such miniature types should be small but showing mature characteristics.

Many **Ferns** are attractive with typical form of plant and leaf at a very early age and retain pleasing lines to maturity. Specimens of **Birdsnest Fern** a foot or less high are particularly attractive. Most house plants have a size and a height at which they are most attractive; before that the stems and leaves appear weak and gawky, after that they appear leggy, awkward and often top heavy. The stems should be of an adequate size and stiffness as is characteristic.

The plant should not be either over-potted or under-potted, the plant size should be in proportion to the container.

Grooming

Sanitation is an important consideration in house plant care. It is difficult to determine the amount of grooming, but the Judge should penalize any grooming which alters the normal characteristics of leaf or plant.

The surface of the soil should be free of debris such as dried leaves, ashes, match sticks and other rubbish.

The pot should be clean and in good condition. The soil should be moist and not appear cracked, dry or worn out. The plant should appear well established in the pot, evidence of recent moving should be penalized to the point of elimination.

All dead leaves and branches should be groomed away, leaving no unsightly stubs. Minor damage can be trimmed away but penalty must be taken if the trimming has altered the form typical of the plant or reduced the size.

The foliage must be wiped clean but not polished. Many schedules state that a plant that has been oiled or otherwise "dressed" to give unnaturally or uncharacteristic gloss will not be judged. In the absence of schedule ruling, the Judge can deduct points under improper grooming and under deviations from normal foliage texture and color to total the degree of fault.

Staking of tall growers is often necessary, the stakes should not be noticeable, they should be of a matching color, not too large or sticking above the plant top. The ties should have been carefully applied at regular intervals along the stem, and not noticeable.

Authorities disagree on the handling and purpose of aerial roots such as appear on **Philodendron**, and some **Succulents**. Some state they are simply used as clinging devices, others that they supply oxygen and relieve drainage problems, thus should not be removed. If dry, ropy roots disfigure the general appearance, deduction may be made.

Labeling

The Judge should be more severe in deductions relative to nomenclature as the main purpose of even the small show is educational and visitors appreciate the opportunity to copy down the names of plants which appeal to them. Just the general family name is not enough as wide differences occur among the species and varieties. Labels should be properly sized, neatly printed and above all, correct.

SUMMARY
Form 25 Points
*compact *full *bushy *even growth *vines controlled *general form typical *well centered in pot *good growth *one plant per pot unless otherwise specified *foliage to pot rim *symmetrical *strong and proportionate stem or stems *short stem internodes

-ungainly -long, bare stems -lopsided -underdeveloped -heavy on one side -stems stringy -lacks symmetry -missing or broken leaves altering symmetry -straggly -uneven growth -dry, ropy aerial roots disfiguring appearance -tall for size, age -sparse foliage -excessive suckering -weedy

Foliage 20 Points
*uniform size, shape, color *strong growth *firm attachment *firm substance *bright, clear, vivid color as is typical to type *turgid *heavily cut (**Monstera**)

-uncharacteristically shiny -lacks substance -weak attachment -limp -imperfect -torn -Monstera stopped splitting

Freedom from Blemish 20 Points
*no scars or blemishes

-diseased -damaged by insect or disease -mechanical damage -yellowing -browning

Size 15 Points
*good relation to pot *is a reasonably mature plant *attractive size

-too small -immature -container too large or small

Grooming 15 Points
*foliage free of dust, soil, residue *soil surface clean *pot clean *well staked *well chosen pot

-stakes too noticeable -ties improperly applied -unsightly length of unused support -debris on soil surface -pot soiled -pot cracked, peeling -artificially dressed, oiled -unsuitable pot texture, color, character, size

Labeling 5 Points
*correct as to genus, species, variety *neat *readable

-name not given -only labeled as to family (i.e succulent, Peperomia, etc.)

Bonsai

SUGGESTED CLASSES (any or all according to anticipated competition)   1-2'
1. Single Trunk Upright
2. Single Trunk Slanting
3. Single Trunk Cascade
4. Single Trunk Gnarled, Twisted

5. On a Stone
6. Two or More Trunks (one stump)
7. Two or More Trees
8. Roots Connected
9. Baby Bonsai, under three inches

Further divisions can be made by making classes for deciduous and evergreens.

BONSAI (pronounced bone-sigh)

While Bonsai are not exhibited in competition in the Orient, classes are becoming more and more popular in America.

Translated as "dwarf or potted dwarf tree", but this is not intended to mean a stunted, deformed, out-of-proportion oddity. Rather, the Bonsai idea is to produce in miniature the natural, graceful, true to scale characteristics of growth habit and reproduction of the genus, species or variety to which the plant belongs and to reproduce a miniature segment of a natural scene that lives, breathes and changes with the seasons.

A Bonsai is distinguished from an ordinary potted plant in that it is considered a work of art to create a "micro-scene" capable of stimulating contemplation and imaginary participation. Bonsai are especially popular among urban population often far from natural beauty; a small scale tree can take one "out" of the city in memory and mind to a country scene of meadow, grove or gorge.

In contrast, the usual pot plant is cultivated for the botanical perfection of the flowers and foliage whereas Bonsai evoke appreciation of aesthetic beauty by their suggestion of some actual spot in nature. This charm and magnetism of a good Bonsai is evident even in pictures to those aesthetically sensitive, even to the point of imagining branches moving and birds singing.

Tray Gardens

Bonsai differ from tray gardens also, in that while a tray garden's function is also to represent a landscape, it does not involve the actual cultivation of plants over an extensive period of time. In the tray garden (Bankei), it makes no difference if the maker uses copies of inanimate or animate objects. The best Bonsai use no added materials, such as miniature bridges, shrines, and the like to carry the impression, but rely entirely on the tree or trees and soil with perhaps a rock or a piece of decorative wood. Thus the location is abstract, could be anywhere in any country, while a pagoda would limit the locale to a single country. Stones are often included for effect and sometimes a stone is placed by itself as an effective exhibit. The Schedule would have to make a place for such to be judged, however.

Earliest record of such tree handling dates from some illustrated thirteenth century Japanese scrolls showing trees and grasses growing in shallow pots as garden ornaments. Bonsai were first seen by the general public at the Chicago World's Fair in 1893 and became popular here after World War Two.

There was a time in Bonsai history when dwarfing was done to create the grotesque, the crippled, the fantastic, but this is not done today. However, Nature does at times produce irregularities in form caused by environmental conditions of wind, snow, storm and other damage and replicas of these natural, gnarled trunks with twisted or bent branches are often aesthetically satisfying.

Many species of trees, shrubs and vines both evergreen and deciduous lend themselves to the restrictive growth without altering any of the normal characteristics. It must be noted that Bonsai are essentially outdoor plants, brought indoors occasionally for show, but must meet the seasonal temperature and conditions in order to naturally express the changing seasons and exhibit perfect health. Some trees will take longer indoor residence, such as the California Redwood, Crab Apples, Chinese Elm, Japanese Maple and the Kumquat. Some authorities recommend at least a four month outdoor residence per year for most types.

SUGGESTED SCALE OF POINTS FOR BONSAI

Overall Artistic Effect According to style   45

Development of a suitable type plant,
. form, as to species   *15*
. branches   *10*
. roots and trunk   *10*
. leaves, fruits or flowers   *10*
Consider proportion and scale of needles, fruit, branches trunk size, branch diameter and spread, height in scale with trunk and taper.

Cultural Perfection   40
Condition and Health   15
. of foliage, branches, fruit, etc.
. of soil surface, moss, etc.
Technique   15
. pruning, wiring
Size and Aged Look   10
Display Effect   15
. container proportion, harmony with tree color and shape
. grooming
. identification

DEVELOPMENT OF A SUITABLE TYPE PLANT

The Judge should expect to find many species of trees, shrubs, plants and vines trained as Bonsai. Specialty nurseries and Bonsai books list Pines, Firs, Larch, Cedar, Beech, Bamboo, Hawthorn, Wisteria, Holly, Maple, Azaleas, Juniper, Willow, Elms, fruit trees such as Cherry, Plum and Persimmon.

The Judge may find that a knowledge of cultural difficulty may be of help in breaking a deadlock. The Red Pine succumbs to smoke-polluted atmosphere and also listed as difficult are the Siberian Pine, Cherry and Camellias. Among the easier ones are the Azalea, Pyracantha, Juneberry, Five-Needle Pine, Maples and Bamboo. The others fall somewhere in between.

American adaptations of the art often include such plants as the geranium, but the feeling of a landscape effect cannot be achieved with these as with true Bonsai which is basically to represent a plant growing in its natural state and forming a smaller-than-life scene. Schedules may make classes for these as short-lived or quasi-Bonsai, however, and the judging criteria should be the same with special attention to leaf size with the Fern-leaved Pelargoniums being considered the most suited. Such short-lived Bonsai entered in a class with regular Bonsai would naturally suffer severe point reduction to the point of elimination.

Generally speaking, any kind of tree is capable of being trained into a Bonsai, the only stipulation being that they should have small leaves and dense twigs. Trees such as the Platanus, Magnolia, Ponderosa Pine, Catalpa, Larger Persimmon are unsuitable because their leaves, needles, trunk, flowers and fruit lack the proper proportion and scale.

Bonsai styles are classifed as to the number and shape of the trunks.

1. Single Upright Trunk

- Japanese name Chokkan
- tall tree standing
- erect, straight trunk
- on level ground
- meadow impression
- usually in a shallow tray or pot
- may also have a rock outcropping

2. Single Trunk Slanting
- Japanese name Shakan

- representing a tree growing at right angles to a slope
- trunk tipped or curved either to right or left
- with lowest branch spread in opposite direction
- top bent slightly forward
- foliage is generally thicker on the side facing the sun
- pots often deeper with less diameter

3. Single Trunk Cascade

- Japanese name Kengai
- represents a tree looking down in a gorge
- main part overhangs the container, tip 1' or more below container
- trunk grows straight up from soil, then turns abruptly downward
- pot often deeper with less diameter

4. Gnarled, Twisted Single Trunk

- Japanese name Hankan
- suggests stunted tree growing
- on top of cliff or wind-swept crag
- trunk grows straight up from soil
- then turns downward
- branches' lowest tips reach below container rim
- not excessively corkscrewed
- sturdy low container

5. On a Stone
- Japanese name Ishi-tsuki

- represents a tree growing on or out of a rock
- usually a gorge over a river or a seascape
- low tray is filled with water, **not soil**
- roots of a tree cling around a rough stone
- stone must not be tippy, but very stable
- or the tree may be planted in a depression in the rock

6. Two or More Trunks

- Japanese name Kobumono
- two or more trunks growing from one stump
- subdivisions: Sokan: two trunks
    sankan: three trunks
    gokan: five trunks
    kubudate: more than six trunks
- no bonsai is cultivated with four trunks
- low container

7. Two or More Trees

- Japanese name Yose-ue
- more than two trees in a pot or container
- subdivisions: nihon-yose: two trees
    gohon-yose: five trees
- may be same species or different
- if different species must be harmonious
- low container

8. Roots Connected

- Japanese name Ne-tsuranari
- several trunks branch up from a crawling root or
- several trunks branch off upright from a recumbent trunk (called raftlike Ikada-buki)
- low container

Form

Bonsai is a symbol of life of austerity and confined as it to a low, shallow container, it must show a balanced growth of trunk, branches and leaves to have an aesthetic value.

Basically the art of Bonsai is to represent a plant growing in its natural state and responding to the seasons. A Judge will find that studying tree-forms as they grow to full size in nature will be a help in judging. Observe deciduous trees when in bloom, enfoliaged and bare-branched. Sketch the forms to imprint the characteristic growth of each species on the mind.

The Judge must evaluate the extent of the exhibitor's skillful trimming and shaping to give the appearance of a full-grown tree or shrub growing on some windswept mountain or a battered tree along a coast or a beautiful specimen left growing in a fertile field. The shape should be suitable for the species, each requires different trimming and shaping.

The Bonsai admonition of first the trunk, second the branches and third the rootage is synonymous with the balanced development of a large tree. In Bonsai shaping the form aims not so much at symmetry as to the beauty of balance in seeming unsymmetry. Trees in their natural state are seldom symmetrical, and in Bonsai as in Japanese landscaping and floral arrangement, aesthetic taste decrees the beauty that comes from a studied violation of symmetry called asymmetrical balance. The result should appear natural, however, not rigid. The tree should be carefully shaped to be free-standing and pleasingly three dimensional when viewed from any angle, with a well-developed front and back which heightens the effect of looking into and through a full-grown tree in its native state.

Miniature growth, old age and historical background are not the only requisites of a good Bonsai. It must have a healthy, shapely grace and beauty. Austerity rather than opulent growth is the rule, and with harmony of foliage to branch; branch to trunk; plant to pot and pot to setting. The plant must seem to have character . . . a personality.

Whether in or out of flowering or foliage season, a deciduous Bonsai loses much if it is not shapely with graceful branch tracery. It is of prime importance that it be of elegant proportions. Many deciduous Bonsai, such as the Elms, Maples, Willows, Cherries and others are admired for this gracefulness of formation of the twigs and the balanced reach of the bare branches as much as when covered with verdant foliage. For this reason deciduous Bonsai are generally considered more elegant and refined than needle-leaved evergreens which show no seasonal changes.

Graceful gestures of the trees
You can't see when there are leaves.

A Judge would be remiss indeed to refuse to judge or award a deserved prize to a deciduous Bonsai shown in its natural dormant period for the enjoyment of those who can appreciate the unclothed structure. The points usually allotted to foliage are simply transferred to branching.

The strictly controlled arrangement of branches according to the rule of three, is observed in some schools, but the present tendency is to respect naturalness. The goal is a natural tree structure and since no law governs the tree growing in its independant way, the Judge should recognize the art of achieving the natural over the art of making a plant conform to man's ruling.

Trunk

The trunk, leaves, roots, fruits and flowers are important aspects of a Bonsai. All these parts combine to make a harmonious whole and any violation of this unity which spoils the tree's appearance is severely penalized. An interestingly textured and shapely trunk is desirable.

Much importance is attached to the size and taper of the trunk. Back in Bonsai history there was a fad for the creation of abnormally short, heavy trunks which were all out of proportion to the natural diameter and length, and it is possible that such aged specimens might be shown, as might another forced type briefly prevalent in which the trunk was twisted like a screw or a much exaggerated "juniper twist". Another form no longer considered desirable is the tako-zukuri or octopus in which the trunk was bent in an unnatural manner. Saba-miki meaning split trunk is a tree in which a great part of the trunk has decayed, leaving only the core, suggesting many decades of survival against the elements and this is an acceptable Bonsai form.

Trunks are often scaly, hoary, cracked and peeling depending upon the age and the natural characteristics of the tree. The trunks of the Japanese Black Pine are expected to be vigorous, gnarled and with a "masculine" appearance. Colors of trunks vary from the white of the birch to the reddish brown of the Red Pine and the smooth color of the beech.

Examine the trunk closely for a grafting scar or joint and if one is noticeable score down accordingly. Bud grafts result in an abruptly crooked stem and most other methods show a difference in trunk size and/or bark color. A generous portion of the trunk should show. The trunk should be in just the right position in the pot to balance the plant. The spread and shape of the branches will determine whether the tree should be set on or off center, as well as the placement on the table or stand. Note the tree positions in the pots in the accompanying sketches.

The Judge should look for ideal natural proportion (in miniature) between trunk and branches. A trunk too slender is penalized as severely as one that is too short or heavy for its height. A chopped-off, blunt top is penalized. The trunk should taper gently toward its top, and at least ⅓ of the total height should be revealed as trunk in the upright forms, particularly. A curve should be displayed to best advantage, no branches should spoil the line of the lower trunk.

Roots

Often the rootage is the margin of difference between a mediocre Bonsai and a superior one. Some species, such as the Trident Maple develop surface roots very readily. A Bonsai with defective root splay is penalized. The roots should be exposed above the soil surface to give a sense of a full-grown tree solidly united with the soil, or the base of the trunk should spread, suggesting roots just below the surface. Aged trees growing in nature have such rootage and this imitation of nature enhances the value of the Bonsai.

There should be several ramifications angling out from the base of the trunk, partly below, partly above the soil surface and a bit of moss gives an even more naturalistic look. A youthful cutting will have less strength to support the trunk than a seedling but continued pot-confinement remedies this defect. After a couple of decades, it is difficult to say a better specimen began from a seedling, cutting, layering or other method.

The roots should appear well established and of a size that seems suitable for the height and age of the tree. Exposed roots which are too fine and weak-appearing or too sparse and spindly are penalized.

Branches

When the branches are arranged in groups according to the Oriental "Rule of 3", the two lowest branches are trained slightly forward, one slightly higher on the best side. Branch number 3 of each group lies between branch one and two and extends to the backside.

The branches must harmonize with the trunk in thickness and length. A tree growing naturally generally has many branches, each one dividing and redividing, getting smaller and finer towards the tip. Such duplication of finely divided tip growth is highly regarded in Bonsai. The top of any aged tree, if it has been properly pinched should be thickly covered with twigs, each with a hoary look clear to the ends.

However, the branches which have developed too thick a crown to be in harmony with the trunk, thus giving the plant a top-heavy, bulky look should be penalized. The branch pattern may be rugged, forceful and masculine or simple, refined and graceful according to the species. There must be no knobs, knots, or breaks on the branches or any other evidence of careless wiring or training techniques. There should be no traces where the top of a trunk or branch have been "lopped off". There should be no u-shaped division at the end of the branches and no parallel branching. Several branches in one place or one branch immediately above another are faults as is opposite branching where a branch on each side of the trunk forms a straight horizontal line.

Bonsai may be exhibited in training wires. Overlong branches can upset the aesthetic balance and this would count against the total score. A dead branch or stub (jin) often occurs in nature and if it adds to the overall effect of age, it should not be scored down. Note Sketch 2. However, a fresh, unhealed stub or scar is to be penalized.

Leaves

Leaf size is important in achieving the illusion of Bonsai, and the trees and plants chosen for Bonsai should be those which have small leaves of fine texture and short needles rather than long. While decades of pot confinement, element exposure and controlled moisture does reduce the leaf size to a certain extent, it is an impossibility to make a Ponderosa Pine needle as short as a Spruce or the coarse, heavy texture of a Catalpa as fine as an Elm or Birch. The Judge must give extra consideration to the artist who has understood the problems of leaf texture and size in these small scale plants. The length and width of leaves and needles must be in harmony (scale) with the size and height of the trunk and the size and sweep of the branches.

Some deciduous trees are valued especially for the beauty of their fall-colored foliage, such as the Maple, the Mountain Ash, and the Pin Oak. There is a nostalgic autumnal charm in such Bonsai exhibited with only a few of the tinted leaves still clinging to the branches with two or three lying on the soil below. The Judge must recognize the extra skill required in maintaining the season-long health of a plant that colors up properly in the fall as unhealthy foliage is apt to fall before coloring.

The Japanese Birch has a natural habit of retaining its dry leaves intact on the twigs until the whitish green shoots appear in the late spring. Maples are favorite Bonsai subjects because they give four-season interest beginning in the spring with shoots of bright color, to comparatively small, deeply divided leaves giving a finely textured summer appearance, autumnal tints of deep-colored leaves which when dropped reveal a fine branch tracery.

Fruit, Flowers

Branches and trunk can be dwarfed by pruning, leaves may become smaller by restriction, but flowers and fruit sizes remain typical of the species. Large flowers and fruits are out of place and scale with miniature trees and achieve an abnormal, grotesque impression. A Magnolia Bonsai in bloom looks like a twig stuck in the pot. Double Camellia flowers are also too large, but the small, single-flowered wild Camellia makes a suitably scaled Bonsai.

Trees with large fruit are also unsuitable. Potted plant enthusiasts often produce apples, oranges, pears, persimmons and other fruits so large and numerous that their total volume is more than that of the soil in the pot, and this would be a most unrealistic condition for a Bonsai. Sometimes wild species have better proportioned fruits and flowers, and the Judge must be sure of his species and varieties before he dogmatically states that an apple or persimmon or some other plant is unsuitably large unless the evidence is right there on the tree. The Judge will upscore a delicate scent in keeping with their miniature grace and beauty rather than a too-powerful scent.

Size and Age of Plant

A size of two feet high and/or two feet in width or less is usually regarded as a convenient size for both handling and enjoyment through staging in a show, home or garden. A Bonsai less than one foot is called katate-mochi which translates to mean "capable of being carried in one hand" and is often seen as an accessory on a desk; baby Bonsai are approximately two and one-half inches and for those who can't resist the very tiny there is the shito, literally "finger-tip", in a pot less than thimble-or small-button-size. The Schedule controls the size specifications of exhibit Bonsai.

As noted, Bonsai size varies, often according to the delicate branch tracery and relative size in nature. Pines approximately two feet; Cherries one foot and so on. However, such large trees as the Five-Needle Pine, the Elm and the Juniper are almost magically amendable to shito "finger-tip" minimizing, living for years as tiny conversation pieces. These wee trees perform their botanical functions in season which adds to their charm and distinction. It is hoped that the Schedule will be so explicit that the Judges will not be forced to judge a two-footer against a two-incher, but if such occasion arises, he should judge each according to its perfection of scale for size. And the tiniest one would not necessarily be the best Bonsai.

The Judge should check the size against the Schedule and against the age given on the label, noting how successfully the size has been controlled for age. There is no definite way of assessing the age of a tree unless the pedigree is handed down as is done in Japan. The age of a naturally stunted plant collected in the wild can only be guessed at or determined by cross section. However, the **impression** of age can be assessed by the Judge and should be. By noting the hoary, gnarled growth of some trunks, the properly exposed roots which occur in nature only in old age and even the pot, if properly chosen, and the appearance of the surface of the soil can carry an impression of age.

Saplings show vigorous growth while old trees possess an austere simplicity and grandeur which is evident even in this miniature size.

Young trees look similar (Oak and Maple look like Hickory, Fir and Spruce like Cedar) and have a general uninteresting symmetrical form. It is only with maturity that characteristic lines develop between types and age, varying growing conditions, accidents and the like, mark the tree and give it character; if there is balance, it is asymmetrical. The impression of youth is given by a slender sapling or a pyramidal or globular mass of leaves, or branches starting very low as in the familiar Christmas-tree shape. Rapid upright growth, straight and without taper is characteristic of youth. Opposite branching is also a juvenile trait that is undesirable. A heavy trunk and short needles add to a mature appearance and give a desirable illusion of a forest giant.

Younger trees and broadleaf evergreens often have nearer-to-normal size foliage while the older Bonsai have more miniature foliage since the long years of pot confinement have reduced the size. White deadwood on Juniper is regarded as a sign of genuine age.

Condition and Health

Bonsai must be healthy appearing, the growth active, even though restrained. The leaves and needles should be of typical color for the species or variety; glossy (if this applies) and free from any insects or disease. A healthy tree will have new or fresh growth during the growing season and well-developed leaf buds during the off season.

Evergreen needles will be firmly attached, naturally green and pliable. Exposure to the elements, sunshine, rain, dew and wind is indispensible to the growth of tree in their natural state and this is often denied Bonsai because they are so easy to move indoors to enjoy. The play of light, fresh wind in the branches strengthens and helps them resist disease. Trees and plant denied this, as well as fresh air, sunshine and night dew often lack vigor. Insufficient exposure to sun is revealed in weakened foliage and large, flimsy leaves with little substance. If a Judge notes that spring bud growth is weak and sickly, he suspects that the Bonsai has been taken abruptly from outdoor winter dormancy into a heated living room. A general weakened, withered appearance may be the result of starvation and should be penalized.

On the other hand, the size of the foliage and amount of growth will be accelerated by excess water and fertilizing, with the result that the trees lose their elegant appearance and all value as Bonsai. A Judge must reward the grower whose touch is so fine that he balances between the weakened appearance of too little food and the lushness of too much. The Judge should also appreciate a vigorous yose-ue Bonsai (clustered trees) as it is difficult to keep all trees equally healthy

Soil Surface

The plant must be well established in the pot, usually deciduous plants are not shown within four months of the last transplanting and *one year is preferable for Pines. Natural, low growing moss on the soil surface indicates that the tree has been in the pot a con-*

siderable time, besides its soft texture is pleasing and unifies the planting. Flat mosses expose the undulations of the surface in a desirable manner.

Fine roots emerging from the drain holes on the bottom are other signs of long tenancy. Soil bulging above the pot rim indicates a rootbound mass and should be penalized.

The soil should look firmly packed, natural and not recently disturbed, but not hard or cement-like either. Of course no weed should be growing in the pot. Rocks used with Bonsai should have character, not be just pebbles. Neither should they be highly colored "specimen" rocks which call attention to themselves as separate from the landscape effect. They should appear as larger than their actual size and be placed in such a way as to suggest a half-buried outcropping balanced by the tree mass. A placement low and flat near the tree trunk or under its exposed roots or as a taller, hollowed "shoulder" for the tree to lean upon add realistic effects.

Container

Bonsai is the art of growing trees and plants in pots or trays containing no more soil than is absolutely necessary and naturally containers must play a very important part, they are often said to be to a Bonsai what a frame is to a picture.

They set off and finish the appearance of the exhibit. An unsuitable, unharmonious pot choice will spoil the appearance of the most perfect Bonsai and should be penalized commeasurate with the severity of the fault.

Pots of startling color or ornate sytle will overwhelm and overshadow the plant. The goal is to have the pot enhance the beauty, elegance and austerity of the plant. Pots vary from flat, shallow tray-like vessels to deeper bowls for Cascades and Slanting styles. Shapes vary from round, oblong, square, rectangular and diamond-shaped. The shape should have been chosen with regard to how well the form balances and complements the shape, size and appearance of the plant it contains.

Subdued, earthy colors of dark brown, grey, black, black-red and dark purple imitate the colors of earth and rocks and the older appearing the pot, the better if the tree also has an aged appearance. Glazed and newly baked pots are more suited to younger saplings and seedlings.

Color selection and texture should be harmonious with the plant color. Generally, evergreens and plants with dark green foliage look best in containers of dark hue. Deciduous plants with light foliage and silvery trunk look well in light colored pots. Brighter hues, glazes and greens are reserved for plants bearing colored fruits or flowers. Dark chocolate brown is a color rarely out of place for Bonsai. Common red clay pots are an unsuitable selection to be penalized.

All Bonsai pots must have drainholes, at least one hole in the smaller size pots and three to five in the larger. The holes or "eyes" should not be clogged. To assure drainage, all Japanese pots have risers, and in some cases these "feet" are inconspicuous, in others they add a decorative touch.

Formal, upright Bonsai look well in flat rectangular and oval containers. Shallow round or oval pots show off light, informal and windswept trees. Thick-trunked and heavy foliaged trees need sturdy, unglazed pots. Cascading Bonsai require deep pots or elevating stands.

Sometimes a Judge finds it easier to assess scale by percentages. An artistic proportion might be approximately 80% plant to 20% pot with a 60 to 40 ratio for low spreading plants. However, the Judge must remember that aesthetics cannot be measured, there are exceptions relative to openness of silhouette, texture of foliage color and depth of pot.

If a stand or base is included in the exhibit, it too is considered and should not either overpower the plant or upset the visual balance. The finish and style should be harmonious with both the pot and the plant.

Grooming

While an aged appearance is an asset to a Bonsai, a bedraggled, unclean, dusty, unkempt look is not. The extreme opposite evidenced by unnaturally glossy foliage is also penalized if the Judge suspects the application of some product to create the shiny look.

Identification

Much interest is attached to the identification of the Bonsai, including the species and variety. Interesting details relative to age and historical background add a great deal to the exhibit. Such labeling should be brief, neatly printed, legible and well-scaled to the exhibit.

SUMMARY

Overall Development 45 Points

Form: *balanced trunk, branch, root development *aesthetically pleasing *free standing *subtly asymmetrical *form suitable to species *three dimensional *pruned to reveal structure

-unnatural -stumpy -awkward -a mere ball of leaves

Trunk: *well proportioned to height and branches *gently tapered *may be split, gnarled showing age

-too heavy -too short -abnormally corkscrewed -unnaturally bent -blunt top -grafting mark -unsteady

Roots: *well exposed *several ramifications *well established

-lacks surface roots -roots too fine and sparse

Branches: *balanced branch reach *twiggy tip *branches in proportion to trunk *elegant tracery *short internodes

-superfluous growth -scraggly tip -crown too thick -knobby -pruning scars -wire weals -twiggy branches too heavy for trunk size -opposite branching -parallel branching -one branch immediately above another -a u-shaped division at branch end

Leaves: *small *short needles *colored *fine texture

-out of scale -needles too long -coarse texture

Fruit, Flowers:

*small scaled *delicate scent

-too large -heavy appearing -scent overwhelming

Cultural Perfection 40 Points

Condition and Health 15 Points *active though restrained growth *foliage, needles, typically colored *multiple trees healthy *free of disease, insects

-lacks vigor -weak foliage -lacks substance, sickly -withered

Soil Surface 5 Points *mossy *settled

-root bound (surface heaving) -rock hard -recently disturbed appearance

Plant Size and Age 10 Points *aged appearance *gnarled trunk, bark *dwarfed foliage *size according to schedule *size controlled for number of years old

-too lush -youthful growth

Technique 15 Points *pruning, wiring

Display Effect 15 Points

Container: *harmonious *well scaled *earthy color *complements plant *aged tree in old, unglazed pot

-overpowering color -too ornate style -lacks proper drain eyes -stand or base upsets visual balance

Grooming: *clean *fresh appearance

-bedraggled -dusty -overgroomed

Identification: *briefly interestingly described *label neat *legible

-lacks indentification -incorrectly labeled -label too large, -messy

Flowering and Fruiting Plants (Potted)

SUGGESTED CLASSES:

1. Flowering Plant, pot size under 7"
2. Flowering Plant, pot size 7-15"
3. Fruiting Plant, pot size up to 15"

Sub-classes may be provided for classification such as listed at the chapter's end or for plants by name such as Fuchsia, Hydrangea, Camellia, African Violet, Geranium.

The Schedule should specify that the plant has been in the exhibitor's possession at least three months with the exception of such annuals as Morning Glory, Alyssum, Balsam, etc.

FLOWERING PLANT

A flowering plant is one grown primarily for the attractiveness and abundance of the flowers. A list of categories for familiar flowering and fruiting house plants appears at the chapter's end

If a potted plant is that of a recognized Plant Society, such as Geranium, Orchid, African Violet, etc., refer to that plant for judging standards and scale.

To be acceptable exhibits, such plants must be in bloom or fruiting; the quality of floriferousness merits thirty points in the scale, a plant lacking flowers would thus forfeit any claim to an award.

Succulents and Cacti present problems as some are grown for their flowers (as the Orchid Cacti, which includes Christmas and Easter), but generally they are grown for their interesting forms. The Judge should refer to the standards and scale for Succulents and Cacti on which the flowers (if present) are included under "Color Interest." The scale for Flowering Plants may optionally be used in the case of Orchid Cacti.

The use of two or more plants in the same pot seldom produces the same effect as the single plant and should be discriminated against.

SCALE OF POINTS

Cultural Perfection	35	Size	20
. form	20	. plant	
. blemishes	10	. flowers	
. grooming	5		
Floriferousness	30	Foliage	10
. color		Label	5
. quality			
. quantity			

CULTURAL PERFECTION

FORM

The shape of the plant should be such as to display the flowers to the best advantage. As a general rule, the plant should be symmetrical and vigorous. The leaves should be regularly and well-spaced on the stems with short internodes and stems proportionate to the plant. The flower stems must be long and strong enough to support the flowers above the foliage.

The pose of some flowers is an important consideration. The tubular blooms of Gloxinias should be held in a horizontal to slightly upright position for best showing.

A well-grown Gloxinia consists of regular whorls of regularly spaced leaves radiating from a common stem forming a plate-like contour. The lower leaves extend beyond and arch slightly down over the pot rim.

Hydrangeas form a rounded or rounded triangular plant when viewed from above. Blind shoots and short, scrubby growth at the base is a serious fault. The stems should be of sufficient strength to support the bloom heads without staking; if staked penalty is taken on Hydrangeas.

Many plants have varieties which have typically varied form such as Fuchsia "CLARET CUP", a trailing basket type and "BERNADETTE", an upright bushy grower. Some varieties are especially adaptable to trellis and standard training. The Judge should penalize any specially trained form if unsuitable varieties are used, or if the result is less than aesthetic.

The top of Cyclamen corms should be well above the soil level. Cyclamen is considered of difficult culture.

The chief defect of Shrimp Plant is its tendency toward gawkiness and bare legs which must be discounted.

Marica, Apostle Plant is so called because the individaul fans or tufts commonly contain twelve leaves. These are about two feet long and a more decorative form is obtained when only one fan is allowed to develop per pot.

Oxalis has a more or less floppy habit of growth and a tendency to sparse foliage and lengthy internodes which must be penalized.

Old plants of Coral Berry, Ardisia crispa (A. crenulata) become leggy and bare at the base; seedlings also show this tendency more than cuttings.

The form of Saxifraga sarmentosa (Strawberry or Geranium Begonia) is particularly effective when kept to a single rosette in a three inch pot with runners trailing over the rim.

Climbing Gloriosa Lily will be stockier, shorter and the stems of less length when it has been grown in full sun.

Blemishes

Refer to Foliage Plants for a detailed listing of general blemishes and their causes. There should be no evidence of nutrient deficiencies, disease, insects, or mechanical damage such as water spots and tears. Mechanical damage is considered a minor fault in judging Gloxinia foliage due to their large size and tendency to brittleness.

Shedding leaves and flower petals indicate overmaturity or cultural upsets to be penalized. Jerusalem Cherry sheds its berries and leaves when moved from greenhouse to home and should be downgraded if shown in this state.

Grooming

Vertical plants such as Amaryllis may be staked, but most spreading, round forms such as Geraniums, Tuberous Begonias, etc. should have stems of sufficient strength so as not to require supplementary support.

Pot and plant should be equally clean; the soil surface should be unlittered and moist. Pots should be in good repair and well chosen for the type of plant they hold. Oiling or artificial dressing will be penalized.

Floriferousness

Floriferousness means an abundance of high quality blooms (fruits) nearing peak condition at optimum color and size for the species or cultivar.

There are some plants which are practically everblooming as for instance, African Violets, Wax Begonias and Patience Plant; some can be made to bloom almost any time after a rest period, such as Calla Lilies; others such as Poinsettias have a regular bloom season and cannot be forced.

Color

The color of the fruits and flowers must be clear, pure and bright as is typical of the plant.

With an abundance of aluminum (acid pH 5.5 or lower) present in the soil, Hydrangea flowers are a clear, true blue. With little or no aluminum (alkaline pH 6.2 to 7.5) the flowers are a true pink but if the aluminum is present in a slightly larger amount (pH 6.0) the flowers are mauve, pinkish blue or may be an unattractive murky color which is to be penalized. Greenish or faded coloring is to be discriminated against.

The color of tall-growing, small flowered Cinerarias are often a displeasing purplish tone without the clear purity found in the dwarf, large flowered types.

Age darkens the colors of many plants such as the brilliant red of the Gloriosa Lily whose coloring is more intense when given sunlight.

Quality

The presence of leaves in a truss of Hydrangea flowers is a serious fault; as is the appearance of a cleft which divides the panicle into two or more parts.

There should be no vegetative growth around the flower buds on Azalea plants. Gloxinias should carry their flowers loosely clustered in the center of the plant, well above the foliage.

Camellias drop unopened flower buds due to lack of light, too much heat, lack of humidity and too little or too much water.

Gardenias drop ther flower buds due to high temperature and are considered difficult to culture.

The waxen ball of five-pointed, double stars of the Hoya carnosa, Wax Plant should be geometrically perfect.

All flowers should be at or nearing peak condition; over-maturity evident in fading or lack of substance, wilting or limpness is to be penalized.

Quantity

The quantity of flowers expected, of course, varies with the plant; a general rule of thumb is that the flower and bud potential should be equal to the leaf area. Flowers and buds should be distributed uniformly over the plant with one-fourth to one-half the flowers open, the rest in bud and various uniform stages of development and color.

An exception is Hydrangea in which 90 per cent of the florets should be open for prime quantity and at least one-half open to escape penalty. The flowers composing each Hydrangea panicle should be uniform in size and stage of openness; and the individual panicles should be of uniform size. Each primary stem on the plant should terminate in a panicle of bloom. There should be a minimum of three panicles on plants in five inch or larger pots.

A Gloxinia tuber may carry as many as 15 flowers and have been reported as producing 35.

Coral Berry plants hang onto the clusters of hollylike berries for two years. A five inch pot of Dwarf Otaheite Orange has been known to carry 10-12 oranges.

SIZE

Plant Size

The size of the plant should be average or slightly above for the species or variety except for miniature types which should be relatively small but showing mature characteristics.

The plant size should be in proportion to the container. Some plants have recommended overall heights such as Hydrangea which is limited to 15-20 inches including the pot.

Cinerarias fall into two main groups, the dwarf, large flowered and the stellata type with smaller flowers, a more open habit of growth and a height up to three feet. All Cinerarias are considered difficult to culture.

Under optimum conditions, some Gloxinias reach astonishing size, such as 26" in diameter in a 6" pot with many leaf blades 9" long.

Many of the flowering plants normally reach dimensions greatly in excess of what would be suitable for home decoration, as for instance, the Chinese Hibiscus, Rose-of-China which is a large shrub or small tree up to 30' in the tropics, but it does not resent hard pruning and produces its large blooms on new wood. Pot confinement and pinching reduces the size of many plants such as the Geranium, so size should be judged as that which is most representative of the plant **AS A HOUSEPLANT!**

The plant should not be so immature as to fail to make an educational and decorative showing of typical characteristics of form, size and floriferousness and yet not so large as to be ungainly, inconvenient and out of proportion in the average home. The problem of appropriate size in flowering plants is mitigated by the fact that blooms do not usually appear until the plant has reached a fairly representative mature state.

Flower Size

The size of the flower must be according to variety and species, and not appear either stunted or gross at the cost of the cultural perfection of foliage and plant size. The flowers of the Night-blooming Cereus Cacti may be one foot long and wide while the Mistletoe Cacti have flowers only one-fourth inch in diameter. Many smaller types of Cacti bear flowers which are larger than the parent plant . . . some bloom when the plant is no more than two inches in diameter.

Large-Flowering Gloxinia hybrids sometimes measure 6-7" blooms; the slipper type has smaller, more delicate flowers. The fruits of the Jerusalem Cherry are normally about one-half inch in diameter.

Like the Poinsettia, the Crown of Thorns and the Dogwood, the most conspicuous part of the Shrimp Plant is the bracts; these are long-lasting and reddish-brown and lengths of six inches are not unusual, the diameter must be correspondingly plump as well.

Some exhibition strains of Cineraria have flowers up to four and five inches across. Camellia flowers range from two to six inches in diameter. Varieties of Ipomea nil (Morning Glory) such as "ROSE MARIE" exceed five inches, while varieties of I. purpurea "HEAVEN-LY BLUE" and "SCARLETT O'HARA" are typically somewhat smaller, approximately 3½ to 5 inches.

Impatiens Plant is expected to have dainty one-two inch blooms. Fuchsias have pendant flowers two to three inches long. The fruit of the Dwarf Otaheite Orange is about one-fourth the size of ordinary oranges, and lemons grown in pots often exceed orchard-grown size.

Foliage

The foliage should be sufficient to clothe the framework of the branches and stems, typically and healthfully colored, lustrous or lush according to texture.

The foliage of some pot plants (Gardenia and Camellia) plays a more important part in the overall effect than that of others (Azaleas). Gloxinia foliage is usually large and ungainly and a true indication of their cultural perfection is the lack of "stretch" in the leaf petioles.

Hairy type leaves should have a lush, deep velvety appearance. Glossy leaves should be lustrous, but naturally so. Any hint of artificial dressing should be penalized as non-typical. Some schedules state that oiled or over-dressed plants will not be judged.

Label

Much of the interest of houseplant exhibits is lost if the viewer is unable to determine the family, species and variety. Correct labeling adds so much to the educational value of the show that Judges should be more severe in their penalties. The labels should be correct, sufficiently sized, but not over-large and neatly printed, not handwritten.

SUMMARY
CULTURAL PERFECTION 35 Points
Form 20 points
*symmetrical plant *plant well foliaged above the soil line *strong stems
*compact *one plant, well centered *pruned for well-balanced framework
*bushy, stocky growth

-multiple plants in pot -top heavy -one sided -leggy -weedy -blind shoots
-short, scrubby growth -grotesque, misshapen form -defoliated -weak stems
-staked Hydrangea -weak, spindly vegetative growth

Blemishes 10 Points
*no blemishes

-shedding fruit or petals -diseased -insect damage -mechanical damage
-water spotting -torn -sun burned, scorched -browning -yellowing

Grooming 5 Points
*pot clean *plant fresh, clean *proper proportion of plant to pot *moist

-dead foliage -dried petals -presence of aged and/or discolored flowers
-soil surface littered -soil dry

Floriferousness 30 Points
Color
*clear *bright *typical *pure *intense or mellow as is typical *uniform

-blurred -murky -faded -off color

Quality
*fresh *turgid *well formed florets *uniform shape
-vegetative growth around Azalea buds -over mature -wilting -lacks substance -leaves in Hydrangea flower head -cleft Hydrangea panicle

Quantity
*flower and bud potential approximately equal to leaf area *uniform dis-
tribution of flowers and buds over plant *Gloxinia flowers loosely clustered in center *floral effect well displayed *reasonably abundant *¼ to ½
flowers open (exception: Hydrangea 50-90%)

-too few flowers open -all buds -less than 3 panicles on Hydrangea -sparse

Size 20 Points
Plant
*representative of the type **As a Houseplant** *reasonably mature *Hydrangea limited to 15-20" including pot

-stunted -over sized Hydrangea -immature

Flowers
*uniform size *uniform cluster size (if present) *optimum size for variety

-stunted -small -not uniform

Foliage 10 Points
*turgid *fresh *healthy

-sparse leaf cover -over long petioles -loose attachment -listless -lacks substance -limp -chlorotic -yellowing -oiled, over-dressed

Label 5 Points
*correct as to genus, species, variety *neat *legible
-name not given -labeled only as to family (geranium, fuchsia, etc.) -care-
lessly written -overlarge

CATEGORIES OF SOME FAMILIAR FLOWERING-FRUITING HOUSE PLANTS

PERENNIAL
ANTHURIUM
SHRIMP PLANT
BEGONIA
BROMELIAD
PATIENCE PLANT
MARICA, APOSTLE PLANT
GERANIUM
AFRICAN VIOLET

SHRUBS AS
HOUSEPLANTS
CAMELLIA
POINSETTIA
FUCHSIA
GARDENIA
HIBISCUS
RHODODENDRONS-
AZALEAS
MINIATURE ROSES

FRUITING
PLANTS
LEMON
ORANGE
POMEGRANATE
JERUSALEM CHERRY
CORAL BERRY

SUCCULENTS
and
CACTI
ORCHID CACTI
including
CHRISTMAS and
EASTER
NIGHT-BLOOMING CEREUS etc.

ORCHIDS
CYPRIPEDIUM
DENDROBIUM
PHALAENOPSIS
CATTLEYA
ONDONTOGLOSSUM
MILTONIA
CYMBIDIUM

ANNUALS or
RAISED AS ANNUALS
FROM CUTTINGS
or
SHORT LIVED
SWEET ALYSSUM
AGERATUM
MARIGOLD
BALSAM
SNAPDRAGONS
STOCKS
CYCLAMEN
LANTANA
CINERARIA
CHRYSANTHEMUMS

BULBS
TUBERS
CORMS
DAFFODILS
HYACINTHS
FREESIA
AMARYLLIS
EASTER LILY
CALLA LILY
TUBEROUS BEGONIA
GLOXINIA

VINES and TRAILERS

MORNING GLORY
PASSION PLANT
CLIMBING NASTURTIUM
FUCHSIA
EPISCIA

GLORIOSA, GLORY LILY
WAX PLANT, HOYA
SAXIFRAGA SARMENTOSA
(called Strawberry Geranium or Begonia)

Religious Themes

The foundation for judging a design with religious connotations is based on the scale of points to be used but behind this and woven into the decision should be consideration for true spirit and sincerity. The design is dealing with, if not actually sacred objects, at least with sacred ideals and any breach of good taste, such as of church customs, gaudiness or coy caricature is most distasteful.

Head-standing angels and baseball playing nuns may be cute and coy, but lack the real significance needed; and their use should suffer a reduction of points.

Religious themes may be expressed in either Traditional or Modern or Abstract without criticism. If the designs observe all the principles and if the concept of the class is communicated and recognizable, the designer should not be penalized for using the medium of contemporary design to express it.

Certainly religion is a **living** thing; a daily, immediate thing (or should be) and if we are to live with our times and express them, we must allow religious convictions to be expressed with today's freedoms.

If the Schedule does not specify that the design be Traditional and the designer chooses Avant Garde, her design must be judged only on its perfection as to the use of the principles, its execution and communicated impact.

A carefully-worded Schedule eliminates problem-causing ambiguities. If a class calls for "A DESIGN USING A BIBLICAL CHARACTER", a figure of St. Francis would be unacceptable and the Judge would deduct points under interpretation of theme and Schedule requirements. St. Francis is not mentioned in the Bible. Figures of angels, shepherds, Madonna, wise men, Peter, etc. would be acceptable as they are mentioned in the Bible.

In a more generalized class such as "ARRANGEMENT WITH A RELIGIOUS THEME", any figure or items which call to mind something pertaining to religious beliefs in any aspect would be acceptable.

Here the Judges would accept St. Francis, the cannonized saint and founder of the Franciscan Order, the Cross, animals, birds, crown of thorns, any items mentioned in the Bible or any items suggested by a Bible quotation.

Cards quoting a Bible verse establish conformity and help communicate and interpret the meaning. Often general objects may be used which in themselves do not have a religious or Biblical connotation, but in combination and context they conform and communicate religious beliefs. A cracked pottery pitcher and a loop of silver cords in themselves convey little meaning until used with appropriate flora materials to express this Biblical quotation ". . . or ever the silver cord be loosed . . . or the pitcher broken by the fountain".

Research into the symbolisms indicated by the Schedule theme is needed by both exhibitor and Judge to be certain the connotation is valid and conveys the proper idea without offense.

Madonna

The posture of the Madonna figures in the communication of the highpoints in Mary's life. An upraised, youthful face and folded hands indicate a reverent pose proper to the young virgin. A standing or kneeling position with arms crossed on the chest can indicate adoration even without the Babe; these postures or standing and seated figures holding the young Child communicate the time of Birth . . . Christmas. A deeply bowed head indicates Easter and an exultant or prayerful pose may also indicate Easter.

A Madonna holding a young child should not be used for an Easter interpretation. It is important to carefully study the pose of the figure or the age of the Child for fitness to the occasion portrayed. The Hogarth line, overused almost to triteness, is sometimes called "the Madonna line" and requires distinctive techniques to lift it above the commonplace.

Out of respect for the reverence of the subject, it is suggested that the feet of a Madonna be elevated above water-level. When using a solid white Madonna the design will have more rhythm and unity if some white materials are included in the plant materials.

Other Figures

The Bible and Christian history contains many other occasions which can be communicated through flora art. Lines, textures and colors should have been chosen to communicate the mood or feeling depicted by the stance of an accessory figure other than the Madonna also. If a figure is used, its texture and character set the fineness of the relationships. Stone, wood, metals, ceramic, terra cotta and glass all call for varying degrees of relationship.

The lines of a figure and the folds of the garments, repeated in plant materials unify a design through dominance and rhythm. (see Accessories)

Designing

Clarity of line, simplicity and restraint are indicated in religious theme designs. The amount of and choice of plant material should be limited to only that which is needed to carry the interpretation. The Madonna figure, because it is a well-known recognizable figure with deep emotional connotations, usually dominates. The design should be so constructed that the removal of any part, including a figure would destroy the design.

The Schedule sets the requirements regarding fresh, dried and artificial materials. A feeling for symbolic rightness will limit the over-use of artificial items which may cheapen the symbolic reverence of Christmas, Easter and other such occasions.

Excessive use of small sizes and intricate forms results in a cluttered look which is to be penalized. Color is God's gift too, and any color can be used but too many contrasting colors or excessive color-play destroys the unity indicated in these designs. A dominant liturgically-symbolic color should carry the design.

Communication of religious themes is strengthened by the use of common symbols and Biblical verses and quotations. Some common symbols of Christian religion are

. the Cross
. Madonna and Child
. serpentine lines
. crown of thorns
. passion flower
. lily, palm
. star shaped flowers
. evergreen (eternity)
. horizontal lines (peace, serenity)
. vertical lines (aspiration, dignity)
. circle (unending love)

. triangle (Trinity)
. treasure ('gifts of gold, frankincense and myrrh')
. liturgical colors such as
. white (purity, innocence, youth)
. blue (truth)
. gold, purple, deep blue (dignity, royalty)
. colors of stained glass
. red (love)
. grey (humility)

SUGGESTED SCALE OF POINTS FOR RELIGIOUS DESIGN

Design   30
Communication   25
  . personal expression

Relationships of Materials 25
  . texture, color
  . character, spirit
Distinction   20

Still Life

Still Life may be defined as a composition in which plant materials (fresh cut or otherwise) and more or less common, inanimate furnishings, objects of everyday life and events are combined and arranged to present a unified, aesthetic grouping. Still Life may be expressive or non-objective with design as its subject, and is allied to one type Assemblage, which see.

The arranger tries to communicate the aesthetic beauty he feels in the rhythmic movement, congenial forms and harmonious textures of ordinary objects which are often overlooked by the average person. The ribbed wartiness of a squash emphasized by the smooth dry whiteness of an onion, itself contrasting with the waxy green petals of the artichoke make the viewer aware of the appeal of texture. A string of raffia-tied garlic looped to a raffia-bound wine bottle emphasizes the smoothness of the bottle and the roughness of the raffia. A few oranges, an orange amaryllis and brown cement blocks emphasize the single-color harmony made exciting by textural and form variations.

The requirements of the class are interpreted more by the objects than by the choice or dominance of the plant materials in contrast to an accessory which merely supplements the story. Unless to fit Schedule requirements, a Still Life need not portray a literal, realistic narrative; its charm lies in the emotional appeal of the varying relationships of line, form, texture and color.

The word "objects" is used in plural when related to Still Life; these objects are chosen for their color, form, texture, size and their helpfulness in the design or in projecting the mood, feeling or message of the theme. In some instances a flower arrangement using an accessory as a theme prop is incorrectly exhibited as a Still Life and penalty must be taken for this lack of understanding of the term. Miniature figures as such are not found in Still Life. The objects are actual size, and true to their function.

To illustrate, a Still Life with Flowers on the theme "Wool" could show items such as uncarded or carded wool, knitting needles, ball of yarn, wool fabric, flowers or stones from the shepherd's meadow but would not contain a miniature of the lamb. The objects accompanying the flowers tell the story without the need of a **realistic** figurine. The arranger should have selected one dominant story and told it briefly.

Objects in Still Life strengthen and interpret the theme or story. They should be in complete harmony (though the contrasts of form, color and textures may be massive) and placed according to the principles of design including depth and a correct and expressive disposition of space.

Still Life may be divided into two categories—Flowers and Objects and Flower-Fruit groupings as indicated by the 17th Century European artists skilled in Still Life paintings. The Japanese Morimono design of flowers, fruits and vegetables have somewhat the feeling of this last category. The cut fruit and food painted so temptingly are unsuitable objects for Flower Show work. Modern trends could establish a third category of Fruit or Flowers with abstracted forms of Still *Life subjects. The type may be scheduled as Conventional or Creative.*

Still Life is often staged in niches, a shelf; hooks for a trompe-l'oeuil effect may be added for a fresh approach. The thoughtful selection and position of the objects spells distinction. Choices and combinations should not be mediocre and commonplace, a mere bowl of fruits — but should have been combined with interesting fabrics, unique jugs, and varied forms. Each object reacts upon and influences all the others. Fruits, flowers and foliage are not restricted to the container as in the traditional flower arrangement but may be laid out in related groupings of varying heights and color value.

A monotonously unvaried silhouette should be deducted. The items chosen should be of various shapes and heights, placed in orderly and expressive juxtaposition. Elevations provided by block, bases, etc. should take their place in the final harmonious design, contributing their own variations in form, texture, color and character.

There may be no single focal area, yet the eye should move easily over the grouping, drawn by the dynamic rhythms of line repetition, color value and textural interest. The number of objects used should be limited by good design and taste. Too many small objects fail to identify, producing a busy, unplanned effect which is penalized. Each object used should have identity, a worth and purpose in the design.

Interest and variety should be provided by the balanced use of round forms, square forms, lone forms . . . of smooth textures, rough or velvety textures. If the textures are all too varying, however, the need for some quiet, plain surfaces may result in a deduction. Textures of the materials used must be compatible. Too sharp a contrast, as from a refined and glossy china vase to rough, dull cement may affect unity and harmony too drastically.

There should be an object of main or dominant interest, floral or otherwise, with other objects and spaces used to relate to it. If the values of color are too nearly the same . . . for example all full chroma, more contrasts should have been provided through darker values and tints. If the design lacks visual unity because of too great a distance between objects lacking adhesive use of space, movement and dynamic balance penalty is taken. The Judge should review the chapter on Abstract for pointers on judging space and depth.

SUGGESTED SCALE FOR STILL LIFE

Relationships	30	Communication	25
. spatial		. of theme (expressive)	
. shapes, textures, colors		. of designer's interest and	
Design	25	delight in form, texture,	
Distinction	20	*color and beauty.*	

Tables

SUGGESTED CLASSES

1. "DINNER AT 8:00"

    Functional. Formal. Settings for Six. Staged in room center. Fresh materials predominating. Table 3x6'. Three entries.

2. "AFTER THE OPERA"

    Functional. Semi-Formal. Settings for Four. Staged in room center. Fresh materials predominating. Table 3x6'. Three entries.

3. "MEAL ON THE MOON"

    Exhibition: logical and illogical placements.

    In niche 36x40". One setting, place mat or cloth, decorative unit. Accessories permitted. Three entries.

4. "COLOR IN CONTRAST"

    Exhibition. Table 3x6'. Fresh materials predominating. Contrasting harmonies. Three entries.

5. *"ONLY ME"*

    Tray, Functional, All fresh plant materials, 3 entries.

TABLES

Flower Show vocabulary includes two types of tables, the Functional logical-use setting upon which food is served, and the Exhibition display where the service of food is given no consideration. These qualities are considered under interpretation and the Schedule should list the type of table expected.

Formerly the hostess concerned herself mostly with what was considered correct; now in many modern settings, there is less formality and convenience and striking decorativeness are major considerations. This relaxation is reflected in the judgment. Taste and imagination play a greater part than expensive appointments. Simplicity and restraint are combined with varying degrees of elegance or formality. Consistency in choice of texture and degree of formality is essential to a blue-ribbon winner. Too many rules in informal classes restrict creativity, the Judge should be guided by fitness, balance and good taste in the combinations.

The Judge should appraise the table first as a complete unit for the overall perfection of design, overall relationships, overall impression of harmony and coordinated spirit according to theme, and then evaluate in detail.

The Judge should assume the position required by the occasion of a functional table (standing for buffet, seated on the floor if necessary) in order to determine if the decorative unit obstructs the view of dining partners, if candle-light shines directly into eyes, and if the close-up, almost eye-level appearance of the decorative unit is as perfect as possible.

For various and sound reasons the American Flag, silverware, candies and food, other than uncut fruit and vegetables are not used on Flower Show Tables.

SUGGESTED SCALE OF POINTS

Functional Table

Overall Design	25
. including all appointments and decorative unit. Harmonious. Attractive	
Overall Compatibility	20
. china . linen . flora . class . color . spirit . textures . accessories	

Perfection of Decorative

Unit	15
. design . color harmony . character, spirit	
Interpretation	20
. according to schedule . functionalism	
Distinction	10
Impeccability & Condition	10

Exhibition Table

Decorative Unit Design	25	*Creative Expression*	20
. *color* . *character* . *texture*		Aesthetic Relationships	20
Design Overall	25	Distinction, Condition	10

Interpretation

The Schedule wording is the foundation for interpretation both of theme and the basic requirements of the class. The Schedule should be definite as to:

1. Theme
2. Style
   . hour (breakfast, noon, dinner)
   . degree of formality
   . *Exhibitional, Full-set Function or Tray*
   . seated or buffet
3. Table dimensions and number of settings
4. Staging (against a wall, room center, niche for exhibition, other)
5. If fresh or dried material is to predominate in the arrangement.

The Judge owes it to the exhibitors and public to understand and take into consideration each technical word in the scheduled class.

Functional Table

The logical function of a meal is to make food available and anything so used is considered a functional item. The two practical requirements which underlie any table setting no matter what the degree of formality, are convenience and a sense of order. The decorative pattern is superimposed upon this pattern of utility.

The Functional table is fully set with the exception of silver and will include dishes, glassware, linens and a decorative unit with or without accessories. Cup, saucer, glass and napkin do not constitute a setting.

Additional functional items might include coffee or tea servers, casseroles, salt-and-pepper servers, serving spoons, ladles, soup tureen, platters, bowls, trivit, chafing dish, wine bucket. All such practical appointments should be properly placed according to overall balance and convenience in use. On a buffet or table set for a specific course, such as main, dessert, tea, the functional items must indicate the course. Enough service items should be used to suggest the food and course being served, but not so many as to interfere with overall design or produce a cluttered look. It is permissible for the exhibitor to state the course represented on a small card.

Napkins are required on a functional table, unless a dessert course is shown when napkins might be in use. A table to show any other course, lacking napkins, should not be awarded a blue ribbon in a functional logical-use class. The functionalism is not influenced by having the fold facing toward or away from the plate and either is acceptable. Any position or fold is acceptable on an informal table as long as it is easy for a diner to unfold and use. On formal tables, the napkin may be placed in the exact center of the service plate. Cups and saucers ordinarily do not appear in first courses, but can for the dessert course. The handles should be placed at the same angle for functional comfort and visual unity.

Trays, buffet and full-set tables all qualify as functional. Formerly napkins on plates were reserved only for most formal settings. However, rules have relaxed to allow such placement even on trays. If the tray title calls for coffee or tea service, tray as well as design must be small or large enough not to cause deduction for balance, scale and proportion. While not inappropriate, a salad plate on a dinner plate on a tray may cause deduction under the principles. Figurines on trays may add whimsical cheer to a bedside or child's tray, but anything used should be compatible with other components. Sprightly colors and fresh materials should be specified. Trays are considered separate from Small Designs (p. 460).

Exhibition Table

The Exhibition Table show exhibit is non-utilitarian, and not related to function. No consideration is given to practical food service. This type is judged as a display planned primarily for decorative effect to show color, texture, shape relationships and new ideas. The appointments need not be functional or realistic, nor placed for logical use, nor in logical serving positions, but impression of dining must be apparent. For instance, napkins might be hung on an upright metal towel server or plates placed on edge or tiers. Objects may be elevated at one or several levels, or hung or placed on the backdrop. The cloth might be used as background with plate mounted, goblet lying on side, balanced by design and other components all placed to form an uncluttered, balanced picture. If the Schedule states Designer's Choice of components, the Exhibitional might include 3 plates, 2 napkins or 3 mats, or one, (i.e. napkin) might be deleted. Schedule governs inclusions or omissions. The balance of interest should be spread and spaced so the composition does not appear either bottom or top-heavy within the space defined by background. The entire composition, not just the decorative unit, must be in proportion and scale to space allowed. May be staged against panels, in niches or triptychs, on small tables, large divided tables or other ways devised by Staging Committees.

The broad interpretation of accessory would be used; that is anything (whether functional or not) which adds to the overall aesthetic effect or theme. Exhibition tables display unique combinations of components. Expect them to be dramatically unusual and usably impractical. However, aesthetic expertise must be apparent. The principles of design govern selections and placement, and are carefully assessed by Judges. Such exhibits are popular classes because they give viewers many new inspirational ideas in limited space with less exhibitor effort.

1. FUNCTIONAL TABLE: 1 setting, linens, decorative unit, functional items placed as for logical use and service.
2. EXHIBITION: 1 setting, linens, decorative unit with any other items of any combination, number or position placed as needed to complete the design.

If the Schedule fails to specify by title or description which type, the exhibit is planned, staged and judged as an aesthetic unit entirely on its design competence. Both types are judged for overall smartness, distinction and creativity, and although the Exhibitional parts may be disparate and illogically placed—the compatibility of form, color and texture should create a unified picture, and promote ideas for combinations suited to full-scale functional tables in viewer homes. Schedule may specify exhibition class for buffet settings.

Degree of Formality

The degree of formality is established by the occasion, the appointments and the placements. Symmetry is synonymous with formality; though an informal table using casual appointments **may be** symmetrical, a formal table **must be!** In a Home Show, the table should be no more formal than the room itself. An informal table may be set at any time of the day or evening. It may use fine quality appointments but the freedom in color selection, decorative unit and seating placement and more casual, relaxed effect make it "informal". Buffet, and outdoor tables are informal no matter what the quality of appointments, placement or color selection. Both types Segments may be scheduled to any degree formality.

Because of the spread of expression possible with regard to refinement and freedom, it is sometimes difficult to draw a line between an informal table using fine appointments and symmetrical balance and a semi-formal table. However, the sophisticated smartness associated with an informal table is often aided by asymmetrical balance which is more interesting, dynamic and lends itself to the unusual placements characteristic of the informal. Refer to the characteristics and requirements of Formal, Semi-formal and Informal at the chapter's end.

Theme Interpretation

The color, period, size and style of the room and shape of the table and occasion or title must be considered under interpretation. The Judge should ask himself if the psychological properties of color have been wisely used for theme conformity and interpretation. For example, a sophisticated theme would not be expressed as well with pastel pink as with dramatic black and white. A low-key scheme dominated by grayed lavender would not appropriately express a cheery theme as would full chroma warm colors. A table for a dramatic personality would use bold forms, contrasting chroma; one for a person well known for charm would make use of soft texture, curved accents and closely related analagous or monochromatic color harmonies.

The psychological properties of line should also have been used to advantage with conformity to theme. Bold lines express modern, nose-gay-like, mounded designs recall the past, zig-zags are exciting, horizontal lines restful, etc.

A table to depict an era should carry through on the theme at least in the obvious details. A "Buffet Table In The Tropics" would not be thematically correct with a damask cloth or a delicately sentimental Victorian-type design. A Victorian Period table would suffer under interpretation if a Modern line design were used. Period tables showing influence of a particular era will be easier to judge after a review of the chapter on Period designs. If a special occasion table is interpreted, it should reflect the spirit of the occasion.

A table depicting a specific personage such as Abraham Lincoln or Madame Pompadour imposes a greater obligation on both exhibitor and Judge in the matter of advance research regarding the tastes and times of the individual.

Coffee table designs should be free-standing (unless otherwise specified in the Schedule) and be presentable from above. The Schedule should specify the coffee table size, as this varies greatly. Generally, the design should be low and fairly compact. Breakfast table decorative units should be small, bright, buoyantly cheerful in effect. No candles would be used. The design may be of mixed or one-kind of flower. The general effect should be more casual, less studied and elaborate than designs for later in the day. Formality increases with the lateness of the dining hour. Bedside and tray designs should be low and not easily over-turned.

OVERALL DESIGN
Proportion

The proportion of unoccupied space to occupied area should be pleasing and should result in an uncluttered look, but not appear bare or lacking in essentials.

A decorative unit, including candles and/or accessories which crowds, detracts from or destroys the unity and harmony of the overall design is discounted. The area occupied by the midtable arrangement on a symmetrically balanced table should not exceed one-third of the length or width of the table. There should be several inches, at least, between it and the settings along either side.

Forward facing or end-of-the-table designs for informal sit-down or buffet tables may be as large as good proportion and space permits. Tea table designs may be elaborate and high, but should not occupy more than one-third of the table area. Bedside and coffee table designs should occupy no more than one-fourth the table surface, leaving room for functional items. T.V. and bed tray designs should not exceed miniature proportions (five inches overall).

The tablecloth which lacks enough "fall" is poorly proportioned and gives a skimpy look which is penalized. The drop should be from 15 to 18" for ideal proportions at a seated table and buffet, tea, wedding and Victorian Period tables may extend to the floor. A table placed on a higher level should probably have a longer cloth overhang to appear to best advantage. The shape of the table might also affect this detail, Judges must take varying points into consideration. There are no rules. The number of items on the table, and the number of place settings should be in proportion to the table area. The table with too many appointments or too many place settings for its size will be penalized.

The area covered by place mats should not be excessive nor appear skimpy. If the mats are so close together they are touching, points are removed. A regular five-branch candelabra is out of proportion on a six-foot table.

Balance

The balance may be symmetrical or asymmetrical, according to the degree of formality, and as long as a pleasing impression of stability results. It becomes easier to assess the balance if one mentally divides the table into thirds; each section should balance the others in interest and use of space, though differing appointments occupy each.

Formal and Semi-formal tables are traditionally symmetrical overall. The Informal table may be either, however, asymmetrical balance is more dynamic and permits more flexibility and freedom of placement. Even though the seating and the decorative unit placement may be unorthodox, it must be balanced and practical. There is no set manner for buffet placement. Orderliness, convenience and design are paramount.

The plates and napkins should be about an inch from the table edge. Placing too far from the edge or even with the edge contributes to an unpleasant sense of imbalance. Room should be left between the plate and napkin for silver even though this is not included on show tables.

Plates or mats should be spaced evenly, the same distance apart; approximately 24" from the center of one mat to the center of the next is practical to give guests room and to balance the table. They should be the same distance from the table edge. Large doilies may drop over the edge a short way. When table mats are used, the napkin is usually placed beside the mat, but the position may vary according to degree of formality and wish.

Small accessories, such as ash trays or place cards or bread and butter plates may be placed above the forks to balance the glass or glasses on the right, but the total effect should remain uncluttered. These items should be grouped or distributed to gain equal attention.

A visually heavy unit of logical-use items on one side of the table should balance an equally heavy unit on the opposite. A single large appointment should be balanced by another of equal visual weight or by a group of small items. Each item should be needed in the overall balance, and its mental removal should create imbalance.

The larger areas of light color (consider the cloth) should be balanced by smaller areas of more intense color.

Some authorities state that in actual practice one candle per diner is required, if no supplemental light is supplied; however balance and proportion control the number of candles on a show table. The Judge should not hold the exhibitor to six or state that two are too few, since information regarding supplemental light is usually incomplete. More than two **may** conceivably create an imbalance in a given design, making penalty necessary.

Scale

The size of the plates in relation to the size of the mats; size of the glasses to size of plates; size of napkins in relation to plates, mats and table size in general are all considerations under scale. The relative size of the flowers to each other, to the container, to the candelabra, accessories and functional items are considered as well. Any item which appears too large or too small in comparison to the rest and to the table should be penalized.

Round mats or doilies should be approximately 15" in diameter, others are usually 12-17". They should be large enough to easily accomodate the setting of china and stemware. The napkin may be placed beside the mat.

Napkins:
> of the 17" size are well scaled to doilies (15")
> of the 20" size are well scaled to mats (12-17")
> of the 17-22" size for dinner plates (10-11")
> of 12-17" size for luncheon plates
> of 11-12" size for tea tables.

A 9-10" plate is properly scaled for a luncheon table though a dinner plate (10-11") is acceptable. A single salad plate is too small and would be penalized.

Capsule classes staged on small tables, in allocated table spaces or in niches should be scaled to the space allowed.

Rhythm

Repetition, gradation and line direction are traditional ways of achieving rhythm in a design and apply as well to table settings.

Transition and movement are strengthened by variations in heights, color relationships and by grouping small items for visual continuity. The eye should be carried over the table from setting to setting, object to object the same as in judging the rhythm of an arrangement.

The dominant color should not be spotted over the table in equally eye-holding areas, or should not hold the eye in one spot, but should be repeated in varying gradations of value overall. This aids the eye in moving easily over the table in rhythmic sequence and progression.

Rhythm can be achieved through repeated use of the same or similar texture, line or form as well as color; or by the measured placement of china, crystal and linen within the designated space (mat, etc.). Rhythmic flow interrupted by spotty placement of small items or color is penalized.

Contrast

Varying heights and lows add rhythm, contrast and transition to a table. A monotonously horizontal "profile", unbroken by different heights of candles, design, stemware and other appointments should be penalized. These vertical heights must be balanced and not all grouped at one end.

Variation in color value and in hue or small amounts of contrasting and strong accent can be used to give the setting personality and character through contrast.

Too much sameness, such as all spike forms in the design, or accessories limited to silver, or color limited to light tints can cause monotony where a bit of contrast would add lively interest and distinction. Contrasts in texture add spark and variety to color, but harmony must prevail. Something dark, something light, something dull, something bright is a helpful little jingle which points up the contrasts involved. Contrasts must be controlled or they will destroy the dominant quality and unity by equalizing interests.

Dominance

Because the repetitious use of the table settings make them dominant, their color, texture and spirit are the keynote establishing the color harmony and degree of formality. Dominance is achieved by the repetition of the keynote color, texture and material.

The table should be unified by one dominating texture and color, but the dominant one must be carefully distributed over the table to avoid a spotty effect.

If the dominant emphasis has been destroyed by too many colors, too large an assortment of materials and textures, too many varied shapes and sizes resulting in a fussy, over-busy appearance, deduction must be made. Salt and pepper servers are optional as are ash trays, place cards and nut dishes. If used, the total effect maintained should not be cluttered or crowded.

If logical grouping of units for practicality and convenience has been ignored and a spotty effect results, penalty is taken. Glasses and pitcher make a logical-use unit for a buffet as does a coffee carafe and cups, a tureen and ladle. One or two such settings should dominate the table.

OVERALL RELATIONSHIPS

Included here are the textural character, color relationships and degree of quality and spirit of all appointments and the decorative unit.

Texture

Texture establishes the degree of formality; the more formal, the finer and smoother the textures of all items including the flowers, should be.

Because of its impact, texture has been called the most important element in table settings and many deductible errors occur in regard to textural relationships. Texture is important in the unification of the whole, including cloth, napkins, flowers, accessories, appointments, place settings and glassware.

While much freedom is allowed in informal tables, penalty must be assessed against the use of china and porcelain with pottery and earthenware, terra cotta figurines with delicate china, a delicate silver epergne on a boldly striped cloth or eggshell-thin china and etched crystal teamed with heavy pottery serving dishes and reed mats all on the same table are extreme examples of unrelated textures.

Good taste and a sense of rightness should be considered in the overall choices. All items must be attractive and acceptable, never garish or vulgar. Blending appointments of this century and that, of this country and that is acceptable for informal tables if their textural spirit is harmonious.

The combination of appointments, as well as those of compound decorative units occupying opposite ends of the table, should be unified through a common material, similar color, same or similar foliage and a pleasing textural relationship.

Textures, colors, quality and spirit of all items need not be identical but should be logical both visually and functionally. Relationships are controlled, restrained on formal and semi-formal tables while those on informal may be striking in design, dramatic in color and unusual in harmony.

Restrictions curb creativity of informal table classes and there always seem to be tasteful exceptions to every rule. For instance, rectangular mats and an oblong container may be just the contrast needed on a certain round table. To say candles are unsuitable outdoors, limits the use of highly decorated modern candles, often used as accessories, and also many highly decorative modern lighting innovations involving candles. There should be no restrictions as to when and where such accessory candles can be used.

Color

Color tie-ins create harmony and unity of relationships. Color adds character; through it can be expressed elegance, gayiety, smartness. Too careful matching can hobble a harmony and leads to monotony where a bit of contrast livens the dominance. Contrast of a pink and white setting with a red tumbler gives a lift where a clear glass would result in triteness. The colors chosen for evening tables should be carefully selected as artificial light is unkind to some hues such as blues and violets which lose value. White and colors on the warm side hold up well under evening conditions.

It is not advisable that the decorative unit repeat all the colors in the china or on the table, this results in destruction of unity and dominance and brings a deduction of points.

When the basic color for the decorative unit is the hue which is featured least in the china, and when multi-colored china is placed on a single color cloth, the color plan is usually satisfying.

The **table covering** should have been selected to dramatize the. china; in formal and semi-formal it remains a subtle background. Both color and texture must be harmonious with the rest of the appointments. While experimentation for interesting effects are encouraged in informal settings, good taste and appropriateness should not be offended.

Napkins may be cloth or paper in keeping with degree of formality. Paper napkins are acceptable with paper mats. Larger lapkins or bibs ingeniously displayed in keeping with the overall design may add interest to informal tables of appropriate theme such as "Clam Bake By the Sea". Interesting napkin holders which echo the theme add a creative touch to informal settings. There are no restrictions on the method of napkin folding, but the fold must be in keeping with the general spirit being interpreted, and must not be too large or fussily displayed. They may be simply folded to show a monogram or design; in squares with two sides turned in; rectangles or triangles, etc.

More fanciful folds are acceptable on informal tables, if convenient, orderly in scale and appropriate to the theme.

A cloth or mat is not mandatory on a table or tray if the surface is wipeable. The Judge must be sure before he criticizes as a seemingly inappropriate surface may be guarded with a soil-retarding finish.

While a table cloth drop is usually 12-18" for sit-down convenience, buffet and special-occasion tables may have floor length. Full length cloths on outdoor tables make them more dominant in the setting and are acceptable if well related.

Wine glasses are optional on formal, semi-formal and informal tables and are usually placed along the top part of an imaginary right-hand crescent or diagonal line from the water glass to the table edge. Style, while often dictated by the type of wine being served should be appropriately related to other appointments in color, fineness of quality and spirit.

Small appointments, such as salt and pepper servers, ashtrays, etc., need not be identical on informal tables if they remain related to the basic plan. Sensitivity to form as well as color is a clue to success, related shapes of plant materials to functional items creates distinctive unity.

Glassware should tie in color-wise with at least one other appointment, and its texture, style and spirit should be in keeping with the other appointments. The etched patterns need not match, but should be similar in detail.

The shape of the container and the plates may be related to the table shape, but this is not mandatory by any means.

The decorative unit should have a definite affinity to either china, linen or glassware in color, texture and spirit.

Perfection of the Decorative Unit

The decorative unit may consist of merely the floral design, or it may include the design, container, base and accessories, including candles or candelabra. In fact, on a functional table, anything not needed in the service of food is considered a part of the decorative unit.

The design and color harmony, including container and material should be expressive of the class theme, and appropriate in spirit and content. All the principles relative to good design must be observed or penalty is taken.

The decorative unit may be given weight, unity and balance through the repetition of color pick-up from the plates or other dominant appointments. Each side of the free-standing design may be different or similar. The design must have a pleasing silhouette and adequate depth. The container and plant material must be in good proportion and the scale relationships of all the items must be consistent. Balance is symmetrical or asymmetrical according to the degree of formality and placement, but the design and the decorative unit as a whole must be visually stabilized. Accessories and design or candles must not be crowded together.

The decorative unit on an informal table may be placed anywhere it will balance the overall design, but it must be of a height or placement so as not to interfere with conversation or service. A design which obstructs diner's view or candles placed so the light would shine directly into diner's eyes must be penalized. If the design is large or high, it should be rather open, in order to reduce mass. It should never be placed directly in front of a place setting. Candles which are the same height as the design are static and immobilize eye movement, a small penalty should be taken.

Decorative units for outdoor porches, terraces and poolside should be substantially constructed so they will not topple in a sudden breeze.

Distinction

Distinction is a combination of beauty, technique and absolute fitness which results in superiority above the commonplace and which has a certain something almost indefinable. Distinction is the child of imagination and craftsmanship. An informal table upon which is used unexpected combinations of colors, unique primitive or rare period pieces with modern in a modern setting or other unconventional combinations or conventional items in unconventional ways gains in distinction.

In table settings, simplicity and restraint are necessary to distinction. The total effect should be uncluttered, a balance of quiet empty areas and occupied space. Only enough materials should have been used to set the mood or complete the picture. Any lack of technique, such as mechanics showing to the point of detracting from the overall design is reason for sacrifice of points under distinction.

Imaginative selection and combination of appointments which stimulates and interests the viewer contributes to distinction. A round design in a round bowl in the center of a round table is the conventional, conservative, "safe" way, but such a setting usually lacks interest unless exciting textures and unusual harmonies relieve the mediocrity and give distinction.

A flippant or unique napkin fold or holder is entirely correct on an informal table, and may earn a point under distinction. Oddly shaped place mats which complement the table shape or the overall placements add distinction. For instance using triangle mats rounded on one side to fit the curve of the rounded table they are used upon. A container contrived from a hat displayer, the unusual textural character of thistle blooms with roses — such things as these contribute to distinction.

Distinctive settings show individuality, personality, imagination and expertise. The Judge must appreciate the observant eye and the adventurous imagination which senses the possibilities of combinations often overlooked by the conservative arranger.

If the scale of points in a Schedule does not list the quality of impeccability or condition, faults such as wrinkles, wilting, etc., are deducted under distinction.

Impeccability and Condition

Anything placed on a table is subject to close scrutiny and should be scrupulously clean, in good repair and arranged with care. Rusty holders, chipped appointments, soiled, over-mature or wilted plant materials are subject to penalty. The use of items which have offensive odors or connotations should be penalized. For instance, frogs, skunk cabbage, immodestly nude figures and others might offend good taste and fastidiousness, therefore are discouraged.

The **table cover** and napkins must be spotlessly clean, crisp and unwrinkled. A single centerfold, lengthwise in the table cloth gives the most impeccable impression. A limp appearance, wrinkles and numerous sharp creases detract from a sense of neatness and must be deducted. The overhang must be perfectly even all around.

The **china and crystal** must be spotless and in good repair, the general effect overall should be one of precision and meticulous care in every detail.

Candles. The problem of whether wicks should be charred or not is a perennial one due to past restrictions, and has received attention all out of proportion to its importance. The rule reputedly came about to "prove" that the candles were functional — there are many other ways of showing functionalism without including the candles which are rightly a part of the decorative unit which is defined as "including arrangement, plus accessories, plus candles". It contains that which is not functional to the service of the meal. Highly decorated candles not meant to be burned should be considered as accessories chosen for what their beauty contributes to the decorative unit and overall design. Functional, ordinary candles should be considered as to what effect their shape, color and holder/s contribute to rhythm, contrast, balance of the decorative unit and the table design overall. Their function in the giving of light is evident whether or not the wick has been burned.

If it is suspected that the candle has been used for a previous occasion, then of course penalty is taken. This could be determined by dripped wax, top depression, less than regular height and probably a scratched, untidy appearance. Wicks can be darkened with a bit of paint, chalk or soot if the exhibitor dislikes the "unfinished" look. It is suggested that a charred or uncharred wick should not carry weight either for or against the design, and the matter should not be given points one way or the other unless it is suspected that the candle actually was re-used, a circumstance hard to imagine.

SUMMARY   (See Scales for number of points)

INTERPRETATION

Functional Table

*functional items indicate food served *placed for convenience and design *napkins present (unless specific dessert course) *napkins easily unfolded for use

-too few items to determine food served *lacking napkins -inconvenient or haphazard placement of functional items -design for small table (coffee, TV, bedside) leaves no room for functional items

Exhibition Table

*all schedule requirements met regarding items to be included

-lacking some schedule-specified items

Degrees of Formality

*characteristics and requirements met *smooth, fine textures and symmetry for formal and semi-formal *color freedom and asymmetrical placements make for informality *all appointments have same degree of formality

-lacks requirements for degree of formality scheduled -too coarse texture for formal, semi-formal -too restrainted and "set" for informal -design too bold for formal table

Theme Interpretation

*theme clearly apparent *color wisely chosen to express interpretation *lines chosen to strengthen interpretation *decorative unit in keeping with theme *textures related to theme
-theme indistinctly expressed -design does not interpret theme -colors inappropriately chosen -design too elaborate for theme -effect too severe and restrained for gaiety of theme -cutwork cloth, cut glass and silver pepper and salts too fine for theme being interpreted

OVERALL DESIGN

Proportion

*occupied and empty space well proportioned and pleasing *decorative unit not exceeding ⅓ table length, width *tablecloth overhang in proportion to table size and height (15-18")

-bare -cluttered -crowded -cloth skimpy -cloth overhang awkward length -place mats occupying too much space -overlapping -overpowering decorative unit -oversize candelabra

Balance

*symmetrical in formal and semi-formal, either for informal *each side or section of the table balances the other *place settings balanced all around *napkins, settings, mats same distance from edge (about 1") 24" from center of one mat to center of next *a single large appointment balancing another or a group of small ones

-one side or end is out of balance -scattered objects if unequal visual weight upset balance -placement of decorative unit unbalances overall design -confusing details

Scale

*no item appears too large or too small in relation to the others *exhibition entry well scaled to space allocated

-overlarge or too small napkins, mats, accessories, glasses, plates, decorative unit, functional items

Rhythm

*eye moves easily over setting *visual continuity through repetition, gradation, line direction, related forms

-color spotted over the table with no real plan -eye-holding objects interrupt rhythm -lacks transitions

Contrast

*tall and round forms varying *pleasing difference in height levels *accents of form, texture and color knowingly used

-monotonously horizontal in profile -lacks color variation and "snap" -unity destroyed by too much contrast -too many patterns -over-busy

Dominance

*one texture, one color emphasized *one or two logical-use items dominate Functional table
-dominance destroyed by too many colors, too many textures, too many varied shapes, sizes -fussy -spotty placements

Overall Relationships

*textures compatible *textures unify whole *good taste exhibited in choices *textures of flowers harmonious with table as a whole and theme *color well used to create harmony and unity *same "spirit" in all appointments *forms of different items harmonious *small appointments related to basic **plan**

-too coarse and too fine textures used together -colors too carefully matched overall -decorative unit not related to general theme -table covering too garish or coarsely textured for other appointments -glassware too refined for other appointments

Perfection of Decorative Unit

*expressive of theme *all principles of design observed *related in color to some other table appointment *pleasing silhouette *one color, form, texture dominant *color combination pleasing *adequate depth *free-standing (if required) *well balanced *candle flame above eye-level *design well placed for conversation and convenience *height and silhouette allow cross-conversation

-more height needed -crowded -off balance -no contrast -bottom heavy -rhythm interrupted by careless placements -flowers out of scale -container too large for design -accessories inappropriate -not free standing (if required) -no color or textural tie-in with other appointments -contrary to spirit and theme -candles same height as design -candle light would shine in diner's eyes -design cuts off a diner's view -accessory unrelated to design in size, shape, placement, feeling

Distinction

*combined superiority and technique *absolute fitness *unique *individual *unexpected color harmony *unconventional "pairing" of parts *unexpected color harmony *has drama *simplicity and restraint observed *stimulating *unusual manner of use in container, functional items, etc. *unusual handling of plant material (clipping, trimming, etc.)

-commonplace -mediocre -lacks impact -conservative -plain -haphazard -lacks skillful appearance -ordinary -trite -lacks finesse -over stated -over matched -pretty but uninspired

Impeccability and Condition

*impeccable *clean *cloth smooth *few creases *pressed *overhang even *one center fold lengthwise is ideal *crisp *fresh *glistening, sparkling *plant material well groomed, turgid

-soiled plant material -overmature material -wilted -insect damaged -wrinkled linens -uneven overhang -limp linen -crumpled -numerous sharp creases -candles, soiled, scratched -finger marks -spots on linen -crooked candles

FORMAL TABLES CHARACTERIZED BY

. limited and subdued color harmony
. pastels
. free standing design

. symmetrical, even-number place settings (number according to schedule)
. geometrical placements
. finest quality appointments
. candle-lit elegance
. lavish use of silver, crystal, shiny textures

Spirit: **Quiet, Dignified, Elegant, Impeccable. Keynote is symmetry.**

Settings
. fine quality china, porcelain
. precise placement, evenly around table, same distance from edge and each other
. bread and butter plates omitted

Glassware
. crystal, fine quality glass
. clear or faintly tinged
. high stem
. wine glasses optional

Table Covering
. linen, damask, lace, organdy
. place mats, doilies acceptable if of fine quality (minimum 24" from center of one mat to center of next)
. single center crease, lengthwise of cloth
. ecru, white, faintly tinged
. overhang (15-18") Exception: Victorian, Wedding

Napkins
. same fabric as cloth. If cloth is lace or organdy, napkins of linen
. same color as cloth
. folded simply, neatly or softly rolled, monogram may be folded to show
. may be to the left of the plate
. fold may face plate (traditional) or away
. if service plate is free of secondary dish for juice, cocktail, soup, the napkin may appear in the exact center of the service plate

Decorative Unit
. fine textured flowers, fresh, crisp. Perfect fruits
. delicate refined design
. symmetrical, conventional
. free standing
. 12-18" tall depending on lightness or mass
. not exceeding one-third table length

Container
. silver, crystal, porcelain
. conventional design

SEMI-FORMAL CHARACTERIZED BY
. only slightly less elegant than formal
. slight deviation from formal
. even number of settings (set by schedule) symmetrically placed
. mid-table decorative unit may be symmetrical or asymmetrically (balanced by accessory or base placement)
. overall design may be symmetrical or asymmetrical (one large object balancing several small ones)
. candle-lit splendor
. beautifully appointed, fine quality
. more leeway in color use, but controlled and dignified

Spirit: Elegant, In good taste, Impeccable, Sumptuous, Lavish.

Settings
. fine quality
. service plates optional
. bread and butter plates, ashtrays, wine glasses, cigarette and matches optional
. dinner plates (10-11")
. 20-24" between settings
. placements exactly same distance from table edge and each other

Glassware
. fine quality glass, crystal
. high stem
. clear or tinted
. patterns need not match exactly

Table Covering
. fine quality linen, damask, lace, other
. runners, mats or full cloth acceptable
. white, ivory, tinted

Napkins
. match or blend with cloth or mats, **Never Contrast**
. simple, neat folds
. fold facing plate (traditional) or away

Decorative Unit
. free standing, midtable
. not over one-third the table length (20-24" for 6' table)
. more leeway in colors, materials and originality than in formal

Container
. fine quality glass, porcelain, silver, fine metals, other
. shape determined by table and design

INFORMAL CHARACTERIZED BY
. variations in seating
. simplicity with flair
. antipathy for the trite and commonplace
. unrestrained color use (may be bold, subtle, conventional, or sentimental)
. unconventional combinations (period pieces in modern settings or combined with modern pieces)
. unbridled creativity
. appointments may match or be combined for utility and effect
. multiple decorative units
. varied asymmetrical or symmetrical decorative unit placements
. may be fine quality or sturdy and casual
. locations including, and other than, the dining room (buffet, terrace, breakfast)

Spirit: Creative, Casual, Stimulating, Gay, Smart, Stylish, Imaginative, Striking, Sophisticated, Intimate, Relaxed, Friendly, Hospitable.

Settings
. range from fine quality to pottery, metals, plastics, glass, earthen ware, others
. may combine unmatched pieces
. may combine styles; objects from other countries
. free forms

Glassware

. range from stemware to tumblers, low-footed goblets or high
. range from delicate to heavy
. range from clear to colored
. wine glasses are optional
. patterns and colors need not match

Table Covering

. range from cork to wood, glass, marble, bare, others
. may be fine quality fabrics or coarse textured
. full size or mats or runners in regular or unusual shapes
. may be any color: bold or subtle; plain white, solid color or patterned (stripe, plaid, others)

Napkins

. color may match, blend or contrast with cloth or mats
. texture may match, blend or contrast
. folds may be unique but must be neat
. unconventional placements and holders

Decorative Unit

. may be symmetrical or asymmetrical
. may be free-standing or other
. may be midtable, ends, side, above, other
. may be restrained, pastel, delicate or vivid, gay, exciting
. may be supplemented with accessories
. may be combined fruits, flowers, dried, other
. may combine objects from different areas of the world
. may be bold, or simple
. may be sentimental, traditional, contemporary or modern

Container

. may be fine quality glass, silver, other
. may be metal, natural (shell, driftwood, pottery, wood, other)
. may be casual, modern, contrived ,free-form or conventional

Terrariums, Bottle Gardens

SUGGESTED SCALE OF POINTS

Cultural Condition	35	Suitability, Compatibility 20

Cultural Condition 35
. established at least 3 months

Landscape Plan 30
. stressing placement, scale, unity, harmony

Suitability, Compatibility 20
. includes scale (foliage size, plant ht.)
. cultural needs

Foliage and/or floral 15
interest

CULTURAL CONDITION

A too-rich soil mixture, or too little light will produce lanky plants which are to be penalized.

Charcoal or crushed rock should have been used in the bottom of the container to facilitate drainage.

The plants must look established, having been growing for some time. Should be at least three months established.

The plants must appear healthy, free of insects or disease. Foliage, clean, thrifty, stem nodes short and typical of variety.

No dirt or mud should be clinging to the glass sides.

Composition of Landscape Plan

All the principles of design should have been observed. The scale of the plants should be right for each other.

The proportion of the plant material to container should be balanced . . . too much or too few and too many tiny plants may draw a penalty.

The foliage should have been thinned out. On the other hand, the exhibit should not be shown until the plants are of a size to make a commendable showing. The placements should be such that the plants show off to best advantage. The tallest plants placed at the back or sides. One small-leaved vine forming a tracery up the side of a slender bottle can be most effective. Keep it simple.

There should be some contrasts, either of texture, leaf size or coloring to add interest.

SUITABILITY, COMPATIBILITY

Terrariums are see-through containers chiefly or wholly closed, containing a grouping of suitable, thriving plants. Dish gardens are uncovered groupings of suitable, thriving plants. Appropriate, in scale accessories may be included. Both are staged in Horticulture Div., but judged for artistic "landscape" effect.

Plants selected should have similar cultural requirements and be able to withstand moist soil, high humidity and low light intensity. The size of the foliages, stems and height of the plant should be scaled to each other and to the container.

Suggested Scale for Dish Gardens, Novelty Scenes

These types are never considered or entered as a design in Artistic Div.

Interpretation of title	25
Arrangement of items used including plants	25
Suitable Relationship of Materials	20
Distinction & Creativity	20
Condition (all parts)	10

Vignettes

The dictionary defines VIGNETTE as a small design decorating a vacant space or an illustration having no definite edges. COMBINE is an art term meaning a grouping of objects according to a plan, implying more space, depth and scope than a Vignette.

In Flower Show parlance, these have come to mean a small section of a room, a corner, entrance, section of wall, often three-sided and complete with full-scale furniture, paintings, draperies, carpet, mantels, floral design according to the Schedule.

Not all these must be or are included in a single exhibit. Vignettes may be quite complete or they may be simply a section of wall or a screen with a chest or table, and the design somewhat in the manner of an enlarged niche (without the emphasis on furnishing, scale) or a Japanese tokonoma.

Detailing and accessories are often more completely furnished in a Combine, somewhat in the manner of a Fair booth. Draperies, chest or table, walls, carpet, chairs, paintings and other wall accessories, plus other items on the table or chest may be included, and such completeness is expected if the Schedule requests a Combine.

The piece of furniture upon which the design is placed dictates the height, width and depth of the design as well as the spirit or style. Hanging or mobile designs must be correctly scaled to the other items. Regardless of the appropriateness of its relationships a flora design which is too large or small will be penalized under design.

The degree of elegance or rustic appearance, formality or informality is established by the theme, occasion and the texture of the furnishings. The finer and smoother the textures, the greater the degree of formality and elegance. The bolder and more startling, the more sophisticated and modern will be the spirit or character.

Theming possibilities are limited only by imagination of the Schedule classes, and the creative and planning ability of the entrants. Judging is done on how well the spirit and character of the theme is expressed by the thoughtful use of an imaginative design and a few pieces of furniture. The type, color of the furniture, draperies, etc. must have been correlated to the spirit, style, color, period and character of the floral design. With but a few elements of a room, a background of draperies or wallpaper, a chest or table upon which the design is placed, the Judge should be able to visualize an entire room. Whether real antiques, copies or contrived, the objects in each Vignette or Combine should tell a convincing story of the home, period or theme depicted.

The arrangement of the elements (furniture, design, etc.) within the allotted space is considered as well as the arrangement of the elements (plant materials, container, base) in the flora design. Each object used is considered a component part of the whole. Any unrelated or misplaced form, color or texture is penalized.

The Schedule may present special problems regarding art objects, sculpture and painting. The flora design may have to be related to a painting (also included) in subject, color, historical period or other category. Such classes require special research for fair decisions.

In judging settings showing Japanese (Oriental influence) a close competition might be resolved by remembering that in Japan the lower (earth) line is placed to lead the eye into the garden. In **adaptations,** this line may stretch out welcomingly toward the door or lead the eye to a davenport, chair, window or fireplace or some other feature.

The Japanese never copied the content of a picture literally, preferring a more subtle interpretation by suggestion. A picture of a pond with cattails would be supplemented with water-loving plants **other** than the cattails; a picture of a bird on a bare cherry branch would be supplemented with a design of cherry branches in bloom.

No matter what style or period, good taste and a sense of rightness should be considered regarding all choices; all items must be acceptable and attractive, in a state of repair.

The chapter on Placement Shows will be of help in judging Vignette and Combine classes.

SUGGESTED SCALE OF POINTS FOR VIGNETTE

Design   30
. consider all elements and principles overall and
. in the flora design
Relationships   25
. color . texture
. spirit . other

Interpretation   25
. of Schedule (is it a Vignette? Combine?)
. of theme (does it communicate the spirit of the theme?)
Distinction   20

Miscellaneous Scales of Points

SCALE 1 — FAIR BOOTH, EDUCATIONAL EXHIBITS

Effectiveness, Educational Value .... 30 Points
. of design beauty and purpose, general interest to public
. educate quickly, briefly, dramatically, accurately; practical; finished product or practice shown, effectively, quickly tell story to moving public.
. perfection of details, simplicity of design, neat, no misspelled public signs
. signs uniform, neat, sizes and print not too small for booth
. color carries, is related, fits subject, adequate lighting
. prime quality and type of materials, everything in good repair, clean
. all items used well chosen for theme
. plant material fresh, prime, not wilted
(Judges stand back to assess total overall effectiveness)

Clarity of Idea and Theme Conformity .... 25 Points
. tie-in between signs, theme, and idea
. clear, concise presentation, easily grasped

Creativity .... 25 Points
. not common, is indivdiual?
. new approach?
. how much effort extended?
. something different?

Design .... 20 Points
. consider balance, proportion, scale, rhythm, contrasts and dominance

Some Fairs have categories which break classes into (1) Educational and (2) Decorative and the judging must be done accordingly. Educational booths must educate quickly. To do this they should:
   . have simplicity, a single dominant, clear theme and should not be
   . a collection of pamphlets which is insufficient or a
   . mere grouping of produce or articles which is uninteresting and ordinary.

It is usually better that one segment of a group's project be covered rather than trying to cover too much which usually confuses rather than instructs and thus draws penalty.

The Judges should note if the presentation is active or is it merely "passive". A passive exhibit is one where nothing is taught, i.e., a beautiful butterfly design made out of all different kinds of seeds does not become educational until it actively teaches by identifying the seeds. A collection of some type plant should be entered under just that . . . a collection. It becomes an educational exhibit only after the factor of "educational value" has been added.

The general public likes to be educated painlessly and the average person will not spend very much time at the display which merely features African Violets unless growing African Violets is already his hobby. His interest must be tittilated by some form of staging or signery . . . to the point where he will leave feeling he has learned something and is interested enough to learn more **on his own!** When that happens, the exhibit is an "active" one, one which teaches; such an exhibit tells succinctly how to do something or how a project is being done.

Any tricks to increase spatial illusion, such as transparency, advancing-receding colors, etc., should be appreciated by the Judges and all principles of design and conditioning of material considered. Protection (glass covering, other) should have been given valuable or poisonous materials.

Touches of whimsey catch the public's fancy and more points for the exhibit, such as the exhibit of mulches which included snow, represented by a big pile of nothing! It had melted on the way to the show. Intriguing titles capture interest and imagination.

The main idea is to sell the idea fast to a moving public and motion is the strongest attraction which can be added to any exhibit, next in line is good lighting . . . the use of spots, or revolving color changes which bring up the third powerful way to attract attention . . . **color!** An exhibit with these three cannot fail to draw the public and coupled with good signs and a dominant and interesting idea, ribbons can be justly awarded.

In judging commercial booths or civic group booths it is well to consider the three leading purposes of advertising which are:
1. tell the story of goods or services
2. stimulate a desire for goods and services
3. develop a feeling of good will through understanding goods or services offered.

Promotions such as visitor contests, samples of a product and demonstrations to dramatize may be inducements but should be in good taste.

Motion of water, spinning or moving parts in any booth is an attention-getter, but must be well-related to the theme or subject covered in that individual booth.

Decorative booths should carry through on one theme. For instance a garden scene to express serenity which has a "nervous", tinkling fountain loses points. "Lawn" must be made of even, straight strips, well mowed. Flora material used must be fresh, turgid. Artificial flowers and foliage are restricted as decorative items in Flower Shows and Floriculture departments. Artificial light (if any) must be meaningful to the design. Over-crowding is a common and serious fault. The center front should be open and/or low in most cases. The whole scene should look natural and inviting.

Proportion and scale are the most commonly violated design principles in booth making. In a garden scene, proportion would concern such items as:

. the amount of lawn to the amount of flower border
. the amount of red to the amount of green (or any other color)

Scale concerns the relative size — a too-big rock, a too-tall sunflower, a too-large sign or one that is too small with too-small print are items to be penalized.

Balance means the booth must be visually balanced on both sides and top and bottom, as well as in depth. A very common fault is too many items in the lower half of the booth and nothing but space above. (See Niche and Vignette judging).

There should be one dominant idea, more of one color, dominance of one item or project. This reduces clutter and makes for distinctive simplicity.

Rhythm means movement. Items should be placed to keep the eye moving from one interesting spot to another. Colors should be rhythmic and harmonious. There should be some contrast and variety of form, colors and textures to add interest.

The upper back, upper sidewalls, center floor and ceiling are often neglected or uncoordinated areas, penalty is taken for this fault.

SCALE 2 — YOUTH HORTICULTURE SCIENCE EXHIBIT

Creative Ability _____ 30 Points
. originality, ingenious uses of materials, purposefulness

Scientific Thought _____ 30 Points
. organization, accurate observation, understanding of the scientific facts

Thoroughness _____ 10 Points
. relating to the completeness of the story

Skill _____ 10 Points
. good workmanship in handling of material, preparation and mounting

Clarity _____ 10 Points
. appropriate labeling, descriptions, sequence of thought to guide visitors

Dramatic Value _____ 10 Points
. overall attractiveness of exhibit. May be on insects, grafting, plant breeding, effects of various kinds of lights, etc. etc.

SCALE 2A — JUDGING YOUTH HORTICULTURAL CLUB ACTIVITY

Give Club Membership

Well Planned Horticultural Program   30
. flower show participation
. flower show practice workshop
. field trip
. indoor gardening
. individual growing projects
. experiments in Horticulture
. others

Civic Activities   20
. outdoor plantings in community
. anti-litter, clean ups, garden therapy, other

Conservation Activities   30
. nature study
. birds
. Arbor Day observance

Other   20
. poster contest, etc.
. at least 6-9 meetings yearly
. year book included

SCALE 3 — YOUTH DEMONSTRATION

Presentation _____ 40 Points
. **arrangement** and use of equipment   10
. **organization** of subject matter   10
. **charts and models** clear, neat, easily read, used effectively   5
. **ability** to work easily and efficiently; skilled, done with ease   10
. **summary** statement brief, important points stressed, all steps clearly seen by the audience   5

Subject Matter _____ 30 Points
. **brief** introduction giving practical value of topic   5
. **interesting, accurate, up-to-date, complete,** practical information   12
. **accurate answers** given to any questions asked   10
. **sources** of information given   3

Demonstrator _____ 15 Points
. voice, clear, words well chosen, natural   5
. appearance neat and proper for the job   5
. poised, friendly manner, posture and action suitable for the job   5

Results _____ 15 Points
. audience interest held throughout   5
. was the product good or was the purpose of the demonstration accomplished? Finished product or practice shown?   5
. was it a "show-how" demonstration? Was the length of the presentation suitable to the subject?   5

SCALE 4 — FAIR QUEEN

Judge's Interview   45
. poise
  -speaking -walking -posture -youth fitness
. personality
  -individual -interesting -pleasant
. appearance
  -neat -harmonious clothing choices -suitable clothing choices

Scholastic Record and Community Activities   30
. grades
. activities at school
. in community
. conduct

Talent   25

SCALE 5 — BEAUTIFICATION PROJECT, (Anti-Litter)

Aesthetic and Practical
Value   35
. to community, city, county, State
. community cooperation secured

Method of Organization
and Progress   25
. History
. Age of project

Permanence of Project   20

Maintenance   20
. neatness
. regular supervision and care provided

SCALE 6 — LANDSCAPE SCALE A

Design of the Whole ————————————————————— 40 Points
. composition
. unity
. scale
. imagination
. ground forms
. color
. circulation
. orientation
. balance
. accents, incidental and focalization

Design of the Details ———————————————————— 30 Points

Construction, perfection of details
. paving . structures . water devices . accessories

Planting
Selection of plant materials
. maturity, size, shape, character
. physical environment as suited to plant
. according to maintenance, minimum care, pest control, winter protection, pruning
. for succession of beauty, seasonability

Placement of plant material, associations
. consider color, forms, textures
. native, semi-native, imported

Design Suitability ——————————————————— 20 Points
. to site   . to purpose, function   . to architecture

Maintenance ————————————————————————— 10 Points
. degree of present perfection
. ease of maintenance, design, selections, placements
. evidence of sustained maintenance (pruning, grass trimmed, etc.)
. practicality

JUDGING SMALL GARDEN DESIGN

We now have in America an International Style of Landscape Design, but the United States is too large and diverse to have a single national style. It has been pointed out that beauty and cost are not related, and that a recognition of beauty is not universal. We all too often merely accept the commonplace.

We must approach any design judgment on the basis of the fundamentals of landscape architecture which is the art of improving land for human use and enjoyment, with three major objectives . . . maximum use, maximum beauty, minimum maintenance.

Some of the many and complex factors and elements that are essential to good landscape design are:

Originality and Distinction — personality, character, never pretentious or with undue elaborateness. Originality should never deteriorate into eccentricity or queerness. Avoidance of what some call "shear horror" or clipped monstrosities. Duplication and sameness of placement, pruning effects, varieties is trite, mundane.

Suitability to Site. Functional Aspects. Maximum Usefulness. Gardens are to be lived in, as well as looked at. Walks and paved areas should seem to belong, be serviceable.

Proportion, Unity, Balance, the greatest of these is unity, the fitted-togetherness!

Incidental Accent and Focalization, closely related to unity and distinction. Accent often accomplished with proper plant selection as well as **Accessories.** The quality and suitability of accents are too often unharmonious with the style of garden. And some, like plastic storks, etc., belong in **no** style garden.

Planting Design. Plant selection and arrangement is next only to general design in importance. It is an invaluable and indispensible requirement in any garden, home grounds, industrial, civic, public property, large or small. Unfortunately, the knowledgeable use of appropriate plant materials is too often the neglected stepchild of the landscape family. Planting design involves far more than just picking up some interesting looking plants at the nursery or supermarket. Practical factors the Judge will consider are:

1. Maturity — the time element and the character and size

2. Physical Environment — sea, winds, shade, tree roots, winter cold, wear and tear, grass and ground covers, soil conditions, moisture

3. Seasonability — a succession of interest and beauty and color

4. Minimum care — pest control, need for winter protection, pruning

5. Plant association — native, semi-native, imported (exotic)

6. Color — research is being done on the impact and use of skillful color harmony. It has been proven that general drabness produces fatigue.

Charm and Appeal. Assess to the garden as a whole. What impression does it give? Does it fit in with the landscape character of the block, area and distant scene? Simplicity is always in good taste.

LANDSCAPE DESIGN B

Suitability of Plant Material, Seasonability _____ 25 Points

. use of trees, bushes, vines for fall color not depending only on flowers for color — 5

. chosen with an eye to house architecture. Fault: tall arborvitae or topiary work by cottage — 7

. chosen with an eye to land topography. Fault: simulated rock garden on flat surface or round flower beds in lawn area — 7

. chosen to give winter interest; interesting twig color, tree form, inclusion of evergreens, other — 6

Placement of Plants ————————————————— 25 Points

. planted in proper relation as to height. Fault: tall zinnias planted
in front of short marigolds 5
. correct distance from house foundation and other plants 4
. proper enclosure 6
A garden should be enclosed with actual fences or trees to stop
the eye from traveling too far. Exceptions are vistas, opened to draw
the eye to an especially scenic view.
. house framed with a few tall trees at back, side-back 4
. plants placed in pleasing sequence. Fault: skimpy borders along
fences, cluttering of an odd assortment of plants 7

Color Harmony ————————————————————— 20 Points

. adjacent color harmonies pleasing. Fault: fuchsia Peonies next
to red-orange Oriental Poppies 8
. colors repeated throughout for rhythm 8
. color of house repeated or related to flower colors creates unity 4

Condition of Plants ———————————————————— 15 Points

. freedom from disease	4	. pruned as needed	3
. freedom from insects	4	. look wellfed, thrifty	4

Maintenance and Cultivation ——————————————— 15 Points

. well weeded	5	weeded, watered, trim-	
. properly mulched	2	med	5
. lawn well mowed,		. ease of maintenance,	
		practicality	3

Special Interest Item ———————————————————5 Extra

SCALE 7 — CEMETERY AND CHURCHYARD

Overall Plan ———————————————————————— 35 Points

. benches, walks, drives conveniently arranged to serve purpose
. materials used in making walks, drives inconspicuous, practical
. family lots accessible and marked
. aesthetic and practical location of
    . flower beds or borders against shrubbery
    . trees and the shrubs
. screening, boundaries, hedges, fences
. lawn thrifty, well-clipped, proportioned to other areas

Maintenance and Upkeep ———————————————————— 30 Points

. neat
. use of native materials, rather than all exotics
. well pruned, and cared for

General Appearance ———————————————————— 35 Points

. unified
. color and textural harmony
. headstones level, straight
. service buildings screened, well kept

SCALE 8 — ROADSIDE DEVELOPMENT AND PARKS SCALE

Location	25	Equipment	25
. attractiveness	15	. tables and benches	10
. convenience to highway,		. water facilities	8
other	10	. garbage cans	7
Landscape Effect	25	Maintenance	25
. plantings composition	10	. neatness	10
. use of native plants	10	. responsible supervision	10
. harmony of combinations	5	. regular inspection	5

SCALE 9 — BIRD SANCTUARY

Year Round Feeder Program   50
. feeders
. fruit, berry plants
. protected from weather, enemies

Housing   25
. natural cover, trees, shrubs

. houses
. selections and building appropriate for desirable birds of the area

Other Features   25
. year round water supply
. bath
. fountain, other

SCALE 10 — HOME VEGETABLE GARDEN

Condition of Plants   30
. consider size for variety
. freedom from insects, disease
. looking well fed and thrifty

Cultivation   30
. well watered
. well weeded
. mulch if used, appropriate, effective

Interest   20
. different varieties or species than usually found in area
. latest and newest varieties
. unique training
. other

Number of Different Kinds   10

Row Width and Plant Placement   10
. according to plant habits
. ease of cultivation
. vining plants separated by upright types

MISCELLANEOUS FLOWER SHOW CLASS SCALES

SCALE 11 — DECORATIVE CUT FOLIAGE

(Broadleaf, Evergreen, etc.)

Characteristic Development   30
. leaf form, placement

Stem   10

Stage Worthiness   50
. color 15 . texture 10
. condition 15 . substance 10

Size   5   Correct Name   5

SCALE 12 — NEEDLELEAF EVERGREENS WITH CONES

Cones   35
. number, general position, beauty

Characteristic Development ·   20
. needles, branch, cones

Choiceness, Novelty, Rarity   15

Stage Worthiness   20
. color . condition

Correct Nomenclature   10

SCALE 13 — BRANCH SPECIMEN, (Fruited, Flowering)

Fruit Quality	30	Characteristic Development 20
. color . condition		
. size . spacing		Choiceness, Rarity, Novelty 15
Stage Worthiness	25	
. general condition,		Labeled Correctly 10
. including foliage		

SCALE 14 — BRANCH SPECIMEN
(Autumn Foliage may be combined with Fruits)

Color of Foliage	30	Color other than Foliage 15
. clarity, trueness to type		. fruit, stem, etc.
Stage Worthiness	20	Characteristic Development 15
. general condition		
. substance, texture		ment
Labeled Correctly	10	Choiceness, Novelty 10

SCALE 15-A — HIBISCUS
(Hibiscus Society)

Size (according to variety)	35
Form, Shape (acc. to variety)	25
Color Trueness	20
Condition of Bloom/s	20
. no spray blemish	
. no insect blemish	
. no weather damage	
. no handling bruises	

SCALE 15-B PROTEAS
(Suggested Scale)

Protea leucospermum lineare

Form	30
Color	25
Condition	25
Stem and Foliage	10
Size	10

Protea Leucodendron grandiflorum

Form	30
. bracts . beard	
Size	25
Color	20
Stem and Foliage	10
Condition	15

BROMELIAD (SOCIETY SCALE)

SCALE 15-c
FLOWERING TYPE
(must have a flower)

Inflorescense		35
. color (includg. plant, bracts, flo)	15	
. size	10	
. conformation of entire inflorescence	10	
Flowers		15
. color	5	
. size	5	
. quantity	5	

Plant Overall		30
. absence of injury	20	
. conformation plant, leaves	10	
. foliage color and/or markings	10	
. size	5	
. labeling correct	5	

FOLIAGE TYPE
(may be in flower)

Conformation	30
. plant, leaves	
Color and/or Markings	30
Size	15
Labeling Correct	5

SCALE 16 — DRIED PLANT MATERIALS
(Air Dried, Borax, Sand, Silica Gel Treated)

Color   30
- . clear . true
- . no streaking, fading or bleaching

Natural Appearance   25
- . in form, texture, size
- . no excessive shriveling of tissues

Variety or Special Interest   15
- . labeled

Technique   20
- . craftsmanship in wiring, taping, shaping during drying
- . care in selection of type suitable for drying

Condition   10
- . free of tears, blemishes, mildew, dust

SCALE 17 — TREATED PLANT MATERIAL
(Glycerin, Color Preserved, Other)

Color   30
- . depth . purity
- . not bleached, streaked

Texture   25
- . flexibility

Condition   10
- . free of blemishes, tears, mildew, dust

Technique   20
- . success of process
- . wiring, taping, shaping, etc.
- . care in selection of suitable type for the process

Variety or Special Interest   15
- . labeled

SCALE 18 — COMPETITIVE CONSERVATION CLASS
(Bird's Christmas Dinner)

Food Value   30

Creativeness   25

Attractive Appearance   20

Practicality   25
- . hangers, holders attached or attachable, other

SCALE 19 — CHRISTMAS TREE (Artificial)

Overall Effect   35

Creativity   35

Technique   30
- . edges well finished
- . well built, neat
- . mechanics hidden

SCALE 20 — SWAGS, WREATHS, OTHER

Design   30
- . proportion . balance
- . color use

Relationship of Materials   20
- . suitability of use

Artistic Effect   25
- . fitted to placement and distance
- . technique

Creativity   25

SCALE 21 — PLAQUE

Defined as constructed by gluing natural materials, pressed flowers, seeds, leaves, stems, etc. onto a background to be hung. Della Robbia influence. Traditional design.

Design   35
- . radial construction
- . focal area
- . vanishing point perspective

Relationship of Material   30

Individuality   20

Theme Interpretation   15

SCALE 22 — BLOOM CYCLE

SUGGESTED CLASSES

A—3 named flowers of the same variety, at three different stages of maturity, showing color from bud to full-blown.

B—3 named varieties (different) of the same species, at three different stages of maturity, showing color from bud to full-blown.

C—3 named species (such as 'PEACE' Rose, 'RADIANCE' Cosmos, etc.). 3 different stages of maturity.

NOTE: Exhibitor to use own container and needlepoint holder as needed. Stems of different lengths with own foliage only, attached if possible. Display to be pleasingly grouped to be viewed from the front. Schedule may allow for interesting seed pod formation, i.e., Clematis or poppy seed head could be one stage of maturity.

SUGGESTED SCALE OF POINTS

Form	15	Placement	20
. true to variety		. pleasing display	
Color	15	Bloom Stage	15
. clear, typical		. good sequence and selection	
Substance	15		
. firm, fresh		Container	10
Condition	10	. suitable in proportion, color, etc.	
. clean, whole			

SCALE 23 — COLLECTION (General)

Cultural Perfection, Quality 40
Number of Different Species or Varieties (Minimum 5) 30
Distinction (newness, superiority, etc.) 10
Nomenclature (correct, suitable, complete as to family, variety) 10
Condition (freedom from blemish, etc.) 10

SCALE 26 — DISPLAY (General)

Arrangement and Effect, General Attractiveness 30
Cultural Perfection 30
Number of Different Species or Varieties (Minimum 5) 20
Nomenclature (Correct, suitable, complete as to family, variety) 10
Condition (freedom from blemish, etc.) 10

SCALE 27 — ROUND FRUITS
(Apples, Pears, Apricots, Peaches, Plums, Etc.)

Prime Eating Quality, Maturity (including size, heavy with juice) 25
Condition, Grooming (freedom from blemish, etc.) 25
Color 20
Uniformity 20
Form (according to species, variety) 10

SCALE 28 — CLUSTER FRUITS (Grapes, Etc.)

Prime Edibility, Maturity For Area 25
Condition, Grooming (freedom from blemish, etc.) 20

SCALE 29—VEGETABLES, VINE FRUITS

(Displayed on plate. Amount and number to be noted in Schedule)

Prime Culinary Quality   50

. taste, texture, smell   20   . color (inside, out)   10
. maturity, substance   10   . weight for size, type, vty. 10

Form   25

. inner: little waste, meaty (pepper, tomato)   20
. outer: typical (impt. in corn, tomatoes, potatoes)   5

Condition   15

. limp . degree of maturity ideal . blemished . groomed . clean

Uniformity   10

. shape . size . color . stage of maturity . length
(if single, apply points to Prime. Impt. in cucumbers, potatoes, etc.)

Note: generally:

Size: medium, typical, ideal edibility

Weight: heavy for size, indicating juice in fruits. A hollow potato or cucumber may weigh less than its size indicates

Substance: tender, crisp, fresh, succulent, not wilted, wrinkled

Color: bright, clear, typical

Condition, Grooming: Wiped clean, not scrubbed, never waxed. Free of blemish,   scars, etc. Well displayed with stems, husks, as per Schedule. Note: Schedule should provide rule allowing Judges to cut and taste one specimen. Rewrap in clear plio.

Asparagus: not white, tips on scales tight

Beans, Peas: not spotted, both ends intact, seeds ½ matured. Sweet Tender

Beets: no off-color rings inside, no scars, darkening, no scaling, cracks, ½" top

Cabbage: solid, heavy; green outer leaves intact.

Cauliflower: white, heavy.

Carrots: muddy, greened, russet, cracked penalized. Top, roots trimmed to 1". No side roots, deduct if removed. Sweet. Small core.

Cantaloupe: Sweet, Not coarse. Thin rind. Fragrant.

Corn: 2" wide strip of husk, silk removed. Wrap in clear film. Ear, kernels well filled. Kernels in milk stage.

Cucumber: Green. ¼" stem attached. Firm. Heavy. Sweet. Not coarse, pithy.

Dill: Green. Fragrant. Full plant shown, tied.

Kohlrabi: Tender. Crisp. Tap root removed. Top trimmed to ½ to ¼".

Lettuce: Clean. Crisp. Tender. Not bitter. ¼" basal plate intact. Leaf type attached to stem. Turgid, not wilted.

Okra: not woody, ½ mature. Stems trimmed ½"

Onion: Green: Crisp. Sweet. Tops 4–6" above white shank. Roots ¼".

Onion: Dry: Neck small. Well cured. Heavy for size. Top ½". Skin intact.

Peppers: Deep color. Firm. Turgid. Heavy. Small seed cavity. Thick walls.

Potatoes: Not hollow. Heavy for size. Sweet not bitter. No greening, hard spots. No deep scars, fissures.

Radishes: Not pithy. Sweet. Turgid, crisp. Clean. Not greening. Top cut to 2", roots intact.

Rhubarb: Pulled, not cut. 1" leaf on stalk. Pungent. Not bitter.

Spinach, Swiss Chard: Bright green. Crisp. Not wilted. Attached to stem, root cut off.

Squash, Winter, Pumpkin: Shell hard, clean, no scars, bleaching. Mature. Heavy for size. 1" stem attached.

Squash, Summer: Not coarse. Sweet. Crisp. Not limp. Even color.

Tomatoes: Firm. Heavy for Size. Meaty. Flavorful. Not overripe. 1" stem

Turnips: Rutabagas: Sweet, not bitter. Not pithy. Color typical. No side roots. Deduct if removed. 1" top.

Watermelon: Symmetrical. Flavorful. Flesh full color. Not coarse, overripe

"GO FORTH MY BOOK AND TAKE

WHATEVER POUNDING THE

HEAVY-FISTED DESTINIES

PREPARE."

— LEONARD BACON, 1887

INDEX